Deadly Arsenals

PUBLICATIONS FROM THE NON-PROLIFERATION PROJECT OF THE CARNEGIE ENDOWMENT FOR INTERNATIONAL PEACE

Nuclear Status Report: Nuclear Weapons, Fissile Material and Export Controls in the Former Soviet Union
Published jointly with Monterey Institute of International Studies
Edited by Jon Brook Wolfsthal, Cristina-Astrid Chuen, Emily Ewell Daughtry, 2001
(Russian edition – May, 2002)

Russia's Nuclear and Missile Complex: The Human Factor in Proliferation
Valentin Tikhonov, 2001

Repairing the Regime: Preventing the Spread of Weapons of Mass Destruction
Edited by Joseph Cirincione, 2000

China's Changing Nuclear Posture: Reactions to the South Asian Nuclear Tests
Ming Zhang, 1999

Proliferation Issue Briefs

WEB-BASED PUBLICATIONS, ONLINE AT **www.proliferationnews.org**

Proliferation News & Resources
The Non-Proliferation Project's daily news site

Carnegie to Go
A downloadable news service for handheld devices

New Leaders, New Directions: Proliferation 2001
A CD based on the 2001 Carnegie International Non-Proliferation Conference

WORKING PAPERS

After the Attacks: U.S. Policy Toward the Subcontinent After 9/11
Lee Feinstein, 2002

The Next Wave: Urgently Needed New Steps to Control Warheads and Fissile Material
Published jointly with the Harvard University's Project on Managing the Atom
Matthew Bunn, 2000

New Challenges in Asia and America
2000 Carnegie International Non-Proliferation Conference Proceedings

The Rise and Fall of START II: The Russian View
Alexander A. Pikayev, 1999

— For these and other publications from the Carnegie Endowment, visit **www.ceip.org/pubs** —

Deadly Arsenals

TRACKING WEAPONS OF MASS DESTRUCTION

Joseph Cirincione

with Jon B. Wolfsthal and Miriam Rajkumar

CARNEGIE ENDOWMENT FOR INTERNATIONAL PEACE

Washington, D.C.

Carnegie Endowment for International Peace
1779 Massachusetts Avenue, N.W., Washington, D.C. 20036
202-483-7600, Fax 202- 483-1840
www.ceip.org

The Carnegie Endowment normally does not take institutional positions on public policy issues; the views and recommendations presented in this publication do not necessarily represent the views of the Carnegie Endowment, its officers, staff, or trustees.

To order, contact Carnegie's distributor:
The Brookings Institution Press
Department 029, Washington, D.C. 20042-0029, USA
1-800-275-1447 or 1-202-797-6258
Fax 202-797-2960, Email bibooks@brook.edu

Library of Congress Cataloging-in-Publication Data

Cirincione, Joseph. / Deadly arsenals : tracking weapons of mass destruction / Joseph Cirincione, with Jon B. Wolfsthal and Miriam Rajkumar.
     p. cm.
Includes bibliographical references.
     ISBN 0-87003-193-7 (paperback)
1. Weapons of mass destruction. 2. Nuclear arms control—Verification. 3. Chemical arms control—Verification. 4. Biological arms control—Verification. I. Wolfsthal, Jon B. II. Rajkumar, Miriam. III. Title.
     U793 .C57 2002
     327.1'74—dc21

2002004867

Front cover inset photos: Royal Navy, UK Ministry of Defence; UN-DPI/H. Arvidsson;
     "Missile Launch Control Room," PhotoDisc
Back cover author photo: Chad Evans Wyatt
Maps: Dave Merrill
Cover & interior design: Cutting Edge Design
Printer: BPS Printing & Graphics, Inc.

09 08 07 06 05 04 03   5 4 3 2   1st Printing 2002

Contents

If there proves to be a silver lining to the terrible events of September 11, it may be that they restored proliferation of weapons of mass destruction to its rightful place at the top of the global security agenda and added a sense of urgency to controlling their continuing spread. The terrorist attacks also highlighted a level of complexity that was present, though not fully appreciated, before that watershed. Non-proliferation policies must distinguish between and effectively address both proliferating states, which are permanent, fixed in place, and by and large deterrable, and terrorist groups, which are not.

Equally, these policies must address the interactions between states and terrorists: most important among them the possibility that fissile materials or weapons might be stolen from or given by states to terrorists. All of the various tools of non-proliferation—formal state-to-state agreements, norms, sanctions, inspections, technology denial, intelligence collection, and military action—have very different application to these profoundly different situations. Effective policies require that distinctions be made between capability and intent—and between the risks that stem from strong or aggressive states and the equally great dangers that can flow from weak or failing ones.

Deadly Arsenals: Tracking Weapons of Mass Destruction is a complete and authoritative resource on the spread of nuclear, chemical, and biological weapons and their means of delivery. Using the most accurate governmental and nongovernmental resources, it presents a clear picture of the risks posed by the proliferation of these weapons of mass destruction, as well as the successes and failures of international efforts to prevent their spread. The authors hope to convey both the seriousness of the threat and the optimism that goes with knowing that tools to deal with these dangers exist and can be effective.

Deadly Arsenals begins with an extended status report on the non-proliferation regime and lucid technical primers on nuclear, chemical, and biological weapons and ballistic missiles. The body of the volume is country-by-country analyses—including the historical and regional influences on a country's decision to pursue, or abandon the pursuit, of weapons of mass destruction. The book has been designed to serve as an easy-to-use working resource for experts, students, journalists, and the interested public. Clear and meticulously researched charts and maps for each country of proliferation concern provide an up-to-date summary of capabilities and risks.

This is the latest volume in a series that began 18 years ago under the former director of the Carnegie Non-Proliferation Project, Leonard Spector. His original volumes set a standard for detail and scholarship that remains the hallmark of the project and its publications. The latest volumes have grown significantly beyond the original series, which focused mainly on nuclear proliferation, to include the entire range of weapons of mass destruction and ballistic missiles. Within this expanded scope the series is still, we believe, the most usable, thorough, complete, and accurate guide to the subject available in a single volume. This edition is a substantially revised and expanded version of its two immediate predecessors in the series—*Tracking Proliferation: A Guide in Maps and Charts, 1998* and *1995*.

We would like to thank the Carnegie Corporation of New York, the Ford Foundation, the Prospect Hill Foundation, and the W. Alton Jones Foundation for their generous support, which makes this book and all the activities of the Non-Proliferation Project possible.

JESSICA T. MATHEWS
President
Carnegie Endowment for International Peace

Acknowledgments

This book stands on the broad shoulders of those who preceded us at the Carnegie Non-Proliferation Project. We are indebted to the project founder, Leonard Spector, and to Rodney Jones, Mark McDonough, Toby Dalton, and Gregory Koblentz, the authors of *Tracking Nuclear Proliferation, 1998*, which formed the basis of our study. We note with great sadness the untimely death of Mark McDonough this year. We, his family, and friends will sorely miss him.

We must acknowledge the international team of experts and scholars who generously gave their time and intellects to review chapters in this book. We would especially like to thank Shai Feldman, Camille Grand, Evan Medieros, Frank Pabian, John Russell, Mark Smith, John Simpson, and our Carnegie colleagues, Rose Gottemoeller, George Perkovich, and Michael Swaine for their valuable amendments and suggestions. We are grateful for Jonathan Tucker's advice and corrections on our chemical and biological proliferation chapters. Avner Cohen did a superb job correcting and expanding the chapter on Israel and Michael Barletta added new insights and interpretations of the nuclear programs of Argentina and Brazil. Judith Perera did a wonderful job editing many of the chapters from her London laptop. Our research is informed by official intelligence assessments, particularly those of the United States and Canada, and discussions with defense and foreign affairs officials in many nations. Data on nuclear weapon arsenals rely heavily on the research of Robert S. Norris and other experts at the Natural Resources Defense Council.

We could not have produced this book without the help of many people at the Carnegie Endowment. Andrew Krepps, Marshall Breit, Maya Pilatowicz, and Sarah Schumaker did a fabulous job dissecting threat assessments, counting missiles, and categorizing biological and chemical warfare threats. Toni Elam came back from maternity leave just in time to provide crucial administrative support. Sherry Pettie and Trish Reynolds patiently shepherded the manuscript through the publications maze to produce the high-quality book you now hold. As always, the library staff of Kathleen Higgs and Chris Henley provided wonderful and timely research. Sally Murray James of Cutting Edge Design gave us a clean, artistic cover and book design, and the professionals at Grammarians produced the book in record time.

None of this would have been possible without the guidance and support of Carnegie's president, Jessica Mathews, whose suggestion launched this book two years ago, and vice presidents Paul Balaran, Tom Carothers, and Carmen MacDougall. We are ever grateful for the faith and generous support of the

Carnegie Corporation, the Ford Foundation, the Prospect Hill Foundation, and the W. Alton Jones Foundation.

With our great appreciation to those who worked to improve the quality of our work also goes our general absolution of any sins; the authors alone accept responsibility for the content and any errors that may remain.

PART ONE
Assessments and Weapons

PREVIOUS PAGE: *The XX-39 CLIMAX, part of Operation Upshot/Knothole, was a 61 kiloton device fired June 4, 1953, at the Nevada Test Site.* (US DEPARTMENT OF ENERGY. ONLINE AT www.nv.doe.gov/news&pubs)

Global Trends

The proliferation of weapons of mass destruction (WMD) is widely recognized as the most serious threat to the national security of the United States and other nations. Official and public attention to proliferation issues, however, has varied over the decades from near-hysteria to apathy. At the beginning of 2002 there seemed to be a balanced appreciation of the urgency of new efforts to prevent proliferation, deter use, and, if necessary, respond to the consequences of attacks involving nuclear, biological, or chemical weapons.

To sustain a balanced policy three aspects to the proliferation problem should be kept in mind: first, the current global situation is dangerous; second, it could have been much worse; and third, the right government policies could make the situation much better.

Weapons of mass destruction are twentieth-century inventions. There is nothing new, of course, about mass destruction. From ancient times a military campaign often meant the slaughter of tens of thousands of soldiers and civilians. As the industrial revolution mechanized warfare, the industrialized nations sought ways to kill more efficiently armored troops or unprotected populations dispersed over wide areas and to annihilate military and economic targets. Military researchers produced weapons that could deliver poison gas, germs, and nuclear explosions with artillery, aerial bombs, and, later, missiles.

Both the Central Powers and the Allies used poison gas for the first time in World War I. Japan inaugurated biological warfare in its attacks against the Chinese at the beginning of World War II, but all the belligerent nations had biological weapon research programs, and Germany used poison gas to kill millions of Jews and other prisoners in its concentration camps. At the end of that war, nuclear weapons were used for the first and last time when the United States struck Japanese cities. Global arsenals peaked during the Cold War decades of the 1960s, 1970s, and early 1980s, when both the NATO nations and the Warsaw Pact perfected and produced tens of thousands of chemical, biological, and nuclear weapons.

Since then, the absolute numbers of these weapons have decreased dramatically. Even before the end of the Cold War the United States and the Soviet Union, with the vast majority of global holdings, agreed to reduce their nuclear arsenals and to eliminate all their chemical and biological weapons. As the threat of global thermonuclear war receded, officials and experts agreed that the propagation of those weapons to other nations posed the most serious remaining threat. In January 1992, for example, the member states of the U.N. Security Council declared that the spread of weapons of mass destruction constituted a "threat to international peace and security." In 1998, the Defense Intelligence Agency (DIA) concluded bluntly in its annual threat assessment, "The proliferation of nuclear, chemical, and biological weapons, missiles, and other key technologies remains the greatest direct threat to U.S. interests world-wide." President George W. Bush, in early 2001, said, "The grave threat from nuclear, biological, and chemical weapons has not gone away with the Cold War. It has evolved into many separate threats, some of them harder to see and harder to answer."[1]

There are two related proliferation risks today: that more nations will acquire these weapons and that subnational or terrorist groups might acquire or use them. For years, policy makers focused on the first risk, most recently involving the suspected programs of a few "rogue states." After September 11, 2001, the terrorist use of weapons of mass destruction seems the more urgent danger, but tension in South Asia reminds us that the acquisition of those weapons, even by established nations, dares catastrophe.

This chapter provides a brief overview of global proliferation threats, describes mass destruction weapons and the nations that have or wish to have them, and the proliferation prospects for the next few years. The national arsenals are the most likely (and for nuclear weapons, the only practical) source for terrorist groups intent on acquiring weapons of mass destruction. Chapter 2 details the major elements of the non-proliferation regime, including the international network of treaties and agreements constructed over the past fifty years to prevent and reduce proliferation. Chapters 3, 4, and 5 describe in greater detail the characteristics of weapons of mass destruction and the specific national programs that exist or that may evolve. Chapters 6 through 22 review the history and status of the most significant national programs, including those countries that have given up nuclear and other weapons of mass destruction. Three of these chapters briefly describe the past and present programs of the United Kingdom, France, and the United States, not because these nations present direct proliferation risks, but to provide information on the recent changes in their policies and postures. The continued existence of large nuclear arsenals increases the perceived desirability of nuclear weapons and the likelihood that other nations will claim equivalent nuclear privileges.

Updates and expansion of the information in this volume, plus the latest developments, debates, and discussions are available on the web site of the Carnegie Endowment.

Proliferation Today

The nations of the world confront serious and immediate threats from the global presence of thousands of nuclear weapons and chemical weapons. They also face the possibility that some nation or group still has or soon could have biological weapons. A wide variety of delivery mechanisms for these weapons exists, including ballistic missiles, cruise missiles, aircraft, artillery, ships, trucks, and envelopes. There is also now a growing recognition of the added danger that terrorist organizations could kill thousands, not just with traditional mass destruc-

Table 1.1: **What Are Weapons of Mass Destruction?**

Nuclear Weapons

A nuclear weapon is a device with explosive energy, most or all of which derives from fission or a combination of fission and fusion processes. Explosions from such devices cause catastrophic damage due both to the high temperatures and ground shocks produced by the initial blast and the lasting residual radiation.

Nuclear fission weapons produce energy by splitting the nucleus of an atom, usually highly enriched uranium or plutonium, into two or more parts by bombarding it with neutrons. Each nucleus that is split releases energy as well as additional neutrons that bombard nearby nuclei and sustain a chain reaction. Fission bombs, such as those dropped on Hiroshima and Nagasaki, are the easiest to make, and they provide the catalyst for more complex thermonuclear explosions. In such weapons a fission explosion creates the high temperatures necessary to join light isotopes of hydrogen, usually deuterium and tritium, which similarly liberate energy and neutrons. Most modern nuclear weapons use a combination of the two processes, called boosting, to maintain high yields in smaller bombs.

Biological Weapons

Biological weapons intentionally disseminate infectious diseases and conditions that would otherwise appear only naturally or not at all. Such agents can be divided into bacteria (such as anthrax), viruses (such as smallpox), rickettsiae (such as Q fever), chlamydia, fungi, and toxins (such as ricin). The features that influence their potential for use as weapons include infectivity, virulence, toxicity, pathogenicity, the incubation period, transmissibility, lethality, and stability. The advent of genetic engineering has had a profound impact on the threat from biological weapons. Agents that are extremely harmful in nature can be modified to increase virulence, the production rate per cell, and survivability under environmental stress, as well as to mask their presence from immune-based detectors. Since most agents are living organisms, their natural replication after dissemination increases the potential impact of a strike, making such weapons even more attractive. Any country possessing a pharmaceutical or food storage infrastructure already has an inherent stabilization and storage system for biological agents. Aerosol delivery is optimal, while explosive delivery is also effective, but to a lesser extent owing to the possibility for organism inactivation because of heat from the blast.

Chemical Weapons

Chemical weapons use the toxic properties, as opposed to the explosive properties, of chemical substances to produce physical or physiological effects on an enemy. Classic chemical weapons, such as chlorine and phosgene, were employed during World War I and consisted primarily of commercial chemicals used as choking and blood agents, which caused respiratory damage and asphyxiation. The advent of such blistering agents as

(Table continues on the following page.)

Table 1.1 (continued)

mustard gas and lewisite, which cause painful burns necessitating medical attention even in low doses, marked the first chemical weapons to produce a significant military effect. Mustard gas, because of its low cost and ability to produce resource-debilitating casualties, has been a popular weapon and was used to inflict numerous casualties during the Iran–Iraq War.

Nerve gases, or anti-cholinesterase agents, were discovered by the Germans in the 1930s and represent the beginning of modern chemical warfare. Such agents block an enzyme in the body that is essential for nervous system function, causing a loss of muscle control, respiratory failure, and eventually death. These gases, which are all liquids at room temperature, are lethal far more quickly and in far lower quantities than are classic agents and are effective both when inhaled and when absorbed through the skin. Nerve gases can be classified as either G-agents (sarin) or V-agents (VX), both of which are exceedingly volatile and toxic. Other types of chemical weapons include mental and physical incapacitants (such as BZ) and binary systems, both of which have undergone limited military development. Chemical weapons can be delivered through bombs, rockets, artillery shells, spray tanks, and missile warheads, which, in general, use an explosion to expel an internal agent laterally.

Radiological Weapons

Radiological weapons use conventional explosives such as dynamite and C–4 to disperse radioactive materials over large areas. The most common conception for their use is explosives surrounded by radioactive material in the form of pellets, powder, or even a radioactive gas. The area of dispersal would depend on the size of the explosion. Victims not injured in the explosion would receive life-threatening levels of radiation exposure. The radiation would inhibit or prevent emergency response teams from aiding the victims, and, depending on the size of the explosion, contaminate large areas for years pending expensive removal operations. Alternatively, a source of radioactive material, such as a nuclear reactor or spent-fuel storage depots, could be targeted with large explosive devices to disperse very high levels of radioactivity into the atmosphere and the surrounding area.

SOURCES

Federation of American Scientists. *Biological Weapons.* Available at www.fas.org/nuke/intro/bw/intro.htm.

Federation of American Scientists. *Chemical Weapons Introduction.* Available at www.fas.org/nuke/intro/cw/intro.htm.

U.S. Department of State. *Biological Weapons Convention.* Available at www.state.gov/www/global/arms/treaties/bwc1.html.

tion weapons, but by destroying or sabotaging critical urban and industrial infrastructures.

Nuclear Weapons

Nuclear weapons are the most deadly weapons ever invented. A single, compact
nuclear weapon can instantly devastate a mid-sized city. Nuclear weapons are
also the most difficult mass destruction weapons to manufacture or acquire.
Today, only eight nations have such weapons. Five nuclear-weapon states are
recognized by the Treaty on the Non-Proliferation of Nuclear Weapons (NPT)
and enjoy special rights and privileges under international law. Listed in order
of the size of their nuclear arsenals, they are: *Russia*, the *United States, China,
France*, and the *United Kingdom*. This group acquired their arsenals during the
twenty years after World War II and remained remarkably stable from 1964,
when China tested its first nuclear weapon, until 1998, when *India* and
Pakistan both detonated nuclear devices and declared their intention to deploy
weapons. India and Pakistan have not yet openly deployed any weapons, but
both are capable of configuring aircraft and missiles with tens of weapons over
the next few years if they so desire. *Israel* is widely believed to have approximately 100 nuclear weapons but neither acknowledges nor denies their existence. India, Pakistan, and Israel are not parties to the NPT.

Apart from these eight countries, three others are known to be actively pursuing nuclear weapon programs. *North Korea* may have accumulated enough
material to construct one or two weapons but agreed in 1994 to freeze and then
transform its nuclear program away from military use. International inspectors
destroyed most of *Iraq*'s nuclear program after the Gulf War, though it has most
likely restarted since Iraq blocked inspections in 1998. Finally, *Iran* is slowly but
steadily pursuing an open civilian nuclear power program and is believed to be
covertly developing expertise for nuclear weapons. All three are member states
of the NPT and, as such, any nuclear weapon programs are illegal and, if
proved, could subject the nations to additional sanctions or even military action
through United Nations resolutions.

In the past twenty years, several major countries have abandoned nuclear
programs, including *Argentina* and *Brazil*, and four others have relinquished
their nuclear weapons to join the NPT as non-nuclear-weapon states. *Ukraine,
Belarus*, and *Kazakhstan* gave up the thousands of nuclear weapons deployed on
their territories when the Soviet Union dissolved. Over a period of two years,
senior officials in both the Bush and Clinton administrations worked with great
dedication to convince these non-Russian republics to renounce their deadly
inheritance. Similarly, *South Africa*, on the eve of its transition to majority rule,
destroyed the six nuclear weapons the apartheid regime had secretly constructed. President Nelson Mandela agreed with the decision, concluding that South
Africa's security was better served in a nuclear-free Africa than in one with several nuclear nations, which is exactly the logic that inspired the original members of the NPT decades earlier. Africa is one of several areas of the world that
have established nuclear-weapon-free zones, where the use or possession of

nuclear weapons is prohibited anywhere on the continent. *Libya* and (to a much lesser extent) *Algeria* have shown interest in nuclear weapons over the years but are not currently considered high-risk states.

Radiological weapons, although not as destructive as nuclear explosive weapons, also pose a serious danger, particularly as a terrorist threat. These are weapons that use conventional explosives, such as dynamite, to disperse radioactive materials, including the highly radioactive waste material from nuclear power reactors or other nonweapon sources. They may be attractive weapons for terrorists owing to the relative ease of their acquisition and use and mass disruption potential. A terrorist act involving the dispersal of radioactive materials would contaminate a wide area, making the treatment of casualties more difficult, exposing many people unhurt in the initial explosion to death and injury from radioactivity, and rendering large areas uninhabitable, pending sizable removal and cleansing operations.[2] As for chemical and biological agents, the invisible and uncertain danger from these weapons would cause widespread fear and horror.

Biological Weapons

Biological weapons, that is, weapons that intentionally use living organisms to kill, are second only to nuclear weapons in terms of their potential to cause mass casualties. Although instances of the deliberate spread of disease go back to the ancient Greeks and Assyrians, the efficient weaponization of biological agents did not occur until the twentieth century. With the exception of the Japanese attacks in China before and during World War II, these weapons have been little used in modern warfare. During the Cold War, the United States and the Soviet Union perfected biological weapons, each developing arsenals capable of destroying all

Table 1.2: **World Nuclear Arsenals**

Russia	20,000
United States	10,500
China	410
France	350
United Kingdom	185
Israel	60–100 suspected
India	10s possible
Pakistan	10s possible

Table 1.3: **Countries Suspected of Developing Nuclear Weapons**

Iran
Iraq
North Korea

human and most plant life on the planet. In 1969, President Richard M. Nixon announced that the United States would unilaterally and unconditionally renounce offensive biological weapons. He ordered the destruction of the entire U.S. biological weapon stockpile and the conversion of all production facilities to peaceful purposes. He reversed 45 years of U.S. reluctance and sought the ratification of the 1925 Geneva Protocol, which prohibited the use of biological and chemical weapons in war (subsequently ratified under President Gerald Ford). Nixon successfully negotiated the Biological and Toxin Weapons Convention (BWC), signed in 1972 and ratified by the Senate in 1975, which prohibits the development, production, stockpiling, acquisition, or transfer of biological weapons. The treaty requires all signatories to destroy all their biological weapons and biological weapon production facilities. The treaty has no verification mechanism, however, and the state parties to the treaty have been trying to negotiate a verification protocol or additional measures to strengthen the BWC.

It is often difficult to get a complete picture of which countries or groups have biological weapons or programs. Milton Leitenberg points out that official assessments rarely distinguish between *suspected, capability, developing*, and *weapon*. Worse, nations with such capabilities or programs are often lumped together in lists with countries with chemical weapon programs or capabilities.[3] In this book we try to desegregate distinct programs and threats. National programs are distinguished by whether they have produced actual weapons, have only research and development programs, or have the basic capability to produce agents. The chapters on specific countries provide the full details of each program.

When the BWC originally entered into force in 1975, there were four nations thought to have biological weapons: the United States, the Soviet Union, China, and South Africa. By the beginning of 2002, 163 nations had signed, ratified, or otherwise acceded to the treaty; however, there are approximately twelve nations suspected of having biological warfare programs. This "dirty dozen" includes Iraq, Iran, Israel, Russia, North Korea, Syria, Libya, and possibly India, Pakistan, China, Egypt, and Sudan. United States officials have publicly identified many of these nations on several occasions, including at the 1996 and 2001 review conferences for the BWC and in annual reports to Congress from the Department of Defense and the former Arms Control and Disarmament Agency. Those nations are all suspected of pursuing offensive biological weapon programs prohibited by the BWC, though not all the countries, such as Israel, are members of the BWC. Almost all the programs are research programs, and only three nations—Iraq, Iran, and Russia—are believed to have

Table 1.4: **Countries Suspected of Retaining Biological Weapons or Programs**

China	Iraq	Pakistan
Egypt	Israel	Russia
India	Libya	Sudan
Iran	North Korea	Syria

produced and stockpiled agents; three others—North Korea, Israel, and China—may have done so.

BIOLOGICAL WEAPON PRODUCTION. *Iraq* remains the most serious proliferation threat. Despite having signed the BWC in 1972 and ratified the accord in 1991, Iraq has clearly pursued an active bioweapons program. After the Gulf War, the U.N. Security Council required Iraq to fully disclose and destroy its program. Iraq denied having a biological weapon program and pursued a policy of obstruction, denial, and evasion to conceal its efforts. Iraqi officials were forced to admit in 1995 that they had produced 30,000 liters of bulk biological agents, some in filled munitions, including Scud missile warheads and aerial bombs. Iraq may have produced up to four times the amount admitted and may have retained 6–16 missiles with biological weapon warheads.[4] Since inspections ended in 1998, Iraq may have reconstituted its program. *Iran* currently maintains an offensive biological weapon program, including active research and the development of agents. In November 2001, Undersecretary of State John Bolton said that Iran had actually produced agents and weapons.[5] Although the *Soviet Union* claimed that it had ended its extensive bioweapons program when it signed the BWC in 1972, President Boris Yeltsin in 1992 disclosed that work had, in fact, continued at substantial levels. There is still considerable uncertainty surrounding Russian weapon facilities, and the possibility exists that agents and weapons remain in Russia.

BIOLOGICAL WEAPON PROGRAMS. *Israel* is believed to have a sophisticated biological weapon program. Israel may have produced anthrax and more advanced agents in weaponized form as well as toxins. United States officials believe that *North Korea* has pursued biological warfare capabilities since the 1960s and has the capability to produce sufficient quantities of biological agents for military purposes within weeks of a decision to do so.[6] *China* has a large, advanced biotechnical infrastructure that could be used to develop and produce biological agents. Chinese officials have repeatedly asserted that the country has never researched or produced biological weapons. United States officials, however, believe that the voluntary BWC declarations submitted by China are inaccurate and incomplete.

POSSIBLE BIOLOGICAL WEAPON RESEARCH PROGRAMS. There is considerable evidence that *Egypt* started a program in the early 1960s that produced weaponized agents.[7] In 1996, U.S. officials reported that by 1972 Egypt had developed biological warfare agents and that there was "no evidence to indicate that Egypt has eliminated this capability and it remains likely that the Egyptian capability to conduct biological warfare continues to exist."[8] Currently, Egyptian officials assert that Egypt never developed, produced, or stockpiled biological weapons.[9] *Syria* has a biotechnical infrastructure capable of supporting limited agent development but has not begun a major effort to produce biological agents or to put them into weapons, according to official U.S. assessments.[10] *Libya* is also believed to have a program, but it has not advanced beyond basic research and development. *India* and *Pakistan* are not believed to have produced or stockpiled offensive biological weapons, although official assessments note that both countries have the resources and capability to support biological warfare research and development efforts.[11] *Sudan* is not believed to have a biological weapon program, but U.S. officials have repeatedly warned of Sudanese interest in developing such a program. Other states of some concern include *South Africa*, which had a bioweapons program that the new unity government says it ended in 1992, and *Taiwan*, which, however, is now rarely mentioned in either official or expert reviews.

BIOTERRORISM. Over the past several decades terrorist attempts to acquire biological agents have fallen short of successful weaponization. Almost all threats to use biological agents, including hundreds of terrorist anthrax hoaxes against abortion clinics and other targets in the United States, have been false alarms. There have been only two significant biological attacks by terrorists in recent times. Some experts contend that the complexity of a biological weapon design for effective dissemination has by and large thwarted bioterrorism. The Japanese religious sect Aum Shinrikyo, for example, tried for several years, and with considerable funding and expertise, to produce and weaponize botulinum toxin and anthrax. The group's extensive efforts failed, and the cult resorted to using the chemical agent sarin for attacks in a Tokyo subway in 1994 and 1995. The first successful terrorist incident involving biological agents occurred in 1984 in Dalles, Oregon, when a religious cult, Rajneesh, disseminated salmonella bacteria in ten restaurants, infecting 750 people, but with no fatalities. When the bioterrorism attack that many had long feared finally came, it was not what the experts had predicted. In October 2001, someone sent letters containing anthrax to members of Congress and the media. The terrorist either did not realize sophisticated dispersal mechanisms were required for mass casualties from anthrax, or simply did not care. The letters killed 5 and infected 18 others. It could have been much worse, but this was the first time that a biological warfare agent was used against the U.S. population. Even this limited attack caused mass disruption and cost billions of dollars in decontamination and prevention expenses.

Chemical Weapons

Experts differ over whether chemical weapons properly belong in the category of "mass destruction weapons." Mass casualties require large amounts of chemical agents relative to either biological or nuclear weapons. Still, 5 metric tons

Table 1.5: **Countries Suspected of Retaining Chemical Weapon Programs**

China	Libya
Egypt	North Korea
India	Pakistan
Iran	Sudan
Iraq	Syria
Israel	

of the nerve gas sarin carried in bombs and dropped by two strike aircraft or the warheads of 36 Scud missiles could kill 50 percent of the people over 4 square kilometers.[12] (By comparison, a Hiroshima-size nuclear bomb of 12-kiloton yield would kill 50 percent of the population over 30 square kilometers.)

Chemical weapons have been used only in isolated instances since World War I, despite (or perhaps because of) the substantial numbers of weapons that are in national arsenals. The 1996 Chemical Weapons Convention (CWC) started a process of "deproliferation" whereby most nations declared their holdings (if any) and began eliminating their arsenals and production facilities. The CWC requires all state parties possessing chemical weapons to destroy them in a safe and environmentally friendly manner not later than ten years after the treaty entered into force, or by April 29, 2007, unless special extensions are granted. The treaty also requires all state parties to destroy or convert all present and past capabilities used to produce chemical weapons by that time. The declarations by the United States and Russia account for the vast majority of known chemical weapon stockpiles.

As of March 2002, 140 of the 145 state parties to the treaty had submitted their initial declarations of chemical weapon holdings and facilities. Four countries—the United States, Russia, India, and South Korea—have declared their possession of chemical weapon stockpiles totaling more than 70,000 metric tons of agents. Russia's 40,000 metric tons is the largest declared stockpile, and that nation's financial difficulties make complete elimination of that stockpile by 2007 impossible. Eleven nations have declared their possession of existing or former chemical weapon production facilities: Bosnia and Herzegovina, China, France, India, Iran, Japan, Russia, South Korea, the United Kingdom, the United States, and Yugoslavia. Thirty-two of the 61 declared facilities were destroyed or converted, 6,000 metric tons of chemical agents were destroyed, and one-fifth of the 8.6 million chemical weapons declared by the four possessor states were eliminated through treaty procedures from 1997 through March 2002.[13]

The most significant remaining national programs, in order of concern, are those in Iraq, North Korea, Iran, India, Israel, China, Syria, Egypt, Libya, Sudan, and perhaps Pakistan.

SUSPECTED CHEMICAL WEAPON STOCKPILES. *Iraq* developed a substantial inventory of chemical weapons, including stockpiles of V-agents, sarin, mustard gas, and tabun. The inspection teams of the United Nations Special Commission (UNSCOM) discovered and destroyed large quantities of these weapons, agents, and production facilities but believe that Iraq still has hidden stores of undisclosed weapons and various precursor chemicals. United States intelligence assessments state that *North Korea* also has had a long-standing chemical warfare program, including the ability to produce bulk quantities of nerve, blister, choking, and blood agents. North Korea is believed to have a large stockpile of these agents and weapons.[14]

Iran's declaration at the May 1998 session of the CWC conference was the first time that that nation had admitted to having had a chemical weapon program, apparently developed in response to Iraqi chemical warfare attacks during the Iran–Iraq War. United States officials say that in the past Iran has stockpiled blister, blood, and choking chemical agents and has weaponized some of these agents into artillery shells, mortars, rockets, and aerial bombs.[15]

Likewise, *India's* declaration under the CWC in June 1997 was the first time that that nation acknowledged it had a chemical warfare production program. While it has pledged to destroy all agents and production facilities, India's activities and exports of dual-use equipment and chemical precursors remain a cause for concern. *China* has ratified the CWC and has declared that it does not possess an inventory of chemical agents. Officials in the United States, however, believe that China has a moderate inventory of traditional agents, an advanced chemical warfare program (including research and development, production, and weaponization capabilities), and a wide variety of potential delivery systems.[16]

Israel is also believed to have an active research and development program for chemical warfare agents and to have produced and stockpiled weapons. *Syria* has not signed the CWC, and U.S. officials believe it has a significant stockpile of the nerve agent sarin. A 1990 intelligence assessment reported that Syria had weaponized these chemicals in 500-kilogram aerial bombs and warheads for its Scud-B missiles.[17] *Egypt* was the first country in the Middle East to obtain chemical weapons and the first to use them. It reportedly employed phosgene and mustard gas against Yemeni royalist forces in the mid-1960s.[18] It is believed still to have a research program and has never reported the destruction of any of its chemical agents or weapons. Israel, Syria, and Egypt are not members of the CWC. *Libya* is suspected of trying to establish an offensive chemical weapon capability and an indigenous production capability for weapons.

CHEMICAL WEAPON RESEARCH PROGRAMS. *Sudan* is also believed to have an active interest in acquiring the capability to produce chemical agents but is not believed to have done so yet. Libya is not a member of the CWC; Sudan is. *Pakistan* sometimes appears on a list of countries with chemical "capabilities" because it has the ability to manufacture chemical weapons should it choose to do so. While Pakistan has imported a number of dual-use chemicals, they are thought to be related to the development of commercial chemical industrial activities and not to a dedicated warfare program. *South Korea* ended its weapon program when it ratified the CWC in 1997 and has been destroying its chemical weapons and production facilities.

Missile Proliferation

Much of the proliferation debate over the past few years has centered not on the weapons themselves, but on one possible means for delivering these weapons: ballistic missiles. It has become common wisdom and a political habit to refer to the growing threat of ballistic missiles. The threat is certainly changing and is increasing according to some measures. Yet by several other important criteria the ballistic missile threat to the United States is significantly smaller than it was in the mid-1980s.

DECREASING ICBM ARSENALS. The number of intercontinental ballistic missiles (ICBM, those with ranges of more than 5,500 kilometers) has decreased dra-

Table 1.6: **Ballistic Missiles**

Twenty-four countries possess only short-range ballistic missiles (that is, with ranges of less than 1,000 kilometers).

Afghanistan	Egypt	Syria
Argentina	Georgia	Taiwan
Armenia	Greece	Turkey
Azerbaijan	Iraq	Turkmenistan
Bahrain	Kazakhstan	Ukraine
Belarus	Libya	UAE
Bulgaria	Slovak Republic	Vietnam
Congo	South Korea	Yemen

Seven countries possess medium-range ballistic missiles (with ranges of 1,000–3,000 kilometers).

China	North Korea
India	Pakistan
Iran	Saudi Arabia
Israel	

One country possesses intermediate-range ballistic missiles (with ranges of 3,000–5,500 kilometers).

China

Five countries possess intercontinental ballistic missiles (with ranges of 5,500+ kilometers).

China	United Kingdom
France	United States
Russia	

matically since the height of the Cold War. In 1987 the Soviet Union deployed 9,378 nuclear warheads on 2,380 long-range missiles aimed at the United States.[19] At the beginning of 2002, Russia had fewer than 5,000 missile warheads deployed on approximately 1,022 missiles.[20] During this period China has maintained a force of about 20 Dong Feng–5 ICBMs. This represents a decrease of 57 percent in the number of missiles capable of striking the continental United States and a decrease of 46 percent in the number of nuclear warheads on those missiles.

These decreases will continue over the next ten years. Russia may decrease its force to as little as 1,000 warheads on its missiles if U.S.–Russian relations continue to improve, or as many as 3,800 warheads if relations deteriorate. Under China's current policy of modernizing its nuclear arsenal, U.S. intelligence predicts that "by 2015, China likely will have tens of missiles capable of reaching the United States,"[21] although that number could increase substantially in response to U.S. missile defense deployments.

IRBM ARSENALS LARGELY ELIMINATED. Since the mid-1980s arms control agreements have nearly eliminated the arsenals of intermediate-range ballistic missiles (those with ranges of 3,000–5,500 kilometers). Presidents Ronald Reagan and Mikhail Gorbachev negotiated in 1997 and implemented the Intermediate-range Nuclear Forces Treaty (INF). The Soviet Union destroyed 660 missiles in this range, eliminating this entire class of missiles from the U.S. and Soviet arsenals. France deactivated and destroyed its 18 land-based and 32 submarine-based IRBMs, while China retains some 20 missiles in the intermediate range. No other nation has developed intermediate-range ballistic missiles, though if North Korea were to launch its developmental Taepo Dong II, it would add a few missiles to this category.

MORE MRBM PROGRAMS. The INF treaty also eliminated all medium-range missiles (those with ranges of 1,000–3,000 kilometers) from the U.S. and Russian arsenals. Although absolute numbers have declined, there is reasonable concern that new missile programs in several countries could threaten international peace. China has 80–100 missiles in the medium range, and several other countries have conducted tests of missiles that do not threaten the territory of the United States but could threaten other nations or deployed forces. North Korea has had one test of its Taepo Dong I missile to 1,320 kilometers. It could extend the range with a third stage and has reportedly deployed 1,300-kilometer No Dong missiles after a single test and may add a longer-range version that is currently under development. Iran has flight-tested the Shahab III, based on the No Dong, with an estimated range of 1,300 kilometers. There are three other programs that are not considered threats to the United States, but some nations view them as threatening. Israel has deployed approximately 50 Jericho II missiles with a range of 1,500 kilometers. India intends to begin production of the Agni II, with a range of about 2,000 kilometers, and may be working on a longer-range (3,500-kilometer) Agni III missile. Pakistan has flight-tested the Ghauri (which has a 1,300-kilometer range) and Ghauri II (in the 2,000-kilometer range) missiles, both based on the No Dong.

AGING SCUD INVENTORIES. Almost all the other nations that possess ballistic missiles have only short-range missiles. For most, their best missiles are aging Scuds that were bought or inherited from the former Soviet Union and that are now declining in military utility as time passes. North Korea is now the primary supplier of Scud-type missiles to the few countries that are interested in the weapon.

FEWER, POORER PROGRAMS. The number of countries trying or threatening to develop long-range ballistic missiles has not changed greatly in 15 years and is somewhat smaller than in the past. The nations now attempting to perfect long-range missiles are also smaller, poorer, and less technologically advanced than were the nations with missile programs 15 years ago.

Only China and Russia have the capability to hit the United States with nuclear warheads on intercontinental land-based ballistic missiles. This has not changed since Russia and China deployed their first ICBMs in 1959 and 1981, respectively. Confusion arises when policy makers speak of missile threats to the United States or to such U.S. interests as forward-deployed troops or allied nations. This merges very short-range missiles, of which there are many, with long-range missiles, of which there are few.

While several programs are a cause for serious concern and could develop into potential international threats, in general the ballistic missile threat is confined, limited, and changing slowly.

Conventional Weapons of Mass Destruction

The terrorist attacks of September 11 may force an expanded definition of weapons of mass destruction to include conventional attacks on critical infrastructure that are capable of causing mass casualties and mass disruption. In most official definitions, the term *weapons of mass destruction* is synonymous with "nuclear, biological, or chemical weapons." However, one definition used by the Federal Bureau of Investigation notes that "a weapon crosses the WMD threshold when the consequences of its release overwhelm local responders."[22] These attacks on critical infrastructure are not a proliferation threat per se, but might be the weapons of choice for some terrorist groups.

There are, for example, 60,000 chemical plants in the United States. A saboteur could turn one of them into an American Bhopal, the town in India where an accident at a Union Carbide pesticide plant released a deadly gas cloud that killed 5,000 people. A trained nuclear engineer could set off a chain reaction at one of the 103 U.S. nuclear power plants, or an airplane could target the plant, triggering a nuclear disaster worse than that at Chernobyl or Three Mile Island. The concern extends beyond reactors to include the 78,000 metric tons of radioactive waste stored in dozens of facilities in the United States.[23] There are 9,300 "high-hazard" dams whose collapse would cause human deaths. Fifty thousand trucks carrying hazardous materials travel on America's highways each day; a truck transporting gasoline or chlorine that explodes in a tunnel could kill hundreds of people. "E-terrorists" could attack some of the 24 government computer networks that the U.S. General Accounting Office recently found to be inadequately protected (including those of the Departments of Defense and the Treasury). Computer hackers could disable power grids, wreaking havoc on American cities.

These are not traditional proliferation problems, but they are now serious national security issues not easily addressed through traditional diplomatic or military measures. Including "conventional" weapons of mass destruction more prominently in threat assessments could force an expanded definition of national security and change traditional views of national defense priorities. If this happened, it would not replace existing proliferation problems (such as the state acquisition of nuclear and biological weapons), but add to them.

In this volume we do not discuss the new threats in any detail but we mark the subject for new research and analysis in the years ahead. Paul Pillar, the former deputy chief of the Counterterrorist Center at the Central Intelligence Agency argues, for example, "The specter of terrorists, especially international terrorists, using chemical, biological, radiological or nuclear means has been overhyped in the sense that it has diverted our attention from what in my view will continue to be the main threat, which is the infliction of loss of life through conventional means."[24] Conventional terrorist attacks can quickly generate fears of WMD terrorism or lead to proposals for state response using advanced military, and even nuclear, weapons. They can also lead to the deployment of additional arms, however inappropriate they may be to the actual threat.

Effective Policies Prevented Worse Dangers

Ever since American scientists detonated the first nuclear bomb at Alamogordo, New Mexico, in July 1945, many officials and experts have feared the future. They worried that proliferation could run out of control, creating a bleak, dangerous world with dozens of nations armed with mass destruction weapons. Several times in the past few decades the public's fear of nuclear war has moved millions of people worldwide to petition for an immediate change in their governments' policies. More than once the very fate of the earth seemed to be at stake, as Jonathan Schell titled his book in 1982.

President John F. Kennedy worried that while only the United States, the Soviet Union, the United Kingdom, and France in the early 1960s possessed

Table 1.7: **Fifteen States with Nuclear, Biological, or Chemical Weapons or with Research Programs**

Country	Nuclear	Biological	Chemical
Russia	W	W	W
China	W	W	W
Israel	W	W	W
United States	W		W
France	W		
United Kingdom	W		
India	W	R	W
Pakistan	W	R	R
Iraq	R	W	W
North Korea	R	W	W
Iran	R	W	W
Egypt		W	W
Syria		R	W
Libya		R	W
Sudan		R	R

Key: Known or suspected Weapons or Agents = W
    Known or suspected Research program = R

nuclear weapons, by the end of the decade, 15 or 20 nations would be able to obtain them. The concern was not that developing countries would acquire the bomb, but rather that the advanced industrial nations would do so, particularly Japan and Germany. Italy, Sweden, and other European nations were already actively pursuing nuclear weapon programs. Neutral Sweden, for example, was then developing plans to build 100 nuclear weapons to equip its air force, army, and navy.

Kennedy moved aggressively to counter those trends. He created the Arms Control and Disarmament Agency in 1961, began negotiations on a treaty to stop the spread of nuclear weapons, and negotiated the Limited Test Ban Treaty, ending nuclear tests in the atmosphere, under water, and in outer space.

United States diplomacy and international efforts to create legal and diplomatic barriers to the acquisition of nuclear weapons, codified in the Treaty on the Non-Proliferation of Nuclear Weapons in 1968, dramatically stopped the rush toward nuclear weapon status. Twenty years after Kennedy's warning, China (with Soviet help) had openly joined the ranks of the new nuclear nations; India had exploded a so-called peaceful nuclear device; and Israel was building a secret nuclear arsenal. All the other nations that had studied nuclear programs in the 1950s and 1960s had abandoned their pursuits. The treaty did little at that time, however, to constrain the nuclear arms race between the two superpowers in the 1960s and 1970s that was sometimes known as vertical proliferation.

Throughout the 1980s and 1990s, however, proliferation experts were again ringing alarms. As Leonard Spector said in 1984 in *Nuclear Proliferation Today* (the first book in the Carnegie Endowment's series on proliferation): "The spread of nuclear weapons poses one of the greatest threats of our time and is among the most likely triggers of a future nuclear holocaust. . . . The spread of nuclear arms also increases the risk of their falling into the hands of dissident military elements or revolutionaries. . . .The threat of nuclear terrorism is also growing."[25]

Non-proliferation efforts have steadily advanced over the past two decades, but never easily and never without serious setbacks. While some nations renounced their weapons of mass destruction programs, others started new programs. Often a majority of nations were able to agree on new treaties and new restraints, only to have other nations block their progress or feign compliance.

After September 11, few doubt the need for urgent government action. President Bush said during his meetings with Russian President Vladimir Putin in November 2001, "Our highest priority is to keep terrorists from acquiring weapons of mass destruction. We will strengthen our efforts to cut off every pos-

Table 1.8: **Countries That Abandoned Nuclear Weapon Programs in the 1990s**

Argentina	Kazakhstan
Belarus	South Africa
Brazil	Ukraine

sible source of biological, chemical, and nuclear weapons material and expertise." These new efforts can be built on the successes of previous actions.

Although nuclear, biological, and chemical arsenals in the United States and the Soviet Union once grew to enormous levels and the technology of these weapons has become increasingly accessible, the world has not been devastated by a thermonuclear war. Moreover, the number of new prospective nuclear nations has shrunk dramatically over the past 20 years, not increased, and the international norm has been firmly established that countries should not, under any circumstances, possess or use either biological or chemical weapons. Global expectations are that the existing stockpiles of nuclear weapons will be greatly reduced, even if their eventual elimination seems but a distant hope.

Only four nations since 1964 have overcome the substantial diplomatic and technical barriers to manufacturing nuclear weapons. The proliferation of biological and chemical weapons is broader, but it is still mainly confined to two regions of the world: the Middle East and Northeast Asia. Most of the world's biological weapons have been destroyed, and the bulk of the global chemical weapon arsenals will likely be eliminated over the next ten years.

With all the serious challenges that exist, the non-proliferation regime has still had a remarkable record of success. But can it hold? Or are international conditions so different today that the regime can no longer work?

Twenty-first Century Proliferation

Some argue that with the end of superpower conflict the world confronts a fundamentally different proliferation problem. While the regime may have worked in the past, they doubt the holdouts can be convinced to adopt the same norms as those held by the regime founders. Many officials in the Bush administration believe that the entire process of negotiating and implementing non-proliferation treaties is both unnecessary and harmful to U.S. national security interests. They argue that some of the treaties, such as the Comprehensive Test Ban Treaty, the Anti-Ballistic Missile Treaty, and the Landmine Treaty, restrict necessary armaments, thus weakening the principal nation that safeguards global peace and security. Other treaties, such as the Chemical Weapons Convention and the Biological Weapons Convention, promote a false sense of security as some nations sign, then cheat on the agreements.

In this view, the construction of a new security paradigm over the next several years must begin by clearing the underbrush of useless and counterproductive treaties. As one influential expert report noted: "The U.S. is highly restricted politically in its capability to withdraw from or even modify established arms control agreements regardless of changes in the strategic environment. . . . Adaptability requires the capacity to both *augment and reduce* U.S. defensive and offensive forces" (emphasis in original).[26] Thus, the Bush administration has withdrawn from or rejected several major treaties, including the Anti-Ballistic Missile Treaty, the START II and III treaties, the Comprehensive Test Ban Treaty, the Small Arms Treaty, and the draft compliance protocol to the Biological Weapons Convention. Officials believe that the United States can provide for its security and for the security of its allies with improved conventional U.S. forces, the deployment of comprehensive missile defenses, new, space-based weapon systems, and fewer—but perhaps newer—nuclear weapons. In this view, international relations will be based on reliable, bilateral agreements and alliance relations, and not on idealist, multi-lateral accords. Nations outside these alliance arrangements will be isolated and contained until democratic regimes can be brought into being. There will most certainly be conflicts, and some may involve weapons of mass destruction, but these can be contained.

In truth, the non-proliferation norm has never been universally recognized. As noted above, several key nations have stayed out of the regime; others are nominally in the regime but have been strongly suspected of cheating on their obligations; and skeptics within many nations criticize what they believe to be the idealistic approach, trying to prevent proliferation with "pieces of paper."

The non-proliferation treaties did not emerge in a diplomatic vacuum. They are an integral part of the political and military balance-of-power and alliance systems of the late twentieth century. Alliance security arrangements, including the promise that the United States would extend a "nuclear umbrella" over Europe and Japan, undoubtedly made it easier for several industrial nations to abandon their nuclear weapon programs. The Soviet Union simply forced non-proliferation on its alliance system. The United States, too, was not adverse to using strong-arm tactics to compel Taiwan and South Korea, for example, to abandon nuclear weapon research. In many developing nations, ambitions ran into formidable financial and technological obstacles to nuclear weapon development, missile engineering, and biological agent weaponization.

At a time when there is increasing interest in unilateral approaches to security arrangements, it is important to point out that financial, technical, and alliance factors have not, in themselves, been sufficient barriers to proliferation. These factors were present in the 1960s and 1970s, but before the signing of the Non-Proliferation Treaty, nuclear proliferation was on the rise; afterward, it was on the decline. The critical importance of the NPT is that it provided the necessary international legal mechanism and established the global diplomatic norm that gave nations a clear path to a non-nuclear future.

Moreover, it is a path that is encouraged and enforced by the dominant political and military powers. The NPT and other treaties do not exist apart from or in opposition to alliance arrangements, rather they embody those arrangements. The non-proliferation regime is thus much more than the sum of pieces of paper. It is a series of agreements that, like the Magna Carta and the Declaration of Independence, capture the political reality of the time and are enforced by the collective political will of the participants.

The political will to constrain proliferation has rarely been stronger. Even before September 11, the joint statement of the ministers of the North Atlantic Council stated: "We continue to place great importance on non-proliferation and export control regimes, international arms control and disarmament as [a] means to prevent proliferation. . . . The Nuclear Non-Proliferation Treaty . . . is the cornerstone of the nuclear non-proliferation regime and the essential foundation for the pursuit of nuclear disarmament."[27]

Table 1.9: **Countries without Weapons of Mass Destruction**

Albania	Czech	Liberia	St. Vincent
Andorra	Republic	Liechtenstein	& the
Angola	Denmark	Lithuania	Grenadines
Antigua &	Djibouti	Luxembourg	Samoa
Barbuda	Dominica	Macedonia	San Marino
Argentina	Dominican	Madagascar	São Tomé &
Armenia	Republic	Malawi	Príncipe
Australia	Ecuador	Malaysia	Saudi Arabia
Austria	El Salvador	Maldives	Senegal
Azerbaijan	Equatorial	Mali	Seychelles
Bahamas	Guinea	Malta	Sierra Leone
Bahrain	Eritrea	Marshall	Singapore
Bangladesh	Estonia	Islands	Slovakia
Barbados	Fiji	Mauritania	Slovenia
Belarus	Finland	Mauritius	Solomon
Belgium	Gabon	Mexico	Islands
Belize	Gambia	Micronesia	South Africa
Benin	Georgia	Moldova	Spain
Bhutan	Germany	Monaco	Sri Lanka
Bolivia	Ghana	Mongolia	Suriname
Bosnia and	Greece	Morocco	Swaziland
Herzegovina	Grenada	Mozambique	Sweden
Botswana	Guatemala	Namibia	Switzerland
Brazil	Guinea	Nauru	Tajikistan
Brunei	Guinea-	Nepal	Tanzania
Bulgaria	Bissau	Netherlands	Thailand
Burkina Faso	Guyana	New Zealand	Togo
Burundi	Haiti	Nicaragua	Tonga
Cambodia	Honduras	Niger	Trinidad &
Cameroon	Holy See	Nigeria	Tobago
Canada	Hungary	Norway	Tunisia
Cape Verde	Iceland	Oman	Turkey
Central	Indonesia	Palau	Turkmenistan
African	Ireland	Panama	Tuvalu
Republic	Italy	Papua New	Uganda
Chad	Jamaica	Guinea	Ukraine
Chile	Japan	Paraguay	United Arab
Colombia	Jordan	Peru	Emirates
Comoros	Kazakhstan	Philippines	Uruguay
Congo	Kenya	Poland	Uzbekistan
Congo	Kiribati	Portugal	Vanuatu
Republic	Kuwait	Qatar	Venezuela
Costa Rica	Kyrgyzstan	Romania	Yemen
Côte d'Ivoire	Laos	Rwanda	Zambia
Croatia	Latvia	Saint Kitts	Zimbabwe
Cuba	Lebanon	and Nevis	
Cyprus	Lesotho	Saint Lucia	

Note: Some nations such as Afghanistan, Ethiopia, Somalia, South Korea, and Vietnam, are not on this list because they may have small numbers of undeclared chemical weapons.

Most allies of the United States share this view of the central importance of treaties (and non-proliferation agreements, in particular) to international security. To most, they are a highly effective (and cost-effective) defense. Even when the treaties are breached, as they have been, weapon use is deterred by the threat of devastating retaliation. The United States by itself has the ability to destroy any opponent with its overwhelming conventional armed forces. Most allies acknowledge an important role for active defensive systems, should nuclear or biological weapons be used. While effective defenses against missiles outside the atmosphere seem impractical (because they could be overwhelmed by lightweight decoys and other countermeasures), defenses against short-range Scuds and Scud derivatives may prove practical and could be deployed to protect troops and defended areas.

It appears, for example, that active diplomacy may very well succeed in eliminating North Korea's nuclear program and the threat that the country will produce or export advanced missile systems. Similarly, if reform elements continue to make progress in Iran and if the United States can both improve relations and convince key nations to eliminate their remaining assistance to missile and nuclear programs, Iran might once again become a regional power having friendly relations with the United States. In many ways, the South Asian programs represent the most difficult challenge, both for the risks of regional war they present and their ripple effect on other Asian states.[28] Even here, though, there remains the possibility that treaties and agreements can be constructed to parallel the NPT regime while taking into account the particularities of the South Asian situation.

As Henry Sokolski points out, "I think it's fair to say the burden is on those who would tear down the traditional arms control regime to show how they would achieve the same goals by other means."[29] It is possible that the powerful moderating mechanisms in the U.S. foreign policy process, realistic appraisals of the continuing importance and successes of international non-proliferation agreements, and the influence and preferences of U.S. allies will combine in the new decade to develop dynamic new approaches to sustain and even expand the regime. If not, future editions of this book may well include a growing list of nuclear nations, and more, not fewer, states with chemical and biological weapons.

NOTES

1. President George Bush, "Remarks by the President to the Troops and Personnel," Norfolk Naval Air Station, Virginia, February 13, 2001.

2. National Council on Radiation Protection and Measurements, "Management of Terrorist Events involving Radioactive Material," Bethesda, Maryland, October 24, 2001.

3. Milton Leitenberg, "Biological Weapons Arms Control," Center for International and Security Studies, University of Maryland, 1996, p. 20. Available at www.ceip.org/files/projects/npp/pdf/leitenberg.pdf.

4. Canadian Security Intelligence Service, "Biological Weapons Proliferation," June 9, 2000, p. 4.

5. John Bolton, Under Secretary for Arms Control and International Security, "Remarks to the Fifth Biological Weapons Convention," Geneva, Switzerland, November 19, 2001.

6. Ibid.

7. Dany Shoham, "Chemical and Biological Weapons in Egypt," *Nonproliferation Review*, spring–summer 1998, pp. 48–58.

8. U.S. Arms Control and Disarmament Agency, "Annual Report to Congress," July 1996.

9. Shoham, "Weapons in Egypt," p. 55.

10. U.S. Department of Defense (DOD), *Proliferation Threat and Response*, January 2001, p. 45.

11. Ibid., pp. 24 and 28.

12. Julian Perry Robinson, "Chemical Weapons Proliferation in the Middle East," in Efraim Karsh, Martin Navias, and Philip Sabin, eds., *Non-Conventional Weapons Proliferation in the Middle East* (Oxford: Clarendon Press, 1993), p. 80.

13. Organization for the Prohibition of Chemical Weapons, *OPCW Synthesis*, March 2002, pp. 1 and 11.

14. U.S. DOD, *Proliferation Threat and Response*, p. 11.

15. Ibid., p. 36.

16. Ibid., p. 15.

17. E. J. Hogendoorn, "A Chemical Weapons Atlas," *Bulletin of the Atomic Scientists*, September/October 1997, p. 37.

18. Ibid., p. 37.

19. Robert Norris and Thomas Cochran, *Nuclear Weapons Databook: U.S.–U.S.S.R./Russian Strategic Offensive Nuclear Forces, 1945–1996* (Natural Resources Defense Council, January 1997), pp. 13 and 46.

20. National Resources Defense Council, "Russian Nuclear Forces 2001," *Nuclear Notebook*, available in *Bulletin of Atomic Scientists*, May/June 2001. Available at www.thebulletin.org/issues/nukenotes/mj01nukenote.html.

21. Foreign Intelligence Council, "Foreign Missile Developments and the Ballistic Missile Threat to the United States through 2015," Central Intelligence Agency, September 1999. Available at www.cia.gov/cia/publications/nie/nie99msl.html#rtoc12.

22. "The FBI and Weapons of Mass Destruction," web site. Available at www.fbi.gov/contact/fo/norfolk/wmd.htm.

23. Eric Pianin, "GAO Challenges Plan for Storage of Nuclear Waste," *Washington Post*, November 30, 2001, p. 3.

24. Steven Hirsch, "Interview: Former CIA Counterterrorist Leader Paul Pillar Discusses Fighting Terrorism," *Global Security Newswire*, December 6, 2001. Available at www.nti.org/d_newswire/issues/newswires/2001_12_5.html#1.

25. Leonard Spector, *Nuclear Proliferation Today* (New York: Vintage Books, 1984), pp. 3–4.

26. "Rationale and Requirements for U.S. Nuclear Forces and Arms Control," National Institute for Public Policy, Washington, D.C., January 2001, p. viii, available at www.nipp.org.

27. "Final Communiqué," Ministerial Meeting of the North Atlantic Council, Budapest, Hungary, May 29, 2001, paras. 76–77.

28. See Joseph Cirincione, "The Asian Nuclear Reaction Chain," *Foreign Policy*, Spring 2000.

29. Quoted in James Kitfield, "Is Arms Control Dead?" *National Journal*, July 14, 2001, p. 223.

CHAPTER 2

The International Non-Proliferation Regime

The global non-proliferation regime is a network of interlocking treaties, organizations, unilateral and bilateral undertakings, and multi-lateral inspections aimed at halting the spread of nuclear, chemical, and biological weapons. The systems in place to control each type of weapon rely on a central agreement that establishes a norm against the possession of weapons and a set of obligations for treaty members.

At the core of this regime are three key treaties. The Treaty on the Non-Proliferation of Nuclear Weapons restrains the spread of nuclear weapons; the Chemical Weapons Convention prohibits the development, possession, or use of chemical weapons; and the Biological and Toxin Weapons Convention bans the development, possession, or use of biological weapons. The nuclear and chemical weapon regimes also involve extensive inspection and verification arrangements and are covered by extensive international export-control arrangements. An effort to negotiate a verification mechanism for biological weapons continues. (See appendixes for the text of each treaty.)

Nuclear Non-Proliferation Regime

The nuclear non-proliferation regime is the oldest and most elaborate of the weapon of mass destruction control systems. It is founded on the basis of the NPT and includes additional treaties that limit the testing and geographical spread of nuclear weapons. It includes a variety of export-control and supplier arrangements, the most important of which is the International Atomic Energy Agency (IAEA).

Nuclear Non-Proliferation Treaty

The NPT helped to establish the international norm against proliferation. Opened for signature in 1968 and entered into force in 1970, the NPT divides member countries into nuclear and non-nuclear-weapon states. "Nuclear-weapon states" are defined by the treaty as countries that detonated a nuclear explosion before January 1, 1967. These include only the United States (first detonation in 1945), the Soviet Union (1949), United Kingdom (1952), France (1960), and China (1964). Russia succeeded to the Soviet Union's status as a nuclear-weapon state under the treaty in 1992; while Ukraine, Kazakhstan, and Belarus, in giving up their nuclear weapons, agreed to become non-nuclear-weapon states. The NPT defines all other countries as non-nuclear-weapon states.[1] Under the NPT:

- Non-nuclear-weapon states pledge not to manufacture or receive nuclear explosives. (Both nuclear weapons and "peaceful nuclear explosives" are prohibited.)

- To verify that they are living up to this pledge, non-nuclear-weapon states also agree to accept IAEA safeguards on all nuclear activities, an arrangement known as *full-scope safeguards.*

- All countries agree not to export nuclear equipment or material to non-nuclear-weapon states except under IAEA safeguards, and nuclear-weapon states agree not to assist non-nuclear-weapon states in obtaining nuclear weapons.

- All countries agree to facilitate the fullest possible exchange of peaceful nuclear technology.

- All countries agree to pursue negotiations in good faith to end the nuclear arms race and to achieve nuclear disarmament under international control.

- A party may withdraw from the treaty on 90 days' notice if "extraordinary events related to the subject matter of the Treaty" have "jeopardized its supreme interests."

The five permanent members of the U.N. Security Council are all members of the NPT. The United States, Russia, and the United Kingdom serve as the treaty's depositary states; China and France did not join until 1992. At the beginning of 2002 the treaty had 182 non-nuclear-weapon state parties, for a total of 187 parties. Only Cuba, India, Israel, and Pakistan have yet to sign the treaty, making it the most widely adhered to arms control treaty in history.

The NPT original term was twenty-five years, with periodic reviews of the treaty occurring every five years. At the NPT Review and Extension Conference held in New York City in April and May 1995, the parties agreed to extend the agreement indefinitely and unconditionally, giving it (for all practical effect) a permanent duration. In addition, the treaty members approved a set of principles and objectives to guide the parties during a strengthened review process in the future. This extension of the treaty was by no means a foregone conclusion, and its indefinite extension was a major victory in international efforts to combat the proliferation of all weapons of mass destruction.

At the May 2000 NPT Review Conference, the participants adopted by consensus a program of action (see appendix A) that includes a series of practical steps, including:

- Early entry into force of START II; the conclusion of START III as soon as possible

- Further unilateral reductions in nuclear arsenals

- Increased transparency by the nuclear-weapon states of their nuclear weapon capabilities

- Further reductions in nonstrategic nuclear weapon stockpiles

- Agreed measures to reduce the operational status of nuclear weapon systems

- Diminishing the role for nuclear weapons in security policies

- Expanding nuclear weapon reductions to other states

- Multilateral controls over fissile material to be removed from warheads

- Creating a subsidiary body with a mandate to deal with nuclear disarmament in the Conference on Disarmament

- A moratorium on nuclear testing pending the entry into force of the Comprehensive Test Ban Treaty

- Application of the principle of irreversibility to nuclear disarmament

International Atomic Energy Agency

Created in 1957, the Vienna-based IAEA is a U.N.-affiliated organization with 132 member countries. Established before the NPT was even negotiated, its principal mission is twofold: to facilitate the use of nuclear energy for peace and to implement a system of audits and on-site inspections (collectively known as safeguards) to verify that nuclear facilities and materials are not being diverted for nuclear explosions. The agency does not offer physical protection and is not a police force; it cannot prevent states from using nuclear materials under its control for use in nuclear weapons. Instead, the safeguards are designed to provide the agency and its members with timely warning should significant quantities of nuclear-weapons-usable materials be diverted for the production of nuclear weapons. It is then up to the agency's members (or the U.N. Security Council, to whom major safeguard violations are reported) to take appropriate action.

The agency's system of inspection was used to form the verification measures of the NPT. Under the treaty, non-nuclear-weapon states must accept "full-scope safeguards" over all nuclear materials—and the facilities that contain those materials—within the jurisdiction of the state in question. The goal of IAEA inspections and monitoring under the NPT is to verify that nuclear materials have not been diverted by the state in question to nuclear weapons or for nuclear explosions of any kind. A state may declare and exempt nuclear materials from IAEA inspection for narrow military purposes, such as fueling naval nuclear reactors, an exemption pointed to by some as a weakness in the IAEA system of verification.

IAEA officials can monitor only those activities connected with the production or use of nuclear materials. The IAEA does not possess the means or the legal authority to search for or investigate activities related to the development or production of nuclear weapons. The activities outside the IAEA's jurisdiction include the fabrication and testing of non-nuclear components of nuclear weapons, high-explosive testing, and nuclear-weapon-design research and development.

In addition to monitoring all peaceful nuclear activities in non-nuclear-weapon state parties to the NPT, the agency also monitors individual facilities and associated nuclear materials in non-NPT parties at the request of these states or their suppliers. Thus, although India, Israel, and Pakistan are not parties to the NPT, several nuclear facilities in each of those countries are subject to IAEA monitoring and cannot be used to support those nations' nuclear weapon programs without detection by the IAEA.

Until 1991, in non-nuclear-weapon state parties to the NPT, the IAEA monitored only those facilities declared by the inspected country and did not seek possible undeclared nuclear installations, lacking a clear political mandate from its members to do so. After the 1991 Gulf War, however, it was learned that Iraq had secretly developed a network of undeclared nuclear facilities as part of an extensive nuclear weapon program. This led the IAEA board of governors in 1991 to reiterate the right of the Agency to exercise its previously unused authority to conduct "special inspections," i.e., to demand access to undeclared sites where it suspected nuclear activities were being conducted. Subsequent measures, including environmental sampling and other holistic safeguard measures, were adopted under Program 93+2, to be implemented in two installments. Part 1, implemented initially in 1996, consisted of measures that could be traced to existing legal authority. Part 2 consisted of measures whose implementation would require complementary legal authority. The IAEA board of governors approved part 2 measures on May 15, 1997.

The Comprehensive Test Ban Treaty

The newest potential element of the regime is the Comprehensive Test Ban Treaty (CTBT), which is a barrier to vertical as well as horizontal proliferation. The conclusion of this treaty fulfilled a preambular commitment of NPT parties to fulfill pledges made in the 1963 Partial Test Ban Treaty "to seek to achieve the discontinuance of all test explosions of nuclear weapons for all time." Opened for signature in New York on September 24, 1996, the CTBT prohibits nuclear test explosions of any size and establishes a rigorous verification system, including seismic monitoring and on-site inspections, to detect any violations.

The CTBT was negotiated at the Geneva Conference on Disarmament (CD), where decisions are usually made by consensus. India temporarily blocked approval of the treaty in mid-August 1996; it objected to the fact that the treaty did not include provisions demanded by India prescribing a "time-bound framework" for the global elimination of nuclear weapons. India also opposed the treaty's entry-into-force provision, which, in effect, would require India's ratification in order to bring the pact into force. To circumvent India's veto, Australia introduced the treaty to the U.N. General Assembly, where decisions are made by majority rather than by consensus. The U.N. General Assembly adopted the CTBT on September 10, 1996, by a vote of 158 to 3 (the negative votes were from India, Bhutan, and Libya).

The U.S Senate rejected ratification of the treaty in October 1999, though the United States and all other participating nations continue to observe the treaty's ban on further tests. The CTBT's entry-into-force provision requires the ratification of 44 "nuclear-capable" nations that possess either nuclear-power or nuclear-research reactors. Three of those nations—India, Pakistan, and North Korea—have not signed the treaty; ten others, including China, Israel, and the United States, have yet to ratify the treaty. In total, 164 nations (including the five nuclear-weapon states and Israel) have signed the treaty, and 89 ratified it by the beginning of 2002. (For more details on the CTBT, see appendix H.)

Supplier Control Mechanisms

Two informal coalitions of nations form a third major element of the non-proliferation regime. They are those nations that voluntarily restrict the export of equipment and materials that could be used to develop nuclear weapons.

Shortly after the NPT came into force in 1970, a number of Western and Soviet-bloc nuclear-supplier states began consultations concerning the procedures and standards that would apply to nuclear exports to non-nuclear-weapon states. The group, known as the NPT Exporters Committee (or the Zangger Committee, so named after its Swiss chairman), adopted a set of guidelines in August 1974. These guidelines included a list of export items that would trigger the requirement for the application of IAEA safeguards in recipient states. These procedures and the "trigger list," updated in subsequent years, represent the first major agreement on the uniform regulation of nuclear exports by current and potential nuclear suppliers. China joined the group in October 1997 and participated in trigger-list discussions for the first time in February 1999.

Following India's nuclear test in 1974, an overlapping group of nuclear-supplier states—in this case including France, which was not then a party to the NPT—met in London to develop export guidelines further. In January 1976, this London group, which became known as the Nuclear Suppliers Group (NSG), adopted guidelines that were similar to those of the NPT Exporters Committee but also extended to transfers of technology and included an agreement to "exercise restraint" in the transfer of uranium-enriched and plutonium-extraction equipment and facilities.

In April 1992, in the wake of the Gulf War, the NSG expanded its export-control guidelines, which until then had covered only uniquely nuclear items, to cover 65 "dual-use" items as well. The group also added as a requirement for future exports that recipient states accept IAEA inspections on all their peaceful nuclear activities. This rule, previously adopted by only some NSG members, effectively precludes nuclear commerce by NSG member states with India, Israel, and Pakistan.

In addition to agreeing to such full-scope safeguards, all nations importing regulated items from NSG member states must promise to furnish adequate physical security for transferred nuclear materials and facilities; pledge not to export nuclear materials and technologies to other nations without the permission of the original exporting nation or without a pledge from the recipient nation to abide by those same rules; and promise not to use any imports to build nuclear explosives. Similar rules, apart from the requirement for full-scope safeguards, apply to exports regulated by the Zangger Committee, which continues to function, although it has been partially eclipsed by the Nuclear Suppliers Group, whose export controls are more far-reaching. The members of the two supplier groups are listed, and more detailed discussion is provided, in appendix F in this volume.

Nuclear-Weapon-Free Zones

Nuclear-weapon-free zones (NWFZs) complement NPT arrangements because they can be geared to specific regional situations. The growing role of NWFZs as part of the non-proliferation regime was reflected in the draft review document of the 1995 NPT Review and Extension Conference: "The establishment of nuclear-weapon-free zones . . . constitutes an important disarmament measure which greatly strengthens the international non-proliferation regime in all its aspects." (See additional information on NWFZs in appendix E in this volume.) NWFZs have been established in Latin America (the Treaty of Tlatelolco, 1967), the South Pacific (SPNFZ, 1996), and Africa (ANWFZ, 1996).

Biological and Chemical Non-Proliferation Regime

Global efforts to contain the spread of biological and chemical weapons center on the Biological and Toxin Weapons Convention (BWC) and the Chemical Weapons Convention. These treaties are not as well developed or long-standing as their nuclear counterparts, but they have made major advances in the past decade and now establish international norms against the development, possession, and use of such weapons. In addition, efforts to expand and improve the implementation of the regimes continue, as witnessed by efforts to negotiate a verification protocol to the BWC.

The Biological and Toxin Weapons Convention

The Geneva Protocol for the Prohibition of the Use in War of Asphyxiating, Poisonous or Other Gases, and of Bacteriological Methods of Warfare of 1925 was limited. It symbolically prohibited the use of both poison gases and bacteriological weapons, but it did not restrict the ability of states to acquire and store chemical and biological weapons, nor did it have verification or enforcement provisions.

The Biological and Toxin Weapons Convention was opened for signature in April 1972 and entered into force on March 26, 1975. The treaty prohibits the development, production, stockpiling, acquisition, or transfer of biological agents or toxins in "quantities that have no justification for prophylactic, protective, and other peaceful purposes."[2] The BWC also specifically bans "weapons, equipment or means of delivery designed to use such agents or toxins for hostile purposes or in armed conflict." The United States, United Kingdom, and the Russian Federation are the three depositary governments for the BWC. At the beginning of 2002, the BWC had 162 signatories and 144 member states. Review conferences are held regularly and have taken place in 1980, 1986, 1991, 1996, and 2000.

When it entered into force, the BWC was the first international treaty to ban an entire class of weapons. However, the treaty lacked effective verification and enforcement measures to ensure compliance. Recognizing these weaknesses, member states established an ad hoc group in 1994 to draft binding verification guidelines for the convention. The ad hoc group is authorized to review four areas: "Definitions of terms and objective criteria; incorporation of existing and further enhanced confidence building and transparency measures, as appropriate, into the regime; a system of measures to promote compliance with the Convention; and specific measures designed to ensure the effective and full implementation of Article X."[3] Yet the BWC's shortcomings continue to restrict its impact. Violations of the convention by Russia, persistent allegations regarding Iraq's biological weapon activities, and a doubling of the number of states suspected of pursuing a biological weapon capability since 1975[4] have raised questions about the convention's utility. Efforts by the ad hoc group to negotiate a legally binding protocol for verification were severely damaged by the withdrawal from the talks by the United States in July 2001 and by a U.S. proposal on December 7, 2001, the last day of the 2001 Review Conference, to disband the ad hoc group.[5]

The Chemical Weapons Convention

Soon after the conclusion of the Biological and Toxin Weapons Convention, draft efforts began for a ban on chemical weapons. Negotiations stalled, however, in seeking agreement on compliance and verification issues. Progress resumed in 1986 when the Soviet Union accepted provisions for systematic inspections at chemical weapon storage and production facilities, the destruction of production facilities, and declarations and routine inspections at commercial industry sites. A year later the USSR also agreed to mandatory short-notice challenge inspections, insisting, however, that all facilities and locations be subject to the procedure. The final catalyst for the completion of a chemical weapons treaty was the use of chemical attacks by both sides during the Iran–Iraq War, demonstrating a clear absence of international means to prevent the acquisition and use of chemical weapons for conflict.

The Chemical Weapons Convention (CWC) entered into force on April 29, 1997. The treaty prohibits the development, production, acquisition, stockpiling, retention or use of chemical weapons, as well as the "transfer, directly or indirectly, [of] chemical weapons to anyone."[6] State parties to the treaty cannot conduct military preparations for the use of chemical weapons, nor can they assist other states in any treaty-banned activity. The CWC also requires members to destroy all chemical weapons and production facilities under its jurisdiction or control, as well as any chemical weapons it may have abandoned on the territory of another state party. Full compliance is expected within ten years of the convention's entry into force. At the beginning of 2002, there were 145 member states to the CWC.

The CWC includes a number of confidence-building measures and ensures transparency through a verification regime that subjects all declared chemical weapons and chemical weapon production facilities to systematic inspections. The Organization for the Prohibition of Chemical Weapons (OPCW) was established to oversee the inspection and verification proceedings. The OPCW maintains a comprehensive web site with the latest information on treaty membership and activities.[7] The convention categorizes chemicals into three "schedules," depending on their applicability for chemical weapon programs and for commercial purposes. Varying levels of control are then applied to the classified chemicals and to their production facilities. Facilities producing chemicals listed in any of the three schedules in quantities in excess of allotted amounts must be declared and will be subject to inspection. The verification provisions of the treaty regulate both the military and civilian chemical industries active in the production, processing, and consumption of chemicals relevant to the convention. Convention provisions authorize a combination of reporting requirements, the routine on-site inspections of declared sites, and short-notice challenge inspections to ensure compliance. The conditions for challenge inspections of any declared or nondeclared facility are also included. The CWC also contains provisions for assistance in the event a member state is attacked or threatened with chemical weapons and for promoting trade in chemicals and related equipment between states for peaceful purposes.

The Australia Group

The Australia Group is an informal association of thirty-three (33) countries that are opposed to the proliferation of chemical and biological weapons (CBW). Its member nations work on the basis of consensus to limit the spread of CBW by the control of chemical weapon precursors, biological weapon pathogens, and CBW dual-use equipment. Measures to address CBW proliferation also include the coordination of national export controls and information sharing on suspicious activities.

The group was established in 1984 after the extensive use of chemical weapons in the Iran–Iraq War. The group initially focused on regulating the export of eight dual-use chemical precursors. By 1991, however, the "warning list" of chemicals subject to control had expanded to include 54 materials (chemicals, pathogens and toxins, and dual-use equipment). Australia Group member states share the group's "warning list" with chemical industries and scientific communities in order to promote an awareness of CBW proliferation risks within individual nations. Enterprises are asked to report any suspicious activities. Many substances used in the production of chemical weapons, however, also have legal industrial purposes, which forces control efforts to strike a difficult balance between security concerns and legitimate trade.

NOTES

1. In this book, Israel, India, and Pakistan are described as non-NPT nuclear-weapon states. The NPT and the non-proliferation regime have no legal category and no provision for additional nuclear-weapon states.

2. Text of Biological Weapons Convention, U.N. Conference on Disarmament, August 23, 2001. Available at www.unog.ch/disarm/distreat/bac_72.htm.

3. United Nations, "Brief Background on the Biological Weapons Convention," August 27, 2001. Available at www.un.org/Depts/dda/WMD/page6.html.

4. Joseph Cirincione, ed., *Repairing the Regime: Preventing the Spread of Weapons of Mass Destruction* (New York: Routledge, 2000).

5. Jenni Rissanen, "Anger after the Ambush: Review Conference Suspended after US Asks for AHG's Termination," *BWC Review Conference Bulletin*, December 9, 2001, available at: www.acronym.org.uk/bwc/revcon8.htm.

6. Text of Chemical Weapons Convention, August 21, 2001. Available at www.opcw.nl/cwc/cwc-eng.htm.

7. See www.opcw.org.

Table 2.1: **Major Treaties and Agreements of the Non-Proliferation Regime**

Non-Proliferation Treaty
Entered into force in 1970 187 member states Under the treaty, the five "nuclear-weapon" states commit to pursue general and complete disarmament, while the remaining "non-nuclear-weapon" states agree to forgo developing or acquiring nuclear weapons.
Chemical Weapons Convention
Entered into force on April 29, 1997 145 member states, 172 signatories The treaty prohibits the production, stockpiling, acquisition, and transfer of chemical weapons.
Biological and Toxin Weapons Convention
Entered into force on March 26, 1975 144 member states, 162 signatories The treaty prohibits the development, production, stockpiling, acquisition, and transfer of pathogens or toxins in weapons systems or other means of delivery.
Comprehensive Test Ban Treaty
Opened for signature on September 24, 1996 89 member states, 164 signatories The treaty prohibits nuclear test explosions of any size and establishes a rigorous global verification system to detect violations.
Missile Technology Control Regime (MTCR)
Announced on April 16, 1987 32 participants This is an informal export-control arrangement designed to regulate the spread of ballistic and cruise missiles capable of delivering a 500-kilogram payload over 300 kilometers or intended to carry weapons of mass destruction.
Agreed Framework
Signed on October 21, 1994 In exchange for North Korea halting and agreeing to dismantle its nuclear program, a U.S.–led coalition agreed to supply North Korea with two proliferation-resistant light-water reactors.

Sources

"Arms Control Agreements." Federation of American Scientists. Available at www.fas.org/nuke/control/index.html.

Cirincione, Joseph, ed. *Repairing the Regime: Preventing the Spread of Mass Destruction*. New York: Routledge, 2000.

"Fact Sheets." Arms Control Association. Available at www.armscontrol.org/ASSORTED/acaff.html.

CHAPTER 3

Nuclear Weapons and Materials

Nuclear weapons have existed for more than fifty years, and the technology required to produce them is well understood and widely available. Nine countries (Britain, China, France, India, Israel, Pakistan, Russia, South Africa, and the United States) have produced nuclear weapons, and more than 40 countries have the technical knowledge and capability of doing so with the application of adequate resources. Even well-organized subnational organizations and terrorist groups, given adequate time and resources, could possibly produce a basic nuclear device.

Despite these realities, nuclear weapons remain highly complex devices and are difficult to produce. Their production requires a significant level of technical capability and a major investment of time and money. By far the most costly, complicated, and observable part of producing a nuclear weapon is acquiring sufficient amounts of weapons-usable nuclear materials from which the explosive power of nuclear weapons derives. If this material can be purchased or stolen, it dramatically reduces—but does not eliminate—the challenges associated with producing a nuclear weapon. Producing specialized nuclear materials and designing and building a well-engineered explosive device requires the construction of large and thus highly visible facilities (those required for nuclear materials production), making the clandestine acquisition of nuclear weapons extremely difficult. The challenge of preventing the spread of nuclear weapons is complicated, however, by the fact that nuclear materials, including weapon-usable materials, have legitimate peaceful uses. These uses include fuel for nuclear power and research reactors and even industrial uses (tritium and plutonium are used in small amounts in smoke detectors and emergency lighting systems). The physical protection of nuclear materials in the civilian sector, therefore, is a critical component of preventing the spread of nuclear weapons. In addition, the international system of safeguards, administered by the International Atomic Energy Agency, can help to deter theft and alert governments if peaceful nuclear materials are diverted for nonlegitimate uses.

Basic Nuclear Concepts

Conventional explosives release energy through the manipulation of molecules, forming and breaking apart clusters of atoms. Nuclear explosions are much more powerful, and harness their energy by splitting or fusing together individual atoms.

Atoms consist of a nucleus of neutrons and protons surrounded by a number of orbiting electrons. Elements are defined by their atomic number, which is equal to the number of protons they possess. Elements can exist in nature in different forms called isotopes, meaning that they have the same atomic number but a different number of neutrons in their nuclei. For example, three forms of hydrogen atoms are found in nature: simple hydrogen, deuterium, and tritium. All three have one proton in their nucleus, but have zero, one, and two neutrons, respectively. Various isotopes interact with other particles (such as other neutrons) and molecules differently. These differences allow some isotopes to be fused together or split apart more easily, creating new (larger or smaller) atoms and releasing various forms of energy and radiation in the form of alpha, beta, gamma or x-rays, and neutrons. It is this splitting or fusing of atoms that produces the energy released in a nuclear reactor or in a nuclear weapon.

The different forms of atoms are designated by their element name (i.e., hydrogen, iron, uranium, and plutonium) and an isotopic number equal to the combined number of neutrons and protons in the nucleus. All atoms, small or large, are referred to in this way. For example, all uranium atoms have 92 protons in their nuclei, but can exist (among other forms) with 143, 145, or 147 neutrons in their nuclei. The different isotopes are referred to as Uranium 233, or U–233 (92 protons plus 143 neutrons), U–235 (92 protons plus 145 neutrons), and U–238 (92 protons plus 147 neutrons). Plutonium (Pu) atoms can exist (among other forms) with 238, 239, and 240 neutrons and protons in their nuclei and are referred to as Pu–238, Pu–239, Pu–240, etc.

Uranium and plutonium are the two main elements that are of relevance when discussing the production of nuclear weapons. (At least one other human-made element, neptunium, can also be used in nuclear weapons, but it exists in very limited quantities globally and is only now being addressed as a proliferation concern.)

Some isotopes can be readily split or fissioned into smaller atoms and are referred to as fissile materials. U–233, U–235, and Pu–239 are all fissile materials that can be used in a nuclear weapon. These atoms split apart after absorbing a neutron into their nucleus. The absorption of the neutron makes the atomic nucleus unstable, and the isotope will then split, seeking a more stable form. Each atom that splits releases energy and additional neutrons that can, in turn, be absorbed by other atoms. These atoms, too, then split and release energy and additional neutrons that go on to split even more atoms. This chain reaction is what enables nuclear materials to be harnessed for various purposes, including the production of heat in a nuclear reactor (for creating steam and then electricity) and the explosive power of a nuclear weapon. In a nuclear reactor, the chain reaction is controlled and limited, while in nuclear weapons the released energy is uncontrolled, enormous, and takes place in a very short time (in tenths of a microsecond).

Basic Nuclear Weapon Concepts

All nuclear weapons rely on a central core of fissile material. The uncontrolled chain reaction releases vast amounts of energy in a small fraction of a second before the central core of nuclear material is blown apart. To create a chain reaction, the core of nuclear material must be formed into a *critical mass*, meaning that enough fissionable material is in a sufficiently small area to enable a self-sustaining number of fissions to take place (that is, more neutrons are released than are absorbed). The amount of material required to produce this mass differs according to the isotopic composition of the material being used (for example, the mass is different for different purity levels of U–235 and Pu–239). A pure form of U–235 (say 90 percent U–235) will have a much smaller critical mass than that of a less pure form (say 45 percent). The IAEA publishes figures on the quantities of material required to produce a nuclear weapon. The "significant quantities" that IAEA specifies are 25 kilograms of highly enriched uranium and 8 kilograms of plutonium. The U.S. Department of Energy and the U.S. National Academy of Sciences have published reports saying that only 4 kilograms of plutonium are required for a basic nuclear weapon. The minimum or exact amount of nuclear material needed to produce nuclear weapons is classified information in all nuclear-weapon states.

Basic Nuclear Weapon Designs

All nuclear weapons use a basic fission chain reaction that is caused by the creation of a critical mass of fissile material. Some weapons rely entirely on this "primary," while others use the primary fission explosion to fuel a second fusion reaction, which can produce much larger explosions. This initial critical mass can be created in one of two ways: by shooting one subcritical mass into another subcritical mass—known as a gun design—or by taking a subcritical sphere of fissile material and compressing it uniformly into a critical mass—known as an implosion weapon.

The gun design is the least complex of the known nuclear weapon designs, having been around for more than a half-century. The nuclear weapon dropped on Hiroshima, Japan, on August 6, 1945, was a gun-type weapon and was so well understood, even at that time, that it was used without being tested beforehand. A gun design shoots a uranium plug into a shaped uranium vessel. The rapid combining of the two parts creates a critical mass, leading to a chain reaction and a nuclear explosion.

The implosion weapon design compresses a subcritical sphere of nuclear material uniformly into a sphere sufficiently small to create a critical mass. The first nuclear explosion (the Trinity test) at Alamogordo, New Mexico, on July 16, 1945, and the nuclear weapon dropped on Nagasaki, Japan, on August 9, 1945, were implosion designs. The implosion design is more complicated but allows for the construction of a more compact weapon, such as those used in missile warheads. The concept is similar to trying to turn a basketball into a baseball with explosives.

Gun-design weapons can only use uranium as a fissile material, since in a gun assembly plutonium will begin producing too many neutrons as the two halves approach each other. These fissions will prevent the formation of a critical mass and result in what is called a fizzle, where only a small amount of energy is released. Because only uranium can be used in the simpler gun design, particular concern surrounds the diversion of produced highly enriched uranium. Both uranium and plutonium can be used in the more complex implosion design.

Design elements in a nuclear weapon can also change the amount of material needed to achieve a critical mass. Adding a basic neutron reflector around the outside of a weapon so that escaping neutrons are reflected back into the mass of material is a common feature used to reduce the amount of material needed to create a nuclear chain reaction.

Advanced Nuclear Designs

Other nuclear weapons "boost" the explosive yield produced by the same amount of fissile materials in a weapon by adding other design elements. This is done mainly by introducing other elements, such as tritium, into the heart of a nuclear explosion. The intense heat and pressures generated by the continuing nuclear explosion result in the fusion of the boosting materials, which in turn release large amounts of energy and additional neutrons that can increase the number of fissile atoms that are split in a reaction. The use of heat to fuse these materials is why these designs are referred to as thermonuclear. The effect is similar to adding gasoline to a campfire—adding fuel to an already occurring series of reactions.

More advanced, or "full-up," thermonuclear weapons use the initial nuclear release from a primary to ignite a fusion reaction. In a fusion reaction, lighter atoms are fused by the heat and radiation released by the primary fission explosion. The first multi-stage, thermonuclear device—also referred to as the hydrogen bomb (because it used liquid deuterium, which is an isotope of hydrogen)—was exploded on November 1, 1952. The explosive used a basic fission primary to produce the heat and radiation necessary to ignite the "secondary" explosive of liquid deuterium. Whereas the first fission nuclear explosions had a force of 20,000 metric tons of TNT (20 kilotons), the first hydrogen explosion had a force of 10,400,000 metric tons of TNT (10.4 megatons).

The Production of Nuclear Materials

Fortunately, from a non-proliferation perspective, fissile materials are not readily found in nature. Uranium–235 is the only naturally occurring fissile material but makes up only .07 percent of the uranium found in nature. This isotope can be increased through a process known as enrichment. To be used in a weapon, uranium must be enriched to at least 20 percent. Weapon-grade uranium is much higher, reaching to and going above 93 percent U–235. All the other fissile materials, including U–233 and plutonium, must be created artificially in a nuclear reactor and subsequently separated in a process referred to as reprocessing, or chemical separation.

Uranium Enrichment

Several methods have been developed for enriching uranium. All of them ultimately rely on differentiating between the isotopes of uranium and isolating material with increased concentrations of U–235. Two principal techniques are in use today: the gaseous diffusion method, in which uranium hexafluoride gas is forced through a selectively porous barrier, and the ultracentrifuge, or gas centrifuge, method, in which uranium hexafluoride gas is swirled in a cylinder that is rotating at extremely high speeds. Electromagnetic isotope separation (EMIS), a process that was used in refining uranium for the first nuclear weapon in the United States and a technology pursued by Iraq in its nuclear weapon program (see chapter 16) separates uranium tetrachloride into different isotopes. EMIS is a highly inefficient but less complex method that was abandoned in the 1950s. Considerable research and development have been conducted on two additional enrichment techniques, the chemical method and laser isotope separation, but neither is used in the commercial production of enriched uranium or for weapon manufacturing. Other methods have been used in weapon programs, including the South African "jet nozzle" design.

Producing highly enriched uranium entails many steps, apart from the enrichment process itself, and many other installations and capabilities are necessary. Nations wishing to obtain highly enriched uranium, without international restrictions prohibiting its use for nuclear explosives, would have to develop an enrichment technology independently or obtain it illegally, since virtually all nuclear exporter states are unwilling to sell nuclear equipment and materials unless the recipients pledge not to use them for nuclear explosives and agree to place them under the inspection system of the International Atomic Energy Agency. (See the appendixes for IAEA safeguards.)

For illustrative purposes, the basic nuclear resources and facilities that would be needed to produce weapons-grade uranium indigenously include:

- uranium deposits

- a uranium mine

- a uranium mill (for processing uranium ore that usually contains less than 1 percent uranium into uranium oxide concentrate, or yellowcake)

- a conversion plant (for purifying yellowcake and converting it into uranium hexafluoride (UF_6) or uranium tetrachloride (UCl_4), the material processed in the enrichment plant)

- an enrichment plant (for enriching the uranium hexafluoride gas or uranium tetrachloride in the isotope U–235), and

- a capability for converting the enriched uranium hexafluoride gas or uranium tetrachloride into solid uranium oxide or metal

Nuclear Reactors

Other fissile materials can be created artificially in nuclear reactors. The United States and other nuclear-weapon states have tended to use dedicated military reactors for the production of these weapon-usable materials, but others (such as India and North Korea) have ostensibly used civilian reactors for the production of plutonium.

In a reactor, uranium fuel (either natural uranium or slightly enriched uranium, depending on the reactor design) is used to create a controlled chain reaction. This reaction releases neutrons that in turn are captured by fertile nuclear materials, such as U–232 or U–238. These materials, with the addition of a new neutron, are converted to U–233 or Pu–239, which are fissile materials. However, the fuel rods containing these materials also contain other reaction by-products through the accumulation of neutrons and the fissioning of elements. Many of these are highly radioactive and require processing to recover the weapon-usable materials.

To do this, "spent" fuel rods are taken to a reprocessing plant, where they are dissolved in nitric acid, and the plutonium is separated from the solution in a series of chemical processing steps. Since the spent fuel rods are highly radioactive, heavy lead casks must be used to transport them. In addition, the rooms at the reprocessing plant where the chemical extraction of the plutonium occurs must have thick walls, lead shielding, and special ventilation to contain radiation hazards.

Although detailed information about reprocessing was declassified by the United States and France in the 1950s and is generally available, it is still a complex procedure from an engineering point of view. Indeed, almost every nation that has tried to develop nuclear weapons by the plutonium route—India, Iraq, Israel, and Pakistan—has sought outside help from the advanced nuclear-supplier countries. North Korea, however, has apparently succeeded in constructing a reprocessing facility at Yongbyon without such foreign assistance.

Like enrichment facilities, however, reprocessing plants can also be used for legitimate civilian purposes because plutonium can be used as fuel in nuclear power reactors. Indeed, through the 1970s it was generally assumed that as the use of nuclear power grew and worldwide uranium resources were depleted, plutonium extracted from spent fuel would have to be recycled as a substitute fuel in conventional power reactors.

In addition, research and development are under way in several nations on a new generation of reactors known as breeder reactors, most notably in France, Japan, and Russia. Breeder reactors use mixed plutonium-uranium fuel surrounded with a "blanket" of natural uranium. As the reactor operates, slightly more plutonium is created in the core and the blanket together than is consumed in the core, thereby "breeding" new fuel. These programs have encountered complex technical and political challenges, not the least of which relate to the overabundance of plutonium and questions about safety and waste produced from these types of reactors and their spent fuel handling. A growing area of research relates to proliferation-resistant reactors that could be used to consume those large amounts of excess plutonium and whose spent fuel would be less well suited for use in the production of plutonium and nuclear weapons.

Like plutonium recycling, the economic advantages of breeders depend on natural uranium's becoming scarce and expensive. Over the past three decades, however, new uranium reserves have been discovered; nuclear power has reached only a fraction of its expected growth levels; and reprocessing spent fuel to extract plutonium (a critical step in the manufacture of plutonium-based fuels) has proved to be far more expensive and complex than anticipated. Moreover, concern has grown over the proliferation risks of the wide-scale use of plutonium as a fuel. These factors led the United States in the late 1970s to abandon its plans to recycle plutonium in light-water reactors and, in the early 1980s, to abandon its breeder reactor development program. Germany has abandoned its breeder reactor program and is phasing out its recycling of plutonium. The United Kingdom, too, has frozen its program to develop breeder reactors, although it is continuing to reprocess spent fuel on a commercial basis for itself and several advanced nations.

The principal proponents of the use of plutonium for civilian purposes are France, Japan, and Russia, which are all continuing to develop the breeder reactor option and are moving forward with sizable plutonium recycling programs. Belgium and Switzerland, although they do not have breeder reactor programs, are using increasing amounts of recycled plutonium in light-water reactors. Broadly speaking, the proponents of nuclear energy in these countries have maintained support for the civil use of plutonium by arguing that, although it may not be economical, it represents an advanced technology that will pay off in the future and reduce a dependence on foreign sources of energy.

Like the production of enriched uranium, the production of plutonium entails many steps, and many installations and capabilities besides the reactor and reprocessing plant are needed. For illustrative purposes, the following facilities and resources would be required for an independent plutonium production capability, assuming that a research or power reactor, moderated by either heavy water or graphite and employing natural uranium fuel, were used:

- uranium deposits

- a uranium mine

- a uranium mill (for processing uranium ore containing less than 1 percent uranium into uranium oxide concentrate, or yellowcake)

- a uranium purification plant (to further improve the yellowcake into reactor-grade uranium dioxide)

- a fuel fabrication plant (to manufacture the fuel elements placed in the reactor), including a capability to fabricate zircaloy or aluminum tubing

- a research or power reactor moderated by heavy water or graphite

- a heavy-water production plant or a reactor-grade graphite production plant, and

- a reprocessing plant

In contrast to heavy-water and graphite-moderated reactors, which use natural uranium as fuel, a light-water moderated reactor would necessitate use of low-enriched uranium, implying that an enrichment capability may be available. If so, highly enriched uranium could, in theory, be produced, obviating the need for plutonium as a weapon material. (It is also possible that a state might import fuel for a light-water reactor under IAEA inspection and, after using the material to produce electricity, reprocess it to extract plutonium. Although IAEA rules would require the country involved to place any such plutonium under IAEA monitoring, the state might one day abrogate its IAEA obligations and seize that material for use in nuclear arms.)

NUCLEAR WEAPON STATUS 2002

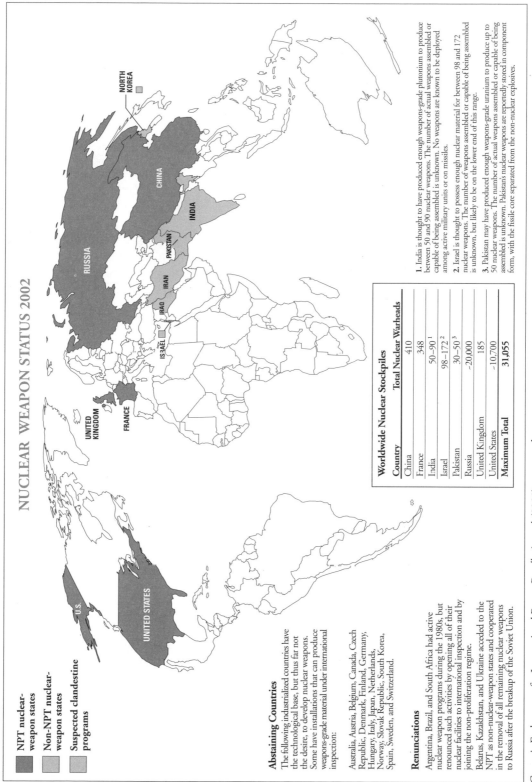

Legend:
- NPT nuclear-weapon states
- Non-NPT nuclear-weapon states
- Suspected clandestine programs

Map labels: U.S., UNITED STATES, UNITED KINGDOM, FRANCE, RUSSIA, CHINA, NORTH KOREA, INDIA, PAKISTAN, IRAN, IRAQ, ISRAEL

Worldwide Nuclear Stockpiles

Country	Total Nuclear Warheads
China	410
France	348
India	50–90 [1]
Israel	98–172 [2]
Pakistan	30–50 [3]
Russia	~20,000
United Kingdom	185
United States	~10,700
Maximum Total	**31,055**

1. India is thought to have produced enough weapons-grade plutonium to produce between 50 and 90 nuclear weapons. The number of actual weapons assembled or capable of being assembled is unknown. No weapons are known to be deployed among active military units or on missiles.

2. Israel is thought to possess enough nuclear material for between 98 and 172 nuclear weapons. The number of weapons assembled or capable of being assembled is unknown, but likely to be on the lower end of this range.

3. Pakistan may have produced enough weapons-grade uranium to produce up to 50 nuclear weapons. The number of actual weapons assembled or capable of being assembled is unknown. Pakistan's nuclear weapons are reportedly stored in component form, with the fissile core separated from the non-nuclear explosives.

Abstaining Countries

The following industrialized countries have the technological base, but thus far not the desire, to develop nuclear weapons. Some have installations that can produce weapons-grade material under international inspection:

Australia, Austria, Belgium, Canada, Czech Republic, Denmark, Finland, Germany, Hungary, Italy, Japan, Netherlands, Norway, Slovak Republic, South Korea, Spain, Sweden, and Switzerland.

Renunciations

Argentina, Brazil, and South Africa had active nuclear weapon programs during the 1980s, but renounced such activities by opening all of their nuclear facilities to international inspection and by joining the non-proliferation regime.

Belarus, Kazakhstan, and Ukraine acceded to the NPT as non-nuclear-weapon states and cooperated in the removal of all remaining nuclear weapons to Russia after the breakup of the Soviet Union.

Carnegie Endowment for International Peace, *Deadly Arsenals* (2002), **www.ceip.org**

CHAPTER 4

Biological and Chemical Weapons, Agents, and Proliferation

Since the mid-1990s, governments and the public have grown increasingly concerned over the threats posed by the proliferation of chemical and biological weapons. The October 2001 anthrax attacks in the United States transformed that concern into demands for substantial government action to respond to and prepare for terrorist attacks using chemical or biological warfare agents. A number of these agents are categorized by experts as weapons of mass destruction because of their potential to inflict massive casualties throughout a broad geographical area. Chemical and biological weapons have also been called "mass casualty weapons . . . [that] do not destroy buildings, cities or transportation. They unfortunately just destroy human lives."[1] Recent technological developments have contributed to the threat posed by chemical and biological weapons. The spread of dual-use chemical technologies has facilitated the surreptitious acquisition of indigenous chemical weapon programs by potential proliferators, while advances in biotechnology could expand the availability and lethality of common biological weapon (BW) agents.

Biological Weapons

Biological weapons distribute pathogenic microorganisms or biologically manufactured toxins to cause illness or death in human, animal, or plant populations.[2] NATO defines a biological agent as a "microorganism (or toxin derived from it) which causes disease in man, plants or animals, or causes deterioration of material."[3] Unlike normal diseases, which appear naturally and spread through contagion, biological weapons are used intentionally to disseminate large quantities of infectious agents to infect a target group. The utility of any biological agent as a weapon is determined by its virulence, infectiousness, sta-

Maya Lena Pilatowicz, a graduate of the Master of Science in Foreign Service Program at Georgetown University and research assistant for the Carnegie Non-Proliferation Project, is co-author of this chapter.

bility, and ease of production. Biological agents can be grouped in four categories: bacterial agents, viral agents, rickettsial agents, and toxins.

- Bacterial agents, such as those that cause anthrax and tularemia, are single cell organisms that either invade host tissue or produce nonliving toxins (poisons). Some bacteria cause disease by both means. Bacterial agents can be cultivated in nutritive solutions. Under specific conditions, some bacteria can transform into spores. Spores are often more resistant to environmental conditions, such as temperature and humidity, than are the original bacteria. Spores "are a dormant form of bacterium, and like the seeds of a plant, they can germinate when conditions are favorable."[4] Because of their resilience, spores are often more effective as biological warfare agents.

- Rickettsial agents include those that cause Q fever and epidemic typhus. Rickettsiae are parasitic microorganisms that live and replicate inside living host cells for survival. They are often highly susceptible to antibiotic treatments.

- Viral agents include smallpox virus, Venezuelan equine encephalitis virus, and various viral hemorrhagic fevers. Viruses are subcellular organisms that are dependent upon host cells for survival. Viral agents act as intracellular parasites, triggering changes within the host cells that eventually lead to cell death. The successful cultivation of viruses is difficult.

- Biological toxins, such as ricin and botulinum toxin, are potent poisons generated by living organisms, i.e., bacteria, fungi, algae, and plants. Unlike bacterial or viral agents, toxins are nonliving, akin to synthetic chemical poisons. As nonliving agents, toxins cannot reproduce or spread and are therefore less deadly relative to living pathogens. Several characteristics, however, differentiate biological toxins from chemical agents. Unlike their chemical counterparts, toxins are not human-made. They are not volatile and thus are unlikely to spread by direct human contact. However, the toxicity of many biological toxins is several orders of magnitude higher than that of chemical nerve agents.[5] Like other biological agents, the effective distribution of toxins generally requires an aerosol system.

The level of technical expertise required to acquire a biological warfare capability remains unclear. Several key traits make pathogens or toxins suitable for use as biological weapons: availability or ease of production; lethality; particle size and weight; ease of dissemination; and stability. To maximize their efficacy, biological agents must be delivered over a widespread area in appropriate doses and under conditions that ensure agent survival. Aerosol delivery—the dispersion of a liquid suspension or dry powder of a microorganism or toxin in an airborne cloud—is optimal. Precise variables such as particle size and the altitude of dissemination are significant determinants of the range and damage that can be caused by a biological weapon attack. Furthermore, to be effectively inhaled by sufficient numbers in the target population, a biological weapon must also disseminate a microbial or toxin agent of an appropriate respirable size. Agent stability must also be maintained during both production and dissemination.

Some experts argue that while agent production is not technically difficult, combining a stable biological agent with an effective dissemination device requires sophisticated technology and expertise. Agent survival is a prerequisite for infection, and biological warfare agents are vulnerable to environmental conditions, including desiccation, humidity, and oxidation. Many agents, particularly live organisms, die when exposed to light or oxygen. Other agents require moisture to survive. Most cannot withstand heat or explosive force. As a result, standard warfare munitions—artillery shells, grenades, rockets, missiles, and bombs—are not effective delivery vehicles for biological weapons.

Other experts argue that developing a crude biological weapon requires only a modest level of expertise. Recent advances in the biological sciences, or the "biotechnology revolution," have increased the availability of dual-use equipment and the number of individuals with the knowledge necessary for biological weapon production. The dissolution of the Soviet Union and the decommissioning of its massive BW program have also added to concerns that rogue states or terrorist organizations may acquire a BW capability. The questionable security at Russian BW storage sites and layoffs or underemployment of BW program workers increase the risk of biological weapon expertise and of components leaking from Russia to potential proliferators. (See the section on chemical and biological weapon programs in chapter 6.)

Once disseminated, aerosols of various pathogenic microorganisms and toxins are often invisible, odorless, and tasteless. With these characteristics, a biological weapon attack could remain undetected until victims began to exhibit symptoms of infection. Depending on the number of victims who inhale the agent, the result could be a massive, simultaneous outbreak of disease.[6] Incubation periods vary from several hours to several days, depending on the specific agent and the amount that has been distributed and inhaled. Pathogenic microorganisms are potential mass casualty weapons because of their ability to multiply within their host. Large quantities of these biological agents, effectively distributed, can cause tens to hundreds of thousands of deaths.

The acquisition of a BW capability requires advanced expertise in various disciplines, including microbiology and aerobiology. Once obtained, however, biological weapons are extremely suitable for covert delivery. As a result, their use by terrorists has been identified as a growing threat to international security. Terrorist intentions involving biological weapons were exposed publicly by the repeated attempts of the Aum Shinrikyo cult to produce and distribute two lethal biological agents in Japan in 1994 and 1995. Despite sustained and well-funded efforts, the group was unsuccessful in producing virulent strains of botulinum toxin and anthrax. The cult's failure demonstrates the technical constraints of biological weapon development.[7] It also reveals the terrorists' recognition of the utility of biological weapons as instruments of mass terror. The potential diversion of biological agents from possible stockpiles in former Soviet states or from states with covert BW programs has elevated concerns over terrorists being able to acquire the weapons.

The October 2001 letter-borne anthrax attacks raised widespread speculation about the methods and potential consequences of covert BW use. The attacks exhibited the range of covert delivery options available to bioterrorists, raised questions about the ease and source of acquisition, and exposed the widespread vulnerabilities of population centers to biological weapons. Recent discussions center on possible methods of protection and appropriate measures for emergency treatment and containment in the event of a large-scale biological weapon attack.

The incidents of biological weapon use in warfare are rare but often dramatic. In the third century, B.C., the Carthaginian leader Hannibal filled pots with poisonous snakes and hurled them onto enemy ships. In 1346, the Tartars catapulted corpses of bubonic-plague victims over the walls of enemy fortresses. British officers engaged in biological warfare in eighteenth-century North America by distributing blankets infected with smallpox to Native Americans.

In the twentieth century, the sophistication of biological warfare was amplified with the emergence of state-sponsored biological weapon programs. In 1940, residents in Chuhsien, China, reportedly contracted the bubonic plague after the Japanese dropped infected fleas and contaminated rice from the air. From 1932 until the end of World War II, Japan developed an extensive biological and chemical weapon program, which included experimentation with biological agents on human subjects in the infamous Units 731 and 100.[8]

Growing capabilities sparked recognition of the destructive potential of biological weapons and were accompanied by international efforts to control their proliferation and use. Nevertheless, the Cold War prompted the development of vast offensive biological weapon programs in the United States and the Soviet Union.

The United States officially ended its offensive biological weapon program in November 1969. President Richard Nixon unilaterally and unconditionally renounced biological weapons and ordered the destruction of all U.S. weapon stockpiles and the conversion of all production facilities to peaceful purposes. At the time, the U.S. biological weapon capability was formidable. The weapon thought most likely to be used was the E133 cluster bomb, which held 536 biological bomblets, each containing 35 milliliters of liquid-suspension anthrax spores. A small explosive charge would, upon impact, turn the liquid into an aerosol to be inhaled by the target population. When the program was dismantled, the United States held in storage some 40,000 liters of anti-personnel biological warfare agents and some 5,000 kilograms of anti-agriculture agents. All were destroyed.

The full extent of the Soviet biological weapon program is still being uncovered. Official disclosure of the program did not occur until 1992, nearly twenty years after the Soviet Union had signed a treaty pledging not to develop or stockpile biological weapons. In U.S. Senate testimony in 1998, former first deputy director of Biopreparat Kenneth Alibek described a Soviet program that employed more than 60,000 people and stockpiled hundreds of anthrax weapon formulations.[9] At its peak, the Soviet biological weapon program supported massive quantities of dry-agent production annually, including: 1,500 metric tons of tularemia bacteria; 4,500 metric tons of anthrax; 1,500 metric tons of bubonic plague bacteria; and 2,000 metric tons of glanders bacteria.[10]

Former Russian President Yeltsin pledged to halt the development of offensive BW capabilities in April 1992. Subsequently, Russia, the United States, and the United Kingdom agreed to a trilateral process of information sharing and mutual site visits to ensure the end of Russia's illegitimate program. By 1994, however, Russia had stopped the exchange of on-site visits, closing numerous facilities to Western observers, which raised questions about the extent of Russia's deactivation of the Soviet BW complex. In spite of such concerns, the United States continues cooperative efforts to help secure the former Soviet Union's vast nuclear, chemical, and biological arsenals, spending close to $5 billion since 1991. Although large numbers of weapons have been successfully destroyed, progress in securing the biological stockpiles is slow.[11] Security remains lax at some Soviet facilities that house lethal biological agents, while the underpayment of Russian bioweapon scientists amplifies the threat of the diversion of biological weapons, agents, and technical expertise.

The exact number and identity of all countries having biological weapon capabilities remain uncertain. Because of the dual-use nature of biotechnology and the ease with which biological weapon development can be camouflaged, the true number of producers and the extent of their capabilities are unknown. Current assessments suggest that approximately twelve nations may have biological weapon warfare programs. In March 2000, the director of the U.S. Central Intelligence Agency stated that "about a dozen states, including several hostile to Western democracies—Iran, Iraq, Libya, North Korea, and Syria— now either possess or are actively pursuing offensive biological and chemical capabilities for use against their perceived enemies. . . . Some countries are pursuing an asymmetric warfare capability. . . . Other states are pursuing BW programs for counterinsurgency use and tactical applications."[12] In February 2001, the director of the U.S. Defense Intelligence Agency told the U.S. Senate that "there are a dozen countries believed to have biological warfare programs."[13]

This dirty dozen includes Iraq, Iran, Israel, North Korea, Syria, Libya, Russia, and possibly India, Pakistan, China, Egypt, and Sudan. Almost all the programs are research programs. Only three nations (Iraq, Iran, and Russia) are believed to have produced and stockpiled agents; three others (Israel, North Korea, and China) may have done so. Other countries that had been of concern include South Africa, which had a bioweapon program that the new unity government says it ended in 1992, and Taiwan, which is now rarely mentioned in either official or expert reviews.

Chemical Weapons

Chemical weapons are lethal human-made substances that can be disseminated as gases, liquids, or solids. The U.S. Army defines a chemical agent as being "a chemical which is intended for use in military operations to kill, seriously injure, or incapacitate man because of physiological effects."[14] The use of such chemical substances against soldiers or civilians constitutes chemical warfare.[15] Chemical weapon agents are produced by mixing various chemicals, called precursors, in specific ratios. Despite the abundance of modern-day toxic substances, only a small number of chemicals are considered suitable for chemical warfare. Throughout the twentieth century, approximately 70 different chemical substances were used and stockpiled as chemical warfare agents. Chemical weapon agents must be highly toxic yet cannot be too difficult to handle. Chemical warfare substances must also be able to withstand prolonged storage without deterioration. Chemical agents must be resistant to atmospheric water and oxygen in order to maintain effectiveness during dispersal. Finally, chemical weapon substances must be able to withstand the high levels of heat that accompany dispersal.

Most substances used in chemical weapons are liquids, although some agents are used in a gaseous form. They may be disseminated by an explosive munition or an aerosol device. Chemical agents may also be allowed to evaporate spontaneously. Chemical weapons are generally categorized in four groups: blood gases, blister agents (or vesicants), choking agents, and nerve agents.

- Blood gases, such as hydrogen cyanide, poison cells by blocking the transport of oxygen in the blood vessels. The most serious effects of cyanide poisoning are caused by a lack of oxygen to the brain.

- Blistering agents, such as mustard gas, phosgene oxime, and lewisite, penetrate body tissues and mucous membranes and react with enzymes, proteins, and DNA to destroy cells. The skin, eyes, and airways are especially vulnerable.

- Choking agents, such as chlorine and phosgene, damage the membrane of the lungs and ultimately cause suffocation. Pulmonary agents must be inhaled to harm the body.

- Nerve agents, such as sarin, VX, and tabun, affect the transmission of nerve impulses in human and animal nervous systems, triggering death. All nerve agents are chemically categorized as organophosphorus compounds.[16] Such chemical warfare agents are highly toxic, spread quickly, and have rapid effects upon skin contact or inhalation.

Chemical weapon delivery requires disseminating the agent in one of two forms: liquid droplets or aerosol. When dispersed, larger droplets fall to the ground, causing ground contamination, whereas the smaller, lighter droplets remain airborne as an aerosol. A chemical cloud is highly susceptible to environmental conditions. Wind velocity necessarily dictates its direction and speed dispersal. Rain and low temperatures may reduce agent effectiveness. Conversely, warm temperatures and high humidity can increase the toxic concentration of the chemical cloud.

A wide variety of possible delivery systems exists for chemical weapon agents. Typical military devices include "artillery shells, aerial bombs (including cluster bombs), spray tanks, missiles, rockets, grenades, and mines. All of these munition types are intended to provide an appropriately sized aerosol that will remain suspended in the air close to the ground[,] where it will be readily inhaled."[17] Sophisticated chemical delivery systems were perfected in the 1960s with the development of binary chemical agents. Previously, chemical weapons were composed of a unitary chemical munition. The chemical agent was manufactured, poured into the munitions, and then stored, ready for use. Binary technology altered weapon design by combining two chemicals of lesser toxicity to create a lethal agent *after* the munition was fired. By delaying the creation of the toxic substance until after the weapon's discharge, binary technology ensured greater safety during transportation, handling, and storage of chemical weapons. Commercial methods of distributing chemical agents are typically less efficient and reliable but can nevertheless be effective. Crop-dusting aircraft, pesticide foggers, and even simple aerosol spray cans offer potential dissemination methods.

The use of chemical agents in warfare can be traced back to the ancient Greeks, who mixed sulfur and pitch resin to engulf enemy troops in toxic fumes during the Trojan War. Chemical weapons have been used or stockpiled by various military forces throughout the twentieth century. The first major instance of chemical warfare occurred on April 23, 1915, when the German army released chlorine gas on Allied troops at Ypres, Belgium. Both the Allies and the Central Powers subsequently employed chemical agents on the battlefield during World War I. By the war's end, an estimated 124,000 metric tons of chemicals had been used on the battlefield by both sides. Mustard gas alone killed 91,000 and injured 1.2 million.[18] After World War I, significant use of chemical warfare occurred in 1935 when Italy used mustard agent in bombs and aerosols against Ethiopia. During World War II, the German chemical weapon program stockpiled 78,000 metric tons of agents, including 12,000 metric tons of tabun and 1,000 pounds of sarin.[19] Japan produced 8,000 metric tons of chemical agents.[20]

Immense quantities of chemical weapons were also produced by both the United States and the Soviet Union throughout World War II and the Cold War. The United States stockpiled an estimated 30,000 metric tons of chemical agents. The destruction of U.S. chemical weapons is in progress at several chemical weapon depots across the nation. Disposal began in 1985.

The Soviet Union officially announced its possession of chemical agents in 1987. The announcement was followed by the deactivation of its chemical weapon production program. In 1988, the United States and the Soviet Union signed the Wyoming Memorandum of Understanding (MOU), launching talks on bilateral verification and an exchange of data about their chemical weapon complexes. Official Russian declarations suggest that the country now has 40,000 metric tons of chemical weapons stored at seven sites and concentrated in central Russia and the Urals. The stockpile includes 32,300 metric tons of sarin, soman, and related nerve gases; 7,700 metric tons of lewisite, mustard gas, and a mixture of both substances; and 5 metric tons of phosgene.[21] The reduction of Russia's chemical weapon arsenal has been stalled in recent years by financial difficulties. Insufficient resources have delayed plans to destroy the weapons by 2007.

Furthermore, some U.S. threat assessments suggest that Russia has not divulged the full extent of its chemical weapon capabilities. Speculation has emerged over the covert Russian development of a new generation of nerve agents, capable of penetrating sophisticated protective gear and detection devices.[22]

Most major states with known chemical weapon stockpiles have pledged to destroy them under the Chemical Weapons Convention. As of March 2002, 140 of the 145 state parties to the treaty had submitted their initial declarations of chemical weapon holdings and facilities. Four countries have declared their possession of chemical weapon stockpiles totaling more than 70,000 metric tons of agents: India, Russia, South Korea, and the United States. Eleven nations have declared their possession of existing or former chemical weapon production facilities: Bosnia and Herzegovina, China, France, India, Iran, Japan, Russia, South Korea, the United Kingdom, the United States and Yugoslavia. Approximately half of the 61 declared facilities have been destroyed thus far.[23]

The most significant national chemical weapon programs are those of China, Egypt, India, Syria, Iraq, Israel, Libya, North Korea, Pakistan, Sudan, and perhaps Iran. Myanmar, Saudi Arabia, South Korea, Taiwan, and Vietnam are also frequently listed as nations with active chemical weapon programs.[24]

Currently, no nonstate actor or substate group is known to possess chemical weapons. Aum Shinrikyo, however, did successfully produce significant amounts of sarin. In 1994, the cult allegedly released a nerve agent in a residential area of Masumoto, Japan, and attacked again in 1995. Those incidents elevated concern over the ability of terrorists to achieve chemical weapon capability.

The September 11 attacks raise a new worry: terrorists may not have to produce chemical agents in order to use chemicals to cause mass casualties. An accident or sabotage at the Union Carbide pesticide plant in Bhopal, India, in 1987 released a cloud of chlorine gas that killed an estimated 5,000 people and injured thousands more. Intentional destruction or sabotage at chemical plants or involving trucks or trains transporting hazardous chemicals could turn industrial facilities into chemical weapons.

Efforts To Control Biological and Chemical Weapons

Global efforts to contain the spread of chemical and biological weapons center upon the Biological and Toxin Weapons Convention and the Chemical Weapons Convention. Initial international efforts to prohibit the use of chemical and biological agents on the battlefield can be traced to the latter part of the nineteenth century. In 1874, the International Declaration concerning the Laws and Customs of War banned the use of poisons on the battlefield.

The extensive use of chemical weapons during World War I led to another attempt by states to establish an international norm against the use of weapons of mass destruction: the 1925 Geneva Protocol. Although it prohibited the use in war of both poison gases and bacteriological weapons, the impact of the Geneva Protocol remained limited. The agreement did not restrict the ability of states to acquire or store chemical and biological weapons, did not have verification or enforcement provisions, and many states reserved the right to respond to a chemical weapon attack in kind. Several nations currently suspected of having a chemical or biological capability have signed the protocol, which also calls into question its ultimate effectiveness. President Richard

Nixon submitted the protocol to the Senate, which ratified the agreement in January 1975 under President Gerald Ford.

The Biological and Toxin Weapons Convention was opened for signature in April 1972 and entered into force on March 26, 1975. The treaty prohibits the development, production, stockpiling, acquisition, and transfer of biological agents or toxins in types or "quantities that have no justification for prophylactic, protective, and other peaceful purposes."[25] The BWC also specifically bans "weapons, equipment or means of delivery designed to use such agents or toxins for hostile purposes or in armed conflict."[26] The United States, the United Kingdom, and the Russian Federation are the three depositary governments for the BWC. At the beginning of 2002, the BWC had 162 signatories and 144 member states. Review conferences are held regularly and have taken place in 1980, 1986, 1991, 1996, and 2001.

When it entered into force, the BWC was the first international treaty to ban an entire class of weapons. However, the treaty lacked effective verification and enforcement measures to ensure compliance. Recognizing these weaknesses, the member states established an ad hoc group in 1994 to draft legally binding verification measures for the convention. The ad hoc group was authorized to negotiate four areas: "Definitions of terms and objective criteria; incorporation of existing and further enhanced confidence-building and transparency measures, as appropriate, into the regime; a system of measures to promote compliance with the Convention; and specific measures designed to ensure the effective and full implementation of Article X."[27]

Efforts to complete a verification protocol ended in July 2001 when the Bush administration announced its opposition to the current approach. The BWC's shortcomings continue to restrict its impact. Violations of the convention by the former Soviet Union, persistent allegations regarding Iraq's biological weapon activities, and a doubling of the number of states suspected of pursuing a BW capability since 1975[28] have raised questions about the convention's effectiveness. Efforts by the ad hoc group to negotiate a legally binding protocol for verification ended when the United States rejected the Draft Protocol and withdrew from the talks in July 2001.[29] The United States claimed that the drafted provisions would have jeopardized the security of U.S. biotechnical and pharmaceutical secrets without effectively detecting treaty violators. The terrorist attacks in New York and Washington, D.C., on September 11, 2001, and the subsequent wave of anthrax attacks have triggered renewed U.S. interest in strengthening the treaty. The Bush administration has proposed a series of measures to be adopted by individual countries to enhance the BWC, including the criminalization of activities prohibited by the BWC, the adoption of regulations to restrict the access and transfer of agents, and the strengthening of existing U.N. procedures for investigating suspicious disease outbreaks or allegations of biological weapon use.

Soon after the conclusion of the Biological and Toxin Weapons Convention, efforts began to negotiate for a ban on chemical weapons. Negotiations stalled, however, over compliance and verification issues. Progress resumed in 1986 when the Soviet Union accepted provisions for systematic inspections at chemical weapon storage and production facilities, the destruction of production facilities, and declarations and routine inspections at commercial industry sites. A year later the USSR also agreed to mandatory short-notice challenge inspections, insisting that all facilities and locations be subject to this procedure. The final catalyst for completion of the chemical weapon treaty was the use of chemical weapons by both sides during the Iran–Iraq War (1980–1988), which demonstrated the clear absence of international means to prevent the acquisition and use of chemical weapons in conflict.

The Chemical Weapons Convention entered into force on April 29, 1997. The treaty prohibits the development, production, acquisition, stockpiling, retention, or use of chemical weapons, as well as the "transfer, directly or indirectly, [of] chemical weapons to anyone."[30] State parties to the treaty cannot conduct military preparations for the use of chemical weapons, nor can they assist other states in any treaty-banned activity. The CWC also requires members to destroy all chemical weapon and production facilities under its jurisdiction or control, as well as any chemical weapons that it may have abandoned on the territory of another state party. Full compliance is expected within ten years of the convention's entry into force. At the beginning of 2002, there were 145 member states to the CWC.

The CWC includes a number of confidence-building measures and ensures transparency through a verification regime that subjects all declared chemical weapon and weapon production facilities to systematic inspections. The convention categorizes chemicals into three "schedules" depending on their applicability for chemical weapon programs and for commercial purposes. Varying levels of control are then applied to the classified chemicals and their production facilities. Facilities producing chemicals listed in any of the three schedules in quantities in excess of specified threshold amounts must be declared and are subject to inspections. The verification provisions of the treaty regulate both the military and civilian chemical industries active in the production, processing, and consumption of chemicals relevant to the convention. Provisions authorize a combination of reporting requirements, routine on-site inspections of declared sites, and short-notice challenge inspections to verify compliance. Conditions for challenge inspections of any declared or nondeclared facility are also included. The Organization for the Prohibition of Chemical Weapons was established to oversee inspection and verification proceedings. The CWC also provides for assistance in the event a member state is attacked or threatened with chemical weapons and for promoting trade in chemicals and related equipment between states for peaceful purposes.

The Australia Group (AG) is an informal association of 33 countries opposed to the proliferation of chemical and biological weapons. Member nations work on the basis of consensus to limit the spread of CBW by the control of chemical weapon precursors, biological weapons pathogens, and CBW dual-use equipment. Measures to address CBW proliferation also include the coordination of national export controls and information sharing about suspicious activities.[31]

The group was established in 1984 after the extensive use of chemical weapons in the Iran–Iraq War. The Australia Group initially focused on regulating the export of eight dual-use chemical precursors. By 1991, however, the "warning list" of chemicals subject to control had expanded to include 54 chemical precursors. The AG began restricting BW-related exports in 1993. Member states share the Australia Group's warning list with chemical industries and scientific communities in order to promote an awareness of CBW proliferation risks within individual nations. Enterprises are asked to report any suspicious activities. Some chemicals used in the production of chemical weapons, however, also have legal industrial purposes, which forces governments to strike a difficult balance between security concerns and legitimate trade.

Notes

1. "Biological Weapons in the Former Soviet Union: An Interview with Kenneth Alibek," conducted by Jonathan B. Tucker, *Nonproliferation Review*, Spring–Summer 1999, p. 1.

2. Richard A. Falkenrath, Robert D. Newman, and Bradley A. Thayer, *America's Achilles Heel* (Cambridge: MIT Press, 1998), p. 15.

3. U.S. Department of the Army, *NATO Handbook on the Medical Aspects of NBC Defensive Operations* (Washington, D.C., 1966), HQ, DA; AmedP-6(B), part 2, p. 1-1. Available at www.fas.org/nuke/guide/usa/doctrine/dod/fm8-9/2ch1.htm.

4. U.S. Army Medical Research Institute of Infectious Diseases, *Medical Management of Biological Casualties Handbook*, 4th ed. (Maryland: Fort Detrick, 2001), p. 13.

5. *FOA Briefing Book on Chemical Weapons*. Available from the Organization for the Prohibition of Chemical Weapons. Available at chemistry.about.com/gi/dynamic/offsite.htm?site= http%3A%2F%2Fwww.opcw.nl%2Fchemhaz%2Fchemhome.htm.

6. Falkenrath, Newman, and Thayer, *America's Achilles Heel*.

7. Milton Leitenberg, "Biological Weapons Arms Control," PRAC paper 16, Center for International and Security Studies, Maryland, May 1996.

8. Edward Eitzen and Ernest Takafuji, "Historical Overview of Biological Warfare," chapter 18, *Medical Aspects of Chemical and Biological Warfare, Part I. The Textbook of Military Medicine* (Office of the Surgeon General, Borden Institute, 1997), p. 416–419.

9. Joseph Cirincione, ed., *Repairing the Regime: Preventing the Spread of Weapons of Mass Destruction* (New York: Routledge, 2000), pp. 7 and 14. See also Kenneth Alibek, "Terrorist and Intelligence Operations: Potential Impact on the U.S. Economy," Statement before the Joint Economic Committee, U.S. Congress, May 20, 1998. Available at www.fas.org/irp/congress/1998_hr/ alibek.htm.

10. Judith Miller, Stephen Engelberg, and William Broad, *Germs: Biological Weapons and America's Secret War* (New York: Simon and Schuster, 2001), p. 254.

11. "Officials Wary about Soviet Arsenal," *Associated Press*, October 30, 2001.

12. George Tenet, director, Central Intelligence, Statement to the Senate Foreign Relations Committee, *Worldwide Threat in 2000: Global Realities of Our National Security*, March 21, 2000. Available at www.cia.gov/cia/public_affairs/speeches/archives/2000/dci_speech_032100.html.

13. V. A. Thomas Wilson, "Global Threat and Challenges through 2015," February 7, 2001.

14. Excluded from consideration are riot control agents, chemical herbicides, and smoke and flame materials. U.S. Department of the Army, *NATO Handbook on the Medical Aspects of NBC Defensive Operations* (Washington, D.C., 1996), HQ, DA; AmedP-6, Part 3; 1-1 Field Manual 8-9.

15. Ibid.

16. *FOA Briefing Book on Chemical Weapons*, Organization for the Prohibition of Chemical Weapons. Available at www.opcw.org/chemhaz/nerve.htm.

17. Frederick Sidell, William Patrick, and Thomas Dashiell, *Jane's Chem-Bio Handbook* (Alexandria: Jane's Information Group, 2000), p. 147.

18. Gert Harigel, *Chemical and Biological Weapons: Use in Warfare, Impact on Society and Environment*, Carnegie Endowment for International Peace. Available at www.ceip.org/files/publications/Harigelreport.asp.

19. Jeffrey Smart, "History of Chemical and Biological Warfare, An American Perspective," Chapter 2, *Medical Aspects of Chemical and Biological Warfare*, op. cit., p. 36.

20. Ibid., p. 37.

21. "Defusing A Toxic Bomb," *Moscow Times*, October 12, 2001, p. 12.

22. U.S. Department of Defense, *Proliferation Threat and Response*, January 2001, pp. 4 and 57.

23. Organization for the Prohibition of Chemical Weapons, Annual Report 2000.

24. OTA, *Proliferation of Weapons of Mass Destruction*, 1995, p. 65. See also E. J. Hogendoorn, "A Chemical Weapons Atlas," *Bulletin on the Atomic Scientists*, September/October 1997, pp. 35–39.

25. Text of the Biological Weapons Convention, U.N. Conference on Disarmament. Available at www.unog.ch/disarm/distreat/bac_72.htm (August 23, 2001).

26. Ibid.

27. United Nations, "Brief Background on the Biological Weapons Convention," available at www.un.org/Depts/dda/WMD/page6html (August 27, 2001).

28. Cirincione, ed., *Repairing the Regime*.

29. "Envoy Tries To Save Pact on Bio-War," *International Herald Tribune*, August 1, 2001.

30. Text of Chemical Weapons Convention. Available at www.opcw.nl/cwc/cwc-eng.htm.

31. "Inventory of International Nonproliferation Organizations and Regimes, 2000 Edition," Center for Nonproliferation Studies, MIIS, August 2000, p. 39.

Table 4.1: **Examples of Biological Warfare Agents**

Biological Warfare Agent (Causative Organism)	Lethality	Incubation Period (Days)	Symptoms/ Clinical Manifestations1	Prophylaxis/ Treatment	Direct Person-to-Person Aerosol Transmission?	Infective Dose
			Bacterial Agents			
Anthrax (*Bacillus anthracis*)	High	1–6	Fever, malaise, and fatigue, which may be followed by an improvement in symptoms for 2–3 days. Alternatively, initial symptoms may progress directly to severe respiratory distress, shock, pneumonia. Death normally follows within 24–36 hours of initiation of symptoms. >90% fatality if untreated.	Vaccine is available. Treatable with high dose of antibiotics administered before onset of symptoms.	No	8,000–50,000 spores
Brucellosis (*Brucella suis*)	Low, incapacitating	5–60	Fever, chills, headache, nausea, weight loss, malaise. Symptoms may last for weeks or months. Fatalities in less than 5% of untreated patients.	No vaccine. Treatable with antibiotics.	No	10–100 organisms
Cholera (*Vibrio cholerae*)	Moderate	1–5	Severe gastroenteritis, diarrhea, vomiting, dehydration. >50% fatality if untreated.	No vaccine. Treatable with antibiotics.	No	10–500 organisms
Glanders (*Burkholderia mallei*)	High	3–5	Fever, sweats, muscle pain, headache, chest pain, and generalized papular/pustular eruptions. >50% fatality rate without treatment. Death in 7–10 days.	No vaccine.	Low	Assumed low

(Table continues on the following page.)

Table 4.1: (continued)

Biological Warfare Agent (Causative Organism)	Lethality	Incubation Period (Days)	Symptoms/ Clinical Manifestations1	Prophylaxis/ Treatment	Direct Person-to-Person Aerosol Transmission?	Infective Dose
Tularemia (*Francisella tularensis*) (rabbit fever or deer-fly fever)	Moderate	2–10	Fever, exhaustion, headache, muscle ache, and weight loss. 30–60% fatality if untreated.	Vaccine is available. Treatable with antibiotics.	No	10–50 organisms
Typhoid fever (*Salmonella typhi*)	Low, incapacitating	7–14	Fever, headache, rose-colored spots on skin, constipation, fatigue. 10–20% fatality if untreated.	Vaccine is available. Treatable with antibiotics.	No	10,000,000 organisms
Plague (Pneumonic) (*Yersinia pestis*)	High	2–3	Pneumonia with malaise, high fever, chills, headache, muscle pain, and productive cough with bloody sputum. Progresses rapidly, resulting in shortness of breath, stridor, bluish discoloration of skin and mucous membranes, and circulatory failure. Death in 1–6 days. 100% fatality if untreated.	Vaccine is available. Treatable if antibiotics are administered within 12–24 hours of onset of symptoms.	Yes, highly infectious	100–500 organisms

Viral Agents

Agent	Lethality	Incubation (days)	Symptoms	Treatment/Vaccine		Infective dose
Smallpox (*Variola major*)	High to moderate	12, on average	Initial symptoms include fever, malaise, vomiting, headache, and backache. Rash and lesions develop in 2–3 days on face, hands, and forearms, followed by the lower extremities and then centrally. 20–40% fatality in unvaccinated individuals.	Vaccine is available.	Yes	10–100 organisms
Venezuelan equine encephalitis (VEE)	Low, incapacitating	2–6	Initial symptoms include general malaise, severe headache, and fever. Nausea, vomiting, cough, and diarrhea may follow. Full recovery usually occurs within 1–2 weeks. Approximately 4% fatality.	Vaccine is available.	No	10–100 organisms
Viral hemorrhagic fevers (RNA viruses from several families, incl.: Filiviridae –Ebola –Marburg Arenaviridae –Lassa –Junin –Machupo Flaviviridae –Yellow Fever Rickertsial Agents	High	4–21	Fever, muscle aches, and exhaustion, vomiting, diarrhea. Can be complicated by easy bleeding, hypotension, flushing of the face and chest, and edema.	No vaccine.[2]	Unclear[3]	1–10 organisms

(*Table continues on the following page.*)

Table 4.1: (continued)

Biological Warfare Agent (Causative Organism)	Lethality	Incubation Period (Days)	Symptoms/Clinical Manifestations1	Prophylaxis/Treatment	Direct Person-to-Person Aerosol Transmission?	Infective Dose
Q Fever (Coxiella burnetti)	Low, incapacitating	14–21	Fever, chills, headache, excessive sweating, malaise, fatigue, loss of appetite, nausea, muscle pain and weight loss. Approximately 1% fatality if untreated.	Vaccine is available. Treatable with antibiotics.	No	1–10 organisms
Epidemic typhus/Endemic typhus (Rickettsia typhil Rickettsia prowazekii)	High	6–16	Fever, headache, weakness, pain, and delirium. 30% fatality rate if untreated. 10–40% fatality if treated.	No vaccine.	No	–
Toxins						
Saxitoxin (paralytic shellfish poisoning)	High	Minutes to hours	Dizziness, numbness, paralysis of respiratory system, followed by death.	No vaccine	No	2–9 micrograms per kilogram of body weight if ingested.
Botulinum toxin (Clostridium botulinum)	High	1–3	Ptosis, generalized weakness, dizziness, dry mouth, blurred vision, and difficulty in speaking and swallowing, Interruption of	Vaccine is available. Treatable with antibiotics if administered early.	No	.001 mg/kg of body weight, if inhaled. 1 mg/kg

Agent	Lethality	Incubation	Signs and symptoms	Vaccine	Transmissible	Lethal dose
			neurotransmission, progression to muscle paralysis and respiratory failure. 65% fatality if untreated.			if ingested.
Ricin (*Ricinus communis*) (castor beans)	High	18–24 hours	Weakness, fever, cough, and pulmonary edema. Progression to severe respiratory distress, hemorrhage, and death within 36–72 hours.	No vaccine.	No	3 mg/kg of body weight, if ingested. (Two castor beans have been fatal to humans.)
Trichothecene (T–2) mcotoxins (*Fusarium tricinetum*)	High to moderate	1–4 hours	Dizziness, nausea, vomiting, blisters, eye pain, necrosis of tissues, hemorrhage, followed by death.	No vaccine.	No	25–50 mg/kg of body weight if inhaled, and 2.4–8 mg/kg through dermal contact.
Staphylococcal enterotoxin B (*Staphylococcus aureus*)	Low, incapacitating	1–6 hours	Sudden onset of fever, chills, headache, muscle pain, nonproductive cough, diarrhea, vomiting, and stomach pain. Fever may last for 2–5 days. Cough may persist for 4 weeks. < 2% fatality rate.	No vaccine	No	.03 mg/kg per person

(Table continues on the following page.)

Table 4.1: (continued)

Sources

Centers for Disease Control and Prevention. *Biological Diseases*. Available at www.bt.cdc.gov/Agent/Agentlist.asp.

Department of the Army. *Textbook of Military Medicine: Medical Aspects of Chemical and Biological Warfare*. Washington, D.C.: Office of the Surgeon General, Borden Institute, 1997. Available at ccc.apgea.army.mil/reference_materials/textbook/HTML_Restricted/index_2.htm.

Departments of the Army, Navy and Air Force. "Annex C: Potential Biological Agents Operational Data Charts." *NATO Handbook on Medical Aspects of NBC Defensive Operations*. AmedP-6(B), part 2, Biological. Washington, D.C., 1996. Available at www.fas.org/nuke/guide/usa/doctrine/dod/fm8-9/2toc.htm.

Federal Emergency Management Agency. *Characteristics and Safety Precautions: Biological and Chemical Agents*. Rapid Response Information System Contents. Available at www.rris.fema.gov/contents.htm#chemagents.

Harry L. Stimson Center. *Chemical and Biological Weapons: Biological Weapons Agents*. Washington, D.C. Available at www.stimson.org/cwc/bwagent.htm.

Chin, James, ed. *Control of Communicable Diseases Manual*. 17th ed. (Washington, D.C.: American Public Health Association, 2000).

Mitretek Systems, *Background on Biological Warfare*. Available at www.mitretek.org/mission/envene/biological/bio_back.html.

Office of the Secretary of Defense. *Anthrax Vaccine Immunization Program*. Available at www.anthrax.osd.mil/Flash_interface/default.html.

Sidell, Frederick R., William C. Patrick, and Thomas R. Dashiell. *Jane's Chem-Bio Handbook*. Alexandria: Jane's Information Group, 1998.

U.S. Army Medical Research Institute of Infectious Diseases. *Medical Management of Biological Casualties Handbook*. 4th ed. February 2001. Available at www.nbc-med.org/SiteContent/HomePage/WhatsNew/MedManual/Feb01/handbook.htm.

Notes

1. Symptoms and clinical manifestations apply to the inhalation of the causative organism.

2. Licensed vaccine is available for yellow fever. A vaccine for Argentine hemorrhagic fever is available as an investigational new drug. This vaccine may provide cross protection against Bolivian hemorrhagic fever.

3. It is unclear how easily filoviruses can be transmitted from human to human. Transmission clearly occurs by direct contact with infected blood, secretions, organs, or semen. Research suggests that the transmission of viruses such as Marburg and Ebola by inhalation is possible, yet consistent evidence has not yet been found.

Table 4.2: **Examples of Chemical Warfare Agents**

Nerve Agents	
NAME AND AGENT IDENTIFICATION	Tabun (GA) Sarin (GB) Soman (GD) Cyclohexyl sarin (GF) VX
MECHANISM OF ACTION	These agents can be absorbed through any body surface: eyes, skin, and respiratory tract. The agents effectively prevent the transmission of nerve signals by inhibiting the enzyme cholinesterase. This enzyme normally breaks down acetylcholine, the neurotransmitter at cholinergic receptor sites. Cholinergic receptor sites are found at smooth and skeletal muscles, the central nervous system, and most exocrine glands. Accumulation of acetylcholine leads to continued stimulation and clinical symptoms such as muscle paralysis.
RATE OF ACTION	*Vapor:* within seconds to several minutes after exposure *Liquid:* within minutes to an hour after exposure. Commonly, there is an asymptomatic period of 1–30 minutes, which is followed by a sudden onset of symptoms.
EFFECTIVE DOSE	*Skin contact:* Tabun (GA), 1,000 mg; Sarin (GB), 1,700 mg; Soman (GD), 50 mg; Cyclohexyl sarin (GF), 30 mg; VX, 10 mg *Inhalation:* (2–10 minutes' exposure): Tabun (GA), 200 mg; Sarin (GB), 70–100 mg; Soman (GD), 70 mg; Cyclohexyl sarin (GF), 75–120 mg; VX, 30 mg
SYMPTOMS	*Vapor:* SMALL EXPOSURE: contraction of pupils, dim vision, headache, mild difficulty breathing LARGE EXPOSURE: sudden loss of consciousness, convulsions, muscular twitching, weakness or paralysis, copious secretions, respiratory failure *Liquid on skin:* SMALL TO MODERATE EXPOSURE: localized sweating, muscle twitching at site of exposure, vomiting, feeling of weakness LARGE EXPOSURE: sudden loss of consciousness, convulsions, muscle twitching, weakness or paralysis, copious secretions, respiratory failure

(Table continues on the following page.)

Table 4.2: (continued)

Vesicants	
NAME AND AGENT IDENTIFICATION	Mustard (H, HD) Lewisite (L) Phosgene oxime (CX)
MECHANISM OF ACTION	Following absorption, the structure of mustard changes. In this form, it is extremely reactive to water and binds with intra- and extracellular enzymes and proteins. Mustard can destroy a large number of cellular substances, thereby influencing numerous processes in living tissue. Lewisite causes an increase in capillary permeability. The exact mechanisms of mustard, lewisite, and phosgene oxime are not known. Phosgene oxime is not a true vesicant; it causes extensive tissue damage and has therefore been called a corrosive agent.
RATE OF ACTION	*Mustard:* binds irreversibly to tissue within several minutes after contact. Clinical signs and symptoms may appear as early as 2 hours after a high-dose exposure or extend to 24 hours after a low-dose vapor exposure. Exposure does not cause immediate pain. *Lewisite:* immediate pain or irritation. Lesions develop within hours. *Phosgene oxime:* Immediate burning and irritation.
EFFECTIVE DOSE	*Skin contact:* Mustard (H, HD), 100 mg/kg; Lewisite (L), 2.8 g *Inhalation:* (2–10 minutes' exposure): Mustard (H, HD), 1,500 mg; Lewisite (L), 1,200–1,500 mg
SYMPTOMS	*Mustard:* Skin, eyes, and airways most commonly affected. Appearance of redness and blisters on skin, irritation, conjunctivitis and corneal opacity and damage in the eyes, irritation of nares, sinus and pharynx, and increasingly severe productive cough if the lower airways are affected. *Lewisite:* Skin and mucous membranes are immediately affected after contact. Redness and blister formation occur more rapidly than following exposure to mustard. Eye exposure causes pain and twitching of the eyelid. Edema of the conjunctiva and lids follow, and eyes may be swollen shut within an hour. Contact with airways leads to similar

	signs and symptoms to mustard. Increased permeability of capillaries resulting in low intravascular volume and shock. May lead to hepatic or renal necrosis with vomiting and diarrhea.
	Phosgene oxime: Redness of skin and appearance of elongated, wheal-like lesions on skin. Damage to eyes similar to that caused by lewisite. Causes pulmonary edema. No other chemical agent produces such immediate onset of symptoms followed by rapid tissue necrosis.
Blood Gases	
NAME AND AGENT IDENTIFICATION	Hydrocyanic acid (AC) Cyanogen chloride (CK)
MECHANISM OF ACTION	Blood gases allow red blood cells to acquire oxygen, but prevent the transfer of this oxygen to other cells. Cyanide ion combines with iron in a component of the mitochondrial cytochrome oxidase complex. This complex is necessary for cellular respiration, an energy-providing process using oxygen. The heart and brain rapidly decay from lack of oxygen and a buildup of carbon dioxide.
RATE OF ACTION	Death occurs 6–8 minutes after inhalation.
EFFECTIVE DOSE	*Skin Contact:* Hydrocyanic acid (AC), 1.1 mg/kg Cyanogen chloride (CK), 200 mg/kg
	Inhalation: (2–10 minutes' exposure): Hydrocyanic acid (AC), 2,500–5000 mg; Cyanogen chloride (CK), 11,000 mg
SYMPTOMS	Central nervous system and heart are most susceptible to cyanide. Fifteen seconds after inhalation of a highly concentrated vapor, there is a period of rapid breathing that is followed in 15–30 seconds by convulsions. Respiratory activity stops 2 3 minutes later, followed by cessation of cardiac activity. Cyanogen chloride also irritates the eyes, nose, and airways.
Pulmonary Agents	
NAME AND AGENT IDENTIFICATION	Chlorine (Cl) Phosgene (CG)
MECHANISM OF ACTION	Pulmonary agents attack lung tissue. Phosgene irritates the alveoli in the lungs and results in the constant secretion of fluids into the lungs. Death results from a lack of oxygen when the lungs are filled with fluid.

(Table continues on the following page.)

Table 4.2: (continued)

RATE OF ACTION	*Chlorine:* Immediate cough and choking sensation. Signs of pulmonary edema may appear within 30 minutes to 4 hours. *Phosgene:* Cough and chest discomfort may appear within 30 minutes of exposure. Pulmonary edema within 2–6 hours. Occasionally, an asymptomatic period can last up to 24 hours.
EFFECTIVE DOSE	*Inhalation:* (2–10 minutes' exposure): Chlorine (Cl), 6,651 ppm/min: Phosgene (CG), 3,200 mg
SYMPTOMS	Corrosion of the eyes, skin, and respiratory tract. Burning sensation in the lungs, choking, coughing, headache, difficulty breathing, nausea, vomiting, sore throat, skin burns, and blurred vision. Accumulation of fluid in lungs leads to fatal choking and pulmonary edema.

SOURCES

Centers for Disease Control and Prevention. *Chemical Agents Listing and Information*. Available at www.bt.cdc.gov/Agent/AgentlistChem.asp.

Department of the Army. *Textbook of Military Medicine: Medical Aspects of Chemical and Biological Warfare*. Office of the Surgeon General. Washington, D.C.: Borden Institute, 1997. Available at ccc.apgea.army.mil/reference_materials/textbook/HTML_Restricted/index_2.htm.

Federal Emergency Management Agency. *Characteristics and Safety Precautions: Biological and Chemical Agents*. Rapid Response Information System Contents. Available at www.rris.fema.gov/contents.htm#chemagents.

Harry L. Stimson Center. *Chemical and Biological Weapons: Chemical Weapons Issues*. Available at www.stimson.org/cwc/cwissues.htm.

Organization for the Prohibition of Chemical Weapons. *An Overview of Chemicals Defined as Chemical Weapons*. Available at www.opcw.org/resp/html/cwagents.html.

CHEMICAL WEAPON STATUS 2002

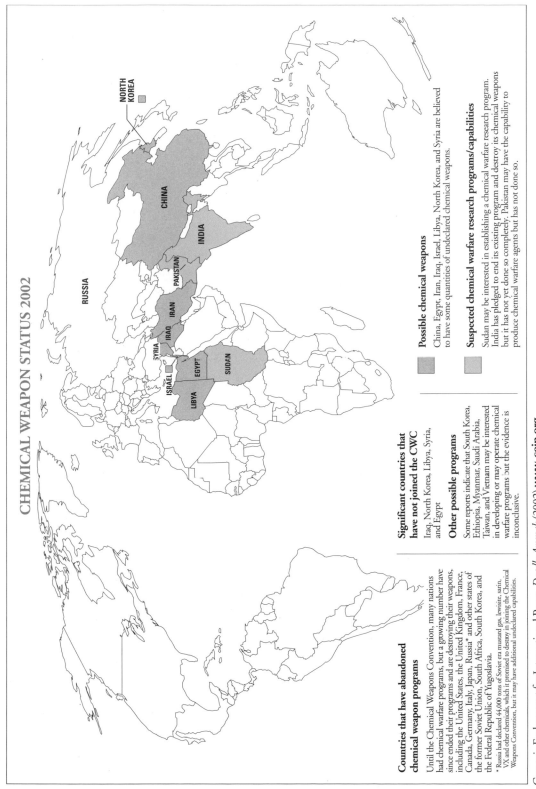

NORTH KOREA

RUSSIA

CHINA

INDIA

PAKISTAN

IRAN

IRAQ

SYRIA

ISRAEL

EGYPT

LIBYA

SUDAN

Countries that have abandoned chemical weapon programs

Until the Chemical Weapons Convention, many nations had chemical warfare programs, but a growing number have since ended their programs and are destroying their weapons, including the United States, the United Kingdom, France, Canada, Germany, Italy, Japan, Russia* and other states of the former Soviet Union, South Africa, South Korea, and the Federal Republic of Yugoslavia.

* Russia had declared 44,000 tons of Soviet era mustard gas, lewisite, sarin, VX and other chemicals, which it promised to destroy in joining the Chemical Weapons Convention, but it may have additional undeclared capabilities.

Significant countries that have not joined the CWC

Iraq, North Korea, Libya, Syria, and Egypt

Other possible programs

Some reports indicate that South Korea, Ethiopia, Myanmar, Saudi Arabia, Taiwan, and Vietnam may be interested in developing or may operate chemical warfare programs but the evidence is inconclusive.

Possible chemical weapons

China, Egypt, Iran, Iraq, Israel, Libya, North Korea, and Syria are believed to have some quantities of undeclared chemical weapons.

Suspected chemical warfare research programs/capabilities

Sudan may be interested in establishing a chemical warfare research program. India has pledged to end its existing program and destroy its chemical weapons but it has not yet done so completely. Pakistan may have the capability to produce chemical warfare agents but has not done so.

Carnegie Endowment for International Peace, *Deadly Arsenals* (2002) **www.ceip.org**

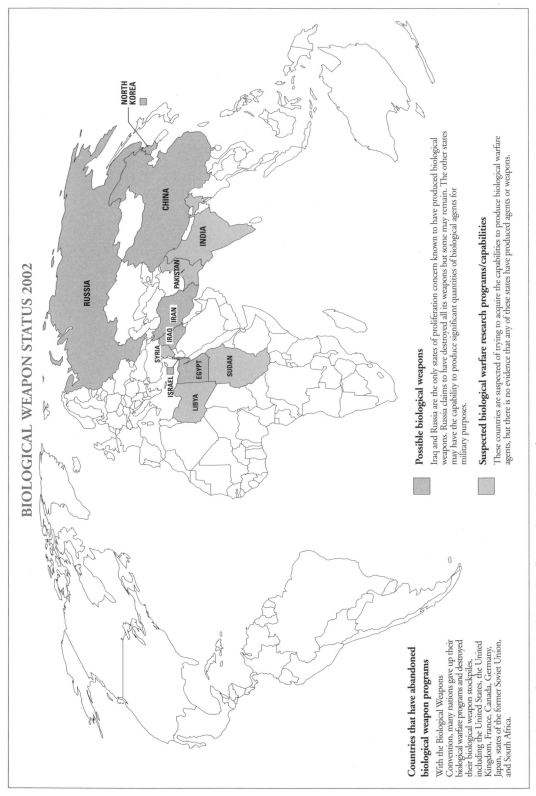

BIOLOGICAL WEAPON STATUS 2002

Possible biological weapons

Iraq and Russia are the only states of proliferation concern known to have produced biological weapons. Russia claims to have destroyed all its weapons but some may remain. The other states may have the capability to produce significant quantities of biological agents for military purposes.

Suspected biological warfare research programs/capabilities

These countries are suspected of trying to acquire the capabilities to produce biological warfare agents, but there is no evidence that any of these states have produced agents or weapons.

Countries that have abandoned biological weapon programs

With the Biological Weapons Convention, many nations gave up their biological warfare programs and destroyed their biological weapon stockpiles, including the United States, the United Kingdom, France, Canada, Germany, Japan, states of the former Soviet Union, and South Africa.

Carnegie Endowment for International Peace, *Deadly Arsenals* (2002), **www.ceip.org**

CHAPTER 5

Missile Proliferation

One of the most important proliferation debates of the past ten years has concerned the assessment of the ballistic missile threat and efforts to deploy missile defenses. When the end of the Cold War largely eliminated the likelihood (if not the capability) of a global thermonuclear war, policy makers turned their attention to the very real danger that weapons of mass destruction could be used in smaller, but still horrifically deadly, numbers. Ballistic missiles garnered the lion's share of attention, though they constitute only one—and perhaps the most difficult—delivery method for those weapons.

The Proliferation Threat

Many experts and officials view ballistic missiles as a particularly menacing, difficult-to-detect, and rapidly proliferating technology. Several threat assessments and reports followed the lead of the 1998 study by the Commission to Assess the Ballistic Missile Threat to the United States (known as the Rumsfeld Commission for its chair, Donald Rumsfeld):

> With the external help now readily available, a nation with a well-developed, Scud-based ballistic missile infrastructure would be able to achieve first flight of a long range missile, up to and including intercontinental ballistic missile (ICBM) range (greater than 5,500 kilometers), within about five years of deciding to do so. During several of those years the U.S. might not be aware that such a decision had been made.[1]

The commission identified two countries as being particularly dangerous: North Korea and Iran.

> The extraordinary level of resources that North Korea and Iran are now devoting to developing their own ballistic missile capabilities poses a substantial and immediate danger to the U.S., its vital interests and its allies. While these nations' missile programs may presently be aimed primarily at regional adversaries, they inevitably and inescapably engage the vital interests of the U.S. as well. . . . Each of these nations places a high priority on threatening U.S. territory, and each is even now pursuing advanced ballistic missile capabilities to pose a direct threat to U.S. territory.[2]

Andrew Krepps, a Junior Fellow with the Non-Proliferation Project at the Carnegie Endowment for International Peace, is co-author of this chapter.

The August 31, 1998, North Korean test of a Taepo Dong I missile/space launch vehicle (SLV) appeared to lend credence to these warnings. The Taepo Dong I failed in its attempt to launch a satellite into orbit and flew only 1,320 kilometers, but it had an enormous impact internationally due to the unexpected use of a third stage on the rocket. As a result of this test and the changing strategic environment, the 1999 National Intelligence Estimate (NIE) included countries other than Russia and China for the first time as ballistic missile threats to the United States. This expanded assessment was used again in the 2001 NIE as well. The most recent NIE concluded that by 2015 the United States

> most likely will face ICBM threats from North Korea and Iran, and possibly Iraq—barring significant changes in their political orientations—in addition to the strategic forces of Russia and China. One agency assesses that the United States is unlikely to face an ICBM threat from Iran before 2015. The threats to the U.S. homeland, nevertheless, will consist of dramatically fewer warheads than today owing to significant reductions in Russian strategic forces. China has been modernizing its long-range strategic missile force since the 1980s. . . . By 2015, the total number of Chinese strategic warheads will rise several-fold, though it will remain still well below the number of Russian or U.S. forces.[3]

Significantly—perhaps reflecting the experiences of September 11—the assessment notes that "U.S. territory is more likely to be attacked with these [chemical, biological, radiological, and nuclear] materials from nonmissile delivery means—most likely from terrorists—than by missiles, primarily because nonmissile delivery means are less costly, easier to acquire, and more reliable and accurate. They can also be used without attribution."[4] The report also cautioned:

> Our assessments of future missile developments are inexact and subjective because they are based on often fragmentary information. . . . States with emerging missile programs inevitably will run into problems that will delay and frustrate their desired development timelines. The impact of these problems increases with the lack of maturity of the program and depends on the level of foreign assistance. Most emerging missile states are highly dependent on foreign assistance at this stage of their development efforts, and disturbance of the technology and information flow to their programs will have discernible short-term effects.[5]

Still, the Quadrennial Defense Review presented to Congress from the Department of Defense on October 1, 2001, argues that "in particular, the pace and scale of recent ballistic missile proliferation has exceeded earlier intelligence estimates and suggests these challenges may grow at a faster pace than previously expected."[6] To compare more completely today's ballistic missile threats to those of the past and to perform a net assessment of the global ballistic missile threat, it is useful to evaluate the threat in its component parts.

Global Ballistic Missile Arsenals

The blurring of short, medium, intermediate, and intercontinental ranges of the world's missile inventory often results in a misinterpretation of the oft-quoted assessment that more than 25 nations possess ballistic missiles. This statement is true, but only China, Russia, and the United States possess the ability to launch nuclear warheads on land-based intercontinental missiles. This has not changed since Russia and China deployed their first ICBMs in 1959 and 1981, respectively.[7] An analysis of global ballistic missile arsenals shows that there are fewer ICBMs, long-range submarine-launched ballistic missiles (SLBMs), and intermediate-range ballistic missiles in the world today than there were during the Cold War. The total number of medium-range ballistic missiles has also decreased, though five new countries have developed or acquired MRBMs since 1989. The number of countries with short-range ballistic missiles (SRBMs) has increased over the past 20 years. Thus, the most accurate way to summarize existing global ballistic missile capabilities is to say that there is a widespread capability to launch short-range missiles. There is a slowly growing, but still limited, capability to launch medium-range missiles. Most important, there are a decreasing number of long-range missiles remaining from the stockpile levels of the Cold War, a fact that is often overlooked.

Long-Range Ballistic Missiles

Force reductions in U.S. and Russian arsenals have dramatically decreased the number of long-range ballistic missiles (missiles with a range of greater than 5,500 kilometers) in the world from their Cold War levels. In 1987, the Soviet Union deployed 2,380 long-range missiles in its combined ICBM and SLBM arsenals.[8] The United States deployed 1,640 long-range missiles.[9] At the end of 2001, Russia had 1,022 long-range missiles,[10] and the United States had 983 long-range missiles.[11] France has reduced its total nuclear arsenal but now has 48 long-range SLBMs that it did not have in 1987.[12] Similarly, the United Kingdom has reduced its arsenal but now holds the title to 58 long-range Trident SLBMs that it did not have in 1987.[13] During this period China has maintained a force of about 20 Dong Feng–5 ICBMs.[14] No other country has

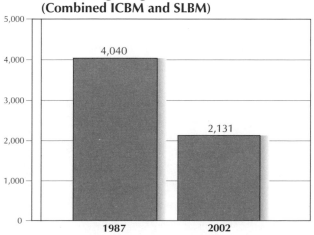

Global Long-Range Ballistic Missile Arsenals (Combined ICBM and SLBM)

developed an ICBM or long-range SLBM during this time. By the beginning of 2002 the total number of long-range ballistic missiles in the world had decreased 47 percent, to 2,131 from the 4,040 that were deployed in 1987.[15]

Intermediate-Range Ballistic Missiles

Intermediate-range ballistic missile arsenals have undergone even more dramatic reductions. The Intermediate-range Nuclear Forces Treaty eliminated this entire class of missiles (with ranges of 3,000 to 5,500 kilometers) from the Soviet/Russian arsenal over a three-year period.[16] Final INF inspections took place on May 31, 2001, verifying the destruction of 660 intermediate-range Soviet ballistic missiles.[17] In 1987 France deployed 18 land-based IRBMs and 32 submarine-based IRBMs, which it has since deactivated and destroyed. China has maintained about 20 DF–4 missiles of this range, and no other nation has developed an IRBM, effectively reducing the current number of IRBMs by 97 percent from Cold War levels.

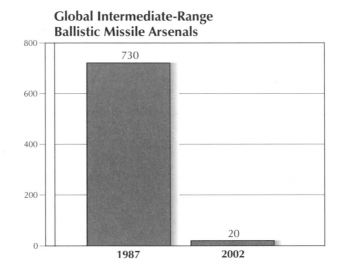

Global Intermediate-Range Ballistic Missile Arsenals

Medium-Range Ballistic Missiles

The broad scope of the INF Treaty also covered medium-range ballistic missiles. Thus, the treaty resulted in the elimination of this class of missile (with a range of 1,000 to 3,000 kilometers) from Soviet/Russian and U.S. ballistic missile arsenals. A total of 149 Russian SS–4 and 234 U.S. Pershing II missiles were destroyed under this treaty.[18] Outside of the treaty, France also eliminated 64 medium-range SLBMs that it possessed in 1987.

The most significant proliferation threat comes from the slow but steady increase in the number of states possessing medium-range ballistic missiles, even though Russia and the United States eliminated their arsenals. This development has attracted great attention and is often cited as evidence of a larger proliferation threat than before. China, India, Iran, Israel, Pakistan, North

Korea, and Saudi Arabia now possess MRBMs. China also possesses a medium-range SLBM capability, although its operational status is in question.[19] Only India, Iran, North Korea, and Pakistan have developed or obtained their missiles since 1989, and of these countries all but India's missiles are based primarily on assistance or technology received from North Korea or China.

Numerically speaking, even though MRBMs are now in the hands of more countries than in 1987, the total number of MRBMs in existence in 2002 is lower than the 547 MRBMs in the combined Chinese, Russian, French, and U.S. forces in 1987.[20] Since then, Israel is believed to have deployed 50 operational Jericho II MRBMs,[21] while Saudi Arabia has deployed 40 CSS–2 MRBMs that it purchased from China.[22] North Korea is believed to have deployed ten No Dong MRBMs,[23] but it has possibly produced up to 100 missiles of this type.[24] MRBMs in India, Iran, and Pakistan and North Korea's Taepo Dong are still in operational testing. Assuming that each of these countries could deploy one to five missiles in a crisis over the next five years, the global total of MRBMs in existence is approximately 310. This represents a 43 percent decrease in global MRBM arsenals from the 1987 level.

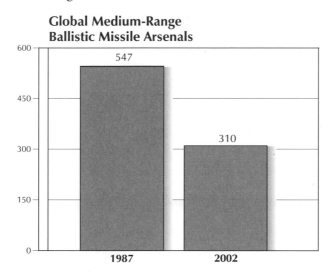

Global Medium-Range Ballistic Missile Arsenals

Short-Range Ballistic Missiles

In addition to the five recognized nuclear-weapon states, there are 30 nations that have ballistic missiles. Of these 30 nations, 24 only have missiles with ranges under 1,000 kilometers. Twenty-two nations only have missiles with an approximate range of 300 kilometers or less. Many of these missiles are old Scud–B systems that have not been well-maintained, and therefore are declining in military utility.

Countries with Ballistic Missile Programs

Another factor by which proliferation can be measured is the number of states with missile development programs. The number of countries with ballistic missile development programs has also decreased from the number of countries pursuing missile development programs during the Cold War. In addition to the five recognized nuclear-weapon states, countries such as Argentina, Brazil, Egypt, India, Iraq, Israel, Libya, and South Africa had programs to develop long-range or medium-range missiles in 1987. By 2002, Argentina, Brazil, Egypt, and South Africa had abandoned their programs, and Libya's remains largely defunct.

Today, the nations that are pursuing long-range missile development programs are also smaller, poorer, and less technologically advanced than were the nations with missile programs 15 years ago. The U.S. threat assessments, such as recent National Intelligence Estimates, note that Iran and North Korea currently have active ballistic missile development programs. With U.N. inspections (now suspended) and sanctions against it, Iraq faces many hurdles to reviving its program. Syria and South Korea have active short-range ballistic missile programs but have not yet demonstrated an interest in or the capability to produce MRBMs. Egypt and Libya may be pursuing purchases of MRBMs (from North Korea) but do not appear to have active development programs. Thus, even with the inclusion of India and Pakistan, the recent NIEs highlight the limited nature of the missile proliferation threat, one that is confined to a few countries whose political evolution will be a determining factor in whether they remain threats to global security.

In South Asia and the Middle East, strategic interest and political dynamics have fueled the continued development of ballistic missile technology as both a means of gaining international prestige as well as obtaining a strategic advantage vis-à-vis regional rivals. Though somewhat limited, this proliferation and the transfer of ballistic missile technology originating in North Korea and China continue to destabilize both regional and global security.

Table 5.1: Countries with Active Ballistic Missile Development Programs over 1,000-km Range*

1987	2002
Argentina	India
Brazil	Iran
Egypt	Iraq
India	Israel
Iraq	North Korea
Israel	Pakistan
Libya	
South Africa	

* Excludes NPT nuclear-weapon states China, France, Russia, and the United States. All of these countries had developed ballistic missiles with ranges greater than 1,000 km by 1987 and were continuing indigenous programs to develop and deploy new missiles that exceeded this range.

Technical Background

Ballistic Missiles, Cruise Missiles, and Unmanned Aerial Vehicles

A ballistic missile is a guided rocket that is powered during the initial part of its flight and then coasts without power—mostly above the atmosphere—along a ballistic path to its target. A cruise missile is an aerodynamic system with jet or rocket propulsion that is powered all the way to its target. An unmanned aerial vehicle (UAV) is a remotely piloted or self-controlled aircraft that can carry cameras, sensors, communications equipment, and other payloads. UAVs are generally powered either by jet or propeller engines.

Ballistic missiles travel at hypersonic speeds, allowing little warning time and making defense difficult. Since the Cold War, ballistic missiles have been considered the most threatening delivery vehicles for nuclear weapons. In the 1988 War of the Cities between Iran and Iraq and in the 1991 Gulf War, Scud ballistic missiles came into prominence with conventional (high-explosive) warheads, and with the threat of chemical and biological warheads. As a result, many commentators interpreted the missile threat to be one of ballistic missiles alone.

Yet cruise missiles are now recognized as a rapidly growing and particularly dangerous proliferation threat. Cruise missile guidance for attacking distant land targets used to be such an expensive and sophisticated technology that, for most countries, cruise missiles could be used with only terminal homing against ships. The past few years, however, have seen the universal availability of inexpensive satellite navigation (the U.S. Global Positioning System and the Russian Glonass), which allows cruise missiles to attack land targets with 100-meter accuracy now and an expected 5-meter (or better) accuracy within ten years.

This accuracy greatly exceeds that available from all but the most sophisticated ballistic missiles. The Scud, for example, is accurate on the order of 1,000 meters, making it ineffective against discrete military targets except with nuclear, biological, or chemical warheads, which cause damage over wide areas. With the high accuracy of cruise missiles, which has already been demonstrated by U.S. Tomahawks, even high-explosive warheads are reliable in destroying their targets. Moreover, compared with ballistic missiles, cruise missiles are:

- cheaper, quicker, and easier to build, and increasingly available on world markets. The Chinese Silkworm, which is already widely disseminated, produced by a number of regional powers, and easily extended in range, may become the Scud of cruise missiles. A proliferator can now acquire many cruise missiles quickly.

- easier to launch from planes and ships. This makes it easier for cruise missiles to reach targets far from an attacker's homeland. It would be possible to use a ship-launched cruise missile to attack North American targets, for example.

- more effective for disseminating chemical and biological agents. Because a cruise missile can release chemical and biological agents in a gradual and controlled fashion (as opposed to a wasteful burst of agent or submunitions with a ballistic missile), each cruise missile can adjust its attack to local conditions, creating a lethal area coverage that is some ten times as great as that from a ballistic missile. With chemical and biological agents being cheaper and more available than nuclear weapons, and with cruise missiles being more affordable than ballistic missiles, cruise missiles with chemical or biological warheads may become more widespread threats than ballistic missiles.

- difficult to defend against. Ballistic missiles (except for the most sophisticated) coast along an observable and predictable path, but cruise missiles can weave around, fly low following the contours of the earth, and attack targets from any direction. Advanced cruise missiles such as the U.S. Tactical Tomahawk cruise missile can now be reprogrammed in flight, allowing the cruise missile to loiter over a battlefield until given a target. In some cases cruise missiles need not fly directly over their targets; they can disseminate chemical and biological agents from a distance upwind. Further, cruise missiles can be small and stealthy. All these factors make cruise missiles difficult to find in flight and therefore difficult to shoot down.

Unmanned aerial vehicles offer many capabilities that are similar to those of cruise missiles, and recent developments in UAV technology demonstrate their rapidly increasing military utility. Though not yet widely used as offensive weapons, UAVs are proving capable of carrying heavier payloads and flying longer distances for extended periods. The April 2001 trans-Pacific flight of the U.S. Global Hawk UAV nonstop from the United States to Australia demonstrated the long-range capabilities of these machines. The Global Hawk, which is capable of carrying a 900-kilogram payload and cruising at a maximum altitude of 19,800 meters, can travel a distance of 2,300 kilometers and survey a given area for 36 hours while preserving the capability to return to its initial base 2,300 kilometers away. The range of the Global Hawk increases if operators change the flight surveillance time of a given mission.

As noted, UAVs are currently used primarily for intelligence and reconnaissance missions. The weaponization of UAVs into unmanned combat aerial vehicles (UCAVs), however, is also progressing. The United States deployed a version of its Predator UAV armed with Hellfire missiles in the war in Afghanistan. The United States has also begun experiments to arm UAVs with "flying plate" weapons that can destroy concrete and steel structures; high-temperature incendiary devices that can create firestorms inextinguishable with water; and "smart" bombs that are capable of penetrating 1.5 meters of concrete.[25] Most important, UAVs could simply be used in the same fashion as cruise missiles, to deliver conventional, chemical, biological, or nuclear payloads. Like their cruise missile counterparts, armed UAVs are easier to launch than ballistic missiles, could be used to disseminate biological or chemical agents more effectively than ballistic missiles, can be recalled and retargeted, and would be difficult to defend against once launched. When developed, basic UAV platforms can be produced to provide a state or group with both armed and unarmed versions, giving a state or actor the capability to expand both its reconnaissance capability and long-range strike capability at the same time. If, for example, the United States were to deploy a missile defense system, China could respond by developing a large fleet of UAVs, providing a nuclear-strike capability difficult to detect by radar that also flies beneath the interceptor ranges of the system.

The operational effectiveness of UAVs, however, is still an issue. While there have been many reports of the use of UAVs in Kosovo and Afghanistan, there is little public information on their effectiveness or, in the case of the Hellfire equipped Predators, their kill rates. The director of the Pentagon's Operational Test and Evaluation noted in a 2001 report, "As tested, the Predator UAV system is not operationally effective or suitable. . . . Poor target location accuracy, ineffective communications, and limits imposed by relatively benign weather, including rain, negatively impact missions such as strike support, combat search and rescue, area search, and continuous coverage."[26]

The production and use of UAVs are already widespread. According to the U.S. Department of Defense, 32 nations manufacture more than 150 models of UAVs, and 55 countries operate some 80 different types of these vehicles.[27] Although many of the UAVs produced and deployed by other nations are no more than cameras attached to jet engines, France, Israel, and Italy possess medium-range, long-endurance UAVs. What is perhaps more alarming is that the current non-proliferation and export-control regime seems unprepared to handle UAV transfers. Unarmed UAVs become armed UAVs simply by changing their payload, meaning that an unarmed UAV purchased for one stated purpose could easily be converted into a weapon. In terms of their classification under the Missile Technology Control Regime (MTCR), analyst Dennis Gormely notes that, unlike ballistic missiles, precise data on the one-way range and payload tradeoff for most UAVs are not readily available. One study cited by Gormely found that more than 80 percent of unarmed UAVs appear capable of exceeding the MTCR's 300-kilometer range Category I threshold.[28]

Range: Payload Tradeoffs

One technical feature of both ballistic and cruise missiles is critical for understanding missile non-proliferation. It is the ability to make tradeoffs between range and payload. Iraq demonstrated this tradeoff in 1987 by reducing the 1,000-kilogram payload of the 300-kilometer range Scud–B, helping to create the Al Hussein missile with twice the range, enough to reach Tehran.[29] Because the MTCR places special restrictions on missiles capable of delivering a 500-kilogram payload to a range of 300 kilometers, some exporters have tried to ignore the range–payload tradeoff. China, for example, once claimed that its M–11 missile, which is capable of delivering an 850-kilogram payload to a range of 280 kilometers, did not have an adequate range to be restricted under the MTCR. A slightly lighter payload (well above 500 kilograms), however, would enable the M–11 to travel more than 300 kilometers. In October 1994, China formally recognized the applicability of this tradeoff.[30] (When only ranges are cited in the remainder of this chapter, they apply to the most commonly cited missile payloads.)

Routes to Proliferation

There are a variety of ways for states seeking ballistic or cruise missiles to acquire them. They can attempt to import entire missile systems, or they can try to build them indigenously—normally using imported components and technology. States need not admit that they are building missiles. Space launch vehicles, scientific research rockets, and large defensive missiles use hardware, technology, and production facilities that are interchangeable with those of ballistic missiles. Various types of UAVs—reconnaissance drones, target drones, and remotely piloted vehicles (some with the stated mission of delivering insecticides)—can be converted to cruise missiles. Moreover, anti-ship cruise missiles can be converted to land-attack cruise missiles.

Missiles, especially ballistic missiles, are complex machines. The medium-range U.S. Pershing II ballistic missile, for example, contained 250,000 parts, each of which needed to work right the first time under high levels of acceleration, vibration, heat, and cold. Thus, the development of missiles is an expensive and time-consuming process, often resulting in an unreliable weapon system.

Moreover, the development of ballistic missiles becomes particularly difficult at a range of about 1,000 kilometers. Above that range, the missile must use two more advanced technologies: staging (firing rockets in a series, with the expended rockets reliably jettisoned from the missiles) and more sophisticated reentry vehicles (to keep the warhead in working order during its fiery descent through the atmosphere).[31] Longer ranges also put a premium on more efficient rocket engines, lighter and stronger materials, more advanced guidance systems, and lighter and more advanced warheads (which is a considerable challenge when nuclear warheads are at issue).

These technical difficulties, compounded with the export controls of the MTCR and active diplomatic efforts by the United States and other concerned governments, offer hope for restraining missile proliferation.

The Dangers of Missile Proliferation

From the point of view of a proliferator, missiles have certain generic advantages over manned warplanes:

- Simplicity. A "pushbutton war" with missiles is much easier for the less technically advanced regional powers than is the development of a trained air force with manned aircraft and a large infrastructure.

- Survivability. Airfields have known locations and are large, vulnerable targets beginning in the first minutes of a war. Manned aircraft, which generally operate from airfields, cannot be expected to last long against the United States and its allies. In contrast, hidden or mobile missiles are difficult to find and destroy.

- Defense penetration. Shooting down a ballistic or a cruise missile in flight is still a challenge even for the United States, which has until recently emphasized the role of protecting against manned aircraft for its active defenses.

- Accuracy. Cruise missiles with satellite navigation and some advanced regional ballistic missile systems are highly accurate. In contrast, the bombing accuracy of manned aircraft depends on equipment and pilot training, which can yield variable results.

- Geopolitics. Long-range and ship-launched missiles will diminish the protective effects of distance. They can project the battle to the rear in regional conflicts and some day even to the United States itself.

- Blackmail or coercive diplomacy. The almost immediate ability to threaten to deliver a nuclear, chemical, or biological weapon by means of a ballistic missile can be used to achieve specific strategic or political goals. This threat can complicate the decision making of adversaries in times of crisis.

The use of missiles in regional conflicts has been demonstrated using conventional high-explosive warheads since the 1970s.[32] Egypt fired a Scud at Israel at the end of the 1973 war, which was merely a gesture. Yet in the 1982 Falkland war, Argentina's French-supplied Exocet cruise missiles sunk the British frigate *Sheffield*. In 1986, after a U.S. air raid, Libya fired three Scuds at the Italian island of Lampadusa, missing the island. The terror of missiles, however, was demonstrated in 1988 in the Iran–Iraq War, with Baghdad and Tehran receiving repeated Scud strikes over several weeks. Starting in 1989, the Soviet-backed government of Afghanistan fired more than 2,000 Scuds against rebel forces. In the 1991 Gulf War, some 88 Iraqi Scuds terrorized Israeli civilians and fell around coalition military bases in Saudi Arabia. The overall military effect was negligible in spite of a strike on a U.S. barracks, which killed 28 soldiers. By contrast, in the Gulf War the United States used three times as many Tomahawk and air-launched cruise missiles, which, because of their high accuracy, had significant military effects. Scuds were used again in the 1994 Yemen civil war. In 1995, Serbia used SA-2 air defense missiles in their secondary role as ballistic missiles.[33]

The record to date has been that, with conventional warheads, ballistic missiles cause terror that can affect an adversary's attitudes toward the continuation of a war, and cruise missiles cause significant damage to specific military targets. Yet missiles are not limited to conventional warheads. After the Gulf War, the United Nations Special Commission discovered Iraqi Scud warheads with chemical and biological agents, and Iraqi plans for nuclear warheads,[34] for remotely piloted vehicles to deliver biological agents,[35] and for ballistic missiles with ranges of up to 3,000 kilometers, which are capable of hitting all of Western Europe.[36]

Global Overview

Despite the advantages of ballistic missiles explored here, few countries have developed this technology. As detailed in table 5.2 at the end of this chapter, almost all of the nations that possess ballistic missiles (24 of 35) have only short-range missiles. In many cases (13 of the 24 countries with only SRBMs) these missiles are Scud or similar systems bought or inherited from Russia or the Soviet Union. Though several states possess modified versions of these missiles with ranges up to 700 kilometers, most of these missiles have a range of 300 kilometers or less. In addition to the five recognized nuclear-weapon states, only six countries (India, Iran, Israel, North Korea, Pakistan, and Saudi Arabia) possess ballistic missiles with ranges greater than 1,000 kilometers. The three non-NPT nuclear states (India, Israel, and Pakistan) have developed and continue to improve SRBM and MRBM systems. There is significant potential for all three to develop intermediate-range missiles in the future, though ICBM development is unlikely. The hard cases of Iran, Iraq, and North Korea possess ballistic missile development programs of significant concern, and are often cited as the states most likely to develop ICBM capabilities by 2015. Questions remain about the missile development programs in Egypt, Libya, and Syria. All three countries may have some interest in developing or obtaining systems that exceed their current short-range capabilities; however, for varying reasons none of the countries is likely to develop such systems in the near future. These countries, therefore, are best classified as countries of moderate proliferation risk.

Non-NPT Nuclear Weapon States

INDIA. India has continued its development of both SRBMs and MRBMs by way of expanding its existing launch platforms. These measures have achieved mixed results. Using the single-stage, liquid-propelled Privthi I as a standard platform, India has attempted to develop three versions of an SRBM. The Privthi I is a road-mobile ballistic missile that is deployed by the Indian army. It has a range of 150 kilometers, with a payload of 1,000 kilograms. The Privthi II, under the control of India's air force, has a range of 250 kilometers, with a payload of 500 kilograms. A sea-based version of the Privthi II that is known as the Dhanush has had a checkered past but now appears to have met its testing requirements. Launched from a surface vessel, the Dhanush was unsuccessfully tested in April 2000 but was successfully tested in late September 2001. Following the test, Indian defense ministry officials said that the missile met its test mission objective and would "soon be operationalized" in the navy.[37]

Building upon the Agni I MRBM-capable "technology demonstrator," which it first tested in 1989, India has successfully developed a rail-mobile version of this MRBM called the Agni II. This missile was tested in April 1999 and again in January 2001. The Agni II has a range of 2,000 kilometers, with a 1,000-kilogram payload. India announced in June 2001 that it has begun limited production of the Agni II and will deploy it under the control of the army some time in 2002.[38] Development continues on the Agni III, an IRBM with an expected range of 3,000 kilometers.

India is also continuing development of sea-based ballistic missile capabilities. The progress of this project, known as Sagarika, remains ambiguous. India still does not possess a submarine on which a missile platform can be based, despite having pursued a nuclear submarine project for some twenty years. A Rand study estimates that an Indian SLBM capability is still another 10–20 years away,[39] and the 2001 NIE lists 2010 as the very earliest deployment date.[40]

India has the technical expertise to pursue an ICBM capability. The Indian Space Research Organization has successfully launched both the Polar Space Launch Vehicle (PSLV), and the Geosynchronous Space Launch Vehicle (GSLV), which could serve as a technological springboard for an ICBM capability. The GSLV is particularly noteworthy because it is the first Indian rocket to possess a cryogenic engine. Although the first versions of the GSLV use cryogenic engines supplied by Russia, India has claimed that it is close to having developed a domestic version.[41]

The potential quest for an ICBM lies in the perceived status and prestige attached to possessing an indigenous ICBM capability. One member of India's National Security Advisory Board has written, "In the final analysis, a country's international standing is founded on the reach of the weapons in its armory. . . . While India has certainly boosted its image by going nuclear, it will truly emerge as an international power only when it tests its first ICBM."[42] However, Indian politicians seem to believe that an ICBM is not necessary.[43] It is likely that India will be content with an intercontinental satellite-launch-vehicle capability.[44]

ISRAEL. As the most capable military power in the region, Israel fields both short-range Jericho I (500 kilometers, with a 500-kilogram payload) and medium-range Jericho II (1,500-kilometer) missiles. Both missiles use a solid propellant and are nuclear-capable. Israel's successful satellite launches using the Shavit SLV suggests that Israel could quickly develop missile platforms with much longer ranges than that of the Jericho II. Israel has little need to develop a longer-range missile system, however, because its current capabilities are adequate to provide a strike capability to its potential adversaries. Development of the single-stage Jericho I missile began in the 1960s with French assistance and was first deployed in 1973. Development of the two-stage Jericho II began in the mid-1970s and was first deployed in 1990. The extended range and 1,000-kilogram payload of the Jericho II makes it a likely nuclear delivery vehicle. Both missiles are land- and rail-mobile. Israel is believed to have deployed a total of 100 Jericho missiles. It continues to test the Jericho II, with the last test having taken place in late June 2001.[45]

PAKISTAN. Pakistan has continued its missile development with heavy reliance upon outside suppliers from North Korea and China. This assistance has proved to be beneficial to Pakistan and has accelerated Pakistan's missile programs past those of its neighbor and rival India. Before 2001 Pakistan used a dual-track approach for its ballistic missile development. Competing development projects pitted the liquid-fueled missiles of Khan Research Laboratories against the solid-fueled missiles of the Pakistan Atomic Energy Commission. The two programs have since been consolidated into the Nuclear Defense Complex.

Since 1998, Pakistan has demonstrated progress in both expanding its SRBM arsenal by way of domestic production and in developing MRBMs that provide it with the capability to strike deep into Indian territory. To complement its arsenal of first-and second-generation Hatf missiles, Pakistan also possesses Hatf III SRBMs, which are now recognized to be M–11 missiles acquired from China.[46] Pakistan first tested this solid-fueled missile under the Hatf III name in July 1997, and this acquisition and test may have aided development of the solid-fueled Shaheen I missile. The Shaheen I is a Pakistani-produced, solid-fuel system that was tested in April 1999. It has a range of 750 kilometers and a payload of 500 kilograms. In early 2001, Pakistan announced that the country had begun the "serial production" of the Shaheen I, adding that this missile had been "inducted" into the army.

Pakistan's MRBM development was initially led by the liquid-fueled Ghauri series. United States intelligence sources have finally confirmed long-held speculation that Pakistan's Ghauri I MRBMs are No Dongs acquired from North Korea.[47] Pakistan first tested the road-mobile Ghauri I MRBM in 1998. It has a range of 1,300 kilometers and is capable of carrying a payload of 700 kilograms. A second version, the Ghauri II, was tested a year later in April 1999 and has a range of 2,000 kilometers. The Shaheen II, a solid-fuel missile with a range of 2,000 kilometers, was displayed in a March 2000 parade, and Pakistan claims to have begun its serial production, but to date the missile has never been flight-tested.

Three Hard Cases

IRAN. Iran has aggressively pursued foreign technology in its development of the Shahab III, an MRBM with a range of 1,300 kilometers. The Shahab III is based on the North Korean No Dong missile, and it is not believed that Iran is capable of domestically producing the missile's engine. Iran flight-tested the Shahab III in July 1998 and in July and September 2000, with the July 2000 test offering conclusive signs of success.[48] The Department of Defense estimates that Iran "has the capability to deploy limited numbers" of the Shahab III.[49] In August 2001 Deputy Director of the CIA John McLaughlin stated that "the Iranians will soon field the 1,300-kilometer range Shahab III,"[50] and press reports in October 2001 indicated that Iran had launched the serial production of this MRBM.[51] Iran has also publicly acknowledged the development of the Shahab IV, which its defense minister originally called a ballistic missile but later categorized as an SLV. The Shahab IV has an estimated range of 2,000 kilometers and is likely a derivative of the Russian SS–4. The Iranian defense minister also announced plans for a Shahab V, but its range remains speculative. As for the long-term goals and capability of Iran's missile program, the CIA states, "Iran is likely sometime in the next 10–15 years to test an ICBM that could hit the United States. . . . Such a test could come as early as 2005, although that is less likely given the ground Iran must still cover."[52] The 2001 NIE notes that Iran is "likely to take until the last half of the decade" to launch an ICBM/SLV, but also notes that one agency judges that Iran will be unlikely to achieve a successful test before 2015.[53]

IRAQ. Under U.N. Security Council Resolution 687, Iraq cannot have missiles with ranges that are greater than 150 kilometers. Although many Iraqi Scuds were destroyed under U.N. supervision, fears remain that several dozen missiles remain unaccounted for and may have escaped destruction. Since December 1998 U.N. inspectors have been unable to monitor Iraqi missile development programs. Furthermore, Iraq's short-range, solid-fueled Ababil 100 and liquid-fueled Al Samoud projects allow it to maintain missile production lines that can be upgraded quickly for longer-range missile production if sanctions are dropped. The CIA also believes that Iraq is hiding a small force of Al Hussein SRBMs, with ranges of 650 kilometers. It also has noted that "Iraq has rebuilt several critical missile production sites" and that, "given the likelihood that missile development work is still going on in Iraq . . . it, too, could develop an ICBM capability some time in the next 15 years with foreign assistance."[54] The 2001 National Intelligence Estimate, however, indicates that in the near term Iraq is likely to focus on rebuilding its regional strike capability rather than on developing a longer-range system. "For the next several years at least, Iraq's ballistic missile initiatives probably will focus on reconstituting its pre–Gulf War capabilities to threaten regional targets and probably will not advance beyond MRBM systems."[55]

NORTH KOREA. North Korea has conducted two known MRBM tests to date, a test of the No Dong MRBM in May 1993 and the August 31, 1998, test of the Taepo Dong I SLV. As previously noted, the 1998 test demonstrated North Korea's progress in its ability to launch a multi-stage missile. The 1,300-kilometer-range No Dong, however, remains the longest-range missile that the country has deployed. The Taepo Dong I last tested likely used a No Dong for its first stage and a Scud–B as its second stage. A "kick motor" of unknown origin is likely to have provided the third stage.

North Korea is also suspected of having developed a longer-range version of the Taepo Dong, known as the Taepo Dong II but has not tested this missile in observance of a self-imposed moratorium on missile flight tests. Development, however, is believed to be continuing. This SLV–ballistic missile is expected to have a range of 3,500–5,000 kilometers, with a payload of 1,000 kilograms. Reducing the payload to several hundred kilograms could give this suspected system an ICBM range of between 10,000 and 15,000 kilometers.[56] North Korea's missile flight moratorium ends in 2003.

North Korea may be the world's leading exporter of ballistic missiles and technology. As detailed in this chapter, the country has sold its missiles, components, and expertise to Egypt, Iran, Libya, Pakistan, Syria, and perhaps others. Talks between the United States and North Korea in 2000 came tantalizingly close to ending both missile tests and exports but have not been aggressively pursued by the Bush administration. Ending the North Korean programs would significantly delay, disrupt, and perhaps end most of the missile programs that are of international concern.

States of Moderate Proliferation Risk

EGYPT. Egypt is not included in U.S. threat assessment reports regarding missile development programs. The CIA, however, states that Egypt "continued its long-standing relationship with North Korea on ballistic missiles."[57] A United Press International report in June 2001 cited a U.S. intelligence official as stating that there are 50–300 North Korean technicians on the ground in Egypt working on a missile program and that Egypt is close to acquiring No Dongs from North Korea. Egyptian officials have repeatedly denied this claim, and the Egyptian ambassador to the United States, Nabil Fahmy, said of the unclassified CIA report to Congress, "The unclassified report talks about stuff from five years ago, it was a limited program, and that's where it stopped."[58] Following the June 21, 2001, bilateral meeting between U.S. Secretary of State Colin Powell and Egyptian Foreign Minister Ahmed Maher, State Department Spokesman Philip Reeker stated that "both countries recognize the importance of maintaining missile control regimes in the region, the importance of focusing on nonproliferation. It's important to the interests of both our countries. And so that will continue to be a subject which we will raise."[59]

LIBYA. The presence of U.N. sanctions from 1992 to 1999 are believed to have severely limited Libya's ability to obtain and develop the proper technology, materials, equipment, and expertise that are critical to MRBM and ICBM development. The U.S. intelligence community has determined that Libya lacks the infrastructure required to develop an ICBM by 2015. Owing to the lack of this infrastructure, Libya's only paths to obtaining this capability would be either the purchase of a completed operational system or the whole-scale importation of the requisite foreign technical and scientific expertise to design, develop, and produce a missile-production infrastructure.[60]

Libya is therefore heavily reliant on foreign suppliers, and its mostly probable route to longer-range missile development will come through upgrades to its aging Scuds or purchases of whole missile systems. Since the removal of sanctions in April 1999, Libya may have stepped up its procurement efforts. In November 1999 a shipment of 32 crates of components for Scud missiles was intercepted by British customs agents on a flight bound for Tripoli by way of Malta.[61] One report stated that the components included parts for a jet propulsion unit that can increase the range of the Scuds to as much as 1,000 kilometers, but this was not confirmed by any other sources. In April 2000, a Taiwanese businessman en route to Tripoli was arrested in Switzerland after missile propulsion components were found in his luggage.[62] Libya has also received ballistic missile–related goods and technical know-how from Russian entities as well as missile-related items, raw materials, and other help from Chinese entities.[63] Serbian and Indian assistance were also cited in an unclassified CIA report to the U.S. Congress.[64]

Reports have also circulated that Libya has purchased No Dong MRBMs from North Korea, but Western defense and intelligence sources have not confirmed such a purchase, acknowledging only that Libya has an interest in acquiring a longer-range missile system. Indigenously, Libya may be continuing its efforts to develop the Al Fatah missile, which the Libyan government claims will have a range of 1,000 kilometers. This missile has yet to be tested, however, and the U.S. Department of Defense assesses the liquid-fueled missile's current range to be only 200 kilometers.[65]

SYRIA. According to the U.S. Defense Department, Syria has continued to work on solid-propellant rocket-motor development with aid from Iran and has also received equipment and assistance for its liquid-fueled missile program from Chinese, North Korean, and Russian entities. The U.S. Department of Defense, however, views Syrian efforts in solid-propellant rocket motors as "laying the groundwork for a future option to develop a modern, solid-propellant SRBM" and does not believe the development program to be indicative of a longer-range program.[66] The 2001 NIE confirmed that Syria is unlikely to gain an interest in ICBM development before 2015 but indicated that strategic imperatives may lead to interest in acquiring an MRBM such as the No Dong.[67] However, with its current arsenal of mobile Scud–B, Scud–C, and SS–21 SRBMs, Syria already possesses the capability to strike deep into the territory of potential regional adversaries such as Iraq, Israel, Jordan, and Turkey.

Syria remains visibly active in its missile development activities and, unlike Libya and Egypt, it has tested new missile technology since 1998. Syria tested a 700-kilometer range Scud–D on September 23, 2000, following a successful test of Israel's Arrow missile defense system.[68] Israel alleges that Syria tested a 300-kilometer-range Scud–B on July 1, 2001, and Israeli newspaper *Ha'aretz Daily* reported that the missile was tested with a chemical warhead.[69] Other reports however, did not corroborate the presence of the chemical tip, and Syrian Defense Minister Mustafa Talas denied that the missile test occurred altogether.[70]

Dealing with Missile Proliferation

The three most prominent instruments for limiting the dangers of missile proliferation are the MTCR, unilateral and bilateral U.S. measures, and missile defenses.

The Missile Technology Control Regime

The MTCR (more fully described in appendix D in this volume) is the only international policy to attempt to limit the proliferation of missiles capable of delivering weapons of mass destruction. It consists of an export-control policy and associated arrangements between member governments.

Unilateral and Bilateral U.S. Measures

Legislatively prescribed sanctions and diplomatic inducement measures are commonly used in a carrot-and-stick fashion to limit the spread of missile technology. Such inducements as benefit packages can be used to help restrain proliferators, while sanctions are used as punitive measures against both those supplying the technology and those receiving it. The U.S. policy toward China and North Korea throughout the 1990s has made use of these tools in an attempt to limit proliferation at its source and punish the countries and entities involved in the distribution and reception of controlled technology.

Although China agreed to "adhere to MTCR Principles" in 1992 and strengthened its export-control mechanisms throughout the 1990s, it continued to provide missile technology components and assistance to Pakistan through the late 1990s and into 2000. In an attempt to discourage this behavior, the United States offered a proposal by which the United States would allow China to resume the launching of U.S.–made satellites. This practice, itself subject to export controls, was halted following allegations in a 1999 report issued by the U.S. House of Representatives Select Committee on U.S. National Security and Military/Commercial Concerns with the People's Republic of China. This report alleged that U.S. firms had transferred controlled missile technology to China while investigating several failed satellite launches. An agreement to allow the resumption of these lucrative satellite launches in exchange for a cessation of proliferation activities was reached in November 2000. China agreed to turn over a list of specific missile components and critical technology that it would ban from export to third countries. As a part of that agreement, China also had to outline how it would enforce the ban.

Continued Chinese assistance to Pakistan's missile complex prevented the accord from ever coming to fruition. After raising formal concerns about continued Chinese missile technology assistance to Pakistan in July 2001, the United States then returned to enacting sanction packages similar to those that it had used during the early 1990s. In September 2001 the Bush administration imposed sanctions on two entities that had been involved in a transfer of missile technology—the China Metallurgical Equipment Corporation and Pakistan's National Development Complex. These two entities were specifically cited for their participation in a transfer from China to Pakistan of missile components controlled under Category II of the MTCR Annex. The resultant penalties are a two-year ban on all new individual export licenses for Commerce Department– or State Department–controlled MTCR Annex items and on all new U.S. government contracts related to MTCR Annex items in both China and Pakistan. United States law also requires a two-year ban on the new licenses for State Department–controlled MTCR exports and on new U.S. government contracts for MTCR items associated with all activities of the Chinese government involved in the development or production of MTCR Annex items, electronics, space systems or equipment, and military aircraft.[71] This stipulation officially ensured that the prohibition of satellite launches on Chinese rockets would continue. Despite the failure to implement the 2000 agreement, the United States continues to raise the issue of Chinese missile-technology transfers to Pakistan and Iran in bilateral meetings.

Since 1998, the United States has also attempted to use diplomatic inducements and sanctions packages in regard to North Korean entities in an attempt to limit the country's ballistic missile proliferation activities. After scoring a qualified success in obtaining a self-imposed moratorium on missile testing from North Korea, the Clinton administration used promises of presidential visits, increases in annual food aid, and offers of free launches for North Korean satellites as bargaining chips in an attempt to secure an agreement. The administration was unable to reach a final agreement before the end of its final term, and the Bush administration has indicated that it will not pursue a "missile-only" agreement. Instead, the Bush administration has stated that it will seek further progress on nuclear and conventional military force issues as well as in the realm of missile proliferation.

Missile Defenses

Missile defense can play a role in an integrated non-proliferation policy. Experts disagree on the exact role, with some arguing that they are the best and perhaps only defense, while others view them as a last line of defense should all other efforts fail. The United States is developing missile defenses in three basic versions: short range, medium range, and long range. Every step up represents a substantial increase in complexity and a lower probability of success. (The newly renamed U.S. Missile Defense Agency groups the programs under boost-phase, mid-course, and terminal defense systems.) Most of the proposed systems employ hit-to-kill interceptors. That is, unlike the Patriot interceptors, which used a proximity fuse and an explosive warhead to scatter pellet-sized fragments in the path of the intended target, the new interceptors will attempt to hit the target head-on, using the kinetic energy of the encounter to destroy the target.

The United States is the only country in the world that is devoting a considerable portion of its defense budget to missile defenses. Israel and Russia are the only other nations with indigenous missile defense efforts. Israel's program is largely funded by the United States (see chapter 13). Russia deployed the world's first operational missile defense system in the 1960s, a set of 100 nuclear-tipped interceptors around Moscow. The interceptors remain, but it appears that the nuclear warheads have been removed.[72] This was always a questionable defensive strategy mandated by the inability of the interceptors to score direct hits, but without the nuclear warheads the system is strictly symbolic. Russia has also upgraded its S–300 air defense missile systems to give them some capability against short-range missiles. The version also known as the SA–12 is being marketed as an alternative to the U.S. Patriot system, but with few, if any sales. A newer S–400 system is comparable to the U.S. THAAD system (described later here) and is intended to intercept medium-range missiles.[73] Some analysts misunderstand the limited nature of these systems and exaggerate Russia's ability to net its systems to provide the accurate and timely tracking of incoming warheads. This sometimes leads to erroneous claims that Russia has an operational national missile defense system.

Finally, Taiwan figures prominently in missile defense discussions. It does not have an indigenous program, but it acquired Patriot missiles from the United States in 1997 to protect its capital, Taipei. Taiwan tested this system for the first time in June 2001.[74] The government is also seeking to upgrade to the Patriot Advanced Capabilities–3 system, with some defense sources claiming that an agreement on the sale of this system has already been reached.[75] These systems would provide some protection against Chinese short-range, conventionally armed ballistic missiles deployed across the Taiwan Straits. A barrage attack, however, using some of the hundreds of missiles that China is deploying would quickly overwhelm the defensive systems.

SHORT-RANGE SYSTEMS. These systems attempt to intercept missiles in their terminal phase as they reenter the atmosphere and close in on a target. Terminal defenses are practical only against short-range missiles since longer-range systems would fly in too fast for any current intercept system. The U.S. system closest to deployment is the improved Patriot system, or PAC–3, designed to intercept Scud-type missiles. These 300- to 1,000-kilometer-range missiles will represent a challenge, but it is one that the PAC–3 should be capable of intercepting under ideal conditions. Although the original Patriot was psychologically important in the Gulf War, it hit few Scuds, as later congressional and Israeli analyses confirmed. The U.S. Army ordered a new missile and selected the Extended Range Interceptor (ERINT) missile after it successfully intercepted two targets in a shoot-off with the original Patriot multi-mode missile in 1993. It has enjoyed a series of successful intercepts in developmental tests against short-range Hera test missiles and cruise missile targets. Operational testing begins in 2002, and some units will be deployed for possible emergency use.

The Navy Area-Wide system was an effort to upgrade the Aegis radar system and Standard missile on the U.S. Navy's destroyers and cruisers. It was similar in concept to the original Patriot system, but on ships. The navy canceled it in December 2001 after the program fell badly behind schedule and over budget. The multi-national Medium Extended Air Defense System (MEADS) program would be based on the new Patriot missile and be a cooperative program with several NATO allies.

Without realistic tests, it is impossible to predict performance, but these short-range systems appear to hold the best possibility for successfully intercepting existing missile threats armed with single warheads. They rely on previously developed radar and hardware systems and, because they intercept their targets within the atmosphere after any decoys that have been deployed would have been stripped away, they do not encounter the difficult discrimination problems that face higher, outside-the-atmosphere interceptors. Countermeasures, such as decoys and submunitions, remain a major unsolved technical barrier to effective missile defense despite decades of effort.

MEDIUM-RANGE SYSTEMS. Two systems are under development to counter medium-range missiles that travel from 1,000 to 3,500 kilometers: the army's Theater High-Altitude Area Defense system (THAAD) and the Navy Theater-Wide (Upper Tier) system, based on Aegis ships with a new Standard–3 missile. Both are now known as Mid-course Interceptor Systems because they attempt to intercept missiles in their mid-course phase, after they have been boosted and are coasting outside the atmosphere. The test record has been disappointing for both systems, with THAAD missing six of its eight attempts, and the Navy Theater-Wide hitting zero in four tests of the LEAP (Lightweight Exo-Atmospheric Projectile) kill vehicle. Both will undergo development and testing over the next few years to reach potential deployments close to 2010.

A third system, the Airborne Laser, is under development to test the idea of deploying a high-energy laser in a modified 747 aircraft. The plane would fly within 300–400 kilometers of missile launch points and attempt to destroy both short- and medium-range missiles in their boost phase by weakening their missile skins through applied laser heat. Intercept tests are scheduled for the middle of the decade.

Some also propose using the Navy Theater-Wide system for boost-phase intercepts, although experts and officials caution that this would require a new and much more powerful interceptor and radar and may pose insurmountable operational problems.

LONG-RANGE SYSTEMS. These systems would also intercept missiles outside the atmosphere in their mid course, but at much longer ranges, using very powerful ground-based interceptors. Current plans involve fielding interceptors in Alaska or other sites to intercept intercontinental-range missiles. From 1999 to the end of 2001, five tests of the system formerly known as the National Missile Defense system have yielded three intercepts. Developmental tests will proceed at the rate of two to four a year through the decade. A few of these interceptors could be deployed in Alaska as early as the end of 2004. The Bush administration has also revived concepts of placing kinetic-energy interceptors in space (formerly known as Brilliant Pebbles) and is investigating again the idea of space-based lasers. Both plans are in the early exploratory stage and are at least a decade away from testing.

Nationally and internationally, a deep divide exists over the threat, technical feasibility, cost, schedule, and strategic consequences of deploying missile defenses. Financially, however, they represent by far the largest component of the U.S. non-proliferation policy, with almost $8 billion allocated for missile defense research in 2002. By comparison, the United States spent $1.7 billion to combat weapons-of-mass-destruction terrorism in 2001 and approximately that amount for all other non-proliferation programs,[76] including the Nunn-Lugar Cooperative Threat Reduction programs.

NOTES

1. Commission To Assess the Ballistic Missile Threat to the United States, "Executive Summary of the Report of the Commission To Assess the Ballistic Missile Threat to the United States." July 15, 1998, p. 5. Available at www.house.gov/hasc/testimony/105thcongress/BMThreat.htm.

2. Ballistic Missile Threat Commission, "Executive Summary," p. 7.

3. National Intelligence Council (NIC), "Foreign Missile Developments and the Ballistic Missile Threat to the United States through 2015," December 2001, p. 6.

4. Ibid., p. 8.

5. Ibid., pp. 3 and 7.

6. Department of Defense (DOD), *Quadrennial Defense Review Report*, Washington, D.C., September 30, 2002, pp. 6–7. Available at www.defenselink.mil/pubs/qdr2001.pdf.

7. France and the United Kingdom acquired intercontinental-range submarine-launched ballistic missiles in 1987 and 1995, respectively.

8. Robert S. Norris and Thomas B. Cochran, *Nuclear Weapons Databook: U.S.–U.S.S.R./Russian Strategic Offensive Nuclear Forces, 1945–1996*, Natural Resources Defense Council, January 1997, p. 13.

9. Norris and Cochran, *Nuclear Weapons Databook*, p. 12.

10. Robert Norris and William Arkin, "NRDC Nuclear Notebook: Russian Nuclear Forces 2001," *Bulletin of the Atomic Scientists*, May/June 2001, vol. 57, no. 3, pp. 78–79.

11. CEIP calculations, based on declarations from the U.S. Department of State, December 5, 2001.

12. Robert Norris and William Arkin, "NRDC Nuclear Notebook: French Nuclear Forces, 2001," *Bulletin of the Atomic Scientists*, July/August 2001, vol. 57, no. 4, pp. 70–71.

13. Robert Norris and William Arkin, "NRDC Nuclear Notebook: British Nuclear Forces, 2001," *Bulletin of the Atomic Scientists*, November/December 2001, vol. 57, no. 6, pp. 78–79.

14. Robert Norris and William Arkin, "NRDC Nuclear Notebook: Chinese Nuclear Forces, 2001," *Bulletin of the Atomic Scientists*, September/October 2001, vol. 57, no. 5, pp. 71–72.

15. In 1987 there were 4,040 U.S., Russian, and Chinese long-range missiles; at the beginning of 2002 there were 2,025 U.S., Russian, and Chinese long-range missiles, plus 58 U.K. and 48 French long-range SLBMs, for a global total of 2,131 long-range ballistic missiles.

16. The U.S. IRBM arsenal had long been eliminated by the time the INF Treaty entered into force. From 1958 to 1963 the United States deployed Thor IRBMs on U.K. territory in a joint agreement with the British government. These missiles were retired in 1963 following improvements in the U.S. ICBM arsenal, and no further IRBMs were produced or deployed.

17. U.S. Department of State, Fact Sheet on 1987 INF Missile Treaty, May 16, 2001. Available at www.usinfo.state.gov/topical/pol/arms/stories/01051701.htm.

18. Ibid.

19. The most recent NIE notes that China possesses this capability, but the NRDC states that as of September 2001, China's lone Xia class submarine is in refit, and the platform and its twelve launchers are therefore not operational. See NIC, "Foreign Missile Developments," p. 9; and Norris and Arkin, "Chinese Nuclear Forces."

20. In 1987, at the time of the signing of the INF Treaty, the United States possessed 234 Pershing II MRBMs, and the Soviet Union posessed 149 SS–4 Sandal MRBMs. China had a force of 40 DF–3 MRBMs, 48 DF–21 MRBMs, and 12 CSS N–3 sea-launched MRBMs.

21. Listed as 50 each of Jericho I and Jericho II missiles in CNS, *Nonproliferation Review* (winter 1996), p. 201. There are "some" Jericho I and II missiles, according to IISS, *The Military Balance, 2000–2001* (London: International Institute of Strategic Studies), p. 142.

22. Ibid., p. 152.

23. Michael Eisenstadt, Kenneth Katzman, Kenneth Timmerman, and Seth Carus, "Iran and Iraq," *Commission To Assess the Ballistic Missile Threat to the United States*, appendix 3, Unclassified Working Papers (Washington, D.C., U.S. GPO, 1998), p. 5. Available at www.fas.org/irp/threat/missile/rumsfeld/pt1_iraq.htm as of 12/19/01.

24. Private discussion with Robert Einhorn, Assistant Secretary for Nonproliferation, U.S. Department of State, September 21, 2001.

25. U.S. Office of the Secretary of Defense, "Unmanned Aerial Vehicles Roadmap: 2000–2025," April 2001, p. 31.

26. U.S. DOD, "Executive Summary: Operational Test Evaluation Report on the Predator Medium-Altitude Endurance Unmanned Aerial Vehicle," Department of Operational Testing and Evaluation, October 31, 2001, p. ii. Available at www.pogo.org/mici/predator.pdf, January 4, 2002.

27. U.S. DOD, "Unmanned Aerial Vehicles Roadmap," p. 12.

28. Veridian Pacific-Sierra Research, "Unmanned Aerial Vehicles: Technical and Operational Aspects of an Emerging Threat," 2000, cited in Dennis Gormely, "Dealing with the Threat of Cruise Missiles," *Adelphi Paper no.* 339, June 2001, p. 34.

29. W. Seth Carus and Joseph Bermudez, "Iraq's Al-Husayn Missile Program," parts 1 and 2, *Jane's Soviet Intelligence Review*, May and June 1990.

30. U.S. Department of State, "Joint Statement of the United States of America and the People's Republic of China on Missile Proliferation," October 4, 1994, distributed by the Office of the Spokesman.

31. Aaron Karp, *Ballistic Missile Proliferation: The Politics and Technics*, SIPRI (New York: Oxford University Press, 1996).

32. Ibid., pp. 44–46.

33. Duncan Lennox, "Ballistic Missiles," *Jane's Defence Weekly*, April 17, 1996, p. 43.

34. U.N. Security Council document S/1996/261, April 11, 1996, p. 7.

35. Barbara Starr, "Iraq Reveals a Startling Range of Toxin Agents," *Jane's Defence Weekly*, November 11, 1995, p. 4.

36. Stewart Stogel, "Missile Plans by Iraq May Aim at Europe," *Washington Times*, February 16, 1996, p. A1.

37. "Dhanush Missile Test-Fired," *Times of India*, September 21, 2001.

38. Rahul Bedi, "Indian Army Will Control Agni II," *Jane's Defence Weekly*, August 22, 2001, p. 5.

39. Gregory Jones, "From Testing to Deploying Nuclear Forces: The Hard Choices Facing India and Pakistan," RAND, Issue Paper 192, 2000.

40. NIC, "Foreign Ballistic Missile Developments," p. 16.

41. S. Srinivasan, "India Developing Launch Engine," *Associated Press*, October 23, 2001.

42. Brahama Chellany, "Load Up!" *Hindustan Times*, February 13, 2001.

43. Ibid.

44. Michael Krepon, Carnegie Proliferation Roundtable, February 16, 2001.

45. Arieh O'Sullivan, "Report: Israel Tested Jericho II," *Jerusalem Post*, July 2, 2001.

46. NIC, "Foreign Ballistic Missile Developments," p. 16.

47. Ibid.

48. Kenneth Katzmann, "Iran: Current Developments and U.S. Policy," CRS Issue Brief for Congress, Congressional Research Service, updated August 1, 2001, p. 2.

49. U.S. DOD, *Proliferation: Threat and Response*, January 2001.

50. John McLaughlin, deputy director, Central Intelligence Agency, "Remarks at the Fourth Annual Space and Missile Defense Conference," Huntsville, Alabama, August 21, 2001. Available at www.cia.gov/cia/public_affairs/speeches/ddci_speech_08232001.html.

51. Andrew Koch and Steve Rodnan, "Iran Begins Serial production of Shahab 3," *Jane's Defence Weekly*, October 10, 2001, p. 8.

52. McLaughlin, "Space and Missile Defense Conference."

53. NIC, "Foreign Ballistic Missile Developments," p. 12.

54. McLaughlin, "Space and Missile Defense Conference."

55. NIC, "Foreign Ballistic Missile Developments," p. 12.

56. Ibid., p. 11.

57. CIA, "Report to Congress on the Acquisition of Technology relating to Weapons of Mass Destruction and Advanced Conventional Munitions, Available at www.cia.gov/cia/publications/bian/bian_sep_2001.htm#11.

58. "Egypt Buys Missiles from North Korea," *UPI*, June 18, 2001.

59. Philip Reeker, U.S. Department of State deputy spokesman, U.S. Department of State Regular News Briefing, June 21, 2001.

60. Ibid., p. 14.

61. "U.K. Warns Libya after Scud Find," *BBC News*, January 9, 2000. Available at news.bbc.co.uk/hi/english/uk/newsid_596000/596088.htm.

62. "Scud Missile Parts Intercepted," *BBC News*, April 12, 2000. Available at news.bbc.co.uk/hi/english/uk/newsid.

63. George Tenet, director, Central Intelligence, "Worldwide Threat 2001: National Security in a Changing World," statement before the Senate Select Committee on Intelligence, February 7, 2001.

64. CIA, "Report to Congress on the Acquisition of Technology relating to Weapons of Mass Destruction and Advanced Conventional Munitions, January–June 2000," released January 30, 2002. Available at www.cia.gov/cia/publications/bian/bian_jun_2002.htm.

65. U.S. DOD, *Proliferation Threat and Response*, January 2001, p. 48.

66. U.S. DOD, *Proliferation Threat and Response*, January 2001, p. 45.

67. NIC, "Foreign Ballistic Missile Developments," p. 15.

68. "Major News Items in Leading Israeli Newspapers," Xinhua (China) General News Service, September 26, 2001.

69. "Syrian Scud Fired with Chemical Warhead," *Ha'aretz*, July 13, 2001.

70. "Syrian Defence Minister Denies Scud Missile Fired towards Israel," *BBC News*, July 3, 2001.

71. U.S. Department of State, *Background Note: China*, September 2001, p. 16.

72. Remarks of Col. General Alexander Yesin, deputy secretary, Security Council of the Russian Federation, and Sergei Rogov, director, Institute of USA and Canada of the Russian Academy of Sciences, at the Carnegie Endowment for International Peace, April 21, 1998, "The Future of U.S.–Russian Strategic Nuclear Relationship. Available at www.ceip.org/files/events/ RussiaEvent42198.asp?p=8&EventID=74.

73. For details on these programs, see the web site of the Federation of American Scientists at www.fas.org/spp/starwars/program/soviet/index.html.

74. Jason Sherman, "Taiwan Officials Prepare for Their First Missile-Defense Test," *Defense News*, June 18–24, 2001, p. 26.

75. Brian Hsu, "Military Still Plans To Buy US Patriot PAC–III Batteries," *Taipei Times*, January 4, 2002.

76. Office of Management and Budget, *Annual Report to Congress on Combating Terrorism*, Executive Office of the President, July 2001. Pursuant to Public Law 105-85. See web site of the Henry L. Stimson Center summary at www.stimson.org/cbw.

Table 5.2: **Countries with Ballistic Missiles**

Country	System Name	Status	Range (km)	Payload (kg)	Origin	Notes
Afghanistan	Scud–B	O	300	1,000	USSR	Operational status questionable
Argentina	Alacran	O	150	400	Domestic	
Armenia	Scud–B	O	300	1,000	Russia[1]	
Azerbaijan	Scud–B	O	300	1,000	USSR	
Bahrain	MGM–140 (ATACMS)	P	165	560	USA	
Belarus	SS–21	O	120	480	USSR	
	Scud–B	O	300	1,000	USSR	
Bulgaria	Scud–B	O	300	1,000	USSR	
	SS–23	O	500	450	USSR	Prohibited by INF Treaty[2]
China	CSS–8	O	230		I	Two-stage: first solid, second liquid; road-mobile
	CSS–X–7	O	300	500	I	Solid-fueled; road-mobile
	CSS–6	O	600	500	I	Solid-fueled; road-mobile
	For China's other ballistic missiles, see chapter 7.					
Congo	Scud–B	O?	300	1,000	Iran	According to press reports[3]
Egypt	Scud–B	O/U	300	1,000	USSR/DPRK	
	Project T	O	450	1,000	I/DPRK	Improved Scud
	Scud–C	O	500	600	DPRK	
	Vector	D	685	?	I/DPRK	Initial project (with Argentina, Iraq) by this name terminated. Some work continues with North Korea?
France	For France's ballistic missiles, see chapter 8.					
Georgia	Scud–B	O	300	1,000	USSR	
Greece	MGM–140 (ATACMS)	O	165	560	USA	
India	Prithvi–150	O	150	1,000	I/USSR	From Russian SA–2; army missile
	Prithvi–250	O	250	500	I/USSR	From Russian SA–2; air force missile
	Dhanush[4]	D/O?	250	500	I	From Prithvi; last tested September 2001; India says it will soon be "operationalized"

(Table continues on the following page.)

Table 5.2: **Countries with Ballistic Missiles** (continued)

Country	System Name	Status	Range (km)	Payload (kg)	Origin	Notes
India (continued)	Sagarika[5]	D?	250–350?	500?	I	From Prithvi
	Prithvi–350	D	350	500	I/USSR	From Russian SA–2
	Agni	T	1,500	1,000	I/US/ France	From Scout; tested February 1994
	Agni II	O/P	2,000	1,000	I/US/ France	India says missile limited production has begun[6]
	Agni III	D	3,000	?	I	
Iran[7]	M–7 (CSS–8)	O	150	190	PRC	Modified SA–2
	Scud–B	O/U	300	1,000	North Korea/ Domestic production	
	Scud–C	O	500	600–700	DPRK	
	Shahab III	T /D?	1,300	1,000?	I/DPRK/ Russia	From No Dong; U.S. intelligence says Iran has a "small number... available for use in a conflict."
	Shahab IV	D	2,000	?	I/Russia	From Russian SS–4?
	Shahab V[8]	D?	3,000–5,500?	?	I/Russia	
Iraq	Al Samoud	D	150	200	I	Liquid-fuel missile; from Scud–B[9]
	Ababil–100	D	150	200	I	Solid-fuel missile; from Scud–B
	Al Hussein	Hidden?	650	500	I	From Scud–B
Israel	Lance	O/S	130	450	US	
	Jericho I	O	500	1,000	France	Road-mobile
	Jericho II	O	1,500	1,000	France/I	Road-mobile
	Jericho III	D	2,500	1,000?	I	
Kazakhstan	Scud–B	O	300	1,000	USSR	
	Tochka–U (modified SS–21)	O	120	480	USSR	
Libya	Scud–B	O/U	300	1,000	USSR	Operational status questionable
	Al Fatah[10]	D/T	200	500	I/?	
North Korea	Scud–B	O/P	300	1,000	USSR	
	Scud–C Variant	O/P	500	600–700	I	
	No Dong	D/T	1,300	700–1,000	I	Single-stage, liquid-fuel missile; tested May 1993
	Taepo Dong I	T	1,500–2,000[11]	1,000	I	Combined No Dong and Scud; tested August 31, 1998

Country	Missile					Notes
	Taepo Dong II	D	3,500–5,500 [12]	1,000	I	
Pakistan	Hatf I	O	80	500	I	
	Hatf II	O	300	500	I/PRC?	
	Hatf III/ M–11	O	600	500	I/PRC	2001 NIE lists the Hatf II to be an M–11
	Shaheen I	P/O	700/750	500	I/PRC?	M–9 derivative? Tested April 1999; solid-fuel missile; Pakistan announced "serial production" of missile October 2000
	Ghauri/ No Dong	T/O	1,300	500–750	I/DPRK	2001 NIE lists the Ghauri to be a No Dong; tested April 6, 1998 [13]
	Ghauri II	D/T	2,000?	700	I/DPRK	From No Dong; tested April 1999
	Shaheen II	D/P	2,000/ 2,500	1,000?	I/DPRK?	Road-mobile; two-stage weapon displayed in March 2000 parade
Russia	Scud–B (SS–1c Mod 1)	O	300	1,000	I	Liquid fuel
	SS–21	O	100–120		I	Solid fuel
	SS–X–26	O	300		I	Solid fuel
	Iskander–E	O	275		I	For export; solid fuel
Saudi Arabia	Dong Feng–3 (CSS–2)	O	2,600	2,150	PRC	Purchased from China in 1987
Slovak Republic	SS–21	O	100–120	480	USSR	
	Scud–B	O	300	1,000	USSR	
South Korea	Nike-Hercules–1	O	180	300	US/I	Modified SAM.
	Nike-Hercules–2	D	250	500	US/I	Modified SAM; tested at reduced range
	MGM–140 (ATACMS)	O	165/300	560	US	Currently fields Block I. Contract for Block IA sale approved; will receive full shipment in 2004
	?	D/T	300	500	I	This yet unnamed missile was tested in November 2001 [14]

(Table continues on the following page.)

Table 5.2: **Countries with Ballistic Missiles** (continued)

Country	System Name	Status	Range (km)	Payload (kg)	Origin	Notes
Syria	SS–21	O	120	480	USSR	Transferred 1983
	Scud–B	O	300	1,000	USSR	
	Scud–C [15]	O	500	600	DPRK	
	Scud–D	T	600–700	?	DPRK	Tested September 2000
Taiwan	Ching Feng	O	130	270	I/Israel?	From Lance
	Tien Chi[16]	D	300	500	I	Modified SAM
Turkey	MGM–140 (ATACMS)	O	165	560	USA	
Turkmenistan	Scud–B	O	300	1,000	USSR	
Ukraine	SS–21	O	120	480	USSR	
	Scud–B	O	300	1,000	USSR	
United Arab Emirates	Scud–B	O	300	1,000	Russia?	
United Kingdom	For the United Kingdom's ballistic missiles, see chapter 9.					
United States	MGM–140 (ATACMS)	O	165	560	I	
	For U.S. nuclear-capable ballistic missiles, see chapter 10.					
Vietnam	Scud–B	O	300	1,000		
Yemen	SS–21	O	100–120	480	USSR	Transferred 1988
	Scud–B	O/U	300	1,000	USSR	Transferred to South Yemen in 1979

KEY		RANGE	
I:	Indigenous	**SRBM**	Short-range ballistic missile (<1,000 km)
D:	in Development	**MRBM**	Medium-range ballistic missile (1,000–3,000 km)
O:	Operational	**IRBM**	Intermediate-range ballistic missile (3,000–5,500 km)
P:	in Production		NOTES
S:	in Storage	**INF Treaty:**	Intermediate-range Nuclear Forces Treaty
T:	Tested	**SAM:**	Surface-to-air missile
U:	Used		

NOTES

1. Russia is thought to have shipped 8 Scud launchers and 24 missiles to Armenia between 1992 and 1995. See Nikolai Novichkov, "Russia Details Illegal Deliveries to Armenia," *Jane's Defence Weekly*, April 16, 1997, p. 15.

2. The International Institute for Strategic Studies lists 8 SS–23 launchers in Bulgaria, despite prohibition of SS–23 missiles by the INF Treaty.

3. Iran reportedly delivered Scud–B and Scud–C missiles to the Democratic Republic of Congo in November 1999. See "DRC Receives Iranian 'Scud' Missiles," *Jane's Defence Weekly*, December 1, 1999, p. 5; and Bill Gertz, "Tehran Sold Scud Missiles to Congolese," *Washington Times*, November 22, 1999.

4. The Dhanush is the naval version of the Prithvi series. "Dhanush Missile Test-fired" *Times of India*, September 21, 2001.

5. The Indian government first acknowledged the existence of the Sagarika in October 1998, identifying it as a 250- to 350-kilometer sea-launched cruise missile derived from the Prithvi. Other sources maintained that the Sagarika program also contained a ballistic missile division. U.S. intelligence reports have classified it as an SLBM.

6. The Agni II test missile traveled more than 1,250 kilometers in an April 1999 test. It was successfully tested (apparently in its final configuration) a second time on January 17, 2001, reportedly to a length of approximately 2,000 kilometers following its firing from a mobile launcher. It is a road-mobile, two-stage missile with a "solid propulsion booster and liquid propulsion upper state" ("Agni–II Testfired in Final Configuration," *Times of India*, January 17, 2001). In a March 7, 2000, letter to Parliament Defense Minister George Fernandes wrote that the Agni–2 had "achieved operationalization stage. . . . The government has decided to induct the missile system based on security needs" ("Indian Missile Set For Production," *International Herald Tribune*, March 8, 2001). On May 31, 2001, The *Times of India* reported that the government had approved the induction of the Agni–2 in 2001–2002 and the development of a longer-range missile. In June of 2001, India announced it had begun limited production of the Agni–2 and that it would be under the control of the army (Rahul Bedi, "Indian Army Will Control Agni II" *Jane's Defence Weekly*, August 22, 2001, p. 15).

7. Iran also produces 125- and 210-kilometer range "Zelzal" missiles.

8. Estimates of the range of this new IRBM are only speculative, drawing upon remarks by the Iranian Defense Minister, who identified the missile as the "Shahab–V." Kenneth Timmerman also suggested that Iran might be developing an IRBM on July 13, 1999, during hearings on the Iran Nonproliferation Act of 1999. See *Hearings of the Subcommittee on Space and Aeronautics*, U.S. House Committee on Science; and Bill Gertz, "Tehran Increases Range on Missiles," *Washington Times*, September 22, 1999.

9. One intelligence report called the Al Samoud a "scaled down Scud." See "Iraq's Weapons of Mass Destruction Programs," U.S. Government White Paper 3050, released February 17, 1998. While this missile has a range of about 150 km (the maximum range allowed for Iraqi missiles by U.N. Security Council resolutions), there are concerns that Iraq continues to devote resources to the Ababil and Al Samoud programs with the intention of quickly transferring these resources back to missiles with longer ranges following the end of sanctions. These concerns are reiterated in the DOD's January 2001 *Proliferation: Threat and Response*: "The Al Samoud is essentially a scaled-down SCUD. . . . We believe that the Al Samoud missile . . . has an inherent potential to exceed the 150-km range restriction imposed under UNSCR 687." The report also registers similar concerns about the Ababil–100. The 2001 NIE noted that a December 2000 parade showcased the Al Samoud on new transporter-erector-launchers, and that it will "be deployed soon."

10. Though intended to have a range of 950 kilometers, the Al Fatah has been successfully tested to only 200 kilometers. See Department of Defense, p. 47–48. The CIA's *Unclassified Report to Congress on the Acquisition of Technology relating to Weapons of Mass Destruction and Advanced Conventional Munitions, 1 January through 30 June* notes that "Libya's current capability remains limited to its aging Scud B missiles, but with continued foreign assistance it may achieve an MRBM capability—a long-desired goal." There are unconfirmed reports that Libya has attempted to purchase longer-range missiles from North Korea (Scud–C and No Dong models have been mentioned).

11. The missile impacted 1,320 kilometers from the launch point. It attempted and failed to put a small satellite into orbit, demonstrating some progress in staging technology. Some experts speculate that an operational third stage and reentry vehicle would allow the Taepo Dong–I to deliver a light payload over 5,500 km.

12. The Taepo Dong–II has not been flight-tested. The 2001 NIE speculates that, with a light payload, it could have a 10,000-km range.

13. Pakistan claimed that the missile impacted 1,100 kilometers from its launch point.

14. See "South Korea Launches Missile in Its First Test Since Last Year," *New York Times*, November 22, 2001.

15. The *Jerusalem Post* reported development of an advanced Syrian modification of the Scud–C (possibly the Scud–D tested September 2000), but this report has not been confirmed by Western sources. See Arieh O'Sullivan, "Syrian Super Scud Ready Soon," *Jerusalem Post*, September 16, 1999.

16. This program was reportedly initiated in autumn 1995 and is based on the Sky Bow II surface-to-air-missile.

BALLISTIC MISSILE PROLIFERATION STATUS 2002

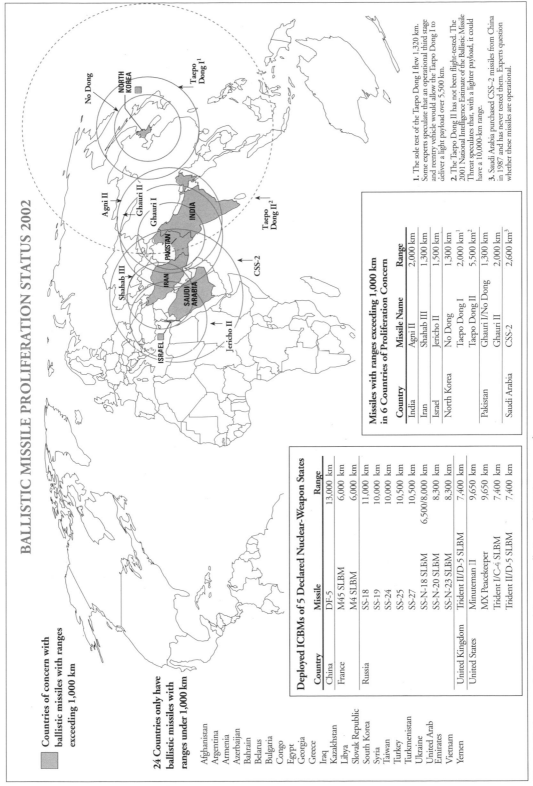

Countries of concern with ballistic missiles with ranges exceeding 1,000 km

24 Countries only have ballistic missiles with ranges under 1,000 km

Afghanistan
Argentina
Armenia
Azerbaijan
Bahrain
Belarus
Bulgaria
Congo
Egypt
Georgia
Greece
Iraq
Kazakhstan
Libya
Slovak Republic
South Korea
Syria
Taiwan
Turkey
Turkmenistan
Ukraine
United Arab Emirates
Vietnam
Yemen

Map labels: No Dong, Taepo Dong I[1], NORTH KOREA, Agni II, Ghauri II, Ghauri I, INDIA, PAKISTAN, Taepo Dong II[2], CSS-2, Shahab III, IRAN, SAUDI ARABIA, Jericho II, ISRAEL

Deployed ICBMs of 5 Declared Nuclear-Weapon States

Country	Missile	Range
China	DF-5	13,000 km
France	M45 SLBM	6,000 km
	M4 SLBM	6,000 km
Russia	SS-18	11,000 km
	SS-19	10,000 km
	SS-24	10,000 km
	SS-25	10,500 km
	SS-27	10,500 km
	SS-N-18 SLBM	6,500/8,000 km
	SS-N-20 SLBM	8,300 km
	SS-N-23 SLBM	8,300 km
United Kingdom	Trident II/D-5 SLBM	7,400 km
United States	Minuteman II	9,650 km
	MX Peacekeeper	9,650 km
	Trident I/C-4 SLBM	7,400 km
	Trident II/D-5 SLBM	7,400 km

Missiles with ranges exceeding 1,000 km in 6 Countries of Proliferation Concern

Country	Missile Name	Range
India	Agni II	2,000 km
Iran	Shahab III	1,300 km
Israel	Jericho II	1,500 km
North Korea	No Dong	1,300 km
	Taepo Dong I	2,000 km[1]
	Taepo Dong II	5,500 km[2]
Pakistan	Ghauri I/No Dong	1,300 km
	Ghauri II	2,000 km
Saudi Arabia	CSS-2	2,600 km[3]

1. The sole test of the Taepo Dong I flew 1,320 km. Some experts speculate that an operational third stage and reentry vehicle would allow the Taepo Dong I to deliver a light payload over 5,500 km.

2. The Taepo Dong II has not been flight-tested. The 2001 National Intelligence Estimate of the Ballistic Missile Threat speculates that, with a lighter payload, it could have a 10,000-km range.

3. Saudi Arabia purchased CSS-2 missiles from China in 1987 and has never tested them. Experts question whether these missiles are operational.

Carnegie Endowment for International Peace, *Deadly Arsenals* (2002), www.ceip.org

Declared Nuclear-Weapon States

Overview

There are five legally acknowledged nuclear-weapon states under the terms of the Treaty on the Non-Proliferation of Nuclear Weapons. All five states, China, France, Russia, the United Kingdom, and the United States are also permanent members of the U.N. Security Council. Combined, the five nations possess more than 20,000 nuclear weapons, the vast majority of these belonging to the United States and the Russian Federation.

Under the terms of the NPT and the commitments taken at five-year review meetings, the five states have agreed to an "unequivocal undertaking by the nuclear-weapon States to accomplish the total elimination of their nuclear arsenals leading to nuclear disarmament,"[1] and to "pursue negotiations in good faith on effective measures relating to cessation of the nuclear arms race at an early date and to nuclear disarmament."[2]

The deployed arsenals of the nuclear-weapon states are declining, with many thousands of nuclear weapons having been withdrawn and eliminated since the end of the Cold War. Several countries, including the United States and Russia, however, now find themselves in possession of huge amounts (hundreds of metric tons) of excess nuclear-weapons-usable materials. This problem adds to global concern regarding the security of nuclear materials, the protection of which is of major importance in preventing the proliferation of nuclear weapons.

A discussion of the five nuclear-weapon states in the following chapters reviews how many nuclear weapons and delivery systems these nations have. It also looks at those issues that affect efforts to prevent the proliferation of nuclear weapons.

NOTES

1. May 1, 2000, Statement by the Five Nuclear Weapon States to the NPT Review Conference.
2. Article 6, Treaty on the Non-Proliferation of Nuclear Weapons.

Russia

Nuclear Weapon Capability

The Russian Federation is a recognized nuclear-weapon state under the Treaty on the Non-Proliferation of Nuclear Weapons and possesses thousands of strategic and tactical nuclear weapons. To support this arsenal, Russia maintains a massive nuclear complex that consists of ten formerly secret nuclear cities that house hundreds of metric tons of weapons-usable nuclear materials and hundreds of thousands of trained scientists and engineers with weapons-related knowledge. Russia is in the process of dramatically reducing the size of its nuclear arsenal and weapons complex owing to changed international security conditions; the negotiation of arms control agreements with the United States; and the retirement of older systems that are reaching the end of their service lives. If current trends continue, Russia may only field some 1,000 strategic nuclear weapons by the end of the decade, although it could maintain a substantially larger nuclear arsenal given adequate resources.

The Soviet Union conducted 715 nuclear weapon tests, the first on August 29, 1949, and the last on October 23, 1990. Russia has signed and ratified the Comprehensive Test Ban Treaty.

Regardless of the size of Russia's future deployed arsenal, its nuclear complex will continue to pose serious non-proliferation risks for many years to come. Significant domestic and international efforts will be required to ensure the safety and security of Russia's current stockpiles of weapons and materials and to ensure that they do not leak into the weapon programs of other states or subnational groups. In addition to Russia's nuclear materials, Russia's nuclear weapon and ballistic missile expertise, in the form of tens of thousands of experienced scientists, engineers, and technicians, poses a particularly challenging non-proliferation concern. Russia has extensive nuclear and missile-related contacts with countries such as Iran and India, and Russian companies and organizations have been repeatedly sanctioned by the United States for assisting the weapon programs of other states. Effective control over Russia's technical complex, including the human dimension, is critical if efforts to prevent the proliferation of nuclear weapons and long-range ballistic missiles to states and organizations of proliferation concern are to succeed.

Since the end of the Cold War, the United States has provided more than $4.7 billion to assist states of the former Soviet Union to secure nuclear weapons and materials, eliminate aging nuclear weapon delivery systems and find alternative, benign employment for its nuclear workforce. Despite these efforts, Russia's nuclear complex continues to pose a serious proliferation risk, and much more remains to be done to adequately secure Russian nuclear materials and expertise. A failure to address the proliferation challenges in Russia effectively could result in the proliferation of weapons of mass destruction to other countries or to subnational groups.

Aircraft, Submarine, and Missile Capabilities

Russia currently deploys approximately 1,000 land- and submarine-based strategic ballistic missiles with intercontinental range, in addition to 80 strategic nuclear-capable bombers. Although most of the major strategic ballistic missile production facilities of the former Soviet Union were located outside Russian territory (especially in Ukraine), Russia continues to possess an advanced and accomplished, albeit currently depressed, missile design and production infrastructure.

Many of Russia's currently deployed strategic missiles are reaching the end of their service lives and are being retired, with the direct assistance of the United States under the Cooperative Threat Reduction program (also called the Nunn-Lugar Program, after its original congressional sponsors). Russia is currently producing limited numbers of its new SS–27 land-based ICBM and continues design work on a new submarine-launched ballistic missile for deployment on its next generation strategic submarine.

Russia's extensive missile experience and expertise, combined with the economic pressures of Russian society as a whole, have raised concerns (mirrored in the nuclear complex) that Russia's missile technology may be assisting other countries. United States intelligence officials have repeatedly alleged that Russian entities are aiding missile programs in other countries, including India and Iran. The United States has levied sanctions against a dozen Russian groups for such cooperation. Russian Government officials deny that any assistance is being provided to the military missile programs of either India or Iran, and Moscow has taken significant steps to improve its export controls over missile-related technology.[1]

Biological and Chemical Weapon Capability

The Soviet Union had vast offensive chemical and biological weapon programs. Today, Russia is a state party to both the Biological Weapons Convention and the Chemical Weapons Convention. However, Russia continues to possess about 40,000 metric tons of chemical weapons, a massive stock of BW samples, and a latent BW production capability. The Soviet program reportedly weaponized plague, anthrax, smallpox, tularemia, brucellosis, and the Marburg virus and developed other possible agents.[2] Russia inherited the vast majority of the Soviet Union's chemical and biological weapon stocks and facilities and is responsible for the elimination of the weapons and stocks in its possession. Russia faces significant problems in complying with its commitments to eliminate these weapons, despite extensive international assistance, and is likely to retain a considerable chemical and biological weapon capability for many years to come. In the meantime, there is much concern over the security of these materials as well as over the experts who are responsible for their production. The risk that chemical or biological weapons or critical production technology may leak out of Russia to proliferant states or terrorist groups remains high and will require a continued investment (domestic or international) to ensure that the Soviet chemical and biological weapon legacy does not lead to further proliferation.

Nuclear Analysis

During the Cold War, the potential, deliberate use of Soviet nuclear weapons posed the main security threat to the United States. In the aftermath of the Cold War, concern over Russia's nuclear arsenal shifted to a new set of concerns. These dangers included the risk that:

- nuclear weapons deployed in Belarus, Kazakhstan, and Ukraine in 1991 might not return to Russian control.

- Russia might lose control of nuclear weapons (especially tactical nuclear weapons) in its inventory.

- Russian nuclear materials and expertise might be bought or stolen and thus assist the efforts of countries or terrorist groups in developing nuclear weapons.

Former U.S. Senator Sam Nunn summed up the risk when he said:

> The old threats we faced during the Cold War, a Soviet strike or an invasion of Europe, were threats made dangerous by Soviet strength. The new threats we face today—increased Russian reliance on early launch and first use and increased reliance on tactical-battlefield nuclear weapons—are threats made dangerous by Russia's weakness. The threats of today go beyond nuclear forces and include terrorist groups. Much of Russia's nuclear, biological, and chemical weapons and materials are poorly secured; its weapons scientists and guards are poorly paid. We can't risk a world where a Russian scientist can take care of his children only by endangering ours.[3]

Those weapons deployed outside Russia when the Soviet Union dissolved have all been returned to Russia. The return of the nuclear weapons deployed in Belarus, Kazakhstan, and Ukraine when the Soviet Union dissolved was a tremendous achievement and helped to save the entire international system of preventing the proliferation of weapons of mass destruction. The creation of three new nuclear-weapon states would have made it all but impossible to convince many other countries to maintain their non-nuclear status. (See chapter 19.)

Strategic Weapons

Russia possesses a large, diverse, and advanced nuclear arsenal of strategic and tactical nuclear weapons. These weapons serve as the ultimate guarantor for

Russian national security, and some elements of Russia's nuclear forces have taken on an enhanced role in Russian security as its conventional military strength has faltered. Russia succeeded the Soviet Union as a nuclear-weapon state and has assumed its legal obligations under arms control agreements, including the NPT, the Strategic Arms Reduction Treaty (START I), the Anti-Ballistic Missile Treaty (ABM), and the Intermediate-range Nuclear Forces Treaty.

Despite its continued importance to Russian security, the Russian arsenal is shrinking. As the majority of Moscow's strategic weapons reach the end of their service lives and are being retired, many suffer from a lack of maintenance funds, raising questions about their long-term reliability and safety. Notwithstanding these concerns, the Russian nuclear arsenal remains formidable (see table 6.1).

It is not yet clear to what level Russia's strategic arsenal will drop over the coming decade. Based on the most optimistic assumptions in terms of Russia's relationship with the United States, the Russian deployed strategic arsenal could drop to a little more than 1,000 weapons by the end of 2010. However, if funding is not available for Russia to effect reductions in its deployed arsenal, and the international situation leads Russia to maintain as large a strategic arsenal as possible, then Russia's deployed nuclear forces could reach close to 4,000 weapons by the end of the year 2010 (table 6.2).

Intercontinental ballistic missiles have historically made up the largest component of the Russian strategic nuclear triad. Yet of the six types of ICBM that Russia deployed in 2001, only one (the SS–27) is expected to be in service by the end of the decade. The rest of the systems—the SS–18, 19, 24 (rail and silo), and 25—are expected to reach the end of their serviceable lives by 2010.[4] It is possible, although unlikely, that Russia could maintain some of these systems longer if needed.[5] It is also not yet certain how many of the new SS–27 land-based ICBMs Russia will produce and deploy. It has produced only limit-

Table 6.1: **Russian Strategic Nuclear Forces**

Type		START I Data September 1990	START I Data January 2002*
ICBMs	Launchers	1,064	742
	Warheads	4,278	3,364
SLBMs	Launchers	940	376
	Warheads	2,804	1,868
Bombers	Launchers	79	80
	Warheads	570	626
Totals	Launchers	2,083	1,198
	Warheads	7,652	5,858

*   START I Memorandum of Understanding Data Exchange, U.S. Department of State, January 31, 2002. Information contained in the January 2002 data exchange is for forces accountable as of July 31, 2001.

Table 6.2: **Projection of Russian Nuclear Forces**

Type		2010 Lower Limit of Warheads	2010 Upper Limit of Warheads
ICBMs	SS–18	0	900
	SS–19	0	432
	SS–25	0	0
	SS–27	230	1,320
SLBMs	Delta III/SS–N–18	96	96
	Delta IV/SS–N–23	448	448
	Borey/?	72	72
Bombers	Bear	120	600
	Blackjack	120	180
Totals		1,086	4,048

ed numbers of that system, although its production capability could reach as high as 50 a year with adequate funding. Median projections suggest that Russia will have 230 SS–27's by the end of the decade. High-end estimates suggest that it could deploy 435 missiles, each with three warheads by 2010.[6]

The Russian submarine force is also in a serious state of decline. The bulk of its submarine force is slated for elimination by the end of the decade, and it is likely that Russia will deploy only seven submarines (all Delta IVs) by 2010. The other submarines in the current arsenal, including the Delta I, II, III, and Typhoon, are slated for retirement by the end of the decade, assuming that enough money is available to implement their elimination. Much of the planned U.S. assistance to Russia over the next ten years will be focused on the elimination of submarines and SLBMs. It is possible that some of these launchers will remain operational in port if necessary or if sufficient funds are not available to dismantle the systems and their associated missiles.

Russia is pursuing work on the next generation of strategic ballistic missile submarines, known as the Borey class. Construction began on the first boat of this class in 1996 but has been delayed owing to funding constraints. It is unlikely that even this first boat, capable of carrying 12 missiles and an undetermined number of warheads, could be deployed by 2007.[7]

The Russian bomber force is likely to remain the most stable component of the Russian strategic triad over the next ten years, although it too will decline in numbers owing to aging systems being retired. The two main bomber types in the Russian military—the Tu–160 Blackjack and the Tu–95 Bear—will provide a basic nuclear deterrent for the Russian Federation, even as the other legs of the triad are dramatically reduced. The number of Bear bombers in particular, however, will begin to decline rapidly at the end of the decade, dropping from an estimated 50 in 2007 to no more than 10 by 2010.

Nuclear Weapons

Since the collapse of the Soviet Union, there has been concern over the security of Russia's nuclear weapons. The possible theft or unauthorized use of a Russian nuclear weapon quickly became a very real threat in the early 1990s, and the international danger posed by the risk resulted in a dramatic set of programs to assist Russia in ensuring the security of its nuclear arsenal. These programs have helped protect Russian nuclear warheads, aiding in their secure transport, and the development of a modern warhead accounting and tracking system. The program demonstrates an unprecedented level of cooperation between two former Cold War adversaries as well as the ability of these enemies to cooperate in addressing common security threats.

Soviet-era warhead accounting and management relied upon the manual (handwritten) tracking of its nuclear arsenal. Through the U.S. CTR program, a new automated system of tracking and accounting is being implemented in Russia. Under the program, the United States has provided Russia with 100 personal computers, as well as software and training. It is also identifying additional needs, including site preparation for the installation of permanent communication equipment. The current program includes plans to install the tracking system at 19 key field and regional sites. The operation of the system is scheduled to begin in 2003; assistance will continue to ensure the system's operation through 2005.[8]

United States government assistance has also resulted in the improvement of Russia's nuclear weapon security at up to 123 storage sites. Initially, 50 sites operated by the 12th Main Directorate, Russia's military division responsible for nuclear weapons, were identified for "quick-fix" security upgrades. Under this rapid upgrade project, CTR provided the 12th MD with 50 kilometers of sensor fencing, 350 sensor alarms, and 200 microwave systems. The shipments of this equipment began in October 1997 and continue. A 1998 request from the Russian Ministry of Defense resulted in the provision of similar equipment for 48 air force and navy storage sites and for 25 Strategic Rocket Force sites.[9] This work continues and has expanded to additional areas. The U.S. Department of Energy has been working since 1998 to improve security at Russian navy sites that contain nuclear weapons. That project is expected to expand in coming years.

CTR assistance has also helped to create the Security Assessment and Training Center (SATC) at Sergiev Posad, a facility built to assist the Ministry of Defense in the design and implementation of security systems throughout the Russian nuclear complex. The site was formally established at a February 1998 ceremony that was attended by then–U.S. Secretary of Defense William S. Cohen and Russian Defense Minister Igor Sergeyev.

Initial Russian weapon security programs focused on helping to protect nuclear warheads during transit, especially those coming from the former Soviet republics to Russia, and to support emergency services in the event of an accident. For this purpose the United States provided Russia with 4,000 Kevlar blankets, 150 supercontainers (used to carry several warheads at a time) for the physical and ballistic protection of nuclear weapons, and 117 special railcar conversion kits (100 cargo, 15 guard, and 2 prototypes) to ensure the security of warheads. In addition, CTR has also provided Russia with five mobile emergency response complexes to deal with accidents. These include rail-mounted and road-mobile cranes, VHF portable radios, portable command and control computers, chemical and fire-fighting protective clothing, personal dosimetry equipment, Violinist III x-ray and gamma-ray instrument kits, and air-sampling monitors. (An additional 150 supercontainers were provided by the United Kingdom in May 1997.) The railcars themselves were produced in Russia using U.S. funds and some U.S. materials; the rest of the equipment was produced in the United States. This program continues, and on November 1, 1999, the U.S. Department of Defense and the Russian Ministry of Defense signed a new memorandum for $41.7 million in additional assistance for the purchase of security systems for railcars. The program's aims have now shifted to the replacement of railcars that are nearing the end of their service lives.[10]

STRATEGIC ARMS CONTROL AND REDUCTIONS. The Strategic Arms Reduction Treaty was signed in Moscow by the United States and the Soviet Union on July 31, 1991. Implementation of the agreement was completed in December 2001, on schedule. START I was the first arms control agreement to actually reduce the levels of deployed strategic weapons; previous agreements had served to cap the expansion of existing arsenals. Under START I, the United States and Russia reduced their strategic accountable nuclear forces to 6,000 warheads each, deployed on no more than 1,600 strategic nuclear delivery vehicles, i.e., intercontinental ballistic missiles, submarine-launched ballistic missiles, and strategic bombers. The sublimits for warheads allow no more than 4,900 weapons to be deployed on either side's ICBMs and SLBMs and, of this subtotal, no more than 1,100 warheads may be deployed on mobile ICBMs. In addition, no more than 1,540 warheads may be deployed on heavy ICBMs.[11]

The entry into force of START I was substantially delayed by the need to secure ratification by each of the four nuclear successor states to the Soviet Union. Belarus, Kazakhstan, Russia, and Ukraine all had nuclear weapons on their territories when the Soviet Union dissolved. Russia was immediately recognized by the international community as the main nuclear successor state of the Soviet Union, but obtaining agreement from the other three states required intensive diplomatic and strategic maneuvering by the United States and Russia, as well as by many other countries. The result was the negotiation of the Lisbon Protocol to the START I agreement, signed on May 23, 1992, by Belarus, Kazakhstan, Russia, and Ukraine. Through the Protocol, the four states agreed to participate jointly in START I as successors of the former Soviet Union and to "implement the Treaty's limits and restrictions" (article 2 of the protocol). In addition, Belarus, Kazakhstan, and Ukraine agreed to "adhere to the Treaty on the Non-Proliferation of Nuclear Weapons" as non-nuclear-weapon state parties "in the shortest possible time" (article 5 of the protocol).

In separate letters to President George H. W. Bush, each of the three presidents of the state parties also agreed to the elimination of all strategic nuclear arms on their territories within the seven-year START I implementation period.

In approving ratification on November 4, 1992, Russia's Supreme Soviet attached a condition that Russia not exchange instruments of ratification until after the other three successor states had acceded to the NPT as non-nuclear-weapon states and carried out their other obligations under the Lisbon Protocol. In Belarus and Kazakhstan, these NPT-related steps proved to be largely uncontroversial. The Belarusian parliament ratified START I on February 4, 1993, and Belarus formally acceded to the NPT on July 22, 1993. The parliament of Kazakhstan ratified START I on July 2, 1992, and Kazakhstan formally acceded to the NPT on February 14, 1994. Ukraine's parliament approved the START I agreement and the NPT in two steps on November 18, 1993, and on February 3, 1994, and on December 5, 1994, deposited its accession to the NPT. All Russian nuclear weapons deployed in Belarus, Kazakhstan, and Ukraine were returned to Russia by the end of 1996. (See chapter 19.)

START II. At the June 1990 Washington summit, Presidents Bush and Gorbachev agreed that following the signing of START I, the two sides would begin new talks on further reductions at the earliest practical date. Those talks began in September 1991. At a subsequent summit in June 1992, Presidents Bush and Yeltsin agreed on the basic principles of START II, including a ban on multiple independently targetable reentry vehicle (MIRV) land-based ICBMs. This was a significant development, since MIRVed ICBMs have been considered "destabilizing" weapons, posing an attractive target for a disarming first strike. In addition, this was a major development since the majority of Russian nuclear arsenals were based on MIRVed ICBMs. Bush and Yeltsin signed the finalized START II agreement in Moscow on January 3, 1993.

START II would have capped the number of deployed strategic warheads in both countries at no more than 3,500 and resulted in the elimination of all land-based MIRVed ICBMs by January 1, 2003. The U.S. Senate ratified START II on January 26, 1996. After more than six years' delay, the Russian Duma ratified the agreement on April 14, 2000. The text of the Russian ratification required the U.S. Senate to approve protocols to the 1972 ABM treaty.

START III. At the March 20–21, 1997, Helsinki Summit, Presidents Yeltsin and Clinton signed a joint statement agreeing to begin negotiations on a START III treaty immediately after START II entered into force and identified certain parameters for that treaty. In addition to agreeing that the pact would limit deployed strategic forces on both sides to between 2,000 and 2,500 warheads by the end of 2007, the presidents agreed that START III would be the first strategic arms control agreement to include measures relating to the transparency of strategic nuclear warhead inventories and the actual destruction of strategic nuclear warheads. In addition, the presidents pledged to explore measures for long-range nuclear sea-launched cruise missiles and tactical nuclear systems. These discussions were to take place apart from, but in the context of, START III negotiations.[12]

Despite several years of informal discussions between U.S. and Russian officials on issues to be addressed in the START III process, no negotiations ever took place and no agreement was ever produced.

During the November 2001 summit with President Putin, President Bush announced that the United States would reduce its strategic nuclear arsenal to between 1,700 and 2,200 nuclear weapons, which represents a major reduction from the 6,000 accountable weapons set by the START I treaty. Although in 2000 President Putin had declared his interest in reducing the Russian nuclear arsenal to 1,500 or fewer weapons, he did not announce a formal Russian target for reductions. In a joint press conference with President Bush after their summit meeting, President Putin did express his interest in having the reductions made part of a formal treaty: "For our part, [Russia is] prepared to present all our agreements in a treaty form, including the issues of verification and control." President Bush followed by saying, "If we need to write it down on a piece of paper, I'll be glad to do that."[13] Officials from both countries indicated in late 2001 and early 2002 that the two sides were working to formalize the proposed cuts in some way in time for the scheduled May meeting between Presidents Bush and Putin in Russia. The exact form that codification would take was unclear. It might include anything from a written political agreement to a formal treaty that requires legislative approval.

This informal agreement and plans to codify it appear to have turned START II and the framework of START III into an historical footnote. The Bush administration has not indicated any interest in reviving and implementing the types of constraints or conditions placed on MIRVed ICBMs—nor the transparency measures discussed in 1997—in a future agreement with Russia.

United States and Russian nuclear deployments are also controlled, in part, by the Intermediate-range Nuclear Forces Treaty signed by Presidents Gorbachev and Reagan on December 8, 1987. The INF treaty required both countries to eliminate all nuclear-capable ground-launched ballistic and cruise missiles in their arsenals with a range of between 500 and 5,500 kilometers no later than June 1, 1991 (three years after the agreement entered into force).[14] This agreement has the unique status of being the only treaty to eliminate an entire class of nuclear weapons. Its implementation resulted, by May 1991, in the verified destruction of 846 long- and short-range U.S. INF missile systems and of 1,846 Soviet missile systems.[15] Under the terms of the agreement, implementation was completed on May 31, 2001, and the two governments announced that they would no longer need to verify the complete elimination of weapon systems covered under the agreement.

Tactical Weapons

Much less is known about the size, composition, and deployment of the Russian arsenal of tactical nuclear weapons. At one point during the Cold War, Russia is believed to have possessed about 30,000 tactical weapons.[16] Russia has substantially reduced its stocks of tactical weapons, and informed estimates suggest that the current stockpile of tactical nuclear weapons range from 3,500 to 8,000. These weapons have taken on greater importance in Russian security planning, however, with the general decline of Russia's conventional military forces.

In October 1991 Soviet President Gorbachev responded to U.S. President Bush's initiative of a month earlier and moved to dramatically reduce the deployment of Russian tactical nuclear weapons. Gorbachev matched the United States by announcing a plan that would eliminate all Soviet nuclear artillery, short-range missile, and land-mine warheads; remove all nuclear weapons for air-defense missiles from deployment areas (for storage or elimination); and remove tactical nuclear weapons from navy forces (ships, submarines, and land-based aircraft). Russian President Yeltsin went further in 1992 when he announced an end to the production of warheads for land-based tactical missiles, artillery, and land mines as well as the decision to eliminate the stockpiles of those weapons. He also announced that Russia would eliminate one-third of its tactical sea-launched nuclear warheads, half of its tactical air-launched nuclear weapons, and half of its nuclear warheads for anti-aircraft missiles.[17]

Russian tactical nuclear weapons deployed in non-Russian republics were returned to Russia in early 1992, and tactical weapon elimination is believed to have continued through the 1990s. There are no formal verification procedures in place or associated with the initiatives, however, to ensure that the systems were in fact removed and destroyed. This uncertainty was reinforced in January 2001 when the *Washington Times* reported that Russia was transferring tactical nuclear weapons to Kaliningrad Oblast, which is an isolated enclave of Russian territory between Poland and Lithuania. Russia denied the claim but in the absence of a formal inspection or other verification procedure, the truth of the allegations cannot be either confirmed or discounted.[18]

Nuclear Materials

The assistance of the United States has been critical to improving the security of both nuclear weapons and nonweaponized nuclear materials in Russia. Nuclear weapons generally enjoy a greater level of security than do Russian nonweaponized nuclear materials (highly enriched uranium and separated plutonium). A significant element of the proliferation threat posed by the breakup of the Soviet Union stems from Russia's vast holdings of these nonweaponized weapons-usable nuclear materials. Even if Russia were to eliminate its nuclear arsenal, the nuclear materials legacy of its Cold War nuclear arsenal would pose a major proliferation concern for decades to come.

Acknowledging this risk during his postsummit news conference with President Putin on November 13, 2001, President Bush said that the "highest priority is to keep terrorists from acquiring weapons of mass destruction." The Bush–Putin statement went on to say, "Both sides agree that urgent attention must continue to be given to improving the physical protection and account-

Table 6.3: **Russian Tactical Nuclear Weapon Stockpiles**

Tactical Weapon Type	Totals in 1991[1]	Total To Remain under 1991 Bush–Gorbachev Agreements	Total Tactical Nuclear Weapon Stockpile, 2000[2]	Deployed Tactical Nuclear Weapons, 2000[3]
Land-based missiles	4,000	0	0	0
Artillery	2,000	0	0	0
Mines	700	0	0	0
Air defense	3,000	1,500	1,500	600
Air force	7,000	3,500	3,500	1,000
Navy	5,000	3,000	3,400	2,000
Total	21,700	8,000	8,400	3,400

NOTES

1. Alexei Arbatov, ed., Yadernye Vooruzheniya Rossii (Moscow: IMEMO, 1997) p. 56.

2. Statement by Russian Minister for Foreign Affairs, Igor Ivanov, before the NPT Review Conference, New York, April 25, 2000. Text of statement is on the Non-Proliferation Project's website, at www.ceip.org/programs/npp/npt2000.htm.

3. Alexei Arbatov, "Deep Cuts and De-alerting: A Russian Perspective," Nuclear Turning Point (Washington, D.C.: Brookings Institution Press, 1999), p. 320.

ing of nuclear materials of all possessor states, and preventing illicit nuclear trafficking."[19]

Russia has the world's largest stocks of weapons-grade and weapons-usable nuclear materials: highly enriched uranium (HEU) and plutonium (Pu). Much of this material is not adequately protected against theft or diversion. An advisory group for the U.S. Department of Energy, chaired by former Senate majority leader and the current ambassador to Japan, Howard Baker, and former White House counsel Lloyd Cutler summed up the issue by saying: "The most urgent unmet national security threat to the United States today is the danger that weapons of mass destruction or weapons-usable material in Russia could be stolen and sold to terrorists or hostile nation states and used against American troops abroad or citizens at home. This threat is a clear and present danger to the international community as well as to American lives and liberties."[20]

Reliable estimates of the total Russian nuclear material stockpile vary, some running as high as 150 metric tons of plutonium[21] and 1,500 metric tons of highly enriched uranium. Of this material, approximately 700 metric tons are thought to be in nuclear weapons. The actual amount of nuclear material produced and held by Russia will never be known with certainty since the production of plutonium and other materials cannot be fully accounted for even under the best circumstances (the United States' own accounting has a margin of accounting error of 1 metric ton).[22]

Nonweaponized materials are scattered throughout Russia at more than 53 sites in hundreds of buildings under varying levels of security and physical protection.[23] Nuclear smuggling from Russian or former Soviet facilities continues to present an acute proliferation risk, and incidents continue to this day despite considerable efforts to improve the security of "loose" Russian materials. The International Atomic Energy Agency has confirmed that more than a dozen cases of smuggled nuclear-weapons-usable materials have occurred, many originating from the former Soviet Union. Hundreds of cases have been reported and investigated over the past decade.

NUCLEAR MATERIAL PROTECTION, CONTROL, AND ACCOUNTING. The Soviet Union relied on antiquated accounting methods and the general security provided by a closed, authoritarian state to help protect its nuclear materials. After the collapse of the Soviet system, Russia was completely unprepared to implement a modern system of nuclear material protection, control, and accounting. Almost immediately instances of smuggling Russian nuclear materials began to be reported in the media, resulting in the development of cooperative international efforts to assist Russia in securing its nuclear materials complex.

United States programs, run primarily by the U.S. Department of Energy, are working to provide enhanced security for those materials, including the consolidation of weapons-usable material into fewer sites to facilitate security upgrades and maintenance. Even after seven years of effort, however, the majority of nonweaponized Russian nuclear materials are not adequately protected. Current U.S. government projects plan to complete initial security upgrades for the materials by the end of 2006 and to complete comprehensive safeguards for the sites by the end of 2010.[24] Even this final level of protection, however, will be below the accepted international standards for the physical protection of nuclear materials. No plans currently exist to provide Russia with the resources needed to reach this level of physical security and accounting.

The Nuclear Material Security Program has received wide congressional support and was funded at the level requested annually by the Clinton administration. Despite the statements of support from the Bush campaign and administration, the first budget request from the Bush administration reduced funding for Russian nuclear material security by about $30 million, from a little more than $170 million in 2001 to $138 million. Additional cuts in Russian non-proliferation programs, including the disposition of nuclear materials and brain drain programs (see below), totaled more than $100 million from the previous year's budget. Congressional action restored funding for nuclear security upgrades for the FY 2002 budget. The Bush administration's budget request for 2003 seems to fully fund the Nuclear Material Security Program at a level of $233 million.

In addition to protecting nuclear materials in place, the United States is also funding the construction of a massive nuclear material storage facility in Russia to securely store nuclear materials that are released from dismantled nuclear weapons. The first wing of the Fissile Material Storage Facility in Mayak—capable of holding 33 metric tons of nuclear material—should begin accepting nuclear materials in 2002. The construction of a second wing is under consideration but will not begin until after the implementation of additional transparency measures to ensure the origin of the nuclear materials to be stored at the facility.[25]

Even the best long-term storage and security of nuclear materials cannot eliminate the proliferation risks associated with these huge stocks. The continued possession of large stocks of excess nuclear materials is a recognized "clear and present danger."[26] Key to reducing the risk that these materials might again be used to produce nuclear weapons (in Russia or by other states or subnational groups) is the disposal of those materials no longer required for defense purposes. To this end, the United States and Russia have been cooperating on two important programs: the HEU purchase agreement and the plutonium disposition program.

The Purchase of Highly Enriched Uranium

On February 18, 1993, Presidents Clinton and Yeltsin agreed that the United States would purchase 500 metric tons of Russian highly enriched uranium from dismantled Russian nuclear weapons.[27] The program reduces the risk of the theft of Russian nuclear material and speeds the dismantlement of Russian nuclear weapons by freeing storage space for released nuclear materials. Under the program, Russia dilutes, or "downblends," weapons-grade HEU into low-enriched uranium, which cannot be used directly in nuclear weapons. This process takes place under intrusive monitoring arrangements. Russia then ships the material to the United States for fabrication into fuel for nuclear power reactors. The entire program is designed to take place over twenty years and was originally expected to pay Russia $12 billion for the material and services. The agreement has since been renegotiated, making the amount paid to Russia contingent on market forces, meaning that Russia will receive less than the original amount envisioned.[28]

Agents appointed by the two governments carry out the pact. The U.S. executive agent is the privatized United States Enrichment Corporation (USEC), and the Russian executive agent is Techsnabexport (Tenex), the commercial arm of the Russian Ministry of Atomic Energy (Minatom). As of September 2001, the United States (through USEC) had purchased the equivalent of 125 metric tons of HEU (3,650 metric tons of LEU fuel) from Russia (enough material to produce 5,000 nuclear weapons), for which Russia received more than $2 billion dollars.[29]

Russia may have 1,000 additional metric tons of HEU not covered by this purchase agreement, much of which could eventually become excess to Russian military needs. Numerous nongovernmental experts have called for an expansion of the HEU agreement to include the purchase of larger amounts of HEU. The economic considerations of such a move are complicated by the fact that the private USEC lacks a financial incentive to expand its purchases. This conflict between national security and financial considerations is a major point of contention between experts and government officials. There are no firm official plans to expand the scope of the purchase agreement, although the issue is reportedly under review by the Bush administration.

Plutonium Disposition

The United States and Russia have both declared large amounts of former defense-purpose plutonium to be excess to defense needs. President Clinton announced that he had designated 50 metric tons of plutonium to be excess on March 1, 1995,[30] and Boris Yeltsin declared that "up to" 50 metric tons of plutonium would be made excess through the nuclear disarmament process in 1997.[31] Collectively, this material is enough to produce 25,000 nuclear weapons, and both countries have pledged to take steps so that the material is never again used for weapons.

These amounts represent significant portions of the plutonium produced in both countries, although both will have large stocks of weapons-usable materials even after these amounts are dispositioned.

The United States and Russia signed an agreement at the June 2000 summit in Moscow to dispose of 34 metric tons each of their excess weapons plutonium. Under the agreement, the two approved methods for the disposal of this material are the irradiation of plutonium in a nuclear reactor and the immobilization of plutonium with high-level radioactive waste (in either glass or ceramic form). The bilateral political agreement calls for both countries to "seek to" begin the operation of "industrial-scale" facilities no later than December 2007, at a disposal rate of 2 metric tons of plutonium per year.[32]

There are several major problems looming over the eventual implementation of the agreement, including technical and political challenges in the U.S. program and a lack of financing for the Russian disposition effort. Facing serious technical challenges and budget constraints, the Bush administration has decided to only pursue reactor-based irradiation of this material and to abandon immobilization. In addition, the Bush administration is looking at investigating the design and construction of advanced reactors for plutonium disposal. In spite of the potential challenges to the disposition program, in December 2001 the Bush administration announced, after a year-long review of U.S. non-proliferation assistance to Russia, that "the Administration remains committed to the agreement with Russia to dispose of excess plutonium."[33]

Russia has stated that it does not possess the funds required to carry out the disposition alone and would simply store the material if international support were unavailable. The United States has already agreed to provide Russia with $200 million to support Russian plutonium disposition efforts.[34] Estimates suggest that the entire Russian disposition effort, including the construction and operation of facilities, could cost $1.7 billion.[35] The first Bush administration budget, submitted to Congress in April 2001, cut funding for the Russian component for plutonium disposition from $39 million in 2001 to $15 million in 2002. Moreover, funding for U.S. plutonium disposition was drastically reduced from earlier program requirements, putting U.S. plans for disposition in jeopardy. The 2003 budget request would raise funding levels for

Russian disposition to $98 million and U.S. disposition efforts to $350 million. Russia would be unwilling and unable to dispose of its excess plutonium unless the United States does so as well. The U.S.–Russian agreement completed at the June 2000 summit in Moscow "recognizes the need for international financing and assistance" in order for Russia to implement its plutonium disposition plans.[36] The July 2000, G–8 summit in Okinawa called upon the G–8 to develop an international financing plan by the 2001 G–8 meeting that was held in Genoa, Italy. This deadline was not met, and no definite plans exist for financing Russia's disposition efforts.

Nuclear Expertise

The breakup of the Soviet Union and prolonged economic strain in Russia also pose serious non-proliferation risks in the form of Russian nuclear weapon expertise and technical know-how. International efforts to prevent the proliferation of nuclear weapons have focused not only on trying to protect Russian nuclear materials, but also on preventing Russian nuclear experts from selling their skills to would-be nuclear-weapon states and organizations.

Russia's nuclear complex is filled with tens of thousands of scientists, engineers, and technicians who are responsible for the construction, maintenance, and dismantlement of Russia's nuclear weapons. Counts vary, but as many as 120,000 workers are directly involved in Russia's nuclear complex today, many of whom have direct access to weapons-usable nuclear materials.[37]

After the collapse of the Soviet Union the employees of Russia's nuclear complex fell on hard times. Formerly the privileged inhabitants of Russia's crowned nuclear cities, these nuclear elite found themselves in geographically remote locations with rapidly dropping living standards and diminishing work orders from the central government.

Collectively referred to as a brain drain, the risk that Russian nuclear experts might be forced by economic necessity to sell their expertise or materials on hand to feed their families rapidly changed the dynamics of Russian and U.S. security considerations. In addition to the possibility of a threat from the inside to the security of nuclear materials, a serious risk of Russian nuclear expertise being transferred to countries or groups seeking nuclear capabilities immediately emerged. A key U.S. Defense Department report stated in 2001 that "numerous scientists and technicians previously involved in key [weapon] programs face severe salary reductions or loss of employment, and they could be the target of recruitment efforts by states or non-state groups trying to establish their own weapons capabilities."[38]

Chief among U.S. government concerns is that Russia's commercial nuclear assistance with Iran might help Tehran acquire nuclear weapons. CIA Director George Tenet testified to the Senate in February 2001 that "Russia . . . remained a key supplier for a variety of civilian Iranian nuclear programs, which could be used to advance its weapons programs as well."[39] The center of these concerns is that legitimate commercial nuclear transactions might provide cover for Iranian efforts to obtain sensitive nuclear technology. Moreover, the

Bushehr plant might put Iranian agents in touch with Russian experts prepared to sell their skills for a price.

The Defense Department's report on proliferation in 2001 went further, stating that "Russia has been a key supplier for civilian nuclear programs in Iran, primarily focused on the Bushehr nuclear power plant project. This assistance provides cover for Iran's nuclear weapon development efforts. Because of the dual-use nature of many nuclear technologies involved, even the transfer of civilian technology may be of use in Iran's nuclear weapons program."[40]

Both the U.S. Department of State and the Department of Energy are involved in efforts to help prevent the brain drain of former Soviet weapon scientists to countries of proliferation concern. These efforts, which are coordinated and supported by other U.S. and international agencies and organizations, consist of projects designed to provide grants for civilian research to scientists and institutions formerly involved in the development of weapons of mass destruction, as well as to help in the conversion and commercialization of former defense industries. The three principal programs in this area are: International Science and Technology Centers, the Initiatives for Proliferation Prevention (IPP), and the Nuclear Cities Initiative (NCI).

The Science Center program is designed to provide temporary support to experts, helping prevent their migration to would-be proliferant countries. The IPP program seeks to develop government–industry partnerships with a view to commercializing the technology from the Russian military complex, and provide temporary employment with a potential for longer-term business development in the Russian nuclear and weapons complex. The NCI seeks to develop permanent jobs and industries for Russian experts, creating the infrastructure and access needed to facilitate direct industry investment in the nuclear cities as their nuclear weapon infrastructure is downsized. This longer-term employment and defense conversion is by far the most difficult challenge in addressing the intellectual legacy of the nuclear arms race, but it is a prerequisite if U.S. support is not a permanent part of the U.S.-Russian relationship. The Bush administration announced plans in 2001 to combine the IPP and NCI programs, but did not release details of what this merger would mean for the two missions.

Science Centers

The State Department manages U.S. participation in both the International Science and Technology Center (ISTC) in Moscow and the Science and Technology Center of Ukraine (STCU). These centers are multi-lateral organizations designed to prevent the spread of weapons of mass destruction and missile technology expertise by providing civilian employment opportunities to former weapon scientists and engineers in the Newly Independent States (NIS).

The ISTC was founded in Moscow in 1992. Its current members are the European Union (EU), Japan, Norway, the Republic of Korea, and the United States as donors. Armenia, Belarus, Georgia, Kazakhstan, the Kyrgyz Republic, and Russia are recipient countries.[41] In July 1995 the STCU, a separate but parallel organization, commenced operations in Kiev. Currently, under the STCU auspices, Canada, the EU, Japan, and the United States fund projects in Ukraine, Georgia, and Uzbekistan. To ensure the full participation of all NIS member states, branch offices of the ISTC have been established in Almaty, Kazakhstan; Yerevan, Armenia; and Minsk, Belarus.[42] The two centers have agreed to establish a joint branch office in Tbilisi, Georgia, since Georgia is a party to both centers. The STCU also has field offices in the Ukrainian cities of Dnipropetrivsk, Kharkiv, and Lviv and has approved plans to open an information office in Tashkent, Uzbekistan.[43]

Since its inception, the ISTC has registered 2,760 project proposals and funded 1,250 projects valued at a total of $335 million. Thirty thousand specialists at more than 400 institutions have received grants from ISTC, making it less likely that they will need to sell their services to would-be proliferators.[44]

Initiatives for Proliferation Prevention and Nuclear Cities Initiative

The U.S. Department of Energy manages and funds IPP and NCI. The Bush administration, however, announced in December 2001 that the programs will be merged into one, "and restructured to focus more effectively on projects to help Russia reduce its nuclear warhead complex."[45] Like the Science Centers, the IPP program aims to provide productive nonmilitary projects for former NIS weapon scientists and engineers. While the longer-term goal is to commercialize technologies through partnerships with industries, a major portion of IPP's efforts is geared to providing the temporary engagement of weapon experts in order to prevent their migration to states of proliferation concern. IPP also seeks to promote the conversion of NIS defense industries to civilian production through the commercialization of NIS technologies and the development of links between NIS institutes and U.S. industrial partners. Unlike the ISTC and the STCU, IPP is exclusively a U.S.–NIS program and does not involve additional international partners. Since its inception, the IPP program has funded more than 700 projects involving more than 10,000 former Soviet weapon scientists at more than 180 institutes.[46]

In 1998, the U.S. Department of Energy launched NCI, designed to assist Russia in the development of nondefense-related industries in Russia's ten "closed" nuclear cities. Those cities, which are geographically isolated, are home to hundreds of thousands of skilled scientists, engineers, and technicians and hundreds of metric tons of weapons-usable nuclear materials. The desperate financial situation of the Soviet Union's remote nuclear complex has sparked a fear that highly skilled nuclear scientists and technicians, with access to nuclear materials and technology, might be forced to sell their wares to would-be nuclear-weapon states. In addition, many supporters of the NCI program hope that the effort will lead to the downsizing of the complex, which would reduce Russia's ability to reconstitute its Cold War nuclear arsenal rapidly, thereby strengthening strategic stability.

The U.S.–Russian Government-to-Government agreement on the Nuclear Cities Initiative was signed by U.S. Secretary of Energy Bill Richardson and

Russian Atomic Energy Minister Yevgeny Adamov on September 22, 1998. The original concept was developed by the U.S. government in cooperation with an initiative from several nongovernmental organizations. According to the agreement, the initiative aims to "create a framework . . . that will provide new jobs for workers displaced from enterprises of the nuclear complex."[47] Since the signing of that agreement, the U.S. Department of Energy and Minatom have agreed to focus initial activities at three of the ten Russian nuclear cities: Sarov (Arzamas-16), Snezinsk (Chelyabinsk-70), and Zheleznogorsk (Krasnoyarsk-26). In addition, Minatom has stated its intention to cease weapon-related activities at Penza-19 and Arzamas-16 by the year 2003.

Biological and Chemical Weapon Analysis

The Soviet Union had active and large-scale chemical and biological weapon programs, the bulk of which were inherited by Russia when the Soviet Union ceased to exist in 1991. Several key biological weapon facilities are located in non-Russian former Soviet Republics, including Kazakhstan and Uzbekistan. Russia's stocks of chemical weapons and biological weapon samples, and the expertise it took to produce them, continue to pose serious proliferation threats. The risk that these materials or the expertise used in their production might leak out of the former Soviet Union and aid countries or terrorist groups in the acquisition or use of chemical or biological weapons is a serious global security concern—a concern that has increased in the wake of the post–September 11 anthrax attacks in the United States. A U.S. administration official testified before the Senate in November 2001 that "the large numbers of stockpiles of chemical agents throughout Russia . . . are not subjected to the best possible physical security measures." The same concerns exist for Russia's biological weapon capabilities. In addition, the same Bush official stated that the United States continues "to have concerns regarding Russia's compliance with the chemical and the biological weapons conventions to which they are a party."[48] Russia continues its efforts, with the assistance of the United States and other countries, to eliminate its chemical and biological weapon capabilities in compliance with its treaty commitments. Progress to date, however, has been slow owing to inadequate funding, poor management, and bureaucratic conflicts.

Chemical Weapons

Russia possesses the largest stocks of chemical weapons in the world. Moscow's holdings include an estimated 40,000 metric tons of chemical weapons at seven storage sites. A major portion (81 percent) of Russia's chemical weapon stockpile consists of nerve agents, including sarin, soman, and VX viral agents. The remaining 19 percent of the stockpile is made up of blistering agents, including lewisite, mustard, and lewisite-mustard mixtures. These materials are stored in both munition containers (including projectiles, rocket warheads, bombs, spray devices, and Scud missile warheads) and bulk storage containers. All the nerve agents are in weaponized form, but some of the blister agents are contained in bulk storage.

Russia is a member of the Chemical Weapons Convention, which requires the elimination of all chemical weapons and the conversion of chemical weapon production facilities. Russia signed the treaty on January 13, 1993, and ratified the pact on November 5, 1997. There are continued suspicions, however, that Russia has not made a full and complete declaration of all its past chemical weapon activities. The terms of the treaty require that all parties eliminate their chemical weapon stockpiles in four phases, completing the destruction of portions of the national stocks within 2, 5, 7, and 10 years of the agreement's entry into force.[49] Russia was the only one of the four declared chemical weapon–possessing states (India, Russia, South Korea, and the United States) that failed to meet the initial deadline for the elimination of 1 percent of its chemical weapons. (Other countries, including Iraq and North Korea, are known to have or are thought to have chemical weapons, but either they have not made official declarations or are not parties to the CWC.) Russia was granted a two-year extension, until April 2002, by the Conference of State Parties to the CWC to meet the deadline.[50]

Russia is unlikely to meet its extended deadline for eliminating the first 1 percent of its weapons, let alone the four-year deadline to eliminate 20 percent of its stockpile. In addition, there is little hope that Russia will be able to comply with the treaty's deadline to eliminate all chemical weapons by 2007. Russia has not yet completed construction on even one of its planned CW destruction facilities and has recently revised its chemical weapon elimination plans.

Table 6.4: **Chemical Weapons by Storage Location and Form**

Chemical Weapons Storage Site	Chemical Type	Percentage of Stockpile	Storage Form
Shchuche	Nerve agent	13.6	Projectiles and rocket warheads
Pochep	Nerve agent	18.8	Air-delivered munitions
Leoniddovka	Nerve agent	17.2	Air-delivered munitions
Gorny	Blister agent/mustard, lewisite, and mixture	2.9	Bulk containers
Maradykovsky	Nerve agent	17.4	Air-delivered munitions
Kizner	Blister agent/lewisite	14.2	Projectiles and rocket warheads
Kambarka	Blister agent/lewisite	15.9	Bulk containers

SOURCE

Smithson, Amy, et al. Chemical Weapons Disarmament in Russia: Problems and Prospects, Report 17, Henry L. Stimson Center, October 1995, Federation of American Scientists web site, www.fas.org/nuke/guide/russia/cbw/cw.htm, November 2001.

The new government plan for the elimination of chemical weapons was approved on July 5, 2001. The new plan calls for the construction of CW elimination facilities at Shchuche, Kambarka, and Gorny and to scale back the cost of the CW destruction efforts from a previous cost of $7 billion to between $3.5 and 4.9 billion. The original plans called for the construction of destruction facilities at each of Russia's seven CW storage sites. The new plan also calls for the construction of material neutralization facilities at Leoniddovka, Maradykovsky, and Pochep to render the nerve agents there safe for transport to Shchuche for final elimination. Shchuche would become the main CW destruction facility for Russian nerve agents, building upon the support provided by the United States and Germany. The other two sites would handle the elimination of Russia's blistering agents.

Russia is receiving considerable assistance from the United States and other countries to facilitate its CW destruction. The United States has agreed to provide funds for the construction of a chemical weapon destruction facility at the CW storage plant in Shchuche. Delayed, in part, by a decision by the U.S. Congress not to fund the construction of this facility in 2000 and 2001, current plans call for the construction of the U.S.–funded plant at Shchuche to begin in 2002. Given the past difficulties with the program, the Department of Defense, which oversees the program, has not yet estimated when the facility will begin operation.[51] Estimates from 1999 predicted the facility would not begin operation until 2006, indicating that the plant is unlikely to go into operation until the end of the decade.[52]

Russia did begin the destruction of "unfilled munitions and devices, and equipment specifically designed for use directly in connection with employment of chemical weapons" in 2000.[53] In addition, Russia has also begun the elimination of its World War I chemical agents, controlled as Category II items under the CWC.[54]

Biological Weapons

The former Soviet Union possessed the world's largest offensive BW program. The program continued to expand even after the USSR signed the Biological Weapons Convention in 1972 and eventually included a network of more than 50 institutes that produced vast amounts (metric tons) of biological agents, including anthrax and smallpox. The Soviet program, however, relied mainly on a surge capability to produce large amounts of weaponized agents in a time of crisis. Russia, according to U.S. and Russian officials and experts, is thought to have destroyed its stocks of offensive weapons, although this destruction cannot be independently verified and significant amounts of offensive stocks may continue to exist in Russia.

Russia is known to maintain a large quantity of biological weapon samples that could be used to grow and produce large amounts of offensive biological agents. In addition, Russia continues to maintain many of the former facilities that would have been used in the production of BW stocks, representing a latent ability to weaponize biological agents. While this residual production capability is of concern to some, the main proliferation risks posed by the former Soviet

BW capability is the risk that the samples of BW agents could be stolen or that the experts responsible for their production might sell their skills to others.

The Soviet BW program produced large amounts of many BW agents. In addition, the Soviet program developed genetically altered strains of weapons to make them resistant to common antibiotics. Thousands of samples of these agents exist in several dozen "libraries" in Russia, each sample of which could be used to grow large amounts of virulent, offensive BW agents.

The non-proliferation threats posed by the former Soviet program are twofold. The first is that the samples of BW agents are not adequately protected against theft. These samples are extremely portable, many consisting merely of test tubes of agents, and an adequate security and tracking system for these agents does not exist. In addition, the official closure of the former BW program by the Russian government means that tens of thousands of experts and employees have been forced to find other ways to support themselves, raising concerns that they may have migrated to help BW programs in other countries.

Missile Analysis

Russia's advanced missile capabilities also pose important proliferation challenges, especially given the continued economic stress in Russian society and in the Russian weapon complex. Just as Russia relied on dedicated nuclear cities in the production of its nuclear arsenal, so too did it construct a series of missile design and production enterprises. Those factories and design bureaus continue to maintain Russia's current missile arsenal and designs; they built the next generation of Russia's strategic missile arsenal, the SS–27 ICBM.

Given the low level of production in Russia, there is a large body of underpaid and underemployed missile-related experts who must find alternative ways to make a living. This, along with the parallel concerns in the nuclear realm, has raised serious concern that Russia's missile expertise may be assisting other countries in the production of advanced ballistic missile capabilities. Chief among these concerns is the possible role of Russia in helping Iran develop long-range missiles. In addition, there continues to be concern over Russia's role in helping India to develop its advanced missile and space-launch capabilities, which are virtually identical to long-range missile programs. These concerns remain, despite the fact that Russia became a member of the Missile Technology Control Regime in 1995 and has adopted internal reforms to tighten controls over missile-related exports. CIA Director Tenet testified in 2001 that

> Russian entities last year [2000] continued to supply a variety of ballistic missile-related goods and technical know-how to countries such as Iran, India, China, and Libya. Indeed, the transfer of ballistic missile technology from Russia to Iran was substantial last year, and in our judgment will continue to accelerate Iranian efforts to develop new missiles and to become self-sufficient in production.[55] Iran's earlier success in gaining technology and materials from Russia has helped to accelerate Iranian development of the *Shahab-3* MRBM, and continuing Russian assistance likely supports Iranian efforts to

develop new missiles and increase Tehran's self-sufficiency in missile production.[56]

Robert D. Walpole, National Intelligence Officer for Strategic and Nuclear Programs, National Intelligence Council, went further in his testimony before the U.S. Senate Governmental Affairs Committee in September 2000, saying that "entities in Russia, North Korea, and China supply the largest amount of ballistic missile-related goods, technology, and expertise to Iran. Tehran is using this assistance to develop new ballistic missiles and to achieve its goal of becoming self-sufficient in the production of existing systems."

What has never been shown conclusively is whether this assistance is carried out by rogue organizations within Russia, operating in violation of Russian government policy and export controls, or whether the assistance was part of a clandestine but official Russian government policy to aid Iran. The goal of the assistance would be to ensure Russia's relation with a key potential ally in the Middle East, especially one with which the United States has no formal relations. Russian officials vigorously deny any formal assistance to Iran's missile or nuclear weapon programs. The failure of continued efforts by the U.S. government to shut down Russia transfers to Iran missile programs, however, raises concern that the transfers might be part of a broader Russian policy toward Iran.

The United States has been highly vocal in its concern that Russian missile expertise is being exported to countries of proliferation concern. United States law, including the Iran Missile Sanctions Act of 1998, requires the president to impose sanctions on companies that provide equipment or technology to Iran's ballistic missile program (see table 6.5). These sanctions prohibit any U.S. government assistance or contracts to the sanctioned entities. Sanctions against two of the entities (INOR and Polyus) were lifted in April 2000.

Table 6.5: **U.S. Missile Sanctions against Russian Firms**

Year	Organization
1998	Baltic State Technical University Europalace 2000 Glavkosmos Grafit INOR Scientific Center MOSO Company Polyus Scientific Production Association
1999	Moscow Aviation Institute Mendeleyev University

SOURCES

Berger, Sandy, national security adviser, speech at Carnegie Endowment International Non-Proliferation Conference, January 12, 1999.

Cirincione, Joseph, ed. *Repairing the Regime: Preventing the Spread of Weapons of Mass Destruction*. New York: Routledge, 2000.

Diamond, Howard. "Clinton Vetoes Sanctions Bill; Sets, Imposes New Sanctions on Russia." *Arms Control Today*, June/July 1998.

Table 6.6: **Russian Nuclear Facilities**

		A. Russian Civilian and Military Nuclear Facilities			
Name	**Location**	**Activity**	**Plutonium**	**Weapons-grade Uranium**	**Comments**
All-Russian Scientific Research Institute of Experimental Physics (VNIIEF)	Sarov	Nuclear weapon design, research, and development	>1,000 kg	>1,000 kg	Non-Proliferation Center
All-Russian Scientific Research Institute of Technical Physics	Snezhinsk	Nuclear warhead research and design	>1,000 kg	>1,000 kg	3 pulse reactors
Avangard Electromechanical Plant	Sarov	Nuclear warhead assembly and dismantlement	>1,000 kg	>1,000 kg	
Beloyarsk Nuclear Power Plant	Zarechnyy	Nuclear power plant	No	>1,000 kg	Bn-600 fast-breeder reactor, fresh- and spent-fuel storage
Bochvar All-Russian Scientific Research Institute of Inorganic Materials	Moscow	Fuel-cycle technology research/ fissile-material processing	<1,000 kg	<1,000 kg	
Electrochemical Plant	Zelenogorsk (formerly Krasnoyarsk-45)	Uranium enrichment, HEU downblending	No	>1,000 kg	Centrifuge enrichment plant
Elektrokhimpribor Combine	Lesnoy (formerly Sverlovsk-45)	Nuclear warhead production and dismantlement facility	>1,000 kg	>1,000 kg	

Facility	Location	Function			Notes
Elektrostal Machine-building Plant	Elektrostal	HEU fuel fabrication for naval propulsion and fast-breeder reactors	No	>1,000 kg	HEU and LEU fuel production lines, 7 critical assemblies
Institute of Medical and Biological Problems	Moscow	Scientific research: medical and biological	No	<100 kg	1 research reactor, under construction
Institute of Physics and Power Engineering	Obninsk	Research and development for nuclear power engineering	>1,000 kg	>1,000 kg	3 research reactors, 2 fast critical assemblies, up to 16 critical assemblies
Institute of Theoretical and Experimental Physics	Moscow	Research on heavy-water applications for nuclear weapon production	No	<1,000 kg	1 decommissioned 2.5-MW heavy-water research reactor
Instrument-making Plant	Trekhgornyy (formerly Zlatoust-36)	Nuclear warhead assembly and dismantlement	>1,000 kg	>1,000 kg	Also produces ballistic missile reentry vehicles
Joint Institute of Nuclear Research	Dubna	International scientific research center	<10 kg	<100 kg	Plutonium-fueled pulsed research reactor
Karpov Scientific Research Institute of Physical Chemistry	Obninsk	Research on chemical applications, medical isotope production	No	<100 kg	
Khlopin Radium Institute	St. Petersburg	Research on reprocessing technologies	<5 kg	<5 kg	Nuclear material storage facility

(Table continues on the following page.)

Table 6.6: **Russian Nuclear Facilities** (continued)

		A. Russian Civilian and Military Nuclear Facilities (continued)			
Name	**Location**	**Activity**	**Plutonium**	**Weapons-grade Uranium**	**Comments**
Khlopin Radium Institute	Gatchina	Research on reprocessing technologies	Gram quantities	Gram quantities	Hot cells
Kurchatov Institute	Moscow	Research in solid-state physics, fusion, and plasma physics	Yes	>1,000 kg	10 research and power reactors, 16 critical assemblies, 2 subcritical assemblies
Luch Scientific Production Association	Podolsk	R&D, production and testing of high-temperature uranium fuel elements	No	>1,000 kg	3 research reactors, 1 central storage facility
Mayak Production Association	Ozersk (formerly Chelyabinsk-65)	Warhead component production, spent-fuel reprocessing	>1,000 kg	>1,000 kg	5 nonoperational plutonium production reactors, 2 HEU-fueled tritium production reactors
Mining and Chemical Combine	Zheleznogorsk (formerly Krasnoyarsk-26)	Spent-fuel reprocessing	>1,000 kg	>1,000 kg	1 operational plutonium production reactor
Moscow Engineering and Physics Institute	Moscow	Educational institution	Small amounts for research	<100 kg	1 2.5-MW research reactor, 5 subcritical assemblies

Novosibirsk Chemical Concentrates Plant	Novosibirsk	HEU fuel fabrication for research reactors	No	>1,000 kg	HEU and LEU fuel production lines
Petersburg Institute of Nuclear Physics	Gatchina	Research on high-energy theoretical physics	No	>100 kg	Operational 18-MW research reactor, 100-MW research reactor under construction
Scientific Research Institute of Atomic Reactors	Dimitrovgrad	Research on power reactors, fuel cycle	>100 kg	>1000 kg	7 operational research reactors, 2 critical assemblies
Scientific Research Institute for Instruments	Lytkarino	R&D of radioelectronic instruments	No	>1,000 kg	5 nonoperational pulsed research reactors
Scientific Research and Design Institute of Power Technology	Moscow	Design of nuclear reactors for power generation, naval propulsion	No	<10 kg	1 inactive (50-kW) research reactor, 3 critical assemblies
Scientific Research and Design Institute of Power Technology	Zarechnyy	Nuclear reactor design and development	No	>100 kg	1 research reactor, 3 critical assemblies, hot cells
Siberian Chemical Combine	Seversk (formerly Tomsk-7)	Largest multi-function compound in the Russian nuclear complex	>1,000 kg	>1,000 kg	2 operational plutonium production reactors, a reprocessing plant, a uranium enrichment plant, plutonium pit fabrication facilities
START Production Association	Zarechnyy (formerly Penza-19)	Nuclear warhead assembly and dismantlement	>1,C00 kg	>1,000 kg	

(Table continues on the following page.)

Table 6.6: **Russian Nuclear Facilities** (continued)

		A. Russian Civilian and Military Nuclear Facilities (continued)			
Name	**Location**	**Activity**	**Plutonium**	**Weapons-grade Uranium**	**Comments**
Tomsk Polytechnical University	Tomsk	Educational institution	No	<100 kg	1 research reactor, fresh-fuel storage vault
Urals Electrochemical Integrated Plant	Novouralsk (formerly Sverdlovsk-44)	Uranium enrichment	No	>1,000 kg	Gas-centrifuge enrichment plant, HEU downblending facilities
		B. Russian Naval Facilities, Northern Fleet			
Ara Bay Naval Base	Vidyayevo	Operational naval base serving nuclear submarines, decom-missioned nuclear submarine storage	No	Unknown amount	
Atomflot	2 km north of Murmansk	Operational nuclear-powered icebreaker base, radioactive waste processing and storage	No	>500 kg	
Gadzhiyevo Naval Base	Gadzhiyevo	Operational naval base serving nuclear submarines, nuclear submarine defueling	No	Unknown amounts	Northern Fleet's largest SSBN base

Gremikha Naval Base	Near Ostrovnoy	Former naval base, nuclear submarine defueling	No	Unknown amounts
Nerpa Shipyard	Snezhnogorsk (formerly Murmansk-60)	START-designated submarine dismantlement facility	No	Approximately 1,000 kg
Northern Machine Building Enterprise	Severodvisnk	START designated submarine dismantlement facility	No	>1,000 kg
Olenya Bay Naval Base	Olenya	Operational naval base serving SSBNs	No	>1,000 kg
Pala Bay Submarine Repair Facility	Polyarnyy	Nuclear submarine repair	No	Unknown amount
Severomorsk Naval Base	Severomorsk	Operational base serving three nuclear-powered battle cruisers	No	>1,000 kg
Sevmorput Naval Shipyard No. 35	Rosta district of Murmansk	Submarine repairs, decommissioned submarine storage	No	Unknown amount
Shkval Naval Yard No. 10	Polyarnyy	Nuclear submarine repair, refueling	No	Unknown amount
Zapadnya Litsa Naval Base	Zaorzersk	Operational naval base serving nuclear submarines	No	Unknown amount
Zvezdochka State Machine Building Enterprise	Yagra Island	START-designated submarine dismantlement facility	No	Unknown amount

(Table continues on the following page.)

Table 6.6: **Russian Nuclear Facilities** (continued)

		C. Russan Naval Facilities, Pacific Fleet			
Name	Location	Activity	Plutonium	Weapons-grade Uranium	Comments
Amurskiy Zavod	Komsomolsk-na-Amure	SSBN and SSN construction	No	Unknown amount	
Cape Sysoyeva	Shkotovo Peninsula	Nuclear submarine waste storage	No	Unknown amount	
Chazhma Ship Repair Facility	Shkotvo Peninsula	Submarine repair and defueling	No	>2,000 kg	
Gornyak Shipyard	Near Vilyuchinsk	Submarine repair and refueling	No	>1,000 kg	
Pavlovsk Bay	Eastern edge of Strelok Bay	Main operational submarine base for Pacific Fleet	No	Unknown amount	
Razboynik Bay	Razboynik Bay	Decommissioned nuclear submarine and reactor compartment storage	No	Unknown amount	
Rybachiy Nuclear Submarine Base	Near Petropavlovsk	Operational naval base serving nuclear submarines	No	Unknown amount	
Zavety Ilyicha	Postavaya Bay	Former operational naval base	No	Unknown amount	

		D. Other Russian Naval Facilities			
Zvezda Far Eastern Shipyard	Bolshoy Kamen	START-designated submarine dismantlement facility	No	Unknown amount	
Admiralteyskiye Verfi Shipyard	St. Petersburg	Construction of submarines and naval vessels	No	Possibly in fresh fuel and critical assembly	
Baltic Shipyard	St. Petersburg	Construction of nuclear-propelled surface vessels	No	Unknown amount	
Central Physical-Technical Institute	Sergiyev Posad (formerly Zagorsk)	Research on nuclear propulsion for naval and space vessels	No	At least 5–10 kg fresh fuel, approximately 90% enrichment	At least 2 pulsed research reactors
Experimental Machine Building Design Bureau	Nizhniy Novgorod	Nuclear reactor design	No	Unknown amount	4 critical assemblies
Krylov Central Scientific Research Institute	St. Petersburg	R&D of nuclear reactors for naval vessels	No	<100 kg	1 0.5-MW research reactor, 2 critical assemblies

Source

Table derived from Wolfsthal, Jon, Cristina-Astrid Cheun, and Emily-Ewell Daughty, ecs., *Nuclear Status Report: Nuclear Weapons, Fissile Material, and Export Controls in the Former Soviet Union.* Washington D.C., 2001.

NOTES

1. Jon Wolfsthal et al., eds., *Nuclear Status Report: Nuclear Weapons, Fissile Material, and Export Controls in the Former Soviet Union* (Washington, D.C.: Carnegie Endowment and Monterey Institute, 2001), p. 175.

2. Amy Smithson, *Toxic Archipelago: Preventing Proliferation from the Former Soviet Chemical and Biological Weapons Complexes*, Report 32, Henry L. Stimson Center, December 1999.

3. Senator Sam Nunn, Acceptance Speech at Eisenhower Institute Awards Dinner, April 26, 2001. Available at www.nti.org/c_press/c_index.html#speeches.

4. Wolfsthal, *Nuclear Status Report*, p. 35.

5. Joseph Cirincione and Jon Wolfsthal, "What If the New Strategic Framework Goes Bad," *Arms Control Today*, November 2001.

6. Wolfsthal, *Nuclear Status Report*, p. 35.

7. Ibid.

8. Interview with U.S. Department of Defense (DOD) officials, September 2001.

9. CTR web page. Available at www.dtra.mil/ctr/project/projrus/ctr_nuclearweapons_proj.html.

10. Discussions with U.S. DOD officials, 2001. See also Wolfsthal, *Nuclear Status Report*, 2001.

11. U.S. Arms Control and Disarmament Agency, *START I Treaty*.

12. White House Fact Sheet, "Joint Statement on Parameters on Future Reduction in Nuclear Forces," Helsinki, Finland, March 21, 1997.

13. White House Press Conference transcript, November 2001.

14. U.S. Arms Control and Disarmament Agency, *Treaty between the United States of America and the Union of Soviet Socialist Republics on the Elimination of their Intermediate-Range and Shorter-Range Missiles*.

15. On-site Inspection Agency (OSIA) fact sheet, "INF Eliminations and Inspectable Sites." Available at www.dtra.mil/news/fact/nw_infelim.html.

16. Table, "USSR/Russian Nuclear Warheads," NRDC web page October 23, 2001. Available at www.nrdc.org/nuclear/nudb/datab10.asp.

17. Stockholm International Peace Research Institute (SIPRI), *Yearbook 1991: World Armament and Disarmament* (New York: Oxford University Press, 1992); Richard Fieldhouse, et al., chap. 2, "Nuclear Weapon Developments and Unilateral Reduction Initiatives," p. 70; SIPRI, *Yearbook 1992: World Armament and Disarmament*, (New York: Oxford University Press, 1993); Dunbar Lockwood and Jon Wolfsthal, chap. 6, "Nuclear Weapon Developments and Proliferation," SIPRI Yearbook, p. 228.

18. Nikolai Sokov, "The Tactical Nuclear Weapons Scare of 2001," Monterey Institute of Strategic Studies web site. Available at cns.miis.edu/pubs/reports/tnw.htm.

19. White House transcript, November 13, 2001.

20. U.S. Department of Energy, "A Report Card on the Department of Energy's Nonproliferation Programs with Russia," Secretary of Energy Advisory Board, January 10, 2000. p. 1.

21. The actual number may not even be known in Russia. The United States Congress appropriated $500,000 for Russia to conduct an internal plutonium inventory.

22. U.S. Department of Energy, "Plutonium: The First Fifty Years," 1994.

23. Wolfsthal, *Nuclear Status Report*, chap. 4; and "Nuclear Facilities in the Former Soviet Union Map."

24. U.S. Department of Energy, MPC&A Program Strategic Plan, July 2001, National Nuclear Security Agency, p. 4.

25. U.S. DOD, *Cooperative Threat Reduction Program Plan*, I–IV–37, 2001.

26. National Academy of Science, *Plutonium Disposition Report*, 1994.

27. For a complete review of this program, refer to *Nuclear Status Report*.

28. Thomas Neff, "Privatizing U.S. National Security: the U.S.–Russian HEU Deal Risk," *Arms Control Today*, August/September 1998.

29. USEC Press Release, September 26, 2001.

30. President Clinton, Speech at the Nixon Center for Peace and Freedom, March 1, 1995.

31. Statement delivered by Minatom Minister Mikhailov at 41st IAEA General Conference, September 26, 1997.

32. U.S. Department of Energy, *Strategic Plan*, Office of Fissile Materials Disposition, June 2000.

33. White House Fact Sheet: "Nonproliferation, Threat Reduction Assistance to Russia," December 27, 2001.

34. FY 1999, *Energy and Water Appropriations Act*.

35. U.S. Department of Energy, "Preliminary Cost Assessment for the Disposition of Weapon-Grade Plutonium Withdrawn from Russia's Military Programs," Office of Fissile Materials Disposition, April 2000.

36. White House Fact Sheet, June 4, 2000.

37. V. Tikhonov, *Russia's Nuclear and Missile Complex* (Washington, D.C.: CEIP, 2001), p. 7.

38. U.S. DOD, *Proliferation Threat and Response*, January 2001, p. 3.

39. George Tenet, Director, Central Intelligence Agency, "Worldwide Threat 2001: National Security in a Changing World," Testimony before the Senate Select Committee on Intelligence, February 7, 2001.

40. U.S. DOD, *Proliferation Threat and Response*, p. 58.

41. International Science and Technology Center (ISTC) Fact Sheet, October 28, 1999. Available at www.istc.ru.

42. In accordance with U.S. policy, the United States has not funded any new projects in Belarus since 1997, although Belarus is still a party to the ISTC.

43. Information about the STCU field offices is available at www.stcu.kiev.ua; the decision to open the joint office in Tbilisi is contained in "Joint Statement: STCU Governing Board Meeting, December 15, 1999." Available at www.stcu.kiev.ua.

44. ISTC Fact Sheet, November 21, 2001. Available at www.istc.ru.

45. White House Fact Sheet, December 27, 2001.

46. Personal communication with U.S. Department of Energy staff, November 2001.

47. *Agreement between the Government of the United States of America and the Government of the Russian Federation on the Nuclear Cities Initiative*, September 22, 1998.

48. Marshall Billingslea, deputy assistant secretary of defense, Testimony before the Senate Governmental Affairs Committee, November 29, 2001.

49. *Convention on the Prohibition of the Development, Production, Stockpiling and Use of Chemical Weapons*, article 4.

50. Organization for the Prohibition of Chemical Weapons, Conference on State Parties, Fifth Session Decision Document C–V/Dec. 14, May 17, 2000. Available at www.opcw.org.

51. Conversation with U.S. DOD personnel, November 2001.

52. U.S. General Accounting Office, "Weapons of Mass Destruction: Effort To Reduce Russian Arsenals May Cost More, Achieve Less Than Planned," NSIAD–99–76, April 13, 1999, p. 3.

53. Category III items under the *Chemical Weapons Convention*, part 4.

54. Jonathan Tucker, "Russia's New Plan for Chemical Weapons Destruction," *Arms Control Today*, July/August 2001.

55. George Tenet, Director, Central Intelligence, Testimony before the Senate Select Committee on Intelligence, "Worldwide Threat 2001: National Security in a Changing World," February 7, 2001. CIA web site, www.cia.gov.

56. *Unclassified Report to Congress on the Acquisition of Technology relating to Weapons of Mass Destruction and Advanced Conventional Munitions*, July 1–December 31, 2000.

NORWAY

SWEDEN

Norwegian Sea

Gadzhiyevo Naval Base

Zapadnaya Litsa

Murmansk

Novaya Zemlya

Baltic Sea

FINLAND

POLAND

LITHUANIA

LATVIA

ESTONIA

Barents Sea

Kara Sea

St. Petersburg

BELARUS

Vypolzovo

Kurchatov Institute
Lytkarino

Moscow

Elektrostal

Kostroma

RUSSIA

Kozelsk

Luch

Teykovo

Obninsk/IPPE

Yurya

Avangard
VNIIEF

Sarov

Yoshkar Ola

Perm

Lesnoy

Zarechnyy

Bershet

Nizhniy Tagil

UKRAINE

Tatishchevo

Dimitrovgrad/NIIAR

Novouralsk

Yekaterinburg

Engels

Mayak

Snezhinsk/VNIITF

Volgograd

Chelyabinsk

Trekhgornyy

Kartaly

Seversk

Dombarovskiy

Novosibirsk

Caspian Sea

GEORGIA

Barnaul

ARMENIA

Aleysk

AZERBAIJAN

Aral Sea

KAZAKHSTAN

IRAN

TURKMENISTAN

UZBEKISTAN

KYRGYZSTAN

CHINA

Carnegie Endowment for International Peace, *Deadly Arsenals* (2002), **www.ceip.org**

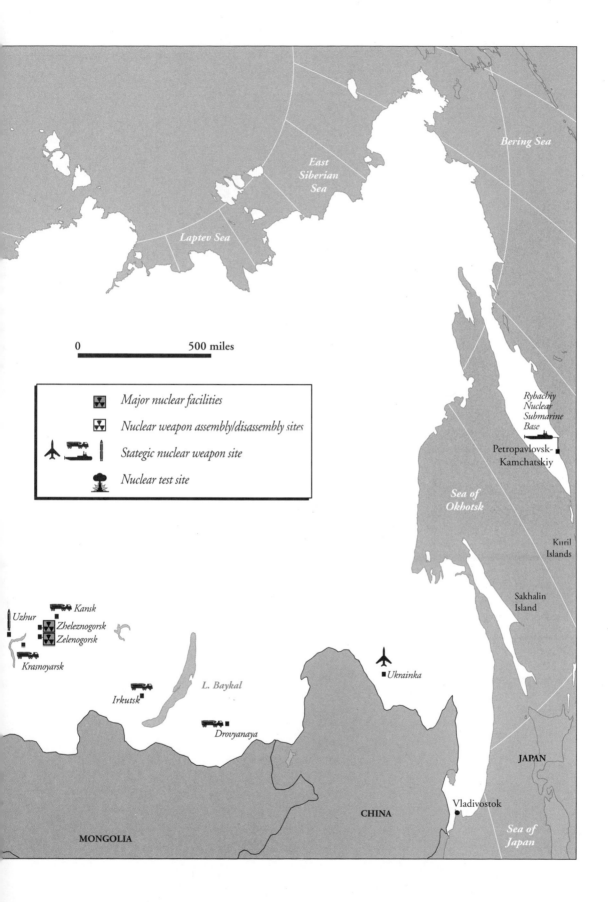

Bering Sea

East
Siberian
Sea

Laptev Sea

0   500 miles

Major nuclear facilities

Nuclear weapon assembly/disassembly sites

Stategic nuclear weapon site

Nuclear test site

Rybachiy
Nuclear
Submarine
Base

Petropavlovsk-
Kamchatskiy

Sea of
Okhotsk

Kuril
Islands

Sakhalin
Island

Uzhur
Kansk
Zheleznogorsk
Zelenogorsk

Krasnoyarsk

L. Baykal

Irkutsk

Ukrainka

Drovyanaya

JAPAN

Vladivostok

CHINA

MONGOLIA

Sea of
Japan

CHAPTER 7

China

Nuclear Weapon Capability

China is a recognized nuclear-weapon state under the Non-Proliferation Treaty and possesses enough nuclear material for hundreds of nuclear weapons. China deploys approximately 400 nuclear weapons on various delivery platforms, mostly short- and medium-range missiles. Approximately 20 Chinese weapons are deployed on systems that can reach the continental United States. Since developing its first nuclear weapon in 1964, China has been a major supplier of sensitive nuclear and missile technology to the developing world. The United States and other countries have worked to draw China step-by-step into the international non-proliferation regime. Over three decades, these efforts have achieved important, though still incomplete, progress. Proliferation issues still complicate the U.S.–China relationship.

China has not officially released details about the size or composition of its nuclear arsenal, making estimates difficult to develop. Much of the unclassified information compiled on China's forces is from unverified media reports and occasional statements by intelligence or government officials. From these it is possible to estimate that China fields approximately 270 warheads on land- and sea-launched missiles, 150 bomber weapons, and 120 weapons on artillery, short-range missiles, and other weapons.[1] Beijing also maintains a fairly extensive nuclear weapon production and research complex. China has conducted 45 nuclear weapon tests, the first of which took place on October 16, 1964, and the last on July 29, 1996. China has signed but not yet ratified the Comprehensive Test Ban Treaty.

Aircraft and Missile Capabilities

China is in the process of modernizing its strategic missile forces. Although China deploys several types of ballistic missiles, only the DF–5 (13,000-kilometer range) is an ICBM by Western standards and is capable of reaching the continental United States. Currently, China deploys approximately 20 DF–5 ICBMs and 20 DF–4 intermediate-range missiles (5,500-kilometer range). The DF–31, a mobile, three-stage solid-fueled ICBM with an estimated range of 8,000 kilometers, is now being developed. Plans to develop another land-based missile, the DF–41, a solid-fueled ICBM with a range of 12,000 kilometers, appear to have been shelved in favor of a more advanced but less developed ICBM.[2] China has conducted three flight tests of the DF–31, the last one on

November 4, 2000. China will likely not be able to field the DF–31 for several years, and a new, longer-range missile will probably not be fielded until the end of the decade. China is also developing the Julang–2, a submarine-launched ballistic missile based on the DF–31. China has only one ballistic missile submarine, however, which has never left coastal waters and is not operational. China's bomber force consists mainly of aging H–6 aircraft based on the Soviet Tu–16 Badger bomber, with a range of 3,000 kilometers. China is purchasing multi-role Su–30 and Su–27 aircraft from Russia, but these are not thought to have been modified for a nuclear role.[3]

Biological and Chemical Weapon Capability

China is believed by U.S. intelligence to possess chemical and biological weapon capabilities, although it is unknown whether it has offensive stocks of such weapons in any significant amount. China is a signatory to the Biological Weapons Convention and the Chemical Weapons Convention and has denied having any biological warfare programs. It declared under the terms of the CWC that it previously had a chemical weapon program but that it destroyed those agents before joining the treaty.

Nuclear Analysis

China is of particular non-proliferation importance in two ways. As a nuclear-weapon state, it has a large nuclear weapon and material production complex. These weapons and materials are of concern to its neighbors, to the United States, and other potential targets. Questions about the security and accountability of the weapons and materials are particularly important. China, however, is also a major supplier of nuclear technology and equipment in the developing world, and its past behavior in the nuclear and missile fields is a significant non-proliferation concern.

Following its first nuclear test in 1964, China began a slow but steady process of developing a full-fledged nuclear weapon infrastructure and strategic and tactical nuclear arsenal.[4] Estranged from the West after the Communist revolution in 1949, China was also isolated from the evolving international framework of peaceful uses of nuclear energy and from the collaboration that produced the IAEA in the 1950s, the NPT in the late 1960s, and the development of nuclear export-control guidelines in the 1970s. As a Communist power during the Cold War, China was also excluded from the establishment of the Missile Technology Control Regime, which originated in 1987 as a Western arrangement to exchange information on and restrain the exports of nuclear-capable missiles and related technology.

In the early years of its isolation from the Western community, China adopted a posture that rhetorically *favored* nuclear weapons proliferation, particularly in the Third World, where this theme once had some appeal as a rallying point for anti-imperialism.[5] Through the 1970s, China's policy was *not to oppose* nuclear proliferation, which it still saw as limiting U.S. and Soviet power.

After China began to open to the West in the 1970s, its rhetorical position gradually shifted to one *that opposes* nuclear proliferation.

China's practical approach to the export of nuclear and military goods did not, however, conform to the standards of the international non-proliferation regime. Major efforts have been made over the past 25 years to persuade China to modify its approach formally, bringing it into closer alignment with the policies of the other nuclear-supplier states. These efforts have produced demonstrable results. A domestic export-control system has developed with constant U.S. encouragement, but it is still a work in progress and has not yet become completely effective.

China's Nuclear Weapons

China is slowly modernizing its strategic nuclear forces but still has the least advanced nuclear arsenal of the five declared nuclear-weapon states. The Chinese doctrine is centered on the maintenance of a "minimum nuclear deterrent" capable of launching a retaliatory strike on a small number of countervalue targets (such as cities) after an adversary's nuclear attack and when its deployments appear consistent with the declared policy. The design and deployment of China's nuclear forces have been shaped by two key concerns: the survival of a second-strike capability and the potential deployment of missile defense systems.

China currently has the capability to strike U.S. cities with a force of approximately 20 long-range Dong Feng–5 missiles, each armed with a single 4- to 5-megaton warhead. The twenty Dong Feng–4 missiles "are almost certainly intended as a retaliatory deterrent against targets in Russia and Asia," according to U.S. intelligence assessments,[6] but the missiles could strike parts of Alaska and the Hawaiian island chain. (China has 80–100 other missiles that could strike targets in Eurasia.) The time needed to launch these liquid-fueled ICBMs, a lack of hardened missile silos, and a lack of missile mobility have raised concern in the Chinese leadership about survivability of these forces. In addition, China's sea-based force (one Xia submarine armed with twelve medium-range ballistic missiles) does not pose a credible threat to either Moscow or Washington. The *Xia* has never sailed outside China's territorial waters, is considered vulnerable to modern anti-submarine warfare techniques, and is not currently operational.[7] To overcome these concerns, China has been pursuing the development of smaller, mobile missiles.

Because of its limited second-strike capabilities, China is particularly concerned about the potential development of missile defenses. A national missile defense covering the United States, together with advanced theater missile defense systems sold to America's Asian allies, would greatly complicate China's nuclear planning. The United States theoretically would then have the ability to destroy or defeat China's deterrent force. Should China's concerns about its security substantially increase, and if military modernization were given preference over economic modernization, it would likely increase its number of deployed warheads, increase its production of planned systems, and develop and deploy (and possibly sell) countermeasures to defeat missile defense systems. China's concerns over the Strategic Defense Initiative announced in 1983 reportedly spurred its plans to develop multiple-warhead technology. The first test of a multiple-warhead missile took place in September 1984. While similar tests have been conducted on several missile types since then (including a November 2000 test of the DF–31 with decoy warheads), no missile currently deployed is thought to carry multiple independently targeted reentry vehicles. China is thought to have been developing smaller warheads when it ended its nuclear test program before signing the CTBT in 1996, and allegations over nuclear espionage by China against the United States, which erupted in 1999, were centered on China's interest in developing smaller warheads for future MIRVed missiles. China plans by 2010 to have completely modernized its nuclear forces, although historically its progress has been slow and has lagged well behind foreign estimates.

ICBMs. The planned improvements of China's land-based forces include the replacement of the aging force of DF–5s, and potentially the DF–4s, with two new, land-based ICBMs.[8] The DF–31 is designed to be a solid-fueled, road-mobile missile with a range of 8,000 kilometers. China conducted a third test of the DF–31 on November 4, 2000, and could field the system as early as the first half of this decade. Plans to develop a 12,000-kilometer land-based missile, the DF–41, appear to have been shelved in favor of a longer-range version of the DF–31, also solid-fueled and road-mobile but less developed.[9] This missile may be deployed near 2010 as the DF–5 leaves service. Some of the newer DF–5's may remain in service past that date.

Exact deployment numbers are unknown, but a recent U.S. National Intelligence Estimate shows that that China could field between 75 and 100 warheads on MIRVed, solid-fueled ICBMs over the next fifteen years, both mobile and in hardened silos, and equipped with various penetration aids to defeat missile defenses.[10] Many reports suggest that the current force consists of about twenty, single-warhead DF–5 missiles.

SLBMs. While China has plans to deploy four to six of its second-generation submarines (the 094), it is unlikely that more than three, if any, will be deployed by 2010. Each submarine could be armed with 12 JL–2 SLBMs, with a range of 8,000 kilometers and a potential MIRV capability. The JL–2 is based on the DF–31 missile and has been under development since the 1980s.[11]

STRATEGIC BOMBERS. The H–6 is China's current medium-range bomber. Based on the Soviet Tu–16 Badger of 1950s' vintage, it has a range of 3,000 kilometers. While the Chinese air force flight-tested a more modern bomber, the H–7, in 1988, most experts believe that it will not have a nuclear role and that only twenty will be built.[12] It is unlikely that China will invest substantial resources in its airborne nuclear capability unless it is able to purchase the T–22M Backfire from Russia. (China is, however, reportedly developing an air-launched cruise missile.)

China's Fissile Material Stockpile

A frequently overlooked proliferation issue in China is its large stockpile of weapons-usable fissile material. Although the situation in China seems stable at present, increased political and economic strain could raise the risk of the diversion of fissile material from China's nuclear complex. Little is known about the state of China's material protection, control, and accounting (MPC&A) system.

The exact size of China's fissile material stock is unknown since Beijing has not disclosed it or the size of its nuclear weapon stockpile. Analysts estimate that China has produced between 2 and 6 metric tons of weapons-grade plutonium and between 15 and 25 metric tons of highly enriched uranium. China is believed to have ended its production of weapons-grade plutonium in 1991 and production of weapons-grade uranium in 1987.[13] Chinese weapons are believed to be heavily dependent on weapons-grade uranium, and it is estimated that China uses 20–30 kilograms per weapon. Plutonium weapons might require 3–4 kilograms on average.[14]

China produced weapons-usable enriched uranium from 1964 until 1987 at two sites, Lanzhou and Heping.[15] Plutonium was also produced at two sites, Jiuquan and Guangyuan, from 1968 until 1991.[16]

China presumably has stored its residual fissile material stocks at various nuclear facilities. Their locations and the amounts of China's nonweaponized fissile material, however, have not been declared and are not specifically known, nor is the level of security at the storage sites. The China National Nuclear Corporation (which has the status of a government ministry) "produces, stores, and controls all fissile material for civilian as well as military applications."[17] It is estimated that about 14 sites associated with China's nuclear weapon program have significant quantities of weapons-usable fissile material. The primary locations of nonweaponized fissile material are believed to be China's facilities for plutonium production and uranium enrichment as well as its research institutes for nuclear weapons and other nuclear fuel-cycle facilities across the country.

Information on China's material protection, control and accounting system is scarce, but the United States has been concerned about it enough to initiate discussions on China's MPC&A (among other issues) between the national nuclear laboratories in both countries. Contacts between the nuclear weapon laboratories in the United States and China were developing beginning in 1994, but they were suspended in the wake of allegations of Chinese nuclear espionage in the Wen Ho Lee case in 1999. Although China's MPC&A system is modeled after the Soviet system, an expert at one of the U.S. national laboratories ranked China's MPC&A system as better than that of the Soviet Union before it collapsed.[18] In 1996, China commissioned a computerized "national nuclear materials accounting system" at about twelve nuclear facilities to improve its ability to prevent the illegal loss, theft, or transfer of nuclear materials.[19] Still, questions remain about the level of protection at China's nuclear facilities.

Alleged Chinese Nuclear and Missile Espionage

United States–China relations were rocked in 1999 by reports that China had stolen the designs of the most advanced U.S. nuclear warheads. The *New York Times* launched the scandal in a March 6, 1999, story that claimed, "Working with nuclear secrets stolen from a U.S. government laboratory, China has made a leap in the development of nuclear weapons: the miniaturization of its bombs. . . . Government investigators have identified a suspect, an American scientist at Los Alamos laboratory."[20] The story was based on leaks from a special investigative committee in the U.S. House of Representatives chaired by Representative Christopher Cox (Republican, California). The committee released a glossy, three-volume, declassified report on May 25, 1999, that concluded:

- These thefts of nuclear secrets from our national weapons laboratories enabled the [People's Republic of China] to design, develop and successfully test modern strategic nuclear weapons sooner than would otherwise have been possible.

- The stolen U.S. nuclear secrets give the PRC design information on thermonuclear weapons on a par with our own. . . . The stolen information includes classified information on seven U.S. thermonuclear warheads."

- The stolen U.S. secrets have helped the PRC fabricate and successfully test modern strategic thermonuclear weapons.[21]

The Committee spent most of its time in 1998 investigating charges that critical technology was transferred to China by major U.S. corporations while using Chinese rockets to launch U.S. satellites. Some political leaders believed the investigation might lead to impeachment charges against then-president Bill Clinton. Although it was a major political issue during much of 1998, it faded in 1999. The committee turned to the matter of Chinese espionage on October 21, 1998, concluded taking testimony on the issue from three witnesses on November 15, and filed its report on January 3, 1999.

The report led to sensational charges. Doctor Wen Ho Lee, a scientist at Los Alamos National Laboratories, was arrested under suspicion of espionage. Doctor Stephen Younger, then–associate director for Nuclear Weapons at Los Alamos, testified at Lee's bail hearing, "These codes and their associated data bases and the input file, combined with someone that knew how to use them, could, in my opinion, in the wrong hands, change the global strategic balance." He added, "They enable the possessor to design the only objects that could result in the military defeat of America's conventional forces. . . . They represent the gravest possible security risk to . . . the supreme national interest."[22]

The Cox committee report recommended that the executive branch conduct a comprehensive damage assessment on the implications of China's acquisition of U.S. nuclear weapon information. The administration did so, forming a team of officials from the intelligence and investigative agencies, including the CIA and FBI, and the nuclear laboratories. An independent panel of nuclear experts, chaired by Adm. David Jeremiah and including Gen. Brent Scowcroft and Dr. John Foster, then reviewed their damage assessment. In April 1999 the panel issued its report. This net assessment reached three critical conclusions:

- China's technical advances have been made on the basis of classified and unclassified information derived from espionage, contact with U.S. and other countries' scientists, conferences and publications, unauthorized media disclosures, declassified U.S. weapons information, and Chinese indigenous development. The relative contribution of each cannot be determined.

- Significant deficiencies remain in the Chinese weapons program. . . . To date, the aggressive Chinese collection effort has not resulted in any apparent modernization of their deployed strategic force or any new nuclear weapons deployment.

- China has had the technical capability to develop a multiple independently targetable reentry vehicle (MIRV) system for its large, currently deployed ICBM for many years, but has not done so.[23]

This assessment contradicted the central claims of the Cox report. As the political fires cooled, most experts agreed with the concerned but cautious independent assessment. The case brought against Dr. Lee, the alleged spy, was dropped in 2001 after he was held for months in solitary confinement. A criminal investigation of the charges was resolved in January 2002 with a fine against the Loral Corporation for its failure to follow proper declassification procedures before providing a report to Chinese officials who sought information on launch failures.[24] Neither the Bush administration, the Senate, nor the House of Representatives has raised anew any of the allegations in the Cox report.

China's Commitment to the Non-Proliferation Regime

Drawing China into the nuclear and missile non-proliferation regimes has been a long-term process. Since opening a dialogue with China in the early 1970s, the United States has used a range of positive incentives and disincentives to encourage China to sign on to the various unilateral and multi-lateral commitments that make up the international non-proliferation regime. During the 1980s and 1990s, China's nuclear-related exports, particularly to Pakistan, were of major international proliferation concern and have continued to cloud bilateral relations between the two countries. China, however, made notable strides in the 1990s by joining formal arms control and non-proliferation regimes, beginning with its accession to the NPT in 1992; its signature (1993) and ratification (1997) of the Chemical Weapons Convention; its cessation of nuclear weapon explosive testing; and its signature of the Comprehensive Test Ban Treaty in September 1996. China has supported multi-lateral negotiations on a fissile material production cut-off convention, and it acceded to the Biological Weapons Convention in 1984.

China has generally stayed away from "informal" multi-lateral control arrangements. It still declines to join the Nuclear Suppliers Group, though it has agreed to observe NSG's published guidelines of 1987. It is still not a full partner to the MTCR and may not be fully observant of the revised guidelines of 1993. It may also have a unilateral interpretation of certain guidelines. In the matter of chemical weapons, China has not joined the Australia Group.

Under direct U.S. pressure, China has moved to establish a domestic legal system to control sensitive nuclear exports by private or semi-private Chinese entities. These steps, while imperfect, were sufficient by 1998 for the United States to certify that China could be trusted to safeguard U.S. sensitive nuclear technology as part of the implementation of the 1985 U.S.–China Agreement for Peaceful Nuclear Cooperation. The certification concluded that "the People's Republic of China has provided clear and unequivocal assurances to the United States that it is not assisting and will not assist any non-nuclear-weapon state, either directly or indirectly, in acquiring nuclear explosive devices or the material and components for such devices."[25]

SENSITIVE NUCLEAR EXPORTS. The continuing nature of China's role as an international supplier of nuclear technology to weapon programs is in question. China disregarded international norms in the 1980s by selling nuclear materials to such countries as Argentina, India, Pakistan, and South Africa, without requiring the items be placed under IAEA safeguards. CIA director George Tenet testified in 2001 that "on the nuclear front, Chinese entities have provided extensive support in the past to Pakistan's safeguarded and unsafeguarded nuclear programs. In May 1996, Beijing pledged that it would not provide assistance to unsafeguarded nuclear facilities in Pakistan; we cannot yet be certain, however, that contacts have ended."[26] Given China's history of exports to weapon programs, any sensitive nuclear exports by China are likely to be interpreted as contradicting its pledges to conform to international standards, even if the items in question are not intended for or were not diverted for non-peaceful ends.

China's nuclear exports to two particular countries, Pakistan and Iran, have been a leading cause of concern. These exports and other issues have provoked several serious crises in U.S.–China relations and triggered repeated congressional demands for sanctions.

PAST EXPORTS TO PAKISTAN. China's assistance to Pakistan's nuclear program over the past 15 years may have been critical to Pakistan's nuclear weapon breakthroughs in the 1980s. In the early 1980s, China was believed to have supplied Pakistan with the plans for one of its earlier nuclear bombs and possibly to have provided enough highly enriched uranium for two such weapons.[27] According to an August 1997 report by the U.S. Arms Control and Disarmament Agency: "Prior to China's [1992] accession [to the NPT], the United States concluded that China had assisted Pakistan in developing nuclear explosives. . . . Questions remain about contacts between Chinese entities and elements associated with Pakistan's nuclear weapons program."[28] China was also believed to be assisting

Pakistan with the construction of an unsafeguarded 50–70 MWt plutonium production reactor at Khusab,[29] and the completion of an unsafeguarded plutonium reprocessing facility at Chasma that had been started with French assistance in the early 1970s. If these facilities were to come on line without safeguards, they would give Pakistan, for the first time, a source of plutonium for use in nuclear weapons.

China has also assisted Pakistan's civilian nuclear program, circumventing the nuclear trade embargo on Pakistan observed by members of the NSG, by helping build a 300-MWe power reactor at Chasma. This reactor will be placed under IAEA safeguards as a condition-of-supply under the existing China–Pakistan agreement for peaceful nuclear cooperation. Pakistan has not, however, accepted full-scope safeguards. Consequently, co-located facilities, such as the partially completed Chasma reprocessing plant, may remain inaccessible to IAEA inspection.

The export of ring magnets to Pakistan disclosed in 1996 seemed to contradict China's claims that it did not help other countries to develop nuclear weapons and that it was tightening its nuclear export controls. According to press reports, the Clinton administration determined in August 1995 that China had sold 5,000 ring magnets valued at $70,000 to the Abdul Qadeer Khan Research Laboratory in Kahuta between December 1994 and mid-1995.[30] This unsafeguarded gas-centrifuge facility can produce weapons-grade, highly enriched uranium. The custom-built ring magnets, made of an advanced samarium-cobalt alloy, would enable Pakistan to upgrade and replace its enrichment centrifuges. Although the ring magnets are not on the nuclear trigger list, they are an integral part of magnetic suspension bearings, which are controlled as dual-use items, by the Zangger Committee. (The committee is an informal association of major nuclear suppliers that regulates nuclear exports and bars its members from exporting any sensitive nuclear material and equipment to such countries as Pakistan that do not accept full-scope safeguards, i.e., regular IAEA inspections of all nuclear materials and activities in its territory.) While Pakistan denied any such transfer occurred, China maintained that its nuclear cooperation with Pakistan was solely for peaceful purposes.[31]

The ring magnet sale resulted in extensive U.S.–Chinese discussions on the issue culminating in a May 10, 1996, announcement that the United States would not impose sanctions against China given three factors: first, the finding that senior-level Chinese officials were unaware of the ring magnet transfer; second, China's public commitment not to "provide assistance to unsafeguarded nuclear facilities;" and, third, China's pledge to engage in a dialogue with the United States on improving export controls.[32] Later reports indicated that the Chinese government had punished the official responsible for the ring magnet transfer.[33] Secretary of State Warren Christopher explained that "senior Chinese officials have explicitly confirmed our understanding that the Chinese policy of not assisting unsafeguarded nuclear facilities would prevent future sales . . . of ring magnets."[34]

China followed these commitments by joining the Zangger Committee and does not appear to have supplied any new technology to Pakistan. Yet U.S.

intelligence officials noted at the end of 2001: "We cannot rule out some continued contacts between Chinese entities and entities associated with Pakistan's nuclear weapons program subsequent to Beijing's 1996 pledge and during this reporting period."[35] China's close ties proved useful in 2001 as Chinese officials played a quiet but—according to U.S. diplomats—crucial role in supporting Pakistan and coordinating with the United States during the anti-terrorism war in Afghanistan.[36]

EXPORTS TO IRAN. China has also been a principal supplier of nuclear technology to Iran. China provided Iran with three zero-power research reactors and one very small (30-kWt) reactor, as well as two or three small calutrons (electromagnetic isotope separation machines). While calutrons in those numbers would not themselves produce fissile uranium in significant quantities, they would serve to train personnel in a sensitive nuclear activity.[37] China and Iran signed a ten-year nuclear cooperation agreement in 1990, and Iran agreed in 1992 to purchase two 300-MWe pressurized-water reactors from China.[38]

The United States has led an international effort to prevent the supply of nuclear technology to Iran and has placed pressure on China (and other suppliers) to cancel nuclear deals with Iran. United States pressure has made a difference. By 1995 there were signs that China's nuclear cooperation with Iran was being scaled back. Another factor in this retrenchment may have been Russia's competition as an alternative supplier. Russia agreed to supply lightwater nuclear reactors to Iran and to help Iran finish construction of the Bushehr nuclear power plant, abandoned by German contractors during the Iran–Iraq War. Opposition from the United States to China's reactor contract probably also played a part.[39] Iranian shortages of capital may have been a third factor. At any rate, in September 1995 China finally agreed to "suspend for the time being" its reactor sale to Iran.[40] A few months later, a Chinese Foreign Ministry spokesman acknowledged that "the implementation of the agreements between China and Iran on nuclear cooperation has ceased."[41]

China continued until 1997, however, to assist Iran in constructing a plant near Esfahan to produce uranium hexafluoride, the material fed into gas centrifuges for enrichment. Chinese technicians were assisting Iran with other parts of the nuclear-fuel cycle, such as uranium mining and processing and fuel fabrication.[42] Yet it seems that these activities were carried out in accordance with the NPT and under IAEA safeguards.

In October 1997 China agreed to end cooperation with Iran on the uranium conversion facility and not to undertake any new cooperation with Iran after completion of the two existing projects—the zero-power reactor and a zirconium production plant. United States intelligence assessments note that "although the Chinese appear to have lived up to these commitments, we are aware of some interactions between Chinese and Iranian entities that have raised questions about its 'no new nuclear cooperation' pledge. According to the State Department, the administration is seeking to address these questions with appropriate Chinese authorities."[43]

EXPORTS TO ALGERIA. China has also pursued a continuing nuclear export relationship with Algeria. The first stage of this cooperation, under an agreement that dates back to 1983, involved the secret construction of the Es Salam 15-MWt research reactor at Ain Oussera.[44] Shortly after the reactor was discovered and publicized in April 1991, Algeria agreed to place it under IAEA safeguards, and an agreement on safeguards for this purpose was signed in February 1992. Thus the reactor has been subject to IAEA inspections since its inauguration in December 1993.

In 1966 China signed agreements with Algeria that covered the second and third stages of nuclear cooperation between the countries.[45] China is helping to construct the Algerian Center of Nuclear Energy Research, which will be placed under IAEA safeguards.

Algeria has also built a hot-cell facility and connected it by a covered canal to the Es Salam research reactor. The hot-cell facility was declared to the IAEA in 1992. If it were used in conjunction with a boosted output of the Es Salam reactor, which could produce up to 5 kilograms of plutonium a year, the hot-cell facility could separate weapons-grade plutonium. By the summer of 1997, IAEA inquiries appeared to satisfy U.S. officials that Algeria will operate the facility under safeguards, allow IAEA environmental sampling, and will not build up an inventory of separated plutonium from spent fuel.[46] Of additional interest is a larger facility nearby that Algeria has not declared to the IAEA as a nuclear facility, but that some Western officials believe may be intended as a large-scale reprocessing facility.

While Algeria formally acceded to the NPT in January 1995 and signed an agreement on safeguards with the IAEA in May 1996, China's nuclear cooperation with the country remains sensitive in light of Algeria's interest in reprocessing facilities and its past lack of candor (see chapter 17).

Sensitive Missile Exports

As with its nuclear exports, China's role as a provider of missile and missile-related technology to several countries has been a controversial issue in overall relations with the United States and other countries. Unlike in the nuclear arena, however, there are no international treaties that prohibit the export of ballistic missiles and related equipment. China was not involved in the creation of the MTCR and for many years resisted being held to its standards. Over time, through the application of sanctions required under U.S. law for the export of missiles and equipment, and with the incentive of licensing the launch of U.S. satellites on Chinese commercial space-launch vehicles, China did agree to abide by some terms of the MTCR. China reportedly has aided the missile programs of Iran, Iraq, Libya, North Korea, Pakistan, Saudi Arabia, and Syria, although the extent of that assistance has been greatly reduced in recent years. CIA Director Tenet testified in 2001 that "last November, the Chinese Foreign Ministry issued a statement that committed China not to assist other countries in the development of ballistic missiles that can be used to deliver nuclear weapons. Based on what we know about China's past proliferation behavior, Mr. Chairman, we are watching and analyzing carefully for any sign that Chinese entities may be acting against that commitment."[47]

PAST EXPORTS TO PAKISTAN. China was believed to have transferred key components for the short-range, nuclear-capable M–11 surface-to-surface missiles to Pakistan in the early 1990s. In June 1991 the United States imposed MTCR Category II sanctions against entities in Pakistan and China for missile technology transfers. These sanctions were lifted in March 1992 after the United States received written confirmation from China that it would abide by the MTCR "guidelines and parameters." Washington took this confirmation to mean that China would not export either the M–9 or the M–11 missile.

But reports surfaced that China had again transferred complete M–11s to Pakistan in late 1992. The Clinton administration again imposed Category II sanctions on Pakistan and China in August 1993. These sanctions were lifted in October 1994 after China again promised not to export M–11 or similar missiles, and to abide by the "guidelines and parameters" of the MTCR.

Press reports in the fall of 1996 revealed new evidence of additional Chinese transfers of complete M–11 missiles to Pakistan. One quoted a recent U.S. National Intelligence Estimate that indicated that Pakistan already had roughly three dozen M–11s stored in canisters at the Sargodha Air Force Base, west of Lahore, along with maintenance facilities and missile launchers.[48] It was said that those missiles, although not "operational," could be unpacked, mated with launchers, and made ready for launch in 48 hours. Even more disturbing in the report was the conclusion that Pakistan, using blueprints and equipment supplied by China, began construction of a factory in late 1995 that was capable of producing short-range, solid-fuel missiles based on the Chinese-designed M–11. The factory, located near Rawalpindi, was then expected to be operational in one or two years.[49]

A Chinese supply of complete missiles, or of the production technology, for missiles covered by the MTCR would be a major violation of MTCR guidelines and, according to U.S. law, would trigger Category I sanctions—which could block all trade between the United States and Chinese aerospace and electronics firms. China and Pakistan both have denied the existence of the missile plant.[50] In April 1997, State Department official Robert Einhorn reiterated Clinton administration concerns over Chinese transfers of missile-related components, technology, and production technology to Pakistan.[51] He also said that the United States could not make the determination that complete, operational missiles had been transferred; such a determination would require a "high evidentiary standard" since the consequences of sanctions on U.S. firms would be highly damaging. The CIA reported in 2001 that "Chinese entities continued to provide significant assistance to Pakistan's ballistic missile program during [the year 2000]."[52]

EXPORTS TO IRAN. China has been a supplier to Iran of anti-ship cruise missiles (Silkworms, C–801s, and C–802s), dating back to the Iran–Iraq War in the

1980s. More recently, China has also played a role in Iran's efforts to set up an indigenous ballistic missile development and production program. In June 1995 the CIA had reportedly concluded that China had delivered guidance systems, rocket fuel ingredients, and computerized machine tools to Iran to assist that country in improving imported ballistic missiles and in producing its own missiles.[53] In August 1996 the China Precision Engineering Institute reportedly agreed to sell missile guidance equipment to Iran.[54] China has transferred short-range CSS–8 ballistic missiles to Iran. In addition, China has sold ten fast-attack craft armed with C–802 anti-ship cruise missiles to Iran, and Iran is modifying additional fast-attack craft to launch the missiles. The CIA reported in 2000 that "China continued to supply crucial ballistic missile–related equipment, technology, and expertise to Iran. Tehran is using assistance from foreign suppliers and entities to support current development and production programs and to achieve its goal of becoming self-sufficient in the production of ballistic missiles."[55]

PAST EXPORTS TO SYRIA. Syria also has received Chinese assistance for its ballistic missile program. A 1988 deal to sell Syria the M–9 missile was apparently canceled under pressure from the United States, but China has supplied Syria with technical expertise for its missile program and ingredients for solid rocket fuel.[56] China has also sold Silkworm anti-ship cruise missiles to Iraq.

PAST EXPORTS TO SAUDI ARABIA. In 1988, China supplied Saudi Arabia with thirty or more DF–3 (CSS–2) intermediate-range ballistic missiles. Although China had deployed these missiles earlier in its own arsenal with nuclear warheads, Chinese and Saudi officials insist that the missiles transferred to Saudi Arabia were equipped only with conventional warheads. Several hundred Chinese technicians maintain the missiles at their bases at Al Sulayyil and Al Leel. These missiles are nearing the end of their operational life, and Saudi Arabia has begun looking for replacements.[57] United States missile sanctions laws could be triggered if China or Saudi Arabia were to arrange transfers of CSS–2 replacements.

Chemical and Biological Weapon Analysis

Official Chinese government statements consistently claim that China never researched, produced, or stockpiled biological weapons. It is widely believed nevertheless that the Chinese declarations are inaccurate and that China retains a limited biological warfare capability despite Beijing's accession to the BWC in 1984. China is believed to have begun its biological weapon program in the 1950s. Its current program is largely based on technology that was developed before it became a state party to the BWC. Nevertheless, China's biotechnical infrastructure and munition production facilities are sufficient to develop, produce, and weaponize biological agents.[58] Research involving biological weapons is also allegedly "being conducted at two ostensibly civilian research facilities known to be under de facto military control."[59] Chinese sales of biological weapon–related technology from China remain a concern. According to former

Secretary of State Madeleine Albright, the United States has received reports that Chinese firms have supplied Iran with dual-use equipment that could be used in a biological weapon program.[60]

China is one of the few countries that has been the victim of biological warfare. In the late 1930s, Japan established a large biological warfare research and testing facility in Manchuria. Known as Unit 731, the program included human testing on Chinese prisoners. Before and during World War II the Japanese successfully disseminated typhus rickettsia, cholera bacteria, and the plague in attacks against Chinese civilians and troops. In October 1940 Japan allegedly launched an airborne attack in the Chinese province of Chekiang in which contaminated rice and fleas were scattered over the city of Chuhsien. An outbreak of the bubonic plague followed the event. A similar Japanese attack in Ning Bo resulted in the death of 500 villagers.[61]

In 1992, China revealed that more than two million chemical weapons had been abandoned in several sites on its territory, a legacy of the former Japanese army's occupation. By the end of 1945 China had suffered an estimated 10,000 fatalities and 80,000 casualties from Japan's use of chemical weapons in China.[62] Joint Sino-Japanese efforts to destroy the stockpiles of mustard, lewisite, and phosgene munitions continue.[63]

Upon ratification of the CWC in April 1997, China acknowledged its former chemical weapon production capability but did not declare possession of a chemical weapon stockpile. There is some evidence that Beijing destroyed its stockpile of chemical weapons before signing the CWC.[64] Other reports contend that China's "current inventory is believed to include the full range of traditional chemical agents."[65] There is little dispute that China retains an extensive chemical weapon capability. A recent report by the U.S. Department of Defense states, "Beijing is believed to have an advanced chemical warfare program including research and development, production and weaponization capabilities."[66] China's chemical industry is able to manufacture numerous chemicals relevant to chemical weapon production. China also maintains a broad range of delivery systems for chemical agents, including artillery rockets, aerial bombs, land mines, mortars, and short-range and medium-range ballistic missiles.

Numerous instances of Chinese chemical weapon materials and technology sales abroad have established China as a serious proliferation concern. Many countries have sought chemicals and technology of Chinese origin. The United States has consistently sanctioned Chinese companies and individuals for chemical weapon proliferation activities. Chemical exports to Iran are of particular concern. During the summer of 1996, China reportedly delivered 400 metric tons of chemicals to Iran, including nerve agent precursors.[67] In May 1997 the United States imposed sanctions on seven Chinese entities for knowingly and materially contributing to Iran's chemical warfare program. These sanctions remained in effect at the beginning of 2002. In June 1998 China announced that it had expanded its chemical export controls to include 10 of the 20 listed by the Australia Group but not prohibited by the Chemical Weapons Convention. Ostensibly, Beijing is seeking to restrain proliferation from within its borders. The results of government enforcement, however, have been mixed.

NOTES

1. William Arkin, Robert Norris, Hans Kristenson, and Joshua Handler, "NRDC Nuclear Notebook: Chinese Nuclear Forces, 2001," *Bulletin of the Atomic Scientists*, September/October 2001, pp. 71–72; International Institute for Strategic Studies, *The Military Balance, 2001–2002* (London: Oxford University Press, 2001), p. 194.

2. Arkin, Norris, Kristenson, and Handler, "Chinese Nuclear Forces."

3. Ibid.

4. See Robert Norris, Andrew Burrows, and Richard Fieldhouse, *Nuclear Weapons Databook, Vol. V: British, French, and Chinese Weapons* (Washington, D.C.: Natural Resources Defense Council, 1994); Ming Zhang, *China's Changing Nuclear Posture* (Washington, D.C.: Carnegie Endowment for International Peace, 1999).

5. See John Wilson Lewis and Xue Litai, *China Builds the Bomb* (Stanford University Press, 1988), p. 36.

6. National Intelligence Council (NIC), "Foreign Missile Developments and the Ballistic Missile Threat through 2015," Unclassified Summary of a National Intelligence Estimate (Washington, D.C.: Central Intelligence Agency, 2002), p. 9.

7. Vice Adm. Thomas Wilson, director, Defense Intelligence Agency, "Global Threats and Challenges through 2015," Statement for the Record, Senate Select Committee on Intelligence, February 7, 2001.

8. NIC, "Foreign Missile Developments," p. 10.

9. Ibid.; and Arkin, Norris, Kristenson, and Handler, "Chinese Nuclear Forces," p. 71.

10. NIC, "Foreign Missile Developments," p. 10.

11. Arkin, Norris, Kristenson, and Handler, "Chinese Nuclear Forces," p. 71.

12. Ibid.

13. David Albright, Frans Berkhout, and William Walker, *Plutonium and Highly Enriched Uranium 1996: World Inventories, Capabilities, and Policies* (Oxford: Oxford University Press, 1997), pp. 76–78 and 128–130.

14. Ibid., pp. 77 and 130.

15. Ann MacLachlan and Mark Hibbs, "China Stops Production of Military HEU," *Nuclear Fuel*, November 13, 1989, p. 5. The 1987 date is based on a personal communication from Mark Hibbs, who was told the date by the head of the China Nuclear Energy Industry Corporation; cited in Albright, Berkhout, and Walker, *Plutonium and Highly Enriched Uranium 1996*, p. 126.

16. Robert Norris, Andrew Burrows, and Richard Fieldhouse, *Nuclear Weapons Databook Vol. V: British, French, and Chinese Nuclear Weapons* (Boulder: Westview Press, 1994), p. 350.

17. Wendy Frieman, "New Members of the Club: Chinese Participation in Arms Control Regimes 1980–1995," *Nonproliferation Review*, spring–summer 1996, p. 18.

18. Interview with U.S. National Laboratory official, June 1996.

19. Tang Bin, "China: Major Advances Realized in Nation's Nuclear Fuel Accounting System," *Zhongguo He Gongye Bao [China Nuclear Industry News]*, September 11, 1996, in FBIS–CST–96–019, November 26, 1996.

20. James Risen and Jeff Gerth, "Breach at Los Alamos: A Special Report"; and "China Stole Nuclear Secrets for Bombs, U.S. Aides Say," *New York Times*, March 6, 1999, p. A1.

21. *Report of the Select Committee on U.S. National Security and Military/Commercial Concerns with the People's Republic of China*, vol. 1 (Washington, D.C.: U.S. GPO, 1999), pp. ii, iii, and 60.

22. "Atomic Scientist Is Taking Case to Court of Public Opinion," *New York Times*, January 9, 2000, p. A16; and "Excerpt from Testimony at Hearing on the Wen Ho Lee Case," *New York Times*, September 27, 2000, p. A16.

23. "The Intelligence Community Damage Assessment on the Implications of China's Acquisition of U.S. Nuclear Weapons Information on the Development of Future Chinese Weapons," April 21, 1999. Available at www.ceip.org/files/projects/npp/resources/ChinaDamageAssessment.htm.

24. "Loral Settles U.S. Probe for $14 Million," *Washington Post*, January 9, 2002, p. A8.

25. Presidential Determination 98-10, issued by the White House, January 15, 1998.

26. George Tenet, "Worldwide Threat 2001: National Security in a Changing World," Senate Select Committee on Intelligence, February 7, 2001.

27. Leslie Gelb, "Pakistan Link Perils U.S.–China Nuclear Pact," *New York Times*, June 22, 1984, p. A1; Leslie Gelb, "Peking Said To Balk at Nuclear Pledges," *New York Times*, June 23, 1984, p. A3; and Gary Milhollin and Gerard White, "A New China Syndrome: Beijing's Atomic Bazaar," *Washington Post*, May 12, 1991, p. C1.

28. Arms Control and Disarmament Agency, *Adherence to and Compliance with Arms Control Agreements*, Washington, D.C., August, 1997, p. 80.

29. Bill Gertz, "China Aids Pakistani Plutonium Plant," *Washington Times*, April 3, 1996.

30. Bill Gertz, "China Nuclear Transfer Exposed," *Washington Times*, February 5, 1996, p. A1; and R. Jeffrey Smith, "U.S. Aides See Troubling Trend in China–Pakistan Nuclear Ties," *Washington Post*, April 1, 1996, p. A14.

31. *Reuters* and *United Press International* reports, February 8, 1996.

32. U.S. Department of State, "Special Briefing on U.S.–China Discussions on Non-Proliferation and Nuclear-related Exports," Washington, D.C., May 10, 1996.

33. Senate Governmental Affairs Committee, International Security, Proliferation, and Federal Services Subcommittee, *Weapons Proliferation in China*, April 10, 1997.

34. Testimony of Secretary of State Warren Christopher before the Commerce, Justice and Judiciary and Related Agencies Subcommittee of the House Appropriations Committee, May 15, 1996.

35. CIA, "Report to Congress on the Acquisition of Technology relating to Weapons of Mass Destruction and Advanced Conventional Munitions, July–December 2000," Washington, D.C., September 2001. Available at www.ceip.org/files/nonprolif/resources/intelligence.asp.

36. Charles Hutzler, "China's Quiet, Crucial Role in the War," *Wall Street Journal*, December 18, 2001, p. A10.

37. Albright, Berkhout, and Walker, *Plutonium and Highly Enriched Uranium 1996*, pp. 359–360.

38. Mark Hibbs, "Russian Industry May Be Key to Iran's Reactor Prospects," Jane's Special Report, *Nucleonics Week*, September 17, 1992, p. 3.

39. Elaine Sciolino, "Iran Says It Plans 10 Nuclear Plants But No Atom Arms," *New York Times*, May 14, 1995, p. 1.

40. "China Softens Stance against Iranian Reactors," *Washington Post*, September 30, 1995.

41. "China–Iran," *Associated Press*, January 9, 1996.

42. Bill Gertz, "Iran Gets China's Help on Nuclear Arms," *Washington Times*, April 17, 1996, p. 1; R. Jeffrey Smith, "China Nuclear Deal with Iran Is Feared," *Washington Post*, April 17, 1995, p. A1; and David Albright, "An Iranian Bomb?" *Bulletin of Atomic Scientists*, July/August 1995, p. 25.

43. CIA, "Report to Congress."

44. Albright, Berkhout, and Walker, *Plutonium and Highly Enriched Uranium 1996*, pp. 363–364.

45. "Algeria Signs Nuclear Draft Agreement with China," *Reuters*, June 2, 1996; and "China: PRC, Algeria To Cooperate in Nuclear Energy Development," *Xinhua*, May 21, 1997, in FBIS–CHI–97–141, May 23, 1997.

46. Mark Hibbs, "Move To Block China Certification," *Nucleonics Week*, August 7, 1997, p. 11.

47. George Tenet, "Worldwide Threat 2001."

48. R. Jeffrey Smith, "China Linked to Pakistani Missile Plant," *Washington Post*, August 25, 1996, p. A1.

49. Ibid.

50. Aurang Zeb, "Pakistan Denies It's Building Missile Factory," *Reuters*, August 26, 1996.

51. Senate Governmental Affairs Committee, *Weapons Proliferation in China*.

52. CIA Report to Congress on the Acquisition of Technology relating to Weapons of Mass Destruction and Advanced Conventional Munitions, July–December 2000, September 7, 2001.

53. Barbara Opall, "U.S. Queries China on Iran," *Defense News*, June 14–25, 1995, p. 1; Elaine Sciolino, "CIA Report Says Chinese Sent Iran Arms Components," *New York Times*, June 21, 1995, p. A1; and "Chinese Shipments Violate Controls," *Jane's Defence Weekly*, July 1, 1995, p. 3.

54. Bill Gertz, "China Sold Iran Missile Technology," *Washington Times*, November 21, 1996, p. 1.

55. CIA Report to Congress.

56. Elaine Sciolino, "China Said To Sell Parts for Missiles," *New York Times*, January 31, 1992, p. A1; and William Safire, "China's 'Hama Rules,' " *New York Times*, March 5, 1992, p. A27.

57. Philip Finnegan, "Saudis Study Missile Buy To Replace Aging Arsenal," *Defense News*, March 17–23, 1997, p. 3.

58. U.S. Department of Defense, *Proliferation: Threat and Response*, January 2001, p. 15.

59. Center for Defense Information. "China," Chemical and Biological Weapons web site. Available at www.cdi.org/issues/cbw/china.html.

60. Bill Gertz, "Albright Concedes 'Concern' over China-Iran Transfers," *Washington Times*, January 24, 1997, p. A6.

61. Edward Eitzen and Ernest Takafuji, "Historical Overview of Biological Warfare," chapter 18, *Medical Aspects of Chemical and Biological Warfare, Part I, The Textbook of Military Medicine*, (Washington, D.C.: Borden Institute, Office of the Surgeon General, 1997), p. 417; and see also Jeffrey Smart, "History of Chemical and Biological Warfare: An American Perspective," chapter 2, *Medical Aspects of Chemical and Biological Warfare, Part I, The Textbook of Military Medicine* (Washington, D.C.: Borden Institute, Office of the Surgeon General, 1997), p. 33.

62. Peter O'Meara Evans, "Destruction of Abandoned Chemical Weapons in China," Paper 13 (Bonn International Center for Conversion, September 1997).

63. "Abandoned Chemical Weapons in China Come to Light," *Jane's Defense Weekly*, July 1, 1998, p. 7.

64. Center for Defense Information. "China," Chemical and Biological Weapons web site. Available at www.cdi.org/issues/cbw/china.html.

65. Federation of American Scientists, "China: Chemical and Biological Weapons." Available at www.fas.org/nuke/juide/china/cbw/index.html.

66. U.S. Department of Defense, *Proliferation: Threat and Response*, January 2001, p. 15.

67. Bill Gertz, "China Sold Iran Missile Technology," *Washington Times*, November 21, 1996, p. 1.

Table 7.1: **China: Nuclear Weapon-related Sites of Proliferation Concern**

Nuclear Weapons Complex[1]	
Name/ Location of facility	**Type/Status**
Northwest Nuclear Technology Institute, in the Scientific Research District outside Malan, Xinjiang	Archive on nuclear explosions, warfare, and weapon research and design; associated with testing at Lop Nur
Jiuquan Atomic Energy Complex (Plant 404), Subei, Gansu	Fabrication of fissile materials into bomb cores, and final weapon assembly; closed
Northwest Institute of Nuclear Technology Xi'an, Shaanxi	Diagnostic support for nuclear test program
Lop Nur Nuclear Weapons Test Base Xinjiang	Nuclear weapon test site and possible nuclear weapon stockpile
Chinese Academy of Engineering Physics (CAEP) Mianyang, Sichuan	Nuclear weapon research, design, and technology complex; called the Los Alamos of China; 11 institutes, 8 located in Mianyang[2]
Institute 905 of CAEP outside Mianyang	Ordnance engineering lab for non-nuclear components of nuclear weapons, "the Chinese Sandia"[3]
Institute of Applied Physics and Computational Mathematics, Beijing	Conducts research on nuclear warhead design computations for CAEP
Shanghai Institute of Nuclear Research Shanghai, Zheijiang	Engaged in tomography, tests solid missile propellants, explosives, and detonation packages for nuclear weapons
Fudan University Shanghai, Zheijiang	Engaged in tomography, tests solid missile propellants, explosives, and detonation packages for nuclear weapons
Harbin, Heilogiang	Possible warhead assembly and production site
Plant 821, Guangyuan, Sichuan	Possible nuclear weapon assembly facility
Plutonium Production Reactors	
Plant 821 Guangyuan, Sichuan	LWGR, nat. U, 1,000-MW; operational Largest plutonium producing reactor in China
Jiuquan Atomic Energy Complex (Plant 404); Subei, Gansu	LWGR, nat. U, 400–500 MW; closed

Research Reactors	
Name/ Location of facility	**Type/Status**
CARR, China Institute of Atomic Energy	60-MW; planned
CFER-CN-0018	65-MW, fast-breeder reactor; under construction
MNSR-SH, Shanghai Testing and Research Institute	30-kW, light-water reactor; operational
HTR-10, Beijing	10-MW, high-temperature gas, pebble bed; operational
NHR-5, Tsinghua University	5-MW, light-water; operational
HFETR Nuclear Power Institute of China, Chengdu, Sichuan	Tank, light-water; HEU (90%), 125-MWt; operational
HFETR critical Nuclear Power Institute of China, Chengdu, Sichuan	Critical assembly, light-water; HEU (90%), 0-MWt; closed
MJTR Nuclear Power Institute of China, Chengdu, Sichuan	Pool, LW; HEU (90%), 5-MWt; operational
MNSR IAE China Institute for Atomic Energy, Tuoli, near Beijing	Tank in pool, light-water; HEU (90%), .027-MWt; operational
MNSR–SD Shandong Geology Bureau, Jinan, Shandong	Tank in pool, light-water; HEU (90%), .03327-MWt; operational
MNSR–SZ Shenzhen University, Guangdong	Tank in pool, light water; HEU (90%), .03027-MWt; operational
Zero Power Fast Critical Reactor Southwest Research Institute, Jianiang/Chengdu, Sichuan	Critical fast; HEU (90%), 0.5-MWt; operational
HWRR–II China Institute for Atomic Energy, Tuoli, near Beijing Under IAEA safeguards.	Heavy-water; LEU (3%), 15-MWt; operational
SPR IAE China Institute for Atomic Energy, Tuoli, near Beijing SPRR–300	Pool, light-water; LEU (10%), 3.5-MWt; operational
Southwest Research Institute, Jianiang/Chengdu, Sichuan Tsinghua Pool	Pool, light-water; LEU (10%), 3.70-MWt; operational

(Table continues on the following page.)

Table 7.1: **China: Nuclear Weapon-related Sites** (continued)

Research Reactors	
Name/ Location of facility	**Type/Status**
Institute of Nuclear Energy Technology, Tsinghua University, Beijing	Pool, two cores, LW; LEU (10%), 2.8-MWt; operational
PPR Pulsing Reactor Nuclear Power Institute of China, Chengdu, Sichuan	Pool, LW; HEU (20%), 1-MWt; operational
Uranium Enrichment	
Heping Uranium Enrichment Plant Heping, Sichuan	Gaseous diffusion plant: estimated to produce 750–2,950 kg HEU/year;[4] operational
Lanzhou Nuclear Fuel Complex Lanzhou, Gansu	Gaseous diffusion plant: estimated to produce at least 150–330 kg HEU/year;[5] decommissioned[6]
Lanzhou Nuclear Fuel Complex Lanzhou, Gansu	Gaseous diffusion plant; new cascade under construction, for LEU export
China Institute of Atomic Energy Tuoli, near Beijing	Laboratory-scale gaseous diffusion: developed enrichment process later installed at Lanzhou
Russian-supplied centrifuge enrichment plant, Lanzhou, Gansu[7]	Large-scale gas centrifuge enrichment facility; under construction, completion in 2005; capacity: 1.5 million SWU/year[8]
Plutonium Reprocessing[9]	
Jiuquan Atomic Energy Complex (Plant 404) Subei, Gansu	Large-scale reprocessing plant, capacity: 300–400 kg Pu/year; and pilot reprocessing plant (both use PUREX method); and nuclear fuel processing plant for refining plutonium into weapons-usable metals; closed
Plant 821 Guangyuan, Sichuan	China's largest plutonium separation facility, capacity: 300–400 kg Pu/year
Nuclear Fuel Component Plant (Plant 812) Yibin, Sichuan	Plutonium fuel-rod fabrication, and plutonium production and processing for nuclear weapons; operating
Lanzhou Nuclear Fuel Complex Lanzhou, Gansu	Pilot spent-fuel reprocessing plant, capacity of 400 kg/HM per day; under construction, completion expected in 2002[10]
Uranium Processing	
Nuclear Fuel Component Plant (202) Baotou, Nei Mongolia province	Fuel-rod fabrication; operating

Uranium Processing (continued)	
Name/ Location of facility	**Type/Status**
Nuclear Fuel Component Plant (Plant 812) Yibin, Sichuan	Fuel-rod fabrication; operating
Jiuquan Atomic Energy Complex (Plant 404), Subei, Gansu	Nuclear fuel processing plant: converts enriched UF_6 to UF_4 for shaping into metal; operational
Tritium, Lithium Deuteride, and Beryllium	
Ningxia Nonferrous Metal Research Institute (Plant 905) Helan Shan, Ningxia	China's main research and production site for beryllium
Nuclear Fuel Component Plant (202) Baotou, Nei Mongolia	Tritium, Li-6 deuterium production; operational
Nuclear Fuel Element Plant (Plant 812) Yibin, Sichuan	Probable production of tritium and Li-6 deuterium

ABBREVIATIONS

HEU	highly enriched uranium
HM	heavy metal
kWt	thousands of watts of thermal output
LEU	low-enriched uranium
LWGR	light-water-cooled graphite-moderated reactor
MT	metric ton
MWt	millions of watts of thermal output
nat. U	natural uranium
SWU	separative work unit

SOURCES

"Datafile: China." *Nuclear Engineering International.* October 1993.

Albright, David, Frans Berkhout, and William Walker. *Plutonium and Highly Enriched Uranium 1996: World Inventories, Capabilities, and Policies.* Oxford: Oxford University Press, 1997.

International Atomic Energy Agency. *Nuclear Research Reactors in the World.* December 1995.

Lewis, John Wilson, and Xue Litai. *China Builds the Bomb.* Stanford: Stanford University Press, 1988.

Norris, Robert S., Andrew S. Burrows, and Richard W. Fieldhouse. *Nuclear Weapons Databook V.* Boulder: Westview Press, 1994.

Nuclear Engineering International. *World Nuclear Industry Handbook 1997.*

Wisconsin Project. "Nuclear Profile: China." *Risk Report.* November 1995, pp. 3–9.

NOTES

1. In addition to the sites listed under Nuclear Weapons Complex, the following sites are engaged in nuclear research, although perhaps they are not explicitly weapon-related: Atomic Research Center, Xingjiang; Institute of Nuclear Energy Technology (INET), Tsinghua University, Beijing; Institute of Nuclear Science and Technology, Sichuan University, Chengdu, Sichuan; Institute of Materials and Elements at the Sichuan Institute of Nuclear Power, Chengdu, Sichuan; China Institute for Radiation Protection (CIRP), Yaiyuan, Shanxi; Beijing Nuclear Engineering Research and Development Academy, Beijing; and Nuclear Research and Development Institute, Tianjin, southeast of Beijing.

2. CAEP is an identical copy of the Northwest Nuclear Weapons Research and Design Academy in Haiyan, the original Chinese weapon design facility that has since been phased out, and the work transferred to CAEP. See Robert Norris, Andrew Burrows, and Richard Fieldhouse, *Nuclear Weapons Databook V* (Boulder: Westview Press, 1994), p. 338.

3. Ibid., p. 348; and *Risk Report*, November 1995, p. 6.

4. U.S. Defense Intelligence Agency, *Soviet and Peoples' Republic of China Nuclear Weapons Employment Policy and Strategy*, TCS–65475–72, March 1972; see discussion in David Albright, Frans Berkhout, and William Walker, *Plutonium and Highly Enriched Uranium 1996: World Inventories, Capabilities and Policies* (New York: Oxford University Press, 1997), p. 126–130.

5. Ibid.

6. Chinese officials opted to replace the aging gaseous diffusion plant at Lanzhou with Russia-built gas centrifuges. Mark Hibbs, "China Moved Centrifuge Complex to Keep Enriching U at Lanzhou," *Nuclear Fuel*, May 17, 1999, p. 11.

7. The first two stages of the facility (each with a 200,000 SWU/year capacity) were built in Hanzhong. Construction of the third and fourth stages was later relocated to Lanzhou. There has been conflicting information as to the exact location of the first two stages of the facility. The most recent reports suggest that the facility is in Hanzhong; see Hibbs, "China Moved Centrifuge Complex." Earlier reports suggested that the facility might be located in Chengdu; see Hibbs, "China Moved Centrifuge Complex," October 6, 1997, and "China's Centrifuge SWU Plant Up and Running, Minatom Says," *Nuclear Fuel*, January 27, 1997, p. 3. The *World Nuclear Industry Handbook 2001* suggests that the plant is at Lanzhou.

8. The first module of the plant began operating in 1998, the second in late September 2000, and the third in November 2001. "Russian Atomic Ministry Delegation to Participate in Launch of Third Line of Gas-Centrifuge Plant in China," *Economic News*, November 13, 2001. Completion of the final module is expected around 2005. Hibbs, "China Moved Centrifuge Complex."

9. Additional military reprocessing facilities are thought to be located at Urumqi, Xinjiang province, and Yumen, Gansu province. "Datafile: China," *Nuclear Engineering International*, October 1993, p. 22.

10. Mark Hibbs, "China Expected Soon to Request Bids for Qinshan Transport Cask," *Nuclear Fuel*, April 30, 2001. See also Mark Hibbs, "Chinese Pu Lab to Operate in 2002, But Interim Storage Now Foreseen," *Nuclear Fuel*, October 30, 2000, p. 9.

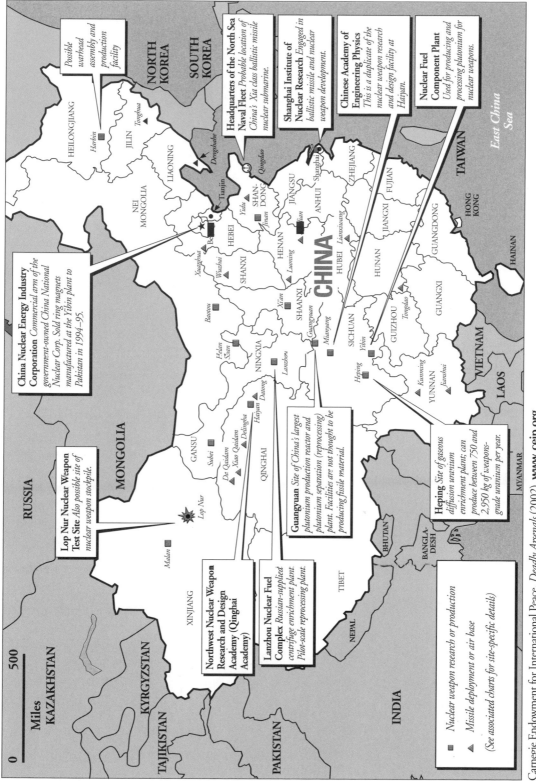

Possible *warhead assembly and production facility.*

China Nuclear Energy Industry Corporation *Commercial arm of the government-owned China National Nuclear Corp. Sold ring magnets manufactured at the Yibin plant to Pakistan in 1994–95.*

Lop Nur Nuclear Weapon Test Site *Also possible site of nuclear weapon stockpile.*

Northwest Nuclear Weapon Research and Design Academy (Qinghai Academy)

Lanzhou Nuclear Fuel Complex *Russian-supplied centrifuge enrichment plant. Pilot-scale reprocessing plant.*

Guangyuan *Site of China's largest plutonium production reactor and plutonium separation (reprocessing) plant. Facilities are not thought to be producing fissile material.*

Heping *Site of gaseous diffusion uranium enrichment plant; can produce between 750 and 2,950 kg of weapons-grade uranium per year.*

Headquarters of the North Sea Naval Fleet *Probable location of China's Xia class ballistic missile nuclear submarine.*

Shanghai Institute of Nuclear Research *Engaged in ballistic missile and nuclear weapon development.*

Chinese Academy of Engineering Physics *This is a duplicate of the nuclear weapon research and design facility at Haiyan.*

Nuclear Fuel Component Plant *Used for producing and processing plutonium for nuclear weapons.*

RUSSIA

KAZAKHSTAN

KYRGYZSTAN

TAJIKISTAN

MONGOLIA

NORTH KOREA

SOUTH KOREA

Harbin HEILONGJIANG

JILIN *Tonghua*

LIAONING *Dengshahe*

NEI MONGOLIA

Tianjin HEBEI SHAN-DONG *Qingdao*

Jinan

Xiaghua *Wuzhai* SHANXI

Yidu

SHAANXI JIANGSU

Xi'an HENAN *Luoyang*

Baotou

NINGXIA *Lanzhou* *Datong* *Helan Shan*

GANSU *Subei* *De Qaidam* *Xiao Quidam* *Delingha* *Haiyan*

QINGHAI

Malan

XINJIANG *Lop Nur*

TIBET

NEPAL

BHUTAN

BANGLA-DESH

INDIA

PAKISTAN

MYANMAR

Guangyuan SICHUAN *Yibin*

Mianyang

CHINA

Lianxiuxiang ANHUI HUBEI ZHEJIANG *Shanghai*

JIANGXI FUJIAN

HUNAN

GUIZHOU *Tongdao*

GUANGDONG HONG KONG

GUANGXI

YUNNAN *Kunming* *Jianshui*

Heping

VIETNAM

LAOS

TAIWAN

HAINAN

East China Sea

Miles
0   500

■ Nuclear weapon research or production

▲ Missile deployment or air base

(See associated charts for site-specific details)

Carnegie Endowment for International Peace, *Deadly Arsenals* (2002), **www.ceip.org**

CHAPTER 8

France

Nuclear Weapon Capability

France is a nuclear-weapon state recognized under the Non-Proliferation Treaty. It deploys approximately 350 nuclear weapons on 84 nuclear-capable aircraft and 48 submarine-launched ballistic missiles on four nuclear submarines (three of them carrying 16 missiles each). France has conducted 210 nuclear weapon tests, the first on February 13, 1960, the last on January 27, 1996. France produced approximately 1,110 nuclear warheads between 1960 and 1992. It has signed and ratified the Comprehensive Test Ban Treaty.

France spent $2.3 billion (15.8 billion francs) on nuclear weaponry in 2001. The budget supported its current forces of 60 Mirage 2000N fighter planes equipped with Air-Sol Moyenne Portée (ASMP) missiles; 24 Super Étendard carrier-based airplanes armed with ASMP missiles, 16 submarine-launched M4A/B missiles, and 32 M45 SLBMs.

Strategic Context

France launched its nuclear program incrementally during the Fourth Republic (1945–1958). In this process, the 1956 Suez crisis was a key turning point. The decision to test a nuclear device was taken during the last weeks of the Fourth Republic in 1958. In February 1960, France tested its first weapon in then-French Algeria. The nuclear arsenal became operational in 1964 with the entry into active service of the first Mirage IVA nuclear bombers.[1]

During the Cold War, France developed a "three-circles" defense policy aimed at protecting its vital interests against external threats (primarily the Soviet Union) through nuclear deterrence, participation in the general defense of Western Europe within the Atlantic Alliance, and by maintaining an active role outside Europe (mainly in Africa and the Middle East).[2] For that purpose, the French arsenal grew to a triad of sea-, air-, and land-based weapon systems with a few hundred warheads, following a national policy of "sufficiency" (*suffisance*) and relying on the threat of massive retaliation.[3]

With the end of the Cold War, France reviewed its nuclear strategy. After the fall of the Soviet Union, France's 1994 defense white paper (the first since 1972) identified French security risks as being the likely increase in the weaponry and military of other nations, including the proliferation of weapons of mass destruction, and Russia's continuing strong military power in Europe.[4] The 1994 white paper also sought to emphasize a reduction in the central role of French nuclear weapons while maintaining a deterrence stance. Nuclear weapons would nevertheless continue to ensure the protection of France's "vital interests," primarily against the "resurgence of a major threat against Western Europe."[5]

In 1995–1996, newly elected Gaullist president Jacques Chirac initiated the restructuring of the French nuclear arsenal. Assuming office after a period of "co-habitation" with a socialist president and a Gaullist prime minister, Chirac faced difficult defense choices.[6] He followed much of the white paper's suggestions for France's defense but changed funding priorities from nuclear weaponry to intelligence, force projection, and a professional army.[7] Against substantial international criticism, Chirac briefly resumed nuclear weapon testing with a series of six tests in 1995–1996 (after a moratorium from 1992 to 1995) and began to restructure the arsenal. He decided to dismantle two ground-to-ground missile systems: the S–3D, based in Albion, and the shorter-range Hades missiles. He continued to effect reductions in nuclear spending from the Cold War level of more than 30 percent of the procurement budget to about 20 percent. There was a debate as policy shifted from the Cold War era "weak to the strong" posture against the Soviet Union to a "strong to the weak," or "strong to the crazy," posture to counter emerging nuclear threats and WMD proliferation. The concept, however, retained its original logic: i.e., preserving French vital interests vis-à-vis all potential threats.[8] President Chirac summarized the current French nuclear doctrine in June 2001:

> Nuclear deterrence is the crux of the resources enabling France to affirm the principle of strategic autonomy from which derives our defense policy. Thanks to the continuous efforts made since the time of General de Gaulle, nuclear deterrence today is an essential foundation of our security and will remain so for many more years in the new strategic context, where it remains fully meaningful and effective.
>
> Nuclear deterrence is above all an important factor of global stability. It is thanks to nuclear deterrence that Europe has been protected for more than 50 years from the ravages it experienced during the twentieth century. By imposing restraint and inciting [others] to exercise reason, a credible nuclear threat commands peace.
>
> Our nuclear forces are not directed against any country, and we have always refused [to accept] that nuclear weapons should be regarded as weapons of war to be used as part of a military strategy.[9]

As suggested in this speech and in previous speeches, France has always given a European dimension to its nuclear forces. France has made several openings to Europeanize its nuclear capabilities more formally, the last mention having been for a "concerted deterrence" (1995). Besides increasing France–U.K. cooperation, these attempts have not, however, been very successful so far.

Nuclear Analysis

As early as the 1930s France began working on a nuclear weapon, but efforts were slowed by a lack of nuclear scientific knowledge and a shortage of uranium. The efforts also suffered heavily from World War II (when France was occupied). French scientists, unlike their American and British colleagues, did not participate in the initial production and testing of the bomb.[10]

In 1945, a French atomic energy commission (Commissariat à l'énergie atomique) was established, but it began focusing on military applications only in the mid-1950s. In 1948, uranium ore was discovered in central France. Four years later, the Parliament set out a five-year plan to produce 50 kilograms of plutonium a year, using natural uranium reactors to fuel nuclear power plants. At the United Nations in 1946 France promised that all its nuclear efforts would be peaceful. At the U.N. General Assembly, France urged the United States and the Soviet Union to discontinue atmospheric nuclear weapon testing. It soon began a secret nuclear weapon development program, however, which became increasingly important throughout the 1950s, until 1958, when the decision to test was finally taken.

In the early stages of the European construction process France discussed the possibility of renouncing nuclear weapons. That idea was soon rejected. After the 1956 Suez crisis, the nuclear program was accelerated, and France initiated plans for its first nuclear test to take place in 1960.[11]

In 1956, France signed the Euratom treaty. Euratom would act as a unifier on European civilian nuclear policy, giving access to nuclear fuel to all members for peaceful purposes. There were parallel exploratory talks with Italy and Germany about military nuclear cooperation, but these were stopped at an early stage when General Charles de Gaulle came back into office in 1958.[12]

When de Gaulle became president, he confirmed the proposed nuclear test date and accelerated the nuclear program. After the 1960 test, France implemented a long-term nuclear plan, ignoring international objectors, and in particular, ignoring criticism made in conjunction with the Partial Test Ban Treaty (1963). France continued atmospheric testing until 1974. In 1968, when other European countries were negotiating the Non-Proliferation Treaty, France avoided the talks even though the NPT recognized its nuclear status. When the treaty was signed, however, France agreed to follow the treaty's regulations without signing it.[13] Even though France became increasingly involved in the logic of nuclear non-proliferation (notably as a founding member of the Nuclear Suppliers Group), France was a longtime critic of the NPT per se. It joined the treaty only in 1992. Ever since it has been an active participant in all NPT debates and a strong supporter of the treaty.

France has used at least nine reactors for plutonium production. It has now ceased plutonium and HEU production (Pu in 1992; HEU in 1996) for military purposes and has started dismantling its fissile material production facilities (the Marcoule reprocessing plant and the Pierrelatte enrichment facility).[14] Paris also deactivated and dismantled the *Plateau d'Albion* missile site in southern France in 1997–1998. Last, but not least, President Chirac also decided to dismantle the South Pacific testing facilities in Mururoa and Fangataufa in 1996. Altogether, the French nuclear forces have been reduced by more than 40 percent since the end of the Cold War.[15]

Missile and Aircraft Analysis

At its peak from 1991 to 1992, France deployed an estimated total of 538 nuclear warheads. The arsenals included 80 ASMPs, which were supersonic wingless guided missiles. Of those missiles, 18 were equipped to the Mirage IVA/P, a low-altitude bomber; 42 missiles were attached to the Mirage 2000N sonic attack aircraft, and 20 armed the carrier-based naval strike aircraft, the Super Étendard. The remainder of France's arsenal included 384 warheads on M4 submarine-based ballistic missiles, 18 land-based intermediate-range S–3 ballistic missiles, and 56 Plutons, which were mobile short-range surface ballistic missiles used by the army.[16]

France conducted its last nuclear test in 1996. That same year President Chirac, having stopped fissile material production, decided to dismantle and discontinue various systems, such as the S–3D intermediate-range missile.[17]

Today, France operates four nuclear-powered ballistic missile submarines in three classes. The country owns two new Triomphant submarines, one L'Inflexible submarine, which carries the M45 SLBM, and one Redoubtable-class submarine (Le Foudroyant), which is equipped with the M4 SLBM. In January 2000, France's second Triomphant-class SSBN officially entered service, equipped with 16 M45 SLBMs and carrying six TN 75–type nuclear warheads each. A third Triomphant-class submarine, Le Vigilant, will be launched in 2002. France has plans to build and deploy a fourth Triomphant submarine by 2008 and is currently testing a new missile, the M–51, to replace in that same year the M45. Carrying up to six warheads, the M–51 will have a range of 8,000–10,000 kilometers.

As part of its airborne nuclear component, today France has 60 nuclear-capable aircraft in its air force, and 24 carrier-based nuclear-capable fighter-bombers in its navy. The Mirage 2000N and Super Étendard aircraft use ASMP air-to-surface nuclear missiles with a range of 250–300 kilometers and armed with warheads of the TN–81 type. France has in service 60 ASMP cruise missiles equipped with a TN–81 warhead, possibly with more inactive weapons stored on board. In early October 1999, France announced the continuation of its development program for the ASMP–A (*Air-Sol Moyenne Portée-Amélioré*) nuclear air-launched cruise missile program, which promises to double the range of the ASMP from 250 kilometers to 500 kilometers. The ASMP–A will also be armed with a new TNA (tête nucléaire aéro-portée) warhead, to be developed by simulation in France's Atomic Energy Commission laboratories. The ASMP–A is scheduled for use in 2007.[18]

Of the three squadrons of Mirage 2000N, two are stationed at Luxeuil and the other at Istres. The Mirage 2000N has some conventional capability in addition to its primary nuclear role. France also retains in service five Mirage IVPs, the Mirage 2000N's nuclear precursor, for reconnaissance missions while other retired Mirage IVPs are stored.[19] France has 50 missiles of the TN–81 type stockpiled for the Mirage 2000N and 10 TN–81 warheads stockpiled for the Super Étendard.

The Rafale (B–301), armed with either the ASMP or the ASMP–A, is being designed for air defense and ground attacks. In 2001, the navy formed a squadron of Rafale M jets in Landivisiau. The air force expects to purchase 234 Rafale's for operation in 2005. In 2003, the Rafale will take the place of the Super Étendard aboard the *Charles de Gaulle* aircraft carrier.

France has built three aircraft carriers: the *Clémenceau*, the *Foch*, and the *Charles de Gaulle*. After its commission in 1961, the *Clémenceau* was modified to carry the AN–52 nuclear gravity bomb and the Super Étendard fleet. The *Foch* began service in 1963 and was then altered to contain nuclear weapons, such as replacement ASMPs for the Super Étendard fighter jets. Both the *Clémenceau* and *Foch* have now been decommissioned. The carrier *Charles de Gaulle*, initially launched in 1994, entered active duty in October 2000. It will eventually be home to several of France's new fighter bombers in the navy and air force. France is considering funding its carrier for the 2003–2008 defense budget.[20]

Previous Chemical Weapon Program

France does not have research or production programs for either chemical or biological weapons. It is a member of the Biological Weapons Convention and the Chemical Weapons Convention. France has declared to the Organization for the Prohibition of Chemical Weapons that it has a stockpile of old chemical weapons on its territory and has opened its facilities for inspection. France stockpiled mustard gas and phosgene before World War II and continued chemical weapon research and testing at B2–Namous in Algeria until the late 1960s. In 1988, President François Mitterrand announced before the United Nations that France had no chemical weapons and had no plans to produce chemical weapons.[21]

NOTES

1. Robert Norris, Andrew Burrows, and Richard Fieldhouse, *British, French, and Chinese Nuclear Weapons, vol. V* (Boulder: Westview Press, 1994), pp. 183–184. On the origins of the French nuclear program, see Lawrence Scheinmann, *Atomic Energy in France under the Fourth Republic* (Princeton University Press), 1969; and Dominique Mongin, *La bombe atomique française, 1945–1958* (Louvain-la-Neuve, Belgium: Bruylant and Paris: LGDJ, 1997).

2. Camille Grand, "A French Nuclear Exception," Occasional Paper 38 (Henry L. Stimson Center, 1998), pp. 12–14.

3. On French nuclear policy during the Cold War, see Marcel Duval and Yves Le Baut, *L'arme nucléaire française: Pourquoi et comment?* (Kronos/S.P.M., 1992).

4. Camille Grand, "France," in *Europe and Nuclear Disarmament: Debates and Political Attitudes in 16 European Countries*, ed. Harald Müller (Brussels: European Interuniversity Press, 1998), p. 39.

5. Grand, "France," p. 40.

6. Grand, "France," p. 35.

7. Grand, "France," p. 35.

8. Grand, "France," p. 38.

9. Transcript of President Jacques Chirac's speech before the Institute of Higher National Defence Studies in Paris, June 8, 2001.

10. Pierre Goldschmidt, "Proliferation and Non-Proliferation in Western Europe: A Historical Survey," *A European Non-Proliferation Policy*, ed. Harald Müller (Clarendon Press: 1987) p. 9.

11. Ibid., p. 12.

12. Ibid.

13. Ibid., p. 24.

14. Norris, Burrows, and Fieldhouse, *British, French and Chinese Nuclear Weapons*, p. 10; and Robert Norris and William Arkin, "Nuclear Notebook." *Bulletin of Atomic Scientists*, June/July 2001, p. 70.

15. For more details about French nuclear arms control policy, see the booklet "Arms Control, Disarmament, and Non-Proliferation: French Policy" (La Documentation française, 2000), pp. 36–56.

16. Norris, Burrows, and Fieldhouse, *British, French and Chinese Nuclear Weapons*, p. 214.

17. Norris and Arkin, "Nuclear Notebook," p. 70.

18. Ibid, p. 71.

19. Ibid.

20. Ibid., p. 70–71.

21. Federation of Atomic Scientists web site on French Chemical and Biological Weapons Capability. Available at www.fas.org/nuke/guide/france/cbw/index.html.

Table 8.1: **French Nuclear Forces, 2001**

	Launcher Type/ Designation	Launchers/ SSBNs	First Deployed	Warheads × yield (kT)	Range (km)	Deployable Warheads
SLBMs	Redoubtable-class SSBN/ M–4A/B	16/1	1985	x 150 kT	6,000	96
	Triomphant-class SSBN/ M–45	32/2	1996	6 x 100 kT	6,000	192
Subtotal, Ballistic Missiles	48/3					288
Aircraft	Super Étendard/ ASMP	24	1978	1 x 300 kT ASMP	650	10
	Mirage 2000N/ ASMP	60	1988	1 x 300 kT ASMP	2,750	0
Total	84					60
Total Strategic Nuclear Forces	132					348

CHAPTER 9

United Kingdom

Nuclear Weapon Capability

The United Kingdom is recognized under the NPT as a nuclear-weapon state. It currently maintains four nuclear-powered ballistic missile submarines, each armed with 16 Trident II missiles and up to 48 warheads. Between 1952 and 1992, the country produced approximately 834 nuclear warheads.[1] The United Kingdom has conducted 44 nuclear weapon tests, the first on October 3, 1952, the last on November 26, 1991. It has signed and ratified the Comprehensive Test Ban Treaty.

Aircraft and Missile Capability

The 1998 Strategic Defense Review (SDR) confirmed that the new nuclear force structure would consist solely of the four Vanguard-class nuclear-powered ballistic missile submarines, only one of which is to be on active patrol duty at any one time. This also required the elimination of Britain's tactical nuclear arsenal. The maximum load of Trident II warheads carried by each submarine was reduced from 96 to 48. Each Vanguard SSBN can carry 16 Trident II D–5 SLBMs. The first submarine, the HMS Vanguard, went on patrol in December 1994. Each Trident II SLBM can carry up to 8 multiple independent reentry vehicles, for a maximum of 128 warheads. The actual force loadings, however, are lower than this because of the Strategic Defense Review, which stipulated that all Trident submarines should carry a maximum of 48 warheads per boat, with each missile downloaded to three warheads. Because the United Kingdom plans to produce only enough warheads for three SSBNs, its total warhead inventory will be not more than 200 warheads for the foreseeable future.[2]

Before the SDR revisions, the Royal Air Force operated eight squadrons of nuclear-capable Tornado GR1/1A bombers armed with WE–177 nuclear gravity bombs. By 1998, all the WE–177 bombs had been dismantled. An air force base in Bruggen, Germany, has closed, and the bombers are being relocated to bases in Lossiemouth, Scotland, and Marham, England.

Biological and Chemical Weapon Capability

The United Kingdom is a member of the Biological Weapons Convention and the Chemical Weapons Convention. The United Kingdom has declared to the Organization for the Prohibition of Chemical Weapons that it has old chemical weapons on its territory and has opened its facilities for inspection.

According to the British Ministry of Defence, the Joint Nuclear, Biological, and Chemical (NBC) Regiment provides "a defence capability" for the air force, navy, and army. Its equipment includes biological and chemical monitoring devices, such as the man-portable chemical agent detector (MCAD) and the Integrated Biological Detection System (IBDS); individual protection equipment; communication and information systems for tracking hazardous material movement and duration; medical research on countermeasures for biological or chemical exposure; and an expanded threat analysis program.[3]

Strategic Context

During the Cold War, the United Kingdom and NATO planned for the worst—a European nuclear war with the Soviet Union and its allies. The close geographical position of the United Kingdom to the Soviet threat created a security environment for nuclear defense and deterrence. The United Kingdom joined NATO in combating the Soviet threat by contributing its land, air, and sea nuclear forces to the Alliance. The United Kingdom manufactured and owned the warheads for its strategic nuclear delivery systems, but other warheads were supplied by the United States under standard NATO nuclear-sharing arrangements.[4]

By 1998, the change in the size and composition of the United Kingdom's nuclear forces had significantly affected its means of implementing deterrence policies from the Cold War era. The United Kingdom's disarmament decision was reached unilaterally, motivated by such issues as the opportunity to reduce the cost of arsenal maintenance and the lack of an imminent Soviet threat. The arsenal was reduced to a single type of warhead and a submarine delivery system. Developing a protégé to the Polaris SSBN became an issue for debate during the Cold War. The British argued over the most cost-effective nuclear defense replacement system for the family of submarines and whether a replacement was necessary. Post–Cold War policies have left NATO as the ultimate defense for the United Kingdom, except for one patrolling nuclear submarine off the British coastline.[5]

Nuclear Analysis

The British were an integral part of helping the United States to develop the bomb. In 1941, the Maud Committee, a group of British scientists dedicated to fission research, estimated that the development of the bomb would take two and a half years. This scientific process slowed during World War II, but following the end of the war in 1946, work was started on plants to produce fissile material.

The United Kingdom wanted a nuclear force as leverage against the Soviets should they obtain weapons. The British also sought greater power after slipping in status as a world leader. The United States clearly showed no interest in sharing atomic knowledge with other countries under its Atomic Energy Act of 1946, which was another reason that the United Kingdom believed that it needed to construct its own nuclear arms. In 1952, the United Kingdom conducted its first nuclear test, called Hurricane, at the Monto Bello Islands off the Australian coast.

The Blue Danube was the first nuclear weapon that Britain produced. Initial models were transferred to the Royal Air Force in November 1953, using plutonium as the fissile material. The smaller and lighter Red Beard entered service in 1958. At the same time, the interim megaton fission bomb Violet Club was produced, followed by its successor, Yellow Sun Mk I. Yellow Sun Mk II was the first British thermonuclear operational gravity bomb with a yield in the megaton range. This came into service in 1962, at the same time as the thermonuclear Blue Steel air-launched cruise missiles. Both used an Anglicized version of the U.S. MK–28 warhead and remained in the stockpiles until 1970. The WE–177, the most recent family of British nuclear-gravity aircraft bombs, entered service with the Royal Air Force strategic bomber force in 1966 and was later deployed on Royal Navy and Air Force attack aircraft and helicopters. The WE–177 was decommissioned between 1992 and 1998.[6]

From the early 1960s to the mid-1990s, the U.K. nuclear stockpile of British-produced warheads is estimated to have been between 250 and 350 warheads. The British stockpile was supplemented by U.S. weapons, which were available under NATO nuclear-sharing arrangements from 1958 to 1991. Three hundred to 400 of these warheads were made available to the United Kingdom in the 1960s and 1970s, and 200–300 warheads in the 1980s. Lance warheads, artillery shells, and depth bombs for land-based maritime patrol aircraft were returned to the United States for dismantlement in 1991.[7]

Nuclear warheads are designed at the Aldermaston facility in Berkshire. Warheads are assembled and disassembled at Burghfield, as are weapon components. The other production facility, at Cardiff, was closed in February 1997. Disassembly of Chevaline warheads is now taking place at the Burghfield facility, scheduled for completion by March 2002.[8]

Missile Analysis

Beginning in 1960, the United Kingdom operated a nuclear-capable land force of Lance missiles and 155-mm howitzers based in Germany with borrowed warheads and delivery devices from the United States under NATO nuclear-sharing arrangements. The Royal Air Force also had access to U.S. depth bombs for its long-range Nimrod aircraft. Bombers such as the Buccaneer, Jaguar, and Tornado were capable of delivering WE–177 bombs. The Royal Navy operated Sea Harriers and anti-submarine helicopters capable of carrying WE–177s.[9]

In 1968, the British launched the first four Polaris (or Resolution-class) submarines carrying 16 A3T SLBMs supplied by the United States. The Polaris A3T missile carried a delivery system that incorporated three warheads, each believed to have a yield of 200 kilotons. The Polaris A3TK or Chevaline missile replaced the A3T in 1982 and was designed to penetrate the Soviet anti-ballistic missile defense system around Moscow. The fleet of Polaris SSBNs was phased out by the end of 1996, and was replaced by the Vanguard SSBNs.[10]

The Trident II D–5 inertially guided submarine-launched ballistic missile has a greater payload capability, range, and accuracy over its precursor, the Polaris SLBM. The three-stage, solid-propellant missile has a range of more than 7,400 kilometers at full payload. The warhead carried by the Trident II D–5 reentry vehicle is believed to have a yield of 100 kilotons.[11]

By October 1991 the United Kingdom's forces were losing diversity: warheads for Lance missiles, Nimrod bombers, and nuclear artillery were transferred from Europe to the United States when NATO's nuclear forces were drastically reduced after the fall of the Soviet Union. In June 1992 the United Kingdom announced the removal of all WE–177 bombs from navy surface ships. The remaining WE–177s were planned for replacement in about 2005 with tactical air-to-surface cruise missiles, but in 1993 the British dropped the idea. In 1998 the Trident missiles aboard the Vanguard SSBNs took over the substrategic role of the WE–177 bombs.[12]

NOTES

1. Robert Norris, Andrew Burrows, and Richard Fieldhouse, *British, French, and Chinese Nuclear Weapons, vol. V* (Boulder: Westview Press, 1994), pp. 63.

2. Robert Norris and William Arkin, "British Nuclear Forces, 2001," *Bulletin of Atomic Scientists*, November/December 2001, vol. 57, no. 6, pp. 78–79.

3. Ministry of Defence, United Kingdom. Available at www.mod.uk/index.php3?page=1920.

4. Darryl Howlett and John Simpson, "The United Kingdom," in *Europe and Nuclear Disarmament: Debates and Political Attitudes in 16 European Countries*, ed. Harald Müller (Brussels: European Interuniversity Press 1998), p. 59.

5. Howlett and Simpson, *Europe and Nuclear Disarmament*, p. 60.

6. Norris, Burrows, and Fieldhouse, *British, French, and Chinese Nuclear Weapons*, pp. 54–60.

7. Ibid., pp. 63–66.

8. Ibid.

9. Howlett and Simpson, "The United Kingdom," p. 59.

10. Norris, Burrows, and Fieldhouse, *British, French, and Chinese Nuclear Weapons*, pp. 100–115.

11. Ibid., pp. 168–169.

12. Howlett and Simpson, "The United Kingdom," pp. 60–61.

Table 9.1: **British Nuclear Forces, 2001**

	Launcher Type/ Designation	Launchers/ SSBNs	First Deployed	Warheads × yield (kT)	Range (km)	Deployable Warheads
SLBMs	Vanguard-class SSBN/ Trident D–5 II	48/4	1994	1–3 100 kt	7,400	185
Total		48/4		55.5 MT		185

CHAPTER 10

United States

Nuclear Weapon Capability

The United States was the first country to develop and test a nuclear weapon and is a recognized nuclear-weapon state under the Non-Proliferation Treaty. The United States continues to maintain the world's largest force of deployed strategic nuclear weapons.[1] Under the accounting rules of the START I treaty, the United States maintains an accountable strategic nuclear arsenal of 1,238 delivery vehicles with 5,949 associated warheads, although the actual number of deployed weapons is larger. The first U.S. nuclear test was conducted on July 16, 1945, after which the United States became the only country to use nuclear weapons in combat, on August 6 and 9, 1945. The last of its 1,030 nuclear weapon tests took place on September 23, 1992. The United States has signed but not ratified the Comprehensive Test Ban Treaty.

Submarine, Aircraft, and Missile Capability

The United States maintains a triad of nuclear forces on board land- and submarine-based missiles and a fleet of strategic nuclear-capable bombers. The United States deploys 50 MX/Peacekeeper intercontinental ballistic missiles armed with ten warheads each and 500 Minuteman III ICBMs (350 armed with three warheads and 150 armed with one warhead each). In addition, Washington maintains 18 nuclear-powered ballistic missile submarines. Each of seven Trident submarines based on the Pacific coast are equipped with the 24 C–4 Poseidon missiles, each of which is loaded with six warheads. Ten Tridents armed with the 24 D–5 missiles each and equipped with eight warheads per missile patrol the Atlantic coast; one is deployed in the Pacific.

The U.S. nuclear bomber force consists of 255 planes, including the B–52, B–1, and B–2 aircraft. Of the 144 B–52's in the U.S. nuclear arsenal, 97 are equipped to carry nuclear air-launched cruise missiles, and 47 are able to carry only air-dropped bombs. The United States has 90 B–1 bombers and 20 B–2's. The United States also maintains nuclear-equipped tactical aircraft.

These forces are in the process of being downsized, and the Bush administration has announced plans to retire the 50 MX missiles, convert four Trident submarines to non-nuclear roles, and to convert permanently the entire force of B–1 bombers to conventional missions.

Biological and Chemical Capability

The United States does not have research or production programs for either chemical or biological offensive weapons. It ratified the Biological Weapons Convention in 1974 and the Chemical Weapons Convention in 1997. The United States has a vast stockpile of chemical weapons that are slated for destruction on its territory and has opened its related facilities for inspection.

Strategic Context

The United States is the most advanced nuclear-weapon state in the world. It maintains a diverse arsenal of strategic and tactical nuclear weapons, as well as large stocks of weapons-grade nuclear materials. After reaching a high point in the mid-1980s, the U.S. nuclear arsenal has been shrinking as part of a negotiated arms reduction process with the Soviet Union and its successor, Russia. In the coming decade, the rationale for the continued deployment and sizing of U.S. nuclear forces should continue to evolve, as highlighted in the Nuclear Posture Review that was released by the Department of Defense on January 9, 2002.[2]

The review outlined plans to continue the already agreed reductions in strategic forces, continue efforts to develop missile defenses, and begin the development of new, low-yield nuclear weapons. The initial warhead reductions parallel those planned during the Clinton administration. By 2007, the Bush administration plans to reduce the deployed arsenal to approximately 3,800 operational strategic warheads. This will include reductions of 500 warheads from the 50 Peacekeeper ICBMs, 768 from the 96 missiles carried on four Trident submarines that will be converted to carry conventional cruise missiles, and 1,000 from the removal of two warheads from each of 500 Minuteman III ICBMs.[3]

The administration plans to field 1,700–2,200 operationally deployed strategic warheads by 2012. This plan represents a slower pace of reduction than that envisioned by the previous administration. In 1997, the United States and Russia agreed on a reduction goal of 2,000–2,500 deployed strategic warheads by the end of 2007 (see "The Effect of Arms Control," below). The lower number proposed by the Bush administration is derived by no longer counting the warheads on submarines or bombers in overhaul as being "operationally deployed." Two Trident submarines, with 192 warheads each, are usually in overhaul at any given time, as are several bombers with dozens of weapons, thus accounting for lower numbers without changing existing nuclear force plans.

Some warheads removed from delivery vehicles will be dismantled, but the majority will be maintained in the active stockpile for potential return to delivery systems on short notice (weeks or months). This is a "responsive reserve" of warheads that can be redeployed should strategic conditions change for the worse. One of the goals of the proposed START III treaty, however, had been to require warhead dismantlement to make future reductions transparent and irreversible. It appears that this is no longer a U.S. goal. The administration also plans to shorten the time required to restart nuclear testing.

United States officials have noted that since the end of the Cold War, the United States has reduced its strategic nuclear systems by more than 50 percent, nonstrategic systems by more than 80 percent, and spending on strategic forces by almost 70 percent.[4] Over the past ten years, the United States has:

- curtailed bomber and ICBM production

- removed all sea-launched nuclear cruise missiles from ships and submarines

- taken all bombers off day-to-day alert

- eliminated the Minuteman II ICBM force

- eliminated all nuclear short-range attack missiles from the bomber force

- eliminated all ground-launched intermediate- and short-range nuclear weapons

- halted underground nuclear testing

- closed major portions of the nuclear weapon production complex

There is considerable resistance from some military and civilian officials for further reductions or policy changes. In the most authoritative public statement on the rationale for maintaining large numbers of deployed forces configured as they were during the Cold War, then–commander-in-chief of the Strategic Command Adm. Richard Mies argued in July 2001 that burden of proof fell on those who advocate reductions to demonstrate exactly how and why such cuts would enhance U.S. security. "There is a tyranny in very deep numerical reductions that inhibits flexibility and induces instability in certain situations," he said. "We must preserve sufficient deterrent capability to respond to future challenges, to provide a cushion against imperfect intelligence and surprises, and to preserve a reconstitution capability as a hedge against unwelcome political or strategic developments."[5]

These views apparently prevailed in the Nuclear Posture Review (NPR). The Bush administration concluded that there will be a need to maintain thousands of deployed nuclear weapons in a triad of bombers, submarines, and land-based missiles for the indefinite future. The diversity is required to "complicate any adversary's offensive and defense planning calculations while simultaneously providing protection against the failure of a single leg of the triad," according to Mies. That is, U.S. forces must remain capable of withstanding a first strike and responding after the attack with an overwhelming and devastating nuclear counterattack. Mies explained:

> Intercontinental ballistic missiles continue to provide a reliable, low-cost, prompt response capability with a high readiness rate. They also promote stability by ensuring that a potential adversary takes their geographically dispersed capabilities into account if contemplating a disarming first strike. . . . The

strategic submarine force is the most survivable leg of the triad, providing the United States with a powerful, assured response capability against any adversary. . . . The United States must preserve a sufficiently large strategic nuclear submarine force to enable two-ocean operations with sufficient assets to ensure an at-sea response force capable of deterring any adversary in a crisis. . . . Strategic bombers . . . allow force dispersal to improve survivability and aircraft recall during mission execution. The low-observable technology of the B–2 bomber enables it to penetrate heavily defended areas and hold high-value targets at risk deep inside an adversary's territory. . . . The B–52 bomber can be employed in a standoff role using long-range cruise missile to attack from outside enemy air defenses.[6]

The Nuclear Posture Review also calls for steps that makes the use of nuclear weapons by the United States more likely, even in response to non-nuclear threats or attacks. The review states that the United States must rely on nuclear weapons to deter and respond to threats from weapons of mass destruction, defined in the review to include not only nuclear weapons, but chemical and biological weapons and even conventional explosives.

Within the new nuclear use policy, there are few if any military contingencies that might not allow the U.S. to respond with nuclear weapons. This policy raises concerns that, by threatening the use of nuclear weapons, even against conventionally armed adversaries, Washington is actually increasing the incentive for states to acquire nuclear weapons, if for no other reason than to deter the use of such weapons by the United States.

Another more subtle, but equally important development in the NPR is the closer integration of conventional and nuclear force planning. The Pentagon states that by more closely linking intelligence, communication, and force operational planning for nuclear and conventional operations, conventional forces can more easily replace operations previously limited to nuclear options, making the use of nuclear weapons less likely. It is possible, however, that this linking of operational capabilities will also work in the reverse, making it easier to target and use nuclear weapons in missions previously reserved for conventional munitions. These changes to operational integration, in combination with more direct planning to consider the use of nuclear weapons against states including China, North Korea, Iraq, Iran, Syria, Libya and others, reverse the trend of de-emphasizing nuclear weapons and could make the use of nuclear weapons far more likely and actually encourage, not discourage, the acquisition of nuclear weapons by additional states.

It remains to be seen what effect, if any, the views of the active military will have on these policies. Traditionally, the uniformed military in the United States has widely resisted anything that would counteract the traditional conventional superiority of the United States, or that might complicate military planning by forcing troops to operate in contaminated battlefields (i.e., chemical or biological weapons or radiation). These concerns have been driving factors in the development in the United States of advanced conventional capabilities as opposed to modern, battlefield nuclear weapons. It is possible that the process of integrating the directives of the NPR will be difficult and that the position of the uniformed military may lead to further modification of these policies.

Nuclear Analysis

The U.S. nuclear arsenal has developed greatly since its inception in 1945. Different strategies have guided the formation of nuclear forces and their possible use as international circumstances and technologies have continued to evolve. This evolution has continued with the collapse of the Eastern bloc and the dissolution of the Soviet Union, America's Cold War nuclear adversary.

From its small-scale beginnings during the Manhattan Project in World War II, the United States constructed a massive nuclear weapon production complex. This system of national laboratories, nuclear material production, and weapon assembly sites also included a large and advanced complex for the production of ballistic missiles, nuclear submarines, and long-range strategic bombers. The cost of producing and maintaining this arsenal since 1940 has been estimated at almost $6 trillion.[7]

The U.S. strategic arsenal now consists of 6,000 accountable nuclear weapons under the terms of the START I treaty. The deployed, operational nuclear arsenal numbers closer to 7,000 nuclear weapons. An exact number is hard to pinpoint, however, since systems are currently undergoing overhaul, conversion, or transfer to other roles. In addition to its deployed, strategic nuclear arsenal, the United States also maintains a smaller number (several hundred) of tactical nuclear weapons, including more than 100 deployed in Europe.[8] The United States also maintains a large reserve of nuclear weapons in storage and inactive reserve. While no official numbers have been released on the size of the total U.S. arsenal, reliable estimates put the stockpile at approximately 10,000 weapons.

To produce nuclear weapons, a country or group must possess special nuclear-weapons-usable materials. During the Cold War, the United States produced an extensive stockpile of weapons-grade uranium and plutonium, a stockpile surpassed only by that of the Soviet Union. The United States ceased its production of highly enriched uranium for weapons in 1964 and ended plutonium production for weapons in 1988.

A report released by the Department of Energy in 1996 documented the past U.S. production of plutonium. The report revealed that before plutonium production ceased in 1988, the United States had produced or acquired from other sources 111.4 metric tons of plutonium. Of this amount, 3.4 metric tons had been used in nuclear weapon tests and in the nuclear weapons used at the end of World War II. Additional amounts were consumed as waste products, through radioactive decay, fission, and transmutation; through inventory differences; supplied to foreign countries; or were transferred to the U.S. civilian industry.[9] The United States has declared 50 metric tons of this material as excess to defense needs and has programs under way, in conjunction with similar efforts in Russia, to dispose of the material.

No official inventory is available on the total stockpile of highly enriched uranium produced by the United States. In 1994, the Department of Energy released an estimate that the nuclear complex had produced 994 metric tons of HEU. It is not clear from this information how much material might have been consumed in nuclear tests or nuclear reactors. In addition, the United States has declared 174 metric tons of HEU to be in excess to defense needs. The material will be diluted and used as fuel for light-water reactors or disposed of as waste.

The Effect of Arms Control

The United States and the Russian Federation reached an important arms control milestone on December 5, 2001, when both sides completed reductions in their strategic nuclear arsenals. Each side reduced its arsenal to 6,000 accountable warheads as required by START I. These are substantial reductions from the nuclear arsenals that both countries deployed when the agreement was signed on July 31, 1991; they demonstrate the role of negotiated, verified arms reduction agreements in U.S. security policy. START I, however, remains the only strategic arms reduction agreement in force. There are no legal agreements now in place to guide or obligate either side to continue making reductions.

The START II treaty signed by President George Bush and Russian President Mikhail Gorbachev in January 1993 was ratified by both nations but has never entered into force. That treaty required reductions to 3,000–3,500 strategic warheads for each nation and eliminated the most destabilizing strategic nuclear systems: multiple-warhead ICBMs. At their March 1997 meeting in Helsinki, President Bill Clinton and Russian President Boris Yeltsin issued a joint statement that established the parameters of future reductions in nuclear force to a general limit of 2,000–2,500 deployed strategic warheads for a future START III treaty, for talks on tactical nuclear weapons, and for increased transparency and irreversibility in the reduction process. The Joint Chiefs of Staff in the United States endorsed those reductions and began planning for a smaller force, including the elimination of the ten-warhead MX missile force. The Department of Defense planned to implement the START II reductions by the end of 2007 and to deactivate by the end of 2003 all strategic nuclear-delivery vehicles planned for elimination, "providing the benefits of a reduced force structure four years prior to the agreed 2007 date for full elimination."[10]

Presidents Bush and Putin have made unilateral statements that each country will reduce their nuclear arsenals to between 1,700 and 2,200 weapons. The two sides are currently engaged in discussions to codify those planned reductions, although the final form of the codification is not yet known.

Through an extensive set of verification and data exchange procedures, as well as the assistance that the United States has provided Russia in implementing cuts to its arsenal, the United States is confident that Russia has achieved START I reductions. Russia, too, is able to verify adequately that the United States has made reductions to the 6,000 level, to treaty sublimits on strategic nuclear-delivery vehicles (missiles and bombers), and to a limit on the number of accountable warheads on ballistic missiles (land- and submarine-launched).

START I does not provide a totally accurate picture of the numbers of nuclear weapons deployed by each side since it attributes systems with weapons that may or may not accurately reflect actual loadings (slightly more are deployed than are reflected under the agreement). The treaty also does not address substrategic (or tactical) nuclear weapons or nondeployed weapons in storage.

The United States Turns from Arms Control Treaties

The United States and Russia continue to field massive offensive nuclear arsenals that the leaders of both countries acknowledge do not reflect the changed nature of their strategic relationship. The negotiated arms reduction process that showed such promise in the early 1990s failed to materialize fully or to make continued strides in reducing the nuclear arsenals of both countries, owing in part to deteriorating U.S.–Russian relations. Key to this blocked progress in the 1990s were internal disputes between the executive and legislative branches of government in both Washington and Moscow that seemed to thwart attempts to break the arms reduction logjam. That stagnation has left both countries with more deployed nuclear weapons than either side needs or wants.

Unilateral statements at the end of 2001 by Presidents Bush and Putin left major security risks unaddressed, including the ability to rearm to Cold War levels as well as the ultimate fate of thousands of weapons and metric tons of nuclear material.

Even with their current, sizable stockpiles, however, the two countries have made substantial progress in reducing arms from their Cold War peaks. (The Russian reductions are detailed in chapter 6.) In 1990, the United States had 10,563 accountable nuclear weapons on 2,246 missiles and bombers. As of January 2002, the United States had 5,949 accountable weapons on 1,238 launchers. These numbers do not reflect the full extent of U.S. nuclear reductions, however. Although no official numbers have ever been provided, reliable estimates from nongovernmental organizations suggest that the United States had 7,657 tactical nuclear warheads in 1990, for a total stockpile of 21,000 warheads.[11] By 2001 the number of tactical weapons had dropped to an estimated 1,160 nuclear sea-launched cruise missiles and air-dropped bombs, with the number of deployed and stockpiled strategic and tactical weapons totaling about 10,000.[12]

Former Biological Weapon Programs

The U.S. biological warfare program was established during World War II under the direction of the War Reserve Service and the Army Chemical Warfare Service. The fledgling program was limited to research and development facilities at Camp Detrick, Maryland, testing facilities in Mississippi and Utah, and a production site in Terre Haute, Indiana. After 1945, research focused on the evaluation of such agents as anthrax, botulinum toxin, brucellosis, psittacosis, and tularemia. The Korean War (1950–1953) prompted an expansion of the program. Large-scale production began in 1954 with the advancement of fermentation, concentration, storage, and weaponization technologies. A biological weapon defense program was established in 1953 and included the development of vaccines and anti-sera to protect troops from biological attack.

Throughout the 1950s other agents were added to the biological weapon research list: cholera, dengue fever, human glanders, plague, Q fever, shigellosis (dysentery), and Venezuelan equine encephalitis (VEE).[13] Efforts were made to develop more virulent and stable strains, agents that were easier and cheaper to produce and weaponize. The testing of agents involved both human and animal subjects. Large-scale open-air tests with live agents were performed on Johnston Atoll in the central Pacific Ocean from 1963 to 1969. American cities— Minneapolis, New York City, Saint Louis, San Francisco, and others— were also subjected to the clandestine testing of dispersal and aerosolization methods involving harmless bacterium.[14] Biological weapon facilities were expanded at Camp Detrick (renamed Fort Detrick in 1956), and in 1954 the army's main center for the production and stockpiling of biological weapon agents and munitions was opened in Pine Bluff, Arkansas.

By 1958 weaponization research yielded "the first missile to carry a BW warhead—the 762-mm Honest John rocket. With a twenty-five-kilometer range, the warhead could deliver 356 4.5-inch (11.5-cm) spherical bomblets. By the early 1960s, the first long-range U.S. missile, the Sergeant, extended the warhead's reach to 120 kilometers and the payload up to 720 spherical bomblets."[15]

The U.S. bioweapon program also involved the development of anti-plant and anti-animal agricultural warfare agents. Bacterial pathogens, toxins, and fungal plant pathogens were developed, as well as herbicides to destroy food crops or defoliate trees, thereby depriving enemy forces of ground cover.

By 1969, the annual budget for chemical and biological warfare research was reported to be $300 million, with $5 million set aside for agricultural-agent development.[16] In November 1969, President Richard Nixon unilaterally and unconditionally renounced offensive biological weapons and ordered the destruction of all U.S. weapon stockpiles and the conversion of all production facilities to peaceful purposes. Biological research was reoriented to the development of defense measures such as vaccines and countermeasures against biological weapon attack. The destruction of the U.S. bioweapon arsenal took place between May 1971 and February 1973 at the Pine Bluff Arsenal, Rocky Mountain Arsenal, and Fort Detrick. The entire anti-crop stockpile was also destroyed. The United States signed the Biological Weapons Convention in 1972.

The U.S. Army Medical Research Institute of Infectious Diseases (USAMRIID) was established to continue research on medical defense against biological weapons. Research at USAMRIID includes the development of countermeasures, defense strategies, vaccines, and medical therapies. All the research is unclassified.

China, North Korea, and the Soviet Union accused the United States of using biological weapons during the Korean War against China and North Korea. The United States denied the allegations and asked for an impartial investigation. China and North Korea, however, rejected World Health Organization and International Red Cross efforts to intervene to mount an investigation. The allegations remain unsubstantiated.

Former Chemical Weapon Programs

The U.S. chemical warfare program was initiated with the establishment of the Chemical Warfare Service (CWS) in 1918. Early agent production focused on chlorine, chloropicrin, mustard gas, and phosgene. Throughout the 1920s and 1930s, the CWS stockpiled chemical shells, mortars, and portable cylinders. The service also began the production and weaponization of the chemical agents tabun and sarin. In 1925, the United States signed the Geneva Protocol, which banned the use of chemical and biological warfare. The U.S. Senate, however, did not ratify the protocol until 1974.

The CWS expanded rapidly during World War II, as the United States deployed more than 400 chemical battalions and companies.[17] Production and storage facilities were also expanded in more than ten states. Between 1940 and 1945, the United States manufactured more than 146,000 metric tons of chemical agents, including cyanogen chloride, hydrogen cyanide, lewisite, and mustard gas.[18] Despite the growth of the U.S. chemical warfare program, President Franklin D. Roosevelt announced a no-first-use policy for chemical weapons. An official statement issued in 1943 declared, "We shall under no circumstances resort to the use of such [chemical] weapons unless they are first used by our enemies."[19]

With the onset of the Korean War the use of chemical weapons was seriously considered, particularly as a means to offset the enemy's superior numbers. Ultimately, the United States did not change its no-first-use policy, although riot-control agents were used on prisoners of war. The development, production, and stockpiling of chemical agents continued. During the 1950s the U.S. chemical warfare program concentrated on the weaponization of sarin. For air delivery, the 1,000-pound M–34 and M–34A1 cluster bombs were developed. Each cluster contained 76 M–125 or M–125A1 10-pound bombs, each holding 2.6 pounds of sarin.[20] In addition, the Chemical Corps (the CWS was renamed in 1946) began the research and development of the nerve agent VX. The VX program reached its height in the 1960s with the weaponization of artillery, rockets, and other delivery systems.

In 1969, Public Law 19-121 imposed restrictions on the testing, transport, storage, and disposal of chemical warfare agents. Combined with President Nixon's reaffirmation of the no-first-use policy for chemical weapons and the resubmission of the Geneva Protocol for Senate ratification, the U.S. chemical weapon program was substantially slowed, though efforts to produce new "binary" weapons continued through the 1980s.

The U.S. arsenal currently consists of unitary lethal chemical munitions that contain blister agents and nerve agents. More than half of the stockpile is in bulk storage containers and the remainder is stored in obsolete munitions.[21] The arsenal is stored at nine U.S. Army sites. Public Law 99-145, passed by

Congress in 1985, requires the army to destroy all obsolete chemical agents and munitions. In 1992, the U.S. Army established the Nonstockpile Chemical Materiel Program to dispose of the materials.[22]

The United States signed the Chemical Weapons Convention in 1993, pledging to dispose of its entire unitary chemical weapon stockpile, binary chemical weapons, recovered chemical weapons, and former chemical weapon production facilities by April 29, 2007.

NOTES

1. For further details, see Thomas B. Cochran, William M. Arkin, Milton Hoenig, *Nuclear Weapons Databook: U.S. Nuclear Forces and Capabilities* (Cambridge, Mass. Ballinger, 1984); Steven Schwartz, ed., *Atomic Audit: The Costs and Consequences of U.S. Nuclear Weapons since 1940* (Washington, D.C.: Brookings Institution Press, 1998); and the web site of the Federation of American Scientists at www.fas.org/nuke/guide/usa/index.html.

2. See U.S. Department of Defense *DefenseLink* web site for transcript of briefing, at www.defenselink.mil/news/Jan2002/t01092002_t0109npr.html. For excerpts of the classified document, see www.globalsecurity.org

3. Walter Pincus, "U.S. To Cut Arsenal To 3,800 Nuclear Warheads," *Washington Post*, January 10, 2002.

4. Statement of Adm. Richard W. Mies, commander in chief, United States Strategic Command, before the Senate Armed Services Committee Strategic Subcommittee, Washington, D.C., July 11, 2001.

5. Ibid.

6. Ibid.

7. Schwartz, ed., *Atomic Audit.*

8. Robert S. Norris and William Arkin, "NRDC Nuclear Notebook: U.S. Nuclear Forces, 2001," *Bulletin of the Atomic Scientists*, March/April, 2001.

9. U.S. Department of Energy, "Plutonium: The First 50 Years," February 1996, pp. 2–3.

10. William S. Cohen, *Annual Report to the President and Congress* (Washington, D.C.: Department of Defense, January 2001), p. 91.

11. Robert S. Norris and Thomas B. Cochran, *U.S.–USSR/Russian Strategic Offensive Nuclear Forces, 1945–1996* (Washington, D.C.: Natural Resources Defense Council, 1997), p. 54.

12. Norris and Arkin, "NRDC Nuclear Notebook," pp. 77–79.

13. Tom Mangold and Jeff Goldberg, *Plague Wars: A True Story of Biological Warfare* (London: Macmillan, 2000), p. 34.

14. Judith Miller, Stephen Engelberg, and William Broad, *Germs: Biological Weapons and America's Secret War* (New York: Simon and Schuster, 2001), p. 42. In late 1950, public health concerns emerged following an experiment using *Serratia marcescens* in San Francisco. Investigation by the Centers for Disease Control and Prevention found no evidence that the experiments posed a public health risk.

15. Mangold and Goldberg, *Plague Wars*, pp. 37–38.

16. Federation of American Scientists (FAS), *United States: Biological Weapons*. Available at www.fas.org/nuke/guide/usa/cbw/bw.htm.

17. Jeffery Smart, "History of Chemical and Biological Warfare: An American Perspective," chap. 2, *Medical Aspects of Chemical and Biological Warfare, Part I. The Textbook of Military Medicine* (Washington, D.C.: Borden Institute, Office of the Surgeon General, 1997), p. 38.

18. Ibid.

19. Ibid., p. 44.

20. Ibid., p. 49.

21. Federation of American Scientists, *United States: Chemical Weapons*. Available at www.fas.org/nuke/guide/usa/cbw/cw.htm.

22. Ibid.

Table 10.1: **U.S. Nuclear Forces**

Deployed Systems					
Name/Type	Launchers	Year Deployed	Range	Warheads/ Launcher	Total War- heads
Intercontinental Ballistic Missiles					
Minuteman III	350	1979	9,650+	3	1,050
Minuteman III	150	1979	9,650+	1	150
MX Peace-keeper	50	1986	9,650+	10	500
ICBM Totals	550				1,700
Submarine-Launched Ballistic Missiles					
	Launchers/Boats				
Trident C–4	168/7	1979	7,360	6	1,008
Trident D–5	264/11	1990	7,360	8	2,112
SLBM Totals	432/18				3,120
Ballistic Missile Totals	982 Missiles				4,820
Strategic Bombers					
B–52H	97	1961	14,000	16	
B–2	21	1994	9,600	16	
Bomber Totals	118				1,660
Total Strategic Launchers and Warheads					
	1100				6,480
Nonstrategic Warheads					
B–61, B–4, B–4, B–10					800
Total Deployed Nuclear Weapons					
	1100+				7,280
Nondeployed Weapons (Hedge, Spares, Inactive)					
					3,376
Total U.S. Nuclear Arsenal					
					10,656

SOURCE

Natural Resources Defense Council. "Faking Nuclear Restraint: The Bush Administration's Secret Plan For Strengthening U.S. Nuclear Forces," February 13, 2002. These numbers estimate actual U.S. nuclear forces and show a more accurate picture than the START I accountable weapon figures exchanged every six months.

Non-NPT Nuclear-Weapon States

Overview

In addition to the five declared nuclear-weapon states under the Treaty on the Non-Proliferation of Nuclear Weapons, three countries possess nuclear weapons: India, Israel, and Pakistan. None of these three countries is a member of the NPT, and all have a significant capability to produce, build, and deliver nuclear weapons.

The drive to create a universal non-proliferation regime is greatly complicated by the nuclear weapon capabilities of the three countries. The NPT defines a nuclear-weapon state as a country that has tested a nuclear weapon device before January 1, 1967 (article 9). None of the countries therefore qualifies under the treaty as a nuclear-weapon state, despite the possession by all three of nuclear weapons. It would be legally impossible for them to join the treaty without its being amended, which would have to be approved by the national procedures of all 187 current members, something that has generally been regarded as an unacceptable and unlikely approach.

The nuclear programs of all three countries demonstrate how regional security affects national decisions to acquire nuclear weapons. Israel's nuclear program was developed in direct response to its insecurity vis-à-vis its Arab neighbors. Pakistan's program was driven by similar concerns about India. India's decision is more complex, but perceived threats from China and Pakistan played an important role.

Efforts to limit and eventually roll back the nuclear programs of the three countries have suffered greatly by a decision in 1998 by India and Pakistan to test nuclear weapons, bringing their nuclear capabilities out of the closet, even while Israel maintains a position of deliberate opacity, neither confirming nor denying its nuclear capabilities. Efforts to reverse nuclear proliferation in the Middle East and South Asia, therefore, are directly tied to regional security and political dynamics.

India

Nuclear Weapon Capability

India possesses the components to deploy a small number of nuclear weapons within a few days and has produced enough weapons-grade plutonium to produce between 50 and 90 nuclear weapons.[1] The Natural Resources Defense Council estimates that India has approximately 30–35 warheads.[2] India is thought to have produced between 225 and 370 kilograms of weapons-grade plutonium and a smaller, but unknown, amount of weapons-grade uranium.[3] Yet three years after India's "Shakti" (strength) nuclear tests, the most striking aspect of the country's weapon program has been its deliberate pace.[4] No nuclear weapons are known to be deployed among active military units or deployed on missiles, and India's nuclear arsenal is believed to be routinely maintained as separate components. India continues to produce nuclear materials for use in weapons and has not officially stated how many weapons it has or plans to produce. India is not a member of the Non-Proliferation Treaty or a signatory of the Comprehensive Test Ban Treaty.

Aircraft and Missile Capability

India has developed several types of ballistic missiles capable of carrying and delivering a nuclear payload. These are the short-range Prithvi and the medium-range Agni. Three variants of the liquid-fueled, road-mobile Prithvi exist, with ranges of 150 kilometers and payloads of 500 kilograms (the army version); 250 kilometers and 500–750 kilograms (the air force version); and 350 kilometers and 500 kilograms (the navy version). The medium-range Agni II, with a declared range of 2,000–2,500 kilometers, was successfully tested in April 1999 and January 2001. Despite its pursuit of ballistic missiles, India's most likely delivery platforms are its fighter-bomber aircraft.[5] These probably include the MiG–27 and Jaguar and potentially the Mirage 2000, MiG–29, and Su–30 aircraft. In a classified internal memo, the Indian Air Force reportedly determined that the country's fighter-bomber aircraft remains the only feasible delivery system until the end of this decade.[6]

Biological and Chemical Weapon Capability

India is a signatory to both the Biological Weapons Convention and the Chemical Weapons Convention. U.S. intelligence assessments maintain, however, that India's significant biotechnical infrastructure and expertise are being used to conduct research on biological warfare defenses.[7] Under the terms of the CWC, India has pledged to destroy all its chemical agents and production facilities, but it retains a sizable indigenous chemical industry, so the activities and sales of Indian firms constitute cause for concern.

The Strategic Context: Policy and Motivations

India's foreign minister, Jaswant Singh, has explained that with the nuclear tests of May 1998 India achieved "a degree of strategic autonomy by acquiring those symbols of power . . . which have universal currency."[8] India's acquisition of nuclear weapons and its public display of this capability can be seen as self-validation and steps toward acquiring the power and status the country believed was its due. These perceptions are reinforced by colonial memories that still underlie much of India's search for status and policy independence.[9] Some of the country's security and political elite often view great-nation status through the prism of nuclear weapons.[10] Many members of the governing BJP party, for example, define power in terms of military power and define military power in terms of nuclear weapon capability. Some observers believe that this perspective has been a driving force of India's weapon program.[11]

In a letter to President Clinton, India's prime minister, Atal Behari Vajpayee, also cited the threat from China as the reason for India's nuclear testing program.[12] Indeed, pronuclear Indian strategists argue that, for India, nuclear weapons make strategic sense only vis-à-vis China. Indian government officials have publicly proclaimed the need for a credible deterrent against Chinese threats.[13] In the 2000–2001 annual report assessing India's security environment, India's Ministry of Defense emphasized, "The asymmetry in terms of nuclear forces is strongly in favor of China, which additionally has helped Pakistan to build missile and nuclear capability."[14]

The Pakistan–China nuclear and missile nexus is also a critical factor in the pronuclear thinking of India's strategists. China has provided major assistance to Pakistan's nuclear and missile programs. This assistance has included a blueprint for a nuclear weapon, missiles, a missile production factory, a plutonium production reactor, and technology and know-how of uranium enrichment (see chapters 7 and 12, on China and Pakistan, respectively). India's concern about China's strategic cooperation with Pakistan is intensified by a perception that the United States has not done all it could to stop Chinese proliferation.[15] Some analysts note that India's decision to test its nuclear weapons may have been hastened by the April 1998 test of the 1,300-kilometer-range Ghauri missile, which demonstrated for the first time Pakistan's capability to hit deep within India's territory.[16]

Indian strategists also saw the 1995 indefinite extension of the NPT as a consolidation of the nuclear status quo, by which India was left out of the nuclear club. Those in India who were eager to test again viewed the nuclear regime as a potential stranglehold that they had to preempt. This feeling set the stage for India's rejection of the CTBT in 1996 and for the tests in 1998.[17]

Despite the argument of the pronuclear lobby in India, there are Indian analysts who argue that nuclear weapons have caused a deterioration in India's security environment, pointing in particular to the fact that the nuclear tests neutralized India's conventional weaponry advantage over Pakistan and solidified the Pakistani–Chinese nexus. They argue that the level nuclear playing field emboldened Pakistan to initiate the Kargil conflict in 1999 and constrained India's ability to respond.[18]

Relations with the United States

From the Indian perspective, the nuclear tests raised the country's visibility and clout in the post–Cold War era. If U.S. attention is a measure of respect and status, then the nuclear tests have ultimately achieved India's objectives. While India's decision probably undermined its chances of obtaining a U.N. Security Council seat, many pronuclear Indian analysts have argued that the resulting increased attention from the sole remaining superpower proved that nuclear weapons were the only way in which to gain international relevance. President Bill Clinton's hugely popular visit to India in March 2000 (delayed in 1997 by the collapse of the government and in 1998 by the Indian tests) set the stage for improved ties. By May 2001, with a newfound self-confidence, New Delhi warmed to the U.S. strategic vision. The government was one of the few that lauded new U.S. plans for missile defenses.

President Clinton's administration had set five benchmarks for the Indian and Pakistani governments to meet before the sanctions it imposed in the aftermath of the nuclear tests would be removed. Those benchmarks were: the signing and ratifying of the Comprehensive Test Ban Treaty; restraint from deploying nuclear weapons and delivery systems; progress toward accepting the fissile-material cut-off treaty (FMCT); formal assurance that nuclear and missile technology exports would be banned; and resumption of a dialogue on Kashmir.[19] Toward the end of his administration, President Clinton had already begun to lift sanctions, even though the benchmarks had not been met. The U.S. government believed that its interests in India extended beyond non-proliferation and, moreover, that sanctions were no longer effective either in deterring proliferation in South Asia or in facilitating better relations with India and Pakistan in general. India's commitment to a test moratorium, its positive record on nuclear export controls, and an expressed willingness to consider the CTBT and FMCT made it more palatable for Washington to ease sanctions in the period after the Clinton visit.

From its inception, the Bush administration has sought to build on the newfound camaraderie with the Indian government. With Republican antipathy toward the CTBT, pressure on India to sign the treaty has disappeared. Benchmarks are no longer discussed. Beyond ensuring that Kashmir does not explode, there is a perception that the Bush administration has decided to downplay nuclear proliferation concerns in order to renew defense ties and establish "strategic" relations with India.[20] India took notice when Deputy Secretary of State Richard Armitage included New Delhi on an Asian trip to "consult" with allies in the region on missile defense. His other stops were allies Japan and South Korea. That gesture was followed by an unprecedented visit by Joint Chiefs of Staff chair Henry Shelton, who promised renewed defense ties. Thus, before September 11, 2001, India was assuming the role of America's "strategic partner" in South Asia, a potential counterweight to China, with Pakistan struggling under the weight of sanctions and isolation.

In this light, the timing for post–September 11 U.S.–Pakistan cooperation seemed inopportune for Indian foreign policy makers. With still vivid memories of Pakistan's close relationship with the United States when the Soviets were in Afghanistan, there was some apprehension in India about the potential dimensions of this renewed relationship between Washington and Islamabad. Zero-sum reasoning still guides South Asian adversaries, particularly when it comes to a relationship with the United States.

The government in New Delhi, however, continues to anticipate a new, more robust relationship with the United States. The lifting of most sanctions imposed on India has opened the way for hitherto unprecedented defense ties. High-level military meetings in December 2001 produced a joint statement that India and the United States would cooperate "to counter threats such as the spread of weapons of mass destruction, international terrorism, narcotics trafficking and piracy." The agreements that were reached reflect a U.S. willingness to sell major weapon platforms to India, something that Washington has not considered since 1984.[21] Among other objectives, Washington hopes that deeper U.S.–Indian relations, may, in fact, serve to moderate New Delhi's nuclear ambitions.

Nuclear Analysis

India was an early beneficiary of the U.S.–sponsored "Atoms for Peace" program launched in 1953. This program was intended to stem the proliferation of nuclear weapons by offering access to civil uses of nuclear technology in exchange for pledges not to apply the technology to weapons. India's nuclear weapon program originated at the Bhabha Atomic Research Center (BARC) in Trombay, which is in western India. Based on the prevailing atmosphere of trust in the early Atoms for Peace years, Canada in 1955 supplied India with the Cirus 40-MWt heavy-water-moderated research reactor (from which India later derived the plutonium for its 1974 "peaceful" nuclear explosion). In lieu of IAEA safeguards (which did not exist until after the IAEA was founded in 1957) Canada required only written "peaceful assurances" that the reactor would be used exclusively for peaceful purposes. The United States sold India some of the heavy water needed for Cirus operations under the same assurances. There was little evidence before the mid-1950s that India had any interest in nuclear weapons.

Led by atomic energy chief Homi Bhabha, India recognized early on the potential dual-use nature of many nuclear technologies, especially of plutonium separation. In 1958, as part of an ambitious scheme to pave the way for breeder reactors, India began to design and acquire the equipment for its Trombay plutonium-reprocessing facility. This facility was commissioned in late 1964, shortly before China detonated its first nuclear explosive device.

When fully operational, the Trombay facility had an estimated capacity to separate up to 10 kilograms of plutonium annually (enough for perhaps two bombs a year). Ten years later, India's nuclear explosion with plutonium that had been generated in Cirus and separated in the Trombay reprocessing facility demonstrated India's nuclear weapon option.

After a testing hiatus of 24 years, India conducted five nuclear tests in May 1998: three on May 11 and two on May 13. The Indian government claims that the May 11 test consisted of a fission device with a 12-kiloton yield, a thermonuclear device with a 43-kiloton yield, and a subkiloton device.[22] On May 13 India tested two more subkiloton devices with a range of between 0.2 and 0.6 kilotons. There is some controversy over whether India successfully tested a thermonuclear device, since the yield recorded and analyzed by Western seismographers was low, leading many in the scientific community to believe that the boosted-fission primary or the thermonuclear secondary did not function as designed.[23]

In its 1999–2000 report, India's Department of Atomic Energy acknowledged, for the first time, that it has implemented a program to develop and deploy nuclear weapons: "Following the successful nuclear tests in May 1998 at Pokharan, implementation of the program to meet the national policy of credible minimum nuclear deterrence in terms of necessary research and development as well as manufacture, is being pursued." BARC is the scientific nerve center of India's nuclear weaponization program. In April 2000 the government ended independent safety oversight at BARC.[24] Some analysts viewed this termination as an indication of accelerated weapon-related activity at BARC.

In 2002 India remains at the formative stages of its overt nuclear policy. The government has cooled its early rhetorical bravado. The nuclear doctrine released in August 1998 remains in the "draft" stages.[25] The government remains committed to weaponization, even if budget and technical realities and international political considerations continue to restrain the pace. India has maintained a self-declared moratorium on further nuclear tests, despite some domestic voices calling for their resumption. The country's testing of short- and medium-range missiles has continued, however.

According to India's Draft Nuclear Doctrine, the authority to use nuclear weapons rests with the prime minister and with a "designated successor." The Draft Nuclear Doctrine also outlines a plan for the command and control of nuclear forces: "An effective and survivable command and control system with requisite flexibility and responsiveness shall be in place. An integrated operational plan, or a series of sequential plans, predicated on strategic objectives and a targeting policy, shall form part of the system."[26]

The Indian military has yet to be fully included in the country's nuclear planning and development.[27] Interservice rivalry has delayed the creation of the post of chief of defense staff to control the country's nuclear forces.[28] The government finally deferred the decision in 2001, saying that the strategic forces that the chief of defense staff would command were not yet in place.[29] The services have proposed the establishment of a National Command Authority (NCA) and the creation of a National Strategic Nuclear Command, comprising military and technical personnel and reporting to the NCA.[30] As of March 2002, there appears to have been little movement on either front. An earlier attempt to set up a national command authority reportedly floundered amid bureaucratic infighting in the country's National Security Council.[31]

India's "Draft" Nuclear Doctrine

A draft report of the National Security Advisory Board (NSAB) on Indian Nuclear Doctrine was released in August 1999, just before national elections. The ruling BJP announced that "this is a draft proposed by the NSAB and has not yet been approved by the Government." Approval would have to wait until after the general elections of 1999.[32] The Draft Doctrine has, however, never been endorsed officially. In fact, the government has decidedly distanced itself from the doctrine, with Foreign Minister Singh calling it a "possible Indian Nuclear Doctrine," which was released for public debate. Saying that the debate was "now under way," Singh added, "It is thus not a policy document of the Government of India."[33]

The Draft Doctrine calls for a "credible minimum nuclear deterrence" based on a policy of "retaliation only," where India "will not be the first to initiate a nuclear strike, but will respond with punitive retaliation should deterrence fail." Deterrence will be a "dynamic concept" and "the "actual size, components, deployment, and employment of nuclear forces" will be determined by "the strategic environment, technological imperatives, and the needs of national security." The Draft Doctrine calls for nuclear forces based on a "triad of aircraft, mobile land-based missiles, and sea-based assets." For this deterrence to work, the doctrine says that India will require "sufficient, survivable, and operationally prepared nuclear forces, a robust command and control system, effective intelligence and early warning capabilities, and comprehensive planning and training for operations in line with the strategy." The doctrine makes no effort to quantify either the deterrence or associated costs.

Some experts argue that India's doctrine is essentially "conservative" in character since its emphasis is on deterrence rather than war fighting, and that ultimately the country's nuclear force will likely be "minimum" rather than "expansive."[34]

Missile Analysis

India's missile capabilities are the result of its Integrated Guided Missile Development Program, which was begun in 1983. In 1998, one of India's prominent nuclear strategic thinkers, retired Indian Air Commodore Jasjit Singh, wrote that the nuclear-capable aircraft's "limitations of range and susceptibility to interception by hostile systems make it critical that the central component of the nuclear arsenal must rest on ballistic missiles."[35]

Yet a potential conflict over the control of delivery systems is evident in a classified internal review conducted by India's air force in the summer of 2001. The review suggests, for example, that all nuclear delivery systems, including the Agni medium-range missile, should be placed under air force control, rather than under the authority of the chief of defense staff. The review submits that "Prithvi is too short to qualify as a nuclear platform. . . . Agni is some distance away from being operational. . . . The only vector is the aircraft and will be so for about a decade. Given the incongruity of tactical nuclear weapons in our nuclear doctrine, the army doesn't need, in fact, may not have, a nuclear role. The third leg of the triad-nuclear submarine is too far away."[36]

Given the Prithvi's range, its role would be restricted to use against Pakistan. As of the summer of 2001, Prithvi is the only nuclear-capable missile in the hands of the Indian military. The army first received the 150-kilometer-range Prithvi missile in 1994. The army is reportedly unenthusiastic about the missile, however; never having been involved in its development, it still has questions about its guidance system.[37] Moreover, because the Prithvi is liquid-fueled, it poses significant operational liabilities as a nuclear delivery system. Prithvi units include numerous vehicles that could be detected once deployed, and hours would be required in the field to prepare the missiles for launch, which would allow interdiction by Pakistan. A nuclear war game exercise staged by the Indian army in the summer of 2001 did not include the Prithvi.[38] There are even reports that the government has decided not to weaponize any Prithvi variant with a nuclear warhead.[39] However, India has continued its tests of the SRBM system. The naval version, the Dhanush, had its first successful test in September 2001.[40] The air force version was successfully tested in December 2001.[41]

India is now concentrating its energy on the Agni II and on the development of an intermediate-range ballistic missile. The Agni medium-range program, begun in the late 1980s, was suspended in 1994 owing to technological problems and diplomatic pressure from the United States. The program resumed under the BJP government in 1998 with a second version of the missile. The Agni II MRBM, with a range of 2,000–2,500 kilometers with a 1,000-kilogram payload, was first tested successfully in April 1999 (just before the BJP faced a no-confidence motion in the Indian Parliament) and then again in January 2001. Indian government officials say that the Agni II is now in production.

The Agni II is an improvement over the "technology demonstrator" Agni I. It is a two-stage, rail- and road-mobile MRBM with a solid-fuel rocket.[42] The Agni I had a liquid-solid motor combination, with the second stage consisting of, essentially, a Prithvi missile. The Agni II could reach all of Pakistan, allowing India to base it deep within the country, thereby increasing the survivability factor against its western neighbor.

The Agni II could reach parts of western China but most of northeast China, including Beijing, remains out of reach, even if the missile were based in northeast India, east of Bangladesh. A Rand study argues that no upgrade of the Agni II is likely to produce a missile with the 3,500–5,000 kilometer range necessary to hold China's most valued assets at risk. Even given India's technical expertise, that range (which will also be a matter of payload) will require the development of a new ballistic missile.[43] Currently, scientists at India's Defense

Research Development Organization (DRDO) are reportedly working to upgrade the Agni II to increase its range and accuracy. They plan to either add a third stage or a second solid-propellant booster to increase its range to 5,000 kilometers with a 1,000-kilogram payload.[44] Foreign assistance, particularly Russian, could allow India to develop its missile capabilities faster.

India has the technical expertise to pursue an ICBM capability, having successfully launched both the Polar Space Launch Vehicle and the Geosynchronous Space Launch Vehicle. The cadre of India's defense scientists who were influential in the nuclear tests would also like to demonstrate India's scientific capability by fielding an ICBM.[45] One member of the National Security Advisory Board has written: "In the final analysis, a country's international standing is founded on the reach of the weapons in its armory. . . . While India has certainly boosted its image by going nuclear, it will truly emerge as an international power only when it tests its first ICBM."[46] Some Indian politicians, however, argue that an ICBM is not necessary for India's defensive needs.[47] It may be that India will be content with an intercontinental satellite-launch-vehicle capability.[48] In any case, many years will be required before India has a test-proven capability to carry nuclear weapons to ranges of 5,000 kilometers or more.

Currently, India has no submarine-launched ballistic missile capability. The Sagarika SLBM project is reportedly continuing with assistance from Russia. Its progress, however, remains ambiguous at best. The Advanced Technology Vessel project was begun in the late 1970s, also with Russian assistance, to develop a nuclear-powered submarine that could be equipped with nuclear-tipped missiles. The program's substantial technical, financial, and bureaucratic problems indicate that there are hurdles ahead for any submarine-based nuclear delivery system.[49] A Rand study estimates that an Indian SLBM capability is still another 10 to 20 years away.[50] Russian assistance would enable faster progress.

India's inventory of nuclear-capable aircraft consist of the Jaguar, which can carry a 1,000-kilogram warhead to a range of 900–1,400 kilometers, the Mirage 2000, and the MiG 27 and 29. Russia is providing 40 nuclear-capable Su–30 aircraft and is leasing four nuclear-capable, navy-based T–22 bombers.[51] India also has a variant of the Russian TU–95, which can carry a heavy nuclear weapon to a range of 5,000–6,000 kilometers.

Biological and Chemical Weapon Analysis

India has many well-qualified scientists and numerous biological and pharmaceutical production facilities that can be used for advanced research or for the development of pathogens. United States intelligence assessments maintain that India's significant biotechnical infrastructure and expertise are being used to conduct research on biological warfare defenses.[52] India ratified the Biological Weapons Convention in 1974.

After ratifying the Chemical Weapons Convention in 1996, India disclosed that it had a chemical weapon production program. This official acknowledgment, made in June 1997, marked the first time that India publicly admitted to be pursuing a chemical warfare capability. While it has pledged to destroy all agents and production facilities, in the past Indian firms have exported a number of items proscribed under Australia Group guidelines, including specific chemical agent precursors and dual-use equipment.[53] These are materials and items that are not themselves weapons but are used to produce chemical agents. Because India has a sizable indigenous chemical industry, its activities and sales remain a cause for concern.

NOTES

1. U.S. Department of Defense, *Proliferation Threat and Response*, January 2001, p. 23; David Albright, "Supplement on Fissile Material and Nuclear Weapons in India and Pakistan," in Joseph Cirincione, ed., *Repairing the Regime: Preventing the Spread of Weapons of Mass Destruction* (Routledge: New York, 2000).

2. NRDC Nuclear Notebook, *Bulletin of the Atomic Scientists*, March/April 2002.

3. Albright, in *Repairing the Regime*.

4. P. R. Chari, "India's Slow Motion Nuclear Deployment," *Carnegie Non-Proliferation Project Issue Brief*, vol. 3, no. 26, September 7, 2000.

5. U.S. DOD, *Proliferation Threat and Response*.

6. Shishir Gupta, "Down to Brasstacks," *India Today*, May 28, 2001.

7. U.S. DOD, *Proliferation Threat and Response*, p. 24.

8. Jaswant Singh, interview with *National Public Radio*, quoted in George Perkovich, *India's Nuclear Bomb: The Impact on Global Proliferation* (Los Angeles: University of California Press, 1999). For a comprehensive discussion of India's motivations, see pp. 404–443.

9. George Perkovich, *India's Nuclear Bomb: The Impact on Global Proliferation* (Los Angeles: University of California Press, 1999), p. 417.

10. George Perkovich, "Dystrophy of Nuclear Muscle," *Outlook India*, October 16, 2000.

11. P. R. Chari, Institute for Peace and Conflict Studies, Carnegie Proliferation Roundtable, February 16, 2001. See also P. R. Chari, "India's Nuclear Doctrine: Confused Ambitions," *Nonproliferation Review*, fall–winter 2000, vol. 7, no. 3.

12. Perkovich, *India's Nuclear Bomb*, p. 419.

13. "Fernandes for Maintaining Parity with China," *Times of India*, October 10, 2000.

14. Ashwani Talwar, "Defense Ministry Beats Less around the Bush," *Times of India*, May 31, 2001.

15. Brahma Chellaney, "Load Up!" *Hindustan Times*, February 13, 2001. Chellaney was one of the strategists on India's Nuclear Security Advisory Board. See also Perkovich, *India's Nuclear Bomb*, p. 421.

16. Perkovich, *India's Nuclear Bomb*, pp. 409–412.

17. George Perkovich, Carnegie Proliferation Roundtable, November 16, 1999.

18. Chari, Carnegie Proliferation Roundtable, February 16, 2001.

19. U.S. Assistant Secretary of State Karl Inderfurth, Testimony to the U.S. Senate Foreign Relations Committee on India and Pakistan, July 13, 1998.

20. Edward Alden and Edward Luce, "A New Friend in Asia: George Bush Is Relegating Concerns about Nuclear Proliferation in order to Win the Friendship of India as a Strategic Ally in the Region," *Financial Times*, August 21, 2001.

21. Celia Dugger, "To Strengthen Military Ties, U.S. Beats Path to India," *New York Times*, December 6, 2001.

22. "Joint Statement by the Chairman of the Atomic Energy Commission and the Scientific Adviser to the Defense Minister," *The Hindu*, May 18, 1998.

23. Perkovich, *India's Nuclear Bomb*, pp. 426–427; Chari, "India's Nuclear Doctrine," pp. 128–129.

24. "Whither Nuclear Safety?" *The Hindu*, July 4, 2000.

25. Draft Report of the National Security Advisory Board on India's Nuclear Doctrine, August 17, 1999. Available at www.meadev.nic.in/govt/opstm-indnucld.htm and also on the Carnegie Non-Proliferation Project's web site at www.ceip.org/npp.

26. Draft Report of National Security Advisory Board on Indian Nuclear Doctrine, August 17, 1999. Available at www.meadev.nic.in/govt/indnucld.htm.

27. Joseph Cirincione, ed., *Repairing the Regime: Preventing the Spread of Weapons of Mass Destruction* (New York: Routledge, 2000), p. 140.

28. Gupta, "Down to Brasstacks."

29. Rahul Datta, "CDS after N-command is Formed," *The Pioneer*, June 12, 2001.

30. Neil Joeck, "Nuclear Relations in South Asia," in Cirincione, ed., *Repairing the Regime*, p. 140.

31. Vivek Raghuvanshi, "Indian Officials Halt Nuclear Command," *Defense News*, November 2000.

32. Brajesh Mishra, India's national security adviser, in opening remarks announcing the release of India's Draft Nuclear Doctrine, August 17, 1999. Available at www.meadev.nic.in/govt/indnucld.htm.

33. C. Raja Mohan, "India Not To Engage in an Arms Race: Jaswant," *The Hindu*, November 29, 1999.

34. Ashley Tellis, "India's Emerging Nuclear Doctrine: Exemplifying the Lessons of the Nuclear Revolution," NBR Analysis, National Bureau of Asian Research, 2001.

35. Jasjit Singh, ed., *Nuclear India*, Institute for Defense Studies and Analyses, New Delhi, 1998, p. 315.

36. Gupta, "Down to Brasstacks."

37. Pravin Sawhney, "Pakistan Scores over India in Ballistic Missile Race," *Jane's Intelligence Review*, November 2000.

38. Harinder Baweja, "Readying for Nukes," *India Today*, May 28, 2001.

39. Atul Aneja, "India Has 'Problems' Managing Nuclear Arms," *The Hindu*, August 14, 2001.

40. "Dhanush Missile Test Fired," *Times of India*, September 21, 2001.

41. "IAF version of Prithvi Passes Test," *Times of India*, December 13, 2001.

42. Mark Hewish, "Ballistic Missile Threat Evolves," *Jane's International Defense Review*, October 2000, p. 41.

43. Gregory Jones, "From Testing to Deploying Nuclear Forces: The Hard Choices Facing India and Pakistan," Issue Paper 192, Rand, 2000.

44. Sawhney, "Pakistan Scores."

45. "ICBMs Any Day, Says Kalam," *Hindustan Times*, September 18, 2000.

46. Chellaney, "Load Up!" *Hindustan Times*, February 13, 2001.

47. Ibid.

48. Michael Krepon, Carnegie Proliferation Roundtable, February 16, 2001.

49. Gopi T. S. Rethiniraj, and Clifford Singer, "Going Global: India Aims for a Credible Nuclear Doctrine," *Jane's Intelligence Review*, February 2001.

50. Jones, "Deploying Nuclear Forces."

51. Jerome Conley, "Indo-Russian Military and Nuclear Cooperation: Implications for U.S. Security Interests," INSS Occasional Paper 31, February 2000; Dinesh Kumar, "Russia Pumps Iron into India's Defense Capability," *Times of India*, October 5, 2000.

52. U.S. DOD, *Proliferation Threat and Response*, p. 24.

53. Ibid., p. 25.

Table 11.1: **India: Nuclear Infrastructure**

Name/Location of Facility	Type and Capacity	Completion or Target Date	IAEA Safeguards
NUCLEAR WEAPON RESEARCH & DEVELOPMENT COMPLEX			
Pokharan Range	Site of nuclear weapon tests in 1998		No
POWER REACTORS: OPERATING			
Tarapur 1	Light-water, LEU and MOX 150-MWe	1969	Yes
Tarapur 2	Light-water, LEU 150-MWe	1969	Yes
Rajasthan, RAPS–1 Kota	Heavy-water, nat. U 90-MWe	1972	Yes
Rajasthan, RAPS–2 Kota	Heavy-water, nat. U 187-MWe	1980	Yes
Madras, MAPS–1 Kalpakkam	Heavy-water, nat. U 170-MWe	1983	No
Madras, MAPS–2 Kalpakkam	Heavy-water, nat. U 170-MWe	1985	No
Narora 1	Heavy-water, nat. U 202-MWe	1989	No
Narora 2	Heavy-water, nat. U 202-MWe	1992	No
Kakrapar 1	Heavy-water, nat. U 170-MWe	1992	No
Kakrapar 2	Heavy-water, nat. U 202-MWe	1995	No
Kaiga 1	Heavy-water, nat. U 202-MWe	2000	No
Kaiga 2	Heavy-water, nat. U 202-MWe	1999	No
Rajasthan, RAPP–3 Kota	Heavy-water, nat. U 202-MWe	2000	No
Rajasthan, RAPP–4 Kota	Heavy-water, nat. U 202-MWe	2000	No
POWER REACTORS: UNDER CONSTRUCTION			
Tarapur 3	Heavy-water, nat. U 500-MWe	2006	No
Tarapur 4	Heavy-water, nat. U 500-MWe	2005	No

Table 11.1 (continued)

Name/Location of Facility	Type and Capacity	Completion or Target Date	IAEA Safeguards
POWER REACTORS: PLANNED AND PROPOSED			
Kaiga 3	Heavy-water, nat. U 220-MWe	–	No
Kaiga 4	Heavy-water, nat. U 220-MWe	–	No
Kaiga 5	Heavy-water, nat. U 220-MWe	–	No
Kaiga 6	Heavy-water, nat. U 220-MWe	–	No
Rajasthan, RAPP–5 Kota	Heavy-water, nat. U 500-MWe	–	No
Rajasthan, RAPP–6 Kota	Heavy-water, nat. U 500-MWe	–	No
Rajasthan, RAPP–7 Kota	Heavy-water, nat. U 500-MWe	–	No
Rajasthan, RAPP–8 Kota	Heavy-water, nat. U 500-MWe	–	No
Koodankulam 1/ Kundankulam 1	Russian VVER–1000/392 Light-water, LEU-1000 MWe[1]	–	Yes
Koodankulam 2/ Kundankulam2	Russian VVER–1000/392 Light-water, LEU-1,000 MWe	–	Yes
RESEARCH REACTORS			
Apsara BARC, Trombay	Light-water, medium-enriched uranium, pool type, 1-MWt	1956	No
Cirus BARC, Trombay	Heavy-water, nat. U 40-MWt	1960	No
Dhruva BARC, Trombay	Heavy-water, nat. U 100-MWt	1985	No
Kamini IGCAR, Kalpakkam	Uranium–233 30-kWt	1996	No
Zerlina BARC, Trombay	Heavy-water, variable fuel; 100-Wt, decommissioned	1961	No
Purnima 1 BARC, Trombay	Fast neutron, critical assembly; zero power, decommissioned	1972	No
Purnima 2 BARC, Trombay	Uranium–233 .005-kWt, dismantled	1984	No
Purnima 3 BARC, Trombay	Uranium–233, decomissioned[2]	–	No

BREEDER REACTORS			
Fast-Breeder Test Reactor (FBTR) IGCAR, Kalpakkam	Plutonium and nat. U 40-MWt	1985	No
Prototype Fast Breeder Reactor (PFBR) IGCAR, Kalpakkam	Mixed-oxide fuel 500-MWe; construction to begin early 2002	2009	No
URANIUM ENRICHMENT			
Trombay	Pilot-scale ultracentrifuge plant, operating	1985	No
Trombay	Laser enrichment research site	early 1980s	No
Rattehalli (Mysore)	Pilot-scale ultracentrifuge plant, operating[3]	1990	No
Center for Advanced Technology, Indore	Laser enrichment research site	1993	No
REPROCESSING (PLUTONIUM EXTRACTION)			
Trombay	Medium-scale, 50 tHM/year; operating	1964/1985	No
Tarapur (Prefre)	Large-scale, 100 (25) tHM/year; operating[4]	1977	Only when safeguarded fuel is present
Kalpakkam	Laboratory-scale, operating	1985	No
Kalpakkam	Large-scale, two lines, 100 tHM/y each- under construction		No
URANIUM PROCESSING			
Rakh, Surda, Mosaboni[5]	Uranium recovery plant at copper concentrator; operating		N/A
Jaduguda, Narwpahar, Bhatin[6]	Uranium mining and milling; operating		N/A
Hyderabad	Uranium purification (UO_2); operating		No
Hyderabad	Fuel fabrication; operating, under expansion		Partial
Trombay	Uranium conversion (UF_6); operating; fuel fabrication[7]		No
Tarapur	Mixed uranium-plutonium oxide (MOX) fuel fabrication; operating		Only when safeguarded fuel is present

Table 11.1 (continued)

Name/Location of Facility	Type and Capacity	Completion or Target Date	IAEA Safeguards
HEAVY-WATER PRODUCTION[8]			
Trombay	Pilot-scale; operational?		–
Nangal	7 tons/year; operating	1962	–
Baroda	67 tons/year; Intermittent operation	1980	–
Tuticorin	71 tons/year; operating	1978	–
Talcher, phase 1	62 tons/year; operating	1980	–
Talcher, phase 2	62 tons/year; operating	1980	–
Kota	100 tons/year; operating	1981	–
Thal-Vaishet	110 tons/year; operating	1991	–
Manuguru	185 tons/year; operating, under expansion	1991	–
Hazira	110 tons/year; operating	1991	–
NUCLEAR WEAPON TEST SITE			
Pokharan Range	Site of nuclear tests conducted in 1998		No

Abbreviations

HEU	highly enriched uranium	MWt	millions of watts of thermal output
LEU	low-enriched uranium	nat. U	natural uranium
MWe	millions of watts of electrical output	kWt	thousands of watts of thermal output
tHM/yr	(metric) tons of heavy metal per year	N/A	not applicable
MOX	mixed oxide fuel		

NOTES

1. See the Australian Nuclear Science and Technology Organization web site, www.ansto.gov.au/info/reports/nucpower/2000notes_mar.html.

2. See the Indian Department of Atomic Energy web site, www.dae.gov.in/publ/persp/radtech/radtech.htm.

3. Mark Hibbs, "India To Equip Centrifuge Plant with Improved Rotor Assemblies," *Nuclear Fuel*, December 1, 1997, p. 7.

4. The Power Reactor Reprocessing Plant (Prefre) has a nominal output capacity of 100 tHM/year but has operated for more than a decade at about 25 tHM/year. Mark Hibbs, "Tarapur–2," *Nuclear Fuel*, September 25, 1995.

5. Sites listed in OECD Nuclear Energy Agency and International Atomic Energy Agency, *Uranium: 1991 Resources, Production, and Demand*, p. 197.

6. These uranium milling sites are located in a 10-kilometer area near Jaduguda. Listed in *Risk Report*, Wisconsin Project, March 1995, p. 9.

7. This is a small plutonium fuel–fabrication facility for Purnima II (5 KWe) that was expanded to produce fuel for the FBTR. David Albright, Frans Berkhout, and William Walker, *Plutonium and Highly Enriched Uranium 1996: World Inventories, Capabilities, and Policies* (Oxford: Oxford University Press, 1997), p. 206.

8. The non-proliferation regime does not include the application of safeguards to heavy-water production facilities, but safeguards are required on the export of heavy water.

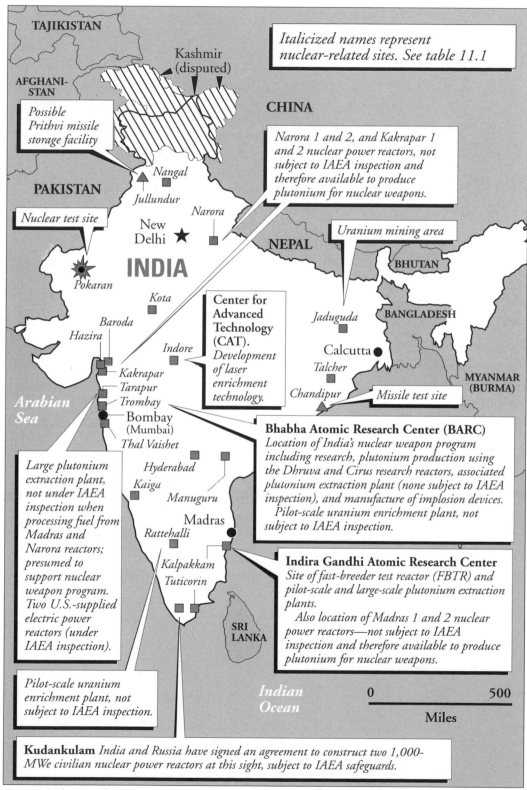

TAJIKISTAN

AFGHANI-STAN

Kashmir (disputed)

Possible Prithvi missile storage facility

CHINA

PAKISTAN

Nuclear test site

Narora 1 and 2, and Kakrapar 1 and 2 nuclear power reactors, not subject to IAEA inspection and therefore available to produce plutonium for nuclear weapons.

Nangal

Jullundur

Narora

New Delhi ★

INDIA

Uranium mining area

NEPAL

BHUTAN

Pokaran

Kota

Baroda

Hazira

Center for Advanced Technology (CAT). *Development of laser enrichment technology.*

Indore

Jaduguda

BANGLADESH

Calcutta ●

Talcher

MYANMAR (BURMA)

Kakrapar
Tarapur
Trombay

Bombay (Mumbai) ●

Thal Vaishet

Arabian Sea

Chandipur

Missile test site

Bhabha Atomic Research Center (BARC)
Location of India's nuclear weapon program including research, plutonium production using the Dhruva and Cirus research reactors, associated plutonium extraction plant (none subject to IAEA inspection), and manufacture of implosion devices.
Pilot-scale uranium enrichment plant, not subject to IAEA inspection.

Large plutonium extraction plant, not under IAEA inspection when processing fuel from Madras and Narora reactors; presumed to support nuclear weapon program. Two U.S.-supplied electric power reactors (under IAEA inspection).

Hyderabad

Kaiga

Manuguru

Madras ●

Rattehalli

Kalpakkam

Tuticorin

Indira Gandhi Atomic Research Center
Site of fast-breeder test reactor (FBTR) and pilot-scale and large-scale plutonium extraction plants.
Also location of Madras 1 and 2 nuclear power reactors—not subject to IAEA inspection and therefore available to produce plutonium for nuclear weapons.

SRI LANKA

Pilot-scale uranium enrichment plant, not subject to IAEA inspection.

Indian Ocean

0   500
Miles

Kudankulam *India and Russia have signed an agreement to construct two 1,000-MWe civilian nuclear power reactors at this sight, subject to IAEA safeguards.*

Italicized names represent nuclear-related sites. See table 11.1

CHAPTER 12

Pakistan

Nuclear Weapon Capability

Pakistan possesses the components and material to assemble a small number of nuclear weapons in a matter of hours or days and has produced enough weapons-grade uranium to produce between 30 and 50 nuclear weapons.[1] In all, Pakistan is thought to have produced between 585 and 800 kilograms of highly enriched uranium and may possess enough weapons-grade plutonium for the production of three to five weapons. Pakistan's nuclear weapons are reportedly stored in component form, with the fissile core separated from the non-nuclear explosives.[2] It is unclear where Pakistan stores its fissile material and warheads. Like India, Pakistan has not joined the Non-Proliferation Treaty or the Comprehensive Test Ban Treaty.

Aircraft and Missile Capability

Pakistan has nuclear-capable missiles with ranges from 280 kilometers to 2,000 kilometers. Pakistan has acquired the bulk of its missile capabilities from China and North Korea. Its missile arsenal includes the Chinese-built and supplied M–11, the liquid-fuel Hatf short-range series, the Ghauri medium-range missiles, and the solid-fuel Shaheen series. Pakistan reportedly possesses about 30 nuclear-capable M–11 surface-to-surface missiles with a range of 280–300 kilometers. In early 2001 Pakistan announced that it had begun the serial production of the Shaheen I, adding that the missile has been "inducted" into the army. The country has also successfully tested the Ghauri I missile that has a range upward of 1,300 kilometers and is capable of carrying a 700-kilogram warhead, and the Ghauri II, a ballistic missile with a range of 2,000 kilometers that can carry a payload of 850 kilograms. The Shaheen II, a solid-fuel missile with a range of 2,000 kilometers, was displayed in a March 2000 parade; Pakistan claims to have begun its serial production. As of March 2002, the Shaheen II has never been tested. The F–16 could be Pakistan's primary nuclear-capable aircraft, capable of carrying a 1,000-kilogram bomb to a distance of 1,400 kilometers.[3] Other delivery vehicles include the French Mirage III fighter-bombers and the Chinese A–5 Fantan.

Biological and Chemical Weapon Capability

Pakistan is believed to have a biotechnical infrastructure sufficient to support a limited biological weapon research and development effort. Although its facilities are less well developed than those of India, they could nonetheless support the production of lethal pathogens. Pakistan is actively seeking foreign assistance to expand its biological and pharmaceutical facilities. It ratified the BWC in 1974 and regularly participates in negotiations to establish an effective verification protocol for the treaty.

Pakistan is actively improving its commercial chemical industry and has imported chemicals with both commercial and weapon utility. It is expected eventually to have the capability to produce a variety of chemical agents because of the dual-use nature of its chemicals and equipment. It is speculated that Pakistan ultimately seeks self-sufficiency in chemical precursor production.[4] Pakistan ratified the CWC in October 1997 and did not declare the possession of any chemical weapons.

Strategic Context

Pakistan's quest for a nuclear deterrent has been motivated principally by fears of domination by India, whose population, economy, and military resources dwarf its own. The country has been locked in a conflict with India since its independence from Britain in 1947. The two countries have fought three full-scale wars since 1947, two of which have been over the disputed territory of Kashmir. The last war, in 1971, led to the dismemberment of Pakistan; its former eastern wing became the independent state of Bangladesh. Pakistan secretly commenced its nuclear weapon program shortly thereafter, convinced that only a nuclear weapon capability would ensure that India did not attempt to eliminate Pakistan as a state. On May 28 and 30, 1998, Pakistan responded to India's May 11 and 13 nuclear tests by conducting tests of its own, declaring itself a nuclear-weapon state.

Since the 1971 India-Pakistan war, relations between Islamabad and New Delhi have alternated between periods of relative peace and periods of considerable tension, punctuated with crises that nearly erupted into war during the winter of 1986–1987 and the spring of 1990. In the latter crisis, there were fears that Pakistan might take steps to deploy its nascent nuclear arsenal. These concerns spurred intensive, and ultimately successful, U.S. diplomatic efforts to defuse the situation. Conflicts in Kargil in 1999 and military mobilizations after terrorist attacks on the Indian government in late 2001 and early 2002 again raised the possibility of war spiraling into a nuclear exchange.

A desire for leadership and status in the Islamic world, popular nationalist sentiment, and bureaucratic pressure have also contributed to Pakistan's bid for nuclear arms. Despite frequent Western (and occasional Pakistani) characterizations of Pakistan's bomb as an Islamic bomb, the Pakistani program is seen most accurately as a nationalistic endeavor. Those who have been involved in its development are largely secular-minded nationalists.[5]

While Pakistani scientists, engineers, and government leaders have proceeded as rapidly as possible since 1972 in developing a nuclear weapon capability, they have always sought to appear as though they were responding to India. Thus, in late 1995, when U.S. agencies detected that India was preparing to conduct a nuclear explosive test, the disclosure triggered a major diplomatic effort by the United States and other countries to dissuade Narasimha Rao, then Prime Minister of India, from proceeding. By early 1996, the threat of a test appeared to have subsided. Nonetheless, testifying before the U.S. Senate in late February, the director of the Central Intelligence Agency, John Deutch, stated, "We are concerned [that] India is considering the possibility of a nuclear test. We have judged that if India should test, Pakistan would follow."[6] Barely two weeks after Deutch's statement, preparations for a Pakistani nuclear test were disclosed. Reportedly, U.S. satellite photographs revealed evidence of Pakistani nuclear test preparations at a site in the Chagai Hills, seemingly as a direct response to India's earlier preparations.

In April 1998, Abdul Qadeer Khan, the self-proclaimed father of the Pakistani nuclear weapon program, declared that as soon as Pakistani scientific teams could "get permission from the government," they were ready and able to test a nuclear weapon.[7] In May 1998, following the Indian nuclear tests, the government of Nawaz Sharif finally gave permission for such a test. On May 28, 2001, after the tests took place at Chagai Hill in western Pakistan, Sharif declared, "Today we have settled a score."[8]

Pakistan's nuclear arsenal offers a sense of military parity with India. It is widely accepted that the May 1998 tests emboldened Pakistan to increase its militancy in the Kashmir valley, confident that it was unlikely to lead to an Indian assault on Pakistan given the country's limited nuclear capability. The summer 1999 incursion into Kargil by Pakistani forces over the line of control that divides Indian and Pakistani-held Kashmir is seen as a direct result of Pakistan's newfound parity.[9]

Relations Between India and Pakistan in the Aftermath of the Tests

When the posttest rhetoric reached alarming levels, India and Pakistan appeared to be moving toward a more stable and constructive set of relations. In February 1999 India's prime minister, Atal Behari Vajpayee, made a widely publicized bus trip to Lahore to meet Prime Minister Sharif, and the two signed the Lahore Agreement, agreeing to "intensify their efforts to resolve all issues, including the issue of Jammu and Kashmir." Both leaders recognized that "the nuclear dimension of the security environment of the two countries adds to their responsibility for avoidance of conflict between the two countries."[10] The Lahore Declaration also included a commitment to "take immediate steps for reducing the risk of accidental or unauthorized use of nuclear weapons and discuss concepts and doctrines with a view to elaborating measures for confidence building in the nuclear and conventional fields, aimed at prevention of conflict." To this effect, the Lahore Declaration issued a Memorandum of Understanding that included specific nuclear confidence-building measures, including prior notification of ballistic missile tests, a continuation of their unilateral moratoria on nuclear testing, and dialogue on nuclear and security issues.

The summer incursion of Pakistani troops into Kargil, however, brought this diplomatic momentum to an abrupt halt. The Kargil conflict was the first between the two neighbors after the nuclear tests of 1998; it destroyed any illusions that the overt nuclear postures of the two countries would act as a restraint on military conflict.[11] Instead, new thinking emerged on a "limited war," which proponents argued could be fought under a nuclear umbrella. Indeed, after the Kargil conflict Indian strategists proffered scenarios of a limited war under the nuclear shadow, precisely because the bomb appeared to have a restraining effect on India. Indian aircraft bombed Pakistani positions in Indian-administered Kashmir, but never over the line of control, largely because Indian political leaders did not want to risk an escalation to a nuclear conflict. They wanted to demonstrate to the world that they were responsible nuclear stewards. On the other hand, having leveled the playing field against an India that has an advantage over Pakistan in terms of conventional weapons, Pakistan was emboldened by the bomb to launch an offensive. Alarmed by the potential for an escalation of the Kargil conflict, the Clinton administration intervened diplomatically. Under U.S. pressure, Nawaz Sharif's government withdrew Pakistani troops from Kargil. This contributed to his downfall, however, when in October 1999 the Sharif government was overthrown in a military coup. The coup brought Gen. Pervez Musharraf to power, and relations with India deteriorated further since the Indians regarded Musharraf as the chief architect of the Kargil incursion.

Nuclear Analysis

Pakistan's nuclear weapon program, secretly launched in 1972, gained new impetus after India's nuclear test in May 1974. The weapons effort was based substantially on the production of highly enriched uranium with technology gained covertly during the late 1970s and 1980s. This was expedited by the return to Pakistan in 1975 of Abdul Qadeer Khan, a German-trained metallurgist who was employed at the classified Urenco uranium-enrichment plant at Anselmo in the Netherlands in the early 1970s. Khan brought to Pakistan personal knowledge of gas-centrifuge equipment and industrial suppliers (especially in Europe) and was put in charge of building, equipping, and operating Pakistan's Kahuta enrichment facility. Khan also reportedly returned to Pakistan with stolen plans for European centrifuges.

The Pakistani nuclear weapon effort relied on a massive smuggling program, which began with the clandestine acquisition of key technology for the Kahuta plant from the Netherlands and included the illicit import of an entire facility from West Germany for producing uranium hexafluoride, as well as many other incidents, some involving duplicitous procurement from the United States.[12]

Since 1979 Pakistan's nuclear program has repeatedly brought the country under U.S. sanctions, which have been intermittently waived as a result of developments in Afghanistan. The 1979 economic and military aid cutoff was made pursuant to the 1977 Glenn-Symington amendment. That amendment requires the termination of assistance to any state that imported uranium-enrichment equipment or technology after 1977 and that has refused to place it under IAEA inspection. In 1981, in the wake of the Soviet occupation of

Afghanistan, the United States suspended the application of the uranium-enrichment sanctions for six years. Instead, Washington provided greatly increased military and economic assistance to Pakistan to create a bulwark against further Soviet expansion and to establish Pakistan as a strategic partner supporting anti-Soviet forces in Afghanistan. Reagan administration officials also argued that the restoration of aid would advance U.S. non-proliferation objectives by enhancing Pakistan's security generally, thereby reducing Islamabad's motivation to acquire nuclear arms.

Pakistan continued its nuclear weapon program, however. The program reached a key milestone in 1985, when, despite numerous pledges to the United States that it would not produce weapons-grade uranium, Pakistan crossed the threshold. By 1986, Pakistan had apparently produced enough material to make its first nuclear device. Although the United States sought to discourage Pakistan from pursuing its nuclear program throughout this period, Washington restrained its pressure on Islamabad because of the need for continued Pakistani cooperation in the campaign to oust Soviet forces from Afghanistan. Pakistani sources now state that the nation acquired its first nuclear explosive capability in 1987.

The Afghanistan-related duality in U.S. policy toward Pakistan was also reflected in the enactment of a 1985 law known as the Pressler amendment. This legislation specified that U.S. aid and government-to-government military sales to Pakistan would be cut off unless the president certified at the beginning of each U.S. fiscal year that Pakistan did "not possess a nuclear explosive device and that the proposed U.S. assistance program would significantly reduce the risk that Pakistan will possess a nuclear explosive device." Despite further Pakistani advances toward nuclear weapons through October 1989 Presidents Reagan and Bush made the certifications necessary to permit U.S. aid and arms sales. The 1989 certification that Pakistan did not possess a nuclear device was, reportedly, made only after Pakistan's prime minister, Benazir Bhutto, agreed to suspend the further production of weapons-grade uranium.

In late 1989 and early 1990, perhaps because of the threat of war with India, Pakistan apparently ended this freeze and fabricated cores for several nuclear weapons from preexisting stocks of weapons-grade uranium. By this time the Soviet army had left Afghanistan, and in October 1990, the Bush administration was unable or unwilling to certify that Pakistan did not possess a nuclear explosive. The United States terminated all aid and government-to-government military sales to Pakistan. At the time, 28 additional F–16s and other military hardware were on order. Since the Pressler sanctions went into effect in 1990, the F–16s were never transferred. Islamabad continued making payments on the purchases after October 1990, hoping to receive these armaments in the event that the prohibition against such U.S. military sales was rescinded.

In late 1991, Prime Minister Sharif reinstated the freeze on the production of weapons-grade uranium, a freeze that held until the spring of 1998.[13] Pakistan continued to produce low-enriched uranium, however, thereby enlarging its total nuclear weapon potential. Other aspects of the Pakistani nuclear program also continued to advance. These included work on nuclear weapon designs; construction of a Chinese-designed and supplied 40-MWt nuclear reactor at Khushab; and the enlargement of Pakistan's capacity to enrich uranium, reportedly through the construction of an enrichment plant at Golra.

Throughout the 1990s Pakistani specialists sought to improve the Kahuta enrichment plant and to expand the country's capacity to enrich uranium. The best-publicized incident was Pakistan's purchase from China of 5,000 custom-made ring magnets, a key component of the bearings that support the high-speed rotation of centrifuges. The shipments of the magnets, which were sized to fit the specific type of centrifuge used at the Kahuta plant, apparently began in December 1994 and continued until the Clinton administration became aware of the transaction in August 1995. It was not clear whether the ring magnets were intended for Kahuta as a "future reserve supply," or whether they were intended to permit Pakistan to increase its number of uranium-enrichment centrifuges, either at Kahuta or at another location.

During the 1990s the United States assisted Pakistan primarily with its refugee and narcotics problems, although congressional amendments allowed for limited military sales to Pakistan. China's ring-magnet assistance to Pakistan, however, undercut the Clinton administration's efforts to restore a measure of non-proliferation influence in its relations with Pakistan. It prevented Pakistan from receiving economic or targeted military aid, which the Clinton administration and many legislators had earlier anticipated extending to Pakistan after the 1999 enactment of the Brown amendment, which sought to modify the Pressler sanctions.

Pakistan actively pursued a plutonium production capability during the 1990s. Its efforts came to fruition in April 1998 when Pakistan announced that the Khushab reactor had begun operation. This facility is not subject to IAEA inspection and is capable of generating enough plutonium for one or two nuclear weapons annually. This plutonium would permit Pakistan to develop smaller and lighter nuclear warheads than it now has. This, in turn, might facilitate Pakistan's development of warheads for ballistic missiles.

Nuclear Tests

In May 1998 Pakistan conducted a series of nuclear tests. There has been no official statement from Pakistan regarding the weapon type that was tested, but it is likely that all the weapons tested were of a simple fission design. The tests are thought to have been successful and appear to have given Pakistan a reliable weapon design with a 10–15 kiloton yield.[14] Pakistan claims to have conducted five tests on May 28. The tests, however, produced only a single seismic signal, possibly the cumulative effect of simultaneous detonations, which indicated a total yield of 6–13 kilotons. The single signal led U.S. scientists to question whether five detonations did take place. The test on May 30, 1998, produced a seismic signal equivalent to a yield of 2–8 kilotons.[15] The tests activated Glenn amendment sanctions, once more ending U.S. government economic assistance and military transfers to Pakistan.

In February 2000 Pakistan established a Nuclear Command Authority, which consists of two committees that advise President Musharraf on the development and employment of nuclear weapons.[16] The following year, Pakistan consolidated the Khan Research Laboratories, previously headed by Abdul Qadeer Khan, and the rival Pakistan Atomic Research Corporation into one Nuclear Defense Complex. Pakistan has yet to enunciate a nuclear doctrine, although, given India's overwhelming superiority in conventional weaponry, the country has rejected the doctrine of no-first-use.

Developments since September 11, 2001, dramatically altered the U.S. policy on nuclear sanctions. Pakistan, once again, became a frontline state in a U.S. battle in Afghanistan, this time against international terrorism. As a result of President Musharraf's decision to respond to the U.S. need for Pakistan's cooperation, all nuclear-related sanctions have been waived. Furthermore, the democracy-related sanctions imposed on Pakistan as a result of the army coup that brought Musharraf to power in October 1999 have also been waived. With this waiver of sanctions, Pakistan is hoping that the United States will transfer the F–16's.[17]

Musharraf informed his public that Pakistan's "strategic assets" were best protected by joining the U.S. coalition against international terrorism. The intimation was that India could take advantage of the military action on Pakistan's western border to launch a preemptive strike on Pakistan's nuclear and missile assets, and that cooperation with the United States would preclude such an event.[18] Ironically, however, the potential for civil unrest as a result of Musharraf's decision has raised U.S. concern over the safety of Pakistan's nuclear strategic assets. Experts urge the United States to consider offering Pakistan assistance in securing its fissile material and weapons.[19] Some analysts argue that some of the fears have been overblown since Pakistan views its nuclear possessions as its "crown jewels" and will go to great lengths to ensure their security.[20]

Missile and Aircraft Analysis

Throughout the 1990s U.S. officials believed that the most likely means of delivering a Pakistani nuclear weapon was the U.S.–supplied F–16s, which had been equipped to arm nuclear weapons in flight. The development of several mature ballistic missile systems—primarily with assistance from China and North Korea—has now given Pakistan the means to deliver nuclear weapons by missile.

Pakistan's efforts to acquire ballistic missiles began in the early 1980s and intensified in the mid-1980s when, with Chinese assistance, it launched a program to develop two short-range ballistic missile systems: the 80-kilometer-range Hatf I and the 300-kilometer range Hatf II. Pakistan also sought to acquire the 280- to 300-kilometer range, nuclear-capable M–11 ballistic missile system and associated equipment from China. Later, Pakistan acquired and developed longer-range systems, including the Ghauri and Shaheen systems, the former derived from North Korean technology and the latter from Chinese.

In its ballistic missile efforts, Pakistan has benefited considerably from Chinese and North Korean assistance,[21] which has put Pakistan's missile development ahead of India's. Competition between the Khan Research Laboratories and the Pakistan Atomic Energy Commission has added momentum to Pakistan's missile program.[22] The Khan Laboratories developed the Ghauris, while the Pakistan Atomic Energy Commission was responsible for the Shaheen series.

In July 1997, in response to India's semi-deployment of the Prithvi short-range missile in Punjab, Pakistan reportedly tested the Hatf III, a 600-kilometer, liquid-fuel ballistic missile.[23] The announced 600-kilometer range and 500-kilogram payload capability of Hatf III suggests that the system is nuclear-capable and capable of reaching New Delhi and other targets deeper in India's interior.

On April 6, 1998, before India's nuclear tests in May, Pakistan tested the Ghauri I missile, which has a range of upward of 1,300 kilometers and carries a 700-kilogram warhead.[24] The Ghauri is a liquid-fuel missile based on North Korea's No Dong and is launched from a road-mobile launcher.[25] With the successful Ghauri I test, Pakistan demonstrated an unprecedented ability to strike deep into Indian territory, taking the Indians by surprise with the pace of Pakistan's missile program.[26] In April 1999, after India's test of the 2,000-kilometer Agni II, Pakistan successfully tested the Ghauri II, a 2,000-kilometer-range ballistic missile that carries a payload of 850 kilograms.

Pakistan also successfully tested the 750-kilometer, solid-fuel, nuclear-capable Shaheen I (also called the Hatf II) in April 1999. This missile is possibly a derivative of the Chinese M–9. The M–9 is reported to have a 600-kilometer range and to be capable of carrying a 500-kilogram payload, which is more than twice the 280-kilometer range claimed by the Chinese for the M–11. While a Pakistani M–11 with a 280-kilometer-range capability would probably not be able to reach India's capital at Delhi from Pakistani territory, the M–9 could target not only Delhi but possibly also reach Mumbai (Bombay), India's largest industrial city. There are unconfirmed reports that Pakistan deployed nuclear warheads on its Shaheen I missiles during the Kargil war in the summer of 1999.[27]

After the tests of the Ghauri II and the Shaheen I in April 1999, Pakistan announced the conclusion—"for now"—of tests of its missiles systems. It called on India to join in a "strategic restraint regime" to limit the development of missile and nuclear weapon technology and deployment.[28] Indeed, Pakistan did not respond to India's test of the Agni II in January 2001, or to the Dhanush test in September 2001, with missile tests of its own. The U.S. Department of Defense, however, asserts that Pakistan has put a "high priority" on its ballistic missile program to counter India's capabilities.[29] It appears unlikely, therefore, that Islamabad will curtail its missile program, given that missiles are central to its nuclear weaponization program and rival those of India.

Foreign Assistance

The precise nature of China's support for Pakistan's ballistic missile program is not known. In the spring of 1995 press reports indicated that Washington believed that China had recently transferred components that could be used with the M–11, and by the summer of 1995 the U.S. intelligence community apparently had concluded that Pakistan had more than 30 complete M–11 missiles on hand. The weapons, which some believe were received as early as November 1992, were said to be sitting in storage crates at the Sargodha Air Force Base, west of Lahore. The Clinton administration declined to impose sanctions on the two countries, however, arguing that it lacked sufficiently firm evidence to support such an action.

The M–11 issue resurfaced in the summer of 1996 when press reports disclosed the conclusion of a U.S. National Intelligence Estimate that, as had been previously estimated, Pakistan had roughly three dozen M–11 missiles.[30] In addition, the document reportedly surmised—based on evidence that Pakistan had been working on such an effort for a number of years—that Pakistan had probably designed a nuclear warhead for the system.[31] In late August 1996 another U.S. intelligence finding was leaked to the press: using blueprints and equipment supplied by China, reportedly Pakistan had in late 1995 begun the construction of a factory to produce short-range missiles based on the Chinese-designed M–11.[32]

None of these China–Pakistan missile-transfer events in 1996 triggered the imposition of U.S. missile-transfer sanctions on China or Pakistan, however. Indeed, throughout this period, modest shipments of U.S. military hardware continued under the Brown amendment.

In the summer of 2001 the United States once again imposed MTCR Category II sanctions on Pakistani and Chinese entities for the sale of sensitive Chinese dual-use technology, assisting Pakistan's missile program.[33] (These sanctions were later rescinded as part of the waiver of sanctions post–September 11.) Chinese assistance has been critical to Pakistan's ballistic missile progress, and the Pentagon estimates that Pakistan will likely require foreign assistance for key technologies for several more years.[34]

NOTES

1. David Albright, "India's and Pakistan's Fissile Material and Nuclear Weapons Inventories, end of 1999," ISIS, Institute for Science and International Security. October 11, 2000. Available at www.isis-online.org.

2. George Perkovich, Carnegie Proliferation Roundtable, "Pakistan's Nuclear Dilemma," September 26, 2001. Available at www.ceip.org/npp.

3. Gregory Jones, "From Testing to Deploying Nuclear Forces: The Hard Choices Facing India and Pakistan," RAND Issue Paper, July 2000.

4. E. J. Hogendoorn, "A Chemical Weapons Atlas," *Bulletin of the Atomic Scientists*, September/October 1997, p. 38.

5. George Perkovich, Carnegie Proliferation Roundtable, "Pakistan's Nuclear Dilemma," September 26, 2001. Available at www.ceip.org/npp.

6. Testimony of John Deutch, director, Central Intelligence Agency, "Current and Projected National Security Threats to the United States and Its Interests Abroad," Select Committee on Intelligence, U.S. Senate (Washington, D.C.: U.S. GPO, February 22, 1996), p. 12.

7. George Perkovich, *India's Nuclear Bomb: The Impact on Global Proliferation* (Berkeley: University of California Press, 1999), p. 413.

8. Ibid., p. 433.

9. Pervez Hoodbhoy, "Nuclear Nirvana," Carnegie Non-Proliferation Project Issue Brief, vol. 3, no. 33, November 16, 2000. Available at www.ceip.org/npp.

10. "The Lahore Declaration," February 21, 1999. Available on the Carnegie Non-Proliferation web site at www.ceip.org/npp.

11. Hoodbhoy, "Nuclear Nirvana."

12. For an overview, see Leonard Spector and Jacqueline R. Smith, *Nuclear Ambitions* (Boulder: Westview Press, 1990), chapters 4 and 7.

13. Jones, "Deploying Nuclear Forces."

14. Ibid.

15. Ibid. See also William J. Broad, "Explosion Is Detected by U.S. Scientists," *New York Times*, May 29, 1998, p. A8; and Michael Hirsh and John Barry, "Nuclear Jitters," *Newsweek*, June 8, 1998, p. 24.

16. U.S. Department of Defense (DOD), *Proliferation Threat and Response*, January 2001.

17. Jason Sherman, "Pakistan Emphasizes Financial over Military Ties," *Defense News*, October 8–14, 2001.

18. Perkovich, at Carnegie Proliferation Roundtable, "Pakistan's Nuclear Dilemma," September 26, 2001.

19. Jon Wolfsthal, "U.S. Needs a Contingency Plan for Pakistan's Nuclear Arsenal," *Los Angeles Times*, October 16, 2001. Also see Seymour Hersh, "Watching the Warheads: Pakistan's Nuclear Weapons at Risk," *New Yorker*, October 26, 2001.

20. Perkovich, at Carnegie Proliferation Roundtable, "Pakistan's Nuclear Dilemma," September 26, 2001.

21. U.S. DOD, *Proliferation Threat and Response*, 2001.

22. Perkovich, *India's Nuclear Bomb*, p. 411.

23. The Prithvi has since been moved to a "strategic" location, to Secunderabad in southern India.

24. "Pakistan Tests Medium-range Missile," *Washington Post*, April 7, 1998.

25. Jones, "Deploying Nuclear Forces."

26. Perkovich, *India's Nuclear Bomb*, p. 410.

27. Mohammed Ahmedullah, "During Kashmir Crises, India, Pakistan Cocked Nuclear Trigger," *Space and Missile Defense Report*, August 3, 2000.

28. U.S. DOD, *Proliferation Threat and Response*, January 2001, p. 30.

29. Ibid.

30. Bill Gertz, "Pakistan Deploys Chinese Missiles," *Washington Times*, June 12, 1996; R. Jeffrey Smith, "Report Cites China-Pakistan Missile Links," *Washington Post*, June 13, 1996.

31. "Pakistan Nuclear Program at a 'Screwdriver Level,'" *Washington Times*, February 20, 1996.

32. R. Jeffrey Smith, "China Linked to Pakistani Missile Plant," *Washington Post*, August 25, 1996; *Time*, vol. 149, no. 26, June 30, 1997.

33. Amir Mateen, "New U.S. Sanctions on China, Pakistan, *The News*, September 2, 2001.

34. U.S. DOD, *Proliferation Threat and Response*, January 2001.

Table 12.1: **Pakistan: Nuclear Infrastructure**

Name/Location of Facility	Type/ Status	IAEA Safeguards
NUCLEAR WEAPON RESEARCH & DEVELOPMENT COMPLEX		
Khan Research Laboratories (KRL) Kahuta	Fabrication of HEU into nuclear weapon	No
Ras Koh	Site of nuclear tests conducted in 1998	No
Kharan Desert	Site of nuclear tests conducted in 1998	No
Pakistan Ordnance Factory, Wah	Possible nuclear weapons assembly site[1]	No
POWER REACTORS		
KANUPP Karachi	Heavy-water, nat. U, 137-MWe; operating	Yes
Chasma-1/ Chasnupp 1	Light-water, LEU, 300-MWe; operating[2]	Yes
Chasma-2/ Chasnupp 2	Light-water, LEU, 310-MWe; planned	Planned
RESEARCH REACTORS		
Pakistan Atomic Research Reactor 1 (PARR 1), Rawalpindi	Light-water, originally HEU, modified to use LEU, 9-MWt; operating (may have been used clandestinely to produce tritium for advanced nuclear weapons)[3]	Yes
PARR 2, Rawalpindi	Pool-type, light-water, HEU, 30-KWt; operating	Yes
Research/Plutonium Production Reactor, Khushab	Heavy-water, nat. U, 40–50-MWt; No operating	
URANIUM ENRICHMENT		
Khan Research Laboratories (KRL), Kahuta	Large-scale ultracentrifuge facility; operating	No
Sihala	Experimental-scale ultracentrifuge facility; operating	No
Golra	Ultracentrifuge plant reportedly to be used as a testing facility; operational status unknown[4]	No
Wah/Gadwal	Enrichment plant[5]	No
REPROCESSING (PLUTONIUM EXTRACTION)		
Chasma	Operating	No

Table 12.1 (continued)

Name/Location of Facility	Type/ Status	IAEA Safeguards
New laboratories, SPINSTECH Rawalpindi	Pilot-scale, "hot cell" facility; design capacity up to 20 kg/year; currently in the process of upgrading[6]	No
PINSTECH Rawalpindi	Experimental-scale laboratory for research on solvent extraction	No
URANIUM PROCESSING		
Baghalchar	Uranium mining; closed	N/A
Dera Ghazi Khan	Uranium mining and milling; operating	N/A
Issa Khel	Uranium ore processing; planned	N/A
Qabul Khel, near Issa Khel	Uranium mining and milling; operating	N/A
Lahore	Milling; operating	N/A
Dera Ghazi Khan	Uranium conversion (UF_6); operating	No
Chasma/Kundian	Fuel fabrication; operating	No
HEAVY-WATER PRODUCTION		
Multan	Operating	No
Karachi	Operating	No

Abbreviations

HEU	highly enriched uranium	MWt	millions of watts of thermal output
LEU	low-enriched uranium	kWt	thousands of watts of thermal output
nat. U	natural uranium	N/A	not applicable
MWe	millions of watts of electrical output		

NOTES

1. See "India Denies Atom-test Plan but then Turns Ambiguous," *New York Times*, December 16, 1996, p. 4.

2. See the International Atomic Energy Agency web site, www.iaea.org/programmes/a2/.

3. See the Federation of American Scientists web site, www.fas.org/nuke/guide/pakistan/facility/rawalpindi.htm.

4. See David Albright, Frans Berkhout, and William Walker, *Plutionium and Highly Enriched Uarnium 1996: World Inventories, Capabilities, and Policies* (Oxford: Oxford University Press, 1997), p. 269ff.

5. A January 4, 1996, article in *The Muslim* reported that during a visit to Islamabad, U.S. official Robert Oakley accused Pakistan of constructing another enrichment facility at Wah with Chinese assistance. Pakistani officials confirmed the existence of the project (see "Pakistan Said Ready To Counter Indian Nuclear Test with Its Own," *Nucleonics Week*, February 29, 1996, p. 14.

6. See the Federation of American Scientists web site, www.fas.org/nuke/guide/pakistan/facility/rawalpindi.htm.

Khan Research Laboratory–Kahuta
Large-scale uranium enrichment plant designed to produce enough weapons-grade uranium for a number of nuclear devices per year; not subject to IAEA inspection.

Possible uranium enrichment R&D facility/pilot plant; not subject to IAEA inspection.

Pakistani Institute of Nuclear Science and Technology (PINSTECH)
Laboratory and pilot-scale plant for plutonium extraction; neither subject to IAEA inspection. PARR-1 (9 MWt) and PARR-2 (30 KWt) research reactors, subject to IAEA safeguards.

Missile production factory

M–11 storage facility

1998 nuclear test sites

40-50 MWt research and plutonium production reactor operational; not under IAEA inspection. In conjunction with the nearby large plutonium extraction plant at Chasma and the pilot-scale plant at Rawalpindi, the reactor could be the source of a significant inventory of unsafeguarded weapons-usable plutonium.

Large plutonium extraction plant; civil works complete; not subject to IAEA inspection. Chinese-supplied 300-MWe nuclear power reactor operational; subject to IAEA inspection. Additional 310-MWe nuclear power reactor planned.

Canadian-supplied KANUPP nuclear power reactor; subject to IAEA inspection.

Italicized names represent nuclear-related sites. See table 12.1

UZBEKISTAN
TURKMENISTAN
TAJIKI-STAN
CHINA
AFGHANISTAN
Kashmir (disputed)
Wah *Golra*
Islamabad *Kahuta*
Tarwanah *Sihala*
Rawalpindi
Isa Khel *Khusab*
Chasma
Sargodha Lahore
Dera Ghazi Khan
Multan
Ras Koh
Kharan Desert
PAKISTAN
IRAN
Karachi
INDIA
Arabian Sea

0   250
Miles

Carnegie Endowment for International Peace, *Deadly Arsenals* (2002), **www.ceip.org**

CHAPTER 13

Israel

Nuclear Weapon Capability

Israel has an advanced nuclear weapon capability and is thought to possess enough nuclear material for between 98 and 172 nuclear weapons.[1] Israel is not a party to the Non-Proliferation Treaty and has not acknowledged that it has nuclear weapons. It is, however, indisputably regarded as a de facto nuclear-weapon state. The exact number of weapons Israel has assembled is unknown but is more likely on the lower end of the possible range. In all, Israel is thought to have produced between 391 and 687 kilograms of weapons-grade plutonium since its nuclear research reactor at Dimona started its operation in early 1964. Plutonium separated from the fuel rods in the reactor allowed Israel to complete the development of its first nuclear device by late 1966 or 1967, becoming the sixth nation in the world to do so.[2] It remains the only nation in the Middle East with nuclear weapons.

Missile and Aircraft Capability

The most capable military power in the region, Israel fields both short-range Jericho I (500 kilometers, with a 500-kilogram payload) and medium-range (1,500 kilometers) Jericho II missiles. Both missiles use solid propellant and are nuclear-capable. Israel's successful satellite launches using the Shavit space launch vehicle directly suggest that Israel could quickly develop missile platforms with much longer ranges then the Jericho II has. Development of the single-stage Jericho I missile began in the early 1960s with French assistance (a contract with the French firm Marcel Dassault for the development of the missile, under the code name MD 620) and was first deployed in 1973. Development of the two-stage Jericho II began in the mid-1970s, with first deployment in 1990. The extended range and 1,000-kilogram payload of the Jericho II makes it a likely nuclear delivery vehicle. Both missiles are land- and rail-mobile. In all, Israel is believed to have deployed 100 Jericho missiles. Israel could also deliver nuclear weapons using its F–4E Phantoms and F–16 Falcons and may also possess artillery-launched nuclear munitions. Israel also has a sizable inventory of cruise missiles that includes the U.S.-origin Harpoon, which can be launched from an aircraft, ship, or submarine. The Harpoons can travel up to 120 kilometers with a payload of 220 kilograms. In May 2000 Israel reportedly carried out a test of a new sea-launched nuclear-capable cruise missile off Sri Lanka. The missiles are said to have hit targets at a range of 1,500 kilometers.[3] It may be a variant on the Israeli Popeye Turbo air-launched cruise missile under development for possible deployment in 2002.[4]

A New Development: Sea-Launched Capability

Probably the most important nuclear-related development in Israel is the formation of its sea-based nuclear arm. By July 2000 Israel completed taking delivery of all three of the Dolphin-class submarines it had ordered at the Thyssen-Nordseewerke shipyard in Kiel, Germany. In doing so, it is widely believed, Israel moved significantly toward acquiring a survivable second-strike nuclear capability. All indications are that Israel is on the way to finalizing a restructuring of its nuclear forces into a triad, like the United States.[5]

Since the early 1980s (and probably even earlier) the Israeli navy (jointly with other governmental agencies) lobbied hard for the notion that Israel should build a small fleet of modern diesel submarines for "strategic purposes," an Israeli euphemism for a sea-launched nuclear capability. Because no American shipyard had the appropriate expertise in building modern diesel, electrical-powered, large submarines, Israel sought a German shipyard as a contractor for the project. After a complex series of negotiations, when a deal was almost signed in early 1990, it was vetoed by Gen. Ehud Barak, then Israel's chief of staff, because of cost. In 1991, in the wake of Iraqi Scud attacks against Israel during the Gulf War, the German government offered to finance the purchase of two submarines fully and to share in the financing of the third to compensate for the role that the German industry played in the development of Iraq's nonconventional weaponry. Israel immediately accepted the German offer for the first two submarines. Shortly after (apparently in a response to alarming reports on Iranian nuclear and missiles projects), it decided to purchase the third one as well. The cost of each submarine is estimated to be about $300 million dollars.

The details of the specific capabilities of the submarines, named *Dolphin*, *Leviathan*, and *Tekumah*, remain highly classified. German leaks indicate that the three 1,900-metric-ton submarines are equipped with ten 21-inch multipurpose tubes, capable of launching torpedoes, mines, and cruise missiles. While under construction in Kiel, Germany, Israel maintained tight security measures and technological oversight on the project. Many of the navigating, communication, and weapon systems in those submarines were reportedly developed, built, and assembled by the Israeli defense industries. It is also believed (but not confirmed) that the most sensitive aspect of the project, the cruise-missile technology that renders the diesel submarines nuclear-capable launching platforms, was developed and built in Israel; the submarines would have to have been assembled only after their arrival in Israel. Speaking at the ceremony for the arrival of the third submarine at its Haifa base in July 2000, the commander of the Israeli navy, Rear Adm. Yedidya Yaari, referred to the new submarine as the finest conventional submarine of its class in the world.[6] It is reported that the Israeli-made cruise missiles have the capability of hitting targets in a range of more than 900 miles.[7]

According to one report in the London *Sunday Times*, by early 2000 Israel had carried out the first launching tests of its cruise missiles, less than two years after the first submarine, *Dolphin*, was delivered to Israel. According to that report, "Elite crews have assembled to man [the submarines]. . . . Five specially selected officers solely responsible for the warheads will be added to each vessel once the missiles are operational."[8]

A strong indication that the acquisition of a sea-launched nuclear capability may be at the center of Israel's nuclear agenda are the recent key appointments in the Israeli nuclear and defense bureaucracy. In 2000 a former deputy commander of the Israeli navy, Brig. Gen. (reserve) Shaul Horev, was recruited to serve as the deputy director general of the Israel Atomic Energy Commission. Horev had previously served as a deputy director of Israel's Defense Ministry "special measures" directorate, reportedly the top-secret organization in charge of nonconventional weaponry. In early 2001, however, having served in the post of deputy director general for five months, Horev was brought back to the Defense Ministry to head the special measures directorate. The changes may also indicate the organizational friction involved.[9]

A fleet of three submarines is believed to be the minimum that Israel needs to have a deployment at sea of one nuclear-armed submarine at all times. Such a survivable deterrent is perceived as essential because of Israel's unique geopolitical and demographical vulnerability to nuclear attack, and one that no potential nuclear enemy of Israel could ignore.

Biological and Chemical Weapon Capability

Israel possesses advanced chemical and biological weapon capabilities, although it is not known what type or how many offensive agents it currently has. Israel is believed to have had sophisticated chemical and biological weapon programs for several decades, centered at the Israel Institute for Biological Research (IIBR) at Ness Ziona, 10 kilometers south of Tel Aviv. There, Israel has reportedly conducted advanced research on both chemical and biological warfare.

Lacking authoritative information, non-Israeli publications have made many claims about Israel's CBW capabilities, from the trivial to the most sensationalist.[10] The government of Israel, as part of its traditional and deliberate policy of ambiguity, has neither confirmed nor denied those reports. Acknowledging the difficulty of assessing Israel's CBW programs and capabilities, Avner Cohen recently characterized them thus: "A near-consensus exists among experts—based on anecdotal evidence and intelligence leaks—that Israel developed, produced, stockpiled, and maybe even deployed chemical weapons at some point in its history."[11] As to biological weapons, however, Cohen appears to be more cautious and tentative: "It would be logical—given the experience with Iraq—that Israel has acquired expertise in most aspects of weaponization, with the possible exception of testing. Although it is probable that Israel has maintained some sort of production capability, it is highly doubtful that Israel engages in the ongoing production or stockpiling of BW agents."[12]

A 1990 DIA study reported that Israel had an operational chemical warfare testing facility. In an oblique reference to Israel, the authoritative *Middle East Military Balance*, which is produced by the Jaffee Center for Strategic Studies in Tel Aviv, notes, "The chemical and biological capabilities of Syria, Iraq, and Iran are matched, according to foreign sources, by Israel's possession of a wide range of such weapons."[13] Israel has signed but not yet ratified the Chemical Weapons Convention and is not a party to the Biological Weapons Convention.

Nuclear Analysis

Unclassified estimates of Israel's nuclear capabilities are based in large part on former Israeli nuclear technician Mordechai Vanunu's revelations in October 1986.[14] Based on Vanunu's information about Israeli plutonium production, the London *Sunday Times* projected that Israel might have as many as 200 nuclear devices.[15] However, most experts who have attempted to harmonize Vanunu's testimony with other relevant information concluded that, given the small size of Israel's only plutonium-producing reactor, located at the Dimona research complex, Israel's nuclear inventory probably contained far fewer weapons. David Albright, Frans Berkhout, and William Walker calculated that, depending on the power level of the Dimona reactor, Israel could have produced 370–650 kilograms of weapons-grade plutonium by the end of 1999.[16] The reactor can produce between 10.6 and 18.6 kilograms of plutonium a year, thus increasing the plutonium supply by the end of 2001 to 391–687 kilograms. Assuming 4 kilograms of plutonium for each warhead, Israel could have enough material for 98–172 weapons at the beginning of 2002, with enough new material for an additional 2–4 new weapons a year. Assuming a more conservative 5 kilograms for each warhead would mean that Israel has enough material for 78–137 weapons.

Vanunu also indicated that Israel had produced tritium and lithium deuteride, suggesting that Israel may have developed "boosted" nuclear weapons, i.e., weapons that use a nuclear-fusion reaction to increase their efficiency. Since Israel is not known to have conducted any nuclear tests (with the possible exception of the 1979 "flash" off South Africa), it is assumed that it has not advanced to the point of producing thermonuclear weapons (hydrogen bombs). Israel is likely to rely on simple, proven designs that would require larger amounts of plutonium than the sophisticated U.S. or Russian designs.

Some experts, however, make different assumptions. A 1991 book by American investigative journalist Seymour Hersh argued that Israel's arsenal was considerably larger and more advanced than even Vanunu's information suggested. Relying largely on interviews with U.S. intelligence analysts and Israelis knowledgeable about the country's nuclear program, Hersh concluded that Israel possessed "hundreds" of low-yield, enhanced-radiation, "neutron"-type warheads, many in the form of artillery shells and land mines, as well as full-fledged thermonuclear weapons.[17]

A 1994 report alleged plausible new details about Israel's nuclear weapon infrastructure, identifying Nahal Soreq as the installation where Israel conducts research on nuclear weapon design. It claimed that Israel's nuclear weapons are assembled at a facility in Yodefat, that Israel's nuclear missile base and bunker for storing nuclear gravity bombs is near Moshav Zekharya, a few kilometers from the town of Beit Shemesh, and that tactical nuclear weapons are stored at Eilabun.[18]

History

Israel's interest in establishing a national nuclear infrastructure, aimed at both security and energy, is as old as the state itself.[19] By 1955, in the wake of David Ben Gurion's return to power in Israel, Shimon Peres (then the director general of the Ministry of Defense) started to explore in earnest the feasibility of a nuclear weapon project. In 1956–1957, out of the forming of the French–Israeli military alliance that reached its climax during the Suez crisis, the Israeli nuclear weapon program was born.[20] At the time, France's socialist government, led by Guy Mollet, was deeply committed to Israel's survival. The two states confronted dangers stemming from Arab nationalism, Israel because of its isolated position in the Middle East and France because of growing unrest in French Algeria. France secretly pledged to assist Israel in developing nuclear arms and agreed to supply a sizable plutonium-producing reactor to be built at Dimona, in the Negev, 40 miles from Beersheba.[21]

In mid-1957, with French Atomic Energy Commission approval, Israel signed an agreement with the French firm of St. Gobain Techniques Nouvelles for the construction of several additional facilities at the Dimona site, including the key installation (where Vanunu would subsequently work) for extracting plutonium from the Dimona reactor's spent fuel. Soon thereafter, France also gave Israel important information on the design and manufacture of nuclear weapons themselves. Francis Perrin, the scientific head of the French Atomic Energy Commission from 1951 to 1970, was intimately involved with the French–Israeli nuclear program. In an on-the-record 1986 interview with the London *Sunday Times*, Perrin acknowledged that France had supplied the Dimona reactor and the plutonium extraction plant and that, for at least two years during the late 1950s, France and Israel had collaborated on the design and development of nuclear weapons.[22]

Recent research by Avner Cohen has revealed that the June 1967 war had an important nuclear dimension. He concludes that by late 1966 Israel had successfully completed the research and development stage of its program. During the tense days of the crisis in late May 1967, just days before the Six-Day War, Israel improvised the assembly of two deliverable nuclear devices and placed them on "operational alert."[23]

No conclusive proof exists that Israel has ever conducted a full-scale nuclear test. Its nuclear arsenal is thought to have been developed in part through the testing of non-nuclear components and computer simulations, and through the acquisition of weapon design and test information from abroad. Israel is thought, for example, to have obtained data from France's first nuclear test, which took place in 1960.[24] It may also have obtained data from U.S. nuclear tests at approximately that time. According to a May 1989 U.S. television documentary, Israel was able to gain access to information concerning U.S. tests from the 1950s and early 1960s. The test data could have included the results of tests of U.S. boosted and thermonuclear weapons that were being developed at the time.[25]

There has been speculation, however, that a signal detected on September 22, 1979, by a U.S. VELA monitoring satellite orbiting over the South Atlantic was in fact the flash from a low-yield nuclear explosive test, possibly from a tactical nuclear weapon or from the fission trigger of a thermonuclear device. Although the official U.S. government scientific review concluded that the most likely explanation was that it was a non-nuclear event, the readings have been attributed by some to a nuclear test conducted by South Africa, and by others to Israel.

Seymour Hersh reports that "according to Israeli officials whose information about other aspects of Dimona's activities has been corroborated," the September 1979 event was indeed an Israeli nuclear weapon test and was the third of a series of tests conducted at that time.[26] The first two tests, Hersh's sources stated, were obscured by storm clouds. The claim that clouds would prevent the detection of an atmospheric nuclear detonation by a VELA satellite has been challenged, however, since the satellite is said to rely in part on infrared sensors that can penetrate cloud cover. Thus, this critical matter remains unresolved.

Motivation and Policy

Israel's pursuit of the nuclear deterrent option as the basis of national survival has been founded primarily on two factors: Israel's lack of territorial strategic depth, which makes it difficult to absorb a conventional attack and respond effectively; and the "preponderance of men and equipment" enjoyed by its Arab neighbors, almost all of whom have been hostile adversaries throughout its history. At the same time, Israel has sought to maintain a margin of qualitative conventional military superiority that would both discourage its foes from resorting to force and ensure victory without the use of nuclear arms in the event of conflict.[27]

Out of this predicament Israel's policy of nuclear ambiguity or nuclear opacity originated. It was first enunciated in a 1963 meeting of Shimon Peres, as Israel's deputy minister of defense, and President John F. Kennedy. Questioned about Israel's nuclear capabilities and intentions, Peres responded that "Israel would not be the first country to introduce nuclear weapons in the [Middle East]."[28]

Beginning in the early 1960s there was continuous friction between the United States and Israel over the question of Israel's nuclear development, culminating in Israel's refusal to join the NPT in 1968.[29] In September 1969, during an official state visit to the United States, Israeli Prime Minister Golda Meir and President Richard Nixon for the first time reached a secret understanding on this sensitive issue that brought an end to the friction. Meir explained to Nixon why Israel had developed nuclear weapons—and hence could not sign the NPT—and why a policy of nuclear opacity (using the old formulation that "Israel will not be the first nation to introduce nuclear weapons to the Middle East") would best serve the interests of both countries. Israel also pledged not to test nuclear weapons or publicly admit to possessing them. Nixon accepted the Israeli position, recognizing that the Israeli bomb was a fait accompli, and ended American pressure on Israel to sign the NPT.[30]

The agreement put an end to a decade of unsuccessful (and at times half-hearted) U.S. efforts to halt the Israeli nuclear program. Since then all Israeli governments have adhered to the agreement. Likewise, while publicly calling on all states to sign the NPT, all subsequent U.S. administrations have not pressured Israel to give up its nuclear weapons. Israeli nuclear opacity was born and cultivated as a symbiotic U.S.–Israeli policy. Over the years, nuclear opacity has become Israel's most distinct contribution to the nuclear age.[31]

A refinement in Israel's defense posture was the Begin doctrine, which became official policy after Israel's air attack on June 7, 1981, on Iraq's pluto-nium-producing Osiraq research reactor. Israeli Prime Minister Menachem Begin then declared that Israel would block any attempt by adversaries to acquire nuclear weapons.[32]

During the 1980s the strategic balance in the Middle East underwent significant changes. Some Arab states undertook or accelerated programs to develop or acquire weapons of mass destruction as well as delivery systems. By the end of the decade, Saddam Hussein was boasting about Iraq's extensive ballistic missile forces and chemical weapon capabilities by declaring (in April 1990) that, if Israel attacked any Iraqi nuclear installations, he would destroy "half of Israel" with chemical weapons. (Iraq had already used chemical weapons in the Iran–Iraq war.)[33] At the same time, Iran, Libya, and Syria were expanding their chemical weapon capabilities, and some of Israel's adversaries were also pursuing the development of biological weapons.

While suspicion of Iraq's nuclear weapon program existed before the 1991 Gulf War, the scale and range of its efforts were not known. It was subsequently revealed that Iraq had embarked not only on a multi-faceted nuclear weapon development program, but also, after its invasion of Kuwait, on a crash program to develop a single nuclear device by April 1991. The emerging WMD threat was demonstrated during the 1991 Gulf War when Israeli cities and sites in Saudi Arabia were attacked by Iraqi extended-range Scud missiles. Although the attacking Scud missiles carried conventional warheads, it was later disclosed that Iraq had stockpiled chemical and biological warheads for such missiles. It is believed that some of the hidden Scud missiles were so armed. Iraq launched a total of 39 Scud missiles against Israel, causing two deaths and hundreds of injuries.[34]

The 1991 Gulf War also demonstrated the difficulties of identifying and striking facilities involved in clandestine proliferation programs. In spite of a massive air campaign, much of Iraq's nuclear weapon infrastructure remained intact. Several nuclear installations had not been identified by the United States or its partners. In some cases, attacked nuclear-related facilities suffered only slight damage, allowing the Iraqis to remove and hide equipment. It was left to the IAEA to discover, in a painstaking effort, the magnitude of the Iraqi nuclear program. The case of Iraq raises important questions over the practicality of the Begin doctrine in the future if potential nuclear infrastructure targets are too distant, hidden too well, and too numerous to be destroyed by air attacks.[35]

Strategic Analysis: A Perspective on Arms Control

The "tacit collaboration between Israel and the Arab members of the anti-Iraq coalition" before and during the Gulf War provided an impetus for the initiation of a peace process in the region, raising the prospect of a transition to arms control.[36] The Middle East Peace Conference, which opened in Madrid on October 30, 1991, under the sponsorship of the United States and the Soviet Union, began sets of bilateral talks between Israel and its neighbors aimed at a comprehensive peace in the region. An additional multi-lateral component of this process was the establishment of five working groups to address regional issues of common interest, one being the Arms Control and Regional Security (ACRS) working group. However, major Israeli antagonists in the region, such as Iran and Syria, did not participate in the talks. The talks were suspended in early 1995 with very limited, if any, concrete accomplishments.

In the context of the April 1995 NPT Review and Extension Conference, the Arab states, led by Egypt, attempted but failed to pressure Israel into renouncing its nuclear option. At the fourth Preparatory Committee (PrepCom) session of the Review and Extension Conference in January 1995, Egypt, as well as Algeria, Libya, and Syria, issued statements indicating that they would consent to an indefinite extension of the NPT only after Israel had agreed to accede to the treaty.[37] Israel's response was embodied in Foreign Minister Shimon Peres' exchange with Egyptian Foreign Minister Amr Mussa: Peres explained that Israel would agree to a nuclear-weapon-free zone (NWFZ) in the Middle East two years after the conclusion of a comprehensive peace accord between all states in the region, including Iran.

From Israel's point of view, security conditions deteriorated rapidly both internally and regionally from 1995 to the end of 2001. During that period, as ballistic missile threats increased, Israel accelerated its development of active ballistic missile defenses. Deploying missile defenses will require an adaptation of Israel's traditional doctrine of "offensive defense." Israel's postulated threat was amplified by Syrian tests of advanced 600-kilometer Scud–C missiles, a system capable of striking Israeli sites from deep within Syria, and possibly with chemical and biological weapons. Iran also posed an increasingly serious threat. In addition to its stockpile of chemical weapons, substantial biological warfare program, and efforts to acquire nuclear weapons, information surfaced that Iran was developing Shahab missiles, with ranges of up to 2,000 kilometers, that would enable Iran to target Israel for the first time (see chapters 5 and 15). Moreover, Israel believed that it continued to face missile threats from Libya, Egypt, Saudi Arabia, and possibly Iraq.

At the same time, the collapse of the peace process established by the 1993 Oslo accords not only undermined efforts to resume the regional arms control talks but also created a deeply pessimistic mood among the Israeli public about peace with anyone. Efforts by Israeli Prime Minister Ehud Barak and Palestinian Authority Chairman Yasser Arafat to negotiate an accord showed promise throughout 1999 but stalled at the end of 2000. A provocative visit by Likud party leader Ariel Sharon to the Temple Mount in September 2000 ignited a new intifada. Since then, hundreds of Palestinians and Israelis have been killed, with only faint prospects in sight for a peaceful resolution to the conflict.

Israel signed the Comprehensive Nuclear Test Ban Treaty on September 25, 1996, the only one of the three non-NPT nuclear-weapon states to do so. From the Israeli perspective, its adherence to the CTBT and its earlier signing of the Chemical Weapons Convention demonstrated Israel's interest in arms control regimes with reliable verification systems that are not subject to abuse or frivolous requests. According to this view, Israel's arms control credentials and policies were also reflected in the active role it played in the negotiations of the CTBT as a primary participant in the drafting of the accord; in its co-sponsorship of the United Nations resolution that opened the CTBT for signature; and in the fact that it was one of its first signatories.[38]

In the early 1990s, both the Bush administration in 1991 and subsequently the Clinton administration in 1993 made proposals to ban the further production of fissile materials for weapons both in the Middle East and globally. The impetus for the 1991 Bush regional proposal was the perception that the "fissban" idea, in addition to the effort to disarm Iraq, could be an important milestone toward an eventual nuclear free zone in the Middle East. In the wake of the Gulf War, it was evident that Israel had to be a part of any effort to reduce the nuclear threat in the Middle East. In this context, advocates of a fissban argued that it offered a realistic compromise: a limited but real constraint on the Israeli nuclear program, coupled with an implicit legitimization of Israel's nuclear status. In 1993 the Clinton administration modified the Bush proposal, calling for a global fissile material cut-off treaty that would ban the further production of plutonium and highly enriched uranium for nuclear weapons as well as the production of such materials outside IAEA safeguards. The cut-off proposal would permit the five nuclear-weapon states and the three de facto nuclear powers (India, Israel, and Pakistan) to retain their existing stocks of unsafeguarded fissile material.[39]

In the early 1990s the Israel government refrained from making an official and public response to the Bush and Clinton initiatives to limit the production of weapons-grade fissile material. Unofficially, however, Israeli officials expressed reservation about the proposals but were careful not to reject them outright. The main concern was that the constraints imposed by the fissban, together with the associated verification modalities, would put Israel on a slippery slope leading to the demise of nuclear opacity and to increased pressure to abandon its nuclear arsenal entirely.[40]

By the mid-late 1990s, following the collapse of ACRS, Israeli opposition to the fissban proposal grew firmer. In 1998 Prime Minister Netanyahu told (and wrote to) President Clinton in unequivocal language that Israel cannot accept the fissban proposal. According to Aluf Benn, *Ha'aretz*'s diplomatic correspondent, in two letters and several conversations Netanyahu told Clinton: "We will never sign the treaty, and do not delude yourselves, no pressure will help. We will not sign the treaty because we will not commit suicide."[41]

Despite India's and Pakistan's declarations of nuclear weapons in 1998, it is unlikely that Israel will follow suit or change its policy of nuclear ambiguity. It appears that only a dramatic change in the nuclear status of Iran or Iraq could trigger a change in the Israeli position. Israeli decision makers will also continue to hold the view, however, that for as long as adversaries in the Middle East region maintain the capability to mount large-scale military attacks against Israel or to threaten Israeli cities with missiles carrying chemical or biological warheads, Israel will need to maintain the nuclear deterrence option. In some respects, one Israeli observer argues, Israel's nuclear posture may have been better understood internationally as a result of its controversy with Egypt before and during the course of the 1995 Review and Extension Conference. In his view, the conflict forced Rabin, Peres, and other Israeli leaders to articulate for the first time "links between the maintenance of the nuclear capability and the continued threats to national survival, linked to the military, geographic and demographic asymmetries in the region."[42]

From the Israeli perspective, a substantive discussion of regional arms control issues is inextricably linked to the achievement of a comprehensive Middle East peace settlement. Such a settlement, however, is unlikely any time soon.

Missile Analysis

Israel currently deploys two nuclear-capable ballistic missile systems: the Jericho I and Jericho II. Up to 50 Jericho I solid-fuel, two-stage missiles with an approximate range of 660 kilometers are thought to be deployed in shelters on mobile launchers, possibly at a facility located midway between Jerusalem and the Mediterranean. The Jericho II solid-fuel, two-stage missile can travel an estimated 1,500 kilometers. Commercial satellite photos indicate that the missile base between Jerusalem and the Mediterranean was enlarged between 1989 and 1993 to allow for Jericho II deployment. Furthermore, a Lawrence Livermore Laboratory study indicates that Israel's Shavit space launch vehicle could be modified to carry 500 kilograms over 7,800 kilometers, in effect giving it the capability of an intercontinental ballistic missile.[43]

Israel now deploys the Arrow II anti-ballistic missile system in a missile battery about 30 miles south of Tel Aviv. The $1.6 billion Arrow system will attempt to intercept short-range Scud-type missiles just as they start reentering the atmosphere after reaching the highest point of their flight trajectory. The program is a joint U.S.–Israeli undertaking begun in 1988 and now sponsored by the U.S. Ballistic Missile Defense Organization. Israel would like to have a fully operational system by 2005, deploying another battery in northern Israel and one more in the south. The system would link operations with Patriot air-defense units.

Israel is also experimenting with another missile interceptor, the Moab, funded in part by the U.S. Ballistic Missile Defense Organization. This system will try to intercept Scud-like missiles soon after launch with an air-to-air missile fired from an unmanned aerial vehicle flying at high altitude. Israel is also developing jointly with the United States the Nautilus, a fixed-site high-energy laser capable of shooting down short-range artillery rockets. This system is intended for deployment, in the near term, in Israel's northern regions to help protect against Hezbollah-directed Katyusha rocket attacks on Israel from southern Lebanon. The follow-on mobile version would be the tactical high-energy laser (THEL) system.

Israel's unmanned aerial vehicle program has been extended to cover cruise missile development, including land-attack cruise missiles (LACM). Reportedly, Israel has three platforms: the Popeye 1, with a range of 100 kilometers and carrying a payload of 360 kilograms; the Delilah, with a 400-kilometer range and a 450-kilogram payload; and the Popeye 3, with a 350-kilometer range and a 360-kilogram payload. The Delilah is said to have been developed with Chinese cooperation, and Israel's armament industries are believed to have extensive ties, including projected cruise missile cooperation with China, India, South Korea, and Turkey.

NOTES

1. Extrapolated from David Albright, Frans Berkhout, and William Walker, *Plutonium and Highly Enriched Uranium 1996: World Inventories, Capabilities, and Policies* (Oxford: Oxford University Press for Stockholm International Peace Research Institute, 1997), p. 263.

2. Avner Cohen, *Israel and the Bomb* (New York: Columbia University Press, 1998), pp. 239 and 273–276.

3. Uzi Mahnaimi and Matthew Campbell, "Israel Makes Nuclear Waves with Submarine Missile Test," *Sunday Times* (London), June 18, 2000.

4. Federation of American Scientists web site, *Israel Special Weapons Guide*, www.fas.org/nuke/guide/israel/missile/popeye-t.htm.

5. See Reuven Pedatzure, "Completing the Deterrence Triangle," Carnegie Proliferation Brief, vol. 3, no.18, June 29, 2000. Available at www.ceip.org/npp.

6. *Ha'aretz*, July 26, 2000.

7. Mahnaimi and Campbell, "Israel Makes Nuclear Waves."

8. Ibid.

9. Aluf Benn, "An Open and Shut Case: Should Israel's Nuclear Policy Continue To Be Kept under Wraps?" *Ha'aretz*, September 26, 2001 (English Internet edition).

10. Many of these sensationalist stories appeared in the *Sunday Times* (London). One of these stories cites a biologist who once held a senior post in the Israeli intelligence as saying that "there is hardly a single known or unknown form of chemical or biological weapon, which is not manufactured at the Institute." Uzi Mahnaimi, "Israeli Jets Equipped for Chemical Warfare," *Sunday Times* (London), October 4, 1998. See also, "Israel's Secret Institute," *Foreign Report*, August 20, 1998; "Israel's Nes[s] Ziona Mystery," *Foreign Report*, February 5, 1998.

11. Avner Cohen, "Israel and CBW: History, Deterrence, and Arms Control," *Nonproliferation Review*, fall 2001, pp.1–20.

12. Ibid.

13. Shai Feldman and Yiftah Shapir, eds., *The Middle East Military Balance 2000–2001*, Jaffee Center for Strategic Studies, Tel Aviv University (Cambridge: MIT Press, 2001), p. 67.

14. "Revealed: The Secrets of Israel's Nuclear Arsenal," *Sunday Times* (London), October 5, 1986.

15. In light of what is known about Israel's nuclear infrastructure, it has long been assumed that its weapons use plutonium rather than highly enriched uranium for their cores.

16. This extrapolation is based on the assumption that the Dimona reactor has been operating reliably at a power level of between 40 and 70 MWt and has not experienced any significant shutdowns nor extended operation at its theoretical upper limit of 150 MWt. See Albright, Berkhout, and Walker, *Plutonium and Highly Enriched Uranium 1996*, pp. 259 and 262; the authors assume in their calculations that Israel uses 5 kg of plutonium for each warhead. The authors of this volume assume that Israel uses 4 kg for each warhead.

17. Seymour Hersh, *The Samson Option* (New York: Random House, 1991), pp. 291, 312, and 319.

18. Harold Hough, "Israel's Nuclear Infrastructure," *Jane's Intelligence Review*, November 1994, p. 508.

19. Cohen, *Israel and the Bomb*, pp. 9–31.

20. Ibid., pp. 41–55.

21. Cohen, *Israel and the Bomb*, chapter 4, pp. 57–68; Leonard Spector, *The Undeclared Bomb* (Cambridge: Ballinger, 1988), pp. 165–187; Pierre Pean, *Les Deux Bombes* (Paris: Fayard, 1981), chapters 5, 7, and 8.

22. "France Admits It Gave Israel A-Bomb," *Sunday Times* (London), October 12, 1986.

23. Cohen, *Israel and the Bomb*, pp. 273–276.

24. Steven Weissman and Herbert Krosney, *The Islamic Bomb* (New York: Times Books, 1981), p. 114.

25. "Israel: The Covert Connection," *Frontline*, PBS Network, May 16, 1989.

26. Hersh, *The Samson Option*, p. 271.

27. Cohen, *Israel and the Bomb* (esp. chapters 1, 12, and 17); Gerald Steinberg, "The Future of Nuclear Weapons: Israeli Perspectives," paper presented at the Ninth Amaldi Conference on Security Questions at the End of the Twentieth Century, Geneva, Switzerland, November 21–23, 1996; revised November 25, 1996.

28. Cohen, *Israel and the Bomb*, pp. 118–119; Barbara Opall, "Peres: Keep Nuclear Details Secret," *Defense News*, July 29–August 4, 1996, p. 3.

29. Cohen, *Israel and the Bomb* (chaps. 5–7, 9–11, and 16–17).

30. Ibid., pp. 336–338; Aluf Benn, "Open Secrets: The Struggle To Keep Nuclear Capabilities Secret," *Ha'aretz*, September 14, 1999 (English Internet edition).

31. Ibid., pp. 341–344; Benn, "Open Secrets."

32. Leonard Spector, with Jacquelin Smith, *Nuclear Ambitions* (San Francisco: Westview Press, 1990), pp. 167 and 188.

33. "Iraq Threatens To Use Chemical Weapons against Israeli Attack," *Financial Times*, April 3, 1990.

34. James Bruce, "Israel's Space and Missile Projects," *Jane's Intelligence Review*, vol. 7, no. 8, 1995, p. 352; and "BRF Israel Missiles," *Associated Press*, January 3, 1997.

35. Avner Cohen, "The Lessons of Osiraq and the American Counterproliferation Debate," in *International Perspectives on Counterproliferation*, ed. Mitchell Reiss and Harald Muller (Washington, D.C.: Woodrow Wilson Center, 1994), Working Paper 99.

36. Efraim Karsh, Efraim Inbar, and Shmuel Sandler, "Arms Control and the New Middle Eastern Environment," *Defense Analysis*, vol. 12, no. 1, 1996, in "Lessons for Arms Control in a Changing Middle East," *Security and Policy Studies*, no. 26 (Ramat Gan, Israel: BESA Center for Strategic Studies, Bar-Ilan University, June 1996), p. 40.

37. Mark Hibbs, "Last NPT PrepCom Moves toward Limited Extension," *Nucleonics Week*, February 2, 1995, p. 6.

38. Gerald Steinberg, "Deterrence and Middle East Stability: An Israeli Perspective," *Security Dialogue*, spring 1997; Steinberg, "The Future of Nuclear Weapons: Israeli Perspectives."

39. Avner Cohen and Marvin Miller, "How To Think About—and Implement—Nuclear Arms Control in the Middle East," *Washington Quarterly* (spring 1993), pp. 101–113; Shai Feldman, *Nuclear Weapons and Arms Control in the Middle East* (Cambridge: MIT Press, 1997); Avner Cohen, "Nuclear Arms Control in the Middle East: Problems and Prospects," paper read in a U.S. Institute of Peace seminar, April 8, 1998; Avner Cohen and Marvin Miller, "The U.S. and the De Facto Nuclear Weapons States: A Post–September 11 Perspective," paper prepared for the Stanley Foundation's Strategy for Peace Conference at Airlie Conference Center, Warrenton, Virginia, October 25–27, 2001, see stanleyfoundation.org/spc/mid_east/.

40. Aluf Benn, "Senior Governmental Officials: Israel Could Live with Clinton's Arms Control Initiative," *Ha'aretz*, October 5, 1993; Cohen and Miller, "De Facto Nuclear Weapons States."

41. Aluf Benn, "Open Secrets," *Ha'aretz*, March 14, 2000; Aluf Benn, "Israel Resists Pressure on Its Nuclear Policy," *Ha'aretz*, May 2, 2000; Aluf Benn, "Sharon Will Stick to Tradition of Nuclear Ambiguity," *Ha'aretz*, February 18, 2001; Cohen and Miller, "De Facto Nuclear Weapons States."

42. Gerald Steinberg, "Middle East Peace and the NPT Extension Decision," *Nonproliferation Review*, vol. 4, no. 1, fall 1996.

43. David Fulghum and Jeffery Lenorovitz, "Israeli Missile Base Hidden in Hill," *Aviation Week and Space Technology*, November 8, 1993, p. 29; Steven Gray, "Israeli Missile Capabilities: A Few Numbers To Think About," Lawrence Livermore National Laboratories, Z Division, October 7, 1988.

Table 13.1: **Israel: Nuclear Infrastructure**

Name/Location of Facility	Type/ Status	IAEA Safeguards
NUCLEAR WEAPONS COMPLEX		
Negev Nuclear Research Center, Dimona	Plutonium production research reactor and plutonium extraction facilities (see below) and other weapon-related infrastructure	No
Moshav Soreq	Nuclear weapon research and design facility	No
Yodefat	Nuclear weapon assembly facility	No
Moshav Zekharya	Nuclear missile base and gravity bomb storage facility	No
Eilabun	Tactical nuclear weapon storage facility	No
RESEARCH REACTORS		
IRR 1, Nahal Soreq	Light-water, pool, HEU, 5-MWt; operating	Yes
IRR 2, Dimona	Heavy-water, nat. U, 40–150-MWt; operating*	No
URANIUM ENRICHMENT		
Dimona	Experimental/pilot-scale (?) laser and centrifuge-enrichment programs; operating	No
REPROCESSING (PLUTONIUM EXTRACTION)		
Dimona	Operating	No
Nahal Soreq	Pilot-scale; operating	No
URANIUM PROCESSING		
Negev area, near Beersheeba	Uranium phosphate mining; operating	N/A
Haifa	Yellowcake produced in two phosphate plants; operating	N/A
Southern Israel	Yellowcake produced in phosphate plant; operating	N/A
Dimona	Uranium purification (UO$_2$), uranium conversion (UF$_6$), and fuel-fabrication facility; all operating	No
HEAVY–WATER PROCESSING		
Rehovot	Pilot-scale plant; operating	No
TRITIUM, LITHIUM DEUTERIDE		
Dimona	Lithium–6 production, allowing the production of both tritium and lithium deuteride; decommissioned	No

Abbreviations

HEU	highly enriched uranium	MWt	millions of watts of thermal output
LEU	low-enriched uranium	kWt	thousands of watts of thermal output
nat. U	natural uranium	N/A	not applicable
MWe	millions of watts of electrical output		

NOTE

* Estimates of the reactor's capacity varies widely. For a good discussion of the reactor power mystery, see David Albright, Frans Berkhout, and William Walker, *Plutonium and Highly Enriched Uranium 1996: World Inventories, Capabilities, and Policies* (Oxford: Oxford University Press, 1997), pp. 257–264.

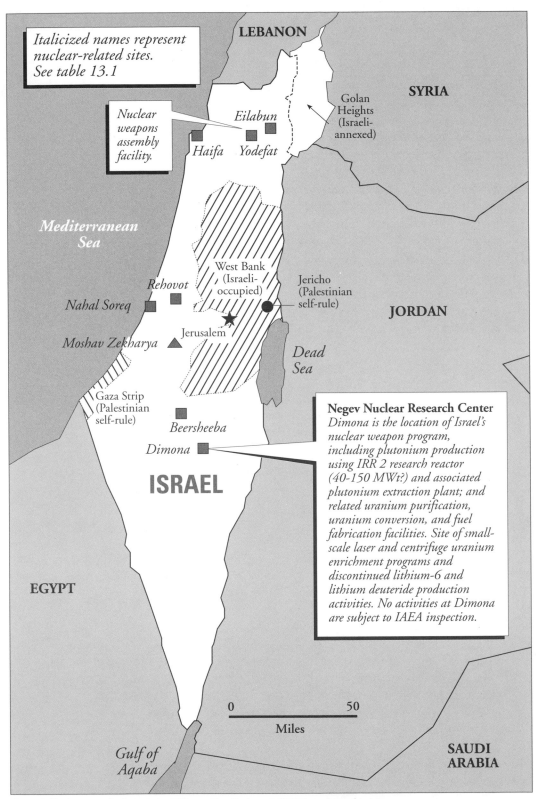

Italicized names represent nuclear-related sites. See table 13.1

LEBANON

SYRIA

Nuclear weapons assembly facility.

Eilabun

Golan Heights (Israeli-annexed)

Haifa *Yodefat*

Mediterranean Sea

West Bank (Israeli-occupied)

Jericho (Palestinian self-rule)

JORDAN

Rehovot

Nahal Soreq

Jerusalem

Moshav Zekharya

Dead Sea

Gaza Strip (Palestinian self-rule)

Negev Nuclear Research Center
Dimona is the location of Israel's nuclear weapon program, including plutonium production using IRR 2 research reactor (40-150 MWt?) and associated plutonium extraction plant; and related uranium purification, uranium conversion, and fuel fabrication facilities. Site of small-scale laser and centrifuge uranium enrichment programs and discontinued lithium-6 and lithium deuteride production activities. No activities at Dimona are subject to IAEA inspection.

Beersheeba

Dimona

ISRAEL

EGYPT

0   50

Miles

Gulf of Aqaba

SAUDI ARABIA

Carnegie Endowment for International Peace, *Deadly Arsenals* (2002), **www.ceip.org**

Three Hard Cases

Overview

While most serious consequences are associated with the proliferation of nuclear, chemical, and biological weapons and ballistic missiles, the number of states aggressively pursuing those capabilities is remarkably limited. In fact, only three additional countries are considered by experts and governments as being capable in the next decade of producing nuclear weapons: Iran, Iraq, and North Korea. These countries are the focus of most non-proliferation efforts and attention in the United States and globally. The success or failure of preventing the acquisition of advanced WMD in those states will help to determine the future effectiveness of the international non-proliferation regime.

Each of the three countries is pursuing WMD capabilities for various reasons. Their motivations need to be understood in order to shape effective non-proliferation policies toward those states. In North Korea, for example, there appear to be opportunities for the United States and other countries to curtail and even roll back nuclear weapon and ballistic missile programs; efforts have already resulted in establishing a freeze on North Korea's nuclear weapon program. In Iran and Iraq, the dynamics are complicated by regional disputes and internal and international political realities that are frustrating efforts to prevent the acquisition of WMD capabilities. Iraq remains under severe economic constraints and sanctions but, in the absence of international inspections, may be advancing with its programs. Iran's efforts are heavily reliant on outside technology and assistance and may be affected in the future by internal political developments.

Lumping countries into groups such as "rogue states" or "axis of evil" tends to prevent the development of effective, finely tuned non-proliferation strategies. Exaggerating proliferation threats and failing to consider individual dynamics has often resulted in ineffective approaches to the problem of the proliferation of weapons of mass destruction.

CHAPTER 14

North Korea

Nuclear Weapon Capability

North Korea may possess enough nuclear material to produce one or perhaps two nuclear weapons. No conclusive evidence exists that North Korea has enough separated material to produce nuclear weapons, but U.S. intelligence agencies believe it to be likely.

North Korea is known to possess 25–30 kilograms of unseparated plutonium in spent fuel produced at its nuclear reactor complex at Yongbyon. This material is under IAEA monitoring. Moreover, North Korea has demonstrated the ability to separate plutonium from spent nuclear fuel. Activities at all the country's declared nuclear facilities—those that are operational and those that were previously under construction—have been frozen under an agreement with the United States that was signed in 1994 (see discussion under "Agreed Framework," below).

Aircraft and Missile Capability

North Korea has the most advanced ballistic missile capability among states of proliferation concern, having tested and deployed missiles with ranges of up to 1,000 kilometers and conducted a single test of a longer-range system that, if fully developed, could deliver a small payload to the United States. Pyongyang continues to abide by a self-imposed missile flight test ban but retains the ability to resume flight tests at any time. North Korea is the leading exporter of ballistic missiles in the world and has sold missiles and missile production capabilities to Egypt, Iran, Libya, Pakistan, and Syria. North Korea may also be gaining important flight test information from missiles being tested in other countries, such as Iran, and continues to conduct ground-based testing of missile engines and components.

Biological and Chemical Weapon Capability

North Korea is believed to possess large stocks of chemical weapons and precursor chemicals, as well as an infrastructure that can be used to produce biological weapons. Although it has acceded to the Biological and Toxin Weapons Convention, it has not signed the Chemical Weapons Convention. United States officials believe that North Korea has pursued biological warfare capabilities since the 1960s and is able to produce sufficient quantities of biological agents for military purposes within weeks of a decision to do so.[1] The United

States Defense Department believes that North Korea would use chemical weapons against U.S. or South Korean troops in combat.

Strategic Context

North Korea is a complex and controversial non-proliferation case, challenging international efforts to prevent the proliferation of weapons of mass destruction. This highly secretive and isolated country has developed a largely indigenous nuclear weapon and ballistic missile production capability. The world outside has only a limited set of tools at its disposal to influence North Korean behavior and convince its leadership to abandon its WMD production and export activities. Despite those limited options, significant progress has been made in curtailing North Korea's nuclear and missile activities and future progress appears possible.

The United States has a long-standing treaty and political commitment to defend its ally South Korea from North Korean attack. The United States deploys 37,000 American troops in South Korea (including one army division and two air force fighter wings). Key to the U.S. approach to stability on the Korean peninsula is to make clear to the North that any attack against the South would fail and present unacceptable costs to Pyongyang.

To date, attempts to restrict North Korea's WMD activities have involved a two-part strategy of deterrence and engagement. The most recent codification of that policy was captured in a report prepared by former Defense Secretary William Perry, released in October 1999.[2] The strategy seeks to test the premise that North Korea's leaders are interested in a better relationship with the West, while at the same time maintaining the military capability to deter and, if necessary, defeat any North Korean aggression against South Korea or the United States.

Since the collapse of the Soviet Union, however, this approach has taken on an important second track of engagement. The first direct high-level talks between North Korea and the United States were held in 1992. Since then the two sides have conducted productive, albeit inconsistent, talks aimed at establishing diplomatic relations and reducing tensions on the peninsula. The talks have generally centered on U.S. efforts to end North Korea's nuclear weapon and ballistic missile programs. North Korea has reciprocated with efforts to obtain financial and diplomatic concessions from the United States.

It is difficult, because of its extreme political isolation, to predict or fully understand the motives for North Korea's diplomatic and military moves. Its leader, Kim Jong-Il, appears to be concerned primarily with the continued survival of his rule and the regime originally established by his father, Kim Il-Sung. This assessment would explain North Korea's pursuit of both nuclear weapons and missiles, since both activities could, from its perspective, increase its ability to deter an attack from outside powers. In the case of its ballistic missile program, it would provide North Korea with an important source of hard currency for its economic survival. This analysis would also explain why North Korea has agreed to abandon its nuclear program and has repeatedly expressed a willingness to scrap its missile program in exchange for diplomatic and financial incentives from the United States. Such steps would accomplish the same goal of improving the chances for the regime's survival.

The Clinton administration pursued an active engagement policy with North Korea, having negotiated the 1994 Agreed Framework and worked on a broader agreement to end the production and export of missiles. The broad outlines of a missile agreement were worked out in late 2000 that would have constrained North Korean missile exports and production in exchange for Korean access to foreign space launch services. The final details, however, were not completed before George W. Bush became president. Among the details not worked out when the new administration entered office was the future status of missiles that had already been built by North Korea. The Bush administration has indicated its willingness to pursue a broader agreement with North Korea, to include the issues of missiles and conventional forces, although President Bush has expressed skepticism regarding negotiations with the North. No substantial progress has been made since late 2000.

Nuclear Analysis

The U.S. intelligence community indicates that North Korea may have enough separated plutonium to produce one or even two nuclear weapons.[3] Moreover, North Korea is known to possess enough plutonium (25–30 kilograms) in spent nuclear fuel irradiated in its 5-MWe research reactor at Yongbyon to produce, perhaps, five or six nuclear weapons.[4] There is no evidence that North Korea possesses a nuclear device, but Pyongyang is thought to be capable of building a first-generation nuclear device, given its current state of technology.

It is not this capability, in itself, that has placed North Korea in the headlines or at the forefront of efforts to prevent the spread of nuclear weapons. North Korea, before the decision to freeze its nuclear program in 1994, was on the verge of becoming a major producer of weapons-grade plutonium outside International Atomic Energy Agency safeguards. Left unchecked, North Korea could have operated reactors, fuel-fabrication, and spent-fuel reprocessing facilities able to produce 200 kilograms of plutonium a year, enough for 50 weapons every year.[5] This would provide North Korea with enough nuclear materials to build its own nuclear arsenals and to export substantial quantities of plutonium to other customer states that in the past have included Iran, Libya, and Syria. It was this export capability that, as much as anything, led to the negotiation of the Agreed Framework in 1994. Moreover, North Korea's signature and then its threatened withdrawal from the NPT had the potential to seriously undermine the international non-proliferation regime if left unchecked.

Previous Plutonium Production

North Korea's nuclear research program is reported to have begun as early as the 1950s,[6] but concerns over North Korea's nuclear weapon program did not fully emerge until the mid-1980s. During this period, U.S. intelligence satellites reportedly photographed the construction of a research reactor and the beginnings of a reprocessing facility in Yongbyon.[7] In 1989 open press sources indicated for the first time that North Korea possessed a plutonium production reactor and extraction capability.[8] It was also in 1989 that North Korea is reported, based on intelligence sources, to have shut down its main research and plutonium production reactor for approximately 100 days.[9] This would have given North Korea enough time to refuel the entire reactor and provided it with a source of enough nuclear material to build a nuclear device. At the time, neither the United States nor any other country took direct action in response to these activities. The strategy pursued was to press North Korea to join and then come into full compliance with its obligations under the NPT, and make that compliance a condition of progress on diplomatic issues.

Pyongyang acceded to the NPT on April 18, 1985, but did not complete the negotiation of a safeguard agreement with the IAEA within the 18 months required by the treaty. It was not until April 9, 1992, that Pyongyang finally approved its safeguard agreement with the agency; initial inspections to verify the accuracy of North Korea's initial declaration began in May 1992. These long-awaited developments came after the United States announced that it would withdraw its nuclear weapons from South Korea as part of a global tactical nuclear withdrawal. North Korea had publicly made the withdrawal of U.S. nuclear weapons from South Korea a condition of its completion of a safeguard agreement.

In all, six official inspection missions took place in North Korea from 1992 to 1993. The initial inspections of North Korea's nuclear facilities included tours of the completed 5-MWe reactor and 50-MWe plant still under construction, as well as of the incomplete "radiochemical laboratory" described by the IAEA as a plutonium reprocessing facility. Subsequent inspections focused mainly on the plutonium reprocessing facilities in North Korea, including some small-scale extraction equipment, referred to as hot cells.

North Korea informed the IAEA as part of this initial inspection process that it had conducted a one-time plutonium extraction experiment on "damaged" fuel rods removed from the 5-MWe reactor at Yongbyon in 1989. The IAEA was given access to the small amount separated by North Korea (approximately 90 grams,[10] or less than 1/40th of the amount required to build a nuclear device). The IAEA's chemical analysis of samples taken from the radiochemical laboratory and hot cells, however, contradicted North Korean claims that it had previously separated only 90 grams of plutonium on one occasion. Instead, the IAEA results indicated that the North had separated plutonium in four campaigns over three years, starting in 1989.[11] The samples taken by the agency showed a variety of radioactive by-products that suggested numerous instances of reprocessing activities. In describing the findings, IAEA Director General Hans Blix explained, "We found two gloves, a waste glove and a plutonium glove, and they don't match."[12] This means that North Korea's statements regarding its past plutonium production are not consistent with what the samples revealed and indicate that North Korea possesses more plutonium than it has declared to the IAEA or to the international community.

The findings added weight to the allegation that North Korea had removed significant amounts of fuel from its 5-MWe reactor during the observed shutdown in 1989. United States intelligence analysts believed that the reactor's core may have been completely replaced during a 100-day-long shutdown. Intelligence information provided to the IAEA also indicated that waste products from the North's plutonium extraction campaigns may be stored at two nearby sites, which appeared to be linked to the radiochemical laboratory by underground pipes capable of transporting liquid wastes. The sites, and the underground pipes, had been unsuccessfully camouflaged by the Koreans.

A long series of discussions and negotiations ensued over these issues, including an unusual visit to North Korea by IAEA Director Blix. Yet the talks were unable to obtain for the IAEA inspectors the unfettered access to sites and information considered necessary to resolve the discrepancies discovered by the IAEA in North Korea's plutonium production declaration. On February 11, 1993, Blix officially requested a "special inspection" of the two suspected waste sites, marking the first time in the agency's history that it had used its right to conduct such visits (see the discussion on Iraq and the aftermath of the Gulf War on the IAEA, chapter 16). Although these sites had been visited by the IAEA during the third inspection mission to North Korea in September 1993, North Korea did not permit full access to the sites, which were not included in its "initial declaration." Ten days later North Korea's Atomic Energy minister informed Blix that the North refused the agency's special inspection request and on March 12, in a letter to the three NPT depositary states and the other NPT members, said that it was exercising its right of withdrawal from the NPT, to take effect in 90 days as spelled out in article 10. This article permits such action on 90 days' notice if a party's "supreme national interests" are jeopardized.

After a round of negotiations with the United States in June 1993, North Korea agreed to "suspend" its withdrawal one day short of the 90-day countdown. However, North Korea asserted that it was no longer a full party to the NPT and that the IAEA no longer had the right to conduct even normal routine and ad hoc inspections. Over the ensuing nine months, Pyongyang severely constrained the IAEA inspection activities that are needed to preserve the "continuity of safeguards." This led Blix to declare in December 1993 that agency safeguards in North Korea could no longer provide "any meaningful assurances" that nuclear materials were not being diverted to weapon uses.[13]

Negotiations between the agency and North Korea continued. In March 1994, as part of a complicated package deal with the United States, North Korea initially agreed to an IAEA inspection of its declared facilities but then blocked the agency from taking key radioactive samples at the plutonium extraction plant at Yongbyon.[14]

More Plutonium

The crisis escalated further in mid-May 1994 when North Korea announced that it was going to defuel its 5-MWe reactor. Gaining access to the fuel to be removed from this reactor immediately became of international concern for two reasons. First, the fuel contained up to 30 kilograms of plutonium, material that could be used to produce several nuclear weapons. Second, by gaining access to the fuel and taking appropriate samples, the IAEA could determine whether the fuel had been in the reactor since its initial operation began in 1986 or whether the fuel was a secondary batch, indicating that North Korea had indeed removed an entire load of fuel from the reactor during the 1989 shutdown.

North Korea steadfastly refused to implement procedures demanded by the IAEA to segregate 300 carefully selected fuel rods from the 8,000-rod core, claiming that it was not a fully bound member of the NPT or of its safeguard agreement.[15] As Pyongyang accelerated and completed the defueling, Hans Blix declared in a letter to the U.N. Security Council on June 2, 1994, that the "agency's ability to ascertain, with sufficient confidence, whether nuclear material from the reactor has been diverted in the past, has been . . . lost."[16] Some controversy surrounds this point, since other ways to determine the reactor's history have since been developed and put forward.

These developments prompted the United States to circulate a proposal to the U.N. Security Council on June 15 calling for two phases of sanctions against North Korea. The first phase of the sanctions, which were to be activated after a grace period, consisted of a worldwide ban on arms imports from, and arms exports to, North Korea, along with a downgrading of diplomatic ties. In the second phase, to be triggered if the North continued to reject the IAEA's demands, a worldwide ban on financial dealings with Pyongyang would be implemented.[17] Moreover, the United States publicly began discussing plans for reinforcing its military presence in South Korea, and there were growing calls for U.S. military action against North Korea to prevent its gaining full access to the plutonium-bearing spent fuel.

The crisis eased after former President Jimmy Carter met with North Korean President Kim Il Sung on June 16–17. The North Korean leader agreed to freeze his country's nuclear program if the United States would resume high-level diplomatic talks. These negotiations took place in July but were suspended until early August because of the sudden death of Kim Il Sung on July 9. These talks eventually led to the negotiation of an "Agreed Statement" on August 12, 1994, under which, in broad terms, North Korea agreed to dismantle the elements of its nuclear program linked to the production of nuclear arms in return for the supply of two, less proliferation-prone, light-water reactors and a number of other energy- and security-related inducements.[18]

The Agreed Framework

The United States and North Korea proceeded with a series of expert-level discussions and another round of high-level talks to work out the modalities of an agreement following the August 12 statement. After several months, they managed to conclude the Agreed Framework, which was signed on October 21, 1994.[19] The accord establishes an intricately linked series of steps that could eventually result in the elimination of North Korea's nuclear weapon program in exchange for the provision of modern reactors and improved diplomatic and economic ties with the outside word. The key points of the framework are given in table 14.1.

At the heart of the framework is a trade between North Korea and the United States and its allies. The United States agreed to the establishment of a multi-national consortium that will finance and supply North Korea with two light-water reactors (LWR) by the target date of 2003. This date has slipped considerably, and the current target date for completing the reactors is estimated for some time in 2009, if not later. In exchange, North Korea agreed to freeze its nuclear program immediately and cease the construction and operation of its nuclear complex (including reactors and reprocessing sites) under

Table 14.1: **Key Elements of the 1994 Agreed Framework**

North Korea	United States
North Korea freezes its operation and construction of nuclear facilities under IAEA supervision.	The United States agrees to provide heavy fuel oil to replace the electrical production potential of the shutdown 5-MW reactor.
North Korea allows the canning and nonreprocessing of spent fuel from its 5-MW reactor under IAEA monitoring. Fuel to be removed from North Korea.	The United States agrees to establish an international consortium to construct two modern, light-water reactors in North Korea.
North Korea agrees to provide all necessary information and access, "including taking all steps that may be deemed necessary by the IAEA" to determine the accuracy of North Korea's initial declaration on past plutonium production	International consortium agrees to complete a significant portion of the reactor complex, not including key components.
North Korea agrees to begin dismantling its finished and incomplete nuclear facilities and to begin removal of spent fuel upon delivery of key reactor components for first light-water reactor.	International consortium to deliver key components for first light-water reactor.
North Korea agrees to complete dismantling of its nuclear facilities and removal of its spent fuel upon delivery of key components for second reactor.	International consortium to deliver key components for second light-water reactor.

IAEA monitoring. Pyongyang also agreed that the plutonium-bearing spent fuel would be removed from North Korea as nuclear components for the first light-water reactor are supplied and that all the facilities where activities are frozen would be dismantled by the time the second LWR is completed.

To offset the energy deficit that North Korea claimed it would face by the "freezing" of its graphite-moderated reactors and related facilities, the United States also agreed to arrange for the delivery to North Korea of heavy oil for heating and electricity to "reach a rate of 500,000 metric tons annually." This grant of heavy fuel oil would stop with the completion of the first LWR.

The agreement requires North Korea to remain a member of the NPT and to come into full compliance with its IAEA safeguard agreement once a "significant portion of the LWR project is completed, but before delivery of key nuclear components." This delay has postponed the IAEA verification of the accuracy and completeness of North Korea's initial report on the nuclear materials in its possession. This leaves open, for now, the question of North Korea's nuclear capabilities, but it does freeze North Korea's program and establish the obligation of North Korea to accept whatever steps the IAEA decides are necessary to verify the accuracy of North Korea's nuclear declaration.

The Agreed Framework also provides for the normalization of relations between North Korea and the United States, U.S. assurances against the threat or use of nuclear weapons against the North, and a North Korean commitment to implement the 1992 North–South Joint Declaration on the Denuclearization of the Korean Peninsula.

Proponents of the Agreed Framework have pointed to its inherent security benefits. They stress that it freezes, and then dismantles, nuclear facilities that would have given North Korea the capability to produce dozens of nuclear weapons each year, some of which might have been exported. Another advantage cited is that North Korea has effectively agreed, for the first time, to the IAEA inspection of the two undeclared waste sites, which will help reveal the history of past plutonium production. Moreover, proponents note that the agreement places restrictions on North Korea beyond those imposed by the NPT by banning the reprocessing of existing spent fuel and requiring the dismantling of North Korea's most sensitive nuclear facilities. As a by-product of the agreement, the construction of the LWRs would require thousands of South Korean engineers, technicians, and laborers to work, live, and socialize in the North for a decade, thereby improving the chances for more normal relations between Pyongyang and Seoul and lifting, at least partially, the veil of secrecy surrounding the North.[20]

On the other hand, critics contend that the agreement guarantees nothing and gives away too much. First, by postponing an IAEA inspection of the two undeclared sites for an extended period (four to six years), the accord delays attaining full compliance with IAEA safeguards and creates an unprecedented "special" safeguard status for North Korea (i.e., it introduces a double standard and a troubling precedent). Postponing inspections, it is argued, compromises the integrity of IAEA safeguards, especially as they relate to the conduct of the agency's special inspections.[21] The accord also will not attempt to rule out, for four to six years, the possibility that North Korea possesses a preexisting stock of plutonium or possibly one or two nuclear weapons. Moreover, the critics stress, the agreement preserves North Korea's ability, for a somewhat longer period, to acquire additional nuclear weapons rapidly, since, if implementation of the pact breaks down, Pyongyang would have immediate access to the stored spent fuel from the 5-MWe reactor, as well as to the Yongbyon reprocessing plant. Finally, the agreement sets a precedent for others to "toy" with the NPT. Iran, for example, has already hinted that it might withdraw from the treaty because of a U.S.–led nuclear embargo.[22]

On balance, it seems clear that the Agreement Framework, although an unorthodox adaptation to North Korea's singular defiance, still provides a credible means of keeping North Korea in the regime and of blocking nuclear weapon manufacture while the time gained is used to construct other incentives and to build constructive working relationships with North Korean authorities.

Since the negotiation of the Agreed Framework, the nuclear arrangement with North Korea has withstood the test of time. North Korea's nuclear program remains frozen and the construction of the light-water reactors, although considerably behind schedule, continues. If North Korea does possess a single nuclear device, it has not explicitly sought to use that fact to its advantage. Had North Korea's nuclear program not been suspended through the terms of the Agreed Framework, North Korea could have been able to produce between 500 and 700 kilograms of weapons-grade plutonium by the end of 2001. This would be enough to produce more than 100 weapons and would have given Pyongyang sufficient amounts of material, conceivably, to export some to other countries while retaining a sizable nuclear arsenal of its own.[23]

Secret Underground Sites

The most significant flare-up over North Korea's nuclear program since the completion of the Agreed Framework were the allegations by the United States that North Korea was building a nuclear facility within Mount Kumchangni. United States intelligence reportedly became concerned about the site near the Yongbyon nuclear facility in 1996 when satellite photos revealed extensive tunneling activities. By 1997 intelligence reports had concluded that the site could be a nuclear-related facility.[24] This assessment was made on the basis of the amount of tunneling being carried out, its proximity to the Yongbyon nuclear site, and the source of water close to the mountain. A determination that the construction site was related to North Korea's nuclear program would have cast the future of the Agreed Framework into doubt, even though the agreement does not prohibit North Korea from constructing other nuclear sites.

Nine months of discussions and negotiations between North Korea and the United States eventually led to an agreement that permitted U.S. experts to inspect the facility in exchange for the United States providing 500,000 metric tons of food aid to North Korea. The final agreement resulted in a U.S. group of 15 experts, including government officials and technical experts from U.S. national laboratories, on a tour of the inside of the Mount Kumchangni from

May 18 to May 24, 1999. The official State Department statement confirmed that the site was not currently housing any nuclear facilities and that its dimensions were not consistent with what would be required to house a nuclear reactor or plutonium reprocessing capability. A second inspection of the site took place in May 2000, with similar conclusions. Some experts have concluded that North Korea conducted tunneling activities at the site specifically to raise concerns in the United States that the North Korean nuclear program had been restarted, in the hope of energizing U.S. efforts to negotiate a broader political and economic agreement with the North. This suggestion, like all others regarding North Korean intentions, however, is impossible to prove or disprove.

Biological and Chemical Weapon Analysis

North Korea possesses chemical weapons and a large amount of chemical precursors for the production of such weapons. It is likely to have the ability to produce "bulk quantities of nerve, blister, choking, and blood agents."[25] North Korea, however, has not signed the Chemical Weapons Convention and has not acknowledged its possession of chemical weapons or agreed to eliminate its holdings. North Korea is thought to possess the means to deliver a chemical agent by ballistic missile, as well as by conventional artillery or aircraft. North Korean troops have also trained to fight in contaminated areas, according to the U.S. Defense Department.[26]

North Korea maintains facilities involved in producing or storing chemical precursors, agents, and weapons. It has at least eight industrial facilities that can produce chemical agents. The production rate and types of munitions, however, are uncertain. Presumably, adamsite, phosgene, prussic acid, sarin, tabun, and a family of mustard gases, constituting the basis of North Korea's chemical weapons, are produced there. In the assessment of U.S. intelligence services, North Korea's reserves, accommodated in perhaps half a dozen major storage sites and in as many as 170 mountain tunnels, are at least 180–250 metric tons, with some estimates of chemical stockpiles running as high as 5,000 metric tons.[27]

North Korea possesses a rudimentary biological weapon capability and has engaged in biological research since the 1960s. Its biological weapon program is not nearly as advanced as its nuclear, chemical, or ballistic missile programs, but North Korea is believed to have the basic infrastructure to produce several biological agents, including anthrax, cholera, and plague. It could deliver such weapons by several means, including artillery or possibly ballistic missiles.[28] North Korea acceded to the Biological and Toxin Weapons Convention in March 1987.

Missile Analysis

North Korea has an extensive ballistic missile program, based primarily on technology derived from Soviet-designed Scud–B missiles. North Korea acquired a number of Scud missiles from Egypt in the 1970s. It either successfully reverse-engineered the system (improving its range and accuracy) or received substantially more equipment and assistance from the Soviet Union than is publicly known. With substantial financing from customer states, including Iran, North Korea has developed and deployed the Scud–Mod B (with a 320- to 340-kilometer range and a 1,000-kilogram payload); the Scud–Mod C (with a 500-kilometer range and a 700-kilogram payload); and the No Dong missiles (with a 1,000-kilometer range and a 700–1,000 kilogram payload). In addition, North Korea tested a space launch vehicle known as the Taepo Dong I on August 31, 1998. Although the third state of the missile failed to boost its payload into orbit, the system demonstrated North Korea's accelerating ability to launch a multi-stage missile and to develop a system with the potential for intercontinental range. The system is believed to use a No Dong missile as its first stage and a Scud–B as its second stage. The third stage is thought to be a solid rocket "kick motor" of unknown origin.

North Korea is also reportedly working on a longer-range Taepo Dong II missile that could enable North Korea to deliver a nuclear-sized payload to the continental United States. North Korea, however, is observing a self-imposed missile flight-test moratorium established as part of its discussions with the United States on a broader agreement to end Pyongyang's missile production and export activities.

North Korea is the leading exporter of ballistic missiles to the developing world, and its exports have continued despite its flight-test moratorium. States that have received missiles from North Korea include Iran, Libya, Pakistan, and Syria. Egypt may also have received some systems from Pyongyang. What is important is that Iran is also believed to have received North Korean assistance in establishing its own missile production capabilities and may intend to enter the missile export market. Iran and Pakistan's missile capabilities are thought to be highly dependent on North Korean technology and equipment.

Notes

1. John Bolton, Under Secretary for Arms Control and International Security, Remarks to the Fifth Biological Weapons Conventional Meeting, Geneva, Switzerland, November 19, 2001.

2. "Review of United States Policy toward North Korea: Findings and Recommendations," Unclassified Report by William Perry, U.S. North Korea Policy Coordinator and Special Adviser to the President and the Secretary of State, Washington, D.C., October 12, 1999.

3. "Unclassified Report to Congress on the Acquisition of Technology relating to Weapons of Mass Destruction and Advanced Conventional Munitions," January 1–June 30, 2000, U.S. Central Intelligence Agency, February 22, 2001.

4. For a full discussion of how much plutonium may have been produced by North Korea, see David Albright, "How Much Plutonium Did North Korea Produce," in David Albright and Kevin O'Neill, eds., *Solving the North Korean Nuclear Puzzle* (Washington, D.C.: Institute for Science and International Security, 2000), pp. 111–126.

5. Statement of Hon. Robert Gallucci, ambassador-at-large to Senate Committee on Foreign Relations, December 1, 1994 (Washington, D.C.: U.S. GPO, 1995).

6. Mike Mazarr, *North Korea and the Bomb: A Case Study in Nonproliferation* (New York: St. Martin's Press, 1995), p. 25.

7. Don Oberdorfer, *The Two Koreas: A Contemporary History* (Massachusetts: Addison-Wesley, 1997), p. 250.

8. John Fialka, "North Korea May Be Developing Ability To Produce Nuclear Weapons," *Wall Street Journal*, July 19, 1989.

9. Les Aspin, *McNeil-Lehrer Newshour*, December 1993.

10. R. Jeffrey Smith, "N. Korea and the Bomb: High-Tech Hide-and-Seek," *Washington Post*, April 27, 1993.

11. Mark Hibbs, "IAEA Special Inspection Effort Meeting Diplomatic Resistance," *Nucleonics Week*, February 18, 1993, p. 16; Smith, "N. Korea and the Bomb"; Hibbs, "U.S. Might Help North Korea Refuel Reactor," *Nuclear Fuel*, November 8, 1993, p. 1; and Smith, "West Watching Reactor for Sign of North Korea's Nuclear Intentions," *Washington Post*, December 12, 1993.

12. Smith, "N. Korea and the Bomb."

13. David Sanger, "U.N. Agency Finds No Assurance North Korea Bans Nuclear Arms," *New York Times*, December 3, 1993. For a detailed examination of the IAEA's relations with the Democratic People's Republic of Korea, see Leon Sigal, *Disarming Strangers: Nuclear Diplomacy with North Korea*, Princeton University Press, Princeton, NJ., 1998.

14. R. Jeffrey Smith, "N. Korean Conduct in Inspection Draws Criticism of U.S. Officials," *Washington Post*, March 10, 1994; R. Jeffrey Smith, "Inspection of North Korea's Nuclear Facilities Is Halted," *Washington Post*, March 16, 1994; David E. Sanger, "North Korea Said To Block Taking of Radioactive Samples from Site," *New York Times*, March 16, 1994; and Michael R. Gordon, "U.S. Goes to U.N. To Increase the Pressure on North Korea," *New York Times*, March 22, 1994. For a comprehensive assessment of the March 1994 inspection, see Sigal, *Disarming Strangers*, pp. 95–108.

15. Mark Hibbs, "Fuel Readiness Means North Korea Can Start Reactors up on Schedule," *Nucleonics Week*, April 7, 1994, p. 14; and R. Jeffrey Smith, "N. Korea Refuses Demand To Inspect Reactor Fuel," *Washington Post*, April 28, 1994.

16. Letter from the Director General of the IAEA Addressed to the Secretary-General of the United Nations relating to North Korea, June 2, 1994.

17. Ann Devroy, "U.S. To Seek Sanctions on N. Korea," *Washington Post*, June 3, 1994; Michael Gordon, "White House Asks for Global Sanctions on North Koreans," *New York Times*, June 3, 1994; David Ottaway, "N. Korea Forbids Inspections," *Washington Post*, June 8, 1994; and Julia Preston, "U.S. Unveils Proposal for Sanctions," *Washington Post*, June 16, 1994.

18. T. R. Reid, "Leaders of 2 Koreas Seek First Summit," *Washington Post*, June 19, 1994; and Michael Gordon, "Back from Korea, Carter Declares the Crisis Is Over," *New York Times*, June 20, 1994. For a detailed account of the Carter-Kim meeting, see Sigal, *Disarming Strangers*, pp. 150–162.

19. Mark Hibbs, "U.S., DPRK To Meet in Berlin on LWR Transfer, Spent Fuel Details," *Nucleonics Week*, September 8, 1994, p.17; "North Korea Rejects Special Nuclear Inspections," *Reuters*, September 16, 1994; and "Agreed Framework between the United States of America and the Democratic People's Republic of Korea," October 21, 1994.

20. Testimony of Leonard Spector, Director of the Nuclear Non-Proliferation Project, Carnegie Endowment for International Peace; and Mitchell Reiss, *Bridled Ambition: Why Countries Constrain Their Nuclear Capabilities* (Washington, D.C.: Woodrow Wilson Center Press: Washington, D.C., 1995), pp. 276–280.

21. The IAEA had previously conducted special inspections in Sweden and Romania, but these were of a fundamentally different nature than the ones proposed for North Korea. See Sigal, *Disarming Strangers*, p. 49.

22. Devroy, "U.S. To Seek Sanctions on N. Korea"; Gordon, "White House Asks for Global Sanctions on North Koreans"; Ottaway, "N. Korea Forbids Inspections"; and Preston, "U.S. Unveils Proposal for Sanctions."

23. Albright and O'Neill, eds., *Solving the North Korean Nuclear Puzzle*, p. 11.

24. Larry Niksch, "North Korea's Nuclear Weapons Program," CRS Issue Brief for Congress, (Washington, D.C.: Congressional Research Service, February 27, 2001).

25. U.S. Department of Defense, *Proliferation: Threat and Response*, January 2001, pp. 11–12.

26. Ibid.

27. Federation of American Scientists, Weapons of Mass Destruction web site, www.fas.org/nuke/guide/dprk/cw/index.html.

28. U.S. DOD, *Proliferation: Threat and Response*.

Table 14.2: **North Korea: Nuclear Infrastructure**

Name/Location of Facility	Type/ Status	IAEA Safeguards
POWER REACTORS		
Sinpo (Kumho)	2 light-water, 1,000-MWe; under construction	Yes
Yongbyon	Gas-graphite, nat. U, 5-MWe; operation frozen	IAEA verifying freeze in operations
Yongbyon	Gas-graphite, nat. U, 50-MWe; construction halted	IAEA verifying construction freeze
Taechon	Gas-graphite, nat. U, 200-MWe; construction halted	IAEA verifying construction freeze
RESEARCH REACTORS		
IRT, Yongbyon	Pool-type, HEU, 4-MWt; operating	Yes
Yongbyon	Critical assembly	Yes
Pyongyang	Subcritical assembly	Yes
REPROCESSING (PLUTONIUM EXTRACTION)		
Yongbyon	Partially completed; operations frozen	Yes
Pyongyang	Soviet-supplied laboratory-scale "hot cells"	No
URANIUM PROCESSING		
Pyongsan	Uranium mining; status unknown	N/A
Pakchon (Sanchon-Wolbingson mine)	Uranium mining; status unknown	N/A
Pyongsan	Uranium milling; status unknown	N/A
Pakchon	Uranium milling; status unknown	N/A
Yongbyon	Uranium purification (UO_2) facility; operating	Yes
Yongbyon	Fuel-fabrication facility; operations frozen	Yes
Yongbyon	Pilot-scale fuel-fabrication facility; dismantled, according to North Korean officials	No

Abbreviations

HEU	highly enriched uranium	MWt	millions of watts of thermal output
LEU	low-enriched uranium	kWt	thousands of watts of thermal output
MWe	millions of watts of electrical output	nat. U	natural uranium
		N/A	not applicable

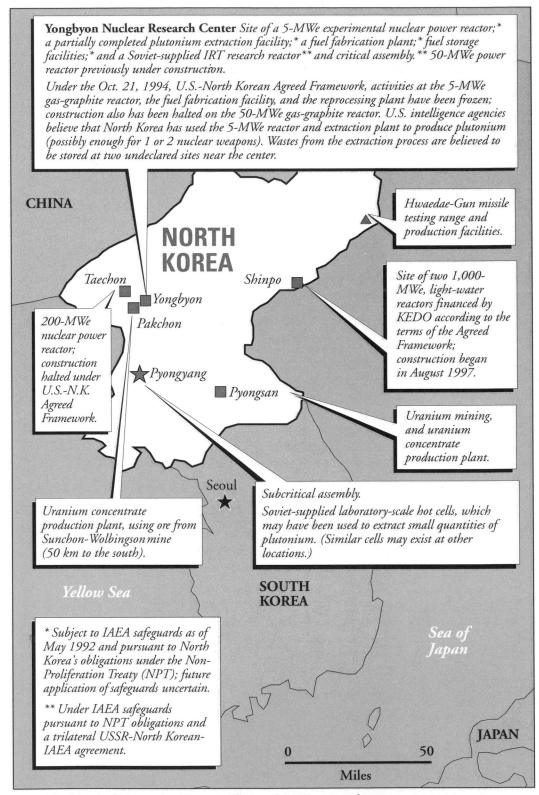

Yongbyon Nuclear Research Center *Site of a 5-MWe experimental nuclear power reactor;* a partially completed plutonium extraction facility;* a fuel fabrication plant;* fuel storage facilities;* and a Soviet-supplied IRT research reactor** and critical assembly.** 50-MWe power reactor previously under construction.*

Under the Oct. 21, 1994, U.S.-North Korean Agreed Framework, activities at the 5-MWe gas-graphite reactor, the fuel fabrication facility, and the reprocessing plant have been frozen; construction also has been halted on the 50-MWe gas-graphite reactor. U.S. intelligence agencies believe that North Korea has used the 5-MWe reactor and extraction plant to produce plutonium (possibly enough for 1 or 2 nuclear weapons). Wastes from the extraction process are believed to be stored at two undeclared sites near the center.

CHINA

NORTH KOREA

Taechon

Yongbyon

Pakchon

Hwaedae-Gun missile testing range and production facilities.

Shinpo

Site of two 1,000-MWe, light-water reactors financed by KEDO according to the terms of the Agreed Framework; construction began in August 1997.

200-MWe nuclear power reactor; construction halted under U.S.-N.K. Agreed Framework.

Pyongyang

Pyongsan

Uranium mining, and uranium concentrate production plant.

Seoul

Uranium concentrate production plant, using ore from Sunchon-Wolbingson mine (50 km to the south).

Subcritical assembly.
Soviet-supplied laboratory-scale hot cells, which may have been used to extract small quantities of plutonium. (Similar cells may exist at other locations.)

Yellow Sea

SOUTH KOREA

Sea of Japan

* Subject to IAEA safeguards as of May 1992 and pursuant to North Korea's obligations under the Non-Proliferation Treaty (NPT); future application of safeguards uncertain.

** Under IAEA safeguards pursuant to NPT obligations and a trilateral USSR-North Korean-IAEA agreement.

JAPAN

0   50

Miles

Carnegie Endowment for International Peace, *Deadly Arsenals* (2002), **www.ceip.org**

CHAPTER 15

Iran

Nuclear Weapon Capability

Iran currently has no nuclear weapon capability, but it is known to be pursuing a nuclear weapon option. The intelligence services of Germany, Israel, the United Kingdom, and the United States have confirmed the existence of a long-term program to manufacture nuclear weapons.[1] The U.S. Department of Defense cites Iran as "one of the countries most active in seeking to acquire NBC [nuclear-, biological-, chemical-] and missile-related technologies."[2] Iran has the basic nuclear technology and infrastructure to build a bomb, and "Iran's success in achieving a nuclear capability will depend, to a large extent, on the supply policies of Russia and China or on Iran's successful illicit acquisition of adequate quantities of weapons-usable fissile material."[3]

Missile Capability

Iran possesses about 300 Scud–Bs with a 300-kilometer range and 1,000-kilogram payload, and approximately 100 Scud–Cs with a 500-kilometer range.[4] Having received North Korean assistance, Iran is now manufacturing Scuds.[5] The country also has 200 Chinese-supplied CSS–8 missiles with an estimated range of 150 kilometers and a payload of 190 kilograms, purchased in late 1989.[6] The short-range series is developed and manufactured primarily as a counterweight against Iraq. Iran has tested the medium-range Shahab III, a derivative of the North Korean No Dong, with a range of 1,300 kilometers and a payload of about 750 kilograms. United States officials assess that Tehran could have the Shahab III on "emergency operational status."[7] This MRBM can reach Israel, although it requires further testing in order to be considered a "reliable threat."[8] The country is also reportedly developing the Shahab IV, with a range of 2,000 kilometers and payload of 1,000 kilograms.[9]

Biological and Chemical Weapon Capability

Although Iran is a member of the Biological Weapons Convention, U.S. intelligence reports claim that Iran currently maintains an offensive biological weapon program. The Iranian program is believed to include active research and development, agent production, and weaponization.[10]

In May 1998, after acceding to the Chemical Weapons Convention, Tehran acknowledged past Iranian involvement in chemical weapon development and production. Like the Iranian BW program, the chemical weapon program began in the 1980s during the war with Iraq. Iranian officials claimed that the Iranian CW program was dismantled at the war's end. United States threat assessments, however, contend that Iran's chemical weapon program remains intact. It is believed that Iran possesses a stockpile of weaponized blood gases and blister and pulmonary agents.

Strategic Context

Iran's experience during the Iran–Iraq War in the 1980s has driven the country's pursuit of weapons of mass destruction. During the war, Iraq used chemical weapons against poorly protected Iranian forces with devastating effect. Iraq's bombardment of Tehran with conventionally armed, extended-range Scud missiles during the spring 1988 War of the Cities was an important factor in leading Iran to accept a cease-fire in October of that year. With the West's conspicuous silence over Saddam Hussein's use of chemical weapons against Iran, the leaders in Tehran decided that acquiring those weapons was the only means of ensuring self-defense. Shortly after the cease-fire, Akbar Hashemi-Rafsanjani, then–speaker of the Iranian parliament and commander-in-chief of Iran's armed forces and later Iran's president, declared:

> With regard to chemical, bacteriological, and radiological weapons training, it was made very clear during the war that these weapons are very decisive. It was also made clear that the moral teachings of the world are not very effective when war reaches a serious stage and the world does not respect its own resolutions and closes its eyes to the violations and all the aggressions which are committed in the battlefield. *We should fully equip ourselves both in the offensive and defensive use of chemical, bacteriological, and radiological weapons.* From now on you should make use of the opportunity and perform this task. (emphasis added)[11]

As Iran looks around its extended neighborhood, it sees Israel, India, and Pakistan with advanced nuclear weapons; inspection-free Iraq; growing ties between Israel and Turkey; an unfriendly, nuclear-armed U.S. Navy; Gulf Arab states that spend vast amounts of money on state-of-the-art, high-tech weaponry and, until recently, a hostile Afghanistan. United States sanctions have helped to diminish Tehran's conventional capabilities and have likely worked toward reaffirming Tehran's belief in the utility of unconventional weapons.[12] Some Iranian leaders have come to see weapons of mass destruction and ballistic and cruise missiles together as their ultimate allies. From Iran's perspective, nuclear weapons may make strategic sense. Iran may well want to maintain a nuclear option, regardless of whether conservatives or moderates are in control in Tehran. Indeed, neither Iran's development of weapons of mass destruction nor its ballistic missile program has abated since Mohammed Khatami was elected president.[13]

Overtly pursuing the nuclear option would of course violate Iran's treaty obligations under the NPT, coming at great political and economic cost. Since President Khatami came to power, Iran has had considerable success in diminishing its isolation and improving relations with much of the world, including its Arab Gulf neighbors and potentially with the United States. Withdrawing from the NPT and manufacturing a bomb would undermine all those success-es. Yet as Saddam Hussein tries to reconstitute Iraq's weapons of mass destruc-tion, including its nuclear program, Iran will feel compelled to match Iraq's progress, despite being a member of the NPT. The absence of weapon inspec-tors in Iraq since December 1998 is undoubtedly a key Iranian security con-cern. A nuclear-armed Iraq could drive Iran toward withdrawing from the NPT and declaring an openly nuclear stance.[14]

On the other side of the spectrum, rapprochement with the United States would probably provide Iran with some space to reconsider exercising its nuclear weapon option.[15] The May 1997 elections that brought President Khatami to power appear to make improved relations with the United States a possibility. While conservatives in Iran continue to resist this possibility, events after September 11, 2001, have seemed to accelerate improved relations. President Bush's "axis of evil" speech ended that process. Moreover, Iran's con-tinued opposition to the Middle East peace process and its support of groups like Hamas will continue to obstruct better U.S.–Iranian relations.

Nuclear Analysis

Estimates about when Iran might acquire nuclear weapons have constantly been pushed back. In 1992–1993, U.S. and Israeli officials had estimated that Iran might have a nuclear bomb by 2000–2002. By 1995, the United States and Israel had readjusted the period to "7–15 years." This "reasonable esti-mate," in then–Defense Secretary William Perry's words, was based on evidence that Iran had revived its nuclear program in the mid-1980s and that following the Gulf War (which revealed the alarming progress of Saddam Hussein's nuclear program), Iran had launched a comprehensive nuclear program with weapon potential.[16] In March 1997, John Holum, at that time the director of the Arms Control and Disarmament Agency, testified before Congress that Iran remained eight to ten years away from acquiring nuclear weapons, which was virtually the same assessment that U.S. officials had given two years earlier. Queried as to whether this meant that Iran's nuclear program was making little progress, Holum replied: "I think they have slipped rather than gained on the timetable. That is my current recollection. I may also want to give you a classi-fied response."[17] According to U.S. assessments, Iran could produce a nuclear weapon in seven to nine years, while Israel estimates that Iran could have the bomb in five to seven years.[18] The uncertainty involved is reflected in the U.S. Defense Department decision not to put a time frame on Iran's nuclear capa-bilities in its 2001 report.[19]

Iran has regularly objected to U.S. efforts to impose a nuclear embargo and to press Russia not to supply Iran with nuclear weapons, arguing that as a mem-ber of the NPT it has treaty rights "to develop research, production and use of nuclear energy for peaceful purposes." In 1991, in an effort to dispel recurring suspicions about its nuclear program, Iran agreed that, in addition to permitting routine IAEA inspections on all nuclear activities as required by the NPT, it would also allow the IAEA to visit any location within the country to check for undeclared nuclear activities. The agency has made two such special visits. A February 1992 visit observed several locations not on Iran's list of declared nuclear sites but found no violations of the NPT. In a follow-up visit in November 1993, IAEA officials viewed facilities in Esfahan, Karaj, and Tehran, but again found no violations of the pact.[20] Nevertheless, the outcomes of the visits have not allayed U.S. concerns.

The revolutionary Islamic regime of Ayatollah Khomeini that came to power in Iran in 1979 inherited two partially completed, German-supplied nuclear power reactors at Bushehr. Khomeini froze construction of these reactors immediately after coming to power.[21] The structures were severely damaged by Iraqi bombing during the 1980–1988 Iran–Iraq War. In 1991 then-President Hashemi Rafsanjani expressed Iran's determination to complete construction of the reactors, but Germany refused to repair or finish the plants because of Iran's apparent interest in nuclear weapons. Iran sought assistance for the task, including from China and Brazil. Finally, in 1995, Tehran signed an $800 million deal with Moscow to finish the first of the two units by 2001.[22] Under the contract, Russia is also to provide low-enriched uranium fuel for a period of ten years, starting in 2001, at an annual cost of $30 million, as well as technical training. In the course of consultation with the United States, however, Russia has dropped its previously contemplated plan to assist Iran in uranium enrichment.

Russia's assistance with the Bushehr nuclear plant is important to Iran's weapon program, although the extent to which that is true is debatable. Its pressurized-water-power reactors are particularly unsuitable to produce weapons-grade material.[23] The 1,000-megawatt nuclear power reactor is under IAEA safeguards and is similar to the light-water reactor supplied by the United States to North Korea under the terms of the Agreed Framework. Bushehr's benefits to Iran's nuclear weapon program are likely to be largely indirect. The project will augment Iran's nuclear technology infrastructure, helping Tehran's nuclear weapon research and development.[24] Iran will also benefit from the presence of thousands of Russian nuclear scientists who are expected to take part in the Bushehr project.[25] Iran might also try to hide illicit transfers of technology and materials in the stream of permitted commerce. Further, Russian "entities" are known to offer nuclear assistance that extends beyond the Bushehr nuclear plant.[26]

The Khomeini regime also inherited a nuclear research base and continued nuclear research activities. The Tehran Research Center, for example, trained specialists and operated a small U.S.–supplied research reactor, which remained under IAEA safeguards.[27] Specialists at the center presumably had access to the research done during the shah's reign, possibly including undeclared nuclear weapon research. In 1984, in the midst of the Iran–Iraq War, Iran opened a new nuclear research center in Esfahan.

By 1992, press reports of Western intelligence findings indicated that Iran had established experimental programs in fissile material production at Sharif University in Tehran and possibly at other locations. These programs reportedly included research and development in both centrifuge uranium enrichment and plutonium reprocessing. Iran was said to be supporting those efforts by means of a clandestine procurement network. It was secretly approaching Western European companies to acquire nuclear-related, dual-use technologies and purchasing a number of small companies (particularly in Germany) to serve as export platforms for sensitive equipment to Iran.[28]

In the spring of 1995 details emerged on Iran's nuclear procurement activities, publicly substantiating suspected efforts to establish a secret gas-centrifuge uranium-enrichment program. Specifically, Western intelligence sources were quoted as stating that, since 1990, Iran had approached German and Swiss firms to purchase balancing machines and diagnostic and monitoring equipment—all dual-use items potentially valuable for laboratory-scale centrifuge development. In addition, Iranian agents were said to have contacted a British company to obtain samarium-cobalt magnetic equipment, potentially useful in the development of centrifuge top bearings.[29] Without foreign assistance, Iran is, many believe, at least five to seven years away from acquiring a nuclear device using indigenous nuclear material, and at least six to nine years away from achieving a nuclear weapon design that can fit in the warhead of a long-range missile.[30]

As noted, Iran continues to remain in good standing with the IAEA, and intelligence agencies have yet to locate a uranium-enrichment plant or a plutonium-reprocessing facility in the country.[31] Tehran has not, however, signed the IAEA's 93+2 protocol, which calls for more intrusive safeguards. That protocol is a result of the 1990 Persian Gulf War, which revealed the extent to which Iraq, an NPT member, had progressed with its clandestine nuclear weapon program. The development of an indigenous capability to produce fissile material might take from eight to ten years, and several unconfirmed reports reveal that Iran has added a second track to its nuclear weapon program, seeking to purchase nuclear expertise and nuclear weapon material illicitly in the former Soviet Union.[32] There have been no reports, however, that Iran succeeded in acquiring whole weapons or nuclear materials on the black market from Russian or other sources. Indeed, there have been no new reported cases involving the smuggling of weapons-usable materials from the former Soviet Union by any party since 1994.[33] On the other hand, hundreds of metric tons of weapons-usable nuclear materials remain poorly secured in Russia and are likely to remain so for many years, despite important U.S.–Russian collaborative efforts to enhance controls over such materials. Thus the potential danger that Iran may be able to obtain the materials will continue.

Most Western nuclear suppliers have adopted, from the regime's earliest days, a U.S.–led embargo on nuclear sales to the Iranian Revolutionary Government. The United States has relied on the Nuclear Suppliers Group to coordinate the Western embargo and has persuaded some states to withhold goods that were regulated under the NSG's core export-control guidelines. NSG rules permit the sale of such items, provided they are subject to IAEA inspection in the recipient state, but Washington has convinced its Western trading partners to adopt the stricter policy in the case of Iran. Russia, though a member, explicitly rejects the U.S.–initiated ban on major nuclear exports to Iran. Moscow argues that the light-water type of reactor that Russia is supplying, which will be under IAEA inspection, is not a proliferation risk.

United States efforts to curtail foreign nuclear sales to Iran intensified during the Bush administration in the aftermath of the 1991 Gulf War. The Iraq experience led the NSG in April 1992 to extend its controls to nuclear dual-use items, those items with both nuclear and non-nuclear end uses—prohibiting the export of items on the list "when there is unacceptable risk of diversion [to the production of nuclear explosives] or when the transfers are contrary to the objective of averting the proliferation of nuclear weapons." Once the new NSG rules were adopted, Washington sought agreement from the leading Western members of the group to prohibit all transfers of nuclear dual-use goods to Iran, but only Germany and the United Kingdom complied. An initially unsuccessful, parallel U.S. proposal, launched in 1992, was to curtail Western sales of (non-nuclear) strategic dual-use items to Iran; the initiative took four years to materialize in the form of the Wassenaar Arrangement in 1996.

U.S. Pressure on China and Russia

For a decade starting in the mid-1980s China was a source of significant assistance to Iran's civil nuclear program.[34] It reportedly trained Iranian nuclear technicians and engineers in China under a ten-year agreement for cooperation signed in 1990. China supplied Iran with two "mini" research reactors installed at Esfahan. China also supplied Iran with a calutron, the type of equipment used in Iraq's EMIS (electromagnetic isotope separation) enrichment program for the separation of weapons-grade uranium. Both countries claim that the aid has been used exclusively for peaceful purposes, in line with Iran's NPT obligations.

In 1992 Washington persuaded China to postpone the sale to Iran of a plutonium-producing research reactor indefinitely and convinced Argentina not to export supporting fuel-cycle and heavy-water production facilities.[35] In March 1992 China agreed to supply two 300-MWe nuclear power reactors to Iran. In the fall of 1995, however, China's reactor sale to Iran was suspended, ostensibly because of difficulties over site selection, although the underlying cause may have been Iran's difficulties in obtaining financing. Other factors may also have been involved. Some reports indicated that China suspended or even terminated the deal because of strong U.S. pressure.[36] In addition, France, Germany, and Japan apparently had declined to supply China with essential components that it might have needed for the reactors it had offered Iran. It is also possible that Iran lost interest in the arrangement once it was confident that Russia would complete the Bushehr project.

In April 1996 the U.S. Department of Defense still regarded China to be Iran's main source of nuclear assistance.[37] In the U.S.–China summit of October 1997, however, China made a commitment to cancel almost all its existing nuclear assistance to Iran and to provide Iran no new nuclear assistance. By 2001, citing that "China appears to be living up to its 1997 commitments," the Department of Defense no longer viewed China as Iran's main nuclear friend, although Chinese missile assistance for Iran continues to pose a proliferation risk.[38] The commitment included a pledge to terminate the sale of a uranium conversion plant to Iran.

During early 1995, Russia proceeded with its contract to help Iran build a nuclear reactor at Bushehr. Tensions rose with Russia when the Clinton administration learned in March–April 1995 that, as part of a secret protocol for the reactor sale contract, Russia had agreed to provide Iran with a gas-centrifuge uranium-enrichment facility. Such a facility, though itself under IAEA inspection and dedicated to the production of low-enriched (non-weapons-grade) uranium, could enable Iran to build and operate a similar plant clandestinely to produce weapons-grade uranium. Other disturbing elements of the protocol were an agreement in principle for Russia to supply a 30–50 MWt light-water research reactor, 2,000 metric tons of natural uranium, and the training of Iranian graduates in the nuclear field in Russia.[39]

Washington has pressured Russia to halt its work on the Bushehr nuclear reactor but has so far met with little success. United States concerns extend even beyond the Bushehr project, as Russian entities are known to be cooperating with Iran beyond the Bushehr project.[40] Throughout the 1990s broader national security concerns have made the United States reluctant to cut off aid to Russia as permitted by U.S. legislation. Under President Vladimir Putin's leadership, Russia has pledged to complete construction of the Bushehr plant. Soon after September 11, 2001, Russia and Iran signed an arms agreement that included an air defense system to be built around the Bushehr reactor.[41]

While the Bushehr project has continued, it has faced significant delays. Initially, Russian officials had estimated that, once construction had begun in early 1996, it would take 55 to 60 months to build the reactor and load it with fuel. However, by the fall of 1996, the project clearly faced complex engineering problems. Specifically, Russian experts were grappling with the incompatibility of the metallurgical specifications of the equipment supplied by Siemens during the 1970s with those of the components to be fitted in the reactor under the Russia–Iran deal.[42] Reportedly, in the fall of 1997, while 200 to 300 Russian experts were still in Iran completing an engineering evaluation at the Bushehr installation, none of the components for the reactor's nuclear steam system had yet been delivered. In January 2001, however, Russia announced that the Bushehr project was 90 percent complete and that operation would begin by 2003.[43]

In addition, Russia's promised sale to Iran of a sizable research reactor, encompassed in the original Bushehr deal, has also faltered. At U.S. urging, Russia refused to provide a heavy-water system—an efficient plutonium producer—as requested by the Iranians. In connection with Russia's reactor sale agreement, the United States was particularly troubled by the arrangements for the disposition of the plutonium-bearing spent fuel from Bushehr. The "take-back" of spent fuel had been a standard feature of Soviet nuclear export agreements. In practice, this means that the plutonium in the spent fuel was returned to the fuel supplier. In Iran's case, spent-fuel returned to Russia could prevent the Iranian diversion of plutonium for weapons. Ultimately, the United

States convinced Russia to stipulate to Iran that spent fuel from the reactor would be returned.[44]

U.S. Sanctions Policy Toward Iran

During the 1980s, the United States imposed a wide range of sanctions on Iran because of its support for international terrorism, its attacks in 1987 on U.S.–flagged Kuwaiti tankers, and other actions that were hostile to U.S. interests. Those sanctions blocked economic and military assistance to Iran, prohibited the importation of Iranian-origin goods, and restricted U.S. contributions to multi-lateral organizations that assist Iran and U.S. Export-Import Bank credits for Iran.

The passage of the 1992 Iran–Iraq Arms Non-Proliferation Act expressly prohibited transfers of nuclear equipment and materials to Iran, as well as exports to Iran of all dual-use commodities and U.S. government and commercial arms sales. The restriction applies both to nuclear dual-use commodities, i.e., those having nuclear and non-nuclear uses and that are regulated internationally by the NSG, and strategic dual-use commodities, i.e., those having military and nonmilitary uses, currently regulated under the Wassenaar Arrangement.

In 1995 and 1996 the United States tightened sanctions on Iran, aiming in part to constrain Tehran's WMD programs.[45] Legislation adopted in February 1996 provided for U.S. economic assistance to Russia to be made upon presidential determination if Russia had terminated its nuclear-related assistance to Iran.[46] The legislation permitted the president to waive this restriction at six-month intervals, however, upon a determination that making U.S. funds available to Russia was in the interest of U.S. national security. In the interests of broader relations with Russia, such waivers have been exercised.[47] In August of 1996, Washington further intensified economic pressure on Iran by imposing secondary sanctions on it and Libya, through the Iran and Libya Sanctions Act of 1996 (ILSA). The law imposes sanctions on foreign enterprises that invest $20 million or more in the energy sector of Iran or Libya. By the fall of 1997 this legislation faced a serious challenge from French, Malaysian, and Russian oil companies that had signed a deal with Iran to help recover and market oil and natural gas. The Clinton administration backed away from imposing the sanctions because of the economic crisis in East Asia and in Russia in the fall of 1997 and spring of 1998, which placed larger U.S. foreign policy interests at stake. The Bush administration has not been enthusiastic about ILSA, but because of congressional support in the summer of 2001, ILSA was extended for a period of five years.

Missile Analysis

Iran's acquisition of ballistic missiles began in the 1980s when, during the Iran–Iraq War, North Korea provided Iran with around 100 Scud–Bs and with facilities that enabled Iran to produce the Scuds indigenously.[48] During the early 1990s, Iran sought to acquire ballistic missile capabilities that could be used for delivering nuclear weapons. It turned to China, Libya, and North Korea for missile systems and related technologies. In the early 1990s Iran reportedly discussed buying the 1,000-kilometer No Dong from North Korea.[49] On March 6, 1992, the United States imposed sanctions, under the missile non-proliferation provisions of the Arms Export Control and Export Administration Acts, against the Iranian Ministry of Defense and Armed Forces Logistics and against two North Korean entities for engaging in missile proliferation activities.

In June 1995, the press cited U.S. intelligence reports as evidence that "strongly implicate[d]" China in the transfer to Iran of equipment, materials, and scientific know-how that could be used in the manufacture of short-range ballistic missiles such as the Chinese M–9 and M–11.[50] China was believed to have transferred "dozens, perhaps hundreds, of missile guidance systems and computerized machine tools" to Iran, as well as rocket propellant ingredients that could be used in its current stockpile of short-range Scud–Mod Bs and Scud–Mod Cs, as well as on Scud variants that Iran might produce in the future.[51] In the final analysis, however, the United States did not find that China's missile transactions with Iran violated China's MTCR–related pledges and declined to impose MTCR-related sanctions against either China or Iran.[52] In 2001, however, the Department of Defense still determined that Chinese, along with Russian, "entities have continued to supply a wide variety of missile-related goods, technology and expertise to Iran."[53]

In 1996, it became clear that North Korea was exporting missile capabilities to Iran. As a result, the United States imposed sanctions on May 26, 1996, on the Iranian Ministry of Defense Armed Forces Logistics, the Iranian State Purchasing Office, and the Korea Mining Development Trading Bureau.[54] The precise nature of the offending transactions remains classified, but U.S. officials indicated that North Korea had sold missile components, equipment, and materials to Iran, although not complete missiles, production technology, or major subsystems.

During 1997, U.S. press reports quoted U.S. and Israeli intelligence findings that Russian enterprises, including cash-strapped Russian technical institutes, research facilities, and defense-production companies, were transferring to Iran Russian SS–4 MRBM technologies. According to these assessments, Iran hoped to employ these SS–4 MRBM technologies to develop two Iranian derivatives of the 1,000-kilometer-range North Korean No Dong missile. The first indigenous missile, the Shahab III, is projected to have a range between 1,300 and 1,500 kilometers. The second such missile is the Shahab IV, which has a 2,000-kilometer range and a 1,000-kilogram payload.

In September 1997 then–Vice President Al Gore raised the issue in Moscow with Prime Minister Viktor Chernomyrdin, as a result of which there was a visible decline in Russian assistance until the summer of 1998.[55] Nevertheless, Russian assistance remains critical to Iran's development of the Shahab series, helping Iran "to save years in its development of the Shahab III"; further it "could significantly accelerate the pace of its ballistic missile development program."[56] The Shahab III was tested in July 1998, July 2000, and September 2000. United States officials believe that only the September 1998 test was successful.[57] In February 1999 Iran said that it was testing the Shahab IV but that it would be used only as a satellite-launch vehicle.[58] Iran has publicly mentioned plans for a Shahab V, with a possible range of 6,000 kilometers.

The U.S. intelligence community has indicated that Iran will likely continue development of IRBM and ICBM systems by initially testing them as space launch vehicle programs. The 2001 National Intelligence Estimate indicated uniform agreement among U.S. intelligence agencies that "Iran *could* attempt to launch an ICBM/SLV about mid-decade although most agencies believe Iran is *likely* to take until the last half of the decade to do so" (emphasis in original).[59] It was also noted that one agency does not find it likely that Iran will achieve a successful test of an ICBM before 2015.

Nevertheless, the 2001 NIE reiterates the importance of the acquisition of complete systems or major subsystems from North Korea or Russia in speeding Iranian ICBM flight-test capability. Thus, even in the aftermath of September 11, the Bush administration is determined to pressure Russia on the issue of Iranian nuclear and missile assistance.[60]

Biological and Chemical Weapon Analysis

Iran's biological weapon program was launched in the early 1980s during the Iran–Iraq War. Despite its ratification of the Biological Weapons Convention in 1973, Iran has allegedly pursued biological weapons under the guise of its extensive biotechnology and pharmaceutical industries. According to U.S. officials, "The Iranian military has used medical, education, and scientific research organizations for many aspects of BW procurement, research, and production."[61] Iran is also actively pursuing dual-use equipment and technology through contacts with Russia and other entities.

During the Iran–Iraq War, Iraq employed chemical weapons against Iranian troops. The primary agents used were mustard gas and the nerve agent tabun. Approximately 50,000 Iranian casualties were reported.[62] In March 1986, U.N. Secretary General Javier Perez de Cuellar formally accused Iraq of using chemical weapons against Iran in violation of the 1925 Geneva Protocol. Iran began its chemical weapon program to deter Iraq's use of chemical weapons. Allegedly, Iran also employed chemical weapons late in the war, but with less success than the Iraqis had.

Continued research on nerve agents presumably continues, as well as the active pursuit of Russian and Chinese expertise to improve chemical precursor production. Iran ratified the Chemical Weapons Convention in 1997.

NOTES

1. Geoffrey Kemp, ed., "Iran's Nuclear Options," in *Iran's Nuclear Weapons Options: Issues and Analysis* (Washington, D.C.: Nixon Center, January 2001), p. 3.

2. U.S. Department of Defense (DOD), *Proliferation: Threat and Response*, January 2001, p. 34.

3. Ibid., p. 35.

4. Shai Feldman and Yiftah Shapir, eds., *The Middle East Military Balance 2000–2001*, Harvard University's BCSIA Studies in International Security and Tel Aviv University's Jaffee Center for Strategic Studies (Cambridge: MIT Press, 2001), p. 134.

5. U.S. DOD, *Proliferation: Threat and Response*, p. 38.

6. Richard Speier, "Iranian Missiles and Payloads," in *Iran's Nuclear Weapons Options: Issues and Analysis*, ed. Geoffrey Kemp (Washington, D.C.: Nixon Center, January 2001), pp. 57–58.

7. U.S. DOD, *Proliferation: Threat and Response*, p. 38.

8. Speier, "Iranian Missiles and Payloads."

9. Ibid.

10. John Bolton, Under Secretary for Arms Control and International Security, "Remarks to the Fifth Biological Weapons Convention," Geneva, Switzerland, November 19, 2001.

11. Tehran Domestic Service, "Hashemi-Rafsanjani Speaks on the Future of the IRGC Iranian Revolutionary Guards Corps," October 6, 1988, in FBIS–NES, October 7, 1988, p. 52.

12. Geoffrey Kemp, Carnegie International Non-Proliferation Conference, June 2001.

13. Kenneth Katzman, "Iran: U.S. Policy and Options," CRS report for Congress, January 14, 2000.

14. Kemp, "Iran's Nuclear Options," p. 14.

15. Ibid.

16. Shai Feldman, *Nuclear Weapons and Arms Control in the Middle East*, Harvard University's BCSIA Studies in International Studies (Cambridge: MIT Press, 1997), p. 47.

17. Testimony of John Holum, director, Arms Control and Disarmament Agency, before the Subcommittee on International Operations and Human Rights, House International Relations Committee, on the Fiscal Year 1998 Authorization for ACDA, March 5, 1997.

18. Aluf Benn, "A New Outlook on Iran's Nuclear Threat," *Ha'aretz*, November 27, 2001.

19. U.S. DOD, *Proliferation: Threat and Response.*

20. Mark Hibbs, "IAEA Explores Iran's Intentions, Minus Evidence of Weapons Drive," *Nucleonics Week*, February 13, 1992, p. 12; "Atomic Team Reports on Iran Probe," *Washington Post*, February 14, 1992; Steve Coll, "Nuclear Inspectors Check Sites in Iran," *Washington Post*, November 20, 1993; Hibbs, "IAEA Says It Found No Non-Peaceful Activity during Recent Iran Visit," *Nucleonics Week*, December 16, 1993, p. 11.

21. Feldman, *Nuclear Weapons.*

22. Ibid.

23. Feldman and Shapir, *The Middle East Military Balance.*

24. U.S. DOD, *Proliferation: Threat and Response*, p. 35.

25. Feldman, *Nuclear Weapons*, p. 48.

26. U.S. DOD, *Proliferation: Threat and Response*, p. 35.

27. Akbar Etemad, "Iran," in Harald Mueller, *European Non-Proliferation Policy* (Oxford: Oxford University Press, 1987). Etemad was chair of the Atomic Energy Organization of Iran under the shah.

28. Mark Hibbs, "U.S. Officials Say Iran Is Pursuing Fissile Material Production Research," *Nuclear Fuel*, December 7, 1992, p. 5; "Iran and the Bomb," *Frontline*, PBS Network, April 13, 1993; Hibbs, "German–U.S. Nerves Frayed over Nuclear Ties to Iran," *Nuclear Fuel*, March 14, 1994, p. 9; Hibbs, "Sharif University Activity Continues Despite IAEA Visit, Bonn Agency Says," *Nuclear Fuel*, March 28, 1994, p. 10; Elaine Sciolino, "Iran Says It Plans 10 Nuclear Plants But No Atom Arms," *New York Times*, May 16, 1995.

29. Thomas Lippman, "Stepped-up Nuclear Effort Renews Alarm about Iran," *Washington Post*, April 17, 1995; Mark Hibbs, "Investigators Deny Iran Smuggled Weapons Material from Germany," *Nucleonics Week*, February 1, 1996, p. 14.

30. Anthony Cordesman, "Iran and Nuclear Weapons," Center for Strategic and International Security, Background paper for the Senate Foreign Relations Committee, March 24, 2000, p. 32. Available at www.csis.org/stratassessment/reports/iranbackground032100.pdf.

31. Feldman and Shapir, eds., *The Middle East Military Balance*, p. 54.

32. Feldman, *Nuclear Weapons*, pp. 52–53.

33. Mark Hibbs, "No Plutonium Smuggling Cases Confirmed by IAEA since Munich," *Nucleonics Week*, March 6, 1997, p. 13.

34. "Iran Confirms Nuclear Cooperation with China," *United Press International*, November 6, 1991; R. Jeffrey Smith, "China-Iran Nuclear Tie Long Known," *Washington Post*, October 31, 1991.

35. Mark Hibbs, "Iran Sought Sensitive Nuclear Supplies from Argentina, China," *Nucleonics Week*, September 24, 1992, p. 2; Steve Coll, "U.S. Halted Nuclear Bid by Iran," *Washington Post*, November 17, 1992.

36. "Source: Nuclear Plans with China Near Collapse," *Al-Sharq Al-Awsat* (London), May 21, 1995, in FBIS–NES–95–099, May 23, 1995, p. 54; "Moscow To Proceed with Nuclear Deal with Iran," *ITAR–TASS* (Moscow), October 2, 1995, in FBIS–SOV–95–191, October 3, 1995, p. 22; Mark Hibbs, "Iran, China Said To Disagree Only on Site Selection for New PWRs," *Nucleonics Week*, October 5, 1995, p. 1; "China/Iran: Reactor Plans Shelved—Again?" *Nucleonics Week*, January 11, 1996, p. 9.

37. U.S. DOD, *Proliferation: Threat and Response*, 1996, p. 14.

38. Ibid., p. 36.

39. "Clinton's Iran Embargo Initiative Impedes U.S. NPT Diplomatic Effort," *Nuclear Fuel*, May 8, 1995, p. 6; Mark Hibbs, "Countering U.S. Claims, Moscow Says Iran Nuclear Program Is Peaceful," *Nucleonics Week*, February 9, 1995, p. 4; Hibbs, "Iran's Arab Neighbors Don't Believe U.S. Has Proof of Weapons Ambitions," *Nucleonics Week*, April 20, 1995, p. 10.

40. U.S. DOD, *Proliferation: Threat and Response*, p. 35.

41. Benn, "Iran's Nuclear Threat."

42. Mark Hibbs, "Russia-Iran Bushehr PWR Project Shows Little Concrete Progress," *Nucleonics Week*, September 26, 1996, p. 3.

43. Kenneth Katzman, "Iran Arms and Technology Acquisition," Congressional Research Service Report, January 2001, p. 13.

44. Michael Eisenstadt, "Halting Russian Aid to Iran's Nuclear and Ballistic Programs," *PolicyWatch*, September 25, 1997.

45. For a detailed look at the sanctions adopted see Kenneth Katzman, "Iran: U.S. Policies and Options," CRS Report for Congress, January 14, 2000, pp. 11–14.

46. "Russia Firm on Iran Reactor Sale; Could Mean Loss of U.S. Aid," *Post-Soviet Nuclear and Defense Monitor*, November 17, 1995, p. 4.

47. "President Clinton Says Aid to Russia Critical to National Security," *Post-Soviet Nuclear and Defense Monitor*, May 31, 1996, p. 1.

48. Katzman, "Iran," p. 18.

49. Ibid.

50. R. Jeffrey Smith, "Iran's Missile Technology Linked to China, Report Says," *Washington Post*, June 17, 1995; Barbara Opall, "U.S. Queries China on Iran," *Defense News*, June 19–25, 1995, p. 1.

51. Elaine Sciolino, "CIA Report Says Chinese Sent Iran Arms Components," *New York Times*, June 21, 1995; "Chinese Shipments Violate Controls," *Jane's Defence Weekly*, July 1, 1995, p. 3.

52. Katzman, "Iran," p. 16.

53. U.S. DOD, *Proliferation: Threat and Response*, p. 36.

54. Federal Register, June 28, 1996, p. 29785; "Daily on U.S. Government Notice of Sanctions against DPRK," Chosun Ilbo (Seoul), June 30, 1996, in FBIS–EAS–96–127, July 3, 1996.

55. Robert Gallucci, "Iran-Russia Missile Cooperation: A U.S. View," in Joseph Cirincione, ed., *Repairing the Regime: Preventing the Spread of Weapons of Mass Destruction* (New York: Routledge, 2000), p. 187.

56. Testimony of John Lauder, director, DCI Nonproliferation Center, before the Senate Committee on Foreign Relations on Russian Proliferation to Iran's Weapons of Mass Destruction and Missile Programs, October 5, 2000.

57. Katzman, "Iran," p. 7.

58. Ibid.

59. National Intelligence Council, "Foreign Missile Developments and the Ballistic Missile Threat through 2015," December, 2001, p. 12.

60. Carol Giacomo, "U.S. To Pressure Russia over Iranian Relations," *Reuters*, December 5, 2001.

61. U.S. Arms Control and Disarmament Agency, *Adherence to and Compliance with Arms Control Agreements*, May 30, 1995, p. 16, as cited in Milton Leitenberg, "Biological Weapons Arms Control," PRAC Paper 16, Center for International and Security Studies at Maryland, May 1996.

62. Office of Technology Assessment, *Proliferation of Weapons of Mass Destruction: Assessing the Risks*, August 1993, p. 10.

Table 15.1: **Iran's Missile Programs**

Missile	Status	Range (km)	Payload (kg)	Suppliers	Notes
M–7 (CSS–8)	O	150	190	PRC	Modified SA–2
Scud–B	O/U	300	1,000	Libya/ Syria	300+ produced
Scud–C	O	500	700	DPRK	60+ produced
Shahab III	O	1,300	750	I/DPRK	From No Dong; tested 22 July 1998
Shahab IV	D	2,000	?	I/Russia	From Russian SS–4
Shahab V	D?	3,000–5,500?	?	I/Russia	

Table 15.2: **Iran: Nuclear Infrastructure**

Name/Location of Facility	Type/ Status	IAEA Safeguards
POWER REACTORS		
Bushehr I	Light-water, LEU, 1,000-MWe; damaged by Iraqi air strikes (1987, 1988). Currently under construction.	Planned
Bushehr II	Light-water, LEU, 1,300-MWe; damaged by Iraqi air strikes (1987, 1988). Facility remains unfinished, and project is currently suspended.	Planned
RESEARCH REACTORS		
Tehran	Light-water, HEU, 5-MWt; operating[1]	Yes
Esfahan	Miniature neutron source reactor (MNSR), 900 grams of HEU, 27-kW operating	Yes
URANIUM ENRICHMENT		
Tehran	Alleged uranium centrifuge research program, Sharif University of Technology	No
REPROCESSING (PLUTONIUM EXTRACTION)		
Tehran	Laboratory-scale hot cells; may not be operational[2]	No
URANIUM PROCESSING		
Yazd Province	Discovery of uranium deposits announced in 1990	N/A
Tehran	Uranium-ore concentration facility; incapacitated.	N/A
Esfahan	Planned uranium conversion plant that could produce UF_4, UF_6, and UO_2. China cancelled its assistance in this area in 1997.	Yes

Abbreviations

HEU	highly enriched uranium	MWt	millions of watts of thermal output
LEU	low-enriched uranium	kWt	thousands of watts of thermal output
MWe	millions of watts of electrical output	N/A	not applicable

NOTES

1. The reactor is located at the Amirabad Technical College, also called Tehran Nuclear Research Center. See "Iran's Weapons of Mass Destruction," *Jane's Intelligence Review*, Special Report No. 6, 1995, p. 10.

2. See David Albright, "An Iranian Bomb?" *Bulletin of the Atomic Scientists*, July/August 1995, p. 25, and "Iran's Weapons of Mass Destruction," *Jane's Intelligence Review*, p. 11.

University of Tehran *U.S.-supplied, Argentine-fueled 5-MWt research reactor, subject to IAEA inspection.*
Sharif University of Technology *Alleged experimental centrifuge uranium enrichment program, and possible research on plutonium separation.*

Esfahan Nuclear Research Center *Chinese-supplied mini research reactors and subcritical assemblies, subject to IAEA inspection. Possible location of nuclear-weapons design research.*

Civilian nuclear research reactors; first inspected by the IAEA in August 1997. The IAEA found no evidence of clandestine or undeclared military nuclear activity at these two facilities.

Yazd province, location of uranium deposits

Partially completed Bushehr 1 and 2 power reactors (1,000 MWe & 1,300 MWe respectively). Damaged during the Iran-Iraq War; construction of Bushehr 1 restarted with Russian assistance.

RUSSIA

KAZAKHSTAN

Aral Sea

Black Sea

GEORGIA

Caspian Sea

UZBEKISTAN

ARMENIA   AZERBAIJAN

TURKEY

AZER.

■ *Bonab*
Ramsar ■

TURKMENISTAN

IRAQ

★ *Tehran*

IRAN

■ *Esfahan*

AFGHANISTAN

KUWAIT

■ *Bushehr*

PAKISTAN

OMAN

Persian Gulf

Gulf of Oman

QATAR   U.A.E.

BAHRAIN   OMAN

SAUDI ARABIA

Arabian Sea

0   400

Miles

YEMEN

Carnegie Endowment for International Peace, *Deadly Arsenals* (2002), **www.ceip.org**

CHAPTER 16

Iraq

Nuclear Weapon Capability

By mid-1997 the International Atomic Energy Agency believed that its dismantlement efforts, regular monitoring and verification efforts, and the damage from Operation Desert Storm had virtually incapacitated Iraq's nuclear weapons infrastructure.[1] United States and British air strikes in Operation Desert Fox during December 1998 inflicted additional damage on Iraq's missile production capabilities. Iraq's ambitions and accumulated nuclear technical expertise remain, however, and with them the capability to restart the program covertly. Without on-site inspectors it is difficult to ascertain the precise extent to which Saddam Hussein has been able to rebuild his nuclear weapon program. According to a U.S. Defense Department 2001 report, "Iraq would need five or more years and key foreign assistance" to rebuild its nuclear facilities to enrich sufficient uranium for a nuclear weapon.[2] Significantly, this time frame has not changed from the five to seven years estimated in the department's 1996 assessment.[3] The time will be considerably shortened if Baghdad acquires fissile material from foreign suppliers. Iraq's greatest asset is the two dozen nuclear scientists and engineers still in Iraq.[4] This expertise, combined with the absence of ground monitors and decreasing support for the U.N. sanctions regime, has led to heightened anxiety about Iraq's program. Iraq may have a workable design for a nuclear weapon, and thus the major obstacle is its acquiring fissile material. If Iraq were to acquire material from another country, it is possible that it could assemble a nuclear weapon in months.[5]

Missile Capability

Under the terms of U.N Security Council Resolution 687, Iraq is not allowed to possess missiles with a range that is beyond 150 kilometers. By the end of 1997, 817 of the 819 prohibited ballistic missiles had been accounted for.[6] Iraq continues to work on the liquid-propelled Al Samoud and the solid-propelled Ababil short-range ballistic missiles, both permitted under U.N. Resolution 687. In July 2000 Iraq successfully tested the Al Samoud, which has a range of 140 kilometers and carries a payload of 300 kilograms. These programs could allow Baghdad to develop technological improvements and an infrastructure that could be applied to a longer-range missile program. The Al Samoud could achieve a low-level operational capability in the near term, and Iraq's solid-propellant program may now be receiving a higher priority.[7] The December 1998 bombing damaged Iraq's ballistic missile infrastructure, but the country retains domestic expertise and sufficient infrastructure to support most missile component production. According to Scott Ritter, who headed the U.N. Special Commission on Iraq Concealment Unit, Iraq probably has between 5 and 25 missile assemblies and missile components for up to 25 missiles salvaged from destroyed stockpiles.[8] The CIA believes that Iraq probably retains a small, covert force of Scud-type missiles.[9] There are no U.N. restrictions on Iraq's development of cruise missiles.

Biological and Chemical Weapon Capability

The absence of U.N. monitoring since 1998 has aroused concerns that Iraq may again have produced some biological warfare agents.[10] Iraq currently maintains numerous science and medical facilities furnished with dual-use equipment where potential biological warfare–related work could easily take place. According to U.N. estimates, Iraq possesses the technology and expertise to reconstitute an offensive biological weapon program within a few weeks or months.[11] Iraq's continual refusal to disclose any details about its biological weapon program has led U.S. officials to conclude that Baghdad maintains an active program, in spite of Iraq's ratification of the Biological Weapons Convention in 1991.[12] In the absence of further monitoring, the current status of the Iraqi chemical weapon program is also unknown. Iraq maintains the expertise to resume chemical agent production within a few weeks or months. However, to attain former levels of production, Iraq would need significant amounts of foreign assistance.

Strategic Context

Saddam Hussein wants Iraq to be the predominant power in the Middle East, and he sees weapons of mass destruction and a ballistic missile program as necessary to achieve that goal. In his strategic calculus, a nuclear bomb would provide him with the ultimate symbol of military power. He believes that it would have been a deterrent against the Coalition forces as the confrontation over Kuwait evolved in 1991.

Iraq's interest in preserving as many of its WMD–related capabilities as possible, in spite of U.N. resolutions, was reflected in its strategy of frustrating and hindering the U.N. inspection process throughout the 1990s, forgoing more than $120 billion in oil revenues, which is an indication of the price Iraq has been prepared to pay to keep as much of its weapon infrastructure as possible.[13]

Troubled relations with Iran have also contributed to the quest for weapons of mass destruction. During the Iran–Iraq War, Saddam Hussein increased pressure on his nuclear scientists to accelerate and expand the nuclear program. He wanted to draw the nuclear weapon program into the framework of the war, including the possibility of using radiation weapons along the border with Iran.[14] Relations with Iran continue to remain problematic. In April 2001, for example, Iran reportedly fired anywhere between 44 and 77 Scud–B missiles against the Mujaihaideen Khalk Organization, which is based in southern and eastern Iraq. Iraq characterized the "aggression" as a coordinated effort by Iran and Saudi Arabia.[15]

For Saddam, the nuclear bomb is a means to prevail in the long term against Iraq's rivals in the region, including Iran, Israel, and Turkey.[16] Israel's destruction of the Osiraq reactor only made Saddam more determined to acquire a nuclear capability. After the Osiraq attack, former Iraqi nuclear scientist Khidhir Hamza says, "We went from 500 people to 7,000 in a timeframe of five years. All done in secret."[17]

In the fall of 1998 Saddam Hussein grew in defiance, having succeeded in gaining sympathy in the Arab world and taking advantage of the sanction rift in the Security Council. By December 15, UNSCOM chief Richard Butler reported that "Iraq's conduct ensured that no progress was able to be made in the fields of disarmament."[18] Saddam Hussein refused to allow inspectors unfettered access inside Iraq without a firm commitment to lift all remaining sanctions. As a result, the standoff led to the withdrawal of all U.N. inspection–related personnel on December 16, 1998, followed by military action that night by the United States and the United Kingdom. U.N. Security Council Resolution 1284, adopted in December 1999, established a follow-up inspection regime in the form of the Monitoring, Verification, and Inspection Commission (UNMOVIC) to continue UNSCOM's work. It has not been able to begin its inspections because of Iraq's refusal to permit them until sanctions are lifted.

Without inspectors on the ground, it is difficult for the United Nations or United States to determine the current state of Iraq's WMD program.[19] The end of inspections has meant not only that there are no inspectors on the ground, but also that the automated video monitoring system that the United Nations installed at known and suspected WMD facilities is no longer operating.[20] The absence of any on-site monitoring in Iraq has raised concerns, therefore, that Saddam Hussein may have begun to reconstitute Iraq's WMD programs, including the nuclear weapon program.

Nuclear Analysis

Iraq ratified the Non-Proliferation Treaty on October 29, 1969, pledging not to manufacture nuclear weapons and agreeing to place all its nuclear materials and facilities under IAEA safeguards. Iraq violated its NPT obligations, however, by secretly pursuing a multi-billion-dollar nuclear weapon program. Iraq's near-term potential to develop nuclear weapons has been curtailed by the implementation of U.N. Security Council Resolution 687, adopted in April 1991, following Iraq's defeat in the 1991 Persian Gulf War. Operation Desert Storm and the inspection and dismantling efforts of the International Atomic Energy Agency, assisted by the U.N. Special Commission on Iraq, are believed to have left no weapons-capable fissile materials and no nuclear-weapons-related production facilities in Iraq. (Note that there is both natural uranium and LEU in Iraq under IAEA safeguards and that Iraq has allowed the IAEA to inspect these materials annually in accordance with its NPT safeguard obligations.)

Iraq's efforts to produce weapons-grade uranium used virtually every feasible uranium-enrichment process, including electromagnetic isotope separation, the use of gas centrifuges, chemical enrichment, gaseous diffusion, and laser isotope separation. The program was initiated in 1982, when the Iraqi authorities decided to abandon Iraq's nuclear reactor program after Israel's June 7, 1981, bombing of the Osiraq research reactor.[21] Until the Israeli attack, Iraq had chosen plutonium over highly enriched uranium as the preferred fissile material for its nuclear weapon program. The Osiraq research reactor, purchased from France in 1976, was unusually large and was therefore capable of irradiating uranium specimens to produce significant quantities of plutonium.[22]

Iraq's EMIS program went undetected because it did not rely on state-of-the-art, imported equipment whose acquisition might have given the effort away.[23] Indeed, the EMIS program might have remained hidden from the IAEA inspection teams but for the fact that it was revealed by an Iraqi nuclear engineer who had defected to U.S. forces after the war.[24] Iraq started its gas-centrifuge program for uranium enrichment later than its EMIS program. It relied heavily on foreign contractors who were willing to circumvent export controls and to sell classified design information on early Western-type centrifuges and high-tensile "maraging" steel for the manufacture of centrifuges.[25]

Iraqi scientists also organized secret attempts to produce and separate small quantities of plutonium in IAEA–safeguarded facilities at Tuwaitha. By 1991 they had acquired a rudimentary ability to separate plutonium, producing approximately 6 grams. Without any changes to the configuration of their radiochemical laboratory, the Iraqis would have been unable to separate more than 60 grams of plutonium a year, a quantity insufficient to produce the 5–8 kilograms needed for a first nuclear device.[26]

Weaponization

The Iraqis focused their efforts on developing an implosion-type weapon,[27] whose basic design involves surrounding a subcritical mass, or core, of fissile material (in this case, highly enriched uranium) with conventional high-explosive charges. The charges are uniformly detonated to compress the nuclear material into a supercritical configuration. Iraq's weaponization program was in its early stages at the time of the Gulf War. In spite of making progress in the high-explosive testing program, Iraqi scientists were still struggling to master the high-explosive charges that must be precisely fabricated in order to produce homogeneous shock waves against the core after ignition.[28]

Disclosures made by Lt. Gen. Hussein Kamel (former Iraqi minister of industry and military industrialization) after his defection to Jordan on August 8, 1995, prompted the Iraqi government to invite then–UNSCOM chair Rolf Ekeus and an IAEA delegation to Baghdad so that it could make new information available about Iraq's former nonconventional weapon activities that had allegedly been withheld by General Kamel. The discussions and subsequent inspections revealed that following the invasion of Kuwait in August 1990, Iraq had embarked on a stepped-up program to develop a nuclear device by extracting weapons-grade material from safeguarded research reactor fuel.[29]

Launched in September 1990, this program provided for such measures as the accelerated design and fabrication of the implosion package, the selection and construction of a test site, and development of a delivery vehicle. The deadline for producing a weapon under this program apparently was April 1991.[30] The program was cut short, however, by the 1991 Gulf War.

The IAEA concluded that the original plan of the Iraqi nuclear weapon program, as set out in 1988, was to produce a small arsenal of weapons, with the first one to be ready in 1991. While the weaponization team made significant progress in designing a workable device, the original deadline could not have been met because progress in the production of HEU—using the EMIS and gas-centrifuge processes—had lagged far behind. The fact that domestically produced HEU would not have been available for some time led Iraq to modify the objective of the original plan and to undertake the accelerated program.

In its October 1996 assessment the IAEA stated that the "industrial infrastructure which Iraq had set up to produce and weaponize special nuclear material has been destroyed." However, the agency was aware "that the know-how and expertise acquired by Iraqi scientists and engineers could provide an adequate base for reconstituting a nuclear-weapons-oriented program."[31]

Sanctions

U.N. Resolution 1284, adopted in December 1999, calls for the streamlining of economic sanctions and for their eventual suspension once UNMOVIC has reported that Iraq is cooperating with U.N. resolutions on dismantling its WMD.[32] This resolution remains the legal basis for continuing to control Iraq's assets, but Iraq has refused to allow UNMOVIC on the ground, insisting that the sanctions should be lifted since it has disarmed to the extent called for by U.N. resolutions.[33] U.N. Resolution 1284 places no limits on the volume of petroleum that Iraq can export for humanitarian needs.[34]

While the sanctions against Iraq have not unraveled altogether, support in the Arab world and from European allies for them has eroded, and China and Russia are eager to resume economic ties with Iraq. An Anglo-American effort in the summer of 2001 to restructure the oil-for-food program failed to receive the support of the Security Council. While lifting most restrictions on Iraq's imports of civilian goods, the proposed resolution sought to diminish Saddam Hussein's ability to circumvent the U.N. escrow account; to tighten the embargo on dual-use technology that could aid Iraq's WMD program; and to continue the blockade on the sale of conventional arms.[35] With Russia set to veto the resolution, the Security Council voted, instead, to continue the existing oil-for-food program.[36]

Disturbing images of the effects of ten years of sanctions against Iraq, combined with escalating violence in Israel and the West Bank, have decisively shifted the sympathies of the "Arab street" to the once-pariah regime of Saddam Hussein. With the backdrop of a collapsing Middle East peace process, sympathy for the Palestinian and Iraqi people has worked in Saddam Hussein's favor, even after September 11. Arab governments have found that their publics are in no mood to continue isolating Saddam Hussein. The United States has recognized that its political success in pursuing its policy toward Iraq is, at least in part, connected to the success of its policy in the Levant.[37]

In public, at least, these governments, including U.S. allies in the region, have begun to be circumspect in their support of the policy of sanctions and no-fly zones. Among the conservative Arab Gulf states, all except Saudi Arabia and Kuwait have flouted the sanctions and shown an interest in resuming ties with Saddam Hussein's regime. Diplomatic and economic relations between even Iraq and Syria have been restored for the first time since the 1990 Gulf War, opening an oil pipeline that adds to Baghdad revenues from illegal oil sales.[38] Iraq also has an oil exchange program with Jordan and Turkey. The United States hopes to reverse this trend with a new hard-line policy to remove Saddam Hussein from power. By early 2002, it appeared that military action was all but certain, hampered only by the continuing conflict in Afghanistan and near-war in Israel.

Missile Analysis

Before the 1991 Gulf War, Iraq had extensive short-range ballistic missile capabilities, including a stockpile of Soviet-supplied, single-stage liquid-fueled Scud–Bs (having a 300-kilometer-range and a 1,000-kilogram payload) and three indigenously produced variants of the Scud–B (the Al Hussein, the Al Hussein Short, and the Al Hijarah) all with an approximate range of 600–650 kilometers. Iraq was developing a domestic manufacturing capability for these modified Scuds, which included a sophisticated missile technology base to reverse-engineer the systems. According to Ambassador Rolf Ekeus, Iraq had the capability to produce Scud-type engines, airframes, and warheads.[39] It had also undertaken a joint venture with Argentina and Egypt to develop a two-stage solid-fueled missile with an intended range of 750–1,000 kilometers, the Badr 2000.[40] UNSCOM concluded that no complete Badr 2000 missile was ever produced in Iraq. (The Argentine version was called Condor.) Baghdad also had plans for a 2,000-kilometer-range missile, called the Tammouz I,[41] which was to have a Scud-derivative first stage and an SA–2 sustainer as the second stage.

Until the Gulf War, Iraq had focused on ballistic missiles as the only truly practicable delivery system for its nuclear weapons. Iraq was apparently pursuing three options. The first option was tailored to the longer-term plan, initiated in 1988, of producing the first of a number of nuclear weapons in 1991. The delivery vehicle would have been based on a modification of the Al Abid satellite launcher and would have had the capability to deliver a 1-metric-ton warhead to a distance of almost 1,200 kilometers.[42] However, since work on the engines for the system did not begin until April 1989, it would not have been ready until 1993. The second option, a fallback position, would have been to put the nuclear warhead on an unmodified Al Hussein missile, which would have limited the range to 300 kilometers. The third option, initiated in August or September 1990 under the accelerated program, was to produce "a derivative of the Al Hussein/Al Abbas short-range missile designed to deliver a warhead of one metric ton to 650 kilometers and to accommodate a nuclear package (80 centimeters in diameter)."[43] The estimated timeframe for completing the third option was six months.

Under the terms of U.N. Security Council Resolution 687, Iraq was obliged to eliminate ballistic missiles with ranges exceeding 150 kilometers. Significantly, Resolution 687 places no limits on Iraqi missile payloads, and range-payload tradeoffs allow missiles with lighter warheads to travel to greater ranges, as Iraq demonstrated in its doubling of the range of the Soviet-supplied Scud missile type.[44]

In early July 1991 UNSCOM destroyed Iraq's known 48 ballistic missiles that had a range capability greater than 150 kilometers and dismantled a large part of the related infrastructure. However, in March 1992 Iraq admitted that it had withheld 85 missiles from UNSCOM's controlled destruction. Iraq had destroyed those missiles in mid-July and October 1991 in a secret operation (after the official destruction of the 48 missiles). UNSCOM inspectors have confirmed that most of Iraq's remaining Scud-based missile force was eliminated, although the clandestine character of Iraq's destruction of the 85 missiles showed that it was desperately trying to preserve missiles and missile components.[45] Furthermore, after Lt. Gen. Hussein Kamel's defection, Iraqi officials admitted that Iraq had carried out research and development work on advanced rocket engines and that it had manufactured rocket engines "made of indigenously produced or imported parts and without the cannibalization of the imported Soviet-made Scud engines."[46]

By early 1995 UNSCOM believed that it had a fairly complete overview of the facilities, equipment, and materials used in Iraq's former missile program. However, because Iraq repeatedly withheld and falsified information, UNSCOM had unresolved issues, partly regarding past research and development activities and partly regarding the numerical accounting of missiles, warheads, and supporting and auxiliary equipment.[47] UNSCOM also found itself in disagreement with the United States over whether all of Iraq's illegal missiles had been accounted for. The U.S. intelligence community believed that Iraq may have successfully hidden up to a hundred such missiles.[48]

In December 1995 UNSCOM reported that some elements of Iraq's final missile declaration were still unaccounted for, including ten missile engine systems that Iraq claimed it had destroyed.[49] Neither was UNSCOM satisfied that it had accounted for the indigenously produced warheads and of "such major components for operational missiles as guidance and control systems, liquid propellant fuels and ground support equipment."[50]

UNSCOM was also concerned that Iraq had resumed the foreign procurement of banned missile technologies and components.[51] Iraq defended those procurement activities as being intended for the legal Ababil–100 missile program. Yet Iraq was ordering the import of equipment and materials without making the required notifications to UNSCOM; that importation would violate the U.N. sanctions in place.[52]

In October 1997 UNSCOM finally reported that it had made significant progress in the missile area, accounting for 817 of the 819 missiles that Iraq had imported from the Soviet Union before the end of 1988. UNSCOM analyzed the remnants of those missiles that Iraq unilaterally destroyed in July and October 1991 and was able to verify that 83 engines of the 85 declared missiles had in fact been destroyed.[53]

Biological and Chemical Weapon Analysis

The United Nations Special Commission in Iraq was created to supervise the destruction of Iraq's biological and chemical weapon and production facilities, pursuant to U.N. Security Council Resolution 687, and to monitor long-term related activities to prevent their reconstruction. In 1991 the Iraqi government declared that it did "not possess any biological weapons or related items."[54] UNSCOM's findings, strengthened by information obtained in 1995 as a result of the Kamel defection, eventually revealed that Iraq's BW program was well developed and highly managed, encompassing all aspects of biological weapon development from research to weaponization.

Until August 1990 the Iraqi BW capability had been expanding and diversifying at a steady pace. The biological weapon program included a broad range of agents and delivery systems. Pathogens produced by the Iraqi program included both lethal agents (e.g., anthrax, botulinum toxin, and ricin) and incapacitating agents (e.g., aflatoxin, mycotoxins, hemorrhagic conjunctivitis virus, and rotavirus). Documents discovered by UNSCOM indicated that Iraq had produced 8,500 liters of anthrax, 20,000 liters of botulinum toxin, 2,200 liters of aflatoxin, and the biological agent ricin.[55] Iraq conducted research to examine the effects of combining biological and chemical agents and also pursued anti-plant agents, such as wheat cover smut.[56]

Biological Weapons

The Iraqi BW program explored and developed a broad range of weapon delivery systems, including aerial bombs, rockets, missiles, and spray tanks. In December 1990 Iraq began the large-scale weaponization of biological agents. More than 160 R–400 aerial bombs and 25 600-kilometer-range Al Hussein missiles were filled with aflatoxin, anthrax, and botulinum toxin. The missiles were deployed in January 1991 to four sites for the duration of the Gulf War.[57]

UNSCOM repeatedly claimed that Iraq had failed to provide a full and correct account of its biological weapon program. Despite its monitoring activities, UNSCOM remained concerned that Iraq may have retained a stock of biological weapons and related manufacturing capabilities as late as 1997. Iraq repeatedly blocked or hindered a number of UNSCOM inspections, culminating in a standoff with the United Nations in late October 1997. Iraq unilaterally ended UNSCOM weapon inspections and monitoring in December 1998; UNSCOM was disbanded shortly thereafter.

Chemical Weapons

In March 1986 U.N. Secretary General Javier Perez de Cuellar formally accused Iraq of using chemical weapons against Iran. Iraq allegedly had used chemical weapons, including mustard and nerve gases, during the Iran–Iraq War, resulting in approximately 50,000 Iranian casualties.[58] Iraq had also used chemical weapons—on its own Kurdish populations in northern Iraq. The CW attack on the city of Halabja on March 16, 1988, has been described as "the largest-scale chemical weapon attack against a civilian population in modern times."[59] During the attack, multiple chemical agents—mustard gas, tabun, sarin, and VX—were delivered by aerial bombs. The exact number of Kurdish casualties is unknown but it is speculated to be high.

Inspections by the United Nations revealed that before the Gulf War, Iraq maintained one of the most extensive chemical weapon capabilities in the developing world. The Iraqi production of chemical weapons began in the early 1980s and continued until December 1990. Iraq had produced sufficient quantities of chemical precursors for almost 500 metric tons of the nerve agent VX. Hundreds of metric tons of tabun, sarin, and the blister agent mustard gas were also produced.[60] Iraq weaponized mortar shells, artillery shells, grenades, aerial bombs, and rockets for chemical use. It also deployed 50 Al Hussein missiles equipped with potent chemical warheads as part of its active forces.

Reportedly, Saddam Hussein fully intended to use chemical weapons and gave local commanders the authority to use them at their discretion. Various explanations have been offered as to why Iraq did not launch a chemical or biological weapon during the war. One is that just before the outbreak of the war, President George Bush vowed that "the American people would demand the strongest possible response . . . and [Iraq] will pay a terrible price" for the use of chemical or biological weapons against the Coalition forces.[61] Another interpretation holds that the U.S. decision to halt the ground war after only four days was influenced by concerns that Iraq might use chemical or biological weapons if Coalition forces closed in on Baghdad. In 1996 Iraqi officials indicated to UNSCOM that they considered their missile-based biological and chemical weapons to be "strategic" capabilities, for potential use against cities in nearby countries. After the Gulf War, allegations of exposure to chemical and biological agents surfaced. Ultimately, nearly 60,000 veterans reported medical problems, prompting an investigation into the so-called Gulf War Syndrome.[62] Research by the U.S. Department of Defense failed to diagnose the problems as symptoms of biological or chemical exposure.

After the Gulf War, UNSCOM, as the U.N.–mandated inspection team, began the detection and destruction of Iraq's chemical weapon stockpiles and production facilities. United Nations specialists destroyed more than 480,000 liters of chemical agents and 1.8 million liters of chemical precursors in the Iraqi arsenal.[63] Because of the size of the Iraqi program, however, it is widely believed that significant quantities of chemical agents and precursors remain stored in secret depots. United Nations officials have publicly expressed their doubts that the entire Iraqi stockpile of chemical weapons was found. Iraq's interest in preserving as many of its biological and chemical weapon capabilities as possible, in spite of U.N. resolutions, was reflected in its strategy of frustrating and hindering the U.N. inspection process. Iraq also repeatedly attempted to import proscribed equipment and tried to hide chemical agents, munitions, and hardware. As a result, UNSCOM reported to the Security Council that "the Commission has serious concerns that a full accounting and disposal of Iraq's holding of prohibited items has not been made."[64] Rough estimates conclude that Iraq may have retained up to 600 metric tons of agents, including mustard gas, VX, and sarin. Approximately 25,000 rockets and 15,000 artillery shells with chemical agents also remain unaccounted for.[65] Iraq is not a state party to the Chemical Weapons Convention.

NOTES

1. Barbara Crossette, "Iraqis Still Defying Arms Ban, Departing U.N. Official Says," *New York Times*, June 25, 1997. Also see Evelyn Leopold, "France Says IAEA Should Close Nuclear File on Iraq," *Reuters*, October 17, 1997.

2. U.S. Department of Defense (DOD), *Proliferation Threat and Response*, January 2001, p. 40.

3. U.S. DOD, *Proliferation Threat and Response*, January 1996.

4. Khidhir Hamza with Jeff Stein, *Saddam's Bombmaker: The Terrifying Inside Story of The Iraqi Nuclear and Biological Weapons Agenda* (New York: Scribner, 2000). Hamza made these comments at a Carnegie Non-Proliferation Roundtable, November 2, 2000.

5. ISIS (Institute for Science and International Security), "Military Strikes in Iraq: Inspections, Sanctions Must Stay in Place To Prevent Nuclear Weapons Program Reconstitution," press release, December 17, 1998, quoted in "Inspecting Iraq," in Joseph Cirincione, ed., *Repairing the Regime: Preventing the Spread of Weapons of Mass Destruction* (New York: Routledge, 2000), p. 183.

6. "Inspecting Iraq," in Cirincione, *Repairing the Regime*, p. 181.

7. Central Intelligence Agency, *Unclassified Report to Congress on the Acquisition of Technology relating to Weapons of Mass Destruction and Advanced Conventional Munitions, January 1 through June 30, 2001*. Released January 2002. Available at www.cia.gov/cia/publications/bian/bian_jan_2002.htm.

8. Scott Ritter, *Endgame* (New York: Simon and Schuster, 1999), p. 217, quoted in "Inspecting Iraq," in Cirincione, *Repairing the Regime*, p. 181.

9. CIA, *Unclassified Report to Congress*.

10. U.S. DOD, *Proliferation Threat and Response*, January 2001, p. 40.

11. Ibid.

12. John Bolton, Under Secretary for Arms Control and International Security, "Remarks to the Fifth Biological Weapons Convention RevCon Meeting," Geneva, Switzerland, November 19, 2001.

13. Rick Marshall, "Ekeus: Weapons of Mass Destruction of Higher Value to Iraq Than Oil," *USIS Washington File*, June 10, 1997.

14. Hamza, Carnegie Proliferation Roundtable, November 2, 2000. Available at www.ceip.org/npp.

15. Amin Tarzi and Darby Parliament, "Missile Messages: Iran Strikes MKO Bases in Iraq," *Nonproliferation Review*, summer 2001, pp. 125–133.

16. Hamza, Carnegie.

17. Ibid.

18. "Inspecting Iraq," in Cirincione, *Repairing the Regime*, p. 181.

19. CIA, *Unclassified Report to Congress*.

20. Ibid.

21. IAEA, *Report on the Fourth IAEA On-site Inspection in Iraq under Security Council Resolution 687*, S/22986, August 28, 1991, p. 5.

22. Rodney Jones and Mark McDonough, with Toby Dalton and Gregory Koblentz, *Tracking Nuclear Proliferation: A Guide in Maps and Charts, 1998* (Washington, D.C.: Carnegie Endowment for International Peace, 1998), pp. 187–194.

23. IAEA, *Report on the Fourth IAEA On-site Inspection*, p. 6; and IAEA, *Report on the Seventh IAEA On-site Inspection*, S/23215, November 14, 1991, annex 4, p. 4.

24. "Iraqi Defector," *Associated Press*, June 14, 1991; R. Jeffrey Smith, "Iraqi Nuclear Program Due Further Inspections," *Washington Post*, June 14, 1991.

25. For descriptions of the Iraqi gas centrifuge program, see IAEA, *Report on the Fourth On-site Inspection*, pp. 3, 9–13; IAEA, *Report on the Seventh On-site Inspection*, pp. 17, 19, and 21, annex 4, pp. 5–10; David Albright and Mark Hibbs, "Iraq's Bomb: Blueprints and Artifacts," *Bulletin of the Atomic Scientists, January/February 1993*, pp. 39–40; Albright and Hibbs, "Iraq's Shop-till-You-Drop Nuclear Program," *Bulletin of the Atomic Scientists*, January/February 1993, pp. 27–37; Albright and Hibbs, "Iraq: Supplier-Spotting," *Bulletin of the Atomic Scientists*, January/February 1993, pp. 8–9.

26. IAEA, *Report on the Fourth On-site Inspection*, pp. 17–19; also see *Report on the Seventh On-site Inspection*, pp. 23 and 27; IAEA, *IAEA Inspections and Iraq's Nuclear Capabilities*, IAEA/PI/A35E, April 1992.

27. See IAEA, *Report on the Eighth On-site Inspection*, p. 15; and IAEA, *Report on the Eleventh IAEA*, S/23947, May 22, 1992, p. 20.

28. IAEA, *First Report on the Sixth IAEA On-site Inspection in Iraq under Security Council Resolution 687 (1991)*, S/23122, October 8, 1991, p. 4; IAEA, *Report on the Seventh On-site Inspection*, pp. 8, 9, 13.

29. IAEA, *Eighth Report of the Director General of the International Atomic Energy Agency on the Implementation of the Agency's Plan for Future Ongoing Monitoring and Verification of Iraq's Compliance with Paragraph 12 of Resolution 687 (1991)*, S/1995/844, October 6, 1995; IAEA, *Report on the Twenty-Eighth IAEA On-site Inspection in Iraq*; IAEA, *Report on the Twenty-Ninth IAEA On-site Inspection in Iraq Under Security Council Resolution 687 (1991)*, S/1996/14, January 10, 1996.

30. Mark Hibbs, "Experts Say Iraq Could Not Meet Bomb Deadline Even with Diversion"; IAEA, *Report on the Twenty-Eighth On-site Inspection*, p. 14; and briefing by Ambassador Rolf Ekeus, Hearings on Global Proliferation, p. 99.

31. IAEA, *Second Consolidated Report of the Director General of the International Atomic Energy Agency under Paragraph 16 of Resolution 1051 (1996)*, S/1996/833, p. 11.

32. Morton Halperin and Geoffrey Kemp, *A Report on U.S. Policy Options toward Iraq* (Washington, D.C.: Nixon Center, June 2001). Available at www.nixoncenter.org/publications/iraqpolicy.htm.

33. "Iraq Resumes WMD Activities, New York Times Reports," Carnegie Analysis, January 22, 2001. Available at www.ceip.org/npp.

34. U.S. DOD, *Proliferation: Threat and Response*, January 2001, p. 39.

35. Halperin and Kemp, *U.S. Policy Options toward Iraq*; and Robert Windrem and Linda Fasulo, "Sanctions Fail To Check Iraqi Military," *MSNBC.com*, August 14, 2001.

36. Colum Lynch, "Russia Threatens Veto of U.N. Iraq Resolution," *Washington Post*, June 26, 2001.

37. Janine Zacharia, "U.S. Pressing Israel To Begin Counting," *Jerusalem Post*, July, 27, 2001.

38. "Iraq and Syria Sign Economic Accords," *Reuters* report in *International Herald Tribune*, August 14, 2001; and Robert Einhorn, "The Emerging Bush Administration Approach to Addressing Iraq's WMD and Missile Programs," keynote address to the Institute for Science and International Security, June 14–15, 2001.

39. Briefing by Ambassador Rolf Ekeus, Hearings on Global Proliferation, p. 93.

40. U.S. DOD, *Proliferation: Threat and Response*, January 1996, p. 21; and UNSCOM, *Report of the Secretary-General on the Status of the Implementation of the Special Commission's Plan for the Ongoing Monitoring and Verification of Iraq's Compliance with Relevant Parts of Section C of Security Council Resolution 687 (1991)*, S/1995/284, April 10, 1995, p. 6.

41. U.S. DOD, *Proliferation: Threat and Response*, January 1996.

42. Ibid.

43. IAEA, *First Consolidated Report of the Director General of the International Atomic Energy Agency under Paragraph 16 of Resolution 1051 (1996)*, S/1996/261, April 11, 1996, p. 7. Also see IAEA, *Report on the Twenty-Eighth On-site Inspection in Iraq*, p. 15, and *Report on the Twenty-Ninth On-site Inspection*, p. 10.

44. R. Jeffrey Smith, "U.N. Finds New Evidence of Iraqi Long-Range Missile Research," *Washington Post*, February 5, 1997.

45. Interview with Rolf Ekeus, spring 1997; UNSCOM, *Report of the Secretary-General on the Activities of the Special Commission Established by the Secretary-General pursuant to Paragraph 9 (b)(i) of Resolution 687 (1991)*, S/1997/774, October 6, 1997, p. 6.

46. UNSCOM, *Report of the Secretary-General on Iraq's Compliance*, October 11, 1995, p. 14.

47. UNSCOM, *Report of the Secretary-General on Iraq's Compliance*, April 10, 1995, p. 6; UNSCOM, *Report of the Secretary-General on Iraq's Compliance*, October 11, 1995, p. 14.

48. David Isby, "Iraq's Residual Scud Force," *Jane's Intelligence Review*, March 1995; Sid Balman, Jr., "CIA: Saddam Building and Hiding Weapons," *United Press International*, September 26, 1994; and Patrick Worsnip, "CIA Chief Attacks Iran, Iraq Weapons Programs," *Reuters*, September 26, 1994.

49. Evelyn Leopold, "U.N. Official Unsatisfied with Iraqi Missile Data," *Reuters*, December 5, 1995.

50. UNSCOM, *Tenth Report of the Executive Chairman*.

51. UNSCOM, *Report of the Secretary-General on Iraq's Compliance*, October 11, 1995, p. 13. Also see UNSCOM, *Tenth Report of the Executive Chairman*; and Barbara Crossette, "U.N. Panel Says Iraq May Still Be Trying To Produce Missiles," *New York Times*, December 22, 1996.

52. UNSCOM, *Report of the Secretary-General on Iraq's Compliance*, October 11, 1995, p. 12.

53. UNSCOM, *Report of the Secretary-General on the Activities of the Special Commission Established by the Secretary-General Pursuant to Paragraph 9 (b)(i) of Resolution 687 (1991)*, S/1997/774, October 6, 1997, pp. 6–8.

54. Ambassador Amir Al-Anabari of Iraq, Letter to U.N. Secretary General, April 18, 1991, as quoted in Michael Crowley, *Disease by Design: De-Mystifying the Biological Weapons Debate*, BASIC (British-American Security Information Council), November 2001.

55. White House Fact Sheet, "Iraq's Program of Mass Destruction: Threatening Security of the International Community," November 14, 1997.

56. *Report of the Secretary-General on the Status of the Implementation of the Special Commission's Plan for the Ongoing Monitoring and Verification of Iraq's Compliance wth Relevant Parts of Section C Of Security Council Resolution 687 (1991) October 11, 1995.*

57. Ibid.

58. Office of Technology Assessment, *Proliferation of Weapons of Mass Destruction: Assessing the Risks*, August 1993, p. 10.

59. Christine M. Gosden, "Chemical and Biological Weapons Threats to America: Are We Prepared?" Testimony before the Senate Select Committee on Intelligence, April 22, 1998.

60. UNSCOM, Seventh Report under Resolution 715, October 4, 1995.

61. Public Papers of George Bush: Book 1, January 1 to June 30, 1991, "Statement by Press Secretary Fitzwater on President Bush's Letter to President Saddam Hussein of Iraq," January 12, 1991. As cited in Michael R. Gordon and Gen. Bernard E. Trainor, *The General's War: The Inside Story of the Conflict in the Gulf* (New York: Little Brown, 1995), p. 493.

62. Jeffery Smart, "History of Chemical and Biological Warfare: An American Perspective," chap. 2, *Medical Aspects of Chemical and Biological Warfare, Part I: The Textbook of Military Medicine* (Washington, D.C.: Office of the Surgeon General, Borden Institute, 1997), p. 73.

63. E. J. Hogendoorn, "A Chemical Weapons Atlas," *Bulletin of the Atomic Scientists*, September/October 1997, p. 37.

64. UNSCOM, *First Consolidated Report of the Secretary-General Pursuant to Paragraph 9*, April 11, 1996, pp. 6–8.

65. Center for Defense Information, "Iraq," Chemical and Biological Weapons web site, www.cdi.org/issues/cbw/Iraq.html.

Table 16.1: **Iraqi Biological Warfare, Chemical Warfare, and Ballistic Missile Programs**

A. Iraqi Biological Warfare Program	
BW AGENT PRODUCTION AMOUNTS[1]	
BW AGENT (ORGANISM)	Anthrax (*Bacillus anthracis*)
DECLARED CONCENTRATED AMOUNT	8,500 liters (2,245 gallons)
DECLARED TOTAL AMOUNT	85,000 liters (22,457 gallons)
COMMENTS	UNSCOM estimated production amounts were actually three to four times more than the declared amounts, but is unable to confirm.
BW AGENT (ORGANISM)	Botulinum toxin (*Clostridium botulinum*)
DECLARED CONCENTRATED AMOUNT	19,400 liters (10x and 20x concentrated) (5,125 gallons)
DECLARED TOTAL AMOUNT	380,000 liters (100,396 gallons)
COMMENTS	UNSCOM estimated production amounts were actually two times more than the declared amounts, but is unable to confirm.
BW AGENT (ORGANISM)	Gas gangrene (*Clostridium perfringens*)
DECLARED CONCENTRATED AMOUNT	340 liters (90 gallons)
DECLARED TOTAL AMOUNT	3,400 liters (900 gallons)
COMMENTS	Production amounts could be higher, but UNSCOM was unable to confirm.
BW AGENT (ORGANISM)	Aflatoxin (*Aspergillus flavus* and *Aspergillus parasiticus*)
DECLARED CONCENTRATED AMOUNT	N/A
DECLARED TOTAL AMOUNT	2,200 liters (581 gallons)
COMMENTS	Production amounts and timeframe of production claimed by Iraq do not correlate.
BW AGENT (ORGANISM)	Ricin (Castor bean plant)
DECLARED CONCENTRATED AMOUNT	N/A
DECLARED TOTAL AMOUNT	10 liters (2.7 gallons)
COMMENTS	Production amounts could be higher, but UNSCOM was unable to confirm.

(Table continues on the following page.)

Table 16.1 (continued)

BW–FILLED AND DEPLOYED DELIVERY SYSTEMS	
DELIVERY SYSTEM	Missile warheads–Al Hussein (modified Scud–B) *Anthrax:* 5 *Botulinum Toxin:* 16 *Aflatoxin:* 4
COMMENTS	UNSCOM could not confirm the unilateral destruction of these 25 warheads because of conflicting accounts provided by Iraq.
DELIVERY SYSTEM	R–400 aerial bombs *Anthrax:* 50 *Botulinum Toxin:* 100 *Aflatoxin:* 7
COMMENTS	Iraq claimed unilateral destruction of 157 bombs, but UNSCOM was unable to confirm that number. UNSCOM has found the remains of at least 23.
DELIVERY SYSTEM	Aircraft aerosol spray tanks (F–1 Mirage modified fuel drop tank) *Anthrax:* 4
COMMENTS	Iraq claims to have produced four but may have manufactured others.
BW AGENT GROWTH MEDIA	
QUANTITY IMPORTED	31,000 kg (68,200 lbs)
UNACCOUNTED FOR AMOUNTS	3,500 kg (7,700 lbs)
B. Iraqi Chemical Warfare Program	
CW AGENT STOCKPILES	
CHEMICAL AGENT	VX *Declared by Iraq:* at least 4 metric tons *Potential based on unaccounted precursors:* 200 metric tons
COMMENTS	Iraq denied producing VX until Hussein Kamil's defection in 1995.
CHEMICAL AGENT	G agents (sarin) *Declared by Iraq:* 100–150 metric tons *Potential based on unaccounted precursors:* 200 metric tons
COMMENTS	Figures include both weaponized and bulk agents.

	CW AGENT STOCKPILES (CONTINUED)
CHEMICAL AGENT	Mustard *Declared by Iraq:* 500–600 metric tons *Potential based on unaccounted precursors:* 200 metric tons
COMMENTS	Figures include both weaponized and bulk agents.

	CW DELIVERY SYSTEMS
DELIVERY SYSTEM	Missile warheads–Al Hussein (modified Scud–B) *Estimated number before the Gulf War:* 75–100 *Munitions unaccounted for:*[2] 45–70
COMMENTS	UNSCOM supervised the destruction of 30 warheads
DELIVERY SYSTEM	Rockets *Estimated number before the Gulf War:* 100,000 *Munitions unaccounted for:*[2] 15,000–25,000
COMMENTS	UNSCOM supervised the destruction of nearly 40,000 chemical munitions (including rockets, artillery, and aerial bombs), 28,000 of which were filled.
DELIVERY SYSTEM	Aerial bombs *Estimated number before the Gulf War:* 16,000 *Munitions unaccounted for:*[2] 2,000
DELIVERY SYSTEM	Artillery shells *Estimated number before the Gulf War:* 30,000 *Munitions unaccounted for:*[2] 15,000
DELIVERY SYSTEMS	Aerial spray tanks *Estimated numbers before the Gulf War:* Unknown *Munitions unaccounted for:*[2] Unknown

C. Iraqi Ballistic Missile Program

ITEM	Soviet-supplied Scud missiles (includes Iraqi modifications of the Scud: the Al Hussein, with a range of 650 km, and the Al-Abbas, with a range of 950 km)
INITIAL INVENTORY	819
COMMENTS	UNSCOM accepted Iraqi accounting for all but two of the original 819 Scud missiles acquired

(Table continues on the following page.)

Table 16.1 (continued)

	C. Iraqi Ballistic Missile Program (continued)
	from the Soviet Union. Iraq has not explained the disposition of major components that it may have stripped from operational missiles before their destruction, and some Iraqi claims—such as of the use of 14 Scuds in ATBM tests—are not believable. Gaps in Iraqi declarations and Baghdad's failure to account fully for indigenous missile programs strongly suggest that Iraq retains a small missile force.
ITEM	Iraqi-produced Scud missiles
INITIAL INVENTORY	Unknown
COMMENTS	Iraq denied producing a completed Scud missile, but it produced or procured and tested all major subcomponents.
ITEM	Iraq-produced Scud warheads
INITIAL INVENTORY	120
COMMENTS	Iraq claims all 120 were used or destroyed. UNSCOM supervised the destruction of 15. UNSCOM inspections found additional CW and BW warheads beyond those currently admitted.
ITEM	Iraqi-produced Scud airframes
INITIAL INVENTORY	2
COMMENTS	Iraq claims testing two indigenous airframes in 1990. It is unlikely that Iraq produced only two Scud airframes.
ITEM	Iraqi-produced Scud engines
INITIAL INVENTORY	80
COMMENTS	Iraq's claim that it melted 63 engines following acceptance tests—53 of which failed quality controls—are unverifiable and not believable. The United Nations is holding this as an open issue.
ITEM	Soviet-supplied missile launchers
INITIAL INVENTORY	11
COMMENTS	UNSCOM doubted Iraq's claim that it unilaterally destroyed five launchers. The Soviet Union may have sold more than the declared 11 launchers.

C. Iraqi Ballistic Missile Program (continued)

ITEM	Iraqi-produced missile launchers
INITIAL INVENTORY	8
COMMENTS	Iraq has the capability to produce additional launchers.

NOTES

1. "Total" refers to the amount of material obtained from the production process, while "concentrated" refers to the amount of concentrated agent obtained after final filtration and purification. The concentrated number is the amount used to fill munitions.

2. All these munitions could be used to deliver CW or BW agents. The numbers for missile warheads include 25 that Iraq claims to have unilaterally destroyed after having filled them with biological agents during the Gulf War. UNSCOM was unable to verify the destruction of these warheads.

Table 16.2: **Iraq: Nuclear Infrastructure**

NAME/LOCATION OF FACILITY	TYPE/STATUS	IAEA SAFEGUARDS[1]
NUCLEAR WEAPONS COMPLEX		
Al Atheer	Prime development and testing complex for nuclear weaponization program; large-scale uranium metallurgy that could produce reflectors, tampers, and other weapons components; location of two isostatic presses (hot and cold) suitable for making shaped charges, plus other remote-controlled machining equipment suitable for production of explosive structures. Operational until damaged by Coalition air attacks (1991); subsequently destroyed by IAEA inspectors.	NPT violation
Al Tuwaitha	Nuclear physics and uranium metallurgy laboratories; research and development (R&D) in triggering system capacitors; possible site for experimental work on neutronic initiators. Operational until damaged by Coalition air attacks (1991); under IAEA monitoring.	NPT violation
Al Qa Qaa	Military R&D facility; development and fabrication of exploding bridge wire detonators and high-explosive lenses (plane and spherical); site of shock-wave and high-explosive experiments; storage of large quantities of HMX high explosive; under IAEA monitoring.	NPT violation
Al Musaiyib (Al Hateen establishment)	High-explosive testing site; facility for hydrodynamic studies; facilities and equipment destroyed by the IAEA	NPT violation
Al Hadre	Open firing range for fuel-air bombs and fragmentation testing, suitable for experimentation with entire non-nuclear explosive structure of an implosion-type nuclear device; damaged by Coalition (1991) air attacks; under IAEA monitoring.	NPT violation
RESEARCH REACTORS		
Osiraq/Tammuz I	Light-water, HEU, 40-MWt; destroyed by Israeli air attack (1981).	Yes
Isis/Tammuz II	Light-water, HEU, 800-KWt; operational until destroyed by Coalition air attack (1991)	Yes
IRT–5000	Light-water, HEU, 5-MWt; operational until destroyed by Coalition air attack (1991)	Yes

URANIUM ENRICHMENT		
Al Tuwaitha	Prototype-scale, electromagnetic isotope separation (EMIS) method; operational until damaged by Coalition air attack (1991)	IAEA violation
Al Tuwaitha	Prototype-scale, gas-centrifuge method; operations relocated to Rashdiya in 1987	IAEA violation
Rashdiya	Prototype-scale, gas-centrifuge method; operations terminated at the outbreak of the 1991 Gulf War; under IAEA monitoring	IAEA violation
Al Tuwaitha	Laboratory-scale, chemical exchange isotope separation method; operational until damaged by Coalition air attack (1991)	IAEA violation
Al Tarmiya	Industrial-scale, EMIS method;[2] partially operational until damaged by Coalition air attack (1991); EMIS–related installations and equipment subsequently destroyed by IAEA	IAEA violation
Ash Sharqat	Industrial-scale, EMIS method; under construction until damaged by Coalition air attack (1991); EMIS–related installations and equipment subsequently destroyed by IAEA	IAEA violation?
Al Furat	Large manufacturing and testing facility for centrifuge production; under construction until it came under IAEA monitoring.	IAEA violation?
REPROCESSING (PLUTONIUM EXTRACTION)		
Al Tuwaitha	Laboratory-scale; three hot cells used for separating plutonium from irradiated uranium; operations terminated as a result of Gulf War (1991); equipment largely escaped damage; destroyed or rendered inoperable subsequently by IAEA inspectors	IAEA violation[3]
URANIUM PROCESSING		
Akashat	Uranium mine; operational until damaged by Coalition air attack (1991)	N/A
Al Qaim	Phosphate plant that produced uranium concentrate (U_3O_8); operational until damaged by Coalition air attack (1991); recovered material under IAEA monitoring	N/A

(Table continues on the following page.)

Table 16.2 (continued)

NAME/LOCATION OF FACILITY	TYPE/STATUS	IAEA SAFEGUARDS[1]
URANIUM PROCESSING (CONTINUED)		
Al Tuwaitha	Laboratory-scale uranium purification facility (UO_2); operational until heavily damaged by Coalition air attack (1991); recovered equipment under IAEA monitoring	IAEA violation
Al Tuwaitha	Laboratory-scale, uranium tetrachloride facility (UCL_4); operational until heavily damaged by Coalition air attack (1991); recovered equipment under IAEA monitoring	IAEA violation
Al Tuwaitha	Laboratory-scale production of uranium hexafluoride (UF_6); operational until damaged by Coalition air attack (1991)	IAEA violation
Al Tuwaitha	Fuel-fabrication laboratory; operational until destroyed by Coalition air attack (1991); recovered nuclear material under IAEA monitoring	IAEA violation
Mosul (Al Jesira)	Industrial-scale, uranium tetrachloride facility (UCL_4); operational until damaged by Coalition air attack (1991)	IAEA violation
Mosul (Al Jesira)	Production-scale uranium purification facility (UO_2); operational until heavily damaged by Coalition air attack (1991); production area sustained greatest damage by subsequent Iraqi deception activities.	IAEA violation

Abbreviations

HEU	highly enriched uranium	MWt	millions of watts of thermal output
LEU	low-enriched uranium	kWt	thousands of watts of thermal output
MWe	millions of watts of electrical output	N/A	not applicable

NOTES

1.   For the purposes of this table, the designations "Yes" and "N/A" ("not applicable") are used to describe the safeguards in place before the 1991 Gulf War at facilities processing or using nuclear materials that were declared by Iraq to the IAEA under Iraq's safeguard agreement with the IAEA (INFCIRC/172). "IAEA violation" denotes clandestine facilities involved in processing or using nuclear materials that were discovered in the course of the postwar IAEA inspections and found by the IAEA to be violations of the IAEA–Iraq safeguard agreement. "NPT violation" denotes clandestine facilities that were discovered in the course of the postwar IAEA inspections and were involved in nuclear weapons-related activities inconsistent with Iraq's NPT pledge not to manufacture nuclear arms.

2.   Component manufacturing facilities for the Iraqi EMIS program were located at: Al Ameen (prototype components); Al Radwan and Al Amir (magnet cores, return irons, ion sources, collector parts); Sehee at Daura (vacuum chamber parts); Salladine (electrical control panel assembly); and Tuwaitha (coil manufacturing).

3.   One of the fuel elements processed was from the IRT–5000 reactor and was exempt from safeguards under article 37 of INFCIRC/172, Iraq's safeguard agreement with the IAEA. The other three were fabricated indigenously from undeclared nuclear material, in violation of the safeguard agreement. A total of 6 grams of plutonium was recovered.

1 **Al Tuwaitha Nuclear Research Center** Tammuz I (Osiraq), Tammuz II (Isis), and IRT-5000 research reactors (the first destroyed by Israel in 1981); subject to IAEA inspection prior to Gulf War.

Site of research and development (R&D) programs in uranium enrichment, including gas centrifuges, electromagnetic isotope separation (EMIS), chemical separation, and gaseous diffusion.*

Location of "hot cells" used for separation of grams of plutonium.* Experimental program for the production of lithium-6 which, if irradiated in a reactor, yields tritium for use in advanced nuclear weapons. Weapons-related R&D activities in nuclear physics, uranium metallurgy, and triggering system capacitors.**

2 **Al Atheer** Prime development and testing site for nuclear weaponization program, including facilities and equipment for large-scale uranium metallurgy and production of weapons components; computer simulations of nuclear weapon detonations; and experiments for the development of an implosion-type explosive structure in nearby "bunker" at Al-Hateen. Possible testing of explosive structures at Al Hadre.**

Al Qa Qaa High Explosives and Propellant Facility Military and nuclear weapons R&D facility; development of exploding bridge wire detonators (EBW) used in the firing system of nuclear weapons; high explosive experiments; storage of large quantities of HMX high explosive used in nuclear weapons.**

4 **Rashdiya** Central site of Iraq's centrifuge research and development efforts.

5 **Al Tarmiya** Industrial-scale complex for EMIS designed for the installation of 70 1,200-millimeter separators plus 20 600-millimeter separators. Eight units were operational prior to Desert Storm bombings; if all separators had been installed, plant could have yielded 15 kg of HEU annually, possibly enough for one nuclear weapon. Replica facilities were under construction at Ash Sharqat.*

6 **Al Furat Project** Large-scale manufacturing and testing facility, designed for the production of centrifuges for uranium enrichment. Site of a planned 100-centrifuge experimental cascade, with an initial operational capability by mid-1993. A 1000-centrifuge cascade was to be built at Taji.*

Al Jesira Large-scale facility for the production of uranium dioxide (UO_2) and uranium tetrachloride (UC_4), feed materials for EMIS. Intended site for the production of uranium hexafluoride (UF_6) to feed the centrifuge enrichment program.*

* Activities found by IAEA to be in violation of Iraq's safeguard agreement with the IAEA.

** Activities found by the United States to be in violation of Iraq's obligations under Article II of the Nuclear Non-Proliferation Treaty (NPT) prohibiting the "manufacture" of nuclear weapons.

Italicized names on map represent nuclear-related sites either declared by Iraq or discovered by IAEA inspectors during implementation of U.N. Security Council Resolution 687 adopted at the end of the 1991 Gulf War. The facilities and equipment at these sites that escaped damage during the war were subsequently dismantled or destroyed by the IAEA or came under IAEA monitoring; sensitive nuclear materials have been removed. See table 16.2

States of Some Concern

Overview

Algeria and Libya do not fit neatly into the proliferation categories set forth in this volume. They are particularly instructive in terms of understanding the complexities associated with the tracking of proliferation programs. The case of Algeria is striking, since even to this day top experts and officials cannot say conclusively whether Algeria's nuclear activities were ever geared to the pursuit of nuclear weapons or whether overzealous intelligence and media services hyped the discovery of previously undeclared nuclear facilities. The full story of this case is discussed in chapter 17. It illustrates how both capabilities and intentions are important factors in tracking proliferation. Likewise, it is not known how seriously Libya pursued the ability to obtain nuclear weapons or whether its change of policy in areas including terrorism extends to its potential pursuit of nuclear capabilities. For this reason we continue to list Algeria and Libya as countries of some concern, since any nuclear developments linked to either country will rekindle concerns about their nuclear intentions.

Algeria

Nuclear Capabilities

Algeria does not possess nuclear weapons or unsafeguarded stocks of nuclear weapons-usable material. It does possess two nuclear research reactors that are capable of producing several kilograms of plutonium each year. Algeria does not have a significant ability to reprocess or separate this plutonium from spent fuel and is not considered a country of active proliferation concern.

Missile and Aircraft Capabilities

Algeria does not have ballistic or cruise missiles or nuclear-capable aircraft.

Chemical and Biological Weapon Capabilities

Algeria does not have research programs for either chemical or biological programs. Algeria acceded to the Biological Weapons Convention in July 2001. It ratified the Chemical Weapons Convention in 1995.

Strategic Context

Suspicions were aroused in 1991 that Algeria might be seeking to develop nuclear weapons through the use of a large, unsafeguarded research reactor. Those fears abated after Algeria agreed to subject the facility to International Atomic Energy Agency inspection in 1991 and acceded to the Nuclear Non-Proliferation Treaty in early 1995. Algeria continues, however, to develop its large nuclear research complex at Ain Oussera in the Atlas Mountains with China's help, and some of those facilities remain outside the inspection regime.

Algeria's existing facilities include two research reactors, one of which (at Ain Oussera) could produce 3–5 kilograms of plutonium a year. Algeria is developing a range of support facilities at the nuclear complex, including hot cell laboratories, large waste storage tanks, and an isotope production plant. While work on a suspected reprocessing facility appears to have stopped, new construction is under way, the precise purpose of which is unclear. A 1998 report from the Spanish intelligence service Cesid concluded that Algeria would soon be in a position to restart a military program if it decided to do so.[1] The threat that continuing political strife might bring a radical government to power makes Algeria's nuclear future a continuing source of concern. Algeria's nuclear activities are likely to remain the focus of international attention in coming years.

Its nuclear baptism came in February 1960 when France detonated its first nuclear device at Reganne, in the Sahara Desert. Even after independence from France in 1962, French nuclear tests continued at Reganne until 1966, when France shifted its test site to the South Pacific.[2] Indigenous nuclear activities in Algeria were minimal until the late 1980s. In 1985, Algeria bought a small, 1-megawatt research reactor from Argentina. The Nur reactor, at Draria, near Algiers, has been subject to IAEA monitoring since it began operating in 1989. Algeria refused to join the NPT, however. As a leader of the Non-Aligned Movement, it viewed the treaty as an instrument of the established nuclear powers to keep non-nuclear nations in a permanent state of inferiority.

In early 1991, U.S. intelligence learned of the research reactor at the Ain Oussera nuclear complex. Because the facility was considered to be too large for Algeria's rudimentary nuclear research program and was not subject to IAEA inspection, Washington feared that it might be part of a nuclear weapon program.[3] Algeria then disclosed that China would supply the nation with a 15-megawatt reactor, Es Salam. It would use low-enriched uranium as fuel and heavy water for the reactor's moderator. Noting the unusually large cooling towers, however, U.S. and other foreign analysts suggested its capacity could be as high as 60 megawatts. The presence of SA–5 surface-to-air missile defense batteries near the facility also pointed to a possible military use. Unconfirmed reports that Algeria was building a reprocessing plant at the complex fueled suspicions that the purpose was to separate weapons-usable plutonium from spent fuel or from uranium targets irradiated in the reactor.[4]

In May 1991, under international pressure, Algeria agreed to place the Ain Oussera reactor under IAEA safeguards.[5] Subsequently, during the December 21, 1993, inauguration of the reactor, Algerian Foreign Minister Salah Dembri said that Algeria would sign the NPT, adding that Algeria "confidently and unequivocally affirms its commitment to the non-proliferation regime."[6] Algeria had completed formalities by late 1994 and on January 12, 1995, formally acceded to the treaty.[7]

A key factor in Algeria's decision was the need for political and economic support from France and other Western powers in the face of a virtual civil war at home. In January 1992 the Algerian army had seized power to prevent a takeover by the radical Islamic Salvation Front (FIS). In response, the FIS, backed by other Islamic extremists, launched a campaign, combining guerrilla warfare and widespread anti-government and anti-secular terrorism.[8]

Algeria joined the NPT just in time to participate in the 1995 Review Conference, where the industrialized nations, led by the United States, pressed strongly for the treaty to be extended indefinitely. Algeria joined a group of Arab states led by Egypt that tried to use the review process to force Israel to joint the NPT and to abandon its nuclear weapon program. Eventually, however, Egypt and its allies agreed to an indefinite NPT extension in return for a resolution calling for a Middle East nuclear-weapon-free zone.

On March 30, 1996, Algeria signed a comprehensive safeguard agreement that provided for IAEA inspections of its nuclear facilities and for IAEA technical assistance. After the agreement went into force on January 7, 1997,

Algeria declared its initial nuclear inventory to the agency. It has not, however, agreed to accept the IAEA's new, more advanced safeguards (the "Additional Model Protocol"), and consequently some facilities at Ain Oussera remain outside the inspection process.[9]

Algeria continued to develop its nuclear ties with China. On June 1, 1996, a draft agreement was signed for a "second stage" of cooperation in nuclear technology.[10] This stage saw the completion of a hot cell facility and the construction of underground waste storage tanks. The draft agreement was followed in October 1996 by a "letter of intent" for phase three of the project, which began in May 1997.[11] Under phase three, China is helping Algeria to construct facilities for the production of radioisotopes for medical, industrial, and agricultural use.[12] It is also providing Algeria with the expertise to operate the hot cell facility. Although hot cells can be used to separate plutonium from irradiated fuel, in declaring the facility to the IAEA, Algeria stated that its aim was to become a leading supplier of medical isotopes.[13] In the context of U.S.–Chinese discussions over the U.S. certification of China's non-proliferation credentials, the United States raised concerns about the possible use of the hot cells for plutonium separation. After IAEA consultations with Algeria, however, the United States was "satisfied" that the hot cells were covered by IAEA safeguards, including environmental sampling.[14] Recent satellite images show other construction taking place at the site that could have military implications.[15]

These developments took place against a backdrop of continuing political turmoil, as Algeria's military-backed government made gains against Islamic fundamentalist rebels. On November 16, 1995, retired General Liamine Zeroual was elected president, winning 61 percent of the vote. A year later, by referendum, 70 percent of the Algerian electorate approved an authoritarian constitution banning religion-based political parties but declaring Islam as the state religion. In parliamentary and municipal elections in 1997 the government made progress in its efforts to gain legitimacy and promote a pluralistic system. Yet sporadic violence has continued, and the government has been slow to implement necessary social and economic reforms.

The prospect that a militant Islamic government might emerge in Algeria—and opt for the development of nuclear weapons to gain legitimacy, prestige, or military power in a hostile international environment—has receded, but it has not entirely disappeared. For the moment, the government is cautiously expanding Algeria's civilian nuclear research program, in compliance with the requirements of the NPT.

NOTES

1. M. Gonzales and J. M. Larraya, "Cesid Warns That in Two Years Algeria Will Have the Capability to Produce Military Plutonium," *El Pais*, August 23, 1998; English translation FBIS–TAC–98–235.

2. "Le Putch des Généraux d'Algier,"*Le Monde*, April 4, 1986; D. G. Brennan, "The Risks of Spreading Weapons: A Historical Case," *Arms Control and Disarmament*, vol. 1 (1968); and Leonard Spector, *Going Nuclear* (Cambridge: Ballinger, 1987), pp. 25–31.

3. Elaine Sciolino and Eric Schmitt, "Algerian Reactor: A Chinese Export," *New York Times*, November 15, 1991, p. A12; "China Helps Algeria Build First Arab Atom Bomb," *Sunday Times*, April 28, 1991; Bill Gertz, "China Helps Algeria Develop Nuclear Weapons," *Washington Times*, April 11, 1991.

4. Ann MacLachlan and Mark Hibbs, "Algeria Confirms Secret Reactor, Questions about Purpose Remain," *Nucleonics Week*, May 2, 1991, p. 3; Barbara Gregory, *Algeria: Contemplating a Nuclear Weapons Option?* (McLean, Va.: Science Applications International Corporation, March 25, 1995); interviews with former U.S. officials.

5. "Algeria: IAEA, Algeria Sign Safeguards Agreement," *Nuclear Fuel*, March 16, 1992, p. 15; "Atomic Energy Inspectors Tour Nuclear Reactor," *Algiers Radio*, January 19, 1992, in FBIS–NES–92–014, January 22, 1992, p. 15.

6. "Algeria Pledges Peaceful Use of PRC–Built Nuclear Reactor," Beijing, *Xinhua Domestic Service*, December 24, 1993, in JPRS–TND–93–003, January 31, 1994, p. 45; "Decision to Join Nuclear Non-Proliferation Treaty Announced," *Radio Algiers Network*, December 21, 1993, in JPRS–TND–94–002, January 18, 1994, p. 12; "Reactions to Dedication of Nuclear Reactor," Algiers, *El Moudjahid*, December 22, 1993, in *JPRS–TND–94–005*, February 25, 1994, p. 10.

7. IAEA, "Algeria Accedes to the Treaty on the Non-Proliferation of Nuclear Weapons," press release PR 95/2 (Vienna, January 13, 1995).

8. James Philips, "The Rising Threat of Revolutionary Islam in Algeria," Heritage Foundation Backgrounder 1060, November 9, 1995.

9. David Albright and Corey Hinderstein, "Algeria: Big Deal in the Desert," *Bulletin of Atomic Scientists*, May/June 2001, p. 45.

10. "Algeria Signs Nuclear Draft Agreement with China," *Reuters*, June 2, 1996; "PRC: Algerian Official Discusses Nuclear Energy Cooperation," Beijing, *Xinhua Domestic Service*, June 3, 1996, FBIS–CHI–96–107, June 3, 1996.

11. Mark Hibbs, "China Attends Zangger Meeting, Might Join Committee after Talks," *Nuclear Fuel*, June 2, 1997, p. 8.

12. "PRC: Talks Held with Algerian Ministers on Medicare, Nuclear Industry," Beijing, *Xinhua*, October 18, 1996, in FBIS–CHI–96–204, October 18, 1996.

13. David Albright, Frans Berkhout, and William Walker, *Plutonium and Highly Enriched Uranium 1996: World Inventories, Capabilities, and Policies* (SIPRI: Stockholm, 1997), p. 363.

14. Mark Hibbs, "Move To Block China Certification Doesn't Concern Administration," *Nucleonics Week*, August 7, 1997, p. 1.

15. Albright and Hinderstein, "Algeria: Big Deal in the Desert."

Table 17.1: **Algeria: Nuclear Infrastructure**

NAME/LOCATION OF FACILITY	TYPE/STATUS	IAEA SAFEGUARDS[1]
RESEARCH REACTORS		
Nur, Draria (Algiers)	Small pool-type, LEU, 1-Mwt; operating.	Yes
Es Salam Ain Oussera	Heavy-water, LEU 15-Mwt; operating	Yes*
REPROCESSING (PLUTONIUM EXTRACTION)		
Ain Oussera	New facility containing hot cells for use in the production of radioactive isotopes	Yes
Draria	Hot cells for use in the production of radioactive isotopes	Yes
URANIUM PROCESSING		
West of Tamanrasset, southern Algeria	Uranium deposits; status unknown	N/A

Abbreviations

HEU   highly enriched uranium
LEU   low-enriched uranium
N/A   not applicable

ADDITIONAL SOURCES

"Algeria: Council of Government Discusses Nuclear Energy Program." Algiers: ENTV Television Network, August 21, 1996, in FBIS–NES–96–165.

"Reports of the Global Activities of the International Atomic Energy Agency." IAEA Newsbriefs, February/March 1994.

Gupta, Vipin. "Algeria's Nuclear Ambitions." International Defense Review, April 1992.

Interviews with former U.S. officials.

NOTE

---

*   On February 27, 1992, Algeria and the IAEA signed a facility-specific safeguard agreement. The agreement provided for the inspection of the reactor, its nuclear fuel, and its heavy water but apparently did not guarantee access to other facilities in the Ain Oussera nuclear research complex. On March 30, 1996, however, pursuant to its obligations under the NPT, Algeria signed a comprehensive inspection agreement with the IAEA that placed all nuclear activities in the country under IAEA safeguards. The agreement entered into force on January 7, 1997.

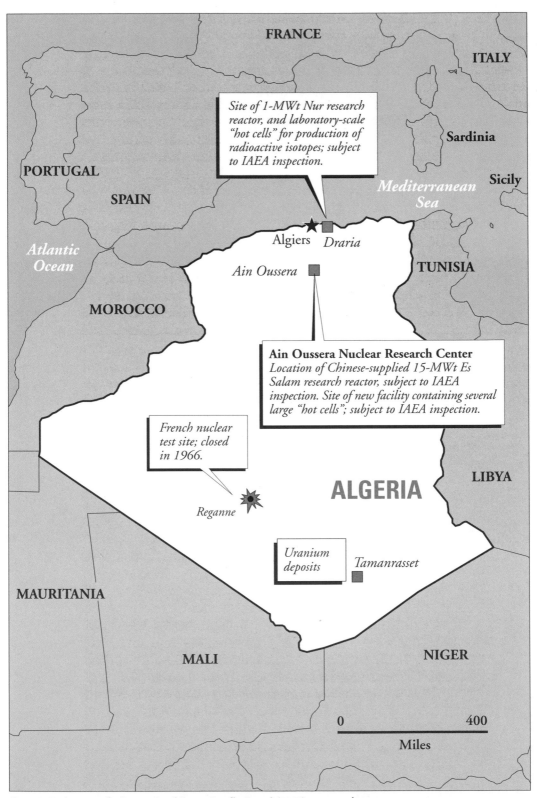

Site of 1-MWt Nur research reactor, and laboratory-scale "hot cells" for production of radioactive isotopes; subject to IAEA inspection.

Ain Oussera Nuclear Research Center
Location of Chinese-supplied 15-MWt Es Salam research reactor, subject to IAEA inspection. Site of new facility containing several large "hot cells"; subject to IAEA inspection.

French nuclear test site; closed in 1966.

Uranium deposits

FRANCE

ITALY

Sardinia

Sicily

Mediterranean Sea

PORTUGAL

SPAIN

Atlantic Ocean

Algiers   *Draria*

Ain Oussera

TUNISIA

MOROCCO

ALGERIA

LIBYA

Reganne

Tamanrasset

MAURITANIA

MALI

NIGER

0   400

Miles

Carnegie Endowment for International Peace, *Deadly Arsenals* (2002), **www.ceip.org**

CHAPTER 18

Libya

Nuclear Weapon Capability

Libya does not possess nuclear weapons or unsafeguarded stocks of nuclear weapons-usable material. Libya operates one 10-megawatt light-water reactor. Its interest in pursuing a nuclear weapon option are unclear.

Biological and Chemical Weapon Capability

Libya is believed to have a biological weapon program, but it has not advanced beyond basic research and development. It may have the capability to produce small quantities of agents, but without foreign assistance and technical expertise, it is not likely to make significant progress beyond its current stage. Libya still appears to have a goal of establishing an offensive chemical weapon capability and an indigenous production capability for weapons.

Missile Capability

Libya currently possesses a limited and aging arsenal of Scud–B missiles that it obtained from the Soviet Union in the 1970s. Libya is struggling to continue its indigenous efforts to develop the Al Fatah missile. Though this missile has a reported range of 950 kilometers, the U.S. Department of Defense assesses its range to be only 200 kilometers.[1] Libya is not believed to possess any aircraft capable of delivering a nuclear payload.

Strategic Context

For thirty years, Libya's mercurial leader, Col. Muammar Qadhafi, has had ambitions to become the leader of the Arab world and to raise Libya's prestige among Islamic and other Third World countries. Until the late 1990s, Libya remained defiant on non-proliferation and arms control issues, especially those related to Israel's nuclear capability. In seeking weapons of mass destruction, it drew constant international condemnation. Its substantial oil wealth, however, has enabled it to buy the technology it needs rather than developing its own. Its nuclear, chemical, and biological weapon programs are all heavily dependent on foreign technology and expertise.

Libya's pursuit of weapons of mass destruction programs, along with its support for terrorist organizations during the 1970s and 1980s, resulted in increasing pressure from the United States and progressively harsher economic sanctions, including international efforts to block the transfer of arms and sensitive technologies. These difficulties have been compounded by problems at home. Since an attempted military coup in 1993, the Qadhafi regime has faced growing dissent, mainly from Islamic fundamentalists, but also from moderates and nationalists, as well as from army officers.[2] There have been reports of violent unrest.[3]

In recent years these pressures—and the difficulties involved in sustaining WMD development programs without any true indigenous capability—appear to have had an effect. Since 1997 Libya has worked to rehabilitate its international image and has made considerable headway since handing over for trial those accused of blowing up a Pan Am aircraft over Scotland in 1988. Qadhafi's anti-terrorist statements since the events of September 11, 2001, and cooperation in supplying intelligence to the United States on those responsible, have confirmed that trend. The United Nations suspended its sanctions against Libya in 1999, and pressure is mounting for the United States to do the same in 2003.

Libya is a party to the Nuclear Non-Proliferation Treaty and to the Biological Weapons Convention. In November 2001 it signed the Comprehensive Test Ban Treaty. Nevertheless, it remains outside the Chemical Weapons Convention, which is a source of concern since Libya's chemical weapon program is the most advanced of all its programs. The suspension of U.N. sanctions has allowed Tripoli to expand its procurement efforts again. According to U.S. intelligence sources, Tripoli reestablished contacts with sources of expertise, parts, and precursor chemicals abroad, primarily in Western Europe.[4] Libya is reviving its defunct civilian nuclear power program through renewed contacts with Russia, but this program will be subject to international inspection. Libya still appears, however, to have a goal of establishing an offensive chemical weapon capability and an indigenous production capability for weapons. It may also be seeking to acquire the capability to develop and produce biological weapon agents. To this extent, Libya remains a country of proliferation concern.

Libya has sought for 30 years to obtain nuclear arms and other weapons of mass destruction to advance the cause of radical Arab nationalism. This pursuit, and Libya's support for terrorist groups in the 1970s and 1980s, led to economic sanctions being imposed on Libya by the United Nations and individual countries. The U.N. sanctions were imposed in 1992 in response to the downing of an airliner over Lockerbie in Scotland in 1988.[5] Some U.S. sanctions were already in place by then, having been imposed in 1986 by President Ronald Reagan. More U.S. sanctions followed in 1992 and 1996.[6] In July 1996, U.S. efforts to block the export of dual-use and military technology to Libya won approval by 33 nations of the Charter of the Wassenaar Arrangement on Export Controls for Conventional Arms and Dual-Use Goods and Technologies. The Wassenaar Arrangement is the successor regime to the Coordinating Committee for Multilateral Export Controls, which was established during the Cold War to prevent the transfer of sensitive technologies with military applications to the Soviet bloc (for the text, see appendix G).[7] In

August 1996 President Bill Clinton signed legislation imposing sanctions on foreign companies that invest more than $40 million for future petroleum ventures in Iran and Libya, as well as companies exporting items to Libya that enhance its WMD and advanced conventional weapon programs.[8] The United Nations suspended its sanctions in 1999, after Libya handed over those responsible for the Lockerbie bombing, but U.S. sanctions remain in place.

Nuclear Analysis

Libya's nuclear ambitions first became evident in 1970, when its attempts to buy nuclear weapons directly from China were rebuffed. In 1977 Libya reportedly turned to Pakistan, offering financial aid and supplies of uranium from Niger, apparently hoping to share in the results of Pakistan's nuclear program. But this also came to nothing, leaving Libya no option but to develop its own nuclear facilities. After Libya ratified the Nuclear Non-Proliferation Treaty in 1975 (signed in 1969 by King Idris), the Soviet Union supplied Libya with a 10-megawatt research reactor, which began operating at Tajoura in 1979. The following year, Libya negotiated a formal safeguard agreement with the International Atomic Energy Agency (IAEA). Plans to have Russia build a power reactor near the Gulf of Sidra were subsequently dropped because of U.S. pressure on potential supplier Belgium and a loss of interest by Moscow.

The true extent of Libya's nuclear ambitions remains unclear. The signals are contradictory. At the 1995 NPT Review and Extension Conference, Libya eventually supported an indefinite extension of the treaty, despite Israel's continued refusal to sign it. Yet in January 1996, Libya's official news agency restated Colonel Qadhafi's position that the Arab states should acquire nuclear weapons to counter Israel's nuclear hegemony in the region.[9] Qadhafi has also asserted that the Arab states would be justified in possessing chemical and biological weapons to counter Israel's nuclear capability.[10] Nevertheless, Libya was among 43 African countries that signed the African Nuclear-Weapon-Free-Zone Treaty (ANWFZ) in April 1996.

The following September, Libya, with Bhutan and India, voted against the Comprehensive Test Ban Treaty at the U.N. General Assembly, arguing that it should provide for nuclear disarmament within a specified time.[11] Nonetheless, Libya finally signed the treaty on November 13, 2001.

In October 1997 Russia reopened nuclear cooperation talks with Libya,[12] and in March 1998 the Atomenergoeksport company signed an $8 million contract involving the partial overhaul of the Tajoura research center. The possibility of cooperation in the construction of a nuclear power station was reportedly under discussion in 1999.[13]

Biological and Chemical Weapon Analysis

Libya's bid to acquire chemical weapons in the late 1980s has been well documented, and it once had a substantial chemical weapon stockpile. It has refused to sign the 1993 Chemical Weapons Convention but in 1971 became party to the 1925 Geneva Protocol forbidding the use in war of chemical and biological weapons. Allegations that Libya used chemical weapons against Chad in 1986 have not been substantiated.

In late 1988, however, Libya finished the construction of a chemical production facility at Rabta, known as Pharma-150, with extensive foreign technical assistance.[14] It produced at least 100 metric tons of blister and nerve agents before it closed in 1990 in the face of U.S.–led international pressure.[15] At the same time a similar plant, Pharma-200, was reportedly being built underground at a military base near Sebha, 650 kilometers south of Tripoli.[16] Little is known about that facility.

Most concern about Libya has focused on what CIA Director John Deutch has described as the "world's largest underground chemical weapons plant" in a mountain at Tarhuna, 40 miles southeast of Tripoli.[17] United States intelligence sources indicated in early 1996 that the plant would be completed "late in this decade" and would be capable of producing the ingredients for tons of poison gas daily.[18] Libya maintained that the plant was part of an irrigation system.[19] Tensions over the Tarhuna plant appeared to ease by late 1996 as reports surfaced that Libya had suspended construction,[20] following comments by U.S. Defense Secretary William Perry that he would not rule out the use of military force to block completion of the plant. Some Pentagon officials suggested that the United States might use a modified version of the B–61 nuclear warhead.[21]

There were also reports in mid-1997 that Libya had received South African equipment for the manufacture of chemical and biological weapons. According to those reports, after the 1994 national elections in South Africa several scientists from the South African military's chemical and biological weapon program (called Project Coast) had sold equipment and perhaps had even traveled to Libya to advise on the project.[22] Libya may still have some chemical weapons.

Libya became party to the Biological Weapons Convention in 1982, but the lack of verification procedures precludes compliance verification. Libya is thought to have sought to establish a biological warfare capability, although a lack of technical expertise has kept the program in the "early research and development stage."[23] The chemical facilities at Rabta, Sebha, and Tarhuna are believed to be involved. Reports suggest, however, that Libya has had to depend on technology and expertise from abroad, in particular from Iraq and South Africa.[24]

Missile Analysis

In the late 1980s and early 1990s Libya made several apparently unsuccessful attempts to purchase foreign missiles, such as the Soviet/Russian SS–23 and SS–21, and the Chinese DF–3A, M–9, and M–11. Libya's limited and antiquated missile arsenal includes basic Scud–Bs bought from the Soviet Union in the mid-1970s. Tripoli continues a program to develop the indigenous Al Fatah missile. On the whole, Libya's missile complex is heavily dependent upon foreign suppliers. The presence of U.N. sanctions from 1992 to 1999 is believed to have severely limited Libya's ability to maintain its Scud–B arsenal and to make further progress in its domestic ballistic missile program, though in recent years several shipments of Scud components have been intercepted en route to Libya.[25] The Central Intelligence Agency has confirmed that Libya has received "ballistic missile-related goods and technical know-how" from Russian entities and "missile-related items, raw materials, or other help" from Chinese entities.[26] Serbian and Indian assistance to Libya's missile program were also cited in an unclassified CIA report to Congress.[27] Reports have circulated that Libya has purchased No Dong MRBMs from North Korea, but Western defense and intelligence sources have not confirmed such a purchase, acknowledging only that Libya has an interest in obtaining a longer-range missile capability.

Notes

1. U.S. Department of Defense (DOD), *Proliferation: Threat and Response*, January 2001, p. 48.

2. Jonathan Wright, "Tripoli Soccer Shooting Spotlights Dissent," *Washington Times*, July 17, 1996.

3. James Bruce, "Col. Qadhafi Dispatches Troops To Quell Unrest," *Jane's Defense Weekly*, April 3, 1996, p. 14.

4. Central Intelligence Agency (CIA), "Report to Congress on the Acquisition of Technology relating to Weapons of Mass Destruction and Advanced Conventional Munitions," July–December 2000, released September 7, 2001.

5. U.N. Security Council, *Resolution 748 (1992)*, S/RES/748, March 31, 1992.

6. *Public Papers of the Presidents of the United States: Ronald Reagan, 1996*, Book I: January 1 to June 27, 1986 (Washington, D.C.: U.S. GPO, 1988), p. 17; and David Hoffman, "President Imposes Boycott on Business with Libya, Qadhafi's Isolation Urged," *Washington Post*, January 8, 1996.

7. "Post–Cocom 'Wassenaar Arrangement' Set To Begin New Export Control Role," *Arms Control Today*, December 1995/January 1996; *Basic Reports: Newsletter on International Security Policy*, February 21, 1996; and Jeff Erlich, "Future of Multinational Export Control Remains in Question," *Defense News*, July 22–28, 1996.

8. Iran and Libya Sanctions Act of 1996, P.L. 104-172, 50 USC 1701; and Eric Pianin, "Clinton Approves Sanctions for Investors in Iran, Libya," *Washington Post*, August 6, 1996. In 1997 the threshold investment was dropped to $20 million.

9. "Arabs Must Get Nuclear Bomb To Match Israel—Libya," *Reuters*, January 27, 1996. Also see "Arabs Need Nuclear Bomb, Qadhafi Says," *Reuters*, May 17, 1995.

10. "Qadhafi Says Arabs Have Right to Germ Warfare Arms," *Reuters*, March 30, 1996; "Qadhafi Tunnels into Trouble Both within and without," *Jane's Defence Weekly*, September 1996, p. 24.

11. United Nations, "Assembly Adopts Comprehensive Nuclear-Test-Ban Treaty," Press Release GA/9083, September 10, 1996.

12. "Russia Ready To Start Talks with Libya on Nuclear Center," Moscow, *Interfax*, October 22, 1997.

13. "Moscow Set To Expand Trade Ties with Libya," Moscow, *Interfax*, April 7, 1999.

14. Stephen Engelberg with Michael Gordon, "Germans Accused of Helping Libya Build Nerve Gas Plant," *New York Times*, January 1, 1989; "Challenges to Peace in the Middle East," address of R. James Woolsey, director, Central Intelligence, to the Washington Institute for Near East Policy, Wye Plantation, Maryland, September 23, 1994, revised.

15. In 1990, by fabricating a fire, Libya tried to give the impression that the facility was seriously damaged. See U.S. DOD, *Proliferation: Threat and Response*, April 1996, p. 26.

16. "Libya," education module on Chemical and Biological Weapons Nonproliferation. Available at SIPRI web site, cbw.sipri.se.

17. Tim Weiner, "Huge Chemical Arms Plant Near Completion in Libya," *New York Times*, February 25, 1996. See also John Diamond, "Watching China," *Associated Press*, February 23, 1996.

18. Weiner, "Huge Chemical Arms Plant Near Completion."

19. "Libya Denies Weapons-Factory Link," *Washington Times*, February 27, 1996; John Lancaster, "Perry Presses U.S. Charge against Libya," *Washington Post*, April 4, 1996; John Lancaster, "Egypt Denies Libyan Chemical Arms Site," *Washington Post*, May 30, 1996.

20. Lancaster, "U.S. Charge against Libya."

21. Robert Burns, "U.S.–Libya," *Associated Press*, April 23, 1996; Charles Aldinger, "U.S. Lacks Conventional Arms To Destroy Libya Plant," *Reuters*, April 23, 1996. Also see Art Pine, "U.S. Hints It Would Bomb Libyan Facility," *Los Angeles Times*, April 19, 1996; Pine, "A-Bomb against Libya Target Suggested," *Los Angeles Times*, April 24, 1996.

22. Peta Thornycroft, "South Africa: Scientists Said to Sell CBW Technology to Libya after 1994," *Johannesburg Mail and Guardian*, February 7, 1997, in FBIS–TAC–97–007; "South Africa: Mandela Fears Chemical Arms Sales to Libya 'Tip of Iceberg,'" *Johannesburg SAPA*, February 11, 1997, in FBIS–TAC–97–007.

23. U.S. DOD, *Proliferation Threat and Response*, April 1996, p. 27; James Adams, "South Africa: Libya Said Seeking Secret Biological Weapons," *London Sunday Times*, February 26, 1995.

24. "Libya," SIPRI education module.

25. "U.K. Warns Libya after Scud Find," *BBC News*, January 9, 2000. Available at news.bbc.co.uk/hi/english/uk/newsid_596000/596088.htm; and "Scud Missile Parts Intercepted," *BBC News*, April 12, 2000. Available at news.bbc.co.uk/hi/english/uk/newsid.

26. George Tenet, director, Central Intelligence Agency, "Worldwide Threat 2001: National Security in a Changing World, " statement before the Senate Select Committee on Intelligence, February 7, 2001.

27. CIA, "Report to Congress on the Acquisition of Technology relating to Weapons of Mass Destruction and Advanced Conventional Munitions, July–December 2000," released September 7, 2001.

Table 18.1: **Libya: Nuclear Infrastructure**

NAME/LOCATION OF FACILITY	TYPE/STATUS	IAEA SAFEGUARDS
RESEARCH REACTORS		
Tajoura	Light-water, HEU, 10-MWt; operating; overhaul planned	Yes
POWER REACTORS		
Gulf of Sidra	Light-water, LEU, 440-MWe; cancelled	N/A

Abbreviations

HEU	highly enriched uranium
LEU	low-enriched uranium
N/A	not applicable

SOURCES

IAEA. *Annual Report 2000.* Vienna, July 2001.

Monterey Institute for International Studies. *Nuclear Developments.* Monterey, Cal., spring 1991.

Spector, Leonard S., with Jacqueline R. Smith. *Nuclear Ambitions.* Boulder: Westview Press, 1990.

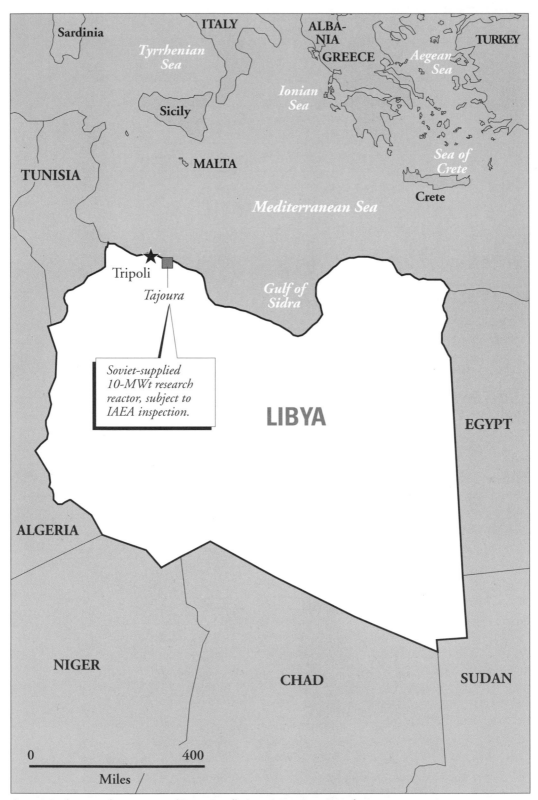

Soviet-supplied
10-MWt research
reactor, subject to
IAEA inspection.

Carnegie Endowment for International Peace, *Deadly Arsenals* (2002), **www.ceip.org**

States That Have Given Up Nuclear Weapons

Overview

O ne of the most striking and underappreciated facts of the nuclear age is the sheer number of countries that either once possessed nuclear weapons or have pursued nuclear capabilities and that now have renounced those ambitions to become established non-nuclear-weapon states.

Before the negotiation on the NPT, more than a dozen states, including Sweden, Switzerland, Turkey, and Egypt, pursued their nuclear weapon options. It was their decisions not to acquire nuclear weapons that, in part, helped establish the international non-proliferation norm. While circumstances differ, in each of those cases where countries gave up their nuclear weapons—including states of the former Soviet Union and South Africa—the international non-proliferation regime was an essential component in locking in their non-nuclear status. Without the international norm against the possession of nuclear weapons and established legal mechanisms, denuclearizing those states may well have proved impossible.

In addition, among the states that have abandoned their nuclear ambitions are Argentina and Brazil, where the establishment of a civilian government was a critical factor in the elimination of weapon efforts. The international non-proliferation regime drew attention to the efforts of those countries to acquire nuclear, biological, and chemical weapons and slowed their pace, buying time for democratic change to take place in those states.

The key factor in all these cases is that all the forms of the non-proliferation regime—the NPT, supplier controls, export controls, and diplomatic pressure—were effective in different ways and helped to prevent the acquisition of nuclear weapons by more countries. While not primary factors in and of themselves, they gave the international community a set of tools to use in different situations to achieve the same result.

CHAPTER 19

Non-Russian Nuclear Successor States: Belarus, Kazakhstan, and Ukraine

Nuclear Capabilities

When the Soviet Union dissolved in 1991, four newly independent republics—Russia, Belarus, Kazakhstan, and Ukraine—had strategic nuclear weapons deployed on their territories as well as significant amounts of nuclear materials. International security and non-proliferation concerns focused immediately on the fate of the nuclear weapons deployed in the non-Russian nuclear republics. As events unfolded, however, international non-proliferation efforts expanded to address the risks posed by stocks of weapons-usable nuclear materials in several non-Russian republics, as well as the fate of nuclear and missile experts whose knowledge could assist other countries or groups seeking to acquire weapons of mass destruction or their means of delivery. In addition, attention also eventually included efforts to reduce the risks associated with the biological and chemical weapon programs of the Soviet Union and the control and disposal of CBW agents. Because of those concerns, all nuclear weapons from the non-Russian republics have been returned to Russia, and programs are being implemented to deal with the other proliferation risks remaining in those countries.

Chemical and Biological Weapon Capabilities

None of the three non-Russian republics has biological or chemical weapon development or production programs. Each is a state party to the Chemical Weapons Convention (Ukraine ratified in 1998, Belarus in 1996, and Kazakhstan in 2000). Belarus and Ukraine are signatories of the Biological Weapons Convention; Ukraine ratified in 1975 and Belarus in 1975. The most serious proliferation concern involves the possible presence of biological agents in the Soviet biological weapon facility in Stepnogorsk, Kazakhstan. Kazakhstan is not a state party to the BWC.

Nuclear Overview

Even after the Soviet Union ceased to exist, Russia's president and military maintained operational control over the Soviet nuclear weapon arsenal. In addition to the weapons deployed on Russian territory, more than 8,000 strategic and tactical nuclear weapons were deployed in the non-Russian republics, the eventual fate of which was uncertain. All of these weapons were eventually returned to Russia, and they and their delivery systems were repatriated or destroyed in a historic achievement for the international non-proliferation regime. At no time did the non-Russian republics obtain operational control or the ability to launch the weapons, but their deployment outside Russia raised the possibility that they might eventually fall under the control of the countries in which they were deployed. That risk, in turn, caused serious international tension and concern. A failure to consolidate nuclear weapons in Russia would have provoked an unparalleled security crisis and dealt a blow to international efforts to prevent the proliferation of weapons of mass destruction.

A combination of political, legal, financial, and technical agreements was used to arrange the return of the nuclear weapons to Russia and to implement the terms of the START I treaty originally signed by the Soviet Union and the United States. That agreement was used as the mechanism by which the weapon systems deployed outside Russia were eliminated. The direct, concerted, and sustained efforts of the United States were critical in locking in the non-nuclear status of the non-Russian republics, ensuring the safe and secure return of the nuclear weapons to Russia, and eliminating nuclear weapon delivery systems controlled by START I.

The return of nuclear weapons to Russia from the three "possessor" states was accomplished using a set of international agreements and commitments, which included:

- *The Alma Ata Declaration*, December 1991. This declaration, made by eleven former Soviet republics, including Russia, Belarus, Kazakhstan, and Ukraine, committed the states to preserve a single control over nuclear weapons pending their consolidation and destruction. The states also committed to return tactical nuclear weapons to Russia no later than July 1, 1992, and strategic nuclear weapons by the end of 1994.

- *The Lisbon Protocol to the START I Treaty*, May 23, 1992. The Lisbon Protocol codified Belarus, Kazakhstan, Russia, and Ukraine as parties to the 1991 Strategic Arms Reduction Treaty as successors to the Soviet Union and to implement collectively the terms of that agreement. Belarus, Kazakhstan, and Ukraine also committed in that Protocol to accede to the Nuclear Non-Proliferation Treaty as non-nuclear-weapon states "in the shortest possible time."[1]

- *The Treaty on the Non-Proliferation of Nuclear Weapons*, July 1, 1968. This agreement defines all countries except those that had tested nuclear weapons before January 1, 1967, as non-nuclear-weapon states. In committing to join this treaty as non-nuclear-weapon states, Belarus, Kazakhstan, and Ukraine pledged not to develop, possess, or control nuclear weapons and to accept full-scope International Atomic Energy Agency safeguards.

These agreements codified Russia's position as the sole nuclear successor state to the Soviet Union and committed the non-Russian republics to return nuclear weapons deployed on their territories to Russia. The implementation of agreements, especially the implementation of the START I, was made possible only through the significant levels of U.S. financial and technical assistance. Those efforts also address the other non-proliferation risks posed by the collapse of the Soviet Union, including the presence of poorly protected nuclear-weapons-usable materials in several non-Russian republics; important former Soviet weapon production and testing facilities located in Ukraine and Kazakhstan; and other dangerous Cold War legacies.

Belarus

Belarus is a non-nuclear-weapon state and no longer has nuclear weapons deployed on its territory. At the time of the Soviet Union's collapse, almost 800 nuclear weapons were deployed in Belarus, including almost 100 warheads for the road-mobile SS–25 ICBMs and 725 tactical nuclear weapons. Russia retained command and control over those nuclear systems, including the arming and launch codes needed to use them. Nonetheless, there was serious concern that Belarus might attempt to assert ownership and control over these nuclear arms and declare itself a nuclear-weapon state.

Belarus signed the Lisbon Protocol to the START I treaty on May 23, 1992, ratified the decision on February 4, 1993, and acceded to the NPT as a non-nuclear-weapon state on July 22, 1993. Relations between the United States and Belarus began to deteriorate after the election of President Alexander Lukashenka in the summer of 1994 and there were hints by officials in Lukashenka's government that Belarus might retain some of the ICBMs on its territory. Despite these "hints," all 54 SS–25 ICBMs and nuclear warheads in Belarus were removed to Russia by November 1996. The removal of the

Table 19.1: **Nuclear Deployments in Non-Russian Republics, 1991**

	Strategic Nuclear Weapons	Tactical Nuclear Weapons
Belarus	~100	725
Kazakhstan	1,400	?
Ukraine	1,900	2,275

SOURCE

Natural Resources Defense Council. 1992 (ACT, January, 1992); discussions with former U.S. government officials, January 2002.

weapons and launchers and the elimination of the nuclear weapon deployment infrastructure all took place with the assistance of the U.S. Cooperative Threat Reduction program. Increasing human rights violations, however, led to the suspension of CTR assistance to Belarus in March 1997. Equipment provided by the United States for the destruction of 81 SS–25 ICBM launch positions was withdrawn, and dismantlement work has ceased. In addition, 1,000 metric tons of liquid rocket fuel and 9,000 metric tons of oxidizer, which were slated for elimination, remain in Belarus. The status of this material is uncertain. The CTR estimates that a total of $36.8 million will be needed to complete all remaining operations in Belarus.

Kazakhstan

Kazakhstan is a non-nuclear-weapon state, and nuclear weapons are no longer deployed on its territory. Non-proliferation concerns stemming from Kazakhstan's independence focused initially on the fate of the more than 1,400 nuclear weapons deployed in Kazakhstan. Attention later shifted to the significant amounts of unprotected nuclear-weapons-usable materials located in the country. Since its independence, however, Kazakhstan has been a model state, cooperating in the removal of nuclear arms from its territory and fully embracing international nuclear non-proliferation norms.

In implementing its arms control and non-proliferation commitments, Kazakhstan has cooperated closely with the United States and received extensive American technical and financial assistance in eliminating its strategic nuclear weapon and delivery systems, in closing the Soviet nuclear test site at Semipalatinsk, and in securing weapons-usable nuclear materials in Kazakhstan.

Nuclear Weapon Systems

Kazakhstan emerged as an independent state in December 1991 with approximately 1,410 strategic nuclear warheads deployed on its territory as well as a still-undisclosed number of tactical nuclear arms. The strategic warheads were deployed on 104 ten-warhead SS–18 intercontinental ballistic missiles and on 370 single-warhead ALCMs, the latter deliverable by Bear–H bombers.[2] The SS–18 was the most capable nuclear weapon system in the Soviet arsenal, each missile capable of carrying ten warheads over a range of 16,000 kilometers.

Kazakhstan's parliament ratified START I on July 2, 1992, and approved Kazakhstan's accession to the NPT on December 13, 1993. Its NPT instrument of ratification was deposited on February 14, 1994. By late January 1992—four months ahead of the schedule established under the Alma-Ata Declaration on Nuclear Arms—all tactical nuclear weapons on Kazakhstan's territory had been withdrawn to Russia.[3] The last strategic nuclear weapons had been removed from Kazakhstan by April 24, 1995.[4]

The U.S. CTR program in Kazakhstan has successfully resulted in the denuclearization of what would have been the world's fourth-largest nuclear weapon state, had its nuclear possessions been consolidated. All offensive strategic arms elimination programs in Kazakhstan have been successfully completed. The CTR program resulted in the return of nuclear warheads, ICBMs, and bombers to Russia and in the destruction of 104 SS–18 silo launchers, launch control centers, and test silos located at Zhangiz-Tobe, Derzhavinsk, Semipalatinsk, and Leninsk. Cooperative Threat Reduction program funds were also used to dismantle seven largely obsolete Bear bombers in Kazakhstan. Forty additional heavy strategic bombers were returned to Russia in February 1994.[5] The CTR program spent a total of $98.3 million in these efforts.

Nuclear Material Security

OPERATION SAPPHIRE. The U.S. government announced on November 23, 1994, that 581 kilograms (1,278 pounds) of highly enriched uranium—previously stored behind only a padlocked door at a uranium conversion and fuel-pellet production facility at Ust-Kamenogorsk, Kazakhstan—had been airlifted secretly to the United States in a program called Operation Sapphire.[6] Although the material had been stockpiled for use as fuel in Soviet naval propulsion reactors rather than for nuclear weapons, the bulk of the HEU was in a form that could be used directly for weapon construction, or weapon fabrication with additional processing.[7] Kazakh officials had become concerned about the material after learning that Iranian government representatives had visited Ust-Kamenogorsk seeking undisclosed nuclear support or materials, according to Bolat Nurgaliyev, then the chief of national security and arms control.[8] Kazakh experts maintained that only about 5 percent of the HEU was pure enough to be used for weapons, while the rest required further processing.

The United States agreed to compensate Kazakhstan for the material, although the transaction was not handled as a straight business deal. The U.S. compensation to Kazakhstan, although undisclosed, was estimated to be between $10 and $20 million, in both cash and in-kind assistance. According to a July 29, 1996, *Nuclear Fuel* report, the U.S. Enrichment Corporation (USEC) planned to sell LEU (on behalf of the U.S. Department of Energy) derived from the Kazakh HEU in mid-1997. After the material was shipped to the Energy Department's plant, USEC hired Babcock and Wilcox's (B&W) Naval Nuclear Fuel Division to downblend the HEU. According to B&W, roughly 90 percent of the material was in the form of uranium mixed with beryllium and a binding agent; the rest was in the form of uranium oxide or metal. The average enrichment was 89–90%. Proceeds from the sale of the blended material were to go to the U.S. Treasury.[9]

OTHER MATERIAL. A second, much larger amount of nuclear-weapons-usable material is still being stored at the former Soviet reactor complex at Aktau, Kazakhstan, on the Black Sea. The BN–350 breeder reactor located there was used in the production of "ivory-grade" plutonium for the Soviet nuclear reactor complex, and more than 3 metric tons of high-grade plutonium is stored there without any clear plan for the material's ultimate disposition. Russia has refused to accept responsibility for the material, and Kazakhstan has worked with the U.S. Department of Energy in securing the site and the material, pending a decision on where to dispose of the material permanently.

The plutonium is contained in fuel rods irradiated in the reactor and has been sealed in large containers with highly radioactive spent-fuel rods to help prevent theft of the material. Four hundred seventy-eight canisters with a mixture of high-grade plutonium-bearing fuel elements and highly radioactive spent fuel are now sealed and monitored by IAEA at the site. The canning project took two and one-half years and cost approximately $40 million. In addition, the Department of Energy provided Kazakhstan with $15 million in assistance to upgrade physical protection at the facility.[10]

SEMIPALATINSK NUCLEAR TEST FACILITY. The former Soviet Semipalatinsk Nuclear Test Site, located in northeastern Kazakhstan, was permanently closed to nuclear explosive tests in August 1991. One undetonated nuclear explosive device (with an expected yield of approximately 0.4 kiloton), however, was left by the Soviet Union in one of the test tunnels 130 meters below the surface of the test site. A Russian–Kazakh commission considered removing the device for dismantlement, but safety considerations precluded unearthing it. Instead, the device was destroyed with conventional explosives on May 31, 1995.[11]

The Cooperative Threat Reduction program provided aid to Kazakhstan in permanently shutting the nuclear test facility at Semipalatinsk. These efforts consisted of helping to seal 13 unused nuclear test holes at the Balapan test field and 181 nuclear weapon test tunnels at the Degelen Mountain tunnel complex.[12]

Biological Weapon Concerns

The Soviet Union had the world's largest offensive biological weapon program, employing at one point 65,000 people (see full discussion in chapter 6). Although the vast majority of production and test facilities were in the Russian Federation, several facilities were located outside the Russian republic. One major facility was built at Stepnogorsk, Kazakhstan. This Soviet production facility "had sufficient capacity to cultivate, process and load into munitions a total of 300 metric tons a day of dry anthrax."[13] This complex of buildings, part of the joint stock company Biomedpreparat, was part of the former Soviet Biopreparat, or "civilian," side of the Soviet BW production infrastructure. It is being dismantled in cooperation with the CTR program. The first several buildings in the complex were eliminated in September 2000, and plans for the final elimination of key facilities are ongoing.[14]

Ukraine

Ukraine is a non-nuclear-weapon state and no longer has nuclear weapons deployed on its territory. At the time of its independence in 1991, Ukraine was the deployment site for more than 1,900 strategic nuclear weapons and between 2,650 and 4,200 tactical nuclear weapons. Gaining operational control over those weapons would have made Ukraine the world's third-largest nuclear-weapon state after Russia and the United States. Following an intensive trilateral diplomatic process with both Russian and Western involvement, however, Ukraine acceded to the Nuclear Non-Proliferation Treaty on December 5, 1994, as a non-nuclear-weapon state. The removal of nuclear weapons was completed in June 1996.[15]

Nuclear Weapons

Ukraine was the deployment site for 46 SS–24 ICBMs, each equipped with ten nuclear warheads (for a total of 460 warheads), 130 SS–19 ICBMs equipped with six warheads each (a total of 780 warheads), 25 Bear–H16 strategic bombers, 19 Blackjack strategic bombers, and more than 600 air-launched cruise and air-to-surface missiles.[16] In addition, between 2,650 and 4,200 Soviet tactical nuclear weapons were estimated to have been deployed or stored in Ukraine when the Soviet Union collapsed.

Ukraine never acquired independent control over the strategic missiles deployed in Ukraine, and Russian military officers and units never relinquished the arming and targeting codes necessary to fire the missiles or detonate the warheads. Nevertheless, shortly after independence, Kiev insisted on the right to block Russia's unilateral use of the weapons that were deployed in Ukraine. In March 1992 Ukraine considered retaining some of the weapons and temporarily halted the transfer of tactical nuclear weapons to Russia.[17] In June 1992, in the first of several steps to establish some control over the nuclear arms on its soil, Ukraine asserted "administrative control" of the strategic bombers, air-launched cruise missiles, and silo-based ICBMs and attempted to replace the Russian soldiers who were guarding them with Ukrainian forces.[18] In late 1992 and early 1993 Ukraine also publicly claimed ownership of warhead components as a means of establishing its right to financial compensation for the energy value of the plutonium and highly enriched uranium they contained. Ukraine also asserted ownership of the strategic delivery vehicles (i.e., bombers and missiles). These efforts to establish control over nuclear weapons in Ukraine coincided with a highly publicized debate in the Ukrainian Rada, Ukraine's parliament, over whether the country should keep nuclear weapons to ensure its security against what many Ukrainians perceived to be a Russian threat to their still fragile independence.

LISBON PROTOCOL TO START I. On May 23, 1992, Ukraine's President Leonid Kravchuk signed the Lisbon Protocol to START I, under which Ukraine agreed to be bound by the treaty—jointly with Belarus, Kazakhstan, and Russia as successors to the obligations of the Soviet Union—and to "implement the Treaty's limits and restrictions" (article 2 of the Protocol). In considering the Lisbon Protocol, the Rada passed a resolution on November 18, 1993, purportedly to ratify START I. Yet it attached qualifications and conditions, some of which attempted to undercut the Lisbon Protocol and Kravchuk's denuclearization commitment—steps unacceptable to Russia and the United States. The resolution declared that only 36 percent of the former Soviet Union's strategic delivery vehicles and 42 percent of its strategic warheads deployed on Ukrainian territory would be subject to elimination under the START treaty, allowing Ukraine to retain the remainder on its territory indefinitely. Furthermore, the Rada made the elimination of the remaining strategic nuclear warheads and delivery vehicles conditional on Ukraine's receiving aid to cover dismantlement costs, compensation for nuclear materials to be extracted from the warheads, and complex security guarantees.

TURNING THE CORNER: THE TRILATERAL STATEMENT. The result of stepped-up negotiations with Ukraine was a deal that satisfied some of Ukraine's practical concerns and that was reflected in the January 14, 1994, Trilateral Statement. Signed by Presidents Kravchuk, Clinton, and Yeltsin, the statement was a key turning point that would lead, eventually, to Ukraine's fulfillment of its denuclearization and non-proliferation pledges. Under its terms, Ukraine would cooperate in the withdrawal to Russia of all remaining nuclear weapons (approximately 1,800 were still on Ukrainian soil) over a period that could not exceed seven years.[19] In Russia, the warheads would be dismantled (a process that the Ukrainians would observe), and the highly enriched uranium extracted from the warheads would be downblended to low-enriched uranium. Some of the LEU, in turn, would be put in the form of pellets in fuel rods and transferred to Ukraine for use in its nuclear power reactors, in compensation for relinquishing the energy value of the uranium in the strategic warheads. In addition to power reactor fuel, Ukraine would also receive U.S. economic aid and U.S. technical assistance for the safe and secure dismantlement of the strategic nuclear arms on its territory. Russia and the United States promised to provide security assurances to Ukraine upon Ukraine's accession to the NPT.

Acting on the deals made in the Trilateral Statement, the Rada on February 3 approved a resolution instructing Kravchuk to exchange the instruments of ratification of START I. The resolution acknowledged that article 5 of the Lisbon Protocol, which called for rapid adherence to the NPT by the three successor states as non-nuclear-weapon states, applied to Ukraine after all. The Rada also implicitly endorsed the Trilateral Statement. At that juncture, however, it did not specifically approve accession to the NPT.[20]

NPT ACCESSION AND START I'S ENTRY INTO FORCE. The summit of the Conference on Security and Cooperation in Europe (CSCE) held in Budapest on December 5, 1994, was chosen as the occasion for Russia, the United Kingdom, and the United States to convey identical security assurances to Ukraine, as well as similar assurances to Kazakhstan and Belarus. France also provided a security assurance to Ukraine at the CSCE summit in a separate document. On the same occasion, Ukraine presented its instruments of accession to the NPT. That action, together with earlier accessions by Belarus and Kazakhstan, satisfied Russia's conditions for exchanging the instruments of ratification for START I. Consequently, at the same meeting Belarus, Kazakhstan,

Russia, Ukraine, and the United States exchanged their START I instruments of ratification, finally bringing the treaty into force.[21]

Missile Program

Ukraine also inherited important components of the Soviet missile production industrial base, which it planned to use to manufacture space launch systems for export. Ukrainian officials estimate that Ukraine's share is about 40 percent of the "Soviet space complex's production capacity."[22] This infrastructure, however, gives Ukraine the capability to produce or export strategic and theater ballistic missiles. Certain space equipment continues to be produced at the Yuzhmash Plant, formerly the SS–18 (heavy) ICBM production facility at Dnipropetrivsk. The Yuzhmash plant was the largest Soviet ICBM factory, where SS–19, SS–20, SS–23, and SS–24 missiles were built. Today, with its two million square feet of floor space, it is the world's largest facility of its kind. It has been reported, however, that its production of military missiles has been suspended since 1991.[23]

Moreover, the former SS–24 production plant at Pavlohrad, which is also believed to be operating, may be engaged in solid-fuel space launch vehicle research and development activities.[24] Although Ukraine agreed in a Memorandum of Understanding signed in Washington on May 13, 1994, to conduct its missile- and space-related exports according to the criteria and standards of the Missile Technology Control Regime, it did not find it easy to meet all the requirements of that regime, including the elimination of its offensive missiles with ranges beyond 300 kilometers. Ukraine was finally admitted to membership in the MTCR in 1998 after agreeing to a U.S. request to cancel the planned export to Iran of electrical turbines destined for the Bushehr reactor.[25]

Comprehensive Threat Reduction Program Assistance

The United States has provided Ukraine with extensive assistance to implement its obligations under START I, including assistance in the elimination of ICBMs, ICBM silos, heavy bombers, and air-launched cruise missiles. Furthermore, going beyond the obligations of the START treaty, the United States is aiding Ukraine's programs to safely dispose of liquid and solid fuel from Soviet ICBMs.

The Cooperative Threat Reduction program provided Ukraine with rapid assistance in the form of $48.1 million for housing deactivated SS–19s and for the early deactivation of SS–24s, as well as providing emergency support assistance. These funds resulted in the elimination of 111 SS–19 ICBMs, 130 missile launch silos, 13 SS–19 launch control silos, and 2 SS–19 training silos.[26] Forty-six SS–24 missiles have been removed from their silos. The missiles (totaling 55 SS–24s, including nine that were never deployed) are being stored at CTR-refurbished or -built facilities at Pervomaysk and Mikhaillenki, pending rocket-motor elimination. The elimination of the SS–24 silos will continue through 2002, although a timetable for final elimination has not been set.[27]

Ukrainian-based SS–19s contained 11,700 metric tons of propellant that required storage and elimination. The CTR provided heavy equipment and 58 "intermodal tank" containers to Ukraine for this purpose and for the construction of a fuel-storage facility at Shevchenkovo for 60 CTR-provided fuel containers. Currently, fuel is being stored at the missile bases at Khmelnitskiy and Pervomaysk. The CTR is also providing assistance in the modification and certification of two fuel incinerators.[28]

Assistance from CTR has also been provided to remove and safely eliminate solid propellant from the 54 SS–24s that were in Ukraine at the time of the Soviet breakup. Initial assistance was provided for the temporary storage of the missiles, and the START I Lisbon Protocol requires the elimination of SS–24 silos by December 4, 2001. Ukraine is currently evaluating fuel-disposal technologies, and CTR estimates that an elimination facility could be operational in the summer of 2002. The Pavlohrad Chemical Plant, the former manufacturing site for these solid-rocket motors, has been selected as the future elimination facility.

Comprehensive Threat Reduction programs also planned to eliminate up to 44 heavy bombers (25 Tu–95/Bears and 19 Tu–160/Blackjacks) by December 4, 2001. Eleven heavy bombers (3 Bear and 8 Blackjacks) were transferred to Russia in February 2000.[29] The remaining 18 bombers were slated for elimination in Ukraine by the end of 2001.

Conclusions

The existence of large numbers of advance nuclear weapons and strategic delivery systems in several non-Russian republics after the demise of the Soviet Union threatened the entire international non-proliferation regime. Moreover, it could have led to the birth of four nuclear-weapon states after the Soviet collapse, instead of just one. Such a situation would have irrevocably changed the international security landscape and increased dramatically the role played by nuclear weapons in global affairs.

The successful denuclearization of Belarus, Kazakhstan, and Ukraine is an unparalleled non-proliferation and security success story, and one that illustrates the value of international norms against the spread of nuclear weapons and other weapons of mass destruction. In addition, the successful implementation of non-proliferation efforts in these three countries could not have been accomplished without the provision of adequate financial, political, and technical resources to implement the removal and elimination of these weapons.

Kazakhstan and Ukraine continue to possess assets that could aid in the production of either nuclear weapons or strategic delivery systems. Nuclear materials, missile production facilities, and civil nuclear infrastructures in both countries remain sources of proliferation concern. These capabilities, however, are not unique in the developed world. Standard approaches, including effective export controls, International Atomic Energy Agency safeguards, and material protection assistance are more than capable of addressing the residual proliferation risks in these countries.

NOTES

1. State Department Fact Sheet, *START I: Lisbon Protocol and the Nuclear Non-Proliferation Treaty*, February 14, 1995, U.S. State Department, Office of Public Affairs.

2. START I Treaty Memorandum of Understanding (MOU) on Data ; Dunbar Lockwood, "New Data from the Clinton Administration on the Status of Strategic Nuclear Weapons Deactivations," Memorandum, Arms Control Association (Washington, D.C., December 7, 1994).

3. See "Chronology of Commonwealth Security Issues," *Arms Control Today*, May 1992, p. 27.

4. Prepared remarks of U.S. Undersecretary of Defense for Policy Walter B. Slocombe before the Senate Armed Services Committee, May 17, 1995.

5. "All Strategic Bombers out of Kazakhstan, Talks on Those in Ukraine," RFE/RL *News Briefs*, vol. 3, no. 9, 2/21–25/94.

6. R. Jeffrey Smith, "U.S. Takes Nuclear Fuel," *Washington Post*, November 23, 1994; Steven Erlanger, "Kazakhstan Thanks U.S. on Uranium," *New York Times*, November 25, 1994.

7. Interviews with U.S. government officials, December 1994.

8. Rowan Scarborough, "Tale Told of How Iran Nearly Got Nuke Gear," *Washington Post*, November 2, 1996.

9. Monterey Institute of International Studies Fact Sheet, November 21, 2001. Available at cns.miis.edu/db/nisprofs/kazakst/fissmat/cfissmat/sapphire.htm.

10. "U.S. Department of Energy (DOE) and the Republic of Kazakhstan Ministry of Energy Mark the Completion of the Packaging of the BN–350 Fast Breeder Reactor Spent Fuel," DOE press release, July 12, 2001.

11. Bruce Pannier, "Kazakhstan Nuclear-Free," *OMRI Daily Digest*, June 1, 1995, p. 3; Douglas Busvine, "Kazakhstan To Blow up Four-Year-Old Nuclear Device," *Reuters*, May 25, 1995; Bruce Pannier, "Kazakhstan To Explode Nuclear Device," *OMRI Daily Digest*, May 24, 1995, p. 2; and Pannier, "Nuclear Bomb To Be Removed from Kazakhstan Test Site," *Komsomolskaya Pravda*, May 13, 1994, in FBIS–SOV–94–093, pp. 13–14.

12. CTR Kazakhstan Accomplishment web site, November 20, 2001, www.dtra.mil/ctr/project/projkaz/ctr_nuclear_elim.html.

13. See Jonathan B. Tucker and Kathleen M. Vogal, "Preventing the Proliferation of Chemical and Biological Weapon Materials and Know-How," *Nonproliferation Review*, spring 2000, vol. 7, no. 1; and Judith Miller et al., *Germs: Biological Weapons and America's Secret War* (New York: Simon and Schuster, 2001).

14. U.S. Department of Defense Fact Sheet, " Biological Weapons Production Facility Dismantlement," December 2001, Defense Threat Reduction Agency web site, www.dtra.mil/ctr/project/projkaz/ctr_bioweap_disman.html.

15. "Kuchma Issues Statement on Removal of Nuclear Weapons," UT–1 Television, June 1, 1996, in FBIS–SOV–96–107, June 5, 1996.

16. See *Treaty between the United States of America and the Union of Soviet Socialist Republics on the Reduction and Limitation of Strategic Offensive Arms*, signed in Moscow on July 31, 1991 (Washington, D.C.: U.S. Arms Control and Disarmament Agency, 1991). Also see *START-related Facilities by Republic as Declared in MOU Data Exchange, September 1, 1990*, Hearings on the START Treaty, Committee on Foreign Relations, U.S. Senate, 102nd Cong., 2nd Sess., February 6, 1992, p. 495.

17. "Ukraine Says Arms Transfer Delay Temporary," *Reuters*, March 25, 1992.

18. "Ukraine Said Seeking Command of Nuclear Forces," *Izvestiya*, June 11, 1992, in FBIS–SOV, June 11, 1992, p. 2.

19. General Roland LaJoie, special briefing on the CTR program. In congressional testimony in October 1994, Assistant Secretary of Defense Ashton Carter reported that there were 1,734 warheads in Ukraine before the initiation of the dismantlement process in January 1994 as opposed to 1,564 warheads as cited in the START I Memorandum of Understanding. See *Testimony of Assistant Secretary of Defense Ashton Carter before the Senate Foreign Relations Committee*, October 4, 1994.

20. John W. R. Lepingwell, "Ukrainian Parliament Removes START I Conditions," Radio Free Europe–Radio Liberty Research Report, February 25, 1994, p. 37.

21. See "Text of Resolution Detailing NPT Reservations," Kiev Radio Ukraine World Service in Ukraine, in FM–FBIS, London, November 16, 1994; "Ukraine Joins Treaty Curbing Nuclear Arms," *Washington Post*, November 17, 1994; and "Ukraine Accedes to NPT Treaty," *United Press International*, December 5, 1994.

22. Gary Bertch and Victor Zaborsky, "Bringing Ukraine into the MTCR: Can U.S. Policy Succeed?" *Arms Control Today*, April 1997.

23. Ibid.

24. U.S. Congress, Office of Technology Assessment, *Technologies Underlying Weapons of Mass Destruction*, OTA–BPISC–I 15, December 1993, p. 12; "Perry Visits Strategic Missile Unit," Moscow, ITAR–TASS, March 22, 1994, in FBIS–SOV–94–056, March 23, 1994, p. 27; "Implementation of Lisbon Protocol," Hearings on the START Treaty, Committee on Foreign Relations, U.S. Senate, 102nd Cong., 2nd Sess., June 23, 1992, p. 199.

25. *Arms Control Reporter*, 2001, p. 706.A.7.

26. CTR Program Plan, P. IV-5, Volodymyr Chumak and Serhey Galaka, "Programma Nann-Lugara v Ukraine" (Nunn-Lugar Program in Ukraine), Kiev, October 1999.

27. Center for Nonproliferation Studies staff correspondence with Volodymyr Chumak, June 2000.

28. CTR Program Plan, p. IV–5.

29. "Zavershena perebroska iz Ukrainy v Rossiyu gruppirovki strategicheskikh bombardirovshchikov," *Interfax*, February 21, 2000, in Center for Nonproliferation Studies' NIS Nuclear Profiles Database, *Russia: Nuclear Weapons*, "Bomber/ALCM Force Developments."

Table 19.2: **Belarus: Nuclear Infrastructure and Other Sites of Proliferation Concern**

NAME/LOCATION OF FACILITY	TYPE/STATUS	IAEA SAFEGUARDS
FORMER NUCLEAR WEAPON FACILITIES		
Lida, former SS–25 missile base		No
Mozyr,* former SS–25 missile base		No
NUCLEAR RESEARCH FACILITIES		
Institute for Power Engineering Problems, Sosny, Minsk	Fresh- and spent-fuel storage; approximately 15 g of plutonium and 370 kg weapons-grade HEU present	Yes
RESEARCH REACTORS		
IRT–M (Institute for Power Engineering Problems)	Pool, HEU, 4–8 MWt; decomissioned	Yes
Critical Assembly 1	Fast critical assembly, LEU; not operating	Yes
Critical Assembly 2	Fast critical assembly, 90% enriched U; not operating	Yes
Experimental reactor, Sosny, Minsk	Neutron generator; operating Yes	

Abbreviations

HEU   highly enriched uranium
LEU   low-enriched uranium
MWt   millions of watts of thermal output

* See Jon Wolfsthal et al., eds., *Nuclear Status Report: Nuclear Weapons, Fissile Material, and Export Controls in the Former Soviet Union* (Washington, D.C.: Carnegie Endowment for International Peace and Monterey, Cal.: Monterey Institute of International Studies, June 2001), p. 158.

Table 19.3: **Kazakhstan: Nuclear Infrastructure and Other Sites of Proliferation Concern**

NAME/LOCATION OF FACILITY	TYPE/STATUS	IAEA SAFEGUARDS[1]
FORMER NUCLEAR WEAPON FACILITIES		
Derzhavinsk	Former SS–18 ICBM base	No
Zhangiz Tobe	Former SS–18 ICBM base	No
Semipalatinsk	Soviet nuclear test range (closed August 1991) Soviet strategic bomber base	
NUCLEAR RESEARCH CENTERS		
Institute of Atomic Energy, Almaty (also Institute of Nuclear Physics)	Hot cell facilities and nuclear material storage; HEU present	Yes
POWER REACTORS		
Aktau	BN–350 (sodium-cooled, fast-breeder), 335-MWe, closed; 3 MT of Pu stored	Yes
RESEARCH REACTORS		
Institute of Nuclear Physics, Almaty	WWR–K, 36% HEU, 10-MWe; operating	Yes
Institute of Nuclear Physics, Almaty	Critical assembly; operating	Yes
IGR (Baikal Test Facility) Semipalatinsk	Graphite-moderated, water-cooled, fueled with 90% HEU; operating; 14 kg of fresh and spent HEU located here	Yes
IVG–1M, Semipalatinsk	60-MWt reactor; 90% HEU; operating	Yes
RA, Semipalatinsk	0.4-MWt experimental reactor, 90% HEU; not operating	Yes
URANIUM PROCESSING		
Stepnogorsk	Uranium mining; operating	Yes
Ulba Metallurgy Plant, Ust-Kamenogorsk	Uranium conversion facility (UO_2) and fuel-pellet production for VVER and RBMK reactors; operating	N/A

Abbreviations

HEU	highly enriched uranium
nat. U	natural uranium
MT	metric ton
Pu	plutonium
MWe	millions of watts of electrical output
MWt	millions of watts of thermal output
N/A	not applicable

NOTES

1. As required by its adherence to the NPT, Kazakhstan signed a full-scope safeguard agreement with the IAEA, which entered into force on August 11, 1995, that subjects all nuclear materials and activities in Kazakhstan to IAEA monitoring.

Table 19.4: **Ukraine: Nuclear Infrastructure and Other Sites of Proliferation Concern**

NAME/LOCATION OF FACILITY	TYPE/STATUS	IAEA SAFEGUARDS
FORMER NUCLEAR WEAPON BASES AND SUPPORT FACILITIES		
Pervomaysk	Former SS–19 and SS–24 missile base; SS–24 missile storage site	
Khmelnitskiy	Former SS–24 missile base; SS–24 missile storage site	
Uzin	Former strategic bomber base and bomber conversion and elimination facility	
Priluki	Former strategic bomber base	
Mikhaylenk	ICBM storage facility	
Pavlograd Machine Plant	Former SS–24 production facility. Future site of ICBM solid-rocket motor elimination	
Yuzhmash Plant, Dnipropetrivsk	Former SS–18 production facility	
Pomerki	Former SS–18 training facility	
Sarny	ICBM conversion and elimination facility	
NUCLEAR RESEARCH FACILITIES		
Institute of Nuclear Research Kiev	Research center and nuclear material storage with HEU in fuel assemblies (see below for research reactors) and small amounts of Pu	Yes
Kharkiv Physics and Technology Institute Kharkiv	Nuclear physics research and nuclear material storage; up to 75 kg of 90% enriched HEU in bulk and item form	Yes
Sevastopol Institute of Nuclear Energy and Industry Sevastopol	Reactor training facility and subcritical assemblies; HEU present (see below for research reactors)	Yes
POWER REACTORS		
Khmelnitskiy Unit 1 Neteshin	VVER–1000, LEU, 950-MWe; operating	Yes
Khmelnitskiy Unit 2, 3, and 4 Neteshin	VVER–1000, LEU, 950-MWe; under construction	Yes
Rovno 1 Kuznetsovsk	VVER–440, LEU, 361 and 384-MWe, operating	Yes
Rovno 2 Kuznetsovsk	VVER–440, LEU, 384-MWe, operating	Yes
Rovno, Unit 3	VVER–1000, LEU, 950-MWe; operating	Yes

Rovno, Unit 4	VVER–1000, LEU, 950-MWe; under construction	Yes
South Ukraine, Units 1, 2, 3 Kostantinovsk	VVER–1000, LEU, 950-MWe; operating	Yes
Zaporozhe, Units 1–6 Energodar	VVER–1000, LEU, 950-MWe; operating	Yes
RESEARCH REACTORS		
WWR–M (Institute of Nuclear Research) Kiev	Tank WWR, 36% and 90% enriched HEU, 10-MWt; operating; 100 kg of HEU on site	Yes
IR–100 (Sevastopol Institute of Nuclear Energy and Industry) Sevastopol	Pool, up to 36% enriched HEU, 200-kWt; shut down	Yes
Subcritical Assemblies Sevastopol	2 subcritical assemblies fueled with up to 36% enriched HEU; operating	Yes
URANIUM PROCESSING		
Zheltiye Vody	Uranium mining and milling; operating	N/A
HEAVY WATER PRODUCTION		
Dnepropetrovsk	Pridneprovsky Chemical Plant; can produce up to 250 metric tons of heavy water/year	Yes

Abbreviations

Pu	plutonium
HEU	highly enriched uranium
LEU	low-enriched uranium
MWe	millions of watts of electrical output
MWt	millions of watts of thermal output
kWt	thousands of watts of thermal output

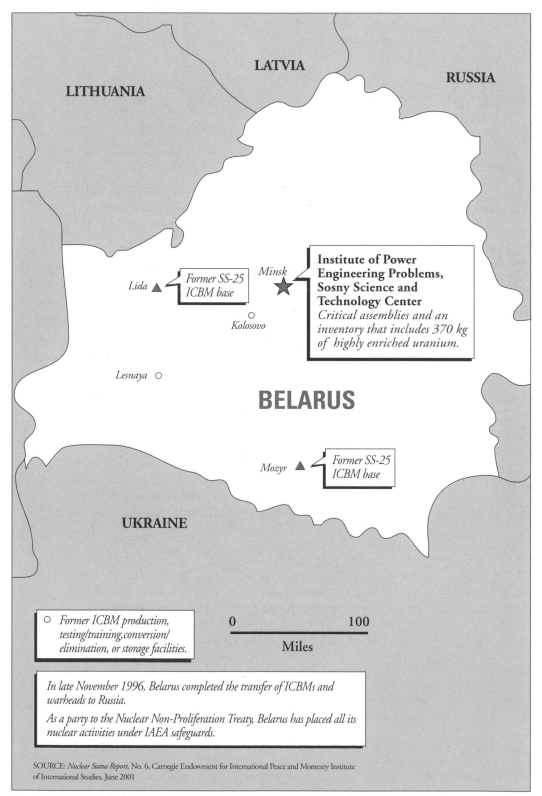

LITHUANIA

LATVIA

RUSSIA

Lida ▲ ┌─────────────┐
    │ *Former SS-25* │
    │ *ICBM base* │

Minsk ★

┌──────────────────────────┐
│ **Institute of Power** │
│ **Engineering Problems,** │
│ **Sosny Science and** │
│ **Technology Center** │
│ *Critical assemblies and an* │
│ *inventory that includes 370 kg* │
│ *of highly enriched uranium.* │
└──────────────────────────┘

○
Kolosovo

Lesnaya ○

BELARUS

Mozyr ▲ ┌─────────────┐
        │ *Former SS-25* │
        │ *ICBM base* │

UKRAINE

┌────────────────────────────┐
│ ○ *Former ICBM production,* │
│   *testing/training,conversion/* │
│   *elimination, or storage facilities.* │
└────────────────────────────┘

0 ──────────────── 100

Miles

┌──┐
│ *In late November 1996, Belarus completed the transfer of ICBMs and* │
│ *warheads to Russia.* │
│ │
│ *As a party to the Nuclear Non-Proliferation Treaty, Belarus has placed all its* │
│ *nuclear activities under IAEA safeguards.* │
└──┘

SOURCE: *Nuclear Status Report*, No. 6, Carnegie Endowment for International Peace and Monterey Institute of International Studies, June 2001

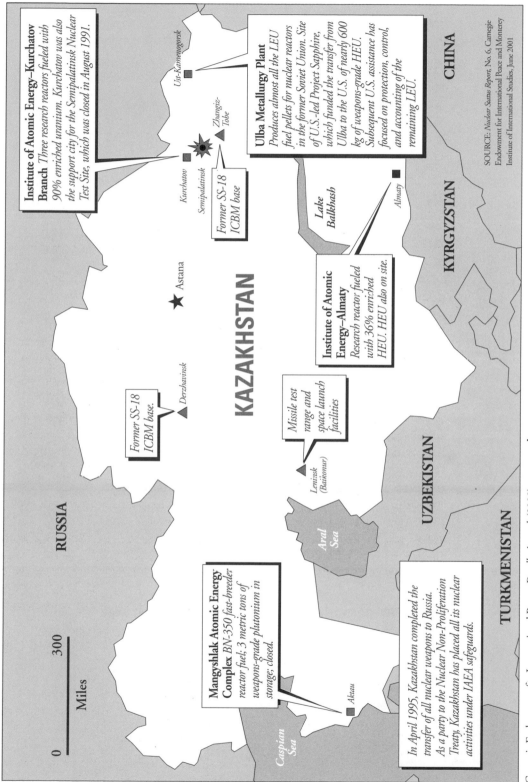

Institute of Atomic Energy–Kurchatov Branch *Three research reactors fueled with 90% enriched uranium. Kurchatov was also the support city for the Semipalatinsk Nuclear Test Site, which was closed in August 1991.*

Ulba Metallurgy Plant *Produces almost all the LEU fuel pellets for nuclear reactors in the former Soviet Union. Site of U.S.-led Project Sapphire, which funded the transfer from Ulba to the U.S. of nearly 600 kg of weapons-grade HEU. Subsequent U.S. assistance has focused on protection, control, and accounting of the remaining LEU.*

Institute of Atomic Energy–Almaty *Research reactor fueled with 36% enriched HEU. HEU also on site.*

Former SS-18 ICBM base

Missile test range and space launch facilities

Former SS-18 ICBM base.

Mangyshlak Atomic Energy Complex *BN-350 fast-breeder reactor fuel; 3 metric tons of weapons-grade plutonium in storage; closed.*

In April 1995, Kazakhstan completed the transfer of all nuclear weapons to Russia. As a party to the Nuclear Non-Proliferation Treaty, Kazakhstan has placed all its nuclear activities under IAEA safeguards.

RUSSIA

CHINA

KYRGYZSTAN

UZBEKISTAN

TURKMENISTAN

KAZAKHSTAN

Ust-Kamenogorsk

Zhangiz-Tobe

Kurchatov

Semipalatinsk

Astana

Derzhavinsk

Leninsk (Baikonur)

Aktau

Almaty

Lake Balkhash

Aral Sea

Caspian Sea

0   300

Miles

SOURCE: *Nuclear Status Report*, No. 6, Carnegie Endowment for International Peace and Monterey Institute of International Studies, June 2001

Carnegie Endowment for International Peace, *Deadly Arsenals* (2002), **www.ceip.org**

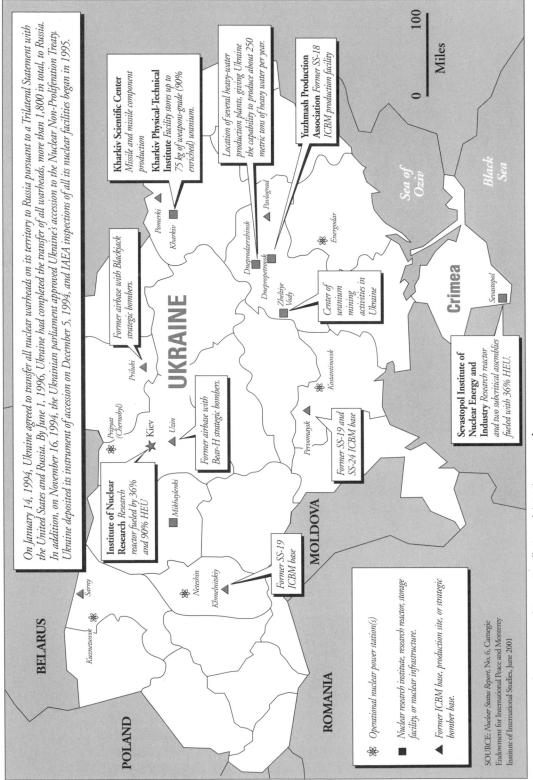

On January 14, 1994, Ukraine agreed to transfer all nuclear warheads on its territory to Russia pursuant to a Trilateral Statement with the United States and Russia. By June 1, 1996, Ukraine had completed the transfer of all warheads, more than 1,800 in total, to Russia. In addition, on November 16, 1994, the Ukrainian parliament approved Ukraine's accession to the Nuclear Non-Proliferation Treaty. Ukraine deposited its instrument of accession on December 5, 1994, and IAEA inspections of all its nuclear facilities began in 1995.

Kharkiv Scientific Center *Missile and missile component production*

Kharkiv Physical-Technical Institute *Facility stores up to 75 kg of weapons-grade (90% enriched) uranium.*

Location of several heavy-water production plants, giving Ukraine the capability to produce about 250 metric tons of heavy water per year.

Yuzhmash Production Association *Former SS-18 ICBM production facility*

Center of uranium mining activities in Ukraine

Sevastopol Institute of Nuclear Energy and Industry *Research reactor and two subcritical assemblies fueled with 36% HEU.*

Former airbase with Blackjack strategic bombers.

Former airbase with Bear-H strategic bombers.

Former SS-19 and SS-24 ICBM base

Institute of Nuclear Research *Research reactor fueled by 36% and 90% HEU*

Former SS-19 ICBM base

UKRAINE

Crimea

BELARUS

POLAND

MOLDOVA

ROMANIA

Sea of Oziv

Black Sea

Sarny

Kaznetsionsk

Netesbin

Khmelnitskiy

Mikhaylenki

Pripyat (Chernobyl)

Kiev

Uzin

Priluki

Pomerki

Kharkiv

Dneprodzerzhinsk

Dnepropetrovsk

Zheltiye Vody

Pavlograd

Energodar

Kostantinovsk

Pervomaysk

Sevastopol

❊ Operational nuclear power station(s)

▪ Nuclear research institute, research reactor, storage facility, or nuclear infrastructure.

▲ Former ICBM base, production site, or strategic bomber base.

SOURCE: *Nuclear Status Report,* No. 6, Carnegie Endowment for International Peace and Monterey Institute of International Studies, June 2001

0   100
Miles

Carnegie Endowment for International Peace, *Deadly Arsenals* (2002), **www.ceip.org**

CHAPTER 20

Argentina

Nuclear Weapon Capability

Today, Argentina does not possess nuclear weapons or unsafeguarded stocks of nuclear-weapons-usable materials, but during the 1960s to 1980s it did have a nuclear development program that many observers feared would be applied to weapon production. Argentina is among the very few countries that have been able to develop a nuclear program without becoming dependent on foreign technology, and it has become a significant exporter of peaceful nuclear technology in its own right. As a full partner in all major elements of the nuclear non-proliferation regime, Argentina has continued to develop its civil nuclear industry. Notably, Argentina joined the Nuclear Suppliers Group and curtailed its nuclear exports to high-risk nations, while still enjoying success in exporting nuclear products and services around the world.

Biological and Chemical Weapon Capability

There is no public information to suggest that Argentina has ever had research or production programs for either chemical or biological weapons. It is a member of the Biological Weapons Convention and the Chemical Weapons Convention.

Nuclear Analysis

The Argentine nuclear program sought to realize several objectives, including the autonomous mastery of advanced technology, energy independence, regional and international prestige, and perhaps to create the option to develop atomic weapons or "peaceful nuclear explosives." Argentine nuclear history was intertwined with that of neighboring rival Brazil, but the complex relationship between the two states included cooperative dimensions in nuclear affairs even at the height of political-strategic tensions in the 1970s.[1] When military rule ended in 1983, Argentina was close to attaining a nuclear weapon option. It has since curtailed activities toward that goal, with potential military applications, and has opened all its nuclear facilities for international inspection.

In late 2001 and in the beginning of 2002, Argentina suffered an acute political-economic crisis, with deadly street riots, a succession of five presidents in just two weeks' time, and a partial default on the country's international loans. After four years of recession, one in five Argentines is unemployed, and more acute national suffering is likely in the future. The severity and resolution of this crisis remain uncertain. Yet, even in this dire time, there is little reason to fear a coup by the armed forces, foreign military adventurism, or any form of nuclear crisis. Recent events offer no reason to doubt that Argentina's commitment to non-proliferation remains firm. Argentina currently has no source of weapons-grade material, lacking both an operational plutonium-separation (chemical reprocessing) plant or a uranium-enrichment facility. The restructuring of the National Atomic Energy Commission (CNEA), which was established in 1950, and commercial success in Argentina's nuclear sector provides further reassurance.

By 1953 the National Atomic Energy Commission had launched a research program and had started mining uranium.[2] Argentina's nuclear program received no outside assistance until 1958, when a U.S.–designed research reactor, the RA–1, was built at Constituyentes following the signing of a nuclear cooperation agreement in 1955.

Using the plans for RA–1, Argentina had built, unaided, three additional research reactors by 1967: the RA–0 at Cordoba, the RA–2 at Constituyentes, and the RA–3 at Ezeiza. By that time, the infrastructure to support a nuclear power plant was also in place, and in 1968 Argentina bought a 320-MWe reactor, Atucha I, from the West German firm Siemens. At the same time, it was pursuing sensitive nuclear development activities, including a laboratory-scale reprocessing facility, which it built at Ezeiza. This facility was closed in 1973, however, after intermittent operation and the extraction of less than 1 kilogram of plutonium from reprocessed spent fuel.[3]

For many years Argentina rejected the International Atomic Energy Agency inspection of its indigenous nuclear facilities, and only at West German insistence was the Atucha plant safeguarded. Following negotiations on the Treaty of Tlatelolco and the NPT in 1967–1968, Argentina refused to join either, on the ground that the treaties would compromise its sovereignty and impose restrictions on its nuclear program (see below under International Cooperation). Argentine officials denounced the NPT as a discriminatory effort by the nuclear-weapon states that amounted to little more than the "disarmament of the disarmed."[4] Argentina also argued that IAEA safeguards did not apply to its indigenously built facilities, and particularly not to the reprocessing laboratory at Ezeiza, even though evidence existed that an Italian firm had participated in its construction.[5]

The drive for nuclear self-sufficiency and, apparently, for a nuclear weapon option, increased after the 1976 coup, which installed a military junta. This ambition was motivated in part by Brazil's 1975 deal with West Germany to acquire the entire nuclear fuel cycle, as well as by the 1978 U.S. Nuclear Non-Proliferation Act, which called into question future supplies of uranium fuel for Argentine reactors.[6] In 1978 the CNEA began to build a second reprocessing facility at Ezeiza with a design capacity of 10–20 kilograms of plutonium a year. Argentina insisted that the facility would be used only for making reactor fuel, but it refused to allow IAEA inspections. Construction ceased, however, in 1990 in the face of U.S. pressure (see table 20.1).

The most serious cause for proliferation concern in Argentina was suddenly revealed in late 1983, just before the inauguration of its first democratically elected government in ten years. The departing military junta revealed that a gaseous-diffusion uranium-enrichment plant had been built since 1978 in complete secrecy at Pilcaniyeu (see map at the end of the chapter). The junta's assurances that the facility was intended for peaceful purposes did not allay suspicions that it was to be part of a clandestine nuclear weapon development program.

The inauguration of Argentine President Raul Alfonsin in December 1983 led to significant policy shifts. The nuclear program, which had been directed by retired navy admirals, was placed under civilian direction, the CNEA budget was cut, and the new government introduced legislation to prohibit the development of nuclear weapons. Nuclear confidence-building measures with Brazil were agreed upon in November 1985. That agreement culminated in reciprocal visits beginning in 1987 to the most sensitive nuclear installations in both countries (i.e., those involved in reprocessing or enrichment and not subject to IAEA inspection). An extensive series of bilateral nuclear cooperation and consultation agreements were also put in place.[7]

The Pilcaniyeu plant is thought to have produced only small amounts of very low enriched uranium and no weapons-grade material (i.e., uranium enriched to 90 percent U–235 or more).[8] Argentina has pledged not to produce HEU in the future, and the plant is subject to close inspection under various international treaties (see below). Commercial decisions now drive Argentina's nuclear program; since 1997 a key concern has been privatization of the nuclear sector. In preparation, the CNEA was restructured with key functions (such as regulation and power generation) now given over to independent bodies.

Argentina–Brazil Rapprochement

Rivalry for regional leadership and military suspicions has fueled the competition between Brazil and Argentina in nuclear development since the early 1950s. As explained earlier here, cooperative elements endured even when bilateral relations were at their worst, notably in nuclear science and diplomacy, and the military governments signed formal cooperation accords in nuclear commerce in 1980.[9] Both countries pursued proliferation-sensitive enrichment and reprocessing activities, as well as civilian research and energy programs. After the transitions from military rule in the mid-1980s, however, Brazil and Argentina took steps that definitively ended their nuclear rivalry. On July 18, 1991, the Argentine and Brazilian foreign ministers signed a bilateral agreement renouncing peaceful nuclear explosives, allowing mutual inspections of nuclear installations, and setting up the Argentine-Brazilian Accounting and Control Commission (ABACC) to implement their commitment. A quadripartite agreement to integrate ABACC's inspection system with that of the IAEA was signed by Argentina, Brazil, the IAEA, and ABACC in Vienna on December 13, 1991. Exchanges of nuclear material inventories and mutual inspections began in late 1992 after the inauguration of ABACC. Argentina's Congress approved the Quadripartite Safeguards Agreement in 1992, but inspections were delayed until it entered into force on March 4, 1994, following approval by Brazil's Congress in February 1994.[10] The agreement made

ABACC and the IAEA responsible for undertaking an initial inventory of all nuclear materials in Argentina as a basis for inspections, a task complicated by years of unsafeguarded activities at Pilcaniyeu.

During 1995 the IAEA's verification of nuclear material and facility design information was "largely completed."[11] ABACC has also successfully implemented its program of ad hoc inspections at nuclear facilities in Argentina, conducting 79 inspections in 1996 and 18 from May to August 2000.[12] The facility of principal concern—the uranium enrichment plant at Pilcaniyeu—has been under an ABACC ad hoc inspection agreement since 1992 and subject to close monitoring and accounting procedures for its materials.[13]

International Cooperation

In January 1994 Argentina acceded to the Treaty for the Prohibition of Nuclear Weapons in Latin America and the Caribbean (the Treaty of Tlatelolco), undertaking not to acquire, manufacture, test, use, or permit the stationing of a nuclear explosive device on its territory and accepting IAEA inspections of all its nuclear activities. That same year it joined the Nuclear Suppliers Group, accepting restrictions on the kinds of nuclear technology it could export. Argentina became a party to the NPT on February 10, 1995.

On February 29, 1996, Foreign Minister Di Tella signed a new agreement for peaceful nuclear cooperation with then–U.S. Secretary of State Warren Christopher. President Clinton submitted the agreement to Congress for statutory review on March 18, 1996, and it came into force on October 16, 1997. A further technical agreement, signed with the CNEA during Clinton's October 1997 trip to Argentina, promotes the exchange of information, cooperative research, and development between Argentine and U.S. nuclear laboratories.[14] The same year a cooperation agreement with Euratom entered into force, replacing an earlier one that had lapsed in 1983.[15] Argentina also has many bilateral nuclear cooperation arrangements with other states, including a wide-ranging agreement signed in 2000 with Australia.[16]

Nuclear Exports

Argentina's comparative self-sufficiency in its nuclear program enabled it to become a major second-tier supplier of nuclear technology and equipment, first to developing nations and later to Europe and Australia. Before Argentina acceded to the NPT, that trend confounded efforts by the United States and others to prevent the spread of a nuclear weapon capability to such countries as Iran and Libya.[17] The return to democratic government in 1983 did little to change Argentina's liberal export policy, especially with respect to North Africa.

In 1974, Argentina concluded a deal to provide Libya with equipment for uranium mining and processing. In 1982, when Argentina was engaged in a war over the Falkland (or Malvina) Islands, Libya supplied $100 million in anti-aircraft and air-to-air missiles. In exchange, Argentina may have provided information or technology for Libya's nuclear weapon program. Close nuclear cooperation is thought to have continued after the Falklands/Malvinas War, with discussions focusing on the possibility of Argentina's exporting reprocessing and enrichment technologies.[18] Reports in 1985 suggested that Argentina was prepared to supply a hot cell facility to Libya, and only U.S. pressure prevented the sale.[19]

In 1985 Argentina and Algeria concluded an agreement under which Argentina exported a 1-megawatt research reactor that went critical in 1989, despite the fact that Algeria was not then a NPT member and had no safeguard agreement with the IAEA. Subsequent plans to sell Algeria an isotope production reactor and hot cell facility were not pursued.[20]

Argentina was also involved in the development of Iran's nuclear program. In 1987 the CNEA joined a consortium set up to complete the Bushehr nuclear power facility, but the project was suspended in 1995. Early in 1992 Argentina was ready to supply Iran with a fuel-fabrication facility and uranium dioxide conversion plant; only last-minute pressure, again from the United States, stopped the shipment. While the facilities were intended for Iran's nuclear power program and would have come under IAEA safeguards, if misused they would have contributed indirectly to weapon development. Iran also sought hot-cell and heavy-water production facilities, but Argentina refused to export the equipment.[21]

Early in his first term, President Carlos Menem took dramatic steps to ally with the United States and to alleviate U.S. concerns regarding Argentine nuclear exports to questionable recipients. In 1992 he put in place a nuclear export-control policy by presidential decree.[22] Two years later Argentina became a member of the Nuclear Suppliers Group.

Exports continue to play an important role in supporting Argentina's nuclear industry. Its decision to comply with NSG guidelines has not had too serious an impact on its export opportunities. Argentina remains a major supplier of nuclear technology and training to the developing world, in particular to Latin America, and it increasingly supplies equipment and services to other customers. Recent clients have included Germany (heavy water in 1997 and 1999), South Korea (heavy water in 1997 and 2000), and Australia (a research reactor in 2000).

Missile Analysis

Today, Argentina has no ballistic missile program or missile stockpile, but for many years it sought to develop a potent medium-range ballistic missile, the Condor II. Although much less reliable information on Argentine missile history exists than on its nuclear affairs, some aspects are noted here.

In the late 1970s the Argentine air force began work on Condor I, a single-stage weather rocket that could be adapted as a short-range tactical missile. After the change of government in 1983, missile development continued, and in 1984 Argentina concluded an agreement with Iraq and Egypt to develop the Condor II, a 1,000-kilometer, two-stage system with a potential payload of 500 kilograms. Argentina was to construct and test the missiles with Iraq providing funding through Egypt, with program managers acquiring technical expertise and equipment from a variety of European sources.[23] The United States and other members of the Missile Technology Control Regime identified the Condor II as being of major concern. Egypt withdrew from the project in September 1989, and in March 1990 Argentina suspended the project because of a lack of funds and cancelled it the next month.[24] After much bureaucratic infighting within the Argentine government, the missile facilities were dismantled and proliferation-sensitive components of the program were physically destroyed, which cleared the way for Argentina to join the MTCR. It did so on November 29, 1994.

Since scrapping the Condor II, Argentina has not undertaken further research and development on medium-range ballistic missiles or on an indigenous space launch vehicle. In early 1997, however, Brazil and Argentina began to discuss the joint design and construction of a commercial rocket for low-altitude satellite launches.[25] Although Brazil was required to give up its development of medium-range missiles when it joined the MTCR, it was allowed to maintain its commercial space launch program.

Biological and Chemical Weapons Analysis

Argentina has no known chemical or biological weapon programs and is a party to both the Biological Weapons Convention and the Chemical Weapons Convention. It has also signed the 1991 Mendoza Accord (Joint Declaration on the Complete Prohibition of Chemical and Biological Weapons), a regional non-proliferation agreement.

NOTES

1. Michael Barletta, "Ambiguity, Autonomy, and the Atom: Emergence of the Argentine-Brazilian Nuclear Regime" (Ph.D. diss., University of Wisconsin, 2000), pp. 101–109.

2. Daniel Poneman, *Nuclear Power in the Developing World* (London: Allen and Unwin, 1982), pp. 68–72.

3. Leonard Spector, *Nuclear Proliferation Today* (New York: Vintage Books, 1984), p. 203.

4. Barletta, "Ambiguity, Autonomy, and the Atom," pp. 115–117; and Julio C. Carasales, *El Desarme de los Desarmados: Argentina y el Tratado de No Proliferación de Armas Nucleares* (Buenos Aires: Pleamar, 1987).

5. Robert Laufer, "Argentina Looks to Reprocessing To Fill Its Own Needs Plus Plutonium Sales," *Nuclear Fuel*, November 8, 1982, p. 3.

6. Carlos Castro Madero and Esteban A. Takacs, *Política Argentina Nuclear: Avance o Retroceso?* (Buenos Aires: El Ateneo, 1991), pp. 79–80, 154–160.

7. Barletta, "Ambiguity, Autonomy, and the Atom," pp. 140–142 and 337–339.

8. David Albright, Frans Berkhout, and William Walker, *Plutonium and Highly Enriched Uranium 1996: World Inventories, Capabilities and Policies* (Oxford: Oxford University Press, 1997), p. 371.

9. Barletta, "Ambiguity, Autonomy, and the Atom," pp. 101–109 and 123–126.

10. Statement by Michael McCurry, "Argentina and Brazil: Ratification of the Quadripartite Safeguards Agreement," U.S. Department of State, March 4, 1994; and John R. Redick, Julio C.

Carasales, and Paulo S. Wrobel, "Nuclear Rapprochement: Argentina, Brazil, and the Non-proliferation Regime," *Washington Quarterly*, vol. 18, no. 1, winter 1995, pp. 107–122.

11. IAEA, *Annual Report 1995*, p. 45.

12. ABACC, "Annual Report 1996," p. 24; *ABACC News*, January/April 1997; *ABACC News*, May/August 2000.

13. ABACC, *Annual Report 1999*.

14. U.S. Department of Energy, press release "U.S.–Argentina Implementing Arrangement for Technical Exchange and Cooperation in the Area of Peaceful Uses of Nuclear Energy," October 18, 1997.

15. Joint Euratom-Argentina press release, October 27, 1997.

16. Australian Nuclear Science and Technology Organization press release June 6, 2000.

17. William Potter, *International Nuclear Trade and Non-proliferation: The Challenge of the Emerging Suppliers* (Lexington: Lexington Books, 1990), pp. 95–109.

18. Spector, *Nuclear Proliferation Today*, p. 157, and Spector, "Brazilian Military Concern over Argentine Talks with Libya," *Correio Braziliense*, May 24, 1983, translated in FBIS/NDP, June 30, 1983, p. 8.

19. Mark Hibbs, "INVAP Seeks Thai Reactor Sale, Syria Expected To Sue for Supply," *Nucleonics Week*, October 27, 1994, p. 1.

20. Richard Kessler, "Menem Government Eyes Isotope Production Reactor for Algeria," *Nucleonics Week*, January 4, 1990, p. 11.

21. Mark Hibbs, "Iran Sought Sensitive Nuclear Supplies from Argentina, China," *Nucleonics Week*, September 24, 1992, p. 2.

22. Gary Marx, "South American Nuclear Threat Fades," *Chicago Tribune*, May 3, 1992, p. 21; and Richard Kessler, "Argentina Unilaterally Adopts Nuclear, Weapons Export Controls," *Nucleonics Week*, April 30, 1992, p. 1.

23. "Nation Joins Missile Technology Control Regime," *Buenos Aires Herald*, November 30, 1994, in JPRS–TND–93–001, January 6, 1994, p. 11; and U.S. Congress, Office of Technology Assessment, *Technologies Underlying Weapons of Mass Destruction*, OTA–BP–ISC–115 (Washington, D.C.: U.S. GPO, December 1993), p. 224.

24. David Ottaway, "Egypt Drops out of Missile Project," *Washington Post*, September 20, 1989; Ottaway, "Is Condor Kaput?" *U.S. News and World Report*, March 5, 1990, p. 20; and Ottaway, "Menem Says Missile Scrapped over U.S. Concern," *Clarin*, April 25, 1990, translated in FBIS–LAT, April 26, 1990, p. 20.

25. Wyn Bowen, Tim McCarthy, and Holly Porteous, "Ballistic Missile Shadow Lengthens," *Jane's IDR Extra*, February 1997, p. 5; "Brazil: Brazil-Argentina Discuss Building Commercial Rocket," *El Mercurio*, March 29, 1997, in FBIS–LAT–97–091, April 1, 1997.

Table 20.1: **Argentina: Nuclear Infrastructure**

NAME/LOCATION OF FACILITY	TYPE/STATUS	IAEA SAFEGUARDS
POWER REACTORS		
Atucha I, Lima	Heavy-water, nat. U, 357-MWe; operating	IAEA/ABACC
Embalse, Cordoba Province	Heavy-water, nat. U, 648-MWe; operating	IAEA/ABACC
Atucha II, Lima	Heavy-water, nat. U, 745-MWe; construction halted[1]	IAEA/ABACC
RESEARCH REACTORS		
RA–0, Cordoba	Light-water, 20% enriched uranium, .01-kWt; operating	IAEA/ABACC
RA–1, Constituyentes	Light-water, 20% enriched uranium, 40-kWt; operating	IAEA/ABACC
RA–2, Constituyentes	Light-water, HEU, less than 0.3 MWt; shut down	IAEA/ABACC
RA–3, Ezeiza	Light-water, LEU, 5-MWt; operating	IAEA/ABACC
RA–4, Rosario	Light-water, 20% enriched uranium, .001-kWt; operating	IAEA/ABACC
RA–6, San Carlos de Bariloche	Light-water, HEU, 500-kWt; operating	IAEA/ABACC
RA–8, Pilcaniyeu	Critical facility, light-water, LEU; operating[2]	IAEA/ABACC
URANIUM ENRICHMENT		
Pilcaniyeu	Gaseous diffusion method; closed for construction	IAEA/ABACC
REPROCESSING (PLUTONIUM EXTRACTION)		
Ezeiza	Construction halted, 1990	N/A
URANIUM PROCESSING		
San Rafael	Uranium mining; operating	N/A
Los Colorados	Uranium mining; operating	N/A
Sierra Pintada	Uranium mining; operations deferred for financial reasons	N/A
Cordoba	Uranium purification (UO_2) plant; operating	IAEA/ABACC
Cordoba	Experimental UO_2 plant; operating	IAEA/ABACC
Cordoba	Uranium purification (UO_2) plant; shut down	IAEA/ABACC
Constituyentes	Uranium conversion (UF_6) plant; operating	IAEA/ABACC
Pilcaniyeu	Uranium conversion (UF_6) facility; operating	IAEA/ABACC

Ezeiza	Fuel fabrication plant (Atucha); operating	IAEA/ABACC
Ezeiza	Fuel fabrication plant (Embalse); operating	IAEA/ABACC
Ezeiza	Plutonium fuel fabrication plant; under construction[3]	IAEA/ABACC
Ezeiza	Enriched uranium laboratory[4]	IAEA/ABACC
Ezeiza	Triple Altura laboratory[5]	IAEA/ABACC
Constituyentes	Pilot-scale plant to fabricate HEU; operating	IAEA/ABACC
Constituyentes	Research reactor fuel-fabrication plant; operating	IAEA/ABACC
Constituyentes	Alpha facility[6]	IAEA
	HEAVY- WATER PRODUCTION	
Arroyito	Production-scale; operating	IAEA/ABACC
Atucha	Pilot-scale; suspended[7]	IAEA/ABACC

Abbreviations

HEU	highly enriched uranium		MWt	millions of watts of thermal output
LEU	low-enriched uranium		kWt	thousands of watts of thermal output
nat. U	natural uranium		N/A	not applicable
MWe	millions of watts of electrical output			

NOTES

1. The plant is about 80 percent completed. Argentina is looking for a foreign partner to complete construction. ("Argentina Wants Foreign Partner To Finish Atucha Plant," *EEE News Service*, January 8, 2001.)

2. Operational since 1997, IAEA research reactor database, www.iaea.org/worldatom/rrdb.

3. David Albright, Frans Berkhout, and William Walker, *Plutonium and Highly Enriched Uranium 1996: World Inventories, Capabilities, and Policies* (Oxford: Oxford University Press for Stockholm International Peace Research Institute, 1997), p. 183. A small plutonium fuel-fabrication plant for Atucha is reportedly under construction. It is possible that this facility is the Triple Altura laboratory listed under "Other Facilities," in IAEA, *Annual Report 1996* (Vienna), p. 87.

4. Listed under "Other Facilities" in IAEA, *Annual Report 2000*.

5. The Triple Altura laboratory, in operation since 1992 according to an ABACC official, is a facility used to recover enriched uranium contained in fuel element scraps.

6. The Alpha facility undertakes research on MOX fuel-rod fabrication and design.

7. *World Nuclear Industry Handbook 1997*, p. 123.

Italicized names represent
nuclear-related sites. See table 20.1

BOLIVIA

PARAGUAY

BRAZIL

ARGENTINA

Pacific
Ocean

Los Colorados

Cordoba

Rio Tercero
(Embalse)   Rosario

Atucha   URUGUAY

San Rafael
Sierra Pintada

Buenos
Aires
(Constituyentes)
(Ezeiza)

CHILE

Arroyito

Uranium enrichment plant
*No known production of
weapons-grade uranium.
Argentina has declared it will
enrich uranium to no more than
20%, precluding its use for
nuclear weapons.*

*Under inspection by the
Argentine-Brazilian Accounting
and Control Commission
(ABACC) pursuant to the
bilateral agreement of July 18,
1991; and under initial ad hoc
inspection by the IAEA under
quadripartite safeguards
agreement between Argentina,
Brazil, ABACC, and the IAEA,
which entered into force on
March 4, 1994.*

Pilcaniyeu

San Carlos
de Bariloche

Atlantic
Ocean

Falkland
Islands
(Br.)

0   500

Miles

Carnegie Endowment for International Peace, *Deadly Arsenals* (2002), **www.ceip.org**

CHAPTER 21

Brazil

Nuclear Weapon Capability

Brazil is a non-nuclear-weapon state and does not possess nuclear weapons or unsafeguarded stocks of weapons-usable material. Brazil has previously sought the option to develop nuclear weapons or "peaceful nuclear explosives" in part in competition with Argentina during the 1970s and 1980s, but primarily in an effort to gain international prestige. By placing its nuclear facilities under international monitoring and signing the NPT in the 1990s, Brazil has assumed an important role in the international non-proliferation regime.

Missile Capability

Brazil has a program to develop a space launch vehicle that is theoretically capable of launching a 500-kilogram warhead up to 3,600 kilometers if it were to be converted for military purposes. Brazil's two test flights in 1997 and 1999 failed to put satellites in orbit.

Biological and Chemical Weapon Capability

There is no public information to suggest that Brazil has ever had research or production programs for either chemical or biological weapons. It is a member of the Biological Weapons Convention and the Chemical Weapons Convention.

Nuclear Analysis

During the 1990s Brazil renounced a secret military program that could have produced weapons-usable material and possibly build a nuclear weapon or PNE. It also completed a series of steps to implement binding non-proliferation commitments. Several decades of nuclear development, much of it through parallel civil and military programs, has resulted in an impressive array of facilities covering the entire nuclear fuel cycle. Some of these—in particular, Brazil's uranium enrichment facilities—still have the technical potential to produce weapons-grade material. Some activities by the military (notably the army's effort to resurrect a research reactor project uncovered in June 1997) and the navy's resumption of its nuclear-powered submarine program in January 2000 indicate that some in the military harbor nuclear ambitions that warrant continued attention. Yet Brazil has unequivocally committed itself to the peaceful development of nuclear energy, and it appears unlikely that it will reverse that stance in the foreseeable future.

Since 1985 Brazil has transformed itself from a cash-strapped nation under authoritarian military rule to a country with a strong market economy, democratically elected leadership, and a prominent international profile. Brazil is now a recognized member of many international nuclear organizations that provide a range of support and assistance. The commercial prospects of its nuclear industry will figure prominently in any future developments. Brazil's second nuclear power reactor, Angra II, finally came on line in July 2000 after years of delay and financial difficulty, and a third reactor is planned. Although nuclear energy does not play a major role in Brazil's energy mix at present, it could become important in the years to come, especially since the country has the necessary supporting facilities for a nuclear power program.

Nuclear Weapon Program

The Brazilian armed forces pursued an unsafeguarded nuclear development program during the 1970s and early 1990s, which aroused suspicions at home and abroad that the military aimed to produce nuclear weapons. Although the effort included activities of serious proliferation concern—especially the navy's development of uranium-enrichment technology and the air force's construction of an apparent nuclear explosive test site—domestic and international pressures helped to isolate the narrow faction that advocated the development of a "Brazilian bomb." The available evidence does not indicate that Brazil had a program dedicated to nuclear weapon production like those of Iraq and South Africa. Instead, there was governmental and military consensus only to develop the technological capacity for the *option* to build atomic weapons, and that even that goal was justified within the military as a PNE project. The military's program efforts were driven as much or more strongly, however, by nonweapon objectives, specifically to develop submarine propulsion, generally to boost Brazil's international standing, and to reach technological autonomy though a mastery of nuclear energy.[1]

Brazilian military interest in sensitive nuclear technology first became evident in 1953, when its National Research Council director, Adm. Álvaro Alberto, went to West Germany to buy experimental ultracentrifuges. The United States blocked the centrifuge deal at the time. Brazil nevertheless signed nuclear cooperation agreements with the United States in 1955, which led in 1957 to Brazil's Comissão Nacional de Energia Nuclear, commissioning its first U.S.–supplied research reactor.

In the early 1960s, Brazil opened negotiations with France for a natural uranium-fueled power reactor, but those negotiations were dropped in 1964. Eventually Brazil acquired its first power plant (Angra I) under a nuclear cooperation agreement signed with the United States in 1965. Brazil ordered this light-water reactor, supplied by the U.S. company Westinghouse, in 1971. Four years later, West Germany agreed to provide Brazil with ten nuclear power plants and the facilities for a complete nuclear fuel cycle, subject to IAEA safeguards. After 15 years, however, Brazil's civilian nuclear sector had little to show for its cooperation with West Germany, apart from an unfinished reactor and an unsuccessful uranium-enrichment program based on the jet-nozzle method. During that same period, however, the Brazilian military was engaged in a parallel program to acquire nuclear weapon capability.

The secret program, reportedly code-named the Solimões Project, started while Brazil was under military rule. It allegedly included research on nuclear weapon design and the excavation of a 300-meter-deep shaft for underground nuclear explosive tests at a military base near Cachimbo in the Amazon jungle. Three different methods to produce weapons-grade fissile material were pursued. Each branch of the military had its own approach, with none subject to IAEA safeguards. The navy, in cooperation with the Institute for Energy and Nuclear Research (IPEN), developed ultracentrifuges for uranium enrichment. The army chose graphite reactors suitable for plutonium production, and the air force undertook research on the laser enrichment of uranium and reportedly on nuclear weapon design and the construction of a nuclear test site.[2] Only the navy–IPEN project succeeded, however, and the navy ultimately dominated the parallel program of the armed forces. Its installations included a laboratory-scale uranium centrifuge plant at IPEN in São Paulo, as well as the initial module of an industrial-scale plant at the navy's Aramar Research Center in Iperó. These installations could have been used to produce uranium enriched to the level needed for nuclear arms, but neither plant is believed to have produced such material.

In a remarkable turnabout in 1990, Brazil renounced its secret program and began a series of steps toward binding non-proliferation commitments. On September 17, 1990, then-President Fernando Collor de Mello closed the Cachimbo test site. He emphasized his decision to end Brazil's nuclear weapon option program by throwing two shovels of lime into the test shaft, symbolically to bury the program. A week later he announced at the United Nations that Brazil was rejecting "the idea of any test that implies nuclear explosions, even for peaceful ends," which was the first time that a Brazilian president had ever renounced PNEs.[3] Brazil subsequently declared its intention to produce only low-enriched uranium, which is not readily suitable for weapons. Aramar director Adm. Othon Pinheiro da Silva declared in March 1993 that his center would not enrich uranium above 20 percent "because of a political decision."[4]

A significant milestone on the non-proliferation path came on May 30, 1994, when Brazil brought into force the Treaty for the Prohibition of Nuclear Weapons in Latin America and the Caribbean (Treaty of Tlatelolco). This included commitments not to acquire, manufacture, test, use, or permit the stationing of nuclear weapons or any nuclear explosive device on its territory and to accept IAEA inspections of all its nuclear activities. Domestic political opposition, however, delayed Brazil's signature of the Nuclear Non-Proliferation Treaty for four more years. By 1994, however, it had accepted the strict international supervision of its nuclear activities.

As a sign of faith in Brazil's commitment to non-proliferation, the United States initialed with Brazil in March 1996 the text of a new nuclear cooperation accord that replaced the earlier, dormant agreement. This agreement was signed in 1997 and entered into force the following year, permitting nuclear commerce for peaceful purposes between the two countries. The United States also supported Brazil's membership in the Nuclear Suppliers Group, which Brazil joined in April 1996 during the plenary session held in Argentina.[5]

Brazil finally signed and ratified both the NPT and the Comprehensive Test Ban Treaty in 1998, following pressure from President Bill Clinton and months of domestic lobbying by President Fernando Henrique Cardoso. At a U.S. State Department ceremony marking the event on September 18, 1998, Brazilian Foreign Minister Luis Lampreia stressed Brazil's "unwavering commitment to the use of nuclear energy for exclusively peaceful purposes."[6]

Nuclear Complex

In July 1991, the Argentine and Brazilian foreign ministers set up the Argentine-Brazilian Accounting and Control Commission (ABACC). An agreement to integrate ABACC's inspection system with that of the IAEA was signed by Argentina, Brazil, the IAEA, and ABACC in Vienna on December 13, 1991. The quadripartite agreement committed the ABACC and the IAEA to establishing an initial inventory of all nuclear materials in Brazil as a basis for future inspections.

The IAEA has no mandate to investigate past weapon-related activities, despite indications that Brazil undertook nuclear weapon research in the 1980s. Completing the inventory was complicated by years of unsafeguarded nuclear activities at IPEN, Iperó, and other sites that contributed to the weapon program. During 1995, however, the IAEA "largely completed" its verification of nuclear material and facility design information in Brazil.[7] Since then, regular IAEA inventory checks and inspections have been carried out to identify any potential diversion, or reversion, of nuclear materials to military use. ABACC also continued its ad hoc inspections, conducting 81 in 1996 and 30 between May and August 2000.[8]

Proliferation concerns were aroused in June 1997 with reports that the Brazilian army had tried to restart the Atlantic Project, involving the construction of a 0.5-megawatt experimental graphite reactor readily suitable for plutonium production in the Guaratiba natural reserve. While President Cardoso was out of the country in November 1996, Vice-President Marco Maciel authorized the project, reportedly under pressure from army officials. After the project was exposed, the army agreed to discontinue it.[9]

Although legally permitted by the NPT and not considered a bellicose application of nuclear technology, nuclear submarine propulsion in Brazil has nevertheless aroused concern that its program might at some point be misused for weapon production, given Brazil's enduring interest. On February 2, 1996, navy minister Adm. Mauro Pereira announced that plans to build a nuclear-powered submarine had been suspended after 17 years of effort. The Aramar Research Center would instead turn its attention to completing the Angra II power reactor and to building conventional submarines. By then, $670 million had been invested at Aramar to develop enriched uranium to fuel submarines.[10] The facility houses about 1,000 ultracentrifuges. The navy wanted to maintain its enrichment program, although it had undertaken not to produce weapons-grade material. The project therefore continued despite a series of setbacks. In 1995–1996, about half of the 2000 employees at the facility, including scientists and researchers, left Aramar.[11] At the end of 1996 the Brazilian press publicized several accidents involving radioactive material and the contamination of personnel over the previous four years.[12] The navy insisted that the incidents had been minor, below the threshold of the IAEA's International Nuclear Events Scale.[13] In January 2000 the Brazilian government allocated funds for the navy to restart its nuclear submarine propulsion project, but the congress subsequently cut the budget. In lobbying legislators to restore funding and to address public suspicions, the navy said that if it produced a nuclear-powered submarine, it would consider allowing ABACC to apply seals to the on-board reactor and use remote monitoring technology to ensure that no diversion of nuclear fuel for weapon purposes took place.[14] At present, the navy continues to face an uphill struggle in gaining sufficient federal funding to realize its nuclear submarine ambitions.[15]

Brazil–Argentina Rapprochement

Although rivalry for regional leadership and military suspicions have fueled the competition between Brazil and Argentina in nuclear development since the early 1950s, the cooperative elements of the relation endured even when bilateral relations were at their worst, notably in nuclear science and diplomacy. The military governments signed formal cooperation accords in nuclear commerce in 1980.[16] Both countries pursued proliferation-sensitive enrichment and reprocessing activities, as well as civilian research and energy programs. After the transition from military rule in the mid-1980s, however, Brazil and Argentina took steps that definitively ended their nuclear rivalry. On July 18, 1991, the Argentine and Brazilian foreign ministers signed a bilateral agreement renouncing PNEs, allowing mutual inspections of nuclear installations, and setting up the ABACC to implement this commitment. Exchanges of nuclear material inventories and mutual inspections began in late 1992 after the inauguration of ABACC. Argentina's congress approved the Quadripartite Safeguards Agreement in 1992, but inspections were delayed until the agreement entered into force on March 4, 1994, following approval by Brazil's congress in February 1994.[17] The agreement made ABACC and the IAEA responsible for performing an initial inventory of all nuclear materials in Argentina as a basis for inspections, a task complicated by years of unsafeguarded activities at Pilcaniyeu.

Missile Analysis

Brazil developed a series of sounding rockets during the 1970s and early 1980s, some of them modified into short-range surface-to-surface missiles for export to Iraq, Libya, and Saudi Arabia. During the early 1990s, however, Brazil terminated its programs to develop more capable missiles. These missiles included the Avibras SS–300 as well as the Orbita–MB/EE–600 and –1000. With ranges of more than 300 kilometers, these missiles are subject to MTCR restrictions. Brazil was widely criticized when the former director of the Brazilian Aerospace Technical Center, Hugo Piva, led a team of missile scientists and technicians to Iraq to assist in the development of Iraq's missile program before the 1990–1991 Persian Gulf War. Objections by the international community led Brazil to introduce export-control legislation, paving the way for later adherence to MTCR export guidelines.[18]

Since 1981 Brazil has been working on a space launch vehicle (SLV) four-stage rocket, designed to place satellites in low-Earth orbit. This project largely depended on foreign missile technology, however, which is restricted under the MTCR. To obtain key missile technology, the Brazilian government announced its decision on February 11, 1994, to comply with MTCR criteria and standards. It agreed to restrict the export of missiles (and key missile components) that are capable of carrying weapons of mass destruction beyond the 300-kilometer threshold.[19] While Brazil stopped exporting sensitive missile technology, it continued to import technology for its civilian space launch program. This activity, and in particular the import of carbon-fiber technology for rocket-motor casings from Russia in early 1995, was technically in violation of MTCR rules. Nevertheless, the United States sought to include Brazil in the MTCR in order to curb its missile program. It therefore waived sanctions relating to the Russian technology deal in return for a pledge from Brazil that it would no longer engage in such activities.[20]

Brazil was admitted to the MTCR in October 1995 and was allowed to maintain its space launch program despite its inherent military capability. The SLV, the centerpiece of the Brazilian space program, can theoretically launch a 500-kilogram warhead up to 3,600 kilometers if it were converted for military purposes. Brazil currently builds its own satellites but must launch them on foreign rockets. The first flight of its space launch vehicle was delayed for many years by MTCR restrictions, financing problems, and programming difficulties until early November 1997. In a serious setback, the maiden launch of the missile on November 2, 1997, was terminated one minute after liftoff because of engine failure. A second attempted launch in December 1999 also failed.

Biological and Chemical Weapon Analysis

Brazil has no known chemical or biological weapon programs and is a party to both the Biological Weapons Convention and the Chemical Weapons Convention. In addition, Brazil is a signatory to the 1991 Joint Declaration on the Complete Prohibition of Chemical and Biological Weapons, a regional non-proliferation agreement also known as the Mendoza Accord.

NOTES

1. Michael Barletta, "Ambiguity, Autonomy, and the Atom: Emergence of the Argentine-Brazilian Nuclear Regime" (Ph.D. diss., University of Wisconsin, 2000), pp. 213–277; and Barletta, "Pernicious Ideas in World Politics: 'Peaceful Nuclear Explosives,' " paper presented at the annual meeting of the American Political Science Association, August 30–September 2, 2001, pp. 29–32. Available at papers.tcnj.edu/papers/019/019013BarlettaMi.pdf.

2. José Casado, "Analyst Views 'Nuclear Explosive Artifacts'," *O Estado De São Paulo*, June 5, 1995, in FBIS–LAT–95–111, June 9, 1995, p. 30; and Helcio Costa, "CPI Sees Bomb Configuration Project at IEAv," *Gazeta Mercantil*, November 29, 1990, in *JPRS–TND–91–001*, January 4, 1991, p. 17.

3. James Brooke, "Brazil Uncovers Plan by Military To Build Atom Bomb and Stops It," *New York Times*, October 9, 1990; David Albright, "Brazil Comes in from the Cold," *Arms Control Today*, December 1990, p. 13, but see Barletta, "Ambiguity, Autonomy, and the Atom," pp. 268–271, who reviews contradictory evidence to suggest that the allegation of a secret military plot to build the bomb may be overblown.

4. Jean Krasno, "Brazil's Secret Nuclear Program," *Orbis*, summer 1994, p. 432.

5. U.S. Department of State, *U.S.–Brazil Agreement on Peaceful Uses of Nuclear Energy*, March 1, 1996; Wyn Bowen and Andrew Koch, "Non-Proliferation Is Embraced by Brazil," *Jane's Intelligence Review*, June 1996, p. 283.

6. U.S. State Department press release, September 18, 1998.

7. *IAEA Annual Report 1996*, p. 46.

8. *ABACC Annual Report 1996*, p. 24; *ABACC News*, May/August, 2000.

9. "Brazil: Army Confirms Gas-Graphite Nuclear Reactor Project," *Jornal do Brasil*, June 5, 1997, in FBIS–LAT–97–156, June 5, 1997; and "Brazil: Ministries Term Nuclear Reactor Project 'Peaceful,'" *Jornal do Brasil*, June 5, 1997, in FBIS–TEN–97–007–L.

10. José Maria Tomazela, "Brazilian Minister: Navy Gave up Nuclear Submarine Plans," *O Estado de São Paulo*, February 7, 1996, in FBIS–LAT–96–028, February 9, 1996, p. 12; and Philip Finnegan, "Brazil Defers Nuclear Sub Plan," *Defense News*, March 11–17, 1996, p. 4.

11. José Maria Tomazela, "Brazil: Iperó Mayor Fears Dismantling of Nuclear Center," *O Estado De São Paulo*, February 14, 1996, in FBIS–LAT–96–036, February 22, 1996, p. 50.

12. "Navy Documents Said To Confirm Leaks of Radioactive Material at Base," *Rede Globo Television*, December 30, 1996, in FBIS–TEN–97–001, January 23, 1997; and Jose Maria Mayrink, "Former Nuclear Plant Employees Report Frequent Past Leaks," *Jornal do Brasil*, January 1, 1997, in FBIS–TEN–97–001.

13. "Navy Communiqué on Radioactive Incidents," *Jornal do Brasil*, December 31, 1996 in FBIS–TEN–97–001.

14. José Maria Tomazela, "Government Resumes Nuclear Submarine Project," *O Estado de Sao Paulo*, February 1, 2000, in FBIS Document ID FTS20000201000871; and Mark Hibbs, "Brazilian Navy To Request More Funds for Nuclear Sub," *Nucleonics Week*, vol. 41, no. 27, July 6, 2000.

15. "Marinha Pede Apoio para Concluir Submarino Nuclear em Iperó," *Cosmo*, January 3, 2002. Available at www.cosmo.com.br/redacao_web/especiais/011018_especial01.shtm.

16. Barletta, "Ambiguity, Autonomy, and the Atom," pp. 101–109 and 123–126.

17. Statement by Michael McCurry, "Argentina and Brazil: Ratification of the Quadripartite Safeguards Agreement," U.S. Department of State, March 4, 1994; and John R. Redick, Julio C. Carasales, and Paulo S. Wrobel, "Nuclear Rapprochement: Argentina, Brazil, and the Non-Proliferation Regime," *Washington Quarterly*, vol. 18, no. 1, winter 1995, pp. 107–122.

18. Maria Helena Tachinardi, "Measures To Control Sensitive Exports Announced," *Gazeta Mercantil*, August 10, 1994, p. 5, as translated in FBIS–LAT–94–162.

19. Raquel Stenzel, "Government Agrees To Comply with Missile Control Pact,'" *Gazeta Mercantil*, February 12, 1994, in JPRS–TND–94–006, March 16, 1994, p. 16.

20. R. Jeffrey Smith, "U.S. Waives Objection to Russian Missile Technology Sale to Brazil," *Washington Post*, June 8, 1995, p. A1.

Table 21.1: **Brazil: Nuclear Infrastructure**

NAME/LOCATION OF FACILITY	TYPE/STATUS	IAEA SAFEGUARDS[1]
NUCLEAR WEAPON-RELATED SITES		
Institute of Advanced Studies, Aerospace Technical Center, San Jose dos Campos	Conducted research on nuclear weapons design	No
Cachimbo	Planned nuclear weapon test site; dismantled, not operational	No
POWER REACTORS		
Angra I	Light-water, LEU, 626-MWe; operating[2]	IAEA/ABACC
Angra II	Light-water, LEU, 1,300-MWe; operating	IAEA/ABACC
Angra III	Light-water, LEU, 1,300-MWe; under construction (currently deferred)[3]	N/A
RESEARCH REACTORS[4]		
IEAR–1, São Paulo	Pool, HEU (20–93% enriched), 2-MWt; operating[5]	IAEA/ABACC
RIEN–1, Rio de Janeiro	Water, 19.9% enriched uranium, .2-KWt; operating	IAEA/ABACC
Triga–UMG, Belo Horizonte	Water, 20% enriched uranium, 100-kWt; operating	IAEA/ABACC
IPEN–Zero Power, São Paulo	Light-water, 4.3% enriched uranium, .1-kWt; operating	IAEA/ABACC
Renap reactors, Aramar Research Center, Ipéro	Experimental, pressurized-water; designed for nuclear-powered submarine; program suspended[6]	IAEA/ABACC
Subcritical assembly, Rio de Janeiro	Graphite, nat. U; operating	IAEA/ABACC
Subcritical assembly, Recife	Light-water, nat. U; operating	IAEA/ABACC
Argonauta	Light-water, .2-kW, operating	IAEA/ABACC
URANIUM ENRICHMENT		
Resende	Pilot-scale, jet-nozzle method; completed; program canceled; possible location of ultracentrifuge equipment relocated from Aramar, construction status deferred*[7]	IAEA/ABACC
Belo Horizonte	Laboratory-scale, jet-nozzle method; shut down	IAEA/ABACC
Aramar Research Center, Isotopic Enrichment Laboratory (LEI), Ipéro	First-stage, industrial-scale plant, ultra-centrifuge method; operating. A nearby pilot-plant using a carbon-fiber rotor design may be under construction.[8]	IAEA/ABACC

Aramar Research Center, Ipéro	Centrifuge production plant; operating	?[9]
IPEN, São Paulo	Laboratory-scale, ultracentrifuge method; operating	IAEA/ABACC
Institute of Advanced Studies (IAEv), Aerospace Technical Center, San Jose dos Campos[10]	Laboratory-scale, laser method; not operational[11]	IAEA/ABACC
REPROCESSING (PLUTONIUM EXTRACTION)		
Resende	Indefinitely postponed	IAEA/ABACC
IPEN, São Paulo	Laboratory-scale; completed; not known ever to have operated[12]	IAEA/ABACC
URANIUM PROCESSING		
Lagoa Real[13]	Uranium mining; operating	N/A
Pocos de Caldas	Uranium mining; operating	N/A
Itataia	Uranium milling; planned	N/A
IPEN, São Paulo	Uranium-purification (UO_2) site	IAEA/ABACC
Aramar Research Center, Ipéro	Laboratory-scale uranium-purification (UO_2) facility; operating	IAEA/ABACC[14]
Resende	Uranium-conversion (UF_6) facility, indefinitely postponed	IAEA/ABACC
IPEN, São Paulo	Pilot-scale uranium-conversion (UF_6) facility; operating	IAEA/ABACC
IPEN, São Paulo	Laboratory-scale uranium-conversion (UF_6) facility; not operating[15]	IAEA/ABACC
Belo Horizonte	Laboratory-scale uranium-conversion (UF_6) facility; operating	IAEA/ABACC
Aramar Research Center, Ipéro	Uranium-conversion (UF_6) plant, construction postponed	IAEA/ABACC[16]
Fuel Elements Factory (FEC), Resende	Fuel-fabrication plant; operating[17]	IAEA/ABACC

* *World Nuclear Industry Handbook*, 2001, p. 241.

Abbreviations

HEU	highly enriched uranium	MWt	millions of watts of thermal output
LEU	low-enriched uranium	kWt	thousands of watts of thermal output
nat. U	natural uranium	N/A	not applicable
MWe	millions of watts of electrical output		

NOTES

1. IAEA and ABACC are conducting parallel inspections at the indicated facilities.

2. On August 1, 1997, the Angra nuclear facility was transferred from Furnas to Nuclen, the state-owned project management organization run by Electrobras, a power-generation holding company. *Nuclear Engineering International*, September 1997, p. 6.

3. The National Energy Council has authorized budgetary studies on restarting the construction. ("Brazil Orders Studies into Third Nuclear Reactor," *Reuters*, December 7, 2001.)

4. ABACC lists Brazil as having three research reactors and three critical or subcritical units. The research reactors are IEAR–1, Triga, and IPEN–Zero Power; the critical/subcritical unit is RIEN–1; and the two subcriticals are at Rio de Janeiro and Recife (Institute for Science and International Security and the Shalheveth Freier Center for Peace, Science, and Technology, "Argentina and Brazil: The Latin American Rapprochement," May 16, 1996, p. 43). The IAEA lists Brazil as having four research reactors: IEAR–1, Triga/IPR–R1, Argonauta, and the IPEN/MB–01 critical assembly. (See IAEA Research Reactor Database, www.iaea.org/worldatom/ rrdb.)

5. Brazil is planning to boost the IEAR–1 reactor to 5 MWe (Ronaldo Mota Sardenberg, "Strategic Affairs Secretary Reviews Nuclear Projects," *Correio Brasiliense*, November 7, 1996, in FBIS–TAC–97–001, February 4, 1997).

6. In January of 2002 the Brazilian government allocated funds to restart the program, but the congress cut the budget. At present the navy faces an uphill battle in gaining sufficient funding to realize its ambitions.

7. In March 1994 Brazil canceled its project to enrich uranium using the German jet-nozzle process. Since then, the facilities using that method at Resende and Belo Horizonte have not been operating, and the Belo Horizonte laboratory has been dismantled (George Vidor, "Jet Nozzle Uranium Enrichment Project Canceled," *O Globo*, Rio de Janeiro, March 19, 1994, in FBIS–LAT–95–056, March 23, 1994, p. 48).

   INB, Brazil Nuclear Industries, may sell 40% of the jet-nozzle enrichment equipment as junk (José Casado, "Article Views Efforts To Revive Nuclear Program," *O Estado de São Paulo*, June 4, 1995 in *FBIS–TAC–95–111*, June 9, 1995, p. 29).

8. David Albright, Frans Berkhout, and William Walker, *Plutonium and Highly Enriched Uranium 1996: World Inventories, Capabilities, and Policies* (Oxford: Oxford University Press for Stockholm International Peace Research Institute, 1997), p. 375. LEI currently has about 725 centrifuges, and the navy plans to install up to 4,000 more in coming years. Eventually, Aramar will produce fuel for Brazil's research reactors (Tania Malheiros, "Aramar Center Manufacturing Equipment To Enrich Uranium," *Jornal do Brasil*, March 19, 1996, in *FBIS–TAC–95–005*, May 8, 1996).

9. According to Marco Marzo, if the IAEA were to ask to visit a centrifuge factory (such as the one at Aramar), the inspectors would be refused because there is no nuclear material present at the site. Whether ABACC can inspect the facilities is not clear (Institute for Science and International Security and Shalheveth Freier Center for Peace, Science, and Technology, "Argentina and Brazil," pp. 51–52).

10. Laser-enrichment research and development were performed at IAEv in San Jose dos Campos by the air force and code-named Sepila (José Casado, "Analyst Views 'Nuclear Explosive Artifacts,'" *O Estado De São Paulo*, June 5, 1995, in FBIS–LAT–95–111, June 9, 1995, p. 30; Helcio Costa, "CPI Sees Bomb Configuration Project at IAEv," *Gazeta Mercantil*, November 29, 1990, in JPRS–TND–91–001, January 4 1991, p. 17). The IAEA lists a laboratory for laser spectroscopy at San Jose dos Campos under safeguards (*Annual Report 1996* [Vienna], p. 84).

11. Although the project has not been officially canceled, few improvements have been made in the past few years (Marco A. Marzo, in Institute for Science and International Security and the Shalheveth Freier Center for Peace, Science, and Technology, "Argentina and Brazil," p. 25.)

12. This facility was reportedly operated with plutonium simulators because Brazil did not have access to unsafeguarded spent fuel. The laboratory is reported to have closed in 1989. German intelligence, however, indicated that Brazil may have irradiated uranium specimens in reactors and reprocessed a very small amount. Also, plans for a pilot

plant (possibly at Resende) never materialized. Albright, Berkhout, and Walker, *Plutonium and Highly Enriched Uranium 1996*, p. 371.

13. Ivo Ribeiro, "Nuclear Company To Sell Gold Mine in Minas Gerais," *Gazeta Mercantil*, November 6, 1995, in FBIS–LAT–95–221.

14. This facility was commissioned and subsequently inspected by ABACC and IAEA officials in early July 1994 (José Maria Tomazela, "IAEA Team Inspects Ipéro Uranium Hexafluoride Plant," *Agencia Estado*, July 29, 1994, in JPRS–TND–94–016, August 19, 1994, p. 19).

15. In its *Annual Report 1996*, p. 84, the IAEA listed the facility at Belo Horizonte as safeguarded but listed the Sao Paulo facility under "Separate Storage Facilities," suggesting that the UF$_6$ production at the latter has ceased.

16. José Maria Tomazela, "IAEA Team Inspects Ipéro"; and Tania Malheiros, "Navy Confirms Project for Hexafluoride Conversion," *Agencia Estado*, August 4, 1994, in JPRS–TND–94–016, August 19, 1994, p. 19.

17. See José Maria Tomazela, "Navy Seeks Funds To Launch Nuclear Submarines by 2007," *Agencia Estado*, November 9, 1995, in FBIS–LAT–95–218, November 13, 1995, p. 36; Tania Malheiros, "Aramar Center Manufacturing Equipment To Enrich Uranium," *Jornal do Brasil*, March 19, 1996, in FBIS–TAC–95–005, May 8, 1996; and Malheiros, "Country to Spend Millions To Manufacture Nuclear Fuel," *Jornal do Brasil*, October 29, 1995, in FBIS–TAC–95–006, December 6, 1995, p. 37.

VENEZUELA

COLOMBIA

GUYANA

SURINAME

FR. GUIANA

Italicized names represent nuclear-related sites. See table 21.1

Missile and space launch test facility

Nuclear test site (dismantled)
Part of nuclear weapon program pursued by Brazil in 1980s until terminated by then-President Fernando Collor de Mello in 1990.

▲ *Alcantara*

■ *Itataia*

☀ *Cachimbo*

■ *Recife*

BRAZIL

PERU

Lagoa Real ■

Atlantic Ocean

Brasilia ★

BOLIVIA

Belo Horizonte ■

Pacific Ocean

Sao Paulo (IPEN)

Pocos de Caldas ■

Resende ■

PARAGUAY

Ipero ■ ■ ■

■ *Rio de Janeiro*

Angra dos Reis

Sao Jose dos Campos

ARGENTINA

Aramar Research Center
First module of industrial-scale centrifuge uranium enrichment plant. No known production of weapons-grade uranium. Facility was apparently a key component of the now-terminated Brazilian nuclear weapon program of 1980s. Brazil has declared that it will enrich uranium to no more than 20%, precluding its use for nuclear weapons.

Under inspection by the Argentine-Brazilian Accounting and Control Commission (ABACC) and pursuant to the bilateral agreement of July 18, 1991; under initial ad hoc inspection by the IAEA under the quadripartite safeguards agreement between Argentina, Brazil, ABACC, and the IAEA, which entered into force on March 4, 1994.

URUGUAY

0   500
Miles

Carnegie Endowment for International Peace, *Deadly Arsenals* (2002), **www.ceip.org**

CHAPTER 22

South Africa

Nuclear Weapon Capability

Since 1991 South Africa has made the transition from a threshold nuclear-weapon state to become a responsible participant in the nuclear non-proliferation regime. It is the first nation to develop and possess nuclear weapons and then renounce them. In a historic reform of South Africa's politics, President F. W. de Klerk ended the country's decades-long policy of racial separation and brought an end to white minority rule. Democratic elections in April 1994 brought Nelson Mandela to the presidency. Mandela's successor, Thabo Mbeki, remains committed to the Nuclear Non-Proliferation Treaty, which South Africa joined in 1991. The highly enriched weapons-grade uranium produced during the 1970s and 1980s remains in South Africa under IAEA inspection. Despite these positive signs, however, some concerns remain. South Africa is estimated to have about 330 kilograms of weapons-grade uranium and another 55 kilograms of 80 percent enriched uranium.[1]

Biological and Chemical Weapon Capability

South Africa has disbanded its former secret biological and chemical warfare programs. It has ratified both the Biological Weapons Convention and the Chemical Weapons Convention.

Nuclear Analysis

South Africa was the first state in the world to give up its nuclear weapon capability voluntarily. When South Africa dismantled its advanced, but clandestine, nuclear weapon program to assume a leading role in the movement for non-proliferation, it reflected the immense political changes that took place during the 1990s. On March 24, 1993, President de Klerk disclosed that South Africa had destroyed six nuclear devices that had been produced as part of its secret nuclear weapon program.[2] By 1994 the government had dismantled the entire associated weapon infrastructure under international inspection. South Africa acceded to the NPT on July 10, 1991, concluding a full-scope safeguard agreement with the International Atomic Energy Agency the following September. All its nuclear plants and all previously produced enriched uranium were placed under IAEA safeguards. South Africa became a member of the Zangger Committee in 1993 and of the Nuclear Suppliers Group in 1995. It played a leading role in the establishment of the African Nuclear Weapons Free Zone

Treaty (the Treaty of Pelindaba) in 1996, becoming one of the treaty's first members in 1997. South Africa signed the Comprehensive Test Ban Treaty in 1996 and ratified it in 1999. Parallel changes took place with respect to its chemical and biological weapon programs.

Although South Africa has declared its fissile material inventory to the IAEA, it has not revealed the exact figures to the public. Moreover, scientists who had previously worked on the nuclear weapon and missile programs constitute a proliferation risk, and reports indicate that some South African scientists are now working in Middle East countries. Other reports suggest that the Atomic Energy Corporation (AEC) secretly sold China equipment from its dismantled nuclear facilities. Until complete transparency is achieved, questions will remain about South Africa's nuclear weapon complex, its continued enrichment activities, and the true extent of its non-proliferation commitment.

Nuclear Development

South Africa's Atomic Energy Corporation was established in Pretoria in 1948 to assess the uranium reserves in southern Africa. The AEC moved to Pelindaba when serious nuclear development began in the late 1960s under the cover of a peaceful nuclear explosives program to bolster South Africa's mining industry. The Nuclear National Research Centre (now the Pelindaba Nuclear Institute) was established at Pelindaba, 30 kilometers west of Pretoria, in 1961. South Africa's 20-megawatt Safari–I nuclear research reactor, acquired from the United States under the Atoms for Peace program, began operating at the center in 1965.

Although initially devoted to peaceful research, the AEC launched a secret project in the early 1960s to develop a unique nozzle (or vortex) enrichment technology. The decision to build an industrial-scale pilot plant was taken in 1969, and the Uranium Enrichment Corporation (UCOR) was set up to construct it at Valindaba (Pelindaba East). The first stages of this "Y" plant were commissioned by the end of 1974, the year in which, according to President de Klerk, the government decided to develop nuclear weapons. Subsequently a commercial-scale "Z" plant enrichment facility was built at Pelindaba. Also as part of this secret program, two nuclear test shafts were completed at a site in the Kalahari Desert in 1977.[3]

In mid-1977 a Soviet observation satellite revealed preparations for an underground nuclear test at the Kalahari site, spurring Washington and Moscow to apply substantial diplomatic pressure on Pretoria, which soon abandoned the site and sealed the boreholes. Nevertheless, efforts continued to produce weapons-grade uranium and to design a nuclear device.[4] The first dummy device, without a core of highly enriched uranium, was produced in August 1977, followed by a smaller version in 1978. By November 1979, once sufficient HEU had been produced, the first operational nuclear device was ready.

South African officials involved with the program deny any intention to use the weapons except as part of a "three-phase nuclear strategy" to deter potential adversaries (especially Soviet-backed forces from neighboring states) and to compel Western involvement should deterrence fail. Phase 1 involved neither confirming nor denying its nuclear capability. In phase 2, faced with imminent attack, Pretoria would reveal its capability to Western leaders to force their intervention. If that failed, phase 3 would involve overt nuclear testing to demonstrate South Africa's ability and willingness to use nuclear weapons.[5] In 1988 South Africa even took the preliminary steps necessary to put phase 3 into effect when it reopened one of the boreholes at the Kalahari test site as part of a contingency plan to help bring an end to the Angolan war.[6]

The weapons, similar to the gun-type design used for the Hiroshima bomb, were designed to be delivered by aircraft, with great attention given to safety, security, and reliability, which suggests that military use had not been ruled out altogether. The still-undeclared phase 4 contingency is further borne out by the substantial investment of South Africa in the development and production of intermediate-range ballistic missiles and the completion in 1989 of the Advena nuclear warhead production facility, which was immediately adjacent to South Africa's original air-deliverable bomb production facility.[7]

The election of de Klerk in September 1989 signaled the end of the nuclear weapon program. On February 26, 1990, he issued internal orders to terminate the effort and to dismantle all weapons. The decommissioning of the uranium-enrichment plant at Pelindaba began in July 1990; six devices were dismantled, and the hardware and technical documents destroyed. Both the original facility (known as the Circle building) and the adjacent Advena complex, the weapon-manufacturing site, were decontaminated and converted for commercial use (and when commercialization failed, the buildings were closed). By early September 1991 all the HEU had been recast and sent back to the Atomic Energy Corporation for permanent storage, ten days before the safeguard agreement was signed with the IAEA. On August 19, 1994, after completing its inspection, the IAEA confirmed that one partial and six complete nuclear devices had been dismantled.[8]

Although the process was completed by 1992, de Klerk did not reveal the program's existence until March 1993. In his speech to parliament he denied that South Africa had received any foreign assistance for its nuclear weapon program or that it had been involved in any nuclear weapon testing, either alone or with another country.[9] In 1997, however, Deputy Foreign Minister Aziz Pahad and former chief of staff Gen. Constand Viljoen said that Israel had supported South Africa's program,[10] supplying tritium for use in boosted fission weapons in return for natural uranium.[11] In 1979 a U.S. satellite detected a flash over the Indian Ocean that was assumed by many analysts to have been a joint Israeli–South African test, although an expert inquiry at the time proved inconclusive.

Conversion to Civilian Programs

Since 1990 the AEC has followed its 2000 Plus Plan, refocusing on commercial rather than strategic activities. It has been renamed the South African

Nuclear Energy Corporation (NECSA) and receives government funding for technology development and industrialization. Safari is now used mainly for vocational training and isotope production. Its continued use of HEU fuel remains a bone of contention with the United States, which has been urging a conversion to low-enriched uranium fuel since June 1994. In 1995 the U.S. Department of Energy and AEC signed an agreement allowing the transfer of American nuclear technology to South Africa to assist in that conversion. South African experts have believed, nevertheless, that the conversion is not economically practical. A NECSA study done in conjunction with the U.S. Argonne National Laboratory was submitted to the South African Department of Minerals and Energy in December 2001, arguing that a conversion to low-enriched silicide fuel would not significantly affect energy production. A decision on the reactor's future is expected by mid-2002.[12]

The restructuring and dismantlement of South Africa's nuclear complex continue. The semi-commercial Z enrichment plant was closed in March 1995,[13] and as of December 2001 it was listed along with the Y enrichment plant as being "partially/fully decommissioned."[14] The research and development of uranium-enrichment technology, however, continues, and in February 1996 the AEC signed a contract with the French nuclear firm Cogema to develop jointly a molecular laser isotope separation (MLIS) enrichment method.[15] A demonstration-scale MLIS facility was to be built at Pelindaba East to enrich uranium for the Koeberg nuclear power plant and other reactors, but the Department of Mineral and Energy has canceled plans for that plant. It was then decided to build a pilot facility inside the plant-Z shell, but in December 1997 funding and technical problems led AEC to cancel the MLIS project altogether.

Non-Proliferation Concerns

Although South Africa emerged as a champion of nuclear non-proliferation at the NPT Extension Conference in 1995, concerns have been raised about its dealings with Iran, which during the apartheid era had good relations with the now-ruling African National Congress (ANC) party. In August 1995 South Africa signed a peaceful nuclear cooperation agreement with Iran,[16] despite a U.S.–led international nuclear embargo. The ANC government announced in June 1996 that it has made no uranium exports to Iran in the past five years.[17] Reports in 1997, however, alleged that AEC head Waldo Stumpf and then-Minister of Mineral and Energy Affairs Pik Botha had met in early 1996 with Gholam Reza Aghazadeh, at the time Iran's oil minister. Aghazadeh reportedly presented Stumpf with a shopping list of items needed to make nuclear weapons. Stumpf has denied that the meeting took place, but Botha confirmed it, adding that South Africa had rejected Iran's request for equipment.[18]

Other reports in the fall of 1997 suggested that the AEC was secretly selling equipment from Pelindaba to the Chinese. Although the transfers appeared to have little relevance to China's weapon program, the secretive nature of the deal raised concerns about the autonomy of AEC's operations.[19]

Missile Analysis

In the 1980s, South Africa's Armscor company developed a medium-range ballistic missile with Israeli assistance under the guise of a space launch vehicle program. It was tested in July 1989. The United States imposed missile proliferation sanctions on Armscor in October 1991.[20] South Africa announced in June 1993 that it was canceling the project,[21] and in October 1994 signed an agreement with the United States pledging to eliminate its MRBM program and abide by the Missile Technology Control Regime.[22] Despite reports suggesting that in 1993 South African engineers and scientists were offering missile expertise to Middle East countries,[23] South Africa was formally admitted to the MTCR in September 1995.[24] In addition to a ballistic missile capability, South Africa has two unmanned aerial vehicles and is developing a land-attack cruise missile, the Skua, capable of traveling 800 kilometers with a 100-kilogram payload.[25]

Biological and Chemical Weapon Analysis

South Africa pursued secret chemical and biological warfare programs during the 1980s (and abandoned them in 1993), despite having joined the Biological Weapons Convention in 1975.[26] It ratified the Chemical Weapons Convention in September 1995, although reports suggested that South African scientists were helping Libya's quest for biological and chemical weapons.[27] In October 1998 the South African Truth and Reconciliation Commission released a report containing 3,500 pages of testimony about human rights violations during the apartheid era.[28] It included a chapter on Project Coast, a clandestine government chemical and biological warfare program conducted during the 1980s and 1990s.

Project Coast started in 1983, ostensibly to produce equipment for defensive purposes, including masks and protective suits. Despite vehement assertions to the contrary, testimony showed that the program went well beyond defensive purposes. Key officials said that Project Coast sponsored the production of chocolates laced with anthrax, umbrellas with poisoned tips, screwdrivers fitted with poison-filled cylinders, and clothing infused with lethal chemicals. Biological and chemical agents were developed to make attacks appear to be the result of natural causes. Other apparently unexecuted ideas included research into drugs to render black women infertile and a plan to poison Nelson Mandela gradually.

NOTES

1. David Albright, Frans Berkhout, and William Walker, *Plutonium and Highly Enriched Uranium 1996: World Inventories, Capabilities and Policies* (New York: Oxford University Press for Stockholm International Peace Research Institute, 1997), p. 391.

2. "De Klerk Tells World South Africa Built and Dismantled Six Nuclear Weapons," *Nuclear Fuel*, March 29, 1993, p. 6; Helmoed-Romer Heitman, "South Africa Built Six Nuclear Weapons," *Jane's Defence Weekly*, April 10, 1993, p. 14.

3. Mark Hibbs, "South Africa's Secret Nuclear Program: From a PNE to a Deterrent," *Nuclear Fuel*, May 10, 1993, p. 3; Mark Hibbs, "South Africa's Secret Nuclear Program: The Dismantling,"

Nuclear Fuel, May 24, 1993, p. 9; Mark Hibbs, "Pretoria Replicated Hiroshima Bomb in Seven Years, Then Froze Design," *Nucleonics Week*, May 6, 1993, p. 16; David Albright, "South Africa and the Affordable Bomb," *Bulletin of the Atomic Scientists*, July/August 1994, p. 37.

4. Mark Hibbs, "South Africa: From PNE to a Deterrent," p. 3; and Albright, "South Africa and the Affordable Bomb," p. 37.

5. Albright, "South Africa and the Affordable Bomb," op. cit., p. 37; Roger Jardine, J.W. de Villers, and Mitchell Reiss, "Why South Africa Gave Up the Bomb," *Foreign Affairs*, November/December 1993; Daryl Howlett and John Simpson, "Nuclearization and Denuclearization in South Africa," *Survival*, Autumn 1993.

6. Frank V. Pabian, "The South African Nuclear Weapons Program: Lessons for U.S. Non-proliferation Policy," *The Non-Proliferation Review*, Monterey Institute of International Studies, fall 1995, p. 9. Available at cns.miis.edu/pubs/npr/pdfs/pabian31.pdf.

7. Albright, "South Africa and the Affordable Bomb," p. 37.

8. "IAEA Confirms All South African Warheads Destroyed," *Reuters*, August 19 1994; Michael Knapik, "South African AEC Head Says Stockpile of HEU Will Be Maintained for Safari," *Nuclear Fuel*, August 16, 1993, p. 5.

9. Yossi Melman, "South Africa Admits: Israel Helped Us Develop Nuclear Weapon," *Ha'aretz*, April 20, 1997. For a good recounting of the story, see David Albright and Corey Gay, "A Flash from the Past," *Bulletin of the Atomic Scientists*, November/December 1997, pp. 15–17.

10. "Israel Reportedly Helped South Africa Develop Nuclear Weapons in the Early 1980s," *Associated Press*, April 20, 1997.

11. Yossi Melman, "Israel-S. African Nuclear Tie," *Ha'aretz*, April 21,1997, in FBIS–NES–97–082.

12. Ann MacLachlan, "New Study Finds Little Financial Loss in Converting Safari to LEU" *Platts Global Energy*, October 1, 2001.

13. Albright, et al., *1996 World Inventories*, p. 383.

14. "Decommissioning of Plants and Buildings" *Nuclear Liabilities Management Online: A Division of the South African Nuclear Energy Corporation Limited* web site, www.radwaste.co.za/closed_down_plant.htm.

15. Lynda Loxton, "France, S. Africa Agree on Nuclear Cooperation," *Reuters*, February 29, 1996; Ann MacLachan, "Cogema To Help South Africa's AEC Develop MLIS Enrichment Process," *Nuclear Fuel*, March 11, 1996, p. 4.

16. "S. Africa Approves Peaceful Nuclear Ties with Iran," *Reuters*, August 21, 1995.

17. "Energy Minister—No Uranium Sent to Iran in Last Five Years," *SAPA* (South Africa), February 21, 1996, in FBIS–TAC–96–007, June 17, 1996.

18. Al J. Venter, "Iran's Nuclear Ambition," *Jane's Intelligence Review*, September 1997, pp. 29–31.

19. "National Party Condemns Nuclear Technology Sale to China," *SAPA* (South Africa), December 14, 1997, in FBIS–AFR–97–348, December 14, 1997; "China-Nuclear," *Associated Press*, December 16, 1997.

20. David Hoffman and R. Jeffrey Smith, "President Waives Sanctions for Israel," *Washington Post*, October 27, 1991.

21. Fred Bridgland, "South Africa Scraps Missile Plan after U.S. Pressure," *Daily Telegraph*, July 1, 1993.

22. "U.S. and South Africa Sign Missile Nonproliferation Agreement," U.S. Department of State press release, October 4, 1994.

23. Henry Sokolski, "Ending South Africa's Rocket Program: A Nonproliferation Success," unpublished paper, August 27, 1996.

24. "South Africa Gains Entrance to MTCR," *Armed Force Newswire*, September 15, 1995.

25. See the report issued by Humphry Crum Ewing, Robin Ranger, David Bosdet, and David Wiencek, *Cruise Missiles: Precision and Countermeasures*, Bailrigg Memorandum 10, 1995, Center for Defense and International Security Studies.

26. Paul Taylor, "Toxic S. African Arms Raise Concern," *Washington Post*, February 28, 1995.

27. James Adams, "Gadaffi Lures South Africa's Top Germ Warfare Scientists," *Sunday Times*, February 26, 1995; Alexandra Zavis, "Mandela Says Chemical Weapons Figures May Be in Libya," *Associated Press*, March 2, 1995; and Lynne Duke, "Drug Bust Exposes S. African Arms Probes," *Washington Post*, February 1, 1997.

28. Truth and Reconciliation Commission Final Report, presented to President Mandela, October 29, 1998.

Table 22.1: **South Africa: Nuclear Infrastructure**

NAME/LOCATION OF FACILITY	TYPE/STATUS	IAEA SAFEGUARDS
FORMER NUCLEAR WEAPON (R&D) COMPLEX		
Pelindaba Nuclear Research Center	Nuclear weapon production and assembly facility; closed[1]	IAEA visited and verified dismantlement
Building 5000 complex (isolated buildings at Pelindaba)	Dedicated to the development and assembly of nuclear explosives; closed[2]	IAEA visited and verified dismantlement
Circle Building/ Advena Central Laboratories	Two generations of buildings involved in nuclear weapon production and assembly; closed[3]	IAEA visited and verified dismantlement
Upington (Vastrap Range), Kalahari	Nuclear test site; closed[4]	IAEA visited and verified sealing of shafts
POWER REACTORS		
Koeberg I	Light-water, LEU, 920-MWe; operating	Yes
Koeberg II	Light-water, LEU, 920-MWe; operating	Yes
RESEARCH REACTORS		
Safari–I, Pelindaba	Tank-type, light-water, HEU, 20-MWt; operating[5]	Yes
URANIUM ENRICHMENT		
Z-Plant Pelindaba East (formerly Valindaba)	Semi-commercial plant able to produce low-enriched uranium, jet-nozzle ("helikon") method; decommissioned	Yes
MLIS plant Pelindaba East	Demonstration-scale MLIS uranium-enrichment plant recently canceled;[6] nuclear materials present	Yes
Y-Plant Pelindaba East	Pilot-scale facility for producing weapons-grade uranium, aerodynamic process; decommissioned[7]	IAEA visited and verified dismantlement
REPROCESSING/ PLUTONIUM EXTRACTION		
Pelindaba	Hot-cell complex; operating	Yes
URANIUM PROCESSING		
Palabora	Uranium mining; operating	N/A
Hartebeestfontein	Uranium mining; operating	N/A
Vaal reefs	Uranium mining; closed	N/A
Western Areas	Uranium mining; closed	N/A
Buffelsfontein	Uranium mining; operating	N/A

Table 22.1: **South Africa: Nuclear Infrastructure**

NAME/LOCATION OF FACILITY	TYPE/STATUS	IAEA SAFEGUARDS
Vaal River	Uranium milling (3 mills); operating	N/A
Pelindaba East	Pilot-scale uranium conversion (UF_6); operating	Yes
Pelindaba East	Semi-commercial-scale uranium conversion plant (UF_6); operating	Yes
Pelindaba	MTR fuel-fabrication plant; operating	Yes
Pelindaba	LEU fuel-fabrication plant; closed (March 1995)	Yes

Abbreviations

HEU	highly enriched uranium	MWt	millions of watts of thermal output
LEU	low-enriched uranium	kWt	thousands of watts of thermal output
MWe	millions of watts of electrical output	N/A	not applicable

ADDITIONAL SOURCES

Boyle, Brendan. "South Africa Testing Laser-Uranium Process." *Reuters*, August 24, 1994.

Datafile. "South Africa." *Nuclear Engineering International*, January 1992.

Hibbs, Mark. "South Africa Reinstatement Ends 18-Year Ban from IAEA Board," *Nucleonics Week*, September 29, 1994.

IAEA. *Annual Report for 1992*. Vienna, July 1993.

MacLachlan, Ann. "South Africa AEC Looking for Partners To Help Fund Laser Enrichment Facility," *Nuclear Fuel*, August 29, 1994.

"South Africa." 1992 *Nuexco Review*, 35.

Spector, Leonard S., with Jacqueline R. Smith. *Nuclear Ambitions*. Boulder: Westview Press, 1990.

NOTES

1. South Africa's first nuclear device was produced at this facility.

2. One critical experiment was conducted at this facility; it is also the site where the first nuclear weapon was produced.

3. Five additional nuclear devices were manufactured at the Circle building between April 1982 and November 1989. When then-President de Klerk canceled the nuclear weapon program, construction of the Advena Central Laboratories had just been completed, and equipment was being moved into the facilities. The laboratories continue to conduct non-nuclear research.

4. The Kalahari test site, which was never used, consisted of two shafts of 385 meters and 216 meters in depth, both 1 meter in diameter. The shafts were sealed with concrete under IAEA supervision.

5. The reactor originally ran on 90% enriched fuel but was downgraded to 45% enriched fuel following the cutoff of fuel supplies by the United States in 1977. In the early 1990s South Africa resumed the use of 90% HEU in the reactor with material from its dismantled nuclear weapons. Studies regarding conversion to LEU continue (Ann MacLachlan, "New Study Finds Little Financial Loss in Converting Safari to LEU," *Nuclear Fuel*, October 2, 2001).

6. "South Africa: Atomic Corporation Abandons French Technology Project," *Sunday Independent*, December 14, 1997, in FBIS–AFR–97–348, December 14, 1997; "South Africa: Pilot Plant To Commercialise Uranium Enrichment Process," *Financial Mail*, November 1, 1996 in FBIS–AFR–96–212, November 1, 1996.

7. According to South Africa's declaration to the IAEA, the plant generated about 1,500 kilograms of enriched uranium while active, ranging from low-enriched uranium to weapons-grade HEU. Out of this inventory, 350 kilograms had been enriched to 90 percent U–235 and above. Each South African nuclear weapon required an estimated 55 kilograms of weapons-grade uranium. South African officials have indicated that they would like to keep at least a portion of the weapons-grade HEU to fuel the Safari–I research reactor.

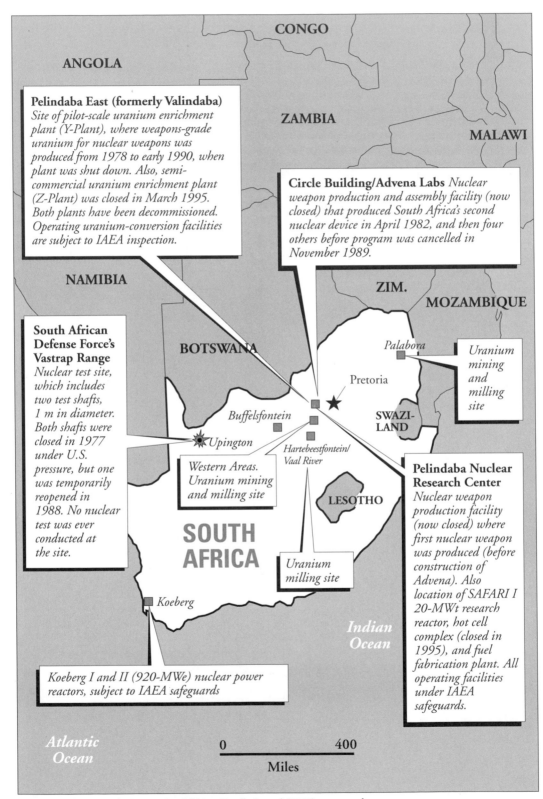

CONGO

ANGOLA

ZAMBIA

MALAWI

Pelindaba East (formerly Valindaba)
Site of pilot-scale uranium enrichment plant (Y-Plant), where weapons-grade uranium for nuclear weapons was produced from 1978 to early 1990, when plant was shut down. Also, semi-commercial uranium enrichment plant (Z-Plant) was closed in March 1995. Both plants have been decommissioned. Operating uranium-conversion facilities are subject to IAEA inspection.

Circle Building/Advena Labs *Nuclear weapon production and assembly facility (now closed) that produced South Africa's second nuclear device in April 1982, and then four others before program was cancelled in November 1989.*

NAMIBIA

ZIM.

MOZAMBIQUE

South African Defense Force's Vastrap Range
Nuclear test site, which includes two test shafts, 1 m in diameter. Both shafts were closed in 1977 under U.S. pressure, but one was temporarily reopened in 1988. No nuclear test was ever conducted at the site.

BOTSWANA

Palabora

Uranium mining and milling site

Pretoria

Buffelsfontein

SWAZI-LAND

🌟 *Upington*

Western Areas. Uranium mining and milling site

Hartebeestfontein/ Vaal River

Pelindaba Nuclear Research Center
Nuclear weapon production facility (now closed) where first nuclear weapon was produced (before construction of Advena). Also location of SAFARI I 20-MWt research reactor, hot cell complex (closed in 1995), and fuel fabrication plant. All operating facilities under IAEA safeguards.

LESOTHO

SOUTH AFRICA

Uranium milling site

Koeberg

Indian Ocean

Koeberg I and II (920-MWe) nuclear power reactors, subject to IAEA safeguards

Atlantic Ocean

0   400

Miles

Carnegie Endowment for International Peace, *Deadly Arsenals* (2002), **www.ceip.org**

Appendixes

The Treaty on the Non-Proliferation of Nuclear Weapons

The Treaty

Signed at Washington, London, and Moscow July 1, 1968
Ratification advised by U.S. Senate March 13, 1969
Ratified by U.S. President November 24, 1969
U.S. ratification deposited at Washington, London, and Moscow March 5, 1970
Proclaimed by U.S. President March 5, 1970
Entered into force March 5, 1970

The States concluding this Treaty, hereinafter referred to as the "Parties to the Treaty,"

Considering the devastation that would be visited upon all mankind by a nuclear war and the consequent need to make every effort to avert the danger of such a war and to take measures to safeguard the security of peoples,

Believing that the proliferation of nuclear weapons would seriously enhance the danger of nuclear war,

In conformity with resolutions of the United Nations General Assembly calling for the conclusion of an agreement on the prevention of wider dissemination of nuclear weapons,

Undertaking to cooperate in facilitating the application of International Atomic Energy Agency safeguards on peaceful nuclear activities,

Expressing their support for research, development and other efforts to further the application, within the framework of the International Atomic Energy Agency safeguards system, of the principle of safeguarding effectively the flow of source and special fissionable materials by use of instruments and other techniques at certain strategic points,

Affirming the principle that the benefits of peaceful applications of nuclear technology, including any technological by-products which may be derived by nuclear-weapon States from the development of nuclear explosive devices, should be available for peaceful purposes to all Parties of the Treaty, whether nuclear-weapon or non-nuclear weapon States,

Convinced that, in furtherance of this principle, all Parties to the Treaty are entitled to participate in the fullest possible exchange of scientific information for, and to contribute alone or in cooperation with other States to, the further development of the applications of atomic energy for peaceful purposes,

Declaring their intention to achieve at the earliest possible date the cessation of the nuclear arms race and to undertake effective measures in the direction of nuclear disarmament,

Urging the cooperation of all States in the attainment of this objective,

Recalling the determination expressed by the Parties to the 1963 Treaty banning nuclear weapon tests in the atmosphere, in outer space and under water in its Preamble to seek to achieve the discontinuance of all test explosions of nuclear weapons for all time and to continue negotiations to this end,

Desiring to further the easing of international tension and the strengthening of trust between States in order to facilitate the cessation of the manufacture of nuclear weapons, the liquidation of all their existing stockpiles, and the elimination from national arsenals of nuclear weapons and the means of their delivery pursuant to a Treaty on general and complete disarmament under strict and effective international control,

Recalling that, in accordance with the Charter of the United Nations, States must refrain in their international relations from the threat or use of force against the territorial integrity or political independence of any State, or in any other manner inconsistent with the Purposes of the United Nations, and that the establishment and maintenance of international peace and security are to be promoted with the least diversion for armaments of the world's human and economic resources,

Have agreed as follows:

Article I

Each nuclear-weapon State Party to the Treaty undertakes not to transfer to any recipient whatsoever nuclear weapons or other nuclear explosive devices or control over such weapons or explosive devices directly, or indirectly; and not in any way to assist, encourage, or induce any non-nuclear weapon State to manufacture or otherwise acquire nuclear weapons or other nuclear explosive devices, or control over such weapons or explosive devices.

Article II

Each non-nuclear-weapon State Party to the Treaty undertakes not to receive the transfer from any transferor whatsoever of nuclear weapons or other nuclear explosive devices or of control over such weapons or explosive devices directly, or indirectly; not to manufacture or otherwise acquire nuclear weapons or other nuclear explosive devices; and not to seek or receive any assistance in the manufacture of nuclear weapons or other nuclear explosive devices.

Article III

1. Each non-nuclear-weapon State Party to the Treaty undertakes to accept safeguards, as set forth in an agreement to be negotiated and concluded with the International Atomic Energy Agency in accordance with the Statute of the International Atomic Energy Agency and the Agency's safeguards system, for the exclusive purpose of verification of the fulfillment of its obligations assumed under this Treaty with a view to preventing diversion of nuclear energy from peaceful uses to nuclear weapons or other nuclear explosive devices. Procedures for the safeguards required by this article shall be followed with respect to source or special fissionable material whether it is being produced, processed or used in any principal nuclear facility or is outside any such facility. The safeguards required by this article shall be applied to all source or special fissionable material in all peaceful nuclear activities within the territory of such State, under its jurisdiction, or carried out under its control anywhere.

2. Each State Party to the Treaty undertakes not to provide: (a) source or special fissionable material, or (b) equipment or material especially designed or prepared for the processing, use or production of special fissionable material, to any non-nuclear-weapon State for peaceful purposes, unless the source or special fissionable material shall be subject to the safeguards required by this article.

3. The safeguards required by this article shall be implemented in a manner designed to comply with Article IV of this Treaty, and to avoid hampering the economic or technological development of the Parties or international cooperation in the field of peaceful nuclear activities, including the international exchange of nuclear material and equipment for the processing, use or production of nuclear material for peaceful purposes in accordance with the provisions of this article and the principle of safeguarding set forth in the Preamble of the Treaty.

4. Non-nuclear-weapon States Party to the Treaty shall conclude agreements with the International Atomic Energy Agency to meet the requirements of this article either individually or together with other States in accordance with the Statute of the International Atomic Energy Agency. Negotiation of such agreements shall commence within 180 days from the original entry into force of this Treaty. For States depositing their instruments of ratification or accession after the 180-day period, negotiation of such agreements shall commence not later than the date of such deposit. Such agreements shall enter into force not later than eighteen months after the date of initiation of negotiations.

Article IV

1. Nothing in this Treaty shall be interpreted as affecting the inalienable right of all the Parties to the Treaty to develop research, production and use of nuclear energy for peaceful purposes without discrimination and in conformity with articles I and II of this Treaty.

2. All the Parties to the Treaty undertake to facilitate, and have the right to participate in, the fullest possible exchange of equipment, materials and scientific and technological information for the peaceful uses of nuclear energy. Parties to the Treaty in a position to do so shall also cooperate in contributing alone or together with other States or international organizations to the further development of the applications of nuclear energy for peaceful purposes, especially in the territories of non-nuclear-weapon States Party to the Treaty, with due consideration for the needs of the developing areas of the world.

Article V

Each party to the Treaty undertakes to take appropriate measures to ensure that, in accordance with this Treaty, under appropriate international observation and through appropriate international procedures, potential benefits from any peaceful applications of nuclear explosions will be made available to non-nuclear-weapon States Party to the Treaty on a nondiscriminatory basis and that the charge to such Parties for the explosive devices used will be as low as possible and exclude any charge for research and development. Non-nuclear-weapon States Party to the Treaty shall be able to obtain such benefits, pursuant to a special international agreement or agreements, through an appropriate international body with adequate representation of non-nuclear-weapon States. Negotiations on this subject shall commence as soon as possible after the Treaty enters into force. Non-nuclear-weapon States Party to the Treaty so desiring may also obtain such benefits pursuant to bilateral agreements.

Article VI

Each of the Parties to the Treaty undertakes to pursue negotiations in good faith on effective measures relating to cessation of the nuclear arms race at an early date and to nuclear disarmament, and on a Treaty on general and complete disarmament under strict and effective international control.

Article VII

Nothing in this Treaty affects the right of any group of States to conclude regional treaties in order to assure the total absence of nuclear weapons in their respective territories.

Article VIII

1. Any Party to the Treaty may propose amendments to this Treaty. The text of any proposed amendment shall be submitted to the Depositary Governments which shall circulate it to all Parties to the Treaty. Thereupon, if requested to do so by one-third or more of the Parties to the Treaty, the Depositary Governments shall convene a conference, to which they shall invite all the Parties to the Treaty, to consider such an amendment.

2. Any amendment to this Treaty must be approved by a majority of the votes of all the Parties to the Treaty, including the votes of all nuclear-weapon States Party to the Treaty and all other Parties which, on the date the amendment is circulated, are members of the Board of Governors of the International Atomic Energy Agency. The amendment shall enter into force for each Party that deposits its instrument of ratification of the amendment upon the deposit of such instruments of ratification by a majority of all the Parties, including the instruments of ratification of all nuclear-weapon States Party to the Treaty and all other Parties which, on the date the amendment is circulated, are members of the Board of Governors of the International Atomic Energy Agency. Thereafter, it shall enter into force for any other Party upon the deposit of its instrument of ratification of the amendment.

3. Five years after the entry into force of this Treaty, a conference of Parties to the Treaty shall be held in Geneva, Switzerland, in order to review the operation of this Treaty with a view to assuring that the purposes of the Preamble and the provisions of the Treaty are being realized. At intervals of five years thereafter, a majority of the Parties to the Treaty may obtain, by submitting a proposal to this effect to the Depositary Governments, the convening of further conferences with the same objective of reviewing the operation of the Treaty.

Article IX

1. This Treaty shall be open to all States for signature. Any State which does not sign the Treaty before its entry into force in accordance with paragraph 3 of this article may accede to it at any time.

2. This Treaty shall be subject to ratification by signatory States. Instruments of ratification and instruments of accession shall be deposited with the Governments of the United States of America, the United Kingdom of Great Britain and Northern Ireland and the Union of Soviet Socialist Republics, which are hereby designated the Depositary Governments.

3. This Treaty shall enter into force after its ratification by the States, the Governments of which are designated Depositaries of the Treaty, and forty other States signatory to this Treaty and the deposit of their instruments of ratification. For the purposes of this Treaty, a nuclear-weapon State is one

which has manufactured and exploded a nuclear weapon or other nuclear explosive device prior to January 1, 1967.

4. For States whose instruments of ratification or accession are deposited subsequent to the entry into force of this Treaty, it shall enter into force on the date of the deposit of their instruments of ratification or accession.

5. The Depositary Governments shall promptly inform all signatory and acceding States of the date of each signature, the date of deposit of each instrument of ratification or of accession, the date of the entry into force of this Treaty, and the date of receipt of any requests for convening a conference or other notices.

6. This Treaty shall be registered by the Depositary Governments pursuant to article 102 of the Charter of the United Nations.

Article X

1. Each Party shall in exercising its national sovereignty have the right to withdraw from the Treaty if it decides that extraordinary events, related to the subject matter of this Treaty, have jeopardized the supreme interests of its country. It shall give notice of such withdrawal to all other Parties to the Treaty and to the United Nations Security Council three months in advance. Such notice shall include a statement of the extraordinary events it regards as having jeopardized its supreme interests.

2. Twenty-five years after the entry into force of the Treaty, a conference shall be convened to decide whether the Treaty shall continue in force indefinitely, or shall be extended for an additional fixed period or periods. This decision shall be taken by a majority of the Parties to the Treaty.

Article XI

This Treaty, the English, Russian, French, Spanish, and Chinese texts of which are equally authentic, shall be deposited in the archives of the Depositary Governments. Duly certified copies of this Treaty shall be transmitted by the Depositary Governments to the Governments of the signatory and acceding States.

IN WITNESS WHEREOF the undersigned, duly authorized, have signed this Treaty.

DONE in triplicate, at the cities of Washington, London and Moscow, this first day of July one thousand nine hundred sixty-eight.

State Parties to the Non-Proliferation Treaty

1. Afghanistan
2. Albania
3. Algeria
4. Andorra
5. Angola
6. Antigua and Barbuda
7. Argentina
8. Armenia
9. Australia
10. Austria
11. Azerbaijan
12. Bahamas
13. Bahrain
14. Bangladesh
15. Barbados
16. Belarus
17. Belgium
18. Belize
19. Benin
20. Bhutan
21. Bolivia
22. Bosnia and Herzegovina
23. Botswana
24. Brazil
25. Brunei Darussalam
26. Bulgaria
27. Burkina Faso
28. Burundi
29. Cambodia
30. Cameroon
31. Canada
32. Cape Verde
33. Central African Republic
34. Chad
35. Chile
36. China
37. Colombia
38. Comoros
39. Congo
40. Costa Rica
41. Côte d'Ivoire
42. Croatia
43. Cyprus
44. Czech Republic
45. Democratic People's Republic of Korea
46. Democratic Republic of the Congo
47. Denmark
48. Djibouti
49. Dominica
50. Dominican Republic
51. Ecuador
52. Egypt
53. El Salvador
54. Equatorial Guinea
55. Eritrea
56. Estonia
57. Ethiopia
58. Fiji
59. Finland
60. France
61. Gabon
62. Gambia
63. Georgia
64. Germany
65. Ghana
66. Greece
67. Grenada
68. Guatemala
69. Guinea
70. Guinea-Bissau
71. Guyana
72. Haiti
73. Holy See
74. Honduras
75. Hungary
76. Iceland
77. Indonesia
78. Iran (Islamic Republic of)
79. Iraq
80. Ireland
81. Italy
82. Jamaica
83. Japan
84. Jordan
85. Kazakhstan
86. Kenya

87. Kiribati
88. Kuwait
89. Kyrgyzstan
90. Lao People's Democratic Republic
91. Latvia
92. Lebanon
93. Lesotho
94. Liberia
95. Libyan Arab Jamahiriya
96. Liechtenstein
97. Lithuania
98. Luxembourg
99. Madagascar
100. Malawi
101. Malaysia
102. Maldives
103. Mali
104. Malta
105. Marshall Islands
106. Mauritania
107. Mauritius
108. Mexico
109. Micronesia (Federated States of)
110. Monaco
111. Mongolia
112. Morocco
113. Mozambique
114. Myanmar
115. Namibia
116. Nauru
117. Nepal
118. Netherlands
119. New Zealand
120. Nicaragua
121. Niger
122. Nigeria
123. Norway
124. Oman
125. Palau
126. Panama
127. Papua New Guinea
128. Paraguay
129. Peru
130. Philippines
131. Poland
132. Portugal
133. Qatar
134. Republic of Korea
135. Republic of Moldova
136. Romania
137. Russian Federation
138. Rwanda
139. Saint Kitts and Nevis
140. Saint Lucia
141. Saint Vincent and the Grenadines
142. Samoa
143. San Marino
144. Sao Tome and Principe
145. Saudi Arabia
146. Senegal
147. Seychelles
148. Sierra Leone
149. Singapore
150. Slovak Republic
151. Slovenia
152. Solomon Islands
153. Somalia
154. South Africa
155. Spain
156. Sri Lanka
157. Sudan
158. Suriname
159. Swaziland
160. Sweden
161. Switzerland
162. Syrian Arab Republic
163. Tajikistan
164. Thailand
165. The former Yugoslav Republic of Macedonia
166. Togo
167. Tonga
168. Trinidad and Tobago
169. Tunisia
170. Turkey
171. Turkmenistan
172. Tuvalu
173. Uganda
174. Ukraine
175. United Arab Emirates

176. United Kingdom of Great
 Britain and Northern Ireland
177. United Republic of Tanzania
178. United States of America
179. Uruguay
180. Uzbekistan
181. Vanuatu

182. Venezuela
183. Viet Nam
184. Yemen
185. Yugoslavia
186. Zambia
187. Zimbabwe

Final Document of the 2000 NPT Review Conference

A Program of Action on Nuclear Non-Proliferation and Disarmament

The final document of the May 2000 Non-Proliferation Treaty Review Conference detailed a program of action on nuclear non-proliferation and disarmament. It was adopted by consensus as part of the final document in Volume I, Part I, Section on Article VI, paragraph 15. The complete text of the final document is available at: www.un.org/Depts/dda/WMD/treaty

The Conference agrees on the following practical steps for the systematic and progressive efforts to implement Article VI of the Treaty on the Non-Proliferation of Nuclear Weapons and paragraphs 3 and 4(c) of the 1995 Decision on "Principles and Objectives for Nuclear Non-Proliferation and Disarmament":

1. The importance and urgency of signatures and ratifications, without delay and without conditions and in accordance with constitutional processes, to achieve the early entry into force of the Comprehensive Nuclear-Test-Ban Treaty.

2. A moratorium on nuclear weapon test explosions or any other nuclear explosions pending entry into force of that Treaty.

3. The necessity of negotiations in the Conference on Disarmament on a non-discriminatory, multilateral and internationally and effectively verifiable treaty banning the production of fissile material for nuclear weapons or other nuclear explosive devices in accordance with the statement of the Special Coordinator in 1995 and the mandate contained therein, taking into consideration both nuclear disarmament and nuclear non-proliferation objectives. The Conference on Disarmament is urged to agree on a program of work which includes the immediate commencement of negotiations on such a treaty with a view to their conclusion within five years.

4. The necessity of establishing in the Conference on Disarmament an appropriate subsidiary body with a mandate to deal with nuclear disarmament. The Conference on Disarmament is urged to agree on a program of work which includes the immediate establishment of such a body.

5. The principle of irreversibility to apply to nuclear disarmament, nuclear and other related arms control and reduction measures.

6. An unequivocal undertaking by the nuclear-weapon states to accomplish the total elimination of their nuclear arsenals leading to nuclear disarmament to which all State parties are committed under Article VI.

7. The early entry into force and full implementation of START II and the conclusion of START III as soon as possible while preserving and strengthening the ABM Treaty as a cornerstone of strategic stability and as a basis for further reductions of strategic offensive weapons, in accordance with its provisions.

8. The completion and implementation of the Trilateral Initiative between the United States of America, the Russian Federation and the International Atomic Energy Agency.

9. Steps by all the nuclear-weapon States leading to nuclear disarmament in a way that promotes international stability, and based on the principle of undiminished security for all:

   • Further efforts by the nuclear-weapon States to reduce their nuclear arsenals unilaterally.

   • Increased transparency by the nuclear-weapon States with regard to their nuclear weapons capabilities and the implementation of agreements pursuant to Article VI and as a voluntary confidence-building measure to support further progress on nuclear disarmament.

   • The further reduction of nonstrategic nuclear weapons, based on unilateral initiatives and as an integral part of the nuclear arms reduction and disarmament process.

   • Concrete agreed measures to further reduce the operational status of nuclear weapons systems.

   • A diminishing role for nuclear weapons in security policies to minimize the risk that these weapons ever be used and to facilitate the process of their total elimination.

   • The engagement as soon as appropriate of all the nuclear-weapon States in the process leading to the total elimination of their nuclear weapons.

10. Arrangements by all nuclear-weapon States to place, as soon as practicable, fissile material designated by each of them as no longer required for military purposes under IAEA or other relevant international verification and arrangements for the disposition of such material for peaceful purposes, to ensure that such material remains permanently outside of military programs.

11. Reaffirmation that the ultimate objective of the efforts of States in the disarmament process is general and complete disarmament under effective international control.

12. Regular reports, within the framework of the NPT strengthened review process, by all States parties on the implementation of Article VI and paragraph 4 (c) of the 1995 Decision on "Principles and Objectives for Nuclear Non-Proliferation and Disarmament," and recalling the Advisory Opinion of the International Court of Justice of 8 July 1996.

13. The further development of the verification capabilities that will be required to provide assurance of compliance with nuclear disarmament agreements for the achievement and maintenance of a nuclear weapon free world.

The further development of the verification capabilities that will be required to provide assurance of compliance with nuclear disarmament agreements for the achievement and maintenance of a nuclear-weapon-free world.

STATEMENT TO THE 2000 NPT REVIEW CONFERENCE H.E. HUBERT DE LA FORTELLE ON BEHALF OF THE UN PERMANENT FIVE NUCLEAR-WEAPON STATES, INTRODUCING THEIR COLLECTIVE STATEMENT

New York, 1 May 2000

Mr Chairman,

I have the honour to take the floor on behalf of the delegations of France, the People's Republic of China, the Russian Federation, the United Kingdom of Great Britain and Northern Ireland and the United States of America.

Willing to contribute in a positive manner to the work of the Review Conference, the five nuclear-weapon States today submit a common statement to the States Parties.

This statement presents some of their positions on issues relating to nuclear disarmament, non-proliferation and peaceful uses, with which the Conference will have to deal.

I draw your attention to paragraph 10 of this statement, which reads:

"Emphasising the essential importance of cooperation, demonstrating and advancing mutual trust among ourselves, and promoting greater international security and stability, we declare that none of our nuclear weapons are targeted at any State."

With this statement, the five nuclear-weapon States reaffirm their willingness to pursue systematic and progressive efforts to reduce nuclear weapons globally, in accordance with decision 2 of 1995.

I have asked that this statement is circulated as an official Conference document.

STATEMENT BY THE DELEGATIONS OF FRANCE, THE PEOPLE'S REPUBLIC OF CHINA, THE RUSSIAN FEDERATION, THE UNITED KINGDOM OF GREAT BRITAIN AND NORTHERN IRELAND AND THE UNITED STATES OF AMERICA

1. The delegations of China, France, Russia, the United Kingdom, and the United States, on the occasion of the sixth Review Conference of the Treaty on the Non-Proliferation of Nuclear Weapons (NPT), formally reiterate the strong and continuing support of our countries for this Treaty, the cornerstone of the international nuclear nonproliferation regime and the essential foundation for nuclear disarmament. We remain unequivocally committed to fulfilling all of our obligations under the Treaty.

2. We welcomed the decision on indefinite extension of the Treaty adopted in 1995 by its member States. We reaffirm our commitment to strengthening the review process of the Treaty and to the principles and objectives for nuclear non-proliferation and disarmament. We reaffirm our commitment to the resolution on the Middle East adopted in 1995. The principles established by those documents will make a continuing contribution to the review process, the Treaty remaining its fundamental guide.

3. The progress of NPT universality has been confirmed after the 1995 conference. We welcome the accession to the Treaty by Chile, Vanuatu, the United Arab Emirates, Comoros, Andorra, Angola, Djibouti, Oman and Brazil. Today, there are 187 member States. We reiterate the need for universal adherence to the NPT and call upon States that have not yet done so to accede to the Treaty at an early date. The nuclear explosions carried out by India and Pakistan in May 1998 were a cause of deep international concern. We continue to call upon both countries to undertake the measures set out in UNSCR 1172. Notwithstanding their nuclear tests, India and Pakistan do not have the status of nuclear-weapon States in accordance with the NPT.

4. We stress that compliance with the NPT by all member States is essential to further the comprehensive goals of the Treaty.

5. We reiterate our unequivocal commitment to the ultimate goals of a complete elimination of nuclear weapons and a treaty on general and complete disarmament under strict and effective international control.

6. A program of action was set out by the 1995 Review and Extension Conference as important in the full realization and effective implementation of Article VI. In pursuit of that program, there have been highly significant multilateral, bilateral and unilateral developments since 1995.

7. The CTBT was opened for signature in New York on 24 September 1996. The five nuclear-weapon States all signed it that very day. Today, 155 States have signed it and 55 of them, including 28 whose ratification is necessary for its entry into force, have deposited their instruments of ratification with the Secretary General of the United Nations, including France and the United Kingdom in a joint ceremony on 6 April 1998. The recent ratification of the CTBT by the Russian Federation is welcome. The Preparatory Commission for the CTBT Organization has been set up in Vienna and is putting into place the international monitoring system of the Treaty. Important progress has been made so far in the setting up of the verification system. We remain committed to ensuring that, at entry into force of the CTBT, the verification regime will be capable of meeting the verification requirements of this Treaty. The first conference of States having ratified the Treaty to consider the issue of its entry into force took place in Vienna in October 1999. No efforts should be spared to make sure that the CTBT is a universal and internationally and effectively verifiable treaty and to secure its early entry into force. There should be no doubt as to the commitment of our five countries to that effect.

8. As one logical multilateral step in the full realization and effective implementation of Article VI, we reaffirm the necessity of a non-discriminatory, universally applicable and internationally and effectively verifiable convention banning the production of fissile material for nuclear weapons or other nuclear explosive devices negotiated in accordance with the 1995 statement of the Special Coordinator of the Conference on Disarmament and the mandate contained therein. We urge the Conference on Disarmament to agree on a program of work as soon as possible, which includes the immediate commencement and early conclusion of negotiations on such a treaty.

9. The contribution of the five nuclear-weapon States to systematic and progressive efforts to reduce nuclear weapons globally has been and will be highlighted by each of us nationally.

10. Emphasising the essential importance of cooperation, demonstrating and advancing mutual trust among ourselves, and promoting greater international security and stability, we declare that none of our nuclear weapons are targeted at any State.

11. Ratification of START II by the Russian Federation is an important step in the efforts to reduce strategic offensive weapons and is welcome. Completion of ratification of START II by the United States remains a priority. We look forward to the conclusion of START III as soon as possible while preserving and strengthening the ABM Treaty as a cornerstone of strategic stability and as a basis for further reductions of strategic offensive weapons, in accordance with its provisions.

12. We are committed to placing as soon as practicable fissile materials designated by each of us as no longer required for defence purposes under

IAEA or other relevant international verification. We have launched a number of significant initiatives to provide for the safe and effective management and disposition of such materials.

13. We welcome the creation of two new nuclear-weapon free zones since 1995 as a significant contribution to the enhancement of regional and international peace and security: South-East Asia and Africa. The five nuclear-weapon States have signed and, in most cases, ratified all the relevant protocols to the treaties of Tlatelolco, Rarotonga and Pelindaba; internal processes are under way to secure the few lacking ratifications. The consultations with States parties to the treaty of Bangkok have recently been accelerated, paving the way for our adherence to the additional protocol. We are looking forward to the successful and early conclusions of those consultations. We encourage the States in Central Asia to pursue successfully their efforts to create a nuclear-weapon free zone in their region. We support and respect the nuclear-weapon free status of Mongolia.

14. We note that the actions of the nuclear-weapon States since 1995 on the relevant additional protocols to Nuclear Weapon Free Zone treaties have increased the number of non-nuclear-weapon States eligible for legally binding Negative Security Assurances to over 100. We reaffirm our commitment to United Nations Security Council resolution 984 adopted in April 1995 on security assurances for NPT non-nuclear-weapon States. According to operative paragraph 10 of resolution 984, the issues addressed in that resolution remain of continuing concern to the Security Council. We are ready to exchange views relating to the positive security assurances referred to in the resolution.

15. We consider the international safeguards system of the International Atomic Energy Agency (IAEA) as one of the essential pillars of the nonproliferation regime. This system acts as a guarantee for stability and the preservation of world peace. We call on all States parties, which are required by Article III of the Treaty and have not yet done so, to sign and bring into force comprehensive safeguards agreements without delay.

16. The development and the implementation of the strengthened safeguards system of the IAEA through new agreements is a significant achievement. We praise the remarkable work carried out by the IAEA in this field and hope that the strengthened system soon spreads across all regions of the world. Here again, universality is the challenge we face. To date, Additional Protocols have been signed by more than fifty non-nuclear-weapon States; nine of them have entered into force. We urge all non-nuclear-weapon States that have not yet done so to sign without delay the additional protocol with a view to its early implementation.

17. As regards States not members of the NPT, one of them has recently signed an Additional Protocol with the IAEA. We encourage the three others to negotiate an Additional Protocol with the IAEA.

18. All the five nuclear-weapon States signed an Additional Protocol with the IAEA and shall seek to ratify their agreements as soon as possible.

19. We support the promotion of transparency in nuclear related export controls within the framework of dialogue and cooperation among all interested States parties to the treaty and we welcome the initiatives taken in order to carry out this objective.

20. We reaffirm the inalienable right of all the parties to the Treaty to develop research, production, and use of nuclear energy for peaceful purposes without discrimination and in accordance with the relevant provisions of the Treaty and the relevant principles on safeguards. Pursuant to our obligation under Article IV, we have provided our support for the technical cooperation programs administered by the IAEA, which has enabled many nations to make progress in the application of nuclear technologies in important fields such as agriculture, hydrology, medicine and environment.

21. We stress the importance of international cooperation in order to maintain the highest practicable levels of nuclear safety. In this regard, we welcome the entry into force and the first review meeting of the convention on nuclear safety as well as the opening for signature of the joint convention on the safety of spent fuel management and on the safety of radioactive waste management. We call on all States which have not yet done so to sign and ratify those two conventions.

22. We are determined to take a forward-looking approach to nuclear non-proliferation and nuclear disarmament. The NPT provides an indispensable framework for future efforts against nuclear proliferation and towards nuclear disarmament. We fully acknowledge our particular responsibility and key role in ensuring continued progress in the implementation of the NPT.

23. The five nuclear-weapon States hope similarly genuine commitment to the pursuit of nuclear non-proliferation and disarmament as a contribution to enhanced peace and security will be shown by all States members of the NPT and States outside the NPT. We will continue to work together and with the non-nuclear-weapon States for the success of the review process.

Convention on The Prohibition of the Development, Production and Stockpiling of Bacteriological (Biological) and Toxin Weapons and on Their Destruction

Signed at Washington, London, and Moscow April 10, 1972
Ratification advised by U.S. Senate December 16, 1974
Ratified by U.S. President January 22, 1975
U.S. ratification deposited at Washington, London, and Moscow March 26, 1975
Proclaimed by U.S. President March 26, 1975
Entered into force March 26, 1975

The States Parties to this Convention,

Determined to act with a view to achieving effective progress towards general and complete disarmament, including the prohibition and elimination of all types of weapons of mass destruction, and convinced that the prohibition of the development, production and stockpiling of chemical and bacteriological (biological) weapons and their elimination, through effective measures, will facilitate the achievement of general and complete disarmament under strict and effective international control,

Recognizing the important significance of the Protocol for the Prohibition of the Use in War of Asphyxiating, Poisonous or Other Gases, and of Bacteriological Methods of Warfare, signed at Geneva on June 17, 1925, and conscious also of the contribution which the said Protocol has already made, and continues to make, to mitigating the horrors of war,

Reaffirming their adherence to the principles and objectives of that Protocol and calling upon all States to comply strictly with them,

Recalling that the General Assembly of the United Nations has repeatedly condemned all actions contrary to the principles and objectives of the Geneva Protocol of June 17, 1925,

Desiring to contribute to the strengthening of confidence between peoples and the general improvement of the international atmosphere,

Desiring also to contribute to the realization of the purposes and principles of the Charter of the United Nations,

Convinced of the importance and urgency of eliminating from the arsenals of States, through effective measures, such dangerous weapons of mass destruction as those using chemical or bacteriological (biological) agents,

Recognizing that an agreement on the prohibition of bacteriological (biological) and toxin weapons represents a first possible step towards the achievement of agreement on effective measures also for the prohibition of the development, production and stockpiling of chemical weapons, and determined to continue negotiations to that end,

Determined, for the sake of all mankind, to exclude completely the possibility of bacteriological (biological) agents and toxins being used as weapons,

Convinced that such use would be repugnant to the conscience of mankind and that no effort should be spared to minimize this risk,

Have agreed as follows:

Article I

Each State Party to this Convention undertakes never in any circumstances to develop, produce, stockpile or otherwise acquire or retain:

(1)   Microbial or other biological agents, or toxins whatever their origin or method of production, of types and in quantities that have no justification for prophylactic, protective or other peaceful purposes;

(2)   Weapons, equipment or means of delivery designed to use such agents or toxins for hostile purposes or in armed conflict.

Article II

Each State Party to this Convention undertakes to destroy, or to divert to peaceful purposes, as soon as possible but not later than nine months after the entry into force of the Convention, all agents, toxins, weapons, equipment and means of delivery specified in article I of the Convention, which are in its possession or under its jurisdiction or control. In implementing the provisions of this article all necessary safety precautions shall be observed to protect populations and the environment.

Article III

Each State Party to this Convention undertakes not to transfer to any recipient whatsoever, directly or indirectly, and not in any way to assist, encourage, or induce any State, group of States or international organizations to manufacture or otherwise acquire any of the agents, toxins, weapons, equipment or means of delivery specified in article I of the Convention.

Article IV

Each State Party to this Convention shall, in accordance with its constitutional processes, take any necessary measures to prohibit and prevent the development, production, stockpiling, acquisition, or retention of the agents, toxins, weapons, equipment and means of delivery specified in article I of the Convention, within the territory of such State, under its jurisdiction or under its control anywhere.

Article V

The States Parties to this Convention undertake to consult one another and to cooperate in solving any problems which may arise in relation to the objective of, or in the application of the provisions of, the Convention. Consultation and cooperation pursuant to this article may also be undertaken through appropriate international procedures within the framework of the United Nations and in accordance with its Charter.

Article VI

(1) Any State Party to this Convention which finds that any other State Party is acting in breach of obligations deriving from the provisions of the Convention may lodge a complaint with the Security Council of the United Nations. Such a complaint should include all possible evidence confirming its validity, as well as a request for its consideration by the Security Council.

(2) Each State Party to this Convention undertakes to cooperate in carrying out any investigation which the Security Council may initiate, in accordance with the provisions of the Charter of the United Nations, on the basis of the complaint received by the Council. The Security Council shall inform the States Parties to the Convention of the results of the investigation.

Article VII

Each State Party to this Convention undertakes to provide or support assistance, in accordance with the United Nations Charter, to any Party to the Convention which so requests, if the Security Council decides that such Party has been exposed to danger as a result of violation of the Convention.

Article VIII

Nothing in this Convention shall be interpreted as in any way limiting or detracting from the obligations assumed by any State under the Protocol for the Prohibition of the Use in War of Asphyxiating, Poisonous or Other Gases, and of Bacteriological Methods of Warfare, signed at Geneva on June 17, 1925.

Article IX

Each State Party to this Convention affirms the recognized objective of effective prohibition of chemical weapons and, to this end, undertakes to continue negotiations in good faith with a view to reaching early agreement on effective measures for the prohibition of their development, production and stockpiling and for their destruction, and on appropriate measures concerning equipment and means of delivery specifically designed for the production or use of chemical agents for weapons purposes.

Article X

(1)   The States Parties to this Convention undertake to facilitate, and have the right to participate in, the fullest possible exchange of equipment, materials and scientific and technological information for the use of bacteriological (biological) agents and toxins for peaceful purposes. Parties to the Convention in a position to do so shall also cooperate in contributing individually or together with other States or international organizations to the further development and application of scientific discoveries in the field of bacteriology (biology) for prevention of disease, or for other peaceful purposes.

(2)   This Convention shall be implemented in a manner designed to avoid hampering the economic or technological development of States Parties to the Convention or international cooperation in the field of peaceful bacteriological (biological) activities, including the international exchange of bacteriological (biological) agents and toxins and equipment for the processing, use or production of bacteriological (biological) agents and toxins for peaceful purposes in accordance with the provisions of the Convention.

Article XI

Any State Party may propose amendments to this Convention. Amendments shall enter into force for each State Party accepting the amendments upon their acceptance by a majority of the States Parties to the Convention and thereafter for each remaining State Party on the date of acceptance by it.

Article XII

Five years after the entry into force of this Convention, or earlier if it is requested by a majority of Parties to the Convention by submitting a proposal to this effect to the Depositary Governments, a conference of States Parties to the Convention shall be held at Geneva, Switzerland, to review the operation of the Convention, with a view to assuring that the purposes of the preamble and the provisions of the Convention, including the provisions concerning negotiations on chemical weapons, are being realized. Such review shall take into account any new scientific and technological developments relevant to the Convention.

Article XIII

(1)   This Convention shall be of unlimited duration.

(2)   Each State Party to this Convention shall in exercising its national sovereignty have the right to withdraw from the Convention if it decides that extraordinary events, related to the subject matter of the Convention, have jeopardized the supreme interests of its country. It shall give notice of such withdrawal to all other States Parties to the Convention and to the United Nations Security Council three months in advance. Such notice shall include a statement of the extraordinary events it regards as having jeopardized its supreme interests.

Article XIV

(1)   This Convention shall be open to all States for signature. Any State which does not sign the Convention before its entry into force in accordance with paragraph (3) of this Article may accede to it at any time.

(2)   This Convention shall be subject to ratification by signatory States. Instruments of ratification and instruments of accession shall be deposited with the Governments of the United States of America, the United Kingdom of Great Britain and Northern Ireland and the Union of Soviet Socialist Republics, which are hereby designated the Depositary Governments.

(3)   This Convention shall enter into force after the deposit of instruments of ratification by twenty-two Governments, including the Governments designated as Depositaries of the Convention.

(4)   For States whose instruments of ratification or accession are deposited subsequent to the entry into force of this Convention, it shall enter into force on the date of the deposit of their instruments of ratification or accession.

(5)   The Depositary Governments shall promptly inform all signatory and acceding States of the date of each signature, the date of deposit of each instrument of ratification or of accession and the date of the entry into force of this Convention, and of the receipt of other notices.

(6)   This Convention shall be registered by the Depositary Governments pursuant to Article 102 of the Charter of the United Nations.

Article XV

This Convention, the English, Russian, French, Spanish and Chinese texts of which are equally authentic, shall be deposited in the archives of the Depositary Governments. Duly certified copies of the Convention shall be transmitted by the Depositary Governments to the Governments of the signatory and acceding states.

IN WITNESS WHEREOF the undersigned, duly authorized, have signed this Convention.

DONE in triplicate, at the cities of Washington, London and Moscow, this tenth day of April, one thousand nine hundred and seventy-two.

PARTIES AND SIGNATORIES OF
THE BIOLOGICAL WEAPONS CONVENTION

STATE (COUNTRY) (163)

Afghanistan
Albania
Algeria
Argentina
Armenia
Australia
Austria
Bahamas
Bahrain
Bangladesh
Barbados
Belarus
Belgium
Belize
Benin
Bhutan
Bolivia
Bosnia and Herzegovina
Botswana
Brazil
Brunei Darussalam
Bulgaria
Burkina Faso
Cambodia (Kampuchea)
Canada
Cape Verde
Chile
China, People's Republic of
Colombia
Congo
Congo, Democratic People's
Republic of
Costa Rica
Croatia
Cuba
Cyprus
Czech Republic
Denmark
Dominica
Dominican Republic
Ecuador

El Salvador
Equatorial Guinea
Estonia
Ethiopia
Fiji
Finland
France
Georgia
Germany
Ghana
Greece
Grenada
Guatemala
Guinea-Bissau
Honduras
Hungary
Iceland
India
Indonesia
Iran
Iraq
Ireland
Italy
Jamaica
Japan
Jordan
Kenya
Korea, Democratic People's Republic of
Korea, Republic of
Kuwait
Kyrgyzstan
Laos
Latvia
Lebanon
Lesotho
Libya
Liechtenstein
Lithuania
Luxembourg
Macedonia, Former Yugoslav
Republic of

Malaysia
Maldives
Malta
Mauritius
Mexico
Monaco
Mongolia
Netherlands
New Zealand
Nicaragua
Niger
Nigeria
Norway
Oman
Pakistan
Panama
Papua New Guinea
Paraguay
Peru
Philippines
Poland
Portugal
Qatar
Romania
Russian Federation
Rwanda
St. Kitts and Nevis
St. Lucia
St. Vincent and the
   Grenadines
San Marino
Sao Tome and Principe
Saudi Arabia
Senegal

Serbia-Montenegro
   (formerly Yugoslavia)
Seychelles
Sierra Leone
Singapore
Slovak Republic
Slovenia
Solomon Islands
South Africa
Spain
Sri Lanka
Suriname
Swaziland
Sweden
Switzerland
Thailand
Togo
Tonga
Tunisia
Turkey
Turkmenistan
Uganda
Ukraine
United Kingdom
United States
Uruguay
Uzbekistan
Vanuatu
Venezuela
Vietnam
Yemen
Zaire
Zimbabwe

SIGNATORY COUNTRIES

Burundi
Central African Republic
Côte d'Ivoire
Egypt
Gabon
Guyana
Haiti
Liberia
Madagascar

Malawi
Mali
Morocco
Myanmar (Burma)
Nepal
Somalia
Syria
Tanzania
United Arab Emirates

The Chemical Weapons Convention Fact Sheet

Released by the U.S. Department of State, Bureau of Arms Control, Washington, DC, November 28, 2000

The Chemical Weapons Convention is a global treaty that bans an entire class of weapons of mass destruction, chemical weapons. The CWC bans the production, acquisition, stockpiling, transfer and use of chemical weapons. It entered into force April 29, 1997.

Chemical weapons pose a threat not just to our military but to innocent civilians, as the 1995 poison gas attack in the Japanese subway showed. Certain aspects of the Chemical Weapons Convention, including its law enforcement requirements and nonproliferation provisions, strengthen existing efforts to fight chemical terrorism. The CWC is a central element of U.S. arms control and nonproliferation policy that strengthens U.S. national security and contributes to global stability.

Under the CWC, each State Party undertakes never, under any circumstances, to:

- develop, produce, otherwise acquire, stockpile or retain chemical weapons, or transfer, directly or indirectly, chemical weapons to anyone;

- use chemical weapons;

- engage in any military preparation to use chemical weapons; and

- assist, encourage or induce, in any way, anyone to engage in any activity prohibited to a State Party under this Convention.

In addition each State Party undertakes, all in accordance with the provisions of the Convention, to:

- destroy the chemical weapons it owns or possesses or that are located in any place under its jurisdiction or control;

- destroy all chemical weapons it abandoned on the territory of another State Party; and

- destroy any chemical weapons production facilities it owns or possesses or that are located in any place under its jurisdiction or control.

Today, we suspect some 20 countries have or may be developing chemical weapons. These weapons are attractive to countries or individuals seeking a mass-destruction capability because they are relatively cheap to produce and do not demand the elaborate technical infrastructure needed to make nuclear weapons. It is therefore all the more vital to establish an international bulwark against the acquisition and use of these weapons.

The CWC is the most ambitious treaty in the history of arms control. Whereas most arms control treaties in the past have only limited weapons, the CWC requires their outright elimination. Parties to the Convention must destroy any and all chemical weapons and chemical weapons production facilities.

The CWC penalizes countries that do not join. Entry into force of the CWC served to isolate the small number of non-participating states as international pariahs and inhibit their access to certain treaty-controlled chemicals. Since many of these chemicals are not only required to make chemical weapons but have important uses in commercial industry, the hold-outs have economic as well as political incentives to join the treaty regime.

The Chemical Weapons Convention and Industry

The CWC is the first arms control treaty to widely affect the private sector. Although the United States does not manufacture chemical weapons, it does produce, process, and consume chemicals that can be used to produce chemical weapons. For example, a solvent used in ballpoint pen ink can be easily converted into mustard gas, and a chemical involved in production of fire retardants and pesticides can be used to make nerve agents. Thus, any treaty to ban chemical weapons must monitor commercial facilities that produce, process, or consume dual-use chemicals to ensure they are not diverted for prohibited purposes.

The CWC provisions covering chemical facilities were developed with the active participation of industry representatives. The verification regime is intrusive enough to give confidence that member states are complying with the treaty, yet it respects industry's legitimate interests in safeguarding proprietary information and avoiding disruption of production.

In testimony before the Senate Foreign Relations Committee, Fred Webber, president and CEO of the Chemical Manufacturers Association, said, "We have studied this treaty in great detail; we have put it to the test. We think the CWC is a good deal for American industry. . . . The Chemical Weapons Convention protects vital commercial interests. I know because we helped design the reporting forms. And I know because we helped develop inspection procedures that protect trade secrets while providing full assurance that chemical weapons are not being produced...The Chemical Weapons Convention makes good business sense and good public policy."

The CWC and the Military

The CWC specifically allows Parties to maintain chemical weapon defensive programs and does not constrain non-CW military responses to a chemical weapon attack. John Shalikashvili, former chair of the Joint Chiefs of Staff, has said in Senate testimony that "Desert Storm proved that retaliation in kind is not required to deter the use of chemical weapons." He explained, "The U.S. military's ability to deter chemical weapons in a post–CW world will be predicated upon both a robust chemical weapons defense capability, and the ability to rapidly bring to bear superior and overwhelming military force in retaliation against a chemical attack." As Defense Secretary Cheney said during the Gulf War, and as former Defense Secretary Perry reiterated, the U.S. response to a chemical weapon attack would be "absolutely overwhelming" and "devastating."

CWC Implementation

With or without the CWC, the United States is already destroying its chemical weapons in accordance with a law passed by Congress more than a decade ago that requires the destruction of the bulk of the U.S. chemical weapon stockpile. That process is under way, with completion slated for the end of 2004. The CWC now requires that all state parties that possess chemical weapons to destroy their stockpiles by April 2007.

The United States is a member of the executive council of the Organization for the Prohibition of Chemical Weapons, in The Hague, which will oversee the implementation of the CWC. United States citizens serve as international inspectors and in other key positions relating to the verification of the treaty. In the United States, the Department of Commerce expects to publish regulations pertaining to CWC verification after the enactment of the CWC Implementation Act.

The CWC puts into place a legally binding international standard outlawing the acquisition and possession, as well as use, of chemical weapons. The convention not only requires states parties to destroy their chemical weapon arsenals but prohibits them from transferring chemical weapons to other countries or assisting anyone in prohibited activities. Combined with restrictions on chemical trade in CWC–controlled chemicals with non-parties, these provisions increase the cost and difficulties of acquiring chemical weapons for states that choose not to participate.

Universal adherence and complete abolition of chemical weapons will not be achieved immediately, but the Convention slows and even reverses chemical weapons proliferation by isolating the small number of rogue states that refuse to join the regime, limiting their access to precursor chemicals and bringing international political and economic pressures to bear if such states continue their chemical weapon programs.

Chemical Weapons Convention Signatories/Ratifiers

The CWC entered into force on April 29, 1997, following ratification by 65
signatories. As of January, 2002, 145 countries have either ratified or acceded
to the CWC. Another 34 are signatories.

Afghanistan
Albania (Ratified 5/11/94)
Algeria (Ratified 8/14/95)
Argentina (Ratified 10/2/95)
Armenia (Ratified 1/27/95)
Australia (Ratified 5/6/94)
Austria (Ratified 8/17/95)
Azerbaijan (Ratified 2/29/00)
Bahamas
Bahrain (Ratified 4/28/97)
Bangladesh (Ratified 4/25/97)
Belarus (Ratified 7/11/96)
Belgium (Ratified 1/27/97)
Benin (Ratified 5/14/98)
Bhutan
Bolivia (Ratified 8/14/98)
Bosnia and Herzegovina (Ratified 2/25/97)
Botswana (Acceded 8/31/98)
Brazil (Ratified 3/13/96)
Brunei Darussalam (Ratified 7/28/97)
Bulgaria (Ratified 8/10/94)
Burkina Faso (Ratified 7/8/97)
Burundi (Ratified 9/4/98)
Cambodia
Cameroon (Ratified 9/16/96)
Canada (Ratified 9/26/95)
Cape Verde
Central African Republic
Chad
Chile (Ratified 7/12/96)
China (Ratified 4/25/97)
Colombia (Ratified 4/5/00)
Comoros
Congo
Cook Islands (Ratified 7/15/94)
Costa Rica (Ratified 5/31/96)
Côte d'Ivoire (Ratified 12/18/95)
Croatia (Ratified 5/23/95)
Cuba (Ratified 4/29/97)

Cyprus (Ratified 8/28/98)
Czech Republic (Ratified 3/6/96)
Democratic Republic of the Congo
Denmark (Ratified 7/13/95)
Djibouti
Dominica (Ratified 2/12/01)
Dominican Republic
Ecuador (Ratified 9/6/95)
El Salvador (Ratified 10/30/95)
Equatorial Guinea (Ratified 4/25/97)
Eritrea (Acceded 2/14/00)
Estonia (Ratified 5/26/99)
Ethiopia (Ratified 5/13/96)
Federal Republic of Yugoslavia (Acceded 4/20/00)
Fiji (Ratified 1/20/93)
Finland (Ratified 2/7/95)
Federal Yugoslav Republic of Macedonia (Acceded 6/20/1997)
France (Ratified 3/2/95)
Gabon (Ratified 9/8/00)
Gambia (Ratified 5/19/98)
Georgia (Ratified 11/27/95)
Germany (Ratified 8/12/94)
Ghana (Ratified 7/9/97)
Greece (Ratified 12/22/94)
Grenada
Guatemala
Guinea (Ratified 6/9/97)
Guinea-Bissau
Guyana (Ratified 9/12/97)
Haiti
Holy See (Ratified 5/12/99)
Honduras
Hungary (Ratified 10/31/96)
Iceland (Ratified 4/28/97)
India (Ratified 9/3/96)
Indonesia (Ratified 11/12/98)
Iran (Ratified 11/3/97)
Ireland (Ratified 6/24/96)
Israel
Italy (Ratified 12/8/95)
Jamaica (Ratified 9/8/00)
Japan (Ratified 9/15/95)
Jordan (Acceded 10/29/97)
Kazakhstan (Ratified 3/23/00)
Kenya (Ratified 4/25/97)
Kiribati (Acceded 9/7/00)

Kuwait (Ratified 5/29/97)
Kyrgyzstan
Laos (P.D.R.) (Ratified 2/25/97)
Latvia (Ratified 7/23/96)
Lesotho (Ratified 12/7/94)
Liberia
Liechtenstein (Ratified 11/24/99)
Lithuania (Ratified 4/15/98)
Luxembourg (Ratified 4/15/97)
Madagascar
Malawi (Ratified 6/11/98)
Malaysia (Ratified 4/20/00)
Maldives (Ratified 5/31/94)
Mali (Ratified 4/28/97)
Malta (Ratified 4/28/97)
Marshall Islands
Mauritania (Ratified 2/9/98)
Mauritius (Ratified 2/9/93)
Mexico (Ratified 8/29/94)
Micronesia (Ratified 6/21/99)
Monaco (Ratified 6/1/95)
Mongolia (Ratified 1/17/95)
Morocco (Ratified 12/28/95)
Mozambique (Acceded 8/15/00)
Myanmar
Namibia (Ratified 11/27/95)
Nauru (Rep of) (11/12/2001)
Nepal (Ratified 11/18/97)
Netherlands (Ratified 6/30/95)
New Zealand (Ratified 7/15/96)
Nicaragua (Ratified 11/5/99)
Niger (Ratified 4/9/97)
Nigeria (Ratified 5/19/99)
Norway (Ratified 4/7/94)
Oman (Ratified 2/8/95)
Pakistan (Ratified 10/28/97)
Panama (Ratified 10/7/98)
Papua New Guinea (Ratified 4/17/96)
Paraguay (Ratified 12/1/94)
Peru (Ratified 7/20/95)
Philippines (Ratified 12/11/96)
Poland (Ratified 8/23/95)
Portugal (Ratified 9/10/96)
Qatar (Ratified 9/3/97)
Republic of Korea (Ratified 4/28/97)

Republic of Moldova (Ratified 7/08/96)
Romania (Ratified 2/15/95)
Russian Federation (Ratified 11/5/97)
Rwanda
Saint Kitts & Nevis
Saint Lucia (Ratified 4/9/97)
Saint Vincent and The Grenadines
Samoa
San Marino (Ratified 12/10/99)
Saudi Arabia (Ratified 8/9/96)
Senegal (Ratified 7/20/98)
Seychelles (Ratified 4/7/93)
Sierra Leone
Singapore (Ratified 5/21/97)
Slovak Republic (Ratified 10/27/95)
Slovenia (Ratified 6/11/97)
South Africa (Ratified 9/13/95)
Spain (Ratified 8/3/94)
Sri Lanka (Ratified 8/19/94)
Sudan (Acceded 5/24/99)
Suriname (Ratified 4/28/97)
Swaziland (Ratified 11/20/96)
Sweden (Ratified 6/17/93)
Switzerland (Ratified 3/10/95)
Tajikistan (Ratified 1/11/95)
Thailand
Togo (Ratified 4/23/97)
Trinidad and Tobago (Acceded 6/24/97)
Tunisia (Ratified 4/15/97)
Turkey (Ratified 5/12/97)
Turkmenistan (Ratified 9/29/94)
Uganda (Ratified 11/30/2001)
Ukraine (Ratified 10/16/98)
United Arab Emirates (Ratified 11/28/00)
United Kingdom of Great Britain and Northern Ireland (Ratified 5/13/96)
United Republic of Tanzania (Ratified 6/25/98)
United States of America (Ratified 4/25/97)
Uruguay (Ratified 10/6/94)
Uzbekistan (Ratified 7/23/96)
Venezuela (Ratified 12/3/97)
Viet Nam (Ratified 9/30/98)
Yemen (Ratified 10/2/00)
Zambia (Ratification 2/9/2001)
Zimbabwe (Ratified 4/25/97)

The Missile Technology Control Regime

The Missile Technology Control Regime was announced in April 1987 by the G–7 governments—Canada, France, the Federal Republic of Germany, Italy, Japan, the United Kingdom, and the United States. The MTCR is an export-control policy together with the institutional measures to implement it.

The impetus for the MTCR came from National Security Decision Directive 70, signed by U.S. President Ronald Reagan in November 1982. That directive made it U.S. policy to "hinder" the proliferation of nuclear-capable missiles and to seek the cooperation of other supplier nations in doing so. More than four years of negotiations were required to reach an agreement on the regime.

Originally, the purpose of the MTCR was to reduce the risk of nuclear proliferation by limiting the spread of ballistic and cruise missiles capable of delivering nuclear weapons. The original export controls focused on rocket and unmanned air vehicle systems capable of delivering a 500-kilogram payload (considered to be the mass of an unsophisticated nuclear warhead) to a range of 300 kilometers (considered to be a strategic distance in the most compact theaters where nuclear weapons might be used).[1]

In January 1993 the G–7 and 15 additional governments that by then had joined the MTCR announced the expansion of the regime's scope to cover missiles capable of delivering not only nuclear weapons but also chemical and biological agents. New export controls applied to unmanned systems capable of delivering any payload to a range of 300 kilometers—and to unmanned systems of any payload or range that were intended for the delivery of nuclear, biological, or chemical (NBC) weapons.

The text of the MTCR appears in a short policy document, the Guidelines, and a longer control list, the Annex.[2]

Functions

The MTCR applies different export-control policies to the most sensitive items (Category I) and to other items that will generally be approved for export unless they contribute to Category I items (Category II). The division of items into two categories enables the regime to target its most stringent restrictions on a limited number of the most dangerous items, while still controlling many of the components, with due account taken of their multi-use nature.

Category I consists of complete rocket and unmanned air vehicle systems capable of exceeding the 500-kilogram and 300-kilometer parameters (including ballistic missiles, space launch vehicles, sounding rockets, cruise missiles, reconnaissance drones, and target drones); their major subsystems; and their production facilities and technology. The parameters of 500 kilograms and 300 kilometers apply to the inherent capability of a system; that is, they take account of the ability to trade off payload and range. Scuds, therefore, with the advertised ability to delivery a 1,000-kilogram payload to a range of 299 kilometers, are included in Category I. As of January 1993, rockets and air vehicles intended for the unmanned delivery of NBC weapons are treated functionally as Category I.

Category II includes lower-level items of hardware and technology, such as gyroscopes, which can be used for various purposes. In January 1993 complete unmanned systems capable of delivering any payload to a range of 300 kilometers were added to Category II.

To guide the export decisions on these items, the MTCR prescribes three levels of export control: prohibitions, presumptions of denial, and case-by-case reviews.

Prohibitions apply to the transfer of complete production facilities or a complete production technology for Category I items. It would undermine the purpose of the regime to export production capabilities and create new suppliers of the most sensitive items targeted for non-proliferation.

A *"strong presumption to deny"* transfers applies to all Category I items regardless of purpose. The presumption also applies to unmanned delivery systems of any payload and range and to Category II items, if the supplier government is persuaded that they are intended for NBC delivery. Transfers of Category I items are to be "rare" and can be made only if the supplier government—not just the recipient—takes responsibility for the end-use. The "strong presumption to deny" forms the core of the regime and is the key innovation in the policy laid down by the MTCR.

A *case-by-case review* must be undertaken before any item of equipment or technology on the MTCR Annex can be approved for export. In the case of Category II items, if the item is likely to contribute to a Category I system, its export will probably be denied. If the item could contribute to an NBC delivery system, it can be exported only on the receipt of credible assurances from the recipient's government. In most cases, a Category II item will be approved for export.

The members of the regime cannot veto one another's export decisions. They can, however, support their common objectives by means of information exchanges. A key element of information exchange is intelligence, particularly the lists of "projects of concern," i.e., Category I systems targeted by the regime. Another element of information exchange is the diplomatic demarche, i.e, the transmission of questions or concerns, usually in regard to a potential or actual export.

The most frequent elements of information exchange are the minutiae of export cases and the technical questions that enable export-control organizations to avoid unintentionally undercutting one another. The regime includes a "no undercut rule," which obliges members generally to reinforce one another's export denials. This rule is an MTCR innovation that has been copied by some other non-proliferation export-control regimes. Because the regime has avoided creating an international institution to administer itself—other than a "point of contact," i.e., the government of France acts as a clearinghouse—the information exchange is the glue that holds the regime together.

A function of the regime has always been to encourage all governments of the world to adopt the regime's export-control policies—whether or not those governments are "members" of the regime, i.e., admitted by consensus to the regime's information exchanges and decision making. Recently, this "outreach" function has become more structured, with members jointly approaching non-members. As the objectives of the regime have gained nearly universal acceptance (with only North Korea, among major missile exporters, officially remaining aloof), the outreach function has gained international weight.

Membership

Between 1989 and 1993, full participation in the regime was awarded to 16 nations that were entitled by treaty arrangements or exceedingly close economic cooperation to many of the items controlled by the regime. These additional 16 members were Australia, Austria, Belgium, Denmark, Finland, Greece, Iceland, Ireland, Luxembourg, the Netherlands, New Zealand, Norway, Portugal, Spain, Sweden, and Switzerland. It was critical to bring those nations into the regime, not only because many of them were missile exporters, but also in order to prevent the reexport of items the sharing of which might be required under such treaty arrangements as NATO, the European Union and the European Space Agency. Under international law, treaties supersede such policies as the MTCR.

Between 1993 and 1995, membership went to five additional nations: Argentina, Brazil, Hungary, Russia, and South Africa. All these nations had indigenous or export programs targeted by the regime. The conditions for membership, therefore, included restrictions on such activities. In 1997 Turkey joined the regime, resulting in all NATO members being MTCR members as well. Since 1998 membership has been extended to the Czech Republic, the Republic of Korea, Poland, and Ukraine. The MTCR now has 33 members.

In 1997 the regime made public the following criteria for membership decisions: whether a prospective new member (1) would strengthen international non-proliferation efforts, (2) demonstrates a sustained and sustainable commitment to non-proliferation, (3) has a legally based, effective export-control system that puts into effect the MTCR guidelines and procedures, and (4) administers and enforces such controls effectively.[3]

In September 1993 the United States formulated a more restrictive public policy toward new members. Because membership must be approved by consensus, this policy has effectively served as a supplement to the criteria listed above. Under this U.S. policy, new members, with the exception of nuclear-weapon states, must renounce "offensive" Category I programs (e.g., the programs of Argentina and South Africa) to develop long-range ballistic missiles. Once accepted into the regime, however, a new member can be considered for Category II assistance that contributes to Category I programs not deemed "offensive," e.g., space launch vehicle development.[4] Brazil was the first nation to benefit from this new policy. However, because the hardware, technology, and facilities for space launch vehicles are interchangeable with those of ballistic missiles, the wisdom of this U.S. policy has been a matter of controversy.

Meanwhile, there is a dispersion of national practices with respect to transfers among members. The United Kingdom, for example, announced in 1989 an Open General Export License that waives the requirement for the case-by-case review of dual-use Category II exports to other MTCR members.

The result of these disparate policies toward intrapartner trade has been the claim by some governments that membership in fact increases their entitlement to missile technology. The regime's partners have explicitly reaffirmed that membership does not involve such an entitlement, nor does it involve any obligation on the part of members to supply missile technology. The "entitlement" view nevertheless persists. It increases the desirability of membership in the reckoning of some governments, but it raises questions as to whether the regime is advancing its non-proliferation objectives. Although membership in the MTCR has never guaranteed access to missile technology, questions remain as to the extent to which membership will facilitate such access.

A growing number of nonmember governments adhere to the export guidelines of the regime. Israel has officially placed MTCR export controls into operation. It is recognized by the U.S. government as an "adherent," gaining advantages under U.S. sanctions laws. Other governments, such as China and Romania, have made unilateral claims of adherence. China's unusual formulation of adherence to the "guidelines and parameters" of the regime has raised questions as to whether China applies MTCR controls only to complete missile systems or also to components and technology, as required by the regime. China's October 1994 agreement to "not export ground-to-ground missiles featuring the primary parameters of the MTCR" left open these questions as well as the question of how China's policy applied to other Category I systems, such as ship-to-ground missiles and space launch vehicles.[5]

Meetings

Policy-making meetings (plenaries) of all the regime members are held roughly every year. The last meetings were held in Budapest in 1998, Noordwijk, Netherlands, in 1999, Helsinki in 2000, and Ottawa in 2001. The next plenary will be held in Poland in September of 2002. These sessions operate by consensus. In conjunction with these policy meetings, there are discussions by technical experts and meetings featuring the sharing of intelligence information.

The past two plenary sessions have been dominated by discussions and deliberations of the Draft International Code of Conduct (ICOC), a politically binding agreement aimed at curbing ballistic missile proliferation among non–MTCR member nations. An augmented draft text was finalized at the 2001 meeting, and universalization of the code will begin in 2002, with France serving as the host of the first negotiation session.

France, the regime's point of contact, distributes the regime's working papers and also hosts monthy intersessional consultations in Paris. The regime also holds technical expert meetings on an ad hoc basis and occasionally hosts outreach seminars regarding export controls and transshipment issues.

Unilateral U.S. Controls

The United States goes beyond the letter of the MTCR in two respects. It has laws requiring the imposition of sanctions for certain transfers that contribute to missile proliferation. It has a catch-all regulation that, in specific cases, extends export controls far beyond the items of the MTCR Annex.

The United States is unique in its legal requirement to impose sanctions.[6] Its missile sanctions were signed into law in 1990 and have been amended several times since.[7] The legislation punishes U.S. and foreign entities for trading (buying, selling, or conspiring to buy or sell) in MTCR–controlled items that contribute to the acquisition, design, development, or production of Category I systems in non–MTCR nations. In the case of companies in MTCR member states (or nonmember states recognized in a bilateral agreement with the United States to apply MTCR controls), the sanctions are applied only if the trade was conducted illegally and enforcement action was not taken by the member or adherent government.

The penalties imposed by the sanction legislation depend on whether the transfer was a Category I or a Category II item. For Category I transfers, the sanctioned entities (both buyer and seller) are banned for a minimum of two years from export license approvals for any U.S. munitions or dual-use item that requires an export license and are banned for the same term from competing for any U.S. government contracts. For Category II transfers, the sanctioned entities are banned for the same minimum term from export license approvals for any U.S. item on the MTCR Annex and are banned from competing for U.S. government contracts for MTCR Annex items. If the United States considers that the penalized transfer has "substantially" contributed to a Category I program, an additional minimum two-year ban may be imposed on all U.S. imports of products from the entities involved. All these sanctions may be waived on national security grounds, and the import bans may be waived on items needed for U.S. defense purposes.

Two amendments to U.S. sanctions law are worth noting. The Helms amendment applies to sanctions against entities in nonmarket economies (principally China and North Korea). It broadens the sanctions, beyond the entities directly involved, to apply to all government electronic, space, and military aircraft activities. A 1994 amendment creates a "rebuttable presumption" that any trade in MTCR items is for use in a Category I system, and is therefore subject to sanctions, if the trade is conducted with a nation designated by the secretary of state as a supporter of international terrorism. The effects of these amendments are to raise the penalties for sanctions against China and to expand the number of Chinese exports that are potential triggers of sanctions when made to such nations as Iran and Syria.

The catch-all regulation was promulgated in 1991 as the U.S. Enhanced Proliferation Control Initiative (EPCI). EPCI requires U.S. exporters to seek an export license for any item or service—whether or not on the published export-control lists—if the exporter has reason to know or is informed by the U.S. government that the item or service is for a missile project in a non–MTCR member nation that appears on a published list of nations with Category I projects. In contrast to the sanction laws, the United States is not alone in administering catch-all controls. An increasing number of MTCR partners have adopted such controls, and in July 1995 the European Union included catch-all controls in its export regulations.[8]

In 1999 Congress passed the fiscal year 2000 National Defense Authorization Act, which required a report on China's adherence to the MTCR. In 2000, Congress passed the Iran Nonproliferation Act, which sanctioned Russian entities for their missile technology cooperation with Iran. In May 2000 Sen. Fred Thompson and Sen. Robert Torricelli introduced the China Nonproliferation Act, which required annual reviews, sanctions, and the use of the U.S. securities market as a policy tool. In September 2000 the Senate passed a motion to table the legislation as an amendment to the bill granting China permanent normal trade relation status. All economic sanctions against China were waived by the State Department following a November 2000 promise by China that it would stop proliferating and would provide an export-control list to the United States. China's failure to produce that list resulted in the reimposition of sanctions against Chinese entities in September 2001.

Effectiveness

Because missile proliferation is obviously occurring, it is easy to conclude that the MTCR, and the U.S. sanctions to enforce it, are ineffective. However, some missile proliferation has not occurred. The unraveling of the Argentine-Egyptian-Iraqi Condor II program—intended to produce a clone of the U.S. Pershing II ballistic missile—and the termination of South Africa's ballistic missile program, are noteworthy examples of the successes of MTCR and sanctions. Other programs have suffered multi-year schedule slippages as a result of MTCR export controls; Brazilian and Indian officials have publicly blamed the MTCR for such problems in their large rocket programs.

Two more sophisticated criticisms of the MTCR are often made. One quotes the second sentence of the Guidelines—"the Guidelines are not designed to impede national space programs or international cooperation in such programs"—to demonstrate that the regime has a huge loophole, that of permitting the proliferation of space launch vehicles, which are interchangeable with ballistic missiles. Although this criticism has been repeated frequently, it fails to take account of the rest of the quoted sentence: "as long as such programs could not contribute to delivery systems for weapons of mass destruction." The criticism also fails to take account of the fact that the MTCR Category I list subjects space launch vehicles to the same "strong presumption to deny" exports as ballistic missiles. In fact, the quoted sentence from the MTCR Guidelines encourages the sale of space launch services and satellites as opposed to the rockets themselves, which permits all nations to obtain the benefits of space activities without access to potential ballistic missiles.

The other sophisticated criticism, far more frequently made, is that the MTCR can only buy time and cannot prevent missile proliferation altogether. Yet the MTCR's export controls not only increase the time required for a missile program but also the cost and unreliability of the program and the international opposition to it. With a missile such as the Pershing II requiring some 250,000 parts, it is not necessary to deny access to all 250,000 in order to damage a missile program substantially.

Even if the MTCR only bought time, that gain would be a valuable accomplishment. Time allows for the preparation of defenses against missiles. And time allows the regime in the proliferator nation to change. A change of regime can be a decisive factor in non-proliferation. The termination of the Condor II program, the South African program, the Category I programs in some Eastern European nations, and the Russian exports that triggered U.S. sanctions all occurred after changes of regimes, after time had been "bought."

Two factors are likely to determine the future effectiveness of the MTCR. One is the willingness of member nations to enforce missile non-proliferation and to persuade nonmembers to do likewise. The other is the extent to which missile-related trade is restrained within—and not only outside—the growing group of MTCR member nations.

NOTES

1. For a description of the original regime, see Richard H. Speier, "The Missile Technology Control Regime," in *Chemical Weapons and Missile Proliferation: With Implications for the Asia/Pacific Region*, ed. Trevor Findlay (Boulder: Lynne Rienner Publishers, 1991), pp. 115–121.

2. The text of the revised MTCR Guidelines is set out in *The Missile Technology Control Regime*, ACDA Fact Sheet, May 17, 1993. The Annex has been revised on average every two years.

3. Press statement adopted at the Tokyo MTCR Plenary (with appendixes), November 6, 1997.

4. White House, "Fact Sheet: Nonproliferation and Export Control Policy," Office of the Press Secretary, September 27, 1993.

5. U.S. Department of State, "Fact Sheet: Joint United States–People's Republic of China Statement on Missile Proliferation," U.S. Department of State, Office of the Spokesman, October 4, 1994.

6. Japan, however, has a policy of taking proliferation concerns into account in decisions on foreign aid.

7. See the *Arms Export Control Act*, chapter 7, and the *Export Administration Act*, section 11B.

8. U.S. Department of Commerce, *Export Administration 1996 Report on Foreign Policy Export Controls*, U.S. Department of Commerce, Bureau of Export Administration, January 1996, section 10.

Plenary Meeting of the Missile Technology Control Regime Press Release

FACT SHEET
Bureau of Nonproliferation
Washington, D.C.
Ottawa, Canada, September 25–28, 2001

The Missile Technology Control Regime (MTCR) held its 16th Plenary Meeting in Ottawa from September 25 [to] 28, 2001, in order to review its activities and strengthen its efforts to prevent missile proliferation. The meeting marked the start of the Canadian chairmanship and was officially opened by the Honorable Dr. Rey Pagtakhan, Secretary of State (Asia-Pacific) of Canada.

The Republic of Korea was warmly welcomed to its first Plenary Meeting.

The MTCR was established in 1987 with the aim of controlling exports of missiles capable of delivering weapons of mass destruction. The 33 countries of the MTCR form an important international arrangement dealing with such missiles, as well as related equipment and technology.[*]

Coordinating their efforts through the MTCR, its member states have contributed significantly to a reduction in the global missile proliferation threat. The Plenary, however, agreed that the risk of proliferation of weapons of mass destruction and their means of delivery remained a major concern for global and regional security, and that more must therefore be done at the national, regional, and global level. The Plenary also noted that the tragic events of September 11, 2001, in the United States only added force to the importance of the MTCR's work in that regard.

The Plenary reemphasized the important role played by export controls, the need to strengthen them further, the need for their strict implementation, and the need for adaptation in the face of technological development.

Partners continued their deliberations on a set of principles, general measures, cooperation, and confidence-building measures in the form of a draft International Code of Conduct against ballistic missile proliferation, taking into account the results of extensive contact on this subject undertaken with countries outside the MTCR since the Helsinki Plenary. The result of these deliberations was an augmented draft text, which will be distributed to all states at an early date.

Universalization of the draft Code should take place through a transparent and inclusive negotiating process open to all states on the basis of equality. In this regard, the Plenary noted with appreciation the offer of France to host the first negotiation session in 2002. France will consult with all states to determine their interest in participating in the process.

This concludes the work of the MTCR per se on the draft Code.

---

*   Argentina, Australia, Austria, Belgium, Brazil, Canada, the Czech Republic, Denmark, Finland, France, Germany, Greece, Hungary, Iceland, Ireland, Italy, Japan, the Republic of Korea, Luxembourg, Netherlands, New Zealand, Norway, Poland, Portugal, Russia, South Africa, Spain, Sweden, Switzerland, Turkey, Ukraine, the United Kingdom, and the United States.

Nuclear Supplier Organizations

Two informal coalitions of nations that voluntarily restrict the export of equipment and materials that could be used to develop nuclear weapons form an important component of the non-proliferation regime. The first group, known as the Non-Proliferation Treaty Exporters Committee (or the Zangger Committee, after its former chair, the Swiss expert Claude Zangger), was formed in the early 1970s to establish guidelines for implementing the export control provisions of article III (2) of the Nuclear Non-Proliferation Treaty.[1] In August 1974 the Zangger Committee adopted a set of guidelines, including a list of export items that would trigger the requirement for the application of International Atomic Energy Agency safeguards in recipient states. The Zangger guidelines and "trigger list" constituted the first mechanism for the uniform regulation of nuclear exports by the principal nuclear supplier states that were NPT parties.

India's nuclear test in 1974 was the catalyst for the formation in January 1976 of the Nuclear Suppliers Group, which first met in London and was called the London Group. France, not then a party to the NPT, joined the NSG. The NSG adopted guidelines that were similar to those of the Zangger Committee but went beyond the Zangger guidelines in restraining transfers of uranium-enrichment and plutonium-extraction equipment and technology.

In April 1992 in the wake of the Gulf War, the NSG expanded its export-control guidelines, which until then had covered only uniquely nuclear items, to cover 65 dual-use items as well. In addition, the group added as a requirement for future exports that recipient states accept IAEA inspection on all their peaceful nuclear activities. This full-scope, or comprehensive, safeguard rule effectively precludes nuclear commerce by NSG member states with states such as India, Israel, and Pakistan, which refuse to accept IAEA safeguards on their entire nuclear infrastructure.[2]

The Zangger Committee: Formation

Shortly after the NPT came into force in 1970 several countries began consultations about the procedures and standards they would apply to nuclear fuel and equipment exports to non-nuclear-weapon states. These consultations were necessary to implement the NPT requirement that such exports and any enriched uranium or plutonium produced through their use be subject to IAEA safeguards in the recipient state. The supplier countries that were engaged in those consultations were parties to the Non-Proliferation Treaty (or have since

413

become parties) and were also exporters or potential exporters of material and equipment for peaceful uses of nuclear energy.

In August 1974 the governments of Australia, Denmark, Canada, Finland, West Germany, the Netherlands, Norway, the Soviet Union, the United Kingdom, and the United States each informed the director general of the IAEA, by individual letters, of their intentions to require IAEA safeguards on their nuclear exports in accordance with certain procedures described in memoranda enclosed with their letters. Those memoranda were identical and included the trigger list of special nuclear materials (enriched uranium and plutonium) and items of equipment "especially designed or prepared" (EDP) for the production of those materials. The memoranda declared that these items would be exported only if the recipient agreed to place them under IAEA safeguards, agreed that they would be used only for peaceful purposes, and agreed not to retransfer such items unless under the same conditions.[3]

Soon afterward, Austria, Czechoslovakia, East Germany, Ireland, Japan, Luxembourg, Poland, and Sweden sent individual letters to the director general, referring to and enclosing memoranda identical to those transmitted by the initial group of governments.

The agreed procedures and trigger list represented the first major agreement on the uniform regulation of nuclear exports by current and potential nuclear suppliers. It had great significance for several reasons. It was an attempt to enforce strictly and uniformly the obligations of article 3, paragraph 2, of the Non-Proliferation Treaty requiring safeguards on nuclear exports. It was intended to reduce the likelihood that states would be tempted to cut corners on safeguard requirements because of competition in the sale of nuclear equipment and fuel-cycle services. In addition, and very important in light of subsequent events, it established the principle that nuclear-supplier nations should consult and agree among themselves on procedures to regulate the international market for nuclear materials and equipment in the interest of non-proliferation. Notably absent from the list of actual participants or potential suppliers, as from the list of parties to the Non-Proliferation Treaty, were France, India, and the People's Republic of China. (The current members of the Zangger Committee are listed below.)

Zangger Committee: Subsequent Developments

Because of advances in technology, the parameters of some of the items on the Zangger Committee trigger list (principally enrichment, reprocessing, and heavy-water production equipment) were subject to substantial clarifications and upgrades during the 1980s. (The Zangger Committee has also been responsible for almost all the clarification and upgrade work later taken up by the NSG.) Prompted by the discovery that Iraq was pursuing various enrichment technologies, the important changes agreed upon by the Zangger Committee in 1993 have added new forms of enrichment technology to the trigger list (including electromagnetic isotope separation and chemical or ion exchange techniques) not previously covered in the enrichment category.

Changes to the trigger list are adopted into controls on a national basis; implementation dates for member states can therefore vary depending on the bureaucratic measures required by each member. Unlike the NSG, the Zangger Committee has controls only on EDP items; it does not control dual-use equipment or technology, nor does it call on participants to exercise particular restraint in the supply of equipment to nuclear facilities that are considered sensitive (i.e., reprocessing and enrichment facilities). Nor do the Zangger Committee guidelines require comprehensive IAEA safeguards as a condition of supply; single-facility arrangements are sufficient. This policy is under review.

The Zangger Committee meets in Vienna twice a year (usually in May and October, with May being considered the main plenary meeting). The United Kingdom provides secretariat services. The committee's detailed deliberations are kept confidential, as are the criteria for membership attendance at policy-making meetings (although NPT adherence, adoption of the committee's guidelines, and adherence to non-proliferation norms are among the requirements for membership).

With the 1992 agreement to harmonize the specifications of the items and equipment on the Zangger trigger list with those of the NSG (see below), some have questioned the relevance of the committee. Member governments recognize some duplication of effort and the overlap with the NSG, but the different memberships and the fact that the committee is a child of the NPT mean that no current members are (yet) willing to suggest that the group be disbanded and its work folded into the NSG.

As of January 2002 there are 33 members of the Zangger Committee: Argentina, Australia, Austria, Belgium, Bulgaria, Canada, China, the Czech Republic, Denmark, France, Finland, Germany, Greece, Hungary, Ireland, Italy, Japan, Luxembourg, the Netherlands, Norway, Poland, Portugal, Romania, Russia, Slovak Republic, South Africa, South Korea, Spain, Sweden, Switzerland, Ukraine, the United Kingdom, and the United States.

The Nuclear Suppliers Group: Formation

In November 1974, within a year of the delivery of the memoranda generated in the Zangger Committee to the IAEA director general, a second series of nuclear supplier negotiations was initiated. This round, convened largely at the initiative of the United States, was a response to three developments: (1) the Indian nuclear test of May 1974, (2) mounting evidence that the pricing actions of the Organization of Petroleum Exporting Countries were stimulating Third World and other nonnuclear states to initiate or accelerate their nuclear power programs, and (3) recent contracts or continuing negotiations by France and West Germany for the supply of enrichment or reprocessing facilities to Third World states, facilities that could provide access to weapons-usable fissile material.

The initial participants in these discussions, conducted in London, were Canada, France, the Federal Republic of Germany, Japan, the Soviet Union, the United Kingdom, and the United States. One of the group's chief accomplishments was to persuade France to join. France, which had not joined the Non-Proliferation Treaty or the Zangger Committee, could have undercut the reforms regarding nuclear supplies. The French, hesitant about becoming involved and uncertain about where the effort might lead, insisted that any meetings be kept confidential. The meetings in London were therefore held in secret. The meetings soon became known, however, which led to suspicion and exaggerated fears about their subject. The group was inaccurately referred to as a cartel. Instead, one of its purposes was to foster genuine commercial competition based on quality and prices, untainted by the bargaining away of proliferation controls.

Two major controversies arose in the series of meetings of what became known as the Nuclear Suppliers Group. These matters were resolved in a new agreement in late 1975. The first concerned whether, and under what conditions, technology and equipment for enrichment and reprocessing, the most sensitive parts of the nuclear fuel cycle from a weapon proliferation perspective, should be transferred to non-nuclear states. The United States and several other participants urged both a prohibition on such transfers and a commitment to reprocessing in multi-national facilities (rather than in installations under the control of individual states). France had already signed contracts to sell reprocessing plants to Pakistan and South Korea, however, and West Germany had agreed to sell to Brazil the technology and facilities for the full fuel cycle (including enrichment and reprocessing). France and West Germany objected to any prohibition.

The second controversy concerned whether transfers should be made to states unwilling to submit all their nuclear facilities to IAEA safeguards, or whether such full-scope safeguards should be a condition of all sales. The NSG came close to reaching consensus on requiring full-scope safeguards as a condition of future supply commitments but was unable to persuade the French and the West Germans. At the time, Argentina, Brazil, India, Israel, Pakistan, and South Africa would have been barred from receiving NSG–controlled exports if the full-scope safeguard rule had been adopted, since each of those developing countries possessed or was developing nuclear installations not subject to IAEA monitoring. While not making full-scope safeguards a condition of nuclear supply, the NSG did act to expand safeguard coverage by adopting a trigger list of nuclear exports, similar to that of the Zangger Committee, which would be permitted only if the exported items were covered by IAEA safeguards in the recipient state.

On January 27, 1976, the seven participants in the NSG negotiations exchanged letters endorsing a uniform code for conducting international nuclear sales. The major provisions of the agreement required that before nuclear materials, equipment, or technology are transferred a recipient state must:

1. pledge not to use the transferred materials, equipment, or technology in the manufacture of nuclear explosives of any kind

2. accept, with no provision for termination, international safeguards on all transferred materials and facilities employing transferred equipment or tech-

nology, including any enrichment, reprocessing, or heavy-water production facility that replicates or otherwise employs transferred technology

3. provide adequate physical security for transferred nuclear facilities and materials to prevent theft and sabotage

4. agree not to retransfer the materials, equipment, or technology to third countries unless they, too, accept the constraints on use, replication, security, and transfer, and unless the original supplier nation concurs in the transactions

5. employ "restraint" regarding the possible export of "sensitive" items (relating to uranium enrichment, spent-fuel reprocessing, and heavy-water production)

6. encourage the concept of multilateral (in lieu of national) regional facilities for reprocessing and enrichment.[4]

The industrialized states of Eastern Europe soon joined the NSG, so that it included virtually all the advanced supplier countries.

The Nuclear Suppliers guidelines extended the Zangger Committee's requirements in several respects. First, France agreed to key points adopted by the NSG, such as the requirement that recipients pledge not to use transferred items for nuclear explosives of any kind and that safeguards on transferred items would continue indefinitely. Second, the NSG went beyond the Non-Proliferation Treaty and the Zangger Committee requirements by imposing safeguards not only on the export of nuclear materials and equipment but also on nuclear technology exports. India had demonstrated the existence of this serious loophole by building its own unsafeguarded replicas of a safeguarded power reactor imported from Canada. The NSG was unable to reach agreement on the application of this reform to reactor technology, however, and so confined its recommended application to sensitive facilities built with the use of exported technology. The group's acceptance of this limited reform was facilitated by the fact that such a condition was incorporated by West Germany in its safeguard agreements for the sale of enrichment and reprocessing facilities to Brazil and by France in its safeguard agreements covering proposed sales of reprocessing plants to the Republic of Korea and Pakistan. (France subsequently canceled both contracts.)

Third, the NSG, while not absolutely prohibiting the export of these sensitive facilities, embodied the participants' agreement to "exercise restraint" in transferring them. Wherever transfers of enrichment plants are involved, the participants agreed to seek recipient-country commitments that such facilities would be designed and operated to produce only low-enriched uranium, not suitable for weapons.

Nuclear Suppliers Group: Subsequent Developments

There was a lull in NSG policy making during the 1980s. In March 1991, however, in the wake of the 1991 Gulf War, the group convened after a ten-year hiatus in The Hague and decided to adopt the clarified and upgraded specifications on the Zangger Committee trigger list. The exercise, which became known as harmonization, was completed in 1992. During 1993 the NSG added another category to its trigger list, uranium conversion plants and equipment, items that are not covered by the Zangger Committee's list.

At U.S. urging, the NSG plenary meeting in Warsaw in March and April of 1992 took a major step. The members agreed that as a condition of supply all members would insist that all contracts of EDP trigger-list items drawn up after April 1992 would require recipient states to accept full-scope safeguards on all their nuclear facilities and on any future facilities. (Previously, some NSG members, including the United States, had required full-scope safeguards as a condition of supply, but the definition of what was covered and the effective date of this requirement were not uniform). Member states adopted this new full-scope safeguard requirement into national legislation during the first half of 1993. The new updated guidelines were issued by the IAEA in July 1993.[5] In 1993 the NSG also agreed to add to its trigger list the additional equipment used for enrichment that had been identified in the Zangger Committee. The NSG set a target date of March 1, 1993, for the implementation of the new category controls. (At the NSG plenary meeting held in Helsinki on April 5–7, 1995, the NSG reviewed the Guidelines for Nuclear Transfers, and some changes were made, particularly with respect to fuel fabrication items.[6])

In a new departure for the NSG, at the Hague meeting of March 1991, members also agreed on the need to expand controls to cover dual-use items that have legitimate non-nuclear uses. (The original NSG and Zangger Committee rules apply only to "nuclear-unique" equipment and material.) The working group established by NSG met under U.S. stewardship in Brussels in June 1991, Annapolis in October 1991, and Interlaken in January 1992 and produced agreement on a list of 65 dual-use items with detailed definitions and a series of guidelines on conditions of transfer. These were formally endorsed by the full plenary meeting of the NSG in Warsaw in April 1992. The NSG members set a target implementation date of the end of 1992 for the part 2 Guidelines, but administrative and national legislative delays have prevented some members from meeting that date.

The dual-use guidelines (known as Guidelines for Transfers of Nuclear-Related Dual-Use Equipment, Material and Related Technology and published by the IAEA in July 1992[7]) require exporting states not to ship items on the list if they are for use by non-nuclear-weapon states in unsafeguarded nuclear fuel-cycle facilities or in nuclear explosive activity. In addition, the dual-use guidelines require states not to transfer items on the list "when there is an unacceptable risk of diversion to such an activity, or when the transfers are contrary to the objective of averting the proliferation of nuclear weapons." Suppliers must obtain a statement from the recipient on the use to which the item will be put and where it will be located, as well as obtain assurances that it will not be used for proscribed purposes and that no retransfer will take place without the consent of the supplier. Decisions on whether a transfer should proceed are also to be guided by additional criteria, such as the recipient's non-proliferation credentials. Although decisions on whether to grant export licenses are left to national discretion, there is a system of consultation among members to ensure uniformity in the implementation of the dual-use guidelines and to guard against commercial disadvantage to a particular state if it denies a transfer request. Members are also encouraged to consult and exchange information on proliferation developments that might be relevant to licensing decisions.[8]

The Japanese (through their mission in Vienna) have taken on the role of administrative secretariat (point of contact) for the trigger list "part 2" dual-use mechanism. They are responsible for the circulation of denial notices, documents, and information to members as well as for arranging meetings. At the 1997 NSG plenary session held in Ottawa on May 8 and 9, 1997, the members agreed to new measures to speed up the sharing of information among themselves and with the point of contact. Specifically, they adopted a parallel-track approach that would combine an improved and secure U.S. computer-based bulletin board system with a European Union secure fax system proposed by France. (The EU system is currently in the demonstration phase with EU members, but not with all NSG members.)[9]

Any state can adhere to either part of the NSG guidelines by notifying the IAEA that it has adopted the necessary legislation to control items on the NSG lists. This does not, however, confer immediate membership in the NSG or the right to attend its policy-making meetings. There are no strict criteria for membership, but potential members must satisfy the existing membership that they have proper credentials. These include a commitment to other non-proliferation norms (e.g., through membership in other agreements, such as the NPT and the Chemical Weapons Convention), the adoption of the necessary legislation to bring the NSG controls into national law, and effective enforcement capabilities. Membership decisions are taken by consensus. The chairmanship of the group rotates.

As of January 2002 the 35 members of the NSG were: Argentina, Australia, Austria, Belgium, Brazil, Bulgaria, Canada, the Czech Republic, Denmark, Finland, France, Germany, Greece, Hungary, Ireland, Italy, Japan, Latvia, Luxembourg, the Netherlands, New Zealand, Norway, Poland, Portugal, Romania, Russia, Slovak Republic, South Africa, South Korea, Spain, Sweden, Switzerland, Ukraine, the United Kingdom, and the United States. Brazil and New Zealand are the only NSG members that do not belong to the Zangger Committee.

SOURCES

Van Doren, Charles N. *Nuclear Supply and Non-Proliferation: The IAEA Committee on Assurances of Supply.* Report for the Congressional Research Service (Rept. 83-202-8), October 1983.

Buchanan, Ewen. *The Non-Proliferation Regime.* Washington, D.C.: Carnegie Endowment for International Peace. Unpublished consultant's report, March 1994.

ADDITIONAL SOURCES

ACDA. "Multilateral Nuclear Export Control Regimes." Factsheet, December 17, 1996, accessed November 8, 1997. Available at www.acda.gov/factshee/exptcon/nuexpcnt.htm.

Davis, Zachary S. "Non-Proliferation Regimes: Policies To Control the Spread of Nuclear, Chemical and Biological Weapons and Missiles." Washington, D.C.: Library of Congress, Congressional Research Service, February 8, 1993.

Gardner, Gary T. *Nuclear Nonproliferation: A Primer.* Boulder: Lynne Rienner Publishers, 1994.

Rauf, Tariq, James Lamson, Swawna McCartney, and Sarah Meek. *Inventory of International Nonproliferation Organizations and Regimes.* Monterey, Cal.: Monterey Institute of International Studies, 1996–1997.

Thorne, Carlton E., ed. *A Guide to Nuclear Export Controls.* Burke, Va.: Proliferation Data Services, 1997.

Timerbaev, Roland, and Lisa Moskowitz. *Inventory of International Nonproliferation Organizations and Regimes.* Monterey, Cal.: Monterey Institute of International Studies, 1994, 1995.

U.S. Congress. *Nuclear Proliferation and Safeguard.* Office of Technology Assessment. Washington, D.C., 1977.

U.S. Congress. Office of Technology Assessment *Proliferation of Weapons of Mass Destruction: Assessing the Risks.* Office of Technology Assessment. Washington, D.C.: GPO, August 1993.

U.S. Department of State. *Report to the Congress Pursuant to Section 601 of the Nuclear Non-Proliferation Act of 1978.* January 1979.

NOTES

1. The Article states: "Each State Party to the Treaty undertakes not to provide: (a) source or special fissionable material, or (b) equipment or material especially designed or prepared for the processing, use or production of special fissionable material, to any non-nuclear-weapon State for peaceful purposes, unless the source or special fissionable material shall be subject to the safeguards required by this Article." See ACDA, "Multilateral Nuclear Export Control Regimes," Factsheet, December 17, 1996 (located at www.acda.gov/factshee/exptcon/nuexpcnt.htm; accessed November 8, 1997).

2. In addition to agreeing to such full-scope safeguards, all nations importing regulated items from NSG members states must promise to furnish adequate physical security for transferred nuclear materials and facilities; pledge not to export nuclear materials and technologies to other nations without the permission of the original exporting nation or without a pledge from the recipient nation to abide by these same rules; and promise not to use any imports to build nuclear explosives. (Similar rules, apart from the full-scope safeguard requirement, apply to exports regulated by the Zangger Committee, which continues to function, although it has been partially eclipsed by the Nuclear Suppliers Group, whose export controls have, in general, been more far-reaching.)

3. The individual letters and the identical memoranda were published by the IAEA in September 1974 in IAEA, INFCIRC/209 (INFCIRC is shorthand for the series of Information Circulars distributed to IAEA members).

4. IAEA, "Guidelines for Nuclear Transfers," INFCIRC/254, part 1 (Vienna).

5. See INFCIRC/254/Rev.1/Part 1.

6. The guidelines were published in the INFCIRC 254, part 1 series; communication with U.S. State Department official, September 4, 1997.

7. INFCIRC/254/Rev.1/Part 2,

8. For further details on the development of the dual-use arrangement and the adoption of full-scope safeguards as a condition of supply, see Carlton E. Thorne, "The Nuclear Suppliers Group: A Major Success Story Gone Unnoticed," *Directors Series on Proliferation* (California: Lawrence Livermore Laboratory), January 5, 1994, p. 29.

9. In the early 1990s the United States suggested a secure computer-based bulletin board system for information sharing that had been in use unofficially, and on a limited basis, among some NSG parties (communication with U.S. State Department official, November 5, 1997).

Wassenaar Arrangement: Dual-Use Export Controls

Background

The Wassenaar Arrangement, established in July 1996, is a voluntary system for coordinating national controls on exports of conventional arms and dual-use technologies that depends on the exchange of information through a consultative forum. Wassenaar is a multi-lateral successor to COCOM, the Coordinating Committee on Multilateral Export Controls. COCOM was organized during the Cold War as a Western allied mechanism for restricting strategic military trade with the Communist blocs, particularly dual-use technologies that could be imported ostensibly for nonmilitary reasons. After the Cold War and collapse of both the Warsaw Pact and the Soviet Union, the West sought through cooperative security and economic policies to foster political and economic reform in the former Communist countries of Eastern Europe and the new states that emerged from the Soviet Union. The promotion of East-West political and security partnership in place of the adversarialism of the previous era required that COCOM, a Western economic warfare institution explicitly targeting the Communist East, be dismantled.

This was best done, however, by rebuilding a mechanism for controls against the export of strategic dual-use items to still-dangerous countries, a mechanism in which reformed, former Communist states could participate as partners. This was the underlying construct for the creation of the Wassenaar Arrangement. Conflict with the countries that were of most urgent non-proliferation attention at the end of the Cold War, especially Iraq and Iran, had a significant impact on the generation of new export-control and sanction policies toward dual-use items, and, in turn, influenced the content of the Wassenaar guidelines. In effect, the Wassenaar dual-use controls are concerned to a considerable extent with dual-use technologies that can facilitate the proliferation of weapons of mass destruction. To the extent that such proliferation may be related to nuclear weapon capabilities, the Wassenaar Arrangement complements (or reinforces) the dual-use controls of the Nuclear Suppliers Group, which focus on equipment, materials, and technologies that are not necessarily intrinsically nuclear but can be used and, indeed, are often critical for developing or manufacturing nuclear weapons.[1]

The Wassenaar Arrangement

The initiative to control strategic dual-use goods by a multilateral mechanism distinct from COCOM was sponsored by the Bush administration at a

421

November 1992 meeting of the major Western industrialized states: Canada, France, Germany, Italy, Japan, the United Kingdom, and the United States, collectively known as the Group of Seven (or G–7). As a consequence of earlier U.S. efforts and the defining experience of the Gulf War, the group had already agreed to refrain from the direct, large-scale sales of military equipment to Iraq and Iran. The new U.S. proposal sought to broaden the scope of the conventional weapon embargo by halting the sale to Iran of dual-use technology that could be used for both military and civilian purposes. This effort was only partially successful, however, with the G–7 agreeing to curtail only those strategic dual-use exports destined for known military end-users. A number of G–7 countries with important commercial links to Tehran and especially to Japan, feared that the United States intended to use the dual-use ban to control all aspects of trade with that country.[2]

The initiative was revived by the Clinton administration in early 1993, when G–7 working groups made progress in identifying core lists of technologies to control because of proliferation concern, although the G–7 continued to fail to agree on a common stand to block Iranian purchases of dual-use goods.

Subsequent Clinton administration efforts to block the export of conventional arms and dual-use military technology to Iran focused on developing a successor regime to COCOM. The charter for the successor regime, known as the Wassenaar Arrangement on Export Controls for Conventional Arms and Dual-Use Goods and Technologies, was approved by 33 nations in the Dutch city of Wassenaar on July 12, 1996. Under the new arrangement participants have agreed not to export conventional arms to four states: Iran, Iraq, Libya, and North Korea; to share information on military sales to other nations; and to regulate the sales of military dual-use items. At the time that Russia agreed to join the arrangement as a founding member, the other organizing states agreed that its substantial preexisting contracts for arms sales with Iran would be exempt from the group's export restrictions.

Although no country is an explicit target of the Wassenaar Arrangement, members are committed to dealing firmly with states whose behavior is a cause for serious concern. There is broad agreement that currently these states are Iran, Iraq, Libya, and North Korea. Wassenaar members deal with these "countries of concern" by preventing, through shared national policies of restraint, their acquisition of armaments and sensitive dual-use goods and technologies for military end-use.[3]

Guidelines

The Wassenaar regime consists of two sets of guidelines, one on conventional weapons and the other on dual-use items and technologies. The guidelines on conventional arms call for regular information exchanges and consultations and reviews of arms transfer or arms export deals. Members agree in principle to exchange information every six months on deliveries of weapons covered by the U.N. Register of Conventional Arms and are supposed to include the details of model and type, together with information on the quantity and the recipient.

The guidelines on exports of dual-use items are based on an agreed list of controlled goods.

The list is further divided into the Basic List (tier 1)—which includes, for example, telecommunication equipment—and annexes, comprising a Sensitive List (tier 2), covering supercomputers, and a Very Sensitive List (a subset of tier 2) that includes, among other things, stealth technology. While exports of dual-use items are at the discretion of national governments, members have agreed to exchange information twice annually on all denials of export licenses for tier 1 items; to notify of denials of licenses for the export of tier 2 items within 60 days; and to provide, twice a year, information on licenses to export any tier 2 items to nonmembers. Members have also agreed to inform other members, within 60 days, of approval of any license that has been denied by another member during the previous three years.

Member Countries[4]

Argentina
Australia

Austria	New Zealand
Belgium	Norway
Bulgaria	Poland
Canada	Republic of Korea
Czech Republic	Romania
Denmark	Russia
Finland	Slovak Republic
France	Spain
Germany	Sweden
Greece	Turkey
Hungary	Ukraine
Ireland	United Kingdom
Italy	United States
Japan	
Luxembourg	
Netherlands	

NOTES

1. Within the United States, exports of both categories of dual-use items are licensed by the Commerce Department, pursuant to the Export Administration Act. Iran-Iraq Arms Nonproliferation Act of 1992, Division A, title XVI, section 1603, P.L. 102-484, 106 Stat. 2571, 50 U.S.C. Section 1701, note (October 23, 1992).

2. See Steve Coll, "Technology from West Floods Iran," *Washington Post*, November 10, 1992; Leslie Helm, "Japan Reluctant To Back Embargo on Iran"; and "Tokyo Distances Itself from Policy on Exports to Tehran," *Los Angeles Times*, November 13, 1992.

3. U.S. Department of State Bureau of Non-Proliferation, "Wassenaar Arrangement," Fact Sheet, August 31, 2001.

4. As of August 31, 2001.

Comprehensive Nuclear Test Ban Treaty

A comprehensive nuclear test ban pledge was embodied in the 1963 Partial Test Ban Treaty and was repeated as a goal in the Nuclear Non-proliferation Treaty preamble in the following terms: "To seek to achieve the discontinuance of all test explosions of nuclear weapons for all time and to continue negotiations to that end." The U.N. General Assembly's adoption of the Comprehensive Test Ban Treaty, on September 10, 1996, fulfilled that pledge and paved the way for a permanent ban on nuclear explosive testing to become an integral part of the nuclear non-proliferation regime.[1]

The rationale for the CTBT was that it would "constrain the development and qualitative improvement of nuclear weapons; end the development of advanced new types of nuclear weapons; contribute to the prevention of nuclear proliferation and the process of nuclear disarmament; and strengthen international peace and security."[2] Some opponents doubted that the treaty would totally prevent qualitative improvements of existing nuclear arsenals or the development of new weapon designs, given the technological capabilities of certain nuclear-weapon states to experiment without fission testing. Other critics objected to the constraints that the treaty might place on the reliability of the U.S. nuclear weapon stockpile or doubted the verifiability of the treaty in other parts of the globe. Yet others have objected to the uncertainties posed by the treaty's complicated entry-into-force provisions. It is widely recognized that the CTBT will be a major advance in arresting the nuclear arms competition and inhibiting nuclear weapon proliferation.

Background

The Conference on Disarmament in Geneva negotiated the CTBT over a period of two-and-a-half years.[3] Negotiations began in January 1994 based on the mandate of a December 1993 U.N. General Assembly consensus resolution (48/70). They continued through 1994 and 1995 and concluded in mid-1996. Ambassador Jaap Ramaker of the Netherlands, chair of the Nuclear Test Ban Committee, faced a deadline to complete the CTBT negotiation in time for its signature at the outset of the 51st session of the General Assembly.[4] The key issues resolved were: the scope of the treaty; whether peaceful nuclear explosions would be permitted; the conditions for verification, including intrusive measures (e.g., challenge inspections); and the terms of entry into force, EIF).

Initially, controversy surrounded the scope of the treaty. Discussions on scope centered, first, on whether the nuclear-weapon states would be allowed any exemptions from the test ban to ensure the safety and reliability of their nuclear stockpiles (i.e., very low yield nuclear tests, or so-called hydronuclear experiments). They also considered China's demand that "peaceful nuclear explosions" be allowed for civil, construction, or commercial purposes. Initially seeking allowances for low-yield tests, the United States had proposed that a test "which released nuclear energy up to the equivalent of 1.8 kg (4 lbs) of TNT explosive power would not be regarded as a violation" of the CTBT.[5] Three other nuclear-weapon states, France, Russia, and the United Kingdom, which lacked the sophisticated testing apparatus and techniques of the United States, proposed that any limit on permissible experiments be set at a higher yield. China officially advocated a ban on any nuclear weapon test explosion but supported an exemption for PNEs.[6]

A breakthrough occurred in August 1995 when France and the United States each declared it would support a "true zero-yield" CTBT, banning any nuclear test explosion. This position would prohibit any hydronuclear experiments. The French decision was influenced by the enormous international criticism of its June 13 announcement of a final series of nuclear tests.[7] The U.S. decision followed the JASON report, commissioned by the U.S. Department of Energy, which concluded that subkiloton nuclear tests would be of little value in ensuring the reliability of the U.S. nuclear stockpile.[8] Nevertheless, in announcing the U.S. commitment to a true zero-yield test ban, President Bill Clinton explicitly reserved the right to exercise "our supreme national interest rights under a comprehensive test ban to conduct necessary testing if the safety and reliability of our nuclear deterrent could no longer be certified."[9] On September 14, 1995, the United Kingdom followed suit by announcing its support for a zero-yield ban. On October 23, in the aftermath of his Hyde Park summit meeting with President Boris Yeltsin, President Clinton announced that Russia had also agreed to seek a zero-yield CTBT.

Another important issue, in the closing stages of the CTBT negotiations in Geneva, concerned the treaty's EIF provisions. The issue arose because China, Russia, and the United Kingdom demanded that the three nuclear weapon threshold states—India, Israel, and Pakistan—become parties to the CTBT before the treaty took effect. Another group of nations, spearheaded by the United States, held a contrasting view and insisted that the EIF provisions facilitate the treaty's EIF as soon as possible, so that no nation, or group of nations, could hold its implementation hostage. After prolonged deliberations, chairman Ramaker came up with a compromise formula according to which a list of 44 nuclear-capable states (as identified by the IAEA) that were members of the expanded Conference on Disarmament, including the five nuclear-weapon states and the three threshold states, would be required to ratify the treaty. If the treaty did not enter into force within three years after it was opened for signature, a conference could be held for those states that had already ratified the treaty to "decide by consensus what measures consistent with international law [could] be undertaken to accelerate the ratification process."[10]

In spite of renewed efforts in the Conference on Disarmament at the end of July to resolve outstanding differences, the full Nuclear Test Ban Ad Hoc

Committee reported, on August 16, 1996, that "no consensus" could be reached, either on adopting the text of the CTBT or on formally passing it to the Conference on Disarmament, owing to objections from India. On August 22, 1996, Australia decided to move that the 50th U.N. General Assembly consider and adopt the CTBT and open the treaty for signature at the earliest possible date. On September 10, 1996, the U.N. General Assembly adopted the treaty by a vote of 158 to 3, with 5 abstentions. The treaty was opened for signature on September 24, 1996, and on that date was signed by 68 nations, including all five nuclear-weapon states.

To enter into force, the CTBT requires that 44 states that were members of the Conference on Disarmament as of June 18, 1996, that had formally participated in the work of 1996 session of the conference, and that have research or power reactors identified by the IAEA, deposit their instruments of ratification.

Synopsis of the CTBT

Preamble: The preamble notes that the treaty serves the goals of both non-proliferation and disarmament and reiterates the international commitment to the "ultimate goal" of eliminating nuclear weapons.

Basic Obligations: The treaty parties agree "not to carry out any nuclear weapon test explosion or any other nuclear explosion." This is the zero-yield formulation that, by not defining a nuclear explosion, seeks to prohibit all of them.

Treaty Organization: To implement treaty provisions, a Comprehensive Test Ban Treaty Organization (CTBTO) has been created in Vienna. The CTBTO includes an executive council, for decision making, and a technical secretariat, for implementing the treaty's verification provisions.[11]

Verification: The treaty has an extensive monitoring system that includes 24-hour-a-day data collection. The International Monitoring System (IMS) will collect four types of data: seismic, radionuclide, hydroacoustic, and infrasound. Information from these sources is collected at the International Data Center (IDC), a component of the CTBT based in Vienna. The IDC provides preliminary analysis of the information for treaty parties. When completed, the seismic data collection system will consist of about 170 seismic stations, including about 50 primary stations that send their signals to the IDC in real time. The radionuclide detection system comprises about 80 stations that collect airborne particulates and test for the presence of by-products of nuclear explosions, such as xenon. These data are relayed to the IDC on a regular basis. The hydroacoustic and infrasound systems will consist of about 70 sensors on land and underwater that detect the sonic signals produced by explosions. These sensors transmit their data in real time to the IDC. In all there will be 337 designated IMS facilities. As of January 2002 legal arrangements already covered 290 sites in 71 host countries; 121 stations had completed construction, with substantial progress on 90 others.

Consultation and Clarification: If a treaty party has questions about "any matter which may cause concern about possible non-compliance," it may request clarification from another party or may request the executive council to investigate. In general, the clarifying nation has one or two days to respond.

On-site Inspections: Any state party may request that the executive council conduct an on-site inspection to help clarify ambiguous events. After receiving such a request, the council must make a decision within 96 hours, with a majority vote of at least 30 of 50 members required to support a challenge inspection. If the council does order such an inspection, the inspection team must arrive in the suspected nation no less than six days after the inspection request was made. In making its request for an on-site inspection, a party may present information gathered both from the treaty's data collection network and from that party's own intelligence information (i.e., information based on national technical means).

Confidence-building Measures: To reduce the possibility of misinterpreting legal chemical explosions, such as mining charges, treaty parties are required to notify (preferably in advance) the technical secretariat of chemical blasts using more than 300 metric tons of TNT or equivalent blasting material.

Compliance: If a suspicious event is inadequately clarified through consultations or on-site inspections, the treaty parties may convene in a special session to "ensure compliance" with the treaty and "to redress and remedy" the situation. The session has three options if it determines that a party has violated the treaty: (1) it can restrict or suspend the party's rights and privileges under the treaty; (2) it can recommend that "collective measures," such as sanctions, be implemented by the remaining treaty parties; and (3), it can bring the matter before the United Nations Security Council. This final option may also be implemented by the executive council if the situation is urgent.

Entry into Force: The treaty will enter into force 180 days after 44 specific nations deposit their instruments of ratification with the United Nations. The 44 nations required for entry-into-force are: Algeria, Argentina, Australia, Austria, Bangladesh, Belgium, Brazil, Bulgaria, Canada, Chile, China, Colombia, Congo (Kinshasa), Egypt, Finland, France, Germany, Hungary, India, Indonesia, Iran, Israel, Italy, Japan, Mexico, Netherlands, North Korea, Norway, Pakistan, Peru, Poland, Romania, Russia, Slovak Republic, South Africa, South Korea, Spain, Sweden, Switzerland, Turkey, Ukraine, United Kingdom, United States, and Vietnam.

Duration: The treaty is of unlimited duration. Any treaty party may withdraw from the pact, giving six-months' notice, if treaty-related events "have jeopardized its supreme interests."

Review: Review conferences will be held every ten years (or more frequently if a majority of parties agree) to examine the operation and effectiveness of the treaty and to consider new technological developments.

Prospects for Entry into Force

On October 13, 1999, the U.S. Senate rejected treaty ratification, 51 to 49. The international reaction was sharp, immediate and—as Sen. Arlen Spector (Republican, Pennsylvania) and others had predicted—harmful to the reputation of the United States. Without U.S. ratification, it is highly unlikely that nonparty states such as India and Pakistan will agree to the treaty. The Bush administration has stated that it will not bring up the treaty for ratification. Nonetheless, international support for the test ban remains strong. United Nations Secretary-General Kofi Annan told the Second Conference on Facilitating the Entry into Force of the Comprehensive Test Ban Treaty that the September 11 terrorist attacks on the Untied States "should have made it clear to everyone that we cannot afford further proliferation of nuclear weapons." Some 50 foreign ministers from a total of 117 nations attended the November 11–13, 2001, conference. All the major allies of the United States, save Israel, have ratified the treaty and attended the conference. The United States boycotted the meeting. The final statement of conference declared that the conduct of nuclear explosions "constitutes a serious threat to global efforts towards nuclear disarmament and non-proliferation" and called for all states that have not done so to ratify the treaty as soon as possible.[12] At the beginning of 2002, 165 nations had signed the treaty, with 89 ratifications. Thirteen of the 44 nuclear-capable states had not yet ratified, including China, Israel, the United States, and three others, North Korea, India and Pakistan, had not yet signed.

Test Ban Treaty Signatories[13]

States that have ratified the treaty [89]:
Argentina, Australia, Austria, Azerbaijan, Bangladesh, Belarus, Belgium, Benin, Bolivia, Brazil, Bulgaria, Cambodia, Canada, Chile, Costa Rica, Croatia, Czech Republic, Denmark, Ecuador, El Salvador, Estonia, Fiji, Finland, France, Gabon, Germany, Greece, Grenada, Guyana, Holy See, Hungary, Iceland, Ireland, Italy, Jamaica, Japan, Jordan, Kenya, Kiribati, Laos, Latvia, Lesotho, Lithuania, Luxembourg, Maldives, Mali, Malta, Mexico, Micronesia, Monaco, Mongolia, Morocco, Namibia, Nauru, Netherlands, New Zealand, Nicaragua, Nigeria, Norway, Panama, Paraguay, Peru, Philippines, Poland, Portugal, Qatar, Republic of Korea, Romania, Russia, Saint Lucia, Senegal, Sierra Leone, Singapore, Slovak Republic, Slovenia, South Africa, Spain, Sweden, Switzerland, Tajikistan, Former Yugoslav Republic of Macedonia, Turkey, Turkmenistan, Uganda, Ukraine, United Arab Emirates, United Kingdom, Uruguay, Uzbekistan

[The 44 states of annex 2 whose ratification is required for entry into force:]
1. States listed in annex 2 to the treaty that have signed and ratified the treaty [31]: Argentina, Australia, Austria, Bangladesh, Belgium, Brazil, Bulgaria, Canada, Chile, Finland, France, Germany, Hungary, Italy, Japan, Mexico, Netherlands, Norway, Peru, Poland, Republic of Korea, Romania, Russia, Slovak Republic, South Africa, Spain, Sweden, Switzerland, Turkey, Ukraine, United Kingdom

2. States listed in annex 2 to the treaty that have signed but not ratified the treaty [10]: Algeria, China, Colombia, Democratic Republic of Congo, Egypt, Indonesia, Iran, Israel, United States, Vietnam

3. States listed in annex 2 to the treaty which have not signed the treaty [3]: Democratic People's Republic of Korea, India, and Pakistan

NOTES

1. In the mid-1970s the United States and the Soviet Union concluded two agreements that placed ceilings on the permitted yield of an underground nuclear explosion at 150 kilotons (1 kiloton is equivalent to the explosive force of 1,000 metric tons of TNT). The 1974 Threshold Test Ban Treaty set this limit for nuclear weapon tests while the 1976 Peaceful Nuclear Explosions Treaty set this limit for peaceful nuclear explosions.

2. ACDA, "Comprehensive Test Ban Treaty," Factsheet, September 11, 1996.

3. For a detailed review and analysis of the CTBT negotiations, see Rebecca Johnson and Sean Howard, "A Comprehensive Test Ban: Disappointing Progress," *Acronym* no. 3, September 1994; Rebecca Johnson, "Strengthening the Non-Proliferation Regime," *Acronym* no. 6, April 1995; Johnson, "Comprehensive Test Ban Treaty: Now or Never," *Acronym* no. 8, October 1995; Johnson, "Endgame Issues in Geneva: Can the CD Deliver the CTBT in 1996?" *Arms Control Today*, April 1996; and Joseph Cirincione, "The Signing of the Comprehensive Test Ban Treaty," ACA press briefing with Spurgeon M. Keeney, Jr., Joseph Cirincione, Richard L. Garwin, Gregory E. van der Vink, and John Isaacs, *Arms Control Today*, September 1996.

4. U.N. General Assembly Resolution 50/65 was adopted by consensus on December 12, 1995.

5. Johnson, "Comprehensive Test Ban Treaty: Now or Never," p. 15.

6. Ibid.

7. Newly elected President Jacques Chirac announced that in September France would resume nuclear testing and conduct eight tests over the following eight months. It would then be ready to sign a CTBT in the fall of 1996. However, in light of mounting international pressure, on January 29, 1996, President Chirac terminated French nuclear testing in the South Pacific.

8. Johnson, "Comprehensive Test Ban Treaty: Now or Never," p. 9.

9. As cited in Johnson, "Endgame Issues in Geneva: Can the CD Deliver the CTBT in 1996? " p. 15.

10. Craig Cerniello, "India Blocks Consensus on CTB, Treaty May Still Go to U.N.," *Arms Control Today*, August 1996, p. 31.

11. The organization maintains a comprehensive web site, www.ctbto.org.

12. Final Declaration, Conference on Facilitating the Entry into Force of the Comprehensive Nuclear Test Ban Treaty, New York, November 11–13, 2001. Available at www.ctbto.org.

13. Accurate as of January 2002, Preparatory Commission for the Comprehensive Nuclear-Test-Ban Treaty Organization, www.ctbto.org/.

Glossary

atomic bomb A bomb whose energy comes from the fission of uranium or plutonium.

beryllium A highly toxic steel-gray metal, possessing a low neutron absorption cross section and high melting point, which can be used in nuclear reactors as a moderator, reflector, or cladding material. In nuclear weapons, beryllium surrounds the fissile material and reflects neutrons back into the nuclear reaction, considerably reducing the amount of fissile material required. Beryllium is also used in guidance systems and other parts for aircraft, missiles, or space vehicles.

blanket A layer of fertile nuclear material, such as uranium–238 or thorium–232, placed around the fuel core of a reactor. During operation of the reactor, material in the blanket absorbs neutrons and decays, with products forming new fissionable , material.

breeder reactor A nuclear reactor that produces somewhat more fissile material than it consumes. The fissile material is produced both in the reactor's core and when neutrons are captured in fertile material placed around the core (blanket). This process is known as breeding. Breeder reactors have not yet reached commercialization, although active research and development programs are being pursued by various countries.

CANDU (Canadian deuterium-uranium reactor) The most widely used type of heavy-water reactor. The CANDU reactor uses natural uranium as a fuel and heavy water as a moderator and a coolant.

centrifuge See *ultracentrifuge*.

chain reaction The continuing process of nuclear fissioning in which the neutrons that are released from a fission trigger at least one other nuclear fission. In a nuclear weapon, an extremely rapid, multiplying chain reaction causes the explosive release of energy. In a reactor, the pace of the chain reaction is controlled to produce heat (in a power reactor) or large quantities of neutrons (in a research or production reactor).

chemical processing The chemical treatment of nuclear materials, usually in irradiated fuel, to separate specific usable constituents. Chemical reprocessing may be carried out with spent (irradiated) fuel to separate fissionable materials and other usable radioactive by-products from the residual fuel. A different kind of chemical processing may occur in preparation for uranium enrichment; natural uranium feedstock is processed chemically to convert it to gaseous form for enrichment operations.

coolant A substance circulated through a nuclear reactor to remove or transfer heat. The most common coolants are water and heavy water.

core The central portion of a nuclear reactor containing the fuel elements, and usually, the moderator. Also the central portion of a nuclear weapon containing highly enriched uranium or plutonium.

critical mass The minimum amount of a concentrated fissionable material required to sustain a chain reaction. The exact mass of fissionable material needed to sustain a chain reaction varies according to the concentration (purity) and chemical form of the material, the particular fissionable isotope present, its geometric properties, and its density. When pure fissionable materials are compressed by high explosives in implosion-type atomic weapons, the critical mass needed for a nuclear explosion is reduced.

depleted uranium Uranium having a smaller percentage of uranium–235 than the 0.7 percent found in natural uranium. It is a by-product of the uranium enrichment process, during which uranium–235 is culled from one batch of uranium, thereby depleting it, and then added to another batch to increase its concentration of uranium–235.

enrichment The process of increasing the concentration of one isotope of a given element (in the case of uranium, increasing the concentration of uranium–235).

feedstock Material introduced into a facility for processing.

fertile material Nuclear material composed of atoms that readily absorb neutrons and decay into other elements, producing fissionable materials. One such element is uranium–238, which decays into plutonium–239 after it absorbs a neutron. Fertile material alone cannot sustain a fission chain reaction.

fission The process by which a neutron strikes a nucleus and splits it into fragments. During the process of nuclear fission, several neutrons are emitted at high speed, and heat and radiation are released.

fissile material A fissionable material that is especially amenable to fission and therefore readily usable for the core of a nuclear weapon. Uranium–235 and plutonium–239 are examples of fissile materials.

fissionable material Material whose atoms are easily split when struck by neutrons and that can easily sustain either a controlled or explosive chain reaction, depending on concentration and other conditions of use; also commonly referred to as fissile material.

fusion The formation of a heavier nucleus from two lighter ones (such as hydrogen isotopes) with the attendant release of energy (as in a hydrogen bomb).

gas-centrifuge process A method of isotope separation in which heavy, gaseous atoms or molecules are separated from light ones by centrifugal force. See *ultracentrifuge*.

gaseous diffusion A method of isotope separation based on the fact that gas atoms or molecules with different masses will diffuse through a porous barrier (or membrane) at different rates. The method is used to separate uranium–235 from uranium–238. It requires large gaseous diffusion plants and significant amounts of electric power.

gas-graphite reactor A nuclear reactor in which a gas is the coolant and graphite is the moderator.

heavy water Water containing significantly more than the natural proportion (1 in 6,500) of heavy hydrogen (deuterium) atoms to ordinary hydrogen atoms. (Hydrogen atoms have one proton; deuterium atoms have one proton and one neutron.) Heavy water is used as a moderator in some reactors because it slows down neutrons effectively and does not absorb them (unlike light, or normal, water) making it possible to fission natural uranium and sustain a chain reaction.

heavy-water reactor A reactor that uses heavy water as its moderator and that typically uses natural uranium as fuel. See *CANDU*.

highly enriched uranium Uranium in which the percentage of uranium–235 nuclei has been increased from the natural level of 0.7 percent to some level greater than 20 percent, usually around 90 percent.

hot cells Lead-shielded rooms with remote handling equipment for examining and processing radioactive materials. In particular, hot cells are used for reprocessing spent reactor fuel.

hydrogen bomb A nuclear weapon that derives its energy largely from fusion. Also known as a thermonuclear bomb.

isotope A form of any element that is identical chemically but different in physical properties from other isotopes of the same element. Isotopes of an element have the same number of protons in the nucleus and therefore the same atomic number, but they have differing numbers of neutrons in the nucleus and therefore different atomic weights. Radioactive elements may have some isotopes that are readily fissionable and others that are not.

kilogram (kg) A metric weight equivalent to 2.2 pounds.

kiloton (kT) The energy of a nuclear explosion that is equivalent to an explosion of 1,000 metric tons of TNT.

laser enrichment method A still-experimental process of uranium enrichment in which a finely tuned, high-power laser is used to differentially excite molecules of various nuclear isotopes. This differential excitation makes it possible, for example, to separate uranium–235 from uranium–238.

light water Ordinary water (H_2O) as distinguished from heavy water (D_2O).

light-water reactor A reactor that uses ordinary water as a moderator and coolant and low-enriched uranium as fuel.

low-enriched uranium Uranium in which the percentage of uranium–235 nuclei has been increased from the natural level of 0.7 percent to less than 20 percent, usually 2 to 6 percent. With the increased level of fissile material, low-enriched uranium can sustain a chain reaction when immersed in light water and is used as fuel in light-water reactors.

medium-enriched uranium Uranium in which the percentage of uranium–235 nuclei has been increased from the natural level of 0.7 percent to between 20 and 50 percent (potentially usable for nuclear weapons, but very large quantities are needed).

megawatt (MW) 1 million watts. Used in reference to a nuclear power plant: 1 million watts of electricity (MWe); used in reference to a research or production reactor: 1 million watts of thermal energy (MWt).

metric ton 1,000 kilograms. A metric weight equivalent to 2,200 pounds or 1.1 tons.

milling A process in the uranium fuel cycle by which ore containing only a very small percentage of uranium oxide (U_3O_8) is converted into material containing a high percentage (80 percent) of U_3O_8, often referred to as yellowcake.

moderator A component (usually water, heavy water, or graphite) of some nuclear reactors that slows neutrons, thereby increasing their efficiency in splitting fissionable atoms dispersed in low-enriched or natural uranium fuel, to release energy on a controlled basis.

natural uranium Uranium as found in nature, containing 0.7 percent of uranium–235, 99.3 percent of uranium–238, and a trace of uranium–234.

neutron An uncharged elementary particle with a mass slightly greater than that of a proton, found in the nucleus of every atom heavier than hydrogen.

nuclear energy The energy liberated by a nuclear reaction (fission or fusion) or by spontaneous radioactivity.

nuclear fuel Basic chain-reaction material, including both fissile and fertile materials. Commonly used nuclear fuels are natural uranium and low-enriched uranium; high-enriched uranium and plutonium are used in some reactors.

nuclear fuel cycle The set of chemical and physical operations needed to prepare nuclear material for use in reactors and to dispose of or recycle the material after its removal from the reactor. Existing fuel cycles begin with uranium as the natural resource and create plutonium as a by-product. Some future fuel cycles may rely on thorium and produce the fissionable isotope uranium–233.

nuclear fuel element A rod, tube, plate, or other mechanical shape or form into which nuclear fuel is fabricated for use in a reactor.

nuclear fuel-fabrication plant A facility where nuclear material (e.g., enriched or natural uranium) is fabricated into fuel elements to be inserted in a reactor.

nuclear power plant Any device or assembly that converts nuclear energy into useful power. In a nuclear electric power plant, heat produced by a reactor is used to produce steam to drive a turbine that in turn drives an electric generator.

nuclear reactor A mechanism fueled by fissionable materials in a controlled nuclear chain reaction that releases heat, which can be used for civic purposes to generate electricity. Since reactors also produce fissionable material (e.g., plutonium) in the irradiated fuel, they may be used as a source of fissile material for weapons. Nuclear reactors fall into three general categories: power reactors, production reactors (for weapons), and research reactors.

nuclear waste The radioactive by-products formed by fission and other nuclear processes in a reactor. Most nuclear waste is initially contained spent fuel. If this material is reprocessed, new categories of waste result.

nuclear weapons A collective term for atomic bombs and hydrogen bombs, weapons based on a nuclear explosion. Generally used throughout the text to mean atomic bombs only, unless used with reference to nuclear-weapon states (all five of which have both atomic and hydrogen weapons).

plutonium–239 A fissile isotope occurring naturally in only minute quantities and manufactured artificially when uranium–238, through irradiation, captures an extra neutron. It is one of the two materials that have been used for the core of nuclear weapons, the other being highly enriched uranium.

plutonium–240 A fissile isotope produced in reactors when a plutonium–239 atom absorbs a neutron instead of fissioning. Its presence complicates the construction of nuclear explosives because of its high rate of spontaneous fission.

power reactor A reactor designed to produce electricity, as distinguished from reactors used primarily for research or for producing radiation or fission.

production reactor A reactor designed primarily for the large-scale production of plutonium–239 by the neutron irradiation of uranium–238.

radioactivity The spontaneous disintegration of an unstable atomic nucleus, resulting in the emission of subatomic particles.

radioisotope A radioactive isotope.

recycle To reuse the remaining uranium and plutonium found in spent fuel. It occurs after those elements have been separated from unwanted radioactive waste products at a reprocessing plant.

reprocessing The chemical treatment of spent reactor fuel to separate plutonium and uranium from unwanted radioactive waste by-products.

research reactor A reactor designed primarily to supply neutrons for experimental purposes. It may also be used for training, the testing of materials, and the production of radioisotopes.

spent fuel Fuel elements that have been removed from the reactor after use because they contain too little fissile material and too high a concentration of unwanted radioactive by-products to sustain reactor operation. Spent fuel is both thermally and radioactively hot.

strategic In modern military usage, the term *strategic* usually implies a war-prosecuting plan, campaign, or combat capability that could be rapidly decisive in defeating an opponent. In the context of this book, *strategic* usually refers to those weapons—long-range offensive nuclear arms, whether missiles or bomber aircraft—that are deployed for nuclear deterrence or retaliation and to corresponding, strategically capable defensive weapons. Although the term is usually associated with *long*-range weapons and operations, in regions consisting of heavily armed small states (e.g., the Middle East), even *shorter*-range offensive systems may be considered strategic if they are nuclear-equipped and capable of striking deep into an opponent's heartland with potentially crippling effects.

tactical In modern military usage, the term *tactical* usually refers to military operations with *shorter*-range weapons systems, on the battlefield, between the front lines of opposing military forces, and to corresponding defensive systems. Tactical weapons and operations may decide the outcome of a battle but normally do not determine the outcome of a war. In this book *tactical* usually refers to *shorter*-range (nonstrategic) missiles and aircraft and to corresponding (non-strategic) defensive systems. Weapon systems that a major power may consider tactical for its operations may be considered strategic by small states in their relations with hostile neighbors.

thermonuclear bomb A hydrogen bomb.

thorium–232 A fertile material.

tritium The heaviest hydrogen isotope, containing one proton and two neutrons in the nucleus, produced most effectively by bombarding lithium–6 with neutrons. In a fission weapon, tritium produces excess neutrons, which set off additional reactions in the weapon's fissile material. In this way, tritium can either reduce the amount of fissile material required or multiply (i.e., boost) the weapon's destructive power as much as five times.

ultracentrifuge A rapidly rotating cylinder that can be used for the enrichment of uranium. The spinning cylinder concentrates the heavier isotope (uranium–238) of uranium hexafluoride gas along the cylinder's walls, while the lighter isotope (uranium–235) concentrates at the center of the cylinder, where it can be drawn off separately.

uranium A radioactive element with the atomic number 92 and, as found in natural ores, an average atomic weight of 238. The two principal natural isotopes are uranium–235 (0.7 percent of natural uranium), which is fissionable, and uranium–238 (99.3 percent of natural uranium), which is fertile.

uranium–233 A fissionable isotope bred in fertile thorium–232. Like plutonium–239, it is theoretically an excellent material for nuclear weapons but is not known to have been used for that purpose. Can be used as a reactor fuel.

uranium–235 The only naturally occurring fissionable isotope. Natural uranium contains 0.7 percent uranium–235; light-water reactors use about 3 percent; and weapons-grade, highly enriched uranium normally consists of 93 percent of this isotope.

uranium–238 A fertile material. Natural uranium is composed of approximately 99.3 percent uranium–238.

uranium dioxide (UO_2) Purified uranium. The form of natural uranium used in heavy-water reactors. Also the form of uranium that remains after the fluorine is removed from enriched uranium hexafluoride (UF_6). Produced as a powder, uranium dioxide is, in turn, fabricated into fuel elements.

uranium oxide (U_3O_8) The most common oxide of uranium found in typical ores. Uranium oxide is extracted from the ore during the milling process. The ore typically contains only 0.1 percent uranium oxide; yellowcake, the product of the milling process, contains about 80 percent uranium oxide.

uranium hexafluoride (UF$_6$) A volatile compound of uranium and fluorine. UF$_6$ is a solid at atmospheric pressure and room temperature, but can be transformed into gas by heating. UF$_6$ gas (alone, or in combination with hydrogen or helium) is the feedstock in all uranium enrichment processes and is sometimes produced as an intermediate product in the process of purifying yellowcake to produce uranium oxide.

vessel The part of a reactor that contains the nuclear fuel.

weapons-grade Nuclear material of the type most suitable for nuclear weapons, i.e., uranium enriched to 93 percent uranium–235 or plutonium that is primarily plutonium–239.

weapons-usable Fissionable material that is weapons-grade or, although less than ideal for weapons, that can still be used to make a nuclear explosive.

yellowcake A concentrate produced during the milling process that contains about 80 percent uranium oxide (U$_3$O$_8$). In preparation for uranium enrichment, the yellowcake is converted to uranium hexafluoride gas (UF$_6$). In the preparation of natural uranium reactor fuel, yellowcake is processed into purified uranium dioxide. Sometimes uranium hexafluoride is produced as an intermediate step in the purification process.

yield The total energy released in a nuclear explosion. It is usually expressed in equivalent metric tons of TNT (the quantity of TNT required to produce a corresponding amount of energy).

zirconium A grayish-white lustrous metal that is commonly used in an alloy form (i.e., zircaloy) to encase fuel rods in nuclear reactors.

Sources

Albright, David, Frans Berkhout, and William Walker. *World Inventory of Plutonium and Highly Enriched Uranium, 1992.* Oxford: Oxford University Press, 1993.

Cochran, Thomas B., William Arkin, Robert S. Norris, and Milton Heonig. *Nuclear Weapons Databook. Vol. 2: U.S. Nuclear Warhead Production.* Cambridge: Ballinger, 1984.

Nero, Anthony V. Jr. *A Guidebook to Nuclear Reactors.* Berkeley: University of California Press, 1979.

Office of Technology Assessment. *Nuclear Power in an Age of Uncertainty.* Washington, D.C., 1984.

U.S. Congress. *Technologies Underlying Weapons of Mass Destruction.* Office of Technology Assessment. Washington, D.C.: U.S. GPO, 1993.

Abbreviations and Acronyms

ABACC	Argentine-Brazilian Accounting and Control Commission
ABM	anti-ballistic missile
ACDA	Arms Control and Disarmament Agency (U.S.)
ACRS	Arms Control and Regional Security
AEC	Atomic Energy Corporation (South Africa)
AG	Australia Group
ALCM	air-launched cruise missiles
ANC	African National Congress
ANWFZ	African Weapon-Free-Zone Treaty
ASMP	Air-Sol Moyenne Portée missiles
BARC	Bhabha Atomic Research Center
BJP	Bharatiya Janata Party (India)
BWC	Biological and Toxin Weapons Convention
CAEP	Chinese Academy of Engineering Physics
CANDU	Canadian deuterium-uranium reactor
CBM	confidence-building measure
CBW	chemical and biological weapons
CD	Conference on Disarmament
CHEN	Comissão Nacional de Energia Nuclear (Brazil)
CIA	Central Intelligence Agency (U.S.)
CIRP	China Institute for Radiation Protection
CNEA	National Atomic Energy Commission (Argentina)
COCOM	Coordinating Committee for Multilateral Export Controls
CSCE	Conference on Security and Cooperation in Europe
CTBT	Comprehensive Test Ban Treaty
CTBTO	Comprehensive Test Ban Treaty Organization
CTR	Cooperative Threat Reduction program
CWC	Chemical Weapons Convention
CWS	Chemical Warfare Service
DIA	Defense Intelligence Agency
DPRK	Democratic People's Republic of Korea
DRDO	Defense Research Development Organization (India)
EDP	especially designed or prepared
EIF	entry into force
EMIS	electromagnetic isotope separation
EPCI	U.S. Enhanced Proliferation Control Initiative
FBTR	fast-breeder test reactor

FEC	Fuel Elements Factory (Argentina)
FIS	Islamic Salvation Front (Algeria)
FMCT	fissile material cut-off treaty
GLCM	ground-launched cruise missiles
GSLV	geosynchronous space launch vehicle
HEU	highly enriched uranium
HNE	hydronuclear experiments
IAEA	International Atomic Energy Agency
IBDS	Integrated Biological Detection System
ICBM	intercontinental ballistic missile
ICOC	International Code of Conduct
IDC	International Data Center
IIBR	Israel Institute for Biological Research
ILSA	Iran and Libya Sanctions Act of 1996
IMS	International Monitoring System
INET	Institute of Nuclear Energy Technology
INF	intermediate-range nuclear forces
IPEN	Institute for Energy and Nuclear Research (Argentina)
IPP	Initiatives for Proliferation Prevention
IRBM	intermediate-range ballistic missile
ISTC	International Science and Technology Center (Moscow)
LACM	land-attack cruise missile
LEAP	Lightweight Exo-Atmospheric Projectile
LEI	Isotopic Enrichment Laboratory (Argentina)
LEU	low-enriched uranium
LWR	light water reactor
MCAD	man-portable chemical agent detector
MEADS	Medium Extended Air Defense System
Minatom	Russian Ministry of Atomic Energy
MIRV	multiple independently targeted reentry vehicle
MLIS	molecular laser isotope separation
MNSR	miniature neutron source reactor
MOD	Ministry of Defense
MOU	Memorandum of Understanding
MOX	mixed oxide fuel
MPC&A	material protection, control, and accounting
MRBM	medium-range ballistic missile
MTCR	Missile Technology Control Regime
NASB	National Security Advisory Board (India)
NATO	North Atlantic Treaty Organization
NBC	Joint Nuclear, Biological, and Chemical Regiment
NCA	National Command Authority
NCI	Nuclear Cities Initiative
NECSA	South African Nuclear Energy Corporation
NIE	National Intelligence Estimate
NIS	Newly Independent States

NISKHI	State Research Institute of Agricultural Science (Kazakhstan)
NPT	Non-Proliferation Treaty
NSG	Nuclear Suppliers Group
NTM	National Technical Means
NWFZ	nuclear-weapon-free zone
OPCW	Organization for the Prohibition of Chemical Weapons
OSI	on-site inspection
PHWR	pressurized heavy-water reactors
PNEs	peaceful nuclear explosives
PSLV	Polar Space Launch Vehicle (Indian)
PWR	pressurized water reactor
SATC	Security Assessment and Training Center
SDI	Strategic Defense Initiative
SDR	Strategic Defense Review
SLBM	submarine-launched ballistic missile
SLV	space launch vehicle
SNOPB	Scientific Experimental and Production Base
SPNFZ	South Pacific nuclear free zone
SRAM	short-range attack missile
SRBM	short-range ballistic missile
SSBN	nuclear ballistic missile submarine
SSN	nuclear-fueled submarine
START	Strategic Arms Reduction Treaty
STCU	Science and Technology Center of Ukraine
SVC	Special Verification Commission
THAAD	Theater High-Altitude Area Defense
THEL	tactical high-energy laser
UAV	unmanned aerial vehicle
UCAV	unmanned combat aerial vehicle
UCOR	Uranium Enrichment Corporation (South Africa)
UNMOVIC	U.N. Monitoring, Verification, and Inspection Commission
UNSC	United Nations Security Council
UNSCOM	U.N. Special Commission
USAMRIID	U.S. Army Medical Research Institute of Infectious Diseases
USEC	United States Enrichment Corporation
VEE	Venezuelan equine encephalitis
VX	V agent
WMD	weapons of mass destruction

Maps

Tables

Index

About the Authors

Joseph Cirincione is the director of the Carnegie Endowment Non-Proliferation Project in Washington, D.C. He is a frequent commentator on proliferation and security issues and is widely quoted in the media. He served for nine years as a national security specialist in the U.S. House of Representatives on the professional staff of the Committee on Armed Services and the Committee on Government Operations. He is the author of numerous articles on nuclear and missile proliferation, the producer of the CD-ROM *New Leaders, New Directions: Proliferation 2001*, and the editor of *Repairing the Regime: Preventing the Spread of Weapons of Mass Destruction* (Routledge, 2000).

Jon B. Wolfsthal is an associate with the Carnegie Endowment Non-Proliferation Project and focuses his research on nuclear-weapon and material security and proliferation. He has written extensively on Russia's nuclear complex and the proliferation challenges arising out of the collapse of the former Soviet Union, as well as on regional security and proliferation in East Asia. Mr. Wolfsthal, who served for five years as an official at the U.S. Department of Energy, is the co-editor of the *Nuclear Status Report: Nuclear Weapons, Fissile Material, and Export Controls in the Former Soviet Union* (Carnegie Endowment/Monterey Institute, 2001).

Miriam Rajkumar is a project associate with the Carnegie Endowment Non-Proliferation Project and focuses her research on proliferation, as well as political and security developments in South Asia and the Persian Gulf. Ms. Rajkumar holds an M.A. in International Relations from the Johns Hopkins University's School of Advanced International Studies in Washington, D.C.

About the Non-Proliferation Project

The Non-Proliferation Project at the Carnegie Endowment for International Peace is an internationally recognized source of information and analysis on efforts to curb the spread of nuclear, chemical, and biological weapons and missile delivery systems. Through publications, conferences and the Internet, the project promotes greater public awareness of these security issues and encourages effective policies to address weapons proliferation and its underlying causes.

The project's ongoing program of research, analysis, and commentary includes articles, working papers, monographs, and books. In addition, project staff maintain an extensive Internet site of documents, maps, charts, and other key resources. Updated hourly, the web site is a prime source of information for journalists and experts worldwide. The project organizes frequent roundtables and briefings, distributes regular *Proliferation Briefs,* and provides the biweekly *Proliferation News Service*, an electronic summary of breaking news. *Carnegie to Go* is a new service that delivers the latest proliferation news, analysis, and data to Palm Pilot, Visor, and other handheld devices.

The project also convenes the annual Carnegie International Non-Proliferation Conference, widely considered one of the premier events in the field. At the Carnegie Moscow Center, the project promotes debate on non-proliferation policies in the former Soviet Union through regular seminars with key Russian experts and officials, major conferences, and publication of two Russian-language periodicals.

Visit the project online at **www.proliferationnews.org**

Carnegie Endowment for International Peace

The Carnegie Endowment is a private, nonprofit organization dedicated to advancing cooperation between nations and promoting active international engagement by the United States. Founded in 1910, its work is nonpartisan and dedicated to achieving practical results.

Through research, publishing, convening, and, on occasion, creating new institutions and international networks, Endowment associates shape fresh policy approaches. Their interests span geographic regions and the relations between governments, business, international organizations, and civil society, focusing on the economic, political, and technological forces driving global change. Through its Carnegie Moscow Center, the Endowment helps to develop a tradition of public policy analysis in the states of the former Soviet Union and to improve relations between Russia and the United States. The Endowment publishes *Foreign Policy,* one of the world's leading magazines of international politics and economics, which reaches readers in more than 120 countries and in several languages.